SOCIETY OF BIBLICAL LITERATURE

1998 Seminar Papers
Part Two

Society of Biblical Literature
Seminar Papers Series

Number 37
Society of Biblical Literature
1998 Seminar Papers
Part Two

Society of Biblical Literature
1998 Seminar Papers
Part Two

One hundred Thirty-fourth Annual Meeting
November 21–24, 1998
Walt Disney World Swan and Walt Disney World Dolphin
Orlando, Florida

Scholars Press
Atlanta, Georgia

Society of Biblical Literature
1998 Seminar Papers
Part Two

Indexed in *Religion Index Two: Multi-Author Works*
published by the American Theological Library Association, Evanston, Illinois.
Indexing also available in the ATLA Religion Database
accessible through Dialog Information Services, Palo Alto, California.
Also available for compact-disk searching through ATLA.

ISBN: 0-7885-0489-4
ISSN: 0145-2711

Printed in the United States of America

Contents

Part One

v

Part Two

POETS, SCRIBES, OR PREACHERS?
THE REALITY OF PROPHECY IN THE SECOND
TEMPLE PERIOD

Lester L. Grabbe
University of Hull
ENGLAND

Late prophetic books such as Zechariah and Haggai describe individuals who deliver prophecies in the name of the God of Israel. Apocalyptic writings such as *1 Enoch* 1-36 and Daniel 7-12 relate the heavenly journeys and the visions (complete with interpretation) of patriarchal figures. Some writings suggest that there were no prophets around to take care of such mundane prophetic tasks as ruling on polluted altar stones (1 Macc 4:44-46); others speak about prophets as if they roamed the streets unhindered and, if not in droves, at least in respectable numbers. This is the *picture*, but what was the reality?

The aim of this paper is to address three questions: (1) the relationship of prophetic literature to social reality; (2) the relationship of apocalyptic literature to prophetic literature and to social reality; and (3) the status of stories about prophets and prophet-like figures. Since each of these topics is potentially large, some of my treatment will be in the nature of a programatic outline. I shall also be building on some of the arguments in my book, *Priests, Prophets, Diviners, Sages*.[1]

The Problems of Definition

In one sense prophets and prophecy are what we say they are. That is, as scholars we can come up with a definition on which we all agree as the basis for communication and further research, regardless of what the ancients meant by the terms. We can decide that a prophet is a four-eyed, one-horned pink and purple people eater who wears an itsy bitsy teeny weeny yellow poka dot bikini, and sleep soundly in our beds at night with a clear conscience, as long as other scholars go along with this. Nevertheless, most definitions pay some lip service to the terminology of the biblical

---

[1]Lester L. Grabbe, *Priests, Prophets, Diviners, Sages: A Socio-historical Study of Religious Specialists in Ancient Israel* (Valley Forge, PA: Trinity Press International, 1995), especially ch. 4 on prophets and pp. 139-41, 183-85, 201-5, 218-20. I shall also be drawing on observations first published in my article, "The Social Setting of Early Jewish Apocalypticism," *JSP* 4 (1989) 27-47.

sources and the definitions given or assumed by the ancient authors. The Hebrew word
נביא has usually lain at the core of the various definitions proposed. The problem we
have for the Second Temple period is that few of our texts discussing prophecy and
prophets are in Hebrew, which means that the characteristic Hebrew term is not present. Instead, we often have to do with the Greek word προφήτης or related words.
Although they generally render נבא/נביא in the Septuagint and other Greek translations,
this does not necessarily mean that they have the same connotation.

Unfortunately, some of the definitions used in scholarship have not
really been purely descriptive but instead incorporated value judgments and carried
theological overtones. Nineteenth-century scholarship produced a definition which
would not be embarrassing to middle-class, liberal *Alttestamentler*, a definition which
continues to be influential.[2] They wanted to distance prophecy from, on the one hand,
the oracles and divination known from the classical and Near Eastern world and, on the
other, from apocalyptic[3] which was alleged to have developed in Judaism when
prophecy degenerated and then replaced it.

No doubt there are differences between a prophet such as Isaiah of
Jerusalem and the Revelation of John or the *Apocalypse of Baruch*. The question is not
whether there are differences, though, but whether these demonstrate a sharp
dichotomy between prophecy and apocalyptic—whether the one ceased and the other
arose as a new entity in its place. One element which the 19th century wanted to
eliminate from prophecy, or at least downplay in importance, was the predictive element. It ignored the fact that prophecy always contained or implied predictions, even
if contingent. Prophets claimed to proclaim messages of God about his plans, but this
inevitably included the future. Prediction was not all there was to prophecy by any
means, but it was certainly there.

One of the main assumptions behind many discussions is that there was a
common "prophetic movement" in ancient Israel. The belief seems to be that the "true,

---

[2]For a discussion of Max Weber's influential definition, see Joseph
Blenkinsopp, *Sage, Priest, Prophet: Religious and Intellectual Leadership in Ancient
Israel* (Library of Ancient Israel; Louisville, KY: Westminister John Knox, 1995) 115-
19.

[3]Some have objected to use of the term "apocalyptic" to refer to the
phenomenon, confining "apocalyptic" to usage as an adjective and preferring
"apocalypticism" for the noun. Although this usage has become fairly widespread in
North America, "apocalyptic" as a noun in English has been around and in respectable
usage for well over a century, and in the UK at least there is no sign that it is being
abandoned. Cf also E. J. C. Tigchelaar, "More on Apocalyptic and Apocalypses," *JSJ*
18 (1987) 137-44, especially 137 n. 2.

classical" prophets were almost a tightly knit group all with the same outlook and characteristics. This owes more to theological prejudice than to data from the OT. There are great differences between the various prophets from Nathan to Malachi. Also, we cannot draw an artificial divide between the "true" and the "false" prophets, which represents only the bias of the text. From a sociological point of view they were all prophets and must be taken into account in any study. Prophets of all sorts were evidently a part of Israelite society from an early time, and they all had certain characteristics which were features of that culture, but this is normal in cultures the world over. There is little evidence of a unified "prophetic school" whose charactistics can be taken as normative in defining prophecy.

Many scholars have seen a gradual shift from prophetic to apocalyptic literature, via "late" or "post-exilic" prophetic books. However, this argument is not as simple as it might first appear because a large amount of the prophetic literature was probably edited during the Persian period, and the present contents of books like Isaiah and Jeremiah are not necessarily pre-exilic. Another problem with accepting such a simple scenario revolves around definitions. For example, Paul Hanson sees a shift from prophecy to "proto-apocalyptic" (Deutero-Isaiah), "early apocalyptic" (Zech 9-11; Isa 56-66), "middle apocalyptic" (Isa 24-27 and Zech 12:1-13), to full-blown apocalyptic writings.[4] This scenario depends on his widely influential differentiation between prophecy and apocalyptic, though he really confines the issues to a discussion of "prophetic eschatology" and "apocalyptic eschatology."[5]

Hanson's distinction between prophecy and apocalyptic is based on his concept of "myth" versus "history": prophecy expects its pronouncements to be worked out in plain history, whereas apocalyptic has abandoned real history for the mythical realm. This looks anachronistic and arbitrary.[6] Hanson begins his definition with what "the prophet has witnessed unfolding in the divine council," but the divine council is itself a mythical concept! To the ancient writers—as to millions of modern-day fundamentalists—the cosmic drama is as historical as the Assyrian invasion. In the same way, it is hard to see that the endtime kingdom foreseen by Daniel differed in any significant way from that of the ideal Davidic rule conceived of by Ezekiel (34:23-30) and others. The vision of Daniel and the other apocalypses is no more fantastic or "other worldly" than that of Isaiah 2:2-4 or Micah 4:1-5 which has the lion lying down with the lamb and even eating straw like a ruminant.

---

[4]Paul D. Hanson, *Dawn of Apocalyptic* (Philadelphia: Westminster, 1973) 11-31, 126-32, 299-315, 368.

[5]Hanson, *The Dawn of Apocalyptic*: 9-12; "Apocalypticism," *IDBSupp* (1976) 29-31.

[6]Cf. J. J. M. Roberts, "Myth Versus History: Relaying the Comparative Foundations," *CBQ* 38 (1976) 1-13.

Many of the other alleged differences between prophetic and apocalyptic writings do not hold up to an actual study of the writings. Are the apocalypses pseudepigraphical? So are many prophetic texts. Do the apocalypses depend a lot on visions? So do many prophecies.[7] Do many apocalypses describe an ideal world to come? So do many prophetic passages. One can of course come up with relatively neutral form critical criteria to distinguish prophetic literary forms from apocalypses.[8] From a form critical perspective many of the old prophetic forms do tend to change or die out, and a new genre of apocalypse arises; however, apocalyptic is not by any means confined to formal apocalypses. In my opinion the sharp distinction between prophecy and apocalyptic is unjustified. For example, there is no reason why the prophetic book of Zechariah 1-8 cannot also be classified as an apocalypse.[9] Indeed, I

---

[7]This may have been the origin of the prophecy even when the vision framework is no longer extant. For the fact that many of the prophecies without visionary frameworks may nevertheless have been received via visions, see the discussion in Grabbe, *Priests, Prophets, Diviners, Sages*: 83, 108-11, 116.

[8]The precise definition of "apocalypse" is still very much debated. A widely used delineation of the genre is that developed by the Society of Biblical Literature seminar whose results appeared in John J. Collins (ed.), *Apocalypse: The Morphology of a Genre* (Semeia 14; Atlanta: Scholars, 1979); see especially p. 9. On the other hand, it has also been challenged or modified by other scholars; e.g., Edward P. Sanders, "The Genre of Palestinian Jewish Apocalypses," in David Hellholm (ed.), *Apocalypticism in the Mediterranean World and the Near East* (Tübingen: Mohr[Siebeck], 1983) 447-59; M. A. Knibb, "Prophecy and the Emergence of the Jewish Apocalypses," in Richard J. Coggins, et al. (ed.), *Israel's Prophetic Tradition: Essays in Honour of Peter R. Ackroyd* (Cambridge University Press, 1982) 155-80, especially 161-65; and James H. Charlesworth (with James R. Mueller), *The New Testament Apocrypha and Pseudepigrapha: A Guide to Publications, with Excursuses on Apocalypses* (Metuchen, NJ/London: Scarecrow, 1987) 20-24. Both Sanders and Charlesworth want a less confining definition, but see Collins' reply to Sanders (*Apocalyptic Imagination: An Introduction to the Jewish Matrix of Christianity* [New York: Crossroad, 1984] 8). The debate continued in the symposium published in *Semeia* 36 (1986); see especially the articles by D. Hellholm (pp. 13-64) and D. E. Aune (pp. 65-96) and the introduction by A. Y. Collins (pp. 1-11). It seems to me that Hellholm's attempt (p. 27) to include a reference to "a group in crisis" is particularly unhelpful. It adds a social component to the definition of a literary genre and thus begs the question of social setting. Cf also Christopher Rowland, *The Open Heaven: A Study of Apocalyptic in Judaism and Early Christianity* (London: SPCK, 1982), Part One, especially pp. 14 and 70; see note 9 below.

[9]See M. A. Knibb ("Prophecy and the Emergence of the Jewish

would rather see apocalyptic as a sub-genre of prophecy than as a separate entity.[10]

For our purposes, however, the genre definitions are not particularly important. What is clear is that the written prophets and the written apocalypses present many of the same problems with regard to relating them to a social context and to social reality. We can debate matters of genre and even definition, but their function seems to have been similar.[11]

Apocalypses": 172-75) for a general discussion of the question. Collins (*The Apocalyptic Imagination*: 19-20, 221 nn. 60-61) still maintains that Zechariah 1-8 and Isaiah 24-27 are not apocalypses.

[10]For a further discussion, see Grabbe, "The Social Setting of Early Jewish Apocalypticism"; *Priests, Prophets, Diviners, Sages*: 106-7, 176-78. As I have already pointed out ("The Social Setting of Early Jewish Apocalypticism": 33-35) apocalypses and related oracular writings can be seen as a type of prophecy. That is, they are presented as a divine message received by a human intermediary to be passed on to a larger audience. Past scholarship has tended to judge all prophecy by what is perhaps a peculiar manifestation at a certain time in Israel's history, the 250 years from about 750 to 500 BCE. Why must the touchstone for defining prophecy for all time be the narrow perspective of a few Israelite prophets at a certain short period of history? It is important to realize that Israelite prophecy during these two and a half centuries was conditioned by several factors, When there was no longer a king and court and the country came under foreign domination, prophecies might well take the form of announcing a divine restoration of these or something even greater such as God's direct rule on a purified earth; alternatively, the idea of a personal afterlife might obviate particular concern for a restored monarchy. In either case, such prophecies might well take the form of an apocalypse or a related genre. Cf also John Barton, *Oracles of God: Perceptions of Ancient Prophecy in Israel after the Exile* (London: Darton, Longman & Todd, 1986) 198-210. Rowland (*The Open Heaven*: 70-71) defines apocalyptic as the "revelation of the divine mysteries through visions or some other form of immediate disclosure of heavenly truths." Apocalyptic literature "should, therefore, be confined to those works which purport to offer disclosures of the heavenly mysteries, whether as the result of vision, heavenly ascent or verbal revelations." However, he does not discuss the fact that a good deal of the prophetic literature would equally fall under this definition. He also strangely excludes such works as the *Testament of Moses* (p. 51), but if its revelation of the subsequent history of Israel is not a "disclosure of heavenly mysteries," I do not know what is.

[11]For a rather more nuanced comparison of prophecy and apocalyptic, which looks at emphases rather than sharp distinctions, see John J. Collins, *Apocalypticism in the Dead Sea Scrolls* (The Literature of the Dead Sea Scrolls; London/New York: Routledge, 1997) 4-8.

But this discussion of definition has quickly and imperceptibly shifted to the context of *literature*, which so often happens, and illustrates an important point that is often overlooked: Israelite prophecy has two aspects to it, a social and a literary. What prophetic figures do is social; what gets written down becomes literary. However, there is a further complication since the prophetic literature also has a social function which needs to be explored. It is also almost entirely from the literature that we know about prophetic figures, their activities and their role in society.[12]

The prophetic corpus of the Hebrew Bible has all sorts of material in it. Some of it describes the activities of prophets and their associates (e.g., Baruch the scribe). Other parts of it concern the prophetic discourses themselves—the prophecies or statements made in the name of Yhwh. We would be foolish indeed to take either sort of material at face value, yet we must ask what the nature of the material implies about prophets and prophecy. The same applies to the non-canonical literature of Second Temple Judaism.

One fact which is far too often overlooked is that some or even a great deal of the prophetic writings did not originate with prophets. Whatever Amos, Isaiah, Jeremiah, and other prophets spoke as oracles from Yhwh, these were at least supplemented by a later generation of tradents. How much of this material is to be assigned to the later tradents is debated and probably varies from book to book. Yet few would claim that the added material was itself primarily oracular material delivered by a fellow prophet; more likely it is poetic (or even prose) material purpose written for its context. The prophetic books as we have them today are, therefore, pseudepigraphic writings with much material contributed by poets and scribes. This is enormously significant for purposes of our discussion: *the prophetic writings and the apocalyptic and relating writings are all scribal works in their present form* and thus present a similar problem when it comes to relating them to their social context.

Survey of Relevant Texts

Ben Sira

Ben Sira is often seen as an opponent of special revelations and all the various practices relating to the future: apocalypticism, divination, astrology, prophetic oracles, and the like (cf. 34:1-8). This is a large question which cannot be dealt with

---

[12]In recent years anthropological studies of prophets and similar figures have been drawn on for analogies to help understand the descriptions in the biblical literature. Although I draw extensively on these in *Priests, Prophets, Diviners, Sages*, they will not be an important part of this article.

in detail here; however, in addition to general references to OT prophets, two passages are of potential value. In 39:1-3 he is describing the ideal sage (i.e., probably his own self-understanding):

> He seeks out the wisdom of all the ancients, and is concerned with prophecies; he preserves the sayings of the famous and penetrates the subtleties of parables; he seeks out the hidden meanings of proverbs and is at home with the obscurities of parables.

This intriguing statement on prophecies is not completely clear, but it indicates that Ben Sira did not see wisdom as confined to the present corpus of wisdom literature or the conventional wisdom tradition. Apparently the sage at a minimum would be interested in interpreting the corpus of prophetic literature. This is further indicated in 36:20-21:

> Bear witness to those whom you created in the beginning, and fulfill the prophecies spoken in your name. Reward those who wait for you and let your prophets be found trustworthy.

In a number of passages he refers to individuals as prophets who are also clearly so labeled in the OT (46:15; 47:1; 48:1; 49:10). Isaiah is said to have seen the future and "revealed what was to occur to the end of time, and the hidden things before they happened" (48:24-25). It is also interesting to find the statement that Joshua "was the successor of Moses in the prophetic office" (46:1), a statement also found in Josephus.

1 Maccabees

One of the main sources for the view that prophecy had ceased is 1 Maccabees. The first passage is 4:44-46:

> They deliberated what to do about the altar of burnt offering, which had been profaned. And they thought it best to tear it down, so that it would not be a lasting shame to them that the Gentiles had defiled it. So they tore down the altar, and stored the stones in a convenient place on the temple hill until a prophet should come to tell what to do with them.[13]

The context does not suggest that prophets were only a phenomenon of the distant past. On the contrary, the context would suggest that although there was no prophet currently available, it was still possible for one to come along in the future. The passage does

---

[13]For convenience, texts from the OT, NT, and Apocrypha are all cited from the NRSV unless other indicated. Texts from Philo, Josephus, and the classical writers are cited from the Loeb Classical Library translations.

not really argue for the cessation of prophecy but only that acceptable prophets were not necessarily common. A similar idea occurs a bit later in the book: "The Jews and their priests have resolved that Simon should be their leader and high priest forever, until a trustworthy prophet should arise" (1 Macc 14:41).

The passage most explicitly stating the view that prophecy had ceased is 1 Maccabees 9:27: "So there was great distress in Israel, such as had not been since the time that prophets ceased to appear among them." According to this, prophets ceased sometime in the past and are no longer extant; however, it agrees with other passages in not ruling out a future prophet.

Qumran Scrolls

Some of the Qumran texts express belief in the appearance of a future prophet who is separate from the Messiah(s) of Aaron and Israel (1QS 9:9-11):

> They should not depart from any counsel of the law in order to walk in complete stubbornness of their heart, but instead shall be ruled by the first directives which the men of the Community began to be taught until the prophet comes, and the Messiahs of Aaron and Israel.

The question is, with whom is this prophet to be identified. A good case can be made that the Teacher of Righteousness was seen by many as this eschatological prophet.[14]

Qumran also did not confine the word נביא in the way that some modern scholars wish to use it. For them, Daniel was also a prophet: "[a]s is written in the book of Daniel, the prophet [הנביא]" (4QFlor frag. 1, II, 3, 24, 5:3).

The *Habakkuk Commentary* makes a statement about the interpretation of prophetic literature which shows an attitude different from what we think of as biblical interpretation (1QpHab 7:3-5):

> And God told Habakkuk to write what going to happen <to> to the last generation, but he did not let him know the consummation of the era. And as for what he says: *Hab 2:2* "So that /may run/ the one who reads it". Its interpretation concerns the Teacher of Righteousness, to whom God has made known all the mysteries of the words of his servants, the prophets.[15]

---

[14]Cf P. Wernberg-Møller, *The Manual of Discipline, Translated and Annotated with an Introduction* (STDJ 1; Leiden: Brill, 1957) 136; A. R. C. Leaney, *The Rule of Qumran and its Meaning: Introduction, Translation and Commentary* (The New Testament Library; Philadelphia: Westminister, 1966) 228.

[15]Translation from Florentino García Martínez and Eibert J. C. Tig-

The Teacher was inspired to interpret prophecies of Habakkuk even though the prophet himself did not understand them. The implication is that interpretation was not just a matter of interpretative rules or techniques; on the contrary, interpretation was a matter of inspiration by the same spirit which had inspired the original prophetic writer.[16]

Philo of Alexandria[17]

Philo discusses the concept of prophecy at some length, especially in *De vita Mosis*. The first is *Vita Mosis* 1.263-99 which recounts the story of Balaam. Philo makes the distinction between augury (which Balaam formerly practised) and prophecy (1.264-68). But then Balaam "straightway became possessed, and there fell upon him the truly prophetic spirit which banished utterly from his soul his art of wizardry . . . . he spake these oracles as one repeating the words which another had put into his mouth."

For Philo Moses is the prophet *par excellence* (προφήτης . . . δοκιμώτατος [2.187]). He distinguishes several sorts of prophecy (2.188-91):

Now I am fully aware that all things written in the sacred books are oracles [χρησμοί] delivered through Moses; but I will confine myself to those which are

---

chelaar (eds and trans), *The Dead Sea Scrolls Study Edition: Volume One 1Q1-4Q273* (Leiden-New York-Köln: Brill, 1997) 17.

[16]In the discussion following a presentation of this paper in Professor Goodman's seminar (see n. 31 below), Dr. Charlotte Hempel kindly mentioned 4Q375 (published by John Strugnell in James VanderKam [ed.], *Discoveries in the Judaean Desert. Volume 19: Qumran Cave 4: XIV Parabiblical Texts, Part 2* [Oxford: Clarendon, 1995] 111-19). I had in fact examined the text in my research for this paper but had not included it because it did not seem to bear on my questions; a subsequent examination of it has not changed my mind.

[17]Studies on this subject include David Winston, "Two Types of Mosaic Prophecy according to Philo," *JSP* 2 (1989) 49-67; John R. Levison, "Two Types of Ecstatic Prophecy according to Philo," *Studia Philonica Annual* 6 (1994) 83-89; "Inspiration and the Divine Sprit in the Writings of Philo Judaeus," *JSJ* 26 (1995) 271-323; David M. Hay, "Philo's View of Himself as an Exegete: Inspired, but not Authoritative," *Heirs of the Septuagint: Philo, Hellenistic Judaism and Early Christianity. Festschrift for Earle Hilgert = Studia Philonica Annual* 3 (1991) 40-52; Sze-kar Wan, "Charismatic Exegesis: Philo and Paul Compared," *Studia Philonica Annual* 6 (1994) 54-82.

more especially his, with the following preliminary remarks. Of the divine utterances, some are spoken by God in His own Person with His prophet for interpreter, in some the revelation comes through question and answer, and others are spoken by Moses in his own person, when possesssed [ἐπιθειάσαντος] by God and carried away [κατασχεθέντος] out of himself. . . . The third kind are assigned to the lawgiver himself: God has given to him of His own power of foreknowlege [προγνωστικῆς] and by this he will reveal future events [τὰ μέλλοντα]. Now, the first kind must be left out of the discussion. They are too great to be lauded by human lips . . . . Besides, they are delivered through an interpreter, and interpretation [ἑρμηνεία] and prophecy [προφητεία] are not the same thing. The second kind I will at once proceed to describe, interweaving with it the third kind, in which the speaker appears under that divine possession [ἐνθουσιῶδες] in virtue of which he is chiefly and in the strict sense considered a prophet.

This included prophesying the future with regard to each of the twelve tribes (2.288):

> Then, indeed, we find him possessed by the spirit, no longer uttering general truths to the whole nation but prophesying to each tribe in particular the things which were to be and hereafter must come to pass.

Philo regards Moses as unique in certain ways. The inspiration of prophets in general is described as follows :

> [*Quis heres* 259-66] Now with every good man it is the holy Word which assures him his gift of prophecy. For a prophet (being a spokesman) has no utterance of his own, but all his utterance came from elsewhere, the echoes of another's voice. The wicked may never be the interpreter of God, so that no worthless person is "God-inspired" [ἐνθουσιᾷ] in the proper sense. The name only befits the wise, since he alone is the vocal instrument of God, smitten and played by His invisible hand. Thus, all whom Moses describes as just are pictured as possessed [κατεχομένους] and prophesying [προφητεύοντας]. . . . But when it comes to its [the sun's = the mind's] setting, naturally ecstasy [ἔκστασις] and divine possession [ἡ ἔνθεος κατοκωχή] and madness [μανία] fall upon us. . . . This is what regularly befalls the fellowship of the prophets. The mind is evicted at the arrival of the divine Spirit, but when that departs the mind returns to its tenancy. . . . For indeed the prophet, even when he seems to be speaking, really holds his peace, and his organs of speech, mouth and tongue are wholly in the employ of Another, to shew forth what He wills.

> [*Spec. leg.* 1.65] A prophet possessed by God will suddenly appear and give prophetic oracles. Nothing of what he says will be his own, for he that is truly under the control of divine inspiration has no power of apprehesion when he speaks but serves as the channel for the insistent words of Another's prompting. For prophets are the interpreters [ἑρμηνεῖς] of God, Who makes full use of their organs of speech to set forth what He wills.

Philo is quite important for another idea: the concept of inspired interpretation. In *Vita Mosis* 2.264-65, 268-69):

> Moses, when he heard of this [that the manna from heaven was doubled on the sixth day and did not evaporate] and also actually saw it, was awestruck and, guided by what was not so much surmise as God-sent inspiration, made announcement of the sabbath. I need hardly say that the conjectures of this kind are closely akin [συγγενεῖς] to prophecies. . . . After this, he uttered a third prophetic saying of truly marvellous import. He declared that on the sabbath the air would not yield the accustomed food . . . . but on the morrow some of the weaker-minded set out to gather the food but were disappointed and returned baffled, reproaching themselves for their disbelief and hailing the prophet as a true seer, an interpreter of God, and alone gifted with foreknowledge of the hidden future.

Interestingly, Philo sees himself as understanding scripture by means of inspiration :

> [*Cher.* 27] But there is a higher thought than these. It comes from a voice in my own soul, which oftentimes is god-possessed [θεοληπτεῖσθαι] and divines where it does not know. This thought I will record in words if I can. The voice told me . . . .

> [*Migr. Abr.* 34-35] I feel no shame in recording my own experience, a thing I know from its having happened to me a thousand times. On some occasions, after making up my mind to follow the usual course of writing on philosophical tenets, and knowing definitely the substance of what I was to set down, I have found my understanding incapable of giving birth to a single idea, and have given it up without accomplishing anything, reviling my understanding for its self-conceit, and filled with amazement at the might of Him that is to Whom is due the opening and closing of the soul-wombs. On other occasions, I have approached my work empty and suddenly become full, the ideas falling in a shower from above and being sown invisibly, so that under the influence of the Divine possession [ὑπὸ κατοχῆς ἐνθέου] I have been filled with corybantic frenzy [κορυβαντιᾶν] and been unconscious of anything, place, persons present, myself, words spoken, lines written. For I obtained language, ideas, an enjoyment of light, keenest vision, pellucid distinctness of objects, such as might be received through the eyes as the result of clearest shewing.

> [*Somn.* 2.164-65] Might it not have been expected, I ask, that these and like lessons would cause even those who were blind in their understanding to grow keen-sighted, receiving from the most sacred oracles the gift of eyesight, enabling them to judge of the real nature of things, and not merely rely on the literal sense? But even if we do close the eye of our soul and either will not take the trouble or have not the power to regain our sight, do thou thyself, O Sacred Guide, be our prompter and preside over our steps and never tire of

anointing our eyes, until conducting us to the hidden light of hallowed words thou display to us the fast-locked lovelinesses invisible to the uninitiate. Thee it beseems to do this; but all ye souls which have tasted divine loves, rising up as it were out of a deep sleep and dispelling the mist, hasten towards the sight to which all eyes are drawn; put away the heavy-footed lingering of hesitation, that you may take in all that the Master of the contexts has prepared in your behoof, for you to see and hear.

Josephus[18]

Josephus's concept of prophecy includes foreknowledge of the future (*Ant.* 8.15.6 §418):

. . . we ought to acknowledge the greatness of the Deity and everywhere honour and reverence Him, nor should we think the things which are said to flatter us or please us more worthy of belief than the truth, but should realize that nothing is more beneficial than prophecy and the foreknowledge [προγνώσεωςε] which it gives, for in this way God enables us to know what to guard against.

Josephus is not afraid to use "prophecy" and "prophet" for figures other than the OT prophets. Daniel is called a prophet (*Ant.* 10.11.4 §§245-49; 10.11.7 §§267-69, 280; 11.7.6 §322). Josephus notes particularly that John Hyrcanus had the gift of prophecy (*War* 1.2.8 §§68-69: *Ant.* 13.10.7 §299). He refers to a number of individuals as "false prophets," indicating that they had the persona of a prophet (*War* 2.13.5 §§261-63; 6.5.2 §285-87; 7.11.1-3 §§437-50; *Ant.* 20.5.1 §97; 20.8.6 §169; 20.8.10 §188; *Life* 76 §§424-25). He also refers to the use of the ephod by the high priests to determine the future as prophecy or prophesing (*Ant.* 6.6.3 §115; 6.12.4-5 §§254, 257; 6.5.6 §359; 7.4.1 §76).

Prophecy is also associated with the interpretation of scripture. The Essenes have those who foretell the future because they are educated (ἐμπαιδοτριβούμενοι) in the holy books and the sayings (ἀποφθέγμασιν) of the prophets from an early age (*War* 2.8.12 §159). Josephus himself is able to foretell the future, which in some way is associated with the written prophecies (*War* 3.8.3 §§351-53):

. . .suddenly there came back into his mind those nightly dreams, in which God had foretold to him the impending fate of the Jews and the destinies of the

---

[18]On Josephus and prophecy in general, see Rebecca Gray, *Prophetic Figures in Late Second Temple Jewish Palestine: The Evidence from Josephus* (Oxford: Clarendon, 1993) (cf. my review in *JTS* 45 [1994] 632-33); Robert Karl Gnuse, *Dreams and Dream Reports in the Writings of Josephus: A Traditio-Historical Analysis* (AGAJU 36; Leiden-New York-Köln: Brill, 1996).

Roman sovereigns. He was an interpreter of dreams and skilled in divining the meaning of ambiguous utterances of the Deity[19]; a priest himself and of priestly descent, he was not ignorant of the prophecies in the sacred books. At that hour he was inspired to read their meaning, and, recalling the dreadful images of his recent dreams, he offered up a silent prayer to God.

A question of particular concern is how Josephus regarded himself. He predicts to Vespasian that he will become emperor and claims that he had a reputation for foretelling correctly the future (*War* 3.8.9 §§399-408):

> He [Vespasian] found, moreover, that Josephus had proved a veracious prophet [ἀτρεκῆ . . . κατελάμβανεν] in other matters . . . he had foretold to the people of Jotapata that their city would captured after forty-seven days and that he himself would be taken alive by the Romans. Vespasian, having privately questioned the prisoners on these statements and found them true, then began to credit those concerning himself.

Why does he not refer to himself as a prophet?[20] There are probably two reasons for this. The lesser is that he identifies himself as a priest and claims to obtain at least part of his skill through this fact. The other is more subtle but also more likely: a blatant claim to be a prophet might cause a reaction. Some people were suspicious of prophets, but there was also preferable that others acclaim him than that he do it himself. It was not a case of modesty, for Josephus is far from modest. But in this case he probably thought that "the wise would understand," and those who did not were probably not important, anyway.

Joseph and Aseneth

Much is still debated about this writing. It is now generally thought to be Jewish, though it has been dated over a wide period of time. Many would have put it before 70, however. In it Levi is said to be a prophet:[21]

---

[19]Many want to disassociate dreams from prophecy; again, this is an artificial dichotomy not based on the biblical and other data (Grabbe, *Priests, Prophets, Diviners, Sages*: 88-89, 108, 116, 145-48).

[20]Although Gray only alludes briefly to this question, she notes that Josephus speaks of himself in prophetic-type language in several passages (*Prophetic Figures*: 37); Gnuse discusses the question at greater length (*Dreams and Dream Reports*: 21-33).

[21]The following passages are from the translation of C. Burchard in James H. Charlesworth (ed.), *Old Testament Pseudepigrapha* (2 vols.; Garden City,

[22:13] And Aseneth loved Levi exceedingly beyond all of Joseph's brethren, because he was one who attached himself to the Lord, and he was a prudent man and a prophet of the Most High and sharp-sighted with his eyes, and he used to see letters written in heaven by the finger of God and he knew the unspeakable (mysteries) of the Most high God and revealed them to Aseneth in secret . . . .

[23:8] And Levi saw the intention of his heart, because Levi was a prophet, and he was sharp-sighted with (both) his mind and his eyes, and he used to read what is written in the heart of men.

[26:6] And Levi, the son of Leah, perceived all these (things) in (his) spirit as a prophet, and he declared the danger (in which) Aseneth (was) to his brothers the sons of Leah.

Liber Antiquitatum Biblicarum (Pseudo-Philo)

The dating of this book is still debated, some willing to put it before 70[22] but the most recent treatment making it post-70 but no later than 150 CE.[23] At the end of his life the judge Cenaz (not in the OT, unless he is to be identified with Othniel's father) prophesies (28:6-10):

When they were sitting, the holy spirit came upon Cenaz and dwelled in him took away his sense, and he began to prophesy . . . . [He describe what he sees, indicating a vision of some sort, as well as giving its meaning.] When Cenaz had spoken these words, he awakened, and his sense came back to him. He however did not know what he had spoken or what he had seen.[24]

This agrees with Philo in envisaging prophecy as the result of the spirit taking possession of the prophet and describing the future.

NY: Doubleday, 1983-85) 2.177-247.

[22]Daniel J. Harrington, Jacques Cazeaux, Charles Perrot, and Pierre-Maurice Bogaert, *Pseudo-Philo: Les antiquités bibliques* (vols. 1-2; SC 229-30; Paris: Cerf: 1976) 2.66-74.

[23]Howard Jacobson, *A Commentary on Pseudo-Philo's* Liber Antiquitatum Biblicarum, *with Latin Text and English Translation* (vols. 1-2 [continuous pagination]; AGAJU 31; Brill: Leiden, 1996) 199-210.

[24]Translation of Jacobson (*Commentary*: 143-44).

Early Christian Writings

The writings of the NT and other early Christian literature give several examples of prophetic activity by living prophets or in some way presuppose that such existed. John the Baptist is identified as a prophet (Mark 6:15; 8:28; 11:32; Mat 11:9; 14:5; 21:26, 46; Luke 7:26; 20:6), as is Jesus (Mat 21:11; Luke 7:16, 39; 24:19; John 4:19; 7:40; 9:17). A passage of particular interest states , "Whoever welcomes a prophet in the name of a prophet will receive a prophet's reward" (Mat 10:41).

1 Corinthians has a number of references to prophets. Men who "pray or prophesy" should have their heads uncovered, while women who do the same should have their heads covered (11:4-5). Prophecy is considered a gift (12:10), though it can fail (13:8). In ch. 14, Paul uses the verb προφητεύζειν several times (vv 1, 3-5, 6, 22, 24, 31, 39) apparently in the sense of "proclaim a divine revelation."[25] Ephesians 2:20 speaks of the church being founded on the "apostles and prophets, with Christ Jesus himself as the cornerstone." 1 Timothy alleges that certain things were prophesied of Timothy before he was born (1:18; 4:14). Exactly what a prophet was is not said, but their existence is taken for granted.

The activities of prophets are described in several passages in Acts:

[11:27-28] At that time prophets came down from Jerusalem to Antioch. One of them named Agabus stood up and predicted by the Spirit that there would be a severe famine over all the the world; and this took place during the reign of Claudius.

[21:8-11] The next day we left and came to Caesarea; and we went into the house of Philip the evangelist, one of the seven, and stayed with him. He had four unmarried daughters who had the gift of prophecy. While we were staying there for several days, a prophet named Agabus came down from Judea. He came to us and took Paul's belt, bound his own feet and hands with it, and said, "Thus said the Holy Spirit, 'This is the way the Jews in Jerusalem will bind the man who owns this belt and will hand him over to the Gentiles.'"

The book of Revelation is an important witness to views about prophecy. The book describes itself as a prophecy (Rev 1:3; 22:10, 18, 19). It also tells about two end-time witnesses who also bear the title "prophet" (Rev 11:3-11):

And I will grant my two witnesses authority to prophesy . . . . They have authority to shut the sky, so that no rain may fall during the days of their

---

[25]*BAGD*: 723.

prophesying . . . . When they have finished their testimony, the beast that comes up from the bottomless pit will make war on them and conquer them and kill them . . . and the inhabitants of the earth will gloat over them and celebrate and exchange presents, because these two prophets had been a torment to the inhabitants of the earth.

Other early Christian literature also mentions prophets. The *Didache* has several instructions which presuppose the existence of such individuals but also tells how to tell the true from the false:[26]

[11:3-12] Now concerning the apostles and prophets. Act in accordance with the precept of the gospel. Every apostle who comes to you should be received as the Lord. But he should not remain more than one day, and if there is some necessity a second as well; but if he should remain for three, he is a false prophet. And when the apostle departs, he should receive nothing but bread until he finds his next lodging. But if he requests money, he is a false prophet. And you must neither make trial of nor pass judgment on any prophet who speaks forth in the spirit. For every (other) sin will be forgiven, but this sin will not be forgiven. And not everyone who speaks forth in the spirit is a prophet, but only if he has the kind of behavior which the Lord approves. From his behavior, then, will the false prophet and the true prophet be known. And every prophet who, in the spirit, orders a table to be spread shall not eat therefrom; but if he does, he is a false prophet. And every prophet who teaches the truth, but does not do the things he teaches, is a false prophet. And every prophet who has met the test—who is genuine—and who performs a worldly mystery of the church but does not teach others to do what he is doing, he shall not be judged by you. For he has his judgment with God—for the ancient prophets also did similarly. And whoever says in the spirit, "Give me money," or anything else, do not listen to him. But if he says that it should be given for others who are in need, let no one judge him.

[13:1-6] And every true prophet who wishes to settle among you deserves his food. Similarly, a true teacher also deserves, like the laborer, his food. Take, therefore, every first fruit . . . and give it to the prophets. For they are your high priests. But if you have no prophet, give to the poor. . . . Similarly with a jug of wine or of oil, take the "first fruit" and give to the prophets.

Finally, Mark 13:14 (//Mat 24:15) refers to Daniel as a prophet. This agrees with usage by Josephus and also fits 4QFlorilegium which puts Daniel alongside the great Israelite prophets (see above).

---

[26]The translations of the *Didache* come from Robert A. Kraft, *The Apostolic Fathers: A New Translation and Commentary, Volume 3 Barnabas and the Didache* (Nw York: Thomas Nelson, 1965).

Analysis

Our survey of the literature illustrates the complex nature of the problem before us. I shall attempt to steer a path through it. The first difficulty is that we seem to have two separate evaluations of the social situation: passages such as 1 Macc 9:27 appear to say that the prophets are in some sense in the past, yet other passages speak of "prophets" who are contemporary with the writer. How can these views be reconciled? We should not necessarily attempt to reconcile them since they may represent two different opposing views in the society of the time. However, we have the rather interesting fact that Josephus seems to exemplify both attitudes. He mentions the gift of prophecy and the existence of prophets (or alleged prophets) long after the biblical period. Yet he also states that the "exact succession of the prophets" (τῶν προφητῶν ἀκριβῆ διαδοχήν) had ceased after the time of Artaxerxes (*Ag. Apion* 1.8 §§40-41).

Although Josephus may not take a completely consistent line on this issue (as he also fails to do on some others), it is not immediately obvious that he is inconsistent in this case. "Succession" is the key word in the context of *Ag. Apion* 1.8 §§40-41, for he is making the point that a line extended from Moses the prophet of prophets to the succeeding prophets as far as the time of Artaxerxes. It was this line which assured the authority of the writings, but when there was no further "exact succession," sacred scripture was no longer written. Josephus's concern in this passage is to explain the status of certain writings; he nowhere suggests that prophecy as such had completely ceased.[27]

1 Maccabees 9:27 (along with 4:44-46; 14:41) seems to be more categorical. However, although it suggests that no prophets were around when it was written and implies that prophets are a thing of the past, it also accepts that there could be future prophets. If the polluted altar stones are hidden away until a prophet comes to tell them what to do, there is clearly no denial of the possibility that prophets could still arise. The writer of 1 Maccabees simply seems to represent the more skeptical view about prophets, in contrast to the more moderate perspective of Josephus who thinks they might even exist in his own time. In fact, Josephus identifies only a few non-biblical figures as prophets, calling a number of those in his own time "false prophets." He may not be that far away from 1 Maccabees, and he probably regarded the biblical prophets (especially Moses) as being in a special category compared to later prophets. Similarly, the Qumran texts do not give much indication of prophets apart from the ones of the Bible, but an endtime prophet seems to be envisaged, perhaps being identified by the community with the Teacher of Righteousness at some point.

---

[27]Cf the discussion in Gnuse (*Dreams and Dream Reports*: 21-27).

Prophets in the early church present a special case. The overwhelming impression is that prophetic figures actually existed (see below). They are spoken of in contexts which take their existence for granted and seem to relate to the actual life of a Christian community. Yet this situation lasts only for about a century as a generally accepted phenomenon. The *Didache* is concerned to make sure that only genuine prophets are supported, as if there were a lot of imposters. Prophetic figures were often problematic, and the developing church quickly outgrew them. Although periodically through history prophetic figures have arisen in the church, they have usually been greeted with suspicion by the hierarchy.

The model of the prophet which emerges from the Second Temple literature includes a number of characteristics. As in the OT, the prophet is someone who claims to have a message from God. He is likewise someone who gives information about the future, which is also the case with many OT prophets. This foreknowledge of the future is an important aspect of being a prophet according to a number of sources we looked at above.

Not only are the known OT prophets given the label "prophet" in the literature, but also Daniel is called a prophet in Josephus (*Ant.* 10.11.4 §§245-49; 10.11.7 §§267-69, 280; 11.7.6 §322) and Matthew 24:15. This label is not confined to Greek literature, for he is also called a נביא in one of the Qumran scrolls (4QFlor frag. 1, II, 3, 24, 5:3). Other OT figures are also called prophets, including Joshua (Sir 46:1; Josephus, *Ant.* 4.7.2 §165) and Noah, Isaac, and Jacob (Philo, *Quis heres* 260-61).

Philo conceived of several sorts of prophecy, but this was in the context of Moses as the supreme prophet. Prophecy was ordinarily thought of in terms of the divine spirit's taking control of the prophet and speaking through him (*Qui heres* 259-66; *Spec. leg.* 1.65). His own mind and speech are displaced by God who uses him as a channel. The prophet was a seer "gifted with foreknowledge of the hidden future" (*Vita Mosis* 2.269; see also 2.188-91, 288). Cenaz's prophecy (*LAB* 28) fits the picture of ordinary prophecy in Philo. Josephus similarly saw prophecy as giving knowledge of the future (*Ant.* 8.15.6 §418). Although he is cagey about referring to himself as a prophet, he claims several successes in predicting what would happen (*War* 3.8.9 §§399-408).

A major question is whether it is legitimate to take those passages which use the term προφήτης, προφετεύειν, and προφητεία as having to do with prophecy in the way so often understood by OT scholars. Most discussions see a difference in meaning between the Hebrew נביא, with the verb נבא (niphal and hitpael), and the Greek words. It is true that two words in different langues seldom have the same precise semantic area. Nevertheless, a study of προφήτης, προφετεύειν, and προφητεία and of נבא and its derivaties shows a large core of overlap. This is not only indicated by the translations of the Septuagint and the Greek Minor Versions but also by origin and usage. προφήτης (προφετεύειν, προφητεία) is usually derived from ἀφίημι (root φημί) which has to do with "speak"; similarly נבא is usually seen to mean "speak" in an etymological sense.[28] Etymology by itself cannot settle the issue, but it can be a clue to usage.

We also find that נביא takes in Daniel and the future prophet expected by the community in some of the Qumran texts (4QFlor frag. 1, II, 3, 24, 5:3). One could argue that this is only a later development and does not give us the right to discuss these developments in terms of "prophecy." If it could be shown that OT prophecy was totally divorced from such usage, that might be a legitimate argument, but the fact is that OT prophecy was itself a complex and multi-faceted phenomenon.

We find three different sources for prophecy during the Second Temple period: First, prophets deliver oracles received from the deity in a variety of ways, including visions and dreams; secondly, prophetic material is written by scribes or sages who may or may not be in a state of "inspiration"; thirdly, prophetic and other material is interpreted via a special sort of inspiration which goes beyond mere intellect or training. We can examine each one of these in more detail.

The prophetic dichotomy between the message delivered orally and the written oracle tended to have its impact in slightly different spheres (though these over-lapped to a large extent, as will be evident). The prophetic figure who stood up in the market place or marched into the official tribunal or made pronouncements in an assembly had an immediate impact. He (less likely, she) might be regarded as mad and rejected as such. Few wanted to take on the burden of possibly interfering with a divine message, however, so it was more likely that the individual was given some sort of hearing even if not an entirely sympathetic one. The exception was likely to be a high government official or ruler, especially if the oracle was a criticism of the ruling power in some way. For this reason, oracles were often viewed with suspicion by those in authority because they were more likely to cause trouble than to support the powers that be.

However, the impact was different when an oracle or prophecy became a part of the tradition, whatever its origin and form. Actual oracles delivered by a prophetic figure were apt to be remembered and circulated at the oral level, over a shorter or longer period of time, to emerge episodically at times when they seemed to be relevant. Such an oracle could also be written down and therefore develop a literary afterlife. In literary form the oracle might not be so widely known among the populace

---

[28]Cf. Helmut Krämer, "προφήτης A. The Word Group in Profane Greek," *TDNT* 6.783-96, especially 783.

(though writing the prophecy down did not prevent its continuing to circulate at a popular level), but it was more likely to have a long life and, since leaders of movements are often from the upper classes and thus literate, it could still serve to fuel popular expectations and attitudes.

But once the utterance of a prophet has been reduced to writing, it does not differ in any significant way from a prophecy or apocalypse created by a scribe. It is not always possible to distinguish prophecy from apocalyptic by formal characteristics; however, even if it is, the impact on the reader and its general credibility may not be any different. The fact that one takes a form already known from the OT prophetic corpus while another belongs to the genre apocalypse or a related form may be of indifference to the reader who sees both as revelation from God giving his will and perhaps hinting at what would come to pass hereafter. Therefore, the debate over the alleged differences is not particularly relevant at this point. They both function in society in much the same way.

It seems clear that some references to prophets and prophecy are literary constructs or at least likely to be. When past figures of Jewish tradition are ascribed attributes which are then said to be characteristics of prophecy, these could be the products of the writer's imagination. This probably applies to the statements in *Joseph and Asenath*. It might even apply to the descriptions of prophets in Acts which is giving an idealization of the early church at many points; however, the references elsewhere in the NT and in the *Didache* suggest that the writer of Acts knew of prophetic individuals in the early church even if the alleged prophecies of Agabus are a complete invention.

Philo is a curious case. He idealizes Moses and may be deducing certain of his description of prophecy from the Bible and from his own desire to make Moses a special sort of prophet. He is also clearly drawing on the ideas of prophecy and possession known in the Greco-Roman world.[29] But he additionally ascribes his own interpretative ability to the operation of the spirit in a way not altogether different from prophecy. He sees himself as an inspired interpreter. In this he seems to be in a similar position to the Teacher of Righteousness in 1QpHab.

This takes us to the next logical question: was there a difference between the writers of prophetic texts and the writers of apocalyptic texts? What was the experience of the writers as they wrote them? It has been suggested that the apocalypticists were not mere scribes toiling at their desks but rather that they had visions or mantic experiences which was the source of the information in their writings.[30] There seems to be no way to confirm this, but it is equally foolish to deny it at least as a possibility.

---

[29]Winston, "Two Types of Mosaic Prophecy" (n. 17 above).

[30]Cf. Rowland (*The Open Heaven*: 226-47) and the references he cites.

Synthesis and Conclusions

1. All our knowledge of prophecy and prophetic figures is literary. We have nothing from archaeology to give us data on the phenomenon, and it is impossible to do anthropological fieldwork on Second Temple Judah. Therefore, any judgments about the social phenomenon of prophets has to be deduced from literary sources. The material is of different sorts, which aids us in making a historical determination, but we have to recognize the state of our information.

2. We get more than one message from the sources about whether prophecy had ceased. Some writers seem to have regarded prophecy as a thing of the past which had long since elapsed; others evidently accept that prophets could exist in the present. The difference between the various writers is not necessarily all that great, however, since all sources seem to accept that a future prophet could arise, perhaps in an eschatological context. Additionally, those texts which accept the present reality of prophets do not usually see them as anything but an exception. Writers seem more willing to accept the presence of false prophets than of true ones. No writing explicitly rules out future prophets even when it seems to think that prophecy ceased at some time in the past.

3. Our sources show that the concept of prophecy in Second Temple writers was rather broader than many OT scholars would allow. Prophecy could especially be used of predictions of the future or messages about what would come to pass hereafter, even though these predictions might take a variety of forms (e.g., oral message from a prophetic figure, vision, dream, written oracle seen as authoritative).

4. Some of our sources talk of prophetic figures other than just those in the OT. These may be labeled "false prophets," but from a sociological viewpoint such a distinction is irrelevant. They show that some claimed the prophetic office and were accepted in such a role by some of the people. Just because those who described them took a different point of view does not oblige us to take over their prejudices uncritically. After all, if the followers of the "false prophets" had written the account preserved to today, we would instead have a picture of a "true prophet."

5. We cannot know for sure how written prophecies and apocalypses came about. In most cases, they do not look like actual oracles received by a prophet and then written down; rather, they look like the work of scribes. It may well be that the writers were reporting actual visions and writing under what they would see as divine inspiration or possession, yet we cannot be sure.

6. Inspired interpretation is a concept which arises during the Second Temple period. It is a new concept, coming about when some writings had become authoritative. Once established it takes its place alongside other forms of claims about prophecy.

7. Whatever the actual differences between prophecy and apocalyptic, at the literary level they seem to have functioned in a very similar way. People read both of them for knowledge of the future. Not only the ancient prophetic literature but also other sections of the Bible, such as the Psalms and even the Torah, were seen as sources for God's plans and a key to the future if the right interpretation could be found. This answer was found not in some sort of exegetical technique or "hermeneutical rules" but in the continued inspiration by the same spirit which had guided the prophets (whose numbers included Moses and David).[31]

---

[31]This paper was prepared for the SBL Sociology of the Literature of the Second Temple Period Group, co-chaired by Professors John Halligan and Philip R. Davies. An earlier draft was read to Professor Martin Goodman's seminar on Judaism in the Greco-Roman Period at Wolfson College, Oxford, 19 May 1998. I thank all three individuals for their invitations to present this paper to their respective groups.

Titus as a Pauline Letter

Donald A. Hagner
Fuller Theological Seminary

What would we make of the Letter to Titus if, contrary to majority opinion, it were accepted as a Pauline letter? This paper accepts Pauline authorship as a working hypothesis, a priori, and proceeds accordingly. Planners of the Theology of the Disputed Paulines Group decided that it would be a sound procedure to treat each of the Pastoral Epistles individually rather than to deal with the corpus as a whole. Earlier papers have thus been devoted to seeing 1 Timothy (Luke Timothy Johnson) and 2 Timothy (Gordon Fee) as Pauline letters. The current paper attempts to explore Titus along similar lines, reading it as a Pauline document.

A word is in order concerning the definition of "Pauline authorship." This expression, as I understand it, does not necessitate that Paul himself penned the letter, but that its content in some meaningful sense actually derives from the apostle himself. Not ruled out here is the possibility that an amanuensis, like Tertius (Rom. 16:22), or an associate of Paul is responsible for the document as it has come down to us, as in the case of most, if not all, of the undisputed letters of Paul. What is assumed by "Pauline authorship" is that Titus is generated by Paul and takes form during the last years of his life.

Although our interest is in the theology of Titus, that is hardly accessible to us apart from the living context in which it is articulated. For this reason the first part of the paper looks at the life-setting of the Letter to Titus. Only due attention to the life-setting of the letter can provide the key to the unusual content (by the standard of the undisputed Paulines) we encounter here. 1 and 2 Timothy have deliberately been excluded from this paper, so as to consider Titus in its own right.

I. The Life-Setting of Titus

We first review the basic data. Accepting Pauline authorship means that we can assume congruence between the narrative or literary world and the contextual or historical world of the letter. Paul writes to Titus, whom he describes as his "true [*gnēsiō*] son according to a common faith," which possibly refers to Titus being a convert of Paul's ministry (no account of this is given in Acts). Titus was a Greek (Gal. 2:3) and is referred to by Paul in 2 Cor. 2:13 as his "brother," and in 2 Cor. 8:23 as "my partner [*koinōnos*]" and "fellow-worker [*synergos*]," "for you [Corinthians]."[1] At the same time, it is clear that the letter has a public character, and will accordingly serve Titus well in accomplishing his mission.

At the conclusion of the letter, Paul writes that he is sending Artemas or Tychichus to Crete and that when that person arrives to take over the work, Titus is to join Paul at Nicopolis, where Paul will spend the winter. Furthermore, Titus is to send on their way both Zenas the lawyer and Apollos (3:12). Artemas and Zenas are nowhere else referred to in the NT. It should be stressed that the only alternative to some form of Pauline authorship that makes any sense of these specific details (or the sending of the letter to Crete), which can hardly have been invented

---

[1] The remaining references to Titus in the NT are: Gal. 2:1; 2 Cor. 7:6, 13, 14; 8:6, 16; 12:18 (bis); and 2 Tim. 4:10.

for the sake of (a too clever) verisimilitude,[2] is possibly some form of the fragment hypothesis, as for example elaborated by P. N. Harrison.[3] It must be admitted that the details of the beginning and end of the letter cannot be fitted into the narrative of Paul's work presented in Acts. On the other hand, Acts makes no claim of being exhaustive in its account of Paul, and the ending of Acts does not itself exclude the possibility of Paul's release and further missionary work.

In a sense, the opening words of 1:5 already define the letter and its contents. Titus has been left by Paul on the island of Crete "for this reason [*toutou charin*], so that you should put in order what remained to be done." What may be regarded as the decisive verb for the entire letter, because it expresses the burden of the document, is found here in the hapax legomenon *epidiorthōsē*, which means approximately "set fully right" or "put in order" (thus NRSV).[4] Paul had not been able to put in place the foundation that he deemed necessary for the ongoing stability and welfare of the churches (note: "in every town," 1:5) he had recently established there. It will be Titus's job to put things (*ta leiponta*, "the things that are lacking") in their proper order for the sake of the future welfare of the churches. Paul does not indicate why he was himself obliged to leave Crete, but Titus, his lieutenant, was left behind and charged with the appropriate responsibilities. This itself is not a procedure that is foreign to us from the undisputed letters.

The first and most important thing that must be accomplished in the putting of things fully in order is the appointing of elders (*presbyterous*) in each church. This leads naturally to the immediate listing of the qualifications required of these leaders (1:5-9). Further directions for the community are then furnished in the form of the Haustafeln of 2:2-10 (specifically to the "older men," "older women," "younger men," and "slaves") and the exhortation to be submissive to "rulers and authorities" (3:1).

Obviously appropriate to the communities of new believers is the repeated stress on the importance of "sound" or "healthy" doctrine (see 1:9, 13; 2:1,2, 8) and the importance of "good works" (1:16; 2:7, 14; 3:1, 8, 14). As Paul contemplates the reality that he will probably not see these Christians again, he puts great stress on these vitally important matters.

The emphasis on correct doctrine and on good works is hardly unknown in the undisputed Pauline letters, but the language and tone here are unique. If Paul writes at the end of his career, and of his life, to an associate charged with carrying on the work that had been done, and if Paul

---

[2]Frances Young argues, to the contrary, that these personal details are "the most compelling evidence for pseudonymity." "Nowhere in the authentic letters," she continues, "do we find Paul worrying about the missing cloaks, but that is just the kind of detail a forger would invent." *The Theology of the Pastoral Letters* (Cambridge: Cambridge University Press, 1994) 139. But why would a skilled forger invent the sort of thing *not* found in the authentic letters? Why furthermore would a forger write to individuals rather than to churches? Why to two different individuals? Why to Titus on Crete?

[3] *The Problem of the Pastoral Epistles* (London: Oxford University Press, 1921). This hypothesis of course has its own set of problems and has not proved attractive to many. More recently J. D. Miller has speculated that the Pastorals were the product of a school that made use of fragments of tradition. *The Pastoral Letters as Composite Documents*, SNTSMS 93 (Cambridge: Cambridge University Press, 1997).

[4]This is obviously analogous to the key expression at the beginning of 1 Timothy according to Luke Timothy Johnson, namely *oikonomian theou tēn en pistei* (1 Tim. 1:4), translated by Johnson, "God's way of ordering reality as it is apprehended by faith." "*Oikonomia Theou*: The Theological Voice of 1 Timothy From the Perspective of Pauline Authorship," presented at the Theology of the Disputed Pauline Letters Group in November, 1996.

made use of an amanuensis, say Luke or Tychicus, for example, then the special character of this material is not only possible from Paul but, indeed, makes quite good sense as coming from Paul. Why the situation assumed in Titus, as sketched here, could only exist in a period some considerable time *after* Paul remains unclear to me. It further remains unclear to me why Paul is regarded as so fixed in his ways that he cannot have written a different kind of letter when new circumstances required it of him.[5] Surely this is not the Paul of the undisputed letters who, if anything, often seems chameleon-like (Romans is hardly like 1 Thessalonians).

Titus and the community face a specific danger from a group described in rather general terms. They are first referred to as the "many insubordinate [*anypotaktoi*; cf. 1:6] men, empty talkers and deceivers, especially the circumcision party [*malista hoi ek tēs peritomēs*]"--that is, among the Jewish converts (1:10). That the majority of converts were Gentiles seems clear from the reference in 3:8 to "those who have come to believe in God." It is probably the Jewish converts who were upsetting entire households by teaching what they should not have (*ha mē de*) and for shameful gain (1:11). They accepted "Jewish myths [*Ioudaïkois mythois*]" and the "commands of men [*entolais anthrōpōn*] who reject the truth" (1:14). These problem people were members of the Christian community, and are to be disciplined: "they must be silenced" (1:11) and rebuked sharply, "in order that they may be sound in the faith [*hygiainōsin en tē pistei*]" (1:13). Probably the same people are in view in the exhortation in 3:9 to "avoid stupid controversies, genealogies, dissensions, and quarrels over the law [*machas nomikas*]." The reference to a factious (*hairetikon*) person in the following verse is, on the other hand, perhaps a more general warning. From this information, it is difficult to know the exact nature of the threat posed by these people, but in view may well be an early form of Jewish gnosticism.[6]

Paul thus writes to an associate, known to us from elsewhere, for the specific purpose of setting right all the things that remain to be done on Crete for the ongoing welfare of the churches. Without question the circumstances presupposed are new. Paul knows that the end of his life may not be far away. He had earlier revised his own earlier personal view that the parousia of Christ was to occur during his lifetime. The parousia, still a real expectation, lay sometime in the indeterminate future and measures were thus required to assure the survival of the churches. This was not a concern in the earlier, undisputed Pauline letters. Now, furthermore, he writes to *an individual* who has the main responsibility to look after matters. This too is unique among the undisputed letters, except for the letter to Philemon, which has its own very specific purpose that makes it atypical compared to the undisputed Pauline letters. Philemon is thus in a way similar to the Pastorals. We encounter in Titus, then, a life-setting that is quite different from the other Pauline letters. The new circumstances constitute a new set of contingencies to which Paul is required to write in a new way.

II. The Theology of Titus

---

[5]E. E. Ellis seems very right to me in his complaint concerning certain scholars who "envision a Paul who is a rather narrow personality unable to combine charism and church order and passionately fixated for life on a very few theological issues. In the end this Paul is too small." "The Pastorals and Paul," *ExpTim* 104 (1992-93) 46.

[6]On the opponents, see Michael Goulder, "The Pastor's Wolves: Jewish Christian Visionaries behind the Pastoral Epistles," *NovT* 38 (1996) 242-256.

There are two passages in Titus that are especially theological in nature, and to these we now turn our attention. We begin with a brief comparison between these passages and Paul's theology.

1.   Titus 2:11-14. For the grace of God has appeared bringing salvation to all, training us to renounce impiety and worldly passions, and in the present age to live lives that are self-controlled, upright, and godly, while we wait for the blessed hope and the manifestation of the glory of our great God and Savior, Jesus Christ. He it is who gave himself for us that he might redeem us from all iniquity and purify for himself a people of his own who are zealous for good deeds.

The initial link between God's grace (charis) and salvation (sōtērios, adj.), is very Pauline in tenor, despite the unique adjectival use of the latter to modify charis. The salvation in view is brought by Jesus Christ who is identified as Savior (sōtēros), the one who gave himself (edōken heauton) in order to redeem (lytrōsētai) us from all iniquity and to cleanse (katharisē) for himself a people of his own (laon periousion).

The eschatological hope of the return of Christ is retained in Titus 2:13 and is typical of Paul (1 Thes. 1:10; Rom. 5:2; Phil. 3:7). Indeed, this passage is very similar to Paul's statement in Phil. 3:20 that "from it (heaven) we await a Savior, the Lord Jesus Christ."

Titus 2:13	Phil. 3:20
prosdechomenoi . . .sōtēros hēmōn	sōtēra apekdechometha
Iēsou Christou	kyrion Iēsoun Christon

What is awaited, more specifically, is "the blessed hope" (tēn makarian elpida), a unique expression in the NT. For "appearance" (epiphaneian) we have the close parallel in 2 Thes. 2:8, which refers to "the manifestation of his coming" (tē epiphaneia tēs parousias autou).

The reference to Christ, who "gave himself" is familiar Pauline idiom (Gal. 1:4) as is the objective of that giving:

Titus 2:14	Gal. 1:4
hos edōken heauton	tou dontos heauton
hyper hēmōn	hyper tōn hamartiōn hēmōn

While Paul does not use the verb lytroomai, he does use the cognate noun apolytrōsis (Rom. 3:24, "the redemption which is in Christ Jesus"; 1 Cor. 1:30). The thought is the same as that conveyed by the verbs agorazō and exagorazō (e.g. Gal. 3:13; 1 Cor. 6:20; 7:23). The verb katharizō is also not used by Paul (but cf. Eph. 5:26, in connection with Christ's giving himself), but the idea of a cleansed or purified people as the result of the work of Christ is not foreign to him (cf. 2 Cor. 11:2; Eph. 5:26). Paul commonly uses the essentially equivalent verb hagiazō for the same idea (e.g. 1 Cor. 1:2; 6:11).

The Old Testament concept referring to "a people of his own" is reflected in Paul's quotation of Lev. 26:12 in 2 Cor. 6:16: "you shall be my people." The reference to good works is also Pauline in character: 2 Cor. 9:8 ("every good [agathon] work"; cf. Col. 1:10; Eph. 2:10). The call to holy living in 2:12 is of course very Pauline (for asebeia, see Rom. 1:18; epithymia is common in Paul; the verb sōphroneō, but not the adverb, is found in Rom. 12:3; 2 Cor. 5:13; dikaiōs and its cognates are common in Paul; eusebōs and its cognates, on the other hand, are not found in Paul).

The christological content of 2:13 is very striking: *tēs doxēs tou megalou theou kai sōtēros hēmōn Iēsou Christou*. If Paul is following the canons of grammar here, then Christ is referred to unambiguously as God. The two nouns, *theou* and *sōtēros*, are governed by a single genitive article, *tou*, and are thus to be understood as referring to a single person.[7] If two distinct persons were in view, this could clearly have been indicated by the use of a second definite article before *sōtēros*. The result of the text as it stands is that Paul is able to refer to Jesus Christ as "our great God and Savior." This is consonant with the alternate references to both God and Christ as *sōtēr* (cf. 1:3-4; 2:10; 3:4, 6).

There is only one place in the Pauline corpus where Christ is referred to as *theos*, namely Rom. 9:5. Here, however, the syntax is ambiguous because of the possibility of punctuating with a full stop after the words *ho christos to kata sarka*, thereby causing the following words to become an independent doxology.[8] Even if Rom. 9:5 does not refer to Christ as *theos*, Paul's high christology makes such a statement quite conceivable (cf., for example, Phil. 2:6; 1 Cor. 8:6; Col. 1:15).

2. Titus 3:4-8a. But when the goodness and loving kindness of God our Savior appeared, he saved us, not because of any works of righteousness that we had done, but according to his mercy, through the water of rebirth and renewal by the Holy Spirit. This Spirit he poured out on us richly through Jesus Christ our Savior, so that, having been justified by his grace, we might become heirs according to the hope of eternal life. The saying is sure.

This hymn-like passage, probably a preformed tradition, presents in exalted language the very heart of Paul's gospel, ending with a formula that emphasizes its importance. It is possible that Paul employs traditional credal elements here as he sometimes does in the undisputed letters.

The word for "goodness" (*chrēstotēs*) is frequent in Paul, and also in reference to God (Rom. 2:4; 11:22; cf. Eph. 2:7). The word for "loving kindness" (*philanthrōpia*), on the other hand, occurs nowhere else in the Pauline corpus. The reference to God as Savior (*sōtēr*) is unique to the Pastorals. (The only undisputed Pauline reference to Christ as *sōtēr* is in Phil. 3:20.) In v. 6 Christ is referred to as "our savior."

The noun *eleos*, referring to the mercy of God, is not used by Paul as often as the cognate verb (for the noun, cf. Rom. 11:30; for the verb, Rom. 9:15, 18; 11:31-32). The verb *sōzō* is, of course, very frequent in Paul, mainly in the passive, with God as the understood subject (an active instance with God as subject can be seen in 1 Cor. 1:21).

The ruling out of salvation by works is prototypically Pauline. Usually countered is "works of the law" (e.g. Rom. 3:20, 28; Gal. 2:16; 3:2, 10). The actual expression here (lit.

---

[7]See M. J. Harris, "Titus 2:13 and the Deity of Christ," in *Pauline Studies*, FS F. F. Bruce, ed. D. A. Hagner and M. J. Harris (Exeter/Grand Rapids: Paternoster/Eerdmans, 1980) 262-277. On epiphany christology, see A. Y. Lau, *Manifest in Flesh: The Epihpany Christology of the Pastoral Epistles*, WUNT 2.86 (Tübingen: J. C. B. Mohr, 1996).

[8] For the interpretation that the words following *ho christos to kata sarka* are best understood as referring to Christ, see B. M. Metzger, "The Punctuation of Rom 9:5," in *Christ and Spirit in the New Testament*, FS C. F. D. Moule, ed. B. Lindars and S. S. Smalley (Cambridge: Cambridge University Press) 95-112.

"works in righteousness" [*ergōn tōn en dikaiosynē*]) is unique, but conceptually Pauline (cf. Rom. 10:3; Phil. 3:9).

The ceremonial washing (*loutron*) of baptism is found elsewhere in the NT only in Eph. 5:26 (but cf. *apolouomai* in 1 Cor. 6:11) and *paliggenesia* is found only in Matt. 19:28, although Gal. 4:29 refers to being born according to the Spirit, and 2 Thes. 2:13 to "sanctification [*hagiasmō*] by the Spirit." The word *anakainōsis* is found elsewhere only in Rom. 12:2 (for the concept, cf. Rom. 6:4), where it refers to the mind (the cognate verb is found in 2 Cor. 4:16; Col. 3:10). The agent of the renewal here is the Holy Spirit. A similar association between baptism and the Spirit is found in 1 Cor. 12:13 and the Spirit makes alive according to 2 Cor. 3:6. Reference to the lavish (*plousiōs*, "richly") pouring out of the Spirit is unique to Titus, but for a similar idea with the same verb, see Rom. 5:5. For the Spirit as the gift of God, see 1 Thes. 4:8. The outpouring of the Spirit[9] is said specifically to be *dia Iēsou Christou tou sōtēros hēmōn*. The agency of Christ is clearly Pauline.

Very Pauline, of course, are the words "having been justified by his grace" (*dikaiōthentes tē ekeinou chariti*), as for example in Rom. 3:24, where the same verb and noun occur together;[10] most common in Paul is the comparable combination of the verb and the noun "faith."[11]

That Christians have become heirs is again Pauline (cf. esp. Rom. 8:17; but also Gal. 3:29; 4:7). Reference to "eternal life" (*zōē aiōnios*) is common in Paul (Rom. 2:7; 6:22-23; Gal. 6:8), as is the more frequent reference simply to "life" with the same meaning. "Hope" (*elpis*) is not used with "eternal life," (as here and in 1:2), but cf. Rom. 5:2, "hope of the glory of God" (cf. Col. 1:27, "the hope of glory;" Col. 1:5, "the hope laid up for you in heaven").[12]

To be noted is the reference in this passage to God, the Holy Spirit, and Jesus--to what would later be called the Trinity (cf. 2 Cor. 13:14).

The words "the saying is trustworthy (*pistos ho logos*)" almost certainly go with what precedes rather than with what follows. The formula is used in the other Pastoral Epistles (1 Tim. 1:15; 3:1; 4:9; 2 Tim. 2:11) where it is placed before the material referred to, and where it is used only for very weighty matters having to do with salvation. It is obviously a rhetorical expression used for emphasis.

In these two passages we encounter theological statements similar to those of the undisputed Pauline letters. These rich passages occur in the midst of the directives that Paul gives to Titus and the communities on Crete. In this way they serve as the indicative that grounds the imperative--exactly as in the other Pauline letters.

When put together, these passages present a basic theology comprising the following

---

[9]On this see Frances Young, *The Theology of the Pastoral Letters*, 68-70.

[10]Dibelius-Conzelmann admit that "as far as the words are concerned, the passage is reminiscent of the genuine Pauline epistles." *The Pastoral Epistles*, Hermeneia (Philadelphia: Fortress, 1972) 150.

[11]See I. H. Marshall, "Salvation, Grace and Works in the Later Writings in the Pauline Corpus," *NTS* 42 (1996) 339-358.

[12]According to P. H. Towner, "On the whole, the already-not yet understanding of salvation expressed by the Pastorals coincides with the Pauline model." *The Goal of Our Instruction: The Structure of Theology and Ethics in the Pastoral Epistles*, JSNTSS 34 (Sheffield: Academic Press, 1989) 140.

elements: God has acted in mercy and loving kindness to bring salvation to the world. This has happened through the appearing of Christ, who gave himself in death to redeem us from our sin. This salvation is a justification by grace and not by works of righteousness that we do. Salvation and the accompanying renewal are experienced through baptism and the Holy Spirit. God thereby purifies for himself a people with the status of heirs, who are to renounce improper behavior and to live in holiness. That people awaits the blessed hope of the appearing of Christ, who is God and Savior, when they will fully realize their inheritance of eternal life.

The Pauline character of this theology is readily apparent.[13] Practically all the constants of Paul's theology isolated by Gordon Fee are to be found here.

       (a) salvation is a divine activity, intiated and carried out by God the Father,

       (b) effected through the death of Christ, who is Son and Lord, and

       (c) made effectual by the gift of the Spirit,

       (d) as an act of pure grace,

       (e) and thus entered and sustained by trusting Christ; moreover, it is

       (f) an eschatological reality that is both "already" and "not yet";

       (g) its primary goal is a people for God's name,

       (h) which involves "turning away from wickedness and doing good."[14]

We may admit that at points the language is not typically Pauline idiom without accepting the conclusion of Dibelius-Conzelmann that we have here "the heiratic language of the Greeks."[15] If, as seems to be the case, we have here Pauline ideas occasionally articulated in vocabulary and ways that are not usual for Paul, that could well be not merely the new situation that is addressed, but the contribution of an amanuensis such as Luke. If the Pauline material here is simply the result of inherited tradition, as Dibelius-Conzelmann assert, one might well expect the language to be more exactly Pauline and not innovative.

III. The Theology of the Practical Instructions of Titus

Theology in Titus is not limited to the two passages just discussed.[16] The opening to the letter is much fuller than the openings of 1 and 2 Timothy, leading J. D. Quinn to conclude that Titus was the first letter in the corpus of the Pastorals, and that the opening was meant to serve as an introduction to the collected form of the three letters.[17] Here after Paul's formulaic reference to himself as *doulos* and *apostolos*, he relates his identity to (*kata*) "the faith [or shall we translate

---

[13] Towner concludes concerning Titus 3:4-7 that "neither the concept of salvation that emerges nor the teaching of justification diverges significantly from Pauline thought." *The Goal of Our Instruction*, 118.

[14] G. D. Fee, "Toward a Theology of 2 Timothy--from a Pauline Perspective," *SBL 1997 Seminar Papers* (Atlanta: Scholars Press, 1997) 737f.

[15] M. Dibelius and H. Conzelmann, *The Pastoral Epistles*, 143.

[16] D. M. Hay correctly remarks that "Because everything in the Disputed Letters is directly or indirectly linked to God's will, nothing in their contents can be ruled 'non-theological.'" "Pauline Theology After Paul," in *Pauline Theology*, vol. 4, "Looking Back, Pressing On," eds. E. E. Johnson and D. M. Hay (Atlanta: Scholars Press, 1997) 182.

[17] J. D. Quinn, *The Letter to Titus*, Anchor Bible (New York: Doubleday, 1990) 7.

pistis "faithfulness" here?] of God's elect" and the "knowledge [*epignōsin*] of the truth in accordance with godliness," "in the hope of eternal life." The rich trio of Pauline verities, faith, knowledge and hope, introduce the letter. The practical concern of godliness (*eusebeia*), proper conduct, is connected with knowledge from the very start. God, who does not lie (*apseudēs*), had promised this eternal life "before the ages" (*pro chronōn aiōniōn*). Verse 3 introduces an anacoluthon stating that "He made manifest at the right time his work in the preaching [*kerygmati*] of his word , which I myself was entrusted, by the command (*kat' epitagēn*; a Pauline expression, cf. Rom. 16:26; 1 Cor. 7:6; 2 Cor. 8:8) of our Savior, God" (1:3). Here Paul refers to his commission to proclaim the gospel through the preaching of God's word. This gospel stems from God who acts as Savior by bringing salvation.

In the next section (1:5-9), Paul presents qualifications for presbyter-bishops. This is the first thing that must be "set in order" (1:5)--indeed, it is basic to all the rest. The appointing of elders is important because Titus will not stay in Crete permanently (cf. 3:12). Others must be installed in leadership positions to carry on the work that Titus has begun. That the appointing of elders was a high priority item for Paul can be indicated by the reference in Acts 14:23 where Paul's revisiting of churches becomes the occasion of the appointing of elders (note: "in every church"). Such "overseers" are also referred to in Acts 20:28 (*episkopoi*), where their responsibility is to "shepherd" the church. They are described as "stewards (*oikonomoi*) of God" (cf. 1 Cor. 4:1). Such *episkopoi* are mentioned in the address of Philippians (1:1). In vv. 6-8 the character of leaders is in view, by means of a listing of vices and virtures. In v. 9 the presbyter-bishop's responsibility for holding to the truth faithfully is emphasized: having "a firm grasp of the word that is trustworthy in accordance with the teaching (*kata tēn didachēn*)," with the result that he is able to promote "sound doctrine" (*en tē didaskalia tē hygiainousē*) on the one hand, and "refute those who contradict it."

The section that follows (1:10-2:1) provides reasons why the appointment of doctrinally sound leaders is so important (*gar*, "for"). Among the threats to the churches of Crete one group is singled out in 1:10: "those of the circumcision" (*hoi ek tēs peritomēs*), who would also seem to be in view in the reference to those who give heed to "Jewish myths or to the commandments of men who reject the truth" (1:14). These are probably those who are influenced by Jewish legalists, hence the reference to the commandments of men (cf. Matt. 15:9). Note too the reference in 3:9 to "quarrels over the law (*machas nomikas*)." There is no typical Pauline polemic, such as in Galatians and Romans, concerning justification by faith. (One might expect an imitator of Paul to feel obligated to introduce one here!) Justification by faith, however, is plainly in view, as we have already seen, in the language of 3:5 and 3:7 (cf. 2:11). But by way of response here, Paul in typical fashion affirms the liberty of the Christian: "To the pure all things are pure" (1:15; cf. Rom. 14:14, 20; 1 Cor. 6:12). These false teachers (1:11b) are to be sharply (*apotomōs*; cf. 2 Cor. 13:10) rebuked "so that they may be sound in the faith (*hygiainōsin en tē pistei*)." Whether these Jewish Christians also have gnostic leanings--hence possibly explaining the reference to myths--is somewhat less certain. Note too, however, the reference to "genealogies (*genealogias*)" in 3:9.

The error of these people was not simply in doctrine, but also had its effect in their conduct. In a way that is similar to 1:15, Paul in 1 Cor. 8:7 can refer to a defiled conscience, where the context also has to do with liberty concerning food offered to idols. Again Jewish Christians might be likely to claim that they knew God (1:16), yet any such knowledge is ruled out by their conduct. They are in the end ill prepared "for every good deed (*pan ergon agathon*)." This Pauline expression (2 Cor. 9:8; 2 Thess. 2:17; Col. 1:10) is used again in 3:1, and is parallel to the more frequent *kalōn ergōn* (2:7, 14; 3:8, 14).

This major section ends in 2:1 with the exhortation to Titus to "teach what is consistent with sound doctrine (*tē hygiainousē didaskalia*). Titus, as a model, is himself (note the emphatic *sy*, and also 2:7, where instruction concerning the younger men is apparently applied to Titus himself) to exhibit the kind of faithfulness to sound doctrine that is required of an *episkopos*. The emphasis on sound doctrine is closely related to the emphasis on conduct befitting the church.

It is no surprise to encounter the *Haustafeln* that begins in 2:2, and continues to 2:10. Part of the setting fully in order that is assigned to Titus, in addition to the directly ecclesiastical, concerns the order of the household (thus addressed in order here are: older men, older women, young women, young men, slaves). The directions continue to contain exhortations to morality and correct doctrine is such a way as to show the close connection between the two.[18] The latter is in view in the following: in 2:2, the older men are to be "sound in faith (*hygiainontas tē pistei*);" in 2:3, the older women to "teach what is good (*kalodidaskalous*);" in 2:7f., younger men are told "in your teaching (*didaskalia*) show integrity, gravity and sound speech (*logon hygiē*)." The pronoun *seauton*, "yourself," in this sentence applies the exhortation also to Titus, who is also called to be a "model of good deeds (*typon kalōn ergōn*)."[19] In Phil. 3:17 Paul refers to himself as a *typos* in his manner of life. Note further that the younger women are to act in such a way "that the word of God may not be discredited (*blasphēmētai*)" (2:5), and that slaves are to act "that in everything they may be an ornament to the doctrine (*tēn didaskalian*) of God our Savior" (2:10). This household code reminds one of Paul not only in the parallel passages in Col. 3:18-4:1 or Eph. 5:22-6:9, but in specific aspects such as the subordination of wives to husbands (1 Cor. 14:34)

The main doctrinal passage that follows is closely linked by the introductory (postpositive) *gar*. The reference to the grace of God that appears for the salvation of all is related to the importance of appropriate conduct: "training (*paideuousa*) us to renounce impiety (*asebeia*) and worldly passions" that we might "live lives that are self-controlled, upright, and godly (*sōphronōs kai dikaiōs kai eusebōs*)." This section ends with reference to the goal of Christ's work: "to redeem us from all iniquity (*anomia*) and and to purify for himself a people of his own who are zealous for good deeds (*zēlōtēn kalōn ergōn*)." The interconnection between theology and exhortation could not be clearer.

2:15 emphasizes the assignment Titus has, if he is to set things in order: "Declare these things; exhort and reprove with all authority. Let no one look down (*periphroneitō*) on you." This leads to more instructions, now to the members of the churches generally. The first of these concerns obedience to rulers and authorities (3:1; cf. Rom. 13:1-7), and then, in 3:2, after other instructions (e.g. to be "gentle" [*epieikeis*]; cf. Phil. 4:5) the exhortation "to be ready for every good work (*pros pan ergon agathon hetoimous*)."[20]

---

[18]Frances Young writes: "Thus for all the parallels and suggested dependencies, the ethical teaching offered in these epistles would only carry conviction in a community that shared the fundamental theological presuppositions which undergird the discourse."*The Theology of the Pastoral Letters*, 39.

[19]See B. Fiore, *The Function of Personal Example in the Socratic and Pastoral Epistles*, AnBib 105 (Rome: Biblical Institute Press, 1986), 211.

[20]Towner rightly: "The modern interpretation's explanation of this concern for respectability, *christliche Bürgerlichkeit* [thus Dibelius], makes far too little of the part played by the mission or witness motive within the

The doctrinal section of 3:4-8a is introduced by a vivid contrast with the general description in 3:3 of the previous state of the readers before they experienced salvation (cf. Gal. 4:3f.; Col. 3:7; Eph. 5:8). A shift to the first person plural here identifies Paul and Titus with the new Cretan Christians as people "who were once foolish, disobedient, led astray, slaves to various passions and pleasures, passing our days in malice and envy, despicable, hating one another."[21] The salvation that brought them out of that state is introduced with an adversative *de* (3:4).

The last section of the body of the letter (3:8b-11) yet again exhorts Titus to diligence in his commission: "I desire that you insist (*diabebaiousthai*) on these things (*peri toutōn*), so that those who have come to believe in God may be careful to devote themselves to good works (*kalōn ergōn*)." To these words is appended the statement "these things are excellent and profitable (*kala kai ōphelima*) to everyone."

In v. 9 again we encounter a general warning (cf. 1:10-16) for Titus and the community to avoid certain things that are "unprofitable and worthless (*anōpheleis kai mataioi*)," namely "stupid controversies, genealogies, dissensions, and quarrels about the law." And in v. 10, directions are given concerning how to deal with a "divisive person (*hairetikon anthrōpon*)." After a first and second admonition (*nouthesian*; cf. Eph. 6:4), they are to reject (*paraitou*) this person from the community (cf. Rom. 16:17). This kind of person "is perverted and sinful, being self-condemned (*autokatakritos*)."

A final bit of exhortation and instruction is found among the concluding lines of the letter, where one last time good works come into view: "let our people learn (*manthanetōsan*) to devote themselves to good works (*kalōn ergōn*), for cases of urgent needs, so that they may not be unfruitful (*akarpoi*)."

From the material surveyed above then we may conclude the following. Paul writes "for the sake of God's elect," with the more specific purpose in mind of "the knowledge of the truth that is in accordance with godliness" (1:1). The last phrase comes to the very heart of the letter for it is precisely this that is the goal of the "setting fully in order" that is Titus's commission in 1:5. It points to the two concerns of theology and conduct and to the interconnection of the two. The teaching, the sound doctrine, the soundness in faith and speech, the adorning of "the doctrine of God our Savior" (2:10), on the one hand, are well balanced in the equal emphasis on being ready for every good work, zealous for good deeds, and stress on devotion to good works, on the other. Specific errors in doctrine are alluded to, as are specific moral failures. The answer to these problems comes in the repeated stress on correct teaching and the importance of good works.[22]

---

ethical structure of the author's thinking. It fails to recognize that social institutions were to be participated in because the Church's mission continued to be vital, *not* because it had diminished in importance or vanished altogether with the hope of the parousia." *The Goal of Our Instruction*, 198f.

[21]There is no need to conclude that Paul identifies himself with every sin that is listed here. *Pace* Young, *The Theology of the Pastoral Letters*, 127. He *is* happy, however, to identify himself as a sinner in need of the same redemption as the Cretans.

[22] The stress on good works in Titus should not be thought of as unPauline. See F. Young, *The Theology of the Pastoral Letters*, 29. As for the integration of theology and ethics, Towner concludes that "If the results of the present study stand, the Pastorals are less easily dissociated from Pauline thought." *The Goal of Our Instruction*, 256.

IV. Some Final Considerations

If the above description of the contents of Titus has shown that this letter contains Pauline theology, no attention has been given to the well-known aspects of the letter that are different from what is usually understood as Pauline--that is, the Paul known to us from the undisputed letters. The position taken here is that the new and unusual can be explained by the following: (1) in contrast to the undisputed letters, Paul here writes towards the end of his career; (2) he writes primarily (but not exclusively) to his lieutenant, who has the task of establishing the churches of Crete for the future, against heresy and unacceptable conduct; (3) he employed an amanuensis who had considerable liberty in formulating the letter.

The life-setting Titus cannot be compared to that of any undisputed letter of Paul. It should be no surprise then that this is *not* the Paul of the earlier letters. After surveying such things as the vocabulary, the style, and the syntax, I. H. Marshall concludes that "this is not the Paul that I know from the genuine letters."[23] That may be true, but it is nonetheless the "real" Paul, if we but allow for the later, different circumstances, and thus the different purpose, of these letters, and add to that an amanuensis--a Luke,[24] or a Tychichus[25]--who could be responsible for some of the more obviously Greco-Roman aspects within the letter.[26]

It is in fact the unique life-setting of Titus (and the other Pastoral letters) that is of fundamental importance in the difference between it and the undisputed letters. As J. C. Beker has taught us well, "Paul's hermeneutic of the gospel is so determined by the contingent situations he addresses that the coherent and abiding elements of his gospel cannot be abstracted from their interplay with these various contingencies."[27] But, according to Beker, the situation is different in the Pastorals: "the delicate balance in Paul between coherence and contingency is here displaced by a coherent structure that has no direct relation to the contingent crisis situation which the *P.E.* must face."[28] Is that really true when one considers the integrated character of the exhortation, theology and ethics that we have seen above? Frances Young puts it correctly when she writes that "any attempt to read these letters soon runs up against the fact that they come from a

---

[23]"Prospects for the Pastoral Epistles," in *Doing Theology for the People of God*, FS J. I. Packer, eds. D. Lewis and A. McGrath (Downers Grove, IL: InterVarsity Press, 1996) 139.

[24]For the classic defense of this conclusion, see S. G. Wilson, *Luke and the Pastoral Epistles* (London: SPCK, 1979). For a critique, however, see J.-D. Kaestli, "Luke-Acts and the Pastoral Epistles: The Thesis of a Common Authorship," in *Luke's Literary Achievement. Collected Essays*, JSNTSS 116, ed. C. M. Tuckett (Sheffield: Academic Press, 1995) 110-126.

[25]This was suggested by J. Jeremias. *Die Briefe an Timotheus und Titus*, NTD 9 (Göttingen: Vandenhoeck & Ruprecht, 1953) 8. But it could perhaps have been Artemus (3:12), about whom we know nothing, or someone whose name does not appear in the letter.

[26]On the role of the secretary in Pauline letters, see O. Roller, *Das Formular der paulinischen Briefe* (Stuttgart: Kohlhammer, 1933), and now, E. R. Richards, *The Secretary in the Letters of Paul*, WUNT 2.42 (Tübingen: J. C. B. Mohr, 1991).

[27]*Heirs of Paul: Paul's Legacy in the New Testament and in the Church Today* (Minneapolis: Fortress, 1991) 20.

[28]Ibid., 46.

particular social context in which there is an encompassing theological perspective which colours all the material which at first sight appears to be ethical or practical rather than theological in its principle thrust."[29]

This is not to deny that Titus (and the Pastorals) reflects a new situation. The question is simply whether that new situation is inconceivable in the 60s and whether it is inconceivable that Paul himself could have written a different type of letter to his deputy than the earlier letters he had written.

All seem to agree that the Pastorals reflect an adaptation of the Pauline tradition to new circumstances. We have here a creative re-expression of Pauline theology for a new situation. Beker refers to "innovative strategies that permit Paul to speak in a fresh manner" and even to "an appropriate reinterpretation and reinstatement of Paul's gospel."[30] Who could do this more effectively than Paul himself? Marshall imagines the kind of rubric that the unknown author could have written over the Pastorals: "These letters represent the kind of thing that I think that Paul would have to say to our churches today if he were still alive. . ."[31] Perhaps if Paul *were* alive and had to write to his assistants, facing these circumstances, he himself would have written more or less these things in more or less this way![32]

Many of the problems usually brought up can be explained on the hypothesis that Paul himself, rather than an imitator, is the adapter of Pauline theology responsible for the letter. Who more than Paul would have been interested in establishing the churches on solid ground, conserving the truth of the gospel, and maintaining conduct befitting the people of God? Towner appropriately suggests that the Pastorals can be understood as reflecting a "transitional stage in Pauline theology," where "the main aspect of transition involves the event of the absence or the departure or imminent departure of the apostle, which points to a transition from first to second generation Christianity."[33]

While it is clear that Titus is to some extent a public document, not enough has been made of the point that Paul writes to a trusted associate. The contents of the letter find their explanation in this balance. Paul does not have to defend his authority to Titus, as he does to the Corinthians. Titus accepts the absolute authority of Paul. The needs of Titus and the Cretan churches dictate the way in which Paul writes. This accounts for the stress on church order and the concern for the protection of orthodoxy, as well as the tone of assurance. Nor does Paul need to explain or elaborate his gospel to Titus. A few succinct references to credal material are sufficient for the purpose. Paul does not need to refute the errors of the opponents, as he does when he writes to the Galatians. Titus knows the errors and the required response; Paul need only allude to them.

---

[29]*The Theology of the Pastoral Letters*, 2.

[30] *Heirs of Paul*, 43; cf. 84.

[31]"Prospects for the Pastoral Epistles," 151.

[32]Cf. D. Guthrie: "the problem still remains to be settled how we may differentiate between a Paulinist steeped in the ten Paulines and Paul echoing his own earlier language, i.e. between a Pauline imitator and the apostle himself." *The Pastoral Epistles and the Mind of Paul* (London: Tyndale Press, 1955) 33.

[33]P. H. Towner, "Pauline Theology or Pauline Tradition in the Pastoral Epistles: The Question of Method," *TynB* 46.2 (1995) 312.

But would Titus be in need of the kind of reminders that Paul provides in his letter? Strictly speaking, the answer would probably be No. But given the importance that Paul put upon the work Titus had to do, these reminders are exactly what we might expect from him. Paul is not averse to repeating what is already known when he regards it as important. And it will not hurt the churches to be acquainted in some detail with the content of the commission that Paul has given Titus.

I have attempted in the above to treat Titus as a letter in its own right, apart from the two letters to Timothy, in the conviction that there are positive gains in doing so. I have therefore avoided mentioning the numerous parallels to those letters, comparing Titus rather with the Pauline letters. Titus has its own authentic life setting which should be taken seriously.[34] In my opinion, however, these letters need ultimately to be considered together. They stem from approximately the same time, in my opinion, were written by the same amanuensis, and address similar situations. The question of their derivation from Paul is finally to be dealt with not individually but for the three together.

In wondering how far the Disputed Letters may actually present Pauline Theology, David Hay asks: "Are there objective criteria on which historians or theologians can agree to decide if these letters re-present 'Pauline theology' or not?"[35] He does not answer his own question. But I suspect an implied negative response. It is perhaps too much to ask for "objective criteria" in this disputed matter. The fundamental problem is simply that there are aspects of these documents that are Pauline and other aspects that are unPauline. Before which of the two words shall we put "seemingly"? The present paper suggests that it be put before "unPauline."

It is, of course, impossible to prove that Titus was written by Paul. But, allowing fully for the necessary differences between this letter and the undisputed Pauline letters, the possibility that Titus stems from Paul through an amanuensis can by no means be confidently ruled out. Indeed, it remains for many a persuasive possibility. We end with the following words of Joachim Jeremias: "Das Entscheidende bleibt: auch hinter diesen Briefen steht als ihr Schöpfer die Gestalt des grossen Heidenapostels."[36]

---

[34]Beker's confidence that the Pastorals "never circulated separately" is hard to understand. *Heirs of Paul*, 36.

[35]"Pauline Theology After Paul," 195.

[36]*Die Brief an Timotheus und Titus*, 8.

The Discourse of Riches and Poverty in the Book of Ben Sira

Benjamin G. Wright III
Lehigh University

The rich and the poor have always been with us, part of the fabric of human society. But how societies have constructed the relative values of wealth and poverty, and how they have treated rich and poor people have varied over time and geography. Certainly contemporary discussions in the U.S. of what to do with the welfare system and how to tax capital gains are witness enough to some of the contemporary issues. The sages of ancient Israel were also aware of the socio-economic disparities between rich and poor, and sapiential literature has as one of its major concerns these disparities and how people ought to respond to them.

In the Wisdom of Ben Sira,[1] the sage's discourses on riches and poverty occur almost exclusively in material that Alexander Di Lella has called "recipe wisdom," that is, wisdom that "deals with everyday attitudes, beliefs, customs, manners, and forms of behavior one should have toward God, one's fellows, and the world at large if one is to live fully and well as a faithful Israelite."[2] For ben Sira riches and poverty are not metaphorical concepts that apply, for instance, to those who are spiritually wealthy or impoverished in the way that the author of the gospel of Matthew redacts the Beatitudes in his Sermon on the Mount. When ben Sira speaks of wealth and poverty, he talks almost exclusively in terms of people who do or do not have material wealth. The ways in which ben Sira constructs his

---

[1]In order to distinguish between ben Sira's book and the Jerusalemite sage himself, I use the Greek form of the book's name, Sirach, to designate the book either in its Hebrew or Greek versions. I denote the sage by his name, keeping in lower case the Hebrew word בן meaning "son of."

[2]Patrick W. Skehan and Alexander A. Di Lella, *The Wisdom of Ben Sira*, AB 39 (New York: Doubleday, 1987) 32.

discourse not only allow one insight into his own attitudes toward these conditions and how he wants his students to respond to them, but they also provide a glimpse into the social world of the sage, the rich and the poor in early second-century BCE Judea.

The Vocabulary of Riches and Poverty in Ben Sira

Since the Wisdom of Ben Sira is not fully extant in Hebrew, one must look both at the surviving Hebrew texts and at the Greek translation of ben Sira's grandson in order to get as complete an understanding as possible of the vocabulary of riches and poverty in the entire book.[3]

In general the terminology in the surviving Hebrew texts is what one would expect to find when one compares it to other wisdom texts like Proverbs, for example.[4] The major terms for poverty all appear in Sirach, ר ש, עני/ענוה, מחסור, דל, אביון. Ben Sira prefers the terms דל and ענוה/עני, however, to indicate poverty. מחסור only occurs once in the extant portions of the Hebrew (40:26), and it means to lack or want.[5]

The Greek translation uses two major word groups to translate the Hebrew words for poverty; these are derived from the stems πτωχ- and ταπειν-. The Greek translator, however, often seems to regard the two roots as synonymous. One example will suffice at this juncture. In Sir 13:20-23 ben Sira writes of the rich and the poor. He notes that "humility (ענוה/ταπεινότης) is an abomination to the proud, likewise the poor (אביץ/πτῶχος) are an abomination to the rich (עשיר)."[6] The surrounding context of the verse shows that the translator was not consistent in his renderings. At the end of v. 19 he rendered דל with πτῶχος. The same Hebrew word, דל, appears in v. 21 as ταπεινός, in v. 22 as ταπεινός again, and in v. 23 as πτῶχος as in v. 19. What complicates matters even more is that the Greek translator, while using these two word groups for *most* of the Hebrew references, also used a variety of other terms to render single instances of the Hebrew words. For instance, in 4:4 θλιβόμενον, one

---

[3]For the Hebrew manuscripts and the places where they are extant, see Pancratius C. Beentjes, *The Book of Ben Sira in Hebrew: A Text Edition of All Extant Hebrew Manuscripts and a Synopsis of All Parallel Hebrew Ben Sira Texts*, SVT 68 (Leiden: Brill, 1997).

[4]On the language of poverty in Proverbs, see J. David Pleins, "Poverty in the Social World of the Wise," *JSOT* 37 (1987) 61-78.

[5]In this single instance, the Greek has ἐλάττωσις.

[6]In Hebrew the passage is only extant in Ms A.

who is afflicted, translates דל. Thus, in those sections of ben Sira where no Hebrew survives, one must use caution when trying to reconstruct what ben Sira may have written in Hebrew in those places.[7]

When ben Sira wants to refer to rich people, he uses the term עשיר, for which the Greek always uses πλούσιος or πλοῦτος.[8] When, however, ben Sira writes about the material goods possessed by the rich, the situation becomes much more complicated. He uses several Hebrew terms indicating material wealth that are rendered by a variety of words in Greek. Other than words from the route עש"ר, ben Sira uses טובה, חרוץ, חיל, הון and מחיר. Unfortunately, the Greek translator did not render any of these terms stereotypically with any single Greek word. The most frequently occurring Greek equivalent is χρῆμα, which renders seven different Hebrew words, including הון, חיל, חרוץ and טובה. At the same time, חיל, for example, is translated by at least six different Greek words. The lack of consistency on the part of the translator for words indicating goods or possessions means that for those parts of the book lacking Hebrew one can get a good idea that such goods are the topic of interest, but what specific Hebrew terms lie behind the Greek may not be altogether certain.

Ben Sira's Attitude Toward Wealth and Poverty

In his analysis of poverty in the biblical book of Proverbs, J. David Pleins argues that the understanding of poverty in this book is quite different from that of the biblical prophets. He remarks that in contrast to the prophetic critique of wealth, "[t]he teachings of the wise support their concerns for social status, class distinction, and the proper use of wealth–concerns which are rooted in the values cultivated by the ruling elite from which the literature comes."[9] Di Lella notes that although Pleins was talking about Proverbs "much of what he writes applies also to such vocabulary in Ben Sira."[10] I will return to the issue of social location below, but in this section I want to look at ben Sira's general attitude

---

[7]For a detailed look at translation technique and the problems of reconstructing the Hebrew of Sirach, see Benjamin G. Wright, *No Small Difference: Sirach's Relationship to Its Hebrew Parent Text*, SBLSCS 26 (Atlanta: Scholars, 1989).

[8]In 13:2 there is a doublet in Greek for the Hebrew עשיר. ἰσχυρός appears in the doublet with πλούσιος.

[9]Pleins, 72.

[10]Alexander A. Di Lella, "The Wisdom of Ben Sira: Resources and Recent Research," *Currents in Research* 4 (1996) 172.

toward wealth and poverty in order to see if it is similar to that which Pleins finds in Proverbs and to provide the background for a discussion of the social location of ben Sira, his students, the rich and the poor.

Ben Sira recognizes that much of everyday living revolves around economic activity. People buy and sell, borrow and lend, acquire wealth and lose it. Yet in this daily activity of acquisition and loss, ben Sira attributes one's fortunes to God. "Good things and bad, life and death, poverty (רישׁ) and wealth, come from the Lord," he says (11:14).[11] In the next breath, however, ben Sira can also claim that "The Lord's gift remains with the devout, and his favor brings lasting success" (ורצנו יצלח לעד Ms A). Whatever success God's favor brings, this verse does not seem to be a blanket endorsement of wealth *per se*. At the least, one's economic condition in this life is fleeting. In this same poem, ben Sira encourages trust in God "for it is easy in the sight of the Lord to make the poor rich, suddenly in an instant" (11:21).

When he speaks about riches, ben Sira is both cautionary and critical. Most of his cautions have to do with the use of wealth and the potentially corrupting nature of money and its acquisition. His criticism of wealth, however, is not directed at simply having money. In fact having wealth can be a good thing; what is important is the behavior of the wealthy person and what is done with wealth. In chap. 40, ben Sira writes about the good things in life. Speaking of wealth he says, "Riches (חיל) and strength build up confidence" (40:26 Ms B). But even though no criticism of wealth is implied in this colon, the next continues "but the fear of the Lord is better than either." These two cola in short epitomize ben Sira's understanding of wealth and riches. "Riches (העושר) are good if they are free from sin" (13:24 Ms A).

Unfortunately, ben Sira realizes, such is all too often not the case, both individually and corporately. International and political strife can be caused by wealth (10:8). Riches and money by their very nature can be corrupting and lead one to transgress, especially where the poor are concerned. Thus, it is the rich person who sins that God despises; he does

---

[11]Most translations are taken from the New Revised Standard Version. In each case, I have consulted both the Hebrew and Greek texts for text-critical difficulties that affect the overall meaning of the passage. In some cases I have also used or adapted the translation given in Skehan and Di Lella's Anchor Bible Commentary.

not hate the rich person because he/she is rich. But, ben Sira knows that "gold has ruined many and has perverted the minds of kings" (8:2).

There is constant temptation in the arena of business. A number of passages in Sirach emphasize caution and proper conduct in commercial activity. One should not be ashamed "of accuracy of scales and weights and acquiring much or little; of profit from dealing with merchants" (42:4-5). Thus, acquiring wealth in business is perfectly acceptable. In fact, ben Sira indicates that becoming wealthy is desirable. Sir 19:1 comes in the middle of a passage on self control. If one lacks self control, ben Sira says, he will not become rich. Business relationships breed sin, however, and gold can be a stumbling block even for the upright. In perhaps his most direct passage on the problems of business, ben Sira says in 26:29-27:3,[12]

26:29 A merchant can hardly keep from wrongdoing,
    nor is the tradesman innocent of sin.
27:1 Many have committed sin for gain,
    and those who seek to get rich will avert their eyes.
27:2 As a stake is driven firmly into a fissure between stones,
    so sin is wedged between selling and buying.
27:3 If a person is not steadfast in the fear of the Lord,
    his house will be quickly overthrown.

The potential pitfalls of wealth are not only present in the process of its acquisition. Once one has wealth numerous difficulties remain. Many who acquire wealth become miserly, and ben Sira condemns the wealthy miser in chap. 14. "Riches (עושר Ms A/ ὁ πλοῦτος) are inappropriate for a small-minded person, and of what use is wealth to a miser...The miser is an evil person; he turns away and disregards people. The eye of the greedy person is not satisfied with his share; greedy injustice withers the soul. A miser begrudges bread, and it is lacking at his table" (14:3, 8-10 Ms A). Chap. 31 contains a long poem on the difficulties of being rich. It begins by noting that wealth creates anxiety and loss of sleep (31:1-2) and goes on

---

[12]Martin Hengel, *Judaism and Hellenism* (Philadelphia: Fortress, 1974) 137, remarks about this passage that ben Sira "is particularly critical of the merchant, who is presumably often still non-Jewish and whose profession, unlike that of divinely sanctioned agriculture (7.15; 20.28), brings with it extreme danger." I am not sure what the evidence is that would establish that these merchants are "presumably often still non-Jewish." Ben Sira is generally critical of thoughtless rushing after wealth. The two passages that Hengel cites here, 7:15 and 20:28, although they speak positively of farm labor and hard work, are not enough, in my estimation, to sustain a social reconstruction of the Jewish farmer versus the largely non-Jewish merchant, which seems to be where Hengel is going in his analysis.

to indict the greedy. "The lover of gold will not be free from sin; whoever pursues profit will be led astray by it. Many have they been who were entrapped by gold, who put their confidence in corals" (31:5-6).[13] Yet for ben Sira, some are rich who are also blameless, and they will be blessed (31:8). But through a series of rhetorical questions at the end of the poem, ben Sira seems to indicate the rarity of someone who is rich and blameless.

> 31:9 Who is he [who is rich and blameless] that we may praise him?
> For he has done wonders among his people.
> 31:10 Who has been tested by it [gold] and found perfect?
> Let it be for him a ground for boasting.
> Who has had the power to transgress and did not transgress,
> and to do evil and did not do it?
> 31:11 His property will be established,
> and the assembly will proclaim his acts of charity.

How then should one respond to having wealth? Ben Sira seems to enjoin two attitudes. The first is implicit in the passages I discussed above. Wealth should be kept in perspective. Human fortune is determined by God, and it can change rapidly (11:14-21). Not all wealth is good, only that acquired justly. The wealthy who unjustly accumulate their riches will both lose what they have gotten and experience God's judgment. "Do not depend on dishonest wealth; it will not benefit you in the day of wrath" (5:8).[14] Wealth gotten dishonestly will "dry up like a river" (40:13). What is more important is the keeping of God's commandments, in ben Sira's language, "the fear of the Lord" (40:26). But even mundane matters, like one's health, may occasionally take precedence over having riches. In Sir 30:14-17, the sage teaches that when it comes to one's health, poverty and health are to be preferred to wealth and sickness.

The second response desired by ben Sira is the proper use of what one has. The primary responsibility of those who have is almsgiving. Ben Sira explicitly connects the obligation to give alms to the poor with the

---

[13]I have followed the translation of Skehan and Di Lella here because of the textual difficulties attached to this section. For an explanation of the problems, see Skehan and Di Lella, 380.

[14]I have followed Hebrew Ms A here for "day of wrath." The Greek has "day of calamity." Sir 5:7 concerns the sudden nature of God's judgment in the "time of punishment" (ביום נקם Ms A, בעת נקם Ms C). The context, then, argues for a picture of God's judgment, not simply an unfortunate circumstance.

biblical commandments. In Sir 29:8-13, a short poem on giving to the poor, ben Sira says that one should help the poor "for the commandment's sake" (v. 9).[15] One should "store up almsgiving in your treasury and it will rescue you from every disaster" (v. 12). The background of this poem is most likely Deut 15:7-11, which promises in v. 10, "Give liberally and be ungrudging when you do, for on this account the Lord your God will bless you in all your work and in all that you undertake." In 17:22 ben Sira compares almsgiving to a "signet ring" with God. In contrast to liberal giving, one is not to take away the little that the poor have. Sirach 4 begins with a short litany of "do not's." Among other things, one should not "cheat the poor of their living," "grieve the hungry," or "turn your face away from the poor," because if one of these should curse you "their creator will hear their prayer."[16] In a more severe indictment of taking from the poor, Sir 34:24-27 calls the one who would impoverish the poor a murderer.

> 34:24 Like one who kills a son before his father's eyes
>   is the person who offers a sacrifice from the property of the poor.
> 34:25 The bread of the needy is the life of the poor;
>   whoever deprives them of it is a murderer.
> 34:26 To take away a neighbor's living is to commit murder.
> 34:27 To deprive an employee of wages is to shed blood.

In much the same way that he did not condemn nor exalt the rich for being wealthy, ben Sira does not despise the poor for being poor, nor does he elevate their status by virtue of their poverty. Ben Sira is very realistic about the place of the poor in his world, and although he nowhere indicates that the poor are pious because they lack an abundance of possessions, in the face of their low status he recognizes that they have some special place in God's eyes. The life of the poor is difficult. Whereas the rich person, when he rests, can enjoy the finer things of life, the poor person "works hard to make a meager living, and if he ever rests he becomes needy"

---

[15]In this short poem, Sirach has the second person pronoun, indicating that ben Sira is speaking to his students. In other passages one finds third person pronouns. Ben Sira's students are probably not to be counted among the wealthy, but they apparently have enough means to warrant ben Sira's encouragement to take care of the poor. More on the social issue will be said below.

[16]This passage most likely has Exod 22:21-23 in the background.

(31:4). Unlike the mourner who recovers from sorrow, "the life of the poor weighs down the heart" (38:19).

In addition to the difficulties inherent in a life of poverty, ben Sira observes that those who are rich often make the lot of the poor worse, and thus, the poor often have hardship piled upon hardship. Sirach 13-14 constitutes a major block of material concerned with rich and poor. One needs to read these two chapters and other passages like them with caution, however, since in the beginning of chap. 13, in which he uses the second person singular "you," ben Sira is addressing his students, who are almost certainly not poor themselves, about the dangers of interacting with rich people.[17] Later in the chapter, beginning in v. 15, he switches to third person singular, which probably indicates more general observations about the nature of the relationship between rich and poor. Vv. 15-24, in which he concentrates on the social predisposition accorded to the rich, contain ben Sira's more universal reflections on this problem. He begins by observing that all creatures prefer their own kind; this includes rich and poor. "What peace is there between rich and poor?" he asks (v. 18). Generally the poor are "an abomination to the rich" (v. 20). The rich, however, receive preferential treatment by those around them.

> 13:21 When the rich person totters, he is supported by a friend,
> but when the poor (דל) falls he is pushed away even by friends.
>
> 13:22 If the rich person slips, many come to the rescue,
> he speaks unseemly words, but they justify him.
> If the poor person (דל) slips, they even criticize him,
> he talks sense, but he is not even given a hearing.
>
> 13:23 The rich person speaks, and all are silent; they extol to the clouds what he says.
> The poor person (דל) speaks and they say, "Who is this fellow?"
> And should he stumble, they even push him down.
>
> 13:24 Riches are good if they are free from sin;
> poverty (העוני) is evil only in the opinion of the ungodly.

---

[17]The mistake of reading passages of this sort as concerning the relationship between rich and poor is made, for example, by Viktor Tcherikover in *Hellenistic Civilization and the Jews* (New York: Atheneum, 1982, reprint of 1959 Jewish Publication Society edition). On p. 147, Tcherikover takes Sir 8:1-2, a passage clearly addressed to ben Sira's students, to indicate the tenuous position of the poor vis-à-vis the rich.

Because of their lowly place in life, ben Sira argues that God, though not counting their poverty as piety, does give them a special hearing when they pray. The "do not's" of chap. 4 conclude with "for if in bitterness of soul some should curse you, their creator will hear their prayer." In a long section of chap. 35, ben Sira is concerned with God's justice, especially toward the poor and oppressed. He insists that God shows no partiality, not even to the poor/humble (דל). It is the prayer of the wronged that he hears. The prayer of the widow and the orphan he will not ignore (vv. 16-17). In v. 21 he returns to the poor. "The prayer of the poor/humble (דל) pierces the clouds, and it will not rest until it reaches its goal. It will not desist until the Most High responds and does justice for the righteous, and executes judgment." It seems as if ben Sira is trying to accomplish two goals in this section while walking a rather thin line. The first is to insist that God does not prefer one person over any other. The second, however, stands somewhat in contrast to the first. He wants to say at the same time that God does, in fact, listen particularly to the prayers of the oppressed and downcast. This latter position affirms the claims made in places like Exodus 22 that God listens and responds to the prayers of the marginalized, and he judges those who oppress them.

Being in poverty, however, is not the worst thing that could happen according to ben Sira. As we saw above, to be poor and healthy is to be preferred to being rich and diseased. In Sir 29:28 ben Sira decries the necessity of living off of borrowed means. In fact, he says in 29:21-22, "The necessities of life are water, bread and clothing, and also a house to assure privacy. Better is the life of the poor (πτωχοῦ) under one's own roof than sumptuous food in the house of others."[18] Poverty is certainly not a desirable condition, but there are apparently worse fates. The one whom ben Sira calls "poor" has *something* at least—a roof, *some* bread or clothing. The kind of destitution that leads to begging is a worse situation than being in poverty. "My child," ben Sira writes, "do not live the life of a beggar; it is better to die than to beg" (40:28). The poor can sometimes do more than just survive; they can find honor as well. Whereas the rich person is accorded honor for wealth, the poor person's knowledge brings

---

[18]The passage is not extant in any of the Hebrew manuscripts.

acclaim. "One who is honored in poverty, how much more in wealth! And one dishonored in wealth, how much more in poverty" (10:31).[19]

When one looks at ben Sira's attitudes toward rich and poor, his outlook is similar to that which Pleins describes for Proverbs. There are occasions where ben Sira recognizes the class conflict that is inherent in his world. There is no peace between rich and poor, he observes. But despite his understanding that the rich and poor are at odds, ben Sira is no social critic. He does not blame the rich for creating the circumstances that oppress the poor, nor does he advocate any measures, other than almsgiving, that would redress the economic disparities that he sees around him. One's place in life is decreed by God, and what sets one person apart from another before God is not station in life, wealth or poverty, but keeping the commandments, fearing the Lord. Ben Sira is not engaging in the kind of social critique that the biblical prophets are.

This situation is somewhat curious when one looks at ben Sira's view of himself, because he clearly sees himself somewhat in the model of the biblical prophet. He understands his own teaching as being "poured out like prophecy" (24:33). The prayer in chap. 36 has a number of prophetic features. The famous section on the sage in chap. 39 also has prophetic elements woven into the role of the sage.[20] But when ben Sira looks at rich and poor as categories of existence, his analysis is pretty standard wisdom fare. He does not seek to change the status quo, but rather he is more pragmatic. He does, however, have the biblical commandments in front of him, and they exhort care for the poor and oppressed. He specifically enjoins his students, who are apparently in a position to do so, to fulfill the commandments, to look out for those who are marginalized. Ben Sira's and his student's own social positions seem to enable them to do little more than that. They are not agents of social change.

---

[19]On the larger poem in which this verse is embedded, see Alexander A. Di Lella, "Sirach 10:19-11:6: Textual Criticism, Poetic Analysis, and Exegesis," in C. L. Meyers and M. O'Connor, eds., *The Word of the Lord Shall Go Forth: Essays in Honor of David Noel Freedman in Celebration of His Sixtieth Birthday* (Winona Lake, IN: ASOR-Eisenbrauns, 1982) 157-164 and Maurice Gilbert S. J., "Wisdom of the Poor: Ben Sira 10,19-11,6," in Pancratius C. Beentjes, ed., *The Book of Ben Sira in Modern Research: Proceedings of the First International Ben Sira Conference 28-31 July 1996 Soesterberg, Netherlands* (Berlin: Walter de Gruyter, 1997) 153-169.

[20]The terminology in 39:6-8 recalls the prophetic image of chap. 24. See Randal A. Argall, *1 Enoch and Sirach: A Comparative Literary and Conceptual Analysis of the Themes of Revelation, Creation and Judgment,* EJL 8 (Atlanta: Scholars, 1995) 87-88.

One potentially fruitful avenue of investigation of ben Sira's attitudes toward rich and poor would be to locate those attitudes in the system of honor and shame evident in other aspects of ben Sira's thought. Claudia Camp understands the notion of honor as "the ability of a man to control the defining attributes of his life over against the challenge of others to subvert that control. The defining attributes may be seen as socially determined signs of value and power: one's women, one's property (i.e. one's household in both personal and impersonal dimensions), one's political influence, one's body, one's reputation or name."[21] Camp has investigated ben Sira's views of women in this regard.[22] Alongside women and reputation, two issues that are important for ben Sira, one could certainly place wealth and poverty. Several of the passages discussed above indicate that one's riches or lack of them, like one's women, carry the potential for honor and shame vis-à-vis the larger community. It is not possible here to give this problem the detailed consideration it deserves, so several examples must suffice. Although wealth and poverty may not make any difference in the eyes of God, they certainly can matter in the eyes of one's fellows. In the series of oppositions in 13:21-23 ben Sira observes that rich people receive recognition from others, even if they "speak unseemly words," while at the same time the poor are ignored when they speak (13:22). Even though a certain social recognition and honor might come as a result of one's material wealth, true honor, for ben Sira, comes in the keeping of the commandments, and that is possible for rich or poor. The righteous rich person of Sirach 31 will be extolled for his acts of charity. Sir 10:30-31, two verses that come at the end of a poem on honor, claim that it is knowledge and wisdom rather than possessions that bring honor to the poor. "The wisdom of the humble (דל) lifts their heads high and seats them among the great" (11:1). Where riches would seem to bring shame for ben Sira is in the improper acquisition and use of

---

[21]Claudia V. Camp, "Honor and Shame in Ben Sira: Anthropological and Theological Reflections," in Beentjes, *The Book of Ben Sira in Modern Research*, 173.

[22]On honor and shame in Sirach, see in addition to the study cited in n. 21 Claudia Camp, "Understanding a Patriarchy: Women in Second Century Jerusalem Through the Eyes of Ben Sira," in A.-J. Levine, ed., *Women Like This: New Perspectives on Jewish Women in the Greco-Roman World*, EJL 1 (Atlanta: Scholars, 1991) 1-39, and David A. deSilva, "The Wisdom of Ben Sira: Honor, Shame and the Maintenance of Minority Cultural Values," paper presented in the Hellenistic Judaism Section, Society of Biblical Literature Annual Meetings (Philadelphia, 1995).

possessions. Wealth is inappropriate for the miser (14:3). "Many have come to ruin because of gold, and their destruction has met them face to face" (31:3). Certain kinds of behavior bring shame on the poor person. In Sir 25:2 ben Sira notes that he hates a "pauper (πτωχόν) who boasts." Perhaps most shameful is having to live by depending on others. "My child, do not lead the life of a beggar; it is better to die than to beg. When one looks to the table of another, one's way of life cannot be considered a life" (40:28-29).[23]

Riches, Poverty and Social Location

Ben Sira's comments on riches and poverty and on relationships with rich and poor people provide important material for trying to sketch his and his students' social location as well as that of the people whom he calls rich and poor, people who occupy social positions different from those of the scribes. Of course ben Sira as a scribe/sage, and one who apparently trains budding sages, has a very elevated view of the role of the sage in Jerusalemite society.[24] It is possible, however, to penetrate some of ben Sira's language to see where he and his trainees fit in the social landscape. Several studies have suggested that the scribe/sage is essentially part of a "retainer" class that is in the employ of the rich and powerful and dependent on them for livelihood.[25] The scribe/sage functions as "a kind of counsellor or technical expert for the powerful; he seems to be ready

---

[23]The Hebrew is very difficult. On the textual problems in Ms B and Masada, see Skehan and Di Lella, 467. They adopt the reading of Masada as corrected by John Strugnell, "Notes and Queries on the 'Ben Sira Scroll from Masada,'" in W. F. Albright Volume, A. Malamat, ed., *Eretz Israel* 9 (1969) 112. The Greek text uses ἐπαίτησις "begging" and ἐπαιτέω "to beg."

[24]Patrick Tiller in an as yet unpublished paper, "Politics and the High Priesthood in Pre-Maccabean Judea" (Dec. 1997 draft; my thanks to the author for making available a copy of the paper), notes that the term "class" is not the most appropriate term to use. Ben Sira is really concerned with power relationships rather than social class in any modern sense. I use the term "class" here for convenience. The term "scribe/sage" is used by Richard Horsley and Patrick Tiller as a description of ben Sira's office. For an explanation see their jointly authored paper, "Ben Sira and the Sociology of the Second Temple," paper presented in The Sociology of the Second Temple Group, Society of Biblical Literature Annual Meetings (San Francisco, 1992). Other scholars prefer either scribe or sage. I use the designation scribe/sage here in order to try to avoid any terminological confusion.

[25]Although he does not use the sociological category "retainer class," this is, in effect, what Daniel J. Harrington seems to suggest in his article "The Wisdom of the Scribe According to Ben Sira," in George W. E. Nickelsburg and John J. Collins, eds., *Ideal Figures in Ancient Judaism*, SCS 12 (Chico, CA: Scholars, 1980) 184-185. Horsley and Tiller explicitly use this language of ben Sira in "Ben Sira and the Sociology of the Second Temple," as does Tiller in "Politics and the High Priesthood in Pre-Maccabean Judea."

and willing to adjudicate disputes even in foreign lands."[26] He also acted as a kind of mediator between his rich and powerful patrons, primarily priests according to Richard Horsley and Patrick Tiller, and ordinary Jews. The scribes/sages devoted themselves to the study of the Jewish law and ancient wisdom and were in that sense guardians of the tradition. Such a position was not achieved by a disinterested study of the text. According to ben Sira, the scribe/sage is set apart by such study. "How different the one who devotes himself to the study of the law of the Most High" (39:1). The sage approaches God in prayer and repentance and "[i]f the Lord is willing, he will be filled with the spirit of understanding. He will pour forth wisdom of his own and give thanks to the Lord in prayer" (39:5-6).[27] His is a divinely inspired wisdom.

In their role as guardians and interpreters of the law, the sages sometimes had obligations to go beyond mediation to advocacy.[28] These two competing functions, service to the sage's aristocratic patrons and guardianship of the Israelite religious tradition, most likely created some rather ticklish situations. It was the sage's responsibility to blunt the desires of the rich and powerful against the poor. In his own life not only must he give to the poor from what he has, but if called upon he must also ensure that the poor are treated justly in the face of pressure to favor the powerful. Ben Sira is very conscious of the inherent dangers. In 4:7 he teaches his students to be deferential to the powerful, "Endear yourself to the congregation; bow your head low to the great (שלטון; μεγιστᾶνες)," but at the same time they should "[r]escue the oppressed from the oppressor and do not be hesitant in giving a verdict." Later in vv. 27-28 he concludes, "Do not subject yourself to a fool or show partiality to a ruler (מושלים; δυνάστης). Fight to the death for truth, and the Lord God will fight for you." But despite such assurances of God's approval, in 7:6, ben Sira can say, "Do not seek to become a judge, or you may be unable to root out injustice; you may be partial to the powerful, and so mar your integrity."

---

[26]Harrington, 185.

[27]On 38:24-39.11 concerning the trades and the sage, see Johannes Marböck, "Sir. 38,24-39,11: Der schriftgelehrte Weise. Ein Beitrag zu Gestalt und Werk Ben Siras," in M. Gilbert, ed., *La Sagesse de l'Ancien Testament*, BETL 51 (Gembloux/Louvain: Duculot/University, 1979) 293-316.

[28]Horsley and Tiller, 29-30; Harrington, 185.

Ben Sira often addresses his students about their attitude toward and behavior in the presence of their social superiors. In these passages he is not talking directly about the conflict between poor and rich; his comments derive from a school context where he is training future scribes and sages in the way that *they* must navigate these treacherous relationships. Ben Sira's students interact with these people as members of a retainer class, not as poor people. It is clear that in ben Sira's thought, the scribe/sage is socially superior to ordinary workers, farmers, smiths, potters and the like (cf. Sir 38:24-34), and it is most likely from among these that ben Sira's poor come. The poor are not necessarily those who are destitute and reduced to begging. As we saw above, they may well have some material means. Ben Sira condemns those who sacrifice "from the property of the poor (ἐκ χρημάτων πενήτων)." It is better to be poor under one's own roof than to depend on the luxuries of others (29:22). Ben Sira and his students clearly stand above these classes of Jews. Sir 4:7 and 7:6 demonstrate the possibility that ben Sira's students could achieve the position of a judge. Sages could sit on the councils, achieve public prominence, expound God's law, sit among rulers (cf. 15:5; 21:17; 39:4); tradespersons and craftspersons could not, even though they "maintain the fabric of the world" (38:31-34).

In the same way, ben Sira and his students do not belong to the class of the rich and powerful. These are clearly a rung above the scribes and sages. The scribes and sages may be closer to the rich than to the poor, but they do not themselves make up the aristocracy.[29] The ability of ben Sira's students to aspire to positions of leadership shows that they were or at least thought themselves to be more akin to the powerful and rich. For ben Sira power and wealth are practically synonymous, and in at least one place he puts the two notions in parallel cola. "Do not contend with a powerful person (איש גדול), lest you fall into his hands. Do not quarrel with a rich person, lest he pay out the price of your downfall" (8:1).[30] For the

---

[29]Patrick Tiller ("Politics and the High Priesthood," 15) shows that ben Sira uses a variety of terms for the ruling elite, but that they all "refer to local rulers of the Judean temple-state." He has an excellent discussion of ben Sira's terms for these powerful rulers and the social reconstructions one can make from them. My brief remarks here depend largely on his analysis.

[30]The translation here depends on Skehan and Di Lella, 209. See their note on p. 210 on the textual difficulties of this verse.

most part, those in the ruling classes and the rich, "would have been members of the priestly aristocracy of Jerusalem or their retainers."[31]

As persons in a social middle position between the rich and powerful and the tradespersons, craftspersons and poor, but mostly beholden to the powerful, ben Sira's advice to his students about dealing with both rich and poor provides a good window into the social world of the sage in third- and second-century BCE Jerusalem. A large portion of ben Sira's advice to his young trainees is about how to deal with those higher up on the social ladder. The practical necessities involved in keeping in the good graces of the rich and powerful and the self-perception that the scribe/sage is more like them than the "lower classes" may also explain the larger proportion of the book that ben Sira devotes to relationships with the powerful than to dealings with social inferiors. Although the relationship of the scribe with the rich and powerful is important, it is not without its inherent dangers, and ben Sira is careful to warn his charges about them. Some of these warnings reflect general circumstances and others involve advice for specific social situations.

In general ben Sira counsels that his students be wary of rich people and their motives. The rich and powerful most often act out of self interest and the sage should not be misled into thinking otherwise. Sir 13:4-7 epitomizes this kind of warning.

> 13:4 A rich person will exploit you if you can be of use to him,
> but if you are in need he will abandon you.
> 13:5 If you own something, he will live with you,
> he will drain your resources without a qualm.
> 13:6 When he needs you he will deceive you and smile at you and
> encourage you;
> he will speak kindly to you and say, "What do you need?"
> 13:7 He will embarrass you with his delicacies until he has drained
> you two or three times,
> and finally he will laugh at you.
> Should he see you afterwards, he will pass you by
> and shake his head at you.[32]

---

[31]Tiller, 16.

[32]I give here the NRSV translation, but the text has a number of problems. See Skehan and Di Lella 248, 251-253 for their translation and textual notes.

One of the apparently more important social situations in which the sage was likely to find himself together with the rich was the banquet, and ben Sira provides extensive advice on one's comportment at such a meal. Two major blocks of material deal with banquets, 31:12-18 and 32:1-13. Sir 13:8-13 may also be concerned with banquets and 41:19 has at the least to do with meal etiquette in general. Sir 31:12-18 advises that the scribe invited to a banquet "at the table of the great" (על שלחן איש גדול)[33] be careful not to be greedy, to eat what is put before him, to be the first to stop and the last to take. To overstep these bounds is to risk causing offense (31:16, 17). 32:1-9 tells the sage in training what to do if the host of the banquet makes him "master of the feast."[34] In this case the advice is not about eating at the banquet, but it concerns the proper times for speaking. The banquet is at the same time an opportunity for enjoyment and praise and a minefield of potential hazards. If the scribe/sage takes care of the banqueters first and fulfills his duties, he can then be seated "so that you may be merry along with them and receive a wreath for your excellent leadership." But he must be careful not to interrupt the music or "display cleverness at the wrong time" (vv. 3-4). He should speak briefly and only if asked (v. 7). When "among the great" (בין שרים)[35] the sage should not be "too forward" (v. 9). 13:8-13 contains a message similar to that of chap. 32, but it does not specifically set the scene as a banquet. The invitation of an important person (נדיב) is an opportunity and a danger. Ben Sira concludes this section, "Be on your guard and be very careful, for you are walking about with your own downfall" (v. 13).[36]

Ben Sira's language of caution in dealing with the rich and powerful appears to be in some tension with his construction of the place of the sage in Jewish society. On the one hand, ben Sira's ideology of the sage should conceivably place him at the top of the social heap. The scribe is endowed with divine inspiration and pours out his teaching like prophecy. He is an

---

[33]I am reading with Ms B^m which corrects Ms B's שלחן גדול to שלחן איש גדול.

[34]This clause is not extant in the Hebrew manuscripts. The Greek has ἡγούμενόν σε κατέστησαν.

[35]The Greek translation ἐν μέσῳ μεγιστάνων in v. 9a indicates that the subject nouns in Ms B probably have been transposed.

[36]The Hebrew and Greek of this verse are very different. I have given the Greek here. Ms A reads "Be on guard and be careful, and do not walk with men of violence."

indispensable advisor and counselor to the powerful. But on the other hand, the reality appears to be that the social position of the scribe/sage is conditioned by the precarious balancing act of proper behavior and support of those who employ him and advocacy on behalf of those who are the socially and economically disadvantaged. The combination of ben Sira's perception of the scribe/sage as fundamental to the functioning of society and the tenuous social position that he in fact occupies might well produce some insecurity, which would necessitate a way of constructing an alternative understanding of the power relationships that create the insecurity. In more specific terms, the sage is the expert in God's law and the guardian of the ancient tradition of wisdom who has a certain power dependent on his knowledge. Yet he still has to be very careful what he says and does when at a banquet, and by rendering fair judgments, he risks alienating people who have power over him. This ambiguous social position could produce a kind of dissonance that had to be resolved.

To describe ben Sira's social situation this way is not to say, however, that there are no social rewards for the scribe/sage.[37] He certainly does achieve a certain social status and recognition. He may become famous as a judge or ambassador (39:4). Like those worthies whom ben Sira describes in chaps 44-50, he may also achieve eternal renown (39:9-11). Yet the temporal social rewards that are accorded to the scribe/sage do not seem to compensate for his lack of power and position when compared to those above him, among them the priests. Patrick Tiller notes,

> From Ben Sira's extensive reflection on the activities of his own "profession" it is clear that the sages were retainers with scribal, legal, cultural and religious functions, some of which may have overlapped with those of the priests. According to Ben Sira's ideology of the priesthood, the function of teaching the law originated with Moses (45:5) and belonged to the Aaronide priesthood (45:17). In second temple Judea the priesthood must have, in effect, over a period of generations, delegated that authority and function to the sages, both with regard to the people generally (37:23), and with regard to the exercise of their own governmental

---

[37]See Michael Stone, "Ideal Figures and Social Context: Priest and Sage in the Early Second Temple Age," in Patrick D. Miller, Jr., Paul D. Hanson, S. Dean McBride, eds., *Ancient Israelite Religions: F. M. Cross Festschrift* (Philadelphia: Fortress, 1988) 575-586.

authority (8:8; 9:17-10:5; 38:32-33; 38:34-39:4). In 9:17-10:5 it seems particularly clear that it is the scribe who stands behind "the wise judge" and "the government of the intelligent one." It appears, in fact, that one of Ben Sira's goals was to enhance the authority and honor of the scribal class. His book is full of claims that the greatest honor is for the wise, those who fear the Lord and obey his commands.[38]

Thus, ben Sira is faced with a real dilemma. He is a strong supporter of the priesthood, at least that in Jerusalem.[39] The priests have been chosen by God to minister before him at the altar. Yet, certain priestly functions, like teaching and interpreting the law have become much more the responsibility of the scribe/sage. In 15:1, ben Sira uses the phrase תופש תורה ("practiced in Torah"), which Jer 2:8 applies to the priests, to refer to the scribe who may not be a priest.[40] As Tiller puts it, "The role of the priests as authoritative interpreters and teachers of the law is being supplanted by the sage."[41] The scribe/sage thus increasingly has a priestly role without the benefits of being a member of the priestly class.

One possible way to enhance the honor, if not the authority, of the scribe/sage would be to maintain that those things which seem to determine the prevalent social order are not in actuality the most meaningful or important, to propose a different hierarchy of values. One of the ways ben Sira accomplishes this goal is through the idea of the "fear of the Lord." This important theme is a complex one in Sirach, but it seems to me that achieving a proper fear of the Lord functions for ben Sira, at least in part, as a mechanism for leveling some of the power and social inequities that he perceives in the social position of the scribe/sage. As ben Sira articulates it, fear of the Lord supersedes all social status and class, and a number of passages suggest that anyone can achieve it. He makes it quite clear in his book, for example, that the fear of the Lord is what truly makes one worthy of honor (10:19). For both rich and poor, "their glory is the fear

---

[38]Tiller, 21-22.

[39]See Benjamin G. Wright III, "'Fear the Lord and Honor the Priest': Ben Sira as Defender of the Jerusalem Priesthood," in Beentjes, *The Book of Ben Sira in Modern Research*, 189-222.

[40]Skehan and Di Lella, 264 cited also in Tiller, 22.

[41]Tiller, 22.

of the Lord" (10:22). "No one is superior to the one who fears the Lord. Fear of the Lord surpasses everything; to whom can we compare who has it?" (25:10-11).

Yet when we look more carefully at ben Sira's discourse about rich and poor, the powerful and the humble, it seems that the scribe/sage is in the best position to achieve such a fear of the Lord. Fear of the Lord for ben Sira is primarily identified with wisdom and fulfilling of the commandments. "The whole of wisdom," he says, "is fear of the Lord, and in all wisdom there is the fulfillment of the Law" (19:20). Who is better able to fulfill the law and learn wisdom than the scribe/sage who is the recognized expert in the law and the guardian of wisdom? The acquisition of wisdom depends on much leisure time and having little business. Those who are laborers and artisans do not have such time (39:24-34). The poor cannot rest because when they do, they find themselves in need (31:4). By contrast, those who have power and wealth and are righteous are a rare breed according to ben Sira. The rich and powerful may have the time, but they find the demands of their wealth and power more pressing. Thus, I find the introduction to the poem on the scribe to be very significant. "How different the one who devotes himself to the study of the Law of the Most High!" (38:34). How different indeed! It may be theoretically possible for all to fear the Lord, but practically the one best able to achieve proper fear of the Lord is the scribe/sage. Ben Sira thus grounds his understanding of himself in a different system of values, his ability to pursue wisdom and fear of the Lord, that which surpasses all else, including riches, poverty and social status. This set of values he holds out to his students as a way for them to understand themselves and to find true honor in their place in life.

Conclusions

The discourse of rich and poor in Sirach is derived from the real-life circumstances of third- and second-century BCE Jerusalem. Viktor Tcherikover expresses it eloquently. "For Ben Sira describes rich and poor, not in the conventional formula known to him in literature, but as an artist who draws the material he needs direct from life."[42] One does not find metaphorical uses of the categories in ben Sira's book. Ultimately ben Sira does not view riches and/or poverty in and of themselves as signs of piety or impiety, of God's favor or disfavor. God may hear the prayer of the poor, but ben Sira maintains that it is not *because* they are poor that God listens. Although they might be rare, ben Sira does not rule out the possibility that rich people could be righteous. What transcends both of these categories is fear of the Lord and the keeping of the commandments.

Because the scribe/sage occupies a sometimes insecure social position and is faced with conflicting loyalties and obligations, the watchword for ben Sira and his students in relating to the rich and powerful is caution. If the scribe/sage remains wary and observes proper etiquette and appropriate behavior he will succeed with the powerful. When it comes to the poor, ben Sira's attitude seems primarily conditioned by his understanding of the covenantal responsibilities to care for the poor, widows, and orphans. Ben Sira exhorts the rich, as well as his students, to fulfill their obligation to the poor through almsgiving. For his budding scribes, he makes clear that if they find themselves in positions of rendering judgments, they must be fair and not prefer the case of the rich because of their influence and power.

The Israelite wisdom tradition was practical as well as philosophical and young scribes/sages needed to learn how to make their way through life. As a result we hear ben Sira reflecting on the everyday realities facing these young men. Through his advice concerning riches and poverty ben Sira has transmitted to us an important snapshot of the social world of Jews in third- and second-century BCE Judea. An analysis of this discourse helps us to see a bit more clearly not only the specific social location of the scribe/sage, but more generally the complex social matrix of real people doing their best to negotiate real lives.

---

[42]Tcherikover, 146. Indeed, Tcherikover suggests on p. 148 that ben Sira "may well have been born and educated in poverty and have gradually climbed to prominence by force of his natural intelligence and of his devotion to the study of Torah and practical wisdom." I do not doubt that ben Sira was gifted intellectually. Given what he says about artisans and tradespersons in chap. 38, I find it less likely that ben Sira's own origins were that humble.

REVISITING THE RICH AND THE POOR
IN 1 ENOCH 92-105 AND THE GOSPEL ACCORDING TO LUKE

George W. E. Nickelsburg
The University of Iowa

In keeping with the theme of this year's sessions of the Wisdom and Apocalypticism Group, I am revisiting the topic of a 1979 article, in which I compared the treatment of riches and the rich in the Epistle of Enoch and the Gospel according to Luke.[1] I argued that the similarities between the two texts indicated that the author(s) of the special Lukan traditions--if not the third evangelist himself--knew these chapters of 1 Enoch, although "the sharp, condemnatory tone in 1 Enoch 92 ff. is somewhat muted in Luke's openness to the possibility of the rich finding salvation through almsgiving, deeds of generosity, and perhaps the wholesale giving up of their riches."[2] Since the Group is studying the relationship between wisdom and apocalypticism, I shall devote the largest part of this paper to 1 Enoch, taking up most of the issues set for the session: the setting of the text; the author's attitudes toward poverty and wealth; his descriptions of the rewards and punishments that will accrue to the rich and poor as a consequence of their present actions and situation; and any prescriptions for the proper use of wealth and poverty. In the second part, I shall offer a comparative analysis of the Third Gospel based on my findings in the first part. I shall argue that both the author of the Epistle and the evangelist *presume* a dualistic world view that is based on revelation, although they embody their material in literary forms that are at home in sapiential literature rather than cloth it in apocalyptic visions. It is a paper still very much in progress.

1. The Epistle of Enoch (1 Enoch 92-105)

The Epistle of Enoch is the last of the five major sections of the text that we know as 1 Enoch.[3] It was composed in the second century B.C.E. as a parenetic conclusion to a literary corpus that had been shaped in the form of an Enochic testament.[4] The major part of the Epistle comprises six addresses directed to the righteous and the sinners. These addresses, in turn, contain strings of Woes against the sinners, Exhortations to the righteous, and Descriptions of events relating to the final judgment. Presumed throughout is the authority of Enoch, which derives from his visions of heaven and the cosmos which were recounted, especially, in chapters 1-36.[5]

According to the *incipit*, Enoch addressed the Epistle "to all my sons who will dwell upon the earth, and to the last generations who will observe truth and peace" (92:1). Apart from some testamentary advice to Enoch's sons (93:2; 94:1-2), the addresses are directed to the members of author's own community, who are designated primarily as "the righteous" (*hoi dikaioi*) and "the pious" (*hoi hosioi / hoi eusebeis*). They are characterized by their observance of God's commandments (construed primarily as walking on the path of truth or righteousness) and their trust in God's vindication of their faithfulness in the midst of oppression.

The counterparts to the righteous and pious are "the sinners" (*hoi hamartoloi*), "the wicked" (*hoi kakoi*), "the unjust *or* unrighteous" (*hoi adikoi*), and "the lawless" (*hoi anomoi*), who divide into two groups. The first are religious teachers, who are said to pervert the truth and lead many astray from the right paths (see, especially, 98:9-99:10; 104:10-11).[6] The second group is described as the oppressors of the righteous and pious, and at a number of points they are identified as being rich and powerful.

1.1 A Profile of the Rich

The Woes in the Epistle of Enoch, typical of the form, are composed of two parts: an indictment and a consequent threat of judgment. Taken together, the initial lines of these Woes provide details about the identity. social location, and actions of the rich. Although the polemical character of this writing mitigates the certainty with which we may describe the historical circumstances that lie behind the text, we may assume that the specific indictments are not spun our of thin air; and in any case, our mandate is to reconstruct the author's perception of the situation, as the text presents it. For the most part my exposition follows the order of the text.[7]

1.1.1 Enoch's First Address (94:6-96:3)

94:6 Woe to those who build iniquity and violence,
    and lay deceit as a foundation;
  for quickly they will be overthrown,
    and they will have no peace.
  7 Woe to those who build their houses with sin;
    for from all their foundations they will be overthrown,
    and by the sword they will fall.
  And those who acquire gold and silver in judgment will quickly perish.
  8 Woe to you, rich, for in your riches you have trusted;
    and from your riches you will depart,
    because you have not remembered the Most High in the days of
      your riches.

This string of Woes begins by using the metaphor of building to describe the dual activity of the sinners: violence and deceit--that is, social and religious transgressions (v 6). The second Woe literalizes the building metaphor and refers to people who construct real houses for themselves in a way that the author construes as sinful (v 7). This could allude to a variety of social injustices: slavery or some kind of impressed labor; non-payment of wages or some other abuse of the employer-employee relationship;[8] or the snatching up of land or materials that do not rightfully belong to the builder. Although nothing in the Woe requires us to identify these builders as "rich," in v 7d--doubtless an addition to the Woe--an editor lumps these people together with others who use the judicial system to acquire substantial wealth (gold and silver). These latter might be judges who take bribes or persons who win heavy lawsuits. The third Woe (v 8) takes up the motif of wealth and criticizes "the rich" (*'ab 'elt* = *hoi plousioi*) for their arrogant dependence on their wealth and their ignoring of God. Lines *a* and *c* may simply express antithetical parallelism, or interpreting the previous Woe, they may imply that the rich disregard the divine command to have compassion on those whom they oppress through the construction of their houses.

95:6 Woe to you, lying witnesses, and those who weigh out injustice;
    for quickly you will be destroyed.

This Woe does not speak of the rich as such, but its reference to the perversion of the judicial system recalls 94:7*d* and indicts not only false witnesses, but crooked judges as well.

1.1.2 Enoch's Second Address (96:4-98:8)

This second major subsection of the Epistle contains the largest concentration of threats against the rich.

96:4 Woe to you, sinners, for your riches make you appear to be righteous,
      but your heart convicts you of being sinners;
   and this word will be a testimony against you,
      a reminder of (your) evil deeds.

5 Woe to you who devour the finest of the wheat,
      and drink <wine from the krater>,[9]
   and tread on the lowly with your might.

6 Woe to you who drink water <from every fountain>;
      for quickly you will be repaid, and cease and dry up,
   because you have forsaken the fountain of life.

7 Woe to you who commit iniquity and deceit and blasphemy;
      it will be a reminder against you for evil.

8 Woe to you, mighty, who with might oppress the righteous one;
      for the day of your destruction will come.

Verse 4 makes a theological rather than a descriptive point. In keeping with Deuteronomic theology, riches are seen as a sign of divine blessing. But in the author's view, the rich are, in fact, sinners, and their inner disposition will serve as an accusing witness against them in the judgment. The second Woe (v 5) draws its language from Amos 5:11 and 6:6. Alongside their sumptuous banqueting, the rich exercise power (*hayl* = *dynamis*; cf. v. 8) that enables them to oppress "the lowly" (*tehutān*). It is the only place in the Epistle that defines the objects of oppression by their social status. The precise referent of v 6 is uncertain; however, in context it suggests that the rich gobble up what they wish and, in so doing, indicate their own moral bankruptcy. After a general Woe (v 7), the author again attacks "the mighty" for using their power (v 5) to oppress, in this case, "the righteous." The section as a whole attacks both the luxury of the upper class and their use of that status and power to abuse the lower class. The emphasis on the luxuriating of the rich recurs in concentrated form in chapter 97.

> 97:7 Woe to you, sinners, who are in the midst of the sea and upon the dry land;
>   there is an evil reminder against you.
>   8 Woe to you who acquire gold and silver unjustly and say,
>   "We have become very wealthy,
>   and we have gotten possessions,
>   and we have acquired all that we wish.
>   9 And all that we wish let us do,
>   for silver we have treasured up in our treasuries,
>   and many goods in our houses;
>   and as water they are poured out."
> 10 You err!
>   For your wealth will not remain,
>   but will quickly ascend from you;
>   for you have acquired everything unjustly,
>   and you will be delivered to a great curse.
> 98:1 And now I swear to you, the wise, and not the foolish,
>   that you will see many things upon the earth.
>   For men will put on adornments as women,
>   and fair colors more than virgins;
>   2   in kingship and majesty and power.
>   And silver and gold will be among them as food,
>   and in their houses they will be poured out like water;
>   3   because they have no knowledge or understanding.

The first of these two passages depicts the immensity of wealth gathered by the rich, which is specified as gold, silver, and "possessions" (*hyparchonta* = Aramaic *nksyn* or *mmwn'*) and "good things" (*agatha*). The reference to "treasuries" (*thēsaurois*) suggests houses that are more like palaces. The expression "sea and dry land" denotes the whole earth and indicates that the author has in mind merchants or persons accustomed to travel.[10] In the author's view, their wealth is not neutral, but has been acquired unjustly,[11] and their sin is exacerbated by their belief that they control their future ("we have acquired all that we wish, and all that we wish let us do").

The second passage continues in their same vein. Again the author refers to the "houses" of the wealthy, where they parade about in fine clothes and jewelry and consume silver and gold like food and water. Their status is indicated in the words "kingship, majesty, and power" (*bas*]*ileia, megalōsynē,* [*exousi*]*a, mangašt, 'ebay, šeltān*). At least in part, the author has the rulers in mind.

> 98:4 I swear to you, sinners,
>> that is was not ordained <for man> to be a slave,[12]
>>> nor was <a decree> given for woman to be a handmaid;
>>> but it happened because of oppression.
>> Thus lawlessness was not sent upon the earth,
>>> but men created it by themselves,
>>> and those who do it come to a great curse.

This anti-deterministic passage is perhaps directed against a misconstrual of the story of the Watchers (1 Enoch 6-11), but is surely meant to undercut any notion that humans are not responsible for their deeds.[13] The first and prime target is the holding of slaves, which is construed as "oppression" (*katadynasteia,* perhaps = *'šq*) and "lawlessness" (*anomia = rš '*).

1.1.3. Enoch's Fourth Address (99:11-100:6)

> 99:12 Woe to you who lay the foundations of sin and deceit,
>> and cause bitterness upon the earth;
>> for because of it they will come to an end.
> 13 Woe to those who build their houses not with their own labors,
>> and they make the whole house of the stones and bricks of sin.
>> Woe to you; you will have no peace.
> 14 Woe to those who reject the foundation and eternal inheritance of their
>> fathers;
>> a spirit of error pursues you
>> You will have no rest.

As in 94:6-7, the notion of building is central. Verse 13 describes the literal building of houses in what is construed as a sinful manner, perhaps through the use of impressed labor, which makes their home a house of sin.[14] The interpretation of the framing Woes is more difficult. "Deceit" may indicate a metaphorical use of the notion of building.[15] Alternatively, it could mean that the wealthy employ deceit to obtain the wealth that allows them to build their houses. Similarly, the final Woe could refer metaphorically to false teaching, which overturns the foundations of the Torah, or it could mean the construction of houses in a way that violates the Torah.[16]

1.1.4 Enoch's Sixth Address (102:4-104:8)

The last of the six addresses in the Epistle of Enoch explicitly takes on the subject of theodicy. The following excerpts are typical of the section. Injustice is described exclusively as oppression suffered by the righteous, and the sinners are typified as the wealthy and the oppressors of the righteous.

102:4 Fear not, souls of the righteous;
       take courage, you pious who have died. . .
    6 When you die, then the sinners say about you,
       "The pious have died according to fate,
       and what have they gained from their deeds? . . .
    9 Therefore it is good for us to eat and drink,
       to plunder and sin and steal
       and get wealth and see good days . . . "

Again, the sinners live the good life, banqueting sumptuously, and the acquisition of wealth is seen to take place at the expense of the righteous.

103:5 Woe to you, dead sinners.
       When you die in the wealth of your sins,
         those who are like you say about you,
       "Blessed are the sinners,
         all their days they have seen.
    6 And now they have died with goods and wealth,
         and affliction and murder they have not seen in their life;
       And they have died in splendor,
         and judgment was not executed on them in their life."

Their sin notwithstanding, the rich prosper. The term "the wealth of your sins" is striking. The author could have said "the multitude of your sins" (Sir 5:6; Ezek 28:6). The use of "wealth" is ironic and perhaps purposely ambiguous, implying a construct chain that means "your sinful (i.e., ill-gotten) riches" (cf. 97:8-9).

> 103:9 Do not say, you who are righteous and pious in life:
> "In the days of our tribulation, we toiled laboriously;
>> and every tribulation we saw, and many evils we found . . . .
> 11 We toiled and labored and were not masters of our labor;
>> we became the food of the sinners.
> And the lawless weighed down their yoke upon us;
> 12   our enemies were our masters,
>> and they goaded us on and penned us in,
>> and to our enemies we bowed our necks,
>> and they had no mercy on us . . . .
> 14 We complained to the rulers in our tribulation,
>> and cried out against those who struck us down and oppressed us;
>> and our complaints they did not receive,
>> nor did they wish to give a hearing to our voice.
> 15 And they did not help us,
>> they did not find (anything) against those who oppressed and devoured us;
> But they strengthened against us
>> them who killed us and made us few;
> And they did not disclose their iniquities,
>> and they did not remove from us the yoke of them who devoured us
>> and dispersed us and murdered us.
> And they did not disclose concerning those who murdered us,
>> nor did they make mention that they raised their hands against us."

In this powerful and poignant passage, "the righteous and pious" complain that the fruits of their labor are taken by their masters, and ironically they describe themselves as becoming both "food for sinners" and draft animals. To make it worse, their enemies conspire with the rulers and judges, who then turn down the complaints of the righteous in court.

1.1.5 Summary

The wealthy who are the object of this author's criticism appear to range from rulers to merchants. They own slaves and build palatial homes through some sort of impressed labor. *They are never spoken of in a positive way.* To the contrary, in their author's view: they oppress the righteous, get their wealth unjustly, and use the courts to their own advantage, all the while banqueting sumptuously and parading about in rich and fine clothes. In addition, they presume that their wealth will secure their future.

Thus, for this author, the rich are, by definition, sinners, and the very form of the Woes that describe their activity indicates that they will suffer the divine judgment that has presently eluded them and which they claim is non-existent (see below § 1.3).

1.2 The Righteous in the Epistle of Enoch

The powerful negative portrayal of the rich in the Epistle indicates a second group, whose description, however, must be implied from the description of the rich. These objects of oppression are slaves, day laborers, persons whose goods and livelihood have been taken unjustly by the rich and powerful. Strikingly, the term "poor" never occurs in 1 Enoch 92-105. The closest we come is a single reference to "the lowly" in 96:5. In the place of a generic term that describes their social or economic status, we find a plethora of references to "the righteous" and "the pious." The usage is not accidental. Although the author is seriously concerned about the circumstances and plight of these people (hence his vivid descriptions of their oppression), he emphasizes the complete *injustice* of their situation. As god-fearing and upright people, they should be experiencing divine blessing. Their suffering, therefore, constitutes a serious religious problem, as chapter 103 so eloquently articulates. This is a deeply existential text, in which the realities of oppression are compounded by the perception that God is not dealing fairly. Thus, the repeated usage of "the righteous" and "the pious" underscores the irony of their situation, and together with the terms "sinners, unjust, and lawless" for those who prosper, it points to the necessity of the divine judgment whose certainty and imminence constitute the great reality of these chapters.

1.3 Judgment in the Epistle of Enoch

As will be evident by now, the issue of poverty and wealth is inextricably bound up with the question of divine justice and judgment. The structure of the Woes allows the author repeatedly to highlight the judgment that will befall the sinners whom he indicts. However, the issue of justice and judgment is complex. The author's enemies and their friends work with the presuppositions of Deuteronomic theology, and from this point of view, the possession of wealth demonstrates divine favor, or at least the lack of divine disfavor (103:5-6). Conversely, these people, who are enemies of the righteous, mock the claims of the suffering righteous:

> 102:6 When you die, then the sinners say about you,
> "The pious have died according to fate,
> and what have they gained from their deeds?
> 7 Behold how they die in grief and darkness,
> and what advantage do they have over us?
> 8 Henceforth let them arise and be saved,
> and they shall forever see <the light>.
> But, behold they have died,
> and henceforth (and) forever they will not see the light,
> 9 Therefore it is good for us to eat and drink,
> to plunder and sin and steal
> and get wealth and see good days.
> 10 Behold those who justify themselves--of what sort their destruction is--
> no righteousness was found in them until their died.
> 11 And they perished and became as those who are not,
> and their souls descended with pain into Sheol."

The righteous, for their part, complain that they have been suffering what are, in effect, the curses of the covenant (103:9-15).[17] Thus, for both the author's own people and their enemies, wealth, prosperity, and the good life, on the one hand, and deprivation and oppression, on the other hand, are the indices of righteousness and sin. Or, possibly more radically, the universe is marked by a profound lack of divine justice.

The author responds to this with a resounding "No!" and refutes these claims, detail by detail.[18] What the righteous miss in this life (102:4-11; 103:9-15) they will receive after death (103:1-4; 104:1-6), and what the rich sinners enjoy in this life (103:5-6) they will be deprived of in their future existence (103:7-8), when the angels report the sins they have witnessed (104:78). Said another way, the righteous and the sinners will receive after death what one another had experienced in this life--exchanging good for evil and vice versa. The message of that judgment runs like a thread through the whole of the Epistle and is built into the structure of the literary forms that constitute the Epistle. It is a post-mortem judgment to be experienced, respectively, in the company of the angels in the heights of heaven (104:4, 6) and in the dark, fiery depths of Sheol (103:7-8).

There is in the Epistle, an exception to this description of the locus of rewards and punishments, namely in the Apocalypse of Weeks (93:1-10; 91:11-17). According to 91:13, at the conclusion of the eighth week of righteousness, the righteous "will acquire possessions in righteousness" (*yqnwn nksyn bqšwt*).[19] This passage, which may well belong to the form of the Enochic corpus to which the Epistle was added,[20] is significant for two reasons. First, it posits an eschatology that features a new heaven and a new earth. In that context, the righteous expect to have possessions, obtained in a righteous manner--as opposed to the ill-gotten riches of their enemies. Secondly, such a this-worldly eschatology, which is not evident in chapters 102-104, is a typical feature of earlier strata.[21] From this we may conclude that: a) in the view of the Epistle as we have it, wealth need not be evil in itself; and b) in the Enochic corpus as a whole, rewards for the righteous may be dispensed on earth, in the material realm.

1.4 Literary Forms in the Epistle of Enoch: Their "Sources" or Parallels

As we have noted, the principal formal components of the Epistle of Enoch are three in number.[22] Their form and content are noteworthy, first, because they focus on issues related to the great judgment. The *Woe* consists of an indictment for sins whose judgment is then asserted or briefly described in the second part. The three component parts of the *Exhortation* are: an appeal to "Fear not" or "Be hopeful"; a reference to the present unjust circumstances of the righteous; and a promise that God will vindicate them. A third form, introduced by the adverbial "then" or "in those days," provides a *Description* of aspects of the judgment.

A second significant fact about these three forms is their "source" in biblical literature. All three of them occur in the classical prophetic literature.[23] Thus, with respect to its form and rhetoric, the warp and weft of the Epistle of Enoch exudes a prophetic ambience.

An equally striking fact about the first two of these forms is, however, their occurrence in the sapiential literature. Ben Sira employs the Woe form (2:12-14; 41:8-9). In a section that imitates Second and Third Isaiah, the author of Baruch employs the exhortation "Have courage" (*tharseite;* 4:5, 21, 27, 30).

In addition to these forms, the Epistle employs four other forms or formulas. 1) Occasionally, we find a refutative form ("Do not say" / quotation / refutation, 98:7-8; 103:9-104:3; 104:7-8; cf. the same idea cast in a Woe in 97:8-10), which is paralleled in the Wisdom of ben Sira (16:17-23). 2) The refutation element in these passages, moreover, is usually introduced by a word that indicates that the author is imparting hitherto unknown information (Know! Be it known! You err!).[24] Sometimes, the author goes so far as to employ an oath (I swear to you, 98:1, 4, 6; 103:1; 104:1). 3) In chapter 101, the author appeals to his readers to "Observe the works of God in the creation." The appeal to nature as the realm of divine revelation is paralleled in Second Isaiah (51:6), but seems here to be drawn from the sapiential tradition, as is evident from its inspiration in 1 Enoch in chapters 2-5.[25] 4) In one instance, the author employs the sapiential form of a Beatitude:

> 99:10 Then blessed will be all who listen to the words of the wise,
> and learn to do the commandments of the Most High;
> and walk in the paths of righteousness,
> and do not err with the erring;
> for they will be saved.

In summary, the author of the Epistle employs literary forms typical of prophetic literature, but also found in sapiential texts. Their substance is the assertion of the coming judgment, and they often imply that the author is transmitting revealed information.

1.5 Revelation, Dualism, and Literary Form in the Epistle of Enoch

This notion of revelation requires brief comment here since we are concerned with a definition of apocalyptic literature. What does this author know, how does he know it, and to what authority does he appeal? The answer, I think, is simple. The author announces the coming judgment, describes certain cosmic and heavenly realia related to it, and undergirds his assertions with the claim, or sometimes, the implication, that he himself has seen these things during his cosmic journeys or his dream visions.

The Apocalypse of Weeks, a review of human history from creation to the *eschaton*, claims as its source Enoch's heavenly vision, the angelic interpretation of it, and the heavenly tablets, which he himself has inspected (93:1-3). Comprised here is the whole of Enoch's journeys, recounted in chapters 12-36, as well as in 81:1-4.[26] Other references to issues relating to the judgment, most of which Enoch affirms as revelation, include his description of the souls of the righteous (102:4--5; cf. chapter 22); his claim to have seen the heavenly tablets on which are written the destiny of the righteous, which he affirms by the divine *kabhod* (103:1-4); and his claim that the angels stand in the presence of that *kabhod*, reminding God of the contents of the register of the righteous (104:1-2).

As I have argued elsewhere, the view of revelation in 1 Enoch is essential to the book's cosmic and temporal dualisms.[27] The author posits a dichotomy, or dualism between the inhabited world, on the one hand, and the outer reaches of the cosmos, on the other hand, and a similar dichotomy between the present time and the hidden future. The world here and now is marked by injustice and evil. In heaven and in the inaccessible parts of the earth, the mechanisms are in place to adjudicate this present injustice and eradicate evil. This adjudication will mark a caesura between the present age and a new age. In this text, the author bridges these dualisms by transmitting the revelations he has received during his journeys through the cosmos in the company of interpreting angels and by means of a night vision about human history and its consummation. Chapters 12-36 + 81 and 85-90 recount these revelations. The Epistle alludes to the journeys and visions without describing them. It *presumes* a dualistic, apocalyptic world view without presenting it in some many words. Granted, this parenetic text was created to be attached to an apocalypse, *its form demonstrates that one can hold an apocalyptic world view and express an eschatology that grows out of it without presenting these ideas in explicit apocalyptic visionary form.*

1.6 The Epistle of Enoch at the Intersection of Prophecy, Wisdom, and Apocalypticism

What does our analysis of the Epistle teach us about the problem with which this Group is concerned? Does it, in any way, help to clarify a distinction between the traditional categories of sapiential and apocalyptic literature, or does it confuse the distinction? I think that it does the latter, and in the process it forces us to rethink our categories. Let us summarize.

The Epistle presumes an apocalyptic world view, which portrays the present world as the locus of profound evil and radical injustice. Sinners use their status, power, and wealth to unjustly oppress the righteous. This situation will be resolved through the direct intervention of the Great Holy God and the divine angelic entourage, which will purify the earth of sin, grant wealth and prosperity to the righteous who have survived, and, additionally, mete out everlasting rewards and punishments in the heights of heaven and the dark recesses of Sheol. The author's claim to revelations of the cosmos and the impending future is the guarantee that this will happen.. Thus, the principal issue for this author is theodicy, and his explication of the problem presumes a set of dualisms bridged by revelation.

Everything I have described thus far applies also to the rest of 1 Enoch, which embodies this world view and message in the explicitly revelatory idioms and in literary forms traditionally associated with biblical prophecy and "classical" apocalyptic literature: oracle; prophetic call and ascent to the heavenly court; cosmic journey; historical review; and dream vision.

Nonetheless, the Epistle differs from these chapters precisely in its use of different idioms and literary forms. It is true that these forms are also drawn, in part, from the biblical prophetic tradition--principally the Woes, Exhortations, and Descriptions of the future. However, the first two of these forms and the rest of the literary forms in the Epistle are closely paralleled in Jewish sapiential literature of the Greco-Roman period, notably, the Wisdom of ben Sira and Baruch. What binds all of these forms together and what characterizes the idiom of the Epistle as a whole is the use of the second person plural as a vehicle for moral parenesis. Different from most of the substance of the other chapters of 1 Enoch--excluding its literary frames--these chapters speak directly and explicitly to an audience, encouraging or admonishing them to right conduct and threatening dire consequences in the absence of such behavior.

In this respect, we may seek some clarification from the traditionally alleged sources of apocalyptic literature, viz., prophecy and wisdom. The claim to direct, personal revelation parallels the biblical prophets and differs from ben Sira. The latter does, indeed, claim that his parenesis and his exhortations are divinely inspired and poured forth like prophecy (24:33). However, this inspiration is not new revelation. Rather, it informs the interpretation of an established prophetic corpus. He is the expositor of the Torah of the greatest of the prophets, who wrote down the words of heavenly wisdom (24:23). Moreover, clearly following the literary order of the *Tanak*, he praises a string of prophets--Joshua (46:1), Samuel (46:13), Nathan (47:1), Elijah (48:1), Elisha (48:8), Isaiah (48:22-25), Jeremiah (49:6-7), Ezekiel (49:8), and the Twelve (49:10)--without presuming to equate his wisdom with theirs.

Summary and Points for Further Discussion

I propose that my findings and observations, both in this paper and in a previous one prepared for this group,[28] offer some points of reference for comparing and contrasting wisdom and apocalypticism.

We have seen the following:

1. Certain sapiential literature of the Greco-Roman period--my point of reference is ben Sira--speaks in the idiom of earlier Israelite sapiential literature (Proverbs) through its use of the proverbial form. At the same time, it employs prophetic literary forms, sets forth moral discourse (including the responsibilities of the rich), indicates high respect for the prophets, and evidences an interest in Israel's history and in the last things, which is typical of much of the prophetic literature.[29] It differs from the prophetic literature in that its prophetic-like sapiential discourse involves the inspired interpretation of an authoritative corpus of prophetic writings.

2. The Enochic corpus is also a child of the prophetic and sapiential traditions, employs literary forms at home in both, speaks in the Epistle in second person moral admonition, focuses on issues of sin and righteousness (with a special emphasis on the irresponsibility of the rich), and takes a long view of Israel's history with a particular focus on the end-time. It differs from ben Sira in three respects, especially. First, it employs a dualistic world view to emphasize the radicality of evil, and its solution in a final eschatological judgment with permanent consequences. Secondly, in connection with this, it does not simply deal with the nexus of human conduct and its consequences, it focuses on the issue of theodicy, the present disparity between conduct and consequences. Thus eschatology is not simply the end of history, it is its solution. Thirdly, it attributes its message to immediate personal revelation rather than inspired interpretation of an authoritative corpus. It is itself the deposit of heavenly wisdom written by the seer.

As we study other texts and deal with other topics, it may be helpful to address the following questions to them:

1. What can we learn about he specifics of the situations to which the texts are addressed and the relationships between the authors and their audiences?

2. Do the texts presume a dualistic world view? In what respects? Is this world view explicit or implicit?

3. Do the texts deal with issues of human deeds and retribution? Do they do so within the context of the problem of theodicy? Do they posit other-worldly judgment. If so, is it a matter of fact or a "necessary" response to the experience of present injustice?

4. Do the texts employ idioms and literary forms typical of prophetic, sapiential, or apocalyptic literature (e.g., 1 Enoch)?

5. Do the texts express or imply a notion of revelation, and, if so, of what sort? Does the author or, in the case of narrative, the speaker claim immediate revelation to undergird statements about the divine and demonic realms and about otherworldly reward and punishment, do such statements imply revelation claimed elsewhere in a corpus of revealed literature, or are the statements made in a matter of fact way with no explicit or implicit claims about direct revelation or revelation one step removed?

2. The Gospel According to Luke

This brief survey of the issue of rich and poor in the Gospel of Luke will address itself to the questions raised in part 1 with a focus on material that is peculiar to that gospel. Because issues relating to the social world of Luke-Acts are immensely complex,[30] I will confine my discussion to an analysis of Luke's *narrative* world. How do Luke and his tradition portray the character and interaction of the rich and the poor? What rewards and punishments await them? What literary forms are employed to discuss these issues? What notions of revelation may be explicit or implicit in these? How does all this impinge on the discussion of wisdom and apocalypticism?

2.1 Negative Portrayals of the Rich

One important strand in Luke's special material and redaction portrays the rich in strongly negative terms that are reminiscent of the Epistle of Enoch.[31] This is explicitly the case in the twin parables in 12:13-34 and 16:19-31. The rich and foolish farmer in the first parable forfeits his future when, in calculated self-interest, he decides to lay up treasures for himself and not be rich toward God. The story illustrates the vice of contentious greed and covetousness (vv 13-15), and Luke comments on it by means of the Q traditions that follow it (12:22-32).[32] With many Enochic resonances, the story of Dives and Lazarus illustrates how another rich man eats and drinks merrily, parades in fine clothes, and ignores his responsibility to care for the poor beggar at his gate. Similarly negative is the Lukan redaction of the Markan account of Jesus and the rich man who seeks eternal life, but refuses to "sell all that you have and distribute it to the poor" (19:22-23). All these stories demonstrate a wrong use of wealth, possessions, and the means of living, that involves withholding them from the poor who need them. Finally, there is the story of the judge and the poor widow (18:1-8). Here the issue is not wealth, but of the abuse of power. Other negative portrayals of the rich are implied in Luke's threats of damnation against them (below § 2.3).

2.2 The Poor in Luke

Luke's treatment of the poor, in analogy to the Epistle of Enoch, is particularly noteworthy for its juxtaposition of poor and rich. They are mentioned together in Mary's hymn (1:48-53) and in the Beatitudes and Woes (6:20-26), albeit without explicitly mentioning any interaction between the two groups. According to the preaching of John the Baptist, the have-nots should be the beneficiaries of those who have something to give, and should not be victimized by the powerful, i.e., tax collectors and soldiers (3:10-14). Similarly, 21:1-4 contrasts the rich and the poor widow. Interaction between rich and poor occurs not only in the stories mentioned in the previous section, but in other pericopes as well. The story of the great banquet illustrates the importance of generosity to the poor and disabled (14:12-14). The parable of the unjust steward serves as a platform for the admonition to make friends by means of one's ill-gotten riches (16:1-33)[33] The story of Zacchaeus recounts how the poor and others who were the victims of this tax collector's oppression were to become the beneficiaries of his generosity (19:1-10). Finally, as I have noted, the poor widow in 19:1-10 is the victim of the cruel judge's indifference..

These Lukan references to the poor offer an interesting foil to the material in 1 Enoch. By and large, it is their poverty and their victimization by the rich and powerful that characterizes them. There are a few exceptions. The Magnificat contrasts "those who fear God" with "the proud," the beatitudes, with the references to their future reward, imply that they are righteous in some sense, and the story of the widow in the temple describes and act of piety (21:1-4). But, in contrast to the Epistle, which focuses on the unjust treatment of "the righteous" and "the pious," Luke employs the term "the poor" or its synonyms more frequently than designations of their status before God.

2.3 Judgment in the Gospel According to Luke

Luke's portrayal of the rewards and punishments of rich and poor parallels quite closely its counterparts in the Epistle of Enoch and the Enochic corpus more generally (above § 1.3). The Magnificat contrasts the punishment of the proud, the mighty, and the rich with the reward of the poor and lowly. In each case, God reverses their situation, giving to the one what had previously been the lot of the other (1:50-53). The Beatitudes and Woes present a similar picture (6:20-26). In the story of the rich farmer, where only the rich person is an active human character, his greedy attempt to secure his future with plenty, at the expense of those who should share in his bounty, results in his loss of that future. Because he intends to "Eat, drink and be merry," tomorrow (after "this night") he is dead.[34] Its paired story, that of Dives and Lazarus, most closely approximates Enochic idiom and imagery (16:19-31). Each of the two major characters receives the opposite of what he had experienced in this life, which is, at the same time, what the other had experienced in his life.[35] Both the parable of the unjust steward (16:19-31) and the story about Zacchaeus promise rewards to the sinful rich who repent and share the wealth with the poor. The initial conclusion to the story of the steward exhorts people with ill-gotten riches to use these to buy friends (presumably the poor) who will welcome them into the "eternal mansions," attesting their generosity (16:9).[36] The story of Zacchaeus illustrates how one such person, a tax-collector and extortionist, brought salvation to his house by giving alms to the poor and repaying and recompensing those whom he had defrauded.[37] Finally, the story of the importunate widow illustrates the ideas expressed in 1 Enoch 103:14-104:13: God will vindicate the cries of the oppressed poor.[38]

Luke has some specific notions about the locus of post-mortem judgment. The story of Dives and Lazarus presents an graphic image of the other world that combines features in the Epistle and in Enoch's journey vision to the realm of the dead (1 Enoch 22). The angels carry Lazarus to Abraham's bosom (cf. 104:1-6), while Dives suffers in the fires of Hades (cf. 103:7-8). The separation of Lazarus, with his access to refreshing water, and Dives and his torture is paralleled to some degree by the notion of separation in 1 Enoch 22.[39] A totally different idea appears in the first Beatitude, albeit one that is also paralleled in 1 Enoch. The poor will inherit *the earth*.

2.4 Luke's Admonitions to the Rich

I have noted that the Epistle paints a highly critical picture of the rich and their oppression of the righteous and anticipates their final punishment. There may be a few exceptions to this in the Epistle. According to 100:6[40]

> Then the wise among men will see the truth,
> > and the sons of the earth will contemplate the words of this epistle,
> > and they will recognize that their wealth cannot save them when iniquity
> > collapses.

It is unclear whether this is a threat of damnation, or whether it allows that some may repent at Enoch's preaching and be saved. Such a hope for "the sons of men" or "sons of (the whole) earth" is expressed in 1 Enoch 10:21; 91:14; and 105:1. Similarly, 101:1-9 appeals to "the sons of men" to follow the example of the sea captains, who throw their goods overboard in order to save their lives from a storm.

These exceptions clarify all the more the message of doom that runs through the Epistle. They also offer a point of contact with Luke, whose expectations of the rich are much more optimistic than the general line taken by the Epistle. The artful linking and pairing of the stories in chapters 16, 18, and 19 illustrate the point. The rich farmer asks "What shall I do," keeps his goods for himself, and is damned. The unjust steward asks the same question and buys himself friends--a parable for the unjustly rich. The tax collector in 18:9-14 repents and is justified. Because the rich ruler who asks, "What shall I do," refuses to give all to the poor, he will be excluded from the kingdom (18:18-15). Zacchaeus exemplifies obedience to Jesus' admonition in 16:9 and buys friends with his ill-gotten riches. As Luke already indicates in his addition to the Baptist's preaching (3:10-14), the big question is: "What shall I/we do," and it is always posed with reference to material goods.[41] He provides examples of people who give both the wrong answer and the right answer. That some give the right answer, and that Luke has Jesus exhort the rich to make the right decision (12:13-15, 22-31; 14:12-14; 16:9-13) suggests to me that for all his parallels to the Epistle of Enoch, Luke is much more hopeful that the rich among his audience--the likes of "Most Excellent Theophilus"--will heed his admonitions.

2.5 Literary Form in the Gospel According to Luke

A discussion of literary form in Luke is perhaps as complex as a treatment of the book's social setting. Here I touch only on matters relating to the gospel's portrayals of rich and poor and its possible connections with apocalyptic and sapiential traditions.

Clearly, the gospel is not an apocalypse, though a few passages have been shaped by traditional visionary forms.[42] Nonetheless, there are some parallels of both form and nuance between the gospel and the Epistle of Enoch. Strikingly they fall into the overlapping area of wisdom, prophecy, and the apocalyptic appropriation of both. Perhaps most notable is Luke's juxtaposition of Beatitudes and Woes. We have already noted the Epistle's use of a Beatitude to carry its message of judgment. Those who listen to the words of the wise and obey God's commandments will be saved (99:10; see above § 1.4). Luke 6:20-23 uses this sapiential form with reference to judgment and the reversal of circumstances. The present oppressive circumstances of the poor and deprived are contrasted with their future reversal. This pattern is underscored by Luke's juxtaposition of these Beatitudes with a string of Woes against the rich that fit precisely the eschatologized pattern of the Enochic Woes. Another formal parallel to the Epistle appears in the story of the rich farmer, which has a counterpart in both 1 Enoch 97:7-10 and Sir 11:18-19.[43] Granted this is a "parable," the Enochic text is a Woe, and the Sirach passage, a brief example beginning with "There is..." However, all three coincide formally in their use of quotation and refutation.

Luke agrees with Enoch against Sirach by depicting the rich man in a bad light and by depicting his demise as divine judgment.

Two aspects of the issue of form are more complicated. The first should be obvious by now. In large part, Luke's discussions of rich and poor are embodied in "parables" (though they are not always called such) that teach right and wrong conduct by exemplifying it in narrative. The term "parable" is, of course, at home in sapiential literature, although I am aware of no such narrative parables in the wisdom literature of the Greco-Roman period. In any case, the striking thing about these Lukan stories about rich and poor is their motif of post-mortem, other-worldly judgment, which is typical of the Epistle of Enoch, but not of Sirach, to use our parade example. A second aspect of form is Luke's frequent use of second person moral exhortation. Often he uses it to frame his exemplifying parables. Grammatically this usage is paralleled in wisdom texts like ben Sira, but it also runs like a thread through the Epistle of Enoch. Where it differs from ben Sira and agrees with the Epistle is in its positing the enactment of post-mortem, otherworldly judgment. This the case in 16:9, but also in the Q saying that follows the story of the rich farmer at 12:33-34.

2.6 Revelation in the Gospel According to Luke

In my discussion of the Epistle, I emphasized that this author *presumed* a dualistic world view mediated by revelation, even though he did not present it in visionary apocalyptic form. I believe that, with some qualification, we can say the same for the author of the third gospel. We have already noted the extent to which his moral exhortations are driven by the expectation of a final judgment, which is sometimes explicitly post-mortem and otherworldly. Luke sees a decisive caesura between this world /age/life and the next. What is the basis for this viewpoint? I suggest that some of his assertions and allusions to this effect are, in fact, based on apocalyptic revelation. I cite two examples for the sake of discussion. First, the story of Dives and Lazarus is based on revelatory traditions in 1 Enoch, as I have suggested above. Secondly, Luke's expectations about the coming of the Son of Man reflect apocalyptic traditions in Daniel and the Parables of Enoch (1 Enoch 37-71) or perhaps the source of the Parables material about the Chosen One/Son of Man.[44] We should qualify these statements. The final form of the Third Gospel comprises multiple layers of tradition: the historical Jesus; the oral creation and development of the Jesus traditions; a variety of written sources; and the final composition itself with its redaction of all of its sources. At what points in this developing process of tradition, the tradents were aware of the apocalyptic character of their traditions and at what point this may have become obscured is a matter to be investigated in the case of each pericope. I wish only to argue: a) that the author of Luke employed what were originally apocalyptic traditions; and b) that the non-apocalyptic *form* of his gospel need not exclude his awareness of the apocalyptic roots of his traditions. One may argue that his depiction of a non-visionary Jesus as the authority for the dominical sayings that constitute most of his text excludes the propriety of employing the term apocalyptic for his gospel. Such a thesis might help to clarify an aspect of our problem. What is the nature of revelatory authority in a given non-apocalypse, and how does it compare with revelatory authority in explicitly apocalyptic texts?

2.7 Summary

Luke's gospel frequently depicts the rich and powerful oppressing, or at least callously disregarding the poor. He posits a decisive judgment at death and/or at the end of the present order, which will reverse the fates of the rich and the poor. The pericopes that embody these ideas have important parallels in 1 Enoch, especially the Epistle, and have been shaped by forms that are at home in both the sapiential and apocalyptic traditions. In what ways they can meaningfully be called sapiential, apocalyptic, or revelatory in some other sense is a matter for further discussion.

3. Conclusion and Some Final Thoughts Relating the Comparative Study of Wisdom and Apocalypticism

Both the Epistle of Enoch and the Gospel according to Luke posit a decisive, post-mortem, otherworldly judgment, and subsequent rewards and punishments as the means adjudicate the present unjust prosperity of the rich and the suffering of the poor whom they oppress or disregard. This great reversal is set within the framework of a spacial and temporal dualism: this world / heaven and Sheol or Hades; the present life or time / its end through a judgment that ushers in a new life or time. Although both texts present these ideas in literary forms that are at home in sapiential texts of the Greco-Roman period, their ultimate source is a visionary revelatory tradition. This is clear enough in the Epistle of Enoch, which constitutes a parenetic application of the visionary traditions to which it is appended. For Luke that revelatory authority is one or several steps removed.

As we consider and compare other themes and their occurrence in Jewish and Christian texts and traditions customarily categorized as "sapiential" or "apocalyptic," it may be helpful to consider whether they are grounded in revelatory authority and, if so, of what sort. The use of sapiential forms does not, in and of itself, indicate a non-apocalyptic world view. Conversely, the use of *topoi* at home in apocalyptic literature does not, in and of itself, justify the term "apocalyptic." We need to be especially cautious about confusing the terms "eschatological" and "apocalyptic" and wary of assuming that a dualistic eschatology (a sharp break between this age and the next) is apocalyptic, since such eschatologies can be found in prophetic writings whose sense of revelation differs substantially from that of the apocalypses.[45] It is my hunch that we will shed helpful light on our project by keeping on our horizon: the continuities and discontinuities between biblical "prophecy" and apocalypticism; the attitudes of the sapiential literature toward prophecy; and the spectrum of notions about revelation evident in all of this literature. Along with all of this we need to focus, as I have not in this paper, on the figure of the alleged and real authors of this literature. What have Enoch, the three hundred years of sages and seers behind the Enochic literature, Jesus of Nazareth, the tradents of the Jesus tradition, and the author of Luke in common with one another as authoritative mouthpieces of God?

NOTES

1 George W. E. Nickelsburg, "Riches, the Rich, and God's Judgment in 1 Enoch 92-105 and the Gospel according to Luke," *NTS* 25 (1979) 324-44.

2 Ibid., 342.

3 On the corpus, see George W. E. Nickelsburg, "Enoch, First Book of," *ABD* 2 (1992) 509-12.

4 Idem, *Jewish Literature Between the Bible and the Mishnah: A Historical and Literary Introduction* (Philadelphia: Fortress, 1981) 150-51.

5 To this should be added 81:1-4, which preserves a remnant of the last of Enoch's journey visions, Randal A. *Argall, 1 Enoch and Sirach: A Comparative Literary and Conceptual Analysis of the Themes of Revelation, Creation, and Judgment* (SBLEJL 8; Atlanta: Scholars Press, 1995) 257-65.

6 George W. E. Nickelsburg, "The Epistle of Enoch and the Qumran Literature," *JJS* 33 (1982) = Essays in Honour of Yigael Yadin, 334-40.

7 Translations from the Epistle are my own and are based the text-critical work in my article, "Enoch 97-104: A Study of the Greek and Ethiopic Texts," in Michael E. Stone, ed., *Armenian and Biblical Studies* (Sion Supp 1; Jerusalem: St. James, 1976) 90-156.

8 Cf. Jer 22:13-14 ("Woe to him who builds his house by unrighteousness and his upper rooms by injustice; who makes his neighbor serve him for nothing and does not give him his wages"), which is the inspiration for 94:7, as well as 99:13 (see below).

9 The Ethiopic of this phrase reads "the strength of the root of the fountain." For the first two nouns I posit a corruption from the Greek verb *kratērizein* to *kratē rizēs*. For the emendation from "fountain" to "wine" and the emenation in v 6, see R. H. Charles, APOT 2 (1913) 267.

10 See J. T. Milik *The Books of Enoch* (Oxford: Clarendon Press, 1976) 50-51.

11 *ouk apo dikaiosynēs / adikōs*; cf. Jer. 22:13, quoted above in n. 8).

12 On the complex text-critical problems of this passage, see Nickelsburg, "Enoch 97-104," 113-17.

13 For a similar passage, cf. Sir 15:11-17:24.

14 Cf. Jer. 22:13-17 and see nn. 9 and 11 above.

15 "Deceit" is a common expression for false teaching in the Epistle; see Nickelsburg, "Epistle," 339.

16 For a similar metaphorical usage, cf. CD 1:16.

17 See George W. E. Nickelsburg, *Resurrection, Immortality, and Eternal Life in Intertestamental Judaism* (HTS 26, Cambridge: Harvard University / London: Oxford University, 1972) 118-19.

18 See George W. E. Nickelsburg, "The Apocalyptic Message of 1 Enoch 92-105," *CBQ* 39 (1977) 318-22.

19 For this Aramaic reading, see 4QEn^g 1 4.17, Milik, *Books of Enoch*, 266.

20 For the possibility that the body of the Epistle was added to a text that already included the Apocalypse of Weeks, see Gabriele Boccaccini, *Beyond the Essene Hypothesis: The Parting of the Ways between Qumran and Enochic Judaism* (Grand Rapids: Eerdmans, 1998) 104-13. I differ from Boccaccini in thinking that the earlier material was attached to the Book of Watchers and did not constitute a "Proto-Epistle."

21 Cf. 1 Enoch 10:16-11:2; 90:28-36; and in the later Book of Parables, e.g., 45:4-5.

22 Nickelsburg, "Apocalyptic Message," 310-13.

23 Ibid., 317-18.

24 Ibid., 315-17.

25 See Argall, *1 Enoch and Sirach*, 101-12.

26 See above, n. 5.

27 "The Apocalyptic Construction of Reality of 1 Enoch," in John J. Collins and James H. Charlesworth, ed., *Mysteries and Revelations: Apocalyptic Studies since the Uppsala Colloquium* (JSPSupp 9; Sheffield: Sheffield Academic Press, 1991) 51-64.

28 "Wisdom and Apocalypticism in Early Judaism: Some Points for Discussion," in SBLASP 1994, 715-32.

29 Ibid., 719-20.

30 See the collection of articles edited by Jerome H. Neyrey, *The Social World of Luke-Acts* (Peabody, MA: Hendrikson, 1991).

31 Nickelsburg, "Riches," 332-43.

32 Ibid., 336-37.

33 On this meaning of the expression, see ibid., 337.

34 For this interpretation, see ibid, 334.

35 For the parallel in 1 Enoch, see above, n. 18.

36 Nickelsburg, "Riches," 337.

37 Ibid., 339-40.

38 For the parallels, see ibid., 339.

39 The specifics of the cosmologies of 1 Enoch 22 and Luke 16:19-31 differ. The former depicts the mountain of the dead, with the souls residing in separate compartments; the latter sees the righteous in Abraham's bosom separated from the netherworld. In common, however, are the notion of separation, the righteous being refreshed by water, and the torture of at least some of the sinners.

40 On the text of this verse, see Nickelsburg, "Enoch 97-104," .

41 On this question in Luke-Acts, see Nickelsburg, "Riches," 341.

42 For Jesus as a visionary, see Luke 10:18, "I saw Satan fall like lightning from heaven" (cf. Rev. 12:7-9). Other texts that reflect the visionary tradition include the stories of Jesus' baptism and transfiguration and the post-resurrection Christophanies.

43 For the parallels, see Nickelsburg, "Riches," 335.

44 On the Synoptic Son of Man traditions and the Parables of Enoch, see George W. E. Nickelsburg, "Son of Man," in *ABD* 6 (1992) 141-46.

45 See Nickelsburg, "Eschatology (Early Jewish)," *ABD* 5 (1992) 593.

The Primal Man in Ezekiel and the Image of God

Dexter E. Callender, Jr.
University of Miami

I

One of hallmarks of the book of Ezekiel is its extensive use of analogical language in its portrayal of humanity. The book also is known to represent a considerable amount of Israel's traditional lore as well as its scripture. One passage that represents the book's use of such imagery is Ezekiel 28:11–19, a text which preserves an oracle against the king of Tyre uttered in the form of a lament. The lament is allegorical and presents a figure to whom the king is likened. Scholarship has long suspected that the passage is a variant tradition of the Yahwist's Eden narrative in Genesis 2–3, and that the figure who forms the basis of the allegory is a variant of the first man. But this is far from certain; the language is difficult, and there are many unanswered questions.

One of the most elusive aspects of the text is the difficult phrase *hôtēm toknît* (v. 12), which literally describes the figure as a "sealer" of the lexically obscure word *toknît*. It is particularly significant because it is the first phrase used to describe the figure. It is arguably an important part of our understanding of the oracle, its relation to the Ezekielian tradition and to the larger canon of the Hebrew Bible. How is this best read and what does it signify? What imagery does it conjure, and how might it be considered an appropriate way to designate the king of Tyre?

The text of Ezek 28:11–19 and my translation are as follows:

11וַיְהִי דְבַר־יְהֹוָה אֵלַי לֵאמֹר: 12 בֶּן־אָדָם שָׂא קִינָה
עַל־מֶלֶךְ צוֹר וְאָמַרְתָּ לּוֹ כֹּה אָמַר אֲדֹנָי יְהֹוִה אַתָּה חוֹתֵם תָּכְנִית מָלֵא
חָכְמָה וּכְלִיל יֹפִי: 13 בְּעֵדֶן גַּן־אֱלֹהִים הָיִיתָ כָּל־אֶבֶן יְקָרָה מְסֻכָתֶךָ
אֹדֶם פִּטְדָה וְיָהֲלֹם תַּרְשִׁישׁ שֹׁהַם וְיָשְׁפֵה סַפִּיר נֹפֶךְ וּבָרְקַת וְזָהָב
מְלֶאכֶת תֻּפֶּיךָ וּנְקָבֶיךָ בָּךְ בְּיוֹם הִבָּרַאֲךָ כּוֹנָנוּ: 14 אַתְּ־כְּרוּב מִמְשַׁח
הַסּוֹכֵךְ וּנְתַתִּיךָ בְּהַר קֹדֶשׁ אֱלֹהִים הָיִיתָ בְּתוֹךְ אַבְנֵי־אֵשׁ הִתְהַלָּכְתָּ:

15 תָּמִים אַתָּה בִּדְרָכֶיךָ מִיּוֹם הִבָּרְאָךְ עַד־נִמְצָא עַוְלָתָה בָּךְ:
16 בְּרֹב רְכֻלָּתְךָ מָלוּ תוֹכְךָ חָמָס וַתֶּחֱטָא וָאֲחַלֶּלְךָ מֵהַר אֱלֹהִים וָאַבֶּדְךָ
כְּרוּב הַסֹּכֵךְ מִתּוֹךְ אַבְנֵי־אֵשׁ: 17 גָּבַהּ לִבְּךָ בְּיָפְיֶךָ שִׁחַתָּ חָכְמָתְךָ
עַל־יִפְעָתֶךָ עַל־אֶרֶץ הִשְׁלַכְתִּיךָ לִפְנֵי מְלָכִים נְתַתִּיךָ לְרַאֲוָה בָךְ:
18 מֵרֹב עֲוֹנֶיךָ בְּעֶוֶל רְכֻלָּתְךָ חִלַּלְתָּ מִקְדָּשֶׁיךָ וָאוֹצִא־אֵשׁ מִתּוֹכְךָ הִיא
אֲכָלַתְךָ וָאֶתֶּנְךָ לְאֵפֶר עַל־הָאָרֶץ לְעֵינֵי כָּל־רֹאֶיךָ: 19 כָּל־יוֹדְעֶיךָ
בָּעַמִּים שָׁמְמוּ עָלֶיךָ בַּלָּהוֹת הָיִיתָ וְאֵינְךָ עַד־עוֹלָם:

(11) And the word of the Lord came to me: (12) "Son of Man, lift up a lamentation over the king of Tyre and say to him, Thus says the Lord God: 'You were a seal, a likeness; full of wisdom and perfect in beauty. (13) You were in Eden, the garden of God, every precious stone was your covering: sardius, topaz, and moonstone; gold topaz, carnelian, and jasper; lapis lazuli, garnet, and emerald; and of gold was its workmanship.[a] Your timbrels and your pipes[b] were established on the day you were created. (14) I placed you with[c] the anointed guardian cherub; you were on the holy mountain of God. Amongst stones of fire you walked. (15) You were blameless in your ways from the day you were created until iniquity was found[d] in you. (16) In the abundance of your trade you filled yourself[e] with violence and you sinned. I cast you as a profane thing from the mountain of God and the guardian cherub drove you from the midst of the stones of fire. (17) Your heart was proud because of your beauty; you corrupted your wisdom for the sake of your splendor. I cast you upon the earth; I set you before kings so they could look upon you.[f] (18) By the multitude of your iniquities in the unrighteousness of your trade you profaned your sanctuaries. So I sent fire from the midst of you. It consumed you and I made you dust on the earth in the eyes of all who see you. (19) All who know you among the

peoples were awestruck over you. You became an object of terror[g] and you ceased to exist forever.[1]

Notes to the Translation

[a]Reading מלאכה for MT singular construct form מלאכת.

[b]Taking MT בך "with you" as a dittograph perhaps arising from the sequence נקביך ביום.

[c]Following LXX, which reflects ʾet kerûb "with the cherub."

[d]The disagreement between the verb nimṣāʾ, which is masculine, and the subject ʿawlātâ, which is feminine, is admissible on the grounds that it frequently occurs when predicate precedes the subject (GKC §145o).

[e]Reading מל(א)ת "you filled" as suggested by LXX επλησας.

[f]Lit. "to look at you."

[g]Following Zimmerli for the difficult ballāhôt hāyîtā "you were calamities."

A primary concern here, as is true for much of the book of Ezekiel, is the text. The grammatical difficulty of the phrase and the appearance of the extremely rare word toknît —a word that arguably reflects a textual corruption—urges us at the outset to seek for a better reading. An interesting example of a commentator who upheld the MT is G. Widengren; he accepted the MT reading ḥôtēm toknît and offered an interpretation of the phrase based on Near Eastern parallels. Widengren argued that the term toknît referred to the high priestly breastpiece, which he construed as the Israelite equivalent to the Mesopotamian "tablet of destiny" (ṭup šîmāti). He interpreted the participle ḥotēm "sealer" on the basis of Enuma Elish iv. 121–22, according to which Marduk seals the tablets of destiny with a seal. Therefore, ḥôtēm toknît is a reference to the

---

[1]This oracle is given as a qînâ, and presumably was originally conceived with some measure of metrical regularity. Nevertheless, the MT is so difficult with respect to text, grammar, and semantics, not to mention alleged glosses, that the editors of BHS opted to forgo metrical arrangement. For convenience of discussion, I have elected to do the same. The latter portions of the oracle yield more obvious signs of parallelism.

protagonist as guardian or keeper of the tablets.[2] Unfortunately, however, one cannot support his understanding of *toknît* on comparative Semitic linguistic grounds.[3] More problematic, however, is the difference in function between the Israelite urim and thummim and the Mesopotamian tablets of destiny. Although Widengren's observation that the tablets of destiny were worn in a pouch on the chest akin to the urim and thummim is intriguing, his statement that the "Primordial Man, the mythical exemplar of both the Phoenician and Israelitic ruler, was wearing the Heavenly Tablets, deciding the destinies of the world" does not accord with the biblical evidence concerning the breastpiece.[4]

The difficulty in making sense of the present MT reading has given rise to numerous proposed emendations to the consonantal text. Among these are J. Smith's "bridegroom of Tanith," reading *hôtēn tanît*; G. A. Cooke's *hākām lĕtaklît* "perfectly wise"; and the reading of P. Cheminant, *tamîm tabnît*, rendered "perfect in form."[5] These examples reveal the difficulty commentators have had in coming to terms with both words in question. For various reasons, some of which are fairly obvious, none of these has garnered scholarly consensus.

This paper will offer an interpretation of the phrase which brings greater clarity to the oracle and which renders it more coherent with related aspects of biblical imagery. I will argue that, given the available evidence, the phrase is best understood in view of the reference to the creation of the first human in the image (*ṣelem*)

---

[2] *The Ascension of the Apostle and the Heavenly Book: King and Savior III* (Uppsala universitetsårsskrift; Uppsala: Lundequists, 1950) 26-27. See also "Early Hebrew Myths and their Interpretation," *Myth, Ritual, and Kingship*, (ed. S.H. Hooke; Oxford: Clarendon, 1958) 167–68: "They were fastened to his breast in a pouch in exactly the same manner as Marduk wore them in Enuma eliš, iv. 121-2 (cf. i. 156-7)."

[3] There is no simple equation of Akkadian *taknitu* with *toknît*, given the unlikely phonological development of Hebrew *o* from an earlier protosemitic **a*, reflected in Akkadian *taknitu*.

[4] "Early Hebrew Myths," 167. Every indication concerning the breastpiece of judgment is that it was understood to reveal the divine will.

[5] J. Smith, *The Book of the Prophet Ezekiel* (London: SPCK, 1931) 75; G.A. Cooke, *A Critical and Exegetical Commentary on the Book of Ezekiel* (ICC; Edinburgh: Clark, 1936); P. Cheminant, *Les Prophéties d'Ezéchiel contre Tyre* (Paris: Letouzey et Ane, 1912).

and likeness (děmût) of God, found in the priestly tradition of Gen 1:26.

II

The form of Ezekiel's oracle concerning the king of Tyre combines lament and classic prophetic judgment speech. It begins with a historical retrospect (11-15) and continues with an indictment and announcement of judgment (16-19), both of which are spoken of as having occurred in the past. As such, the oracle tells a story about the king of Tyre that directs the reader's attention to the myth upon which it is based. There are several features of the oracle that indicate that the tradition the oracle draws upon is that of the primal man. By "primal man" I refer to the biblical concept of a first human who forms a link or interface between humanity and the divine. The clearest attestation of this tradition is found in three places in the biblical canon. Genesis 1-3 present the most direct presentation of the tradition. Job 15:7ff provides an indirect witness when Eliphaz asks Job:

> "were you born the first man?"
> were you brought forth before the hills?
> Did you listen in the council of God,
> and do you limit wisdom to yourself?

Here, the "first man" is alluded to by way of analogy or metaphor. Such appears to be the case in Ezek 28:11-19 as well. The first feature indicative of the primal man tradition comprises several allusions in Ezek 28:11-19 which suggest a connection with J's Eden narrative of Genesis 3. The setting is Eden, the fecund primordial garden which, among other things, provides a staging area for human/divine contact. In Ezekiel's oracle it is referred to as ʿēden gan ʾĕlōhîm, "Eden, the garden of God." The mention of a "guardian cherub" in Ezekiel 28 is likewise suggestive. Here, it drives the protagonist from among the stones of fire, whereas in Gen 3:24, it guards the way to the garden's tree of life.[6] The

---

[6] The MT phrase ʾatt kerûb "you were the cherub," immediately suggests that the protagonist and the cherub are one and the same. This position is accepted by Tryggve Mettinger, *King and Messiah: The Civil and Sacral Legitimation of the Israelite Kings* (Lund: Gleerup, 1976), and most recently by M. Greenberg *Ezekiel 21-37: a New Translation with Introduction and*

recurring emphasis in Ezek 28:15-18 on "sin" and the subsequent judgment announced by God reflects the decision of the human couple in Genesis to disregard the prohibition of Yahweh and the subsequent curses he placed upon them.

There are other, more subtle, allusions which suggest that the protagonist in Ezek 28:11-19 is a human figure akin to what is preserved in Genesis 2–3. One is expressed in the judgment portion of the oracle and recounts the reduction of the protagonist "to ashes."[7] This is reminiscent of the curse placed on Adam in Gen 3:19 "you are dust and to dust you shall return." Also, the lament makes allusion to the apparent divine knowledge of the protagonist. This is seen in the reference to the stones of the high priestly breastpiece (v. 13). Here too, wisdom is understood within the context of the protagonist's humanity—the stones signify divine knowledge in the hands of a human. The reference recalls the human acquisition of "the knowledge of good and evil" in Genesis 2–3, shorthand for higher knowledge more properly belonging to the realm of the divine.[8]

Next, the placement of the lament alongside the oracle against the prince of Tyre (vv. 1-10) likewise suggests a perceived connection with Genesis 2–3 on the part of the redactors of Ezekiel.[9] In the immediately preceding oracle, the prince of Tyre is berated by means

---

Commentary (AB; New York: Doubleday, 1997) 579–84. In view of the material in Genesis 3 and the generally acknowledged corruptions of the MT of Ezekiel, it is likely that LXX represents an earlier text.

[7]The fact that the term *ʾēper* is used, as opposed to *ʿāpār* of the Genesis account, is of little consequence. The two terms are interchangeable as far as they regard the composition of the human body. Job likened his tragic situation to death, saying that he had been cast into the clay (*ḥomer*) and had "become like dust (*ʿāpār*) and ashes (*ʾēper*)," all three words vividly expressing his physical constitution (Job 30:19). In Gen 18:27, Abraham expresses a state of humility before God with the words "I have set out to speak to the Lord, though I am but dust (*ʿāpār*) and ashes (*ʾēper*)." It is clear that no distinction is to be made here between the two terms *ʾēper* and *ʿāpār*.

[8]I am inclined to understand the phrase *daʿat tôb wārāʿ* as a merismus, expressing what might be referred to as "the knowledge of all things." For a discussion of various interpretations of the phrase, see H. Wallace, *The Eden Narrative* (Atlanta: Scholars Press, 1985), 120ff.

[9]This was observed earlier by Hermann Gunkel in his *Genesis*, (Göttinger Handkommentar zum alten Testament, ed. W. Nowack; Göttingen: Vandenhoeck und Ruprecht, 1910) 34.

of metaphoric reference to a mythical figure which shows signs of being a variant expression of the ideas found in Genesis 2–3. The protagonist is explicitly identified as a human (ʾattā ʾādām). Just as Adam is placed in Eden, where Yahweh freely strolls about (cf. Gen 3:8), so too is the protagonist in Ezek 28:1–10 set within a locus for divine activity, called the "dwelling of the gods" (môšab ʾelôhîm; v. 2). In Ezek 28:1-10, allusion is made to the apparent divine knowledge of the protagonist, which is construed within the context of the protagonist's humanity ("you have made your mind like the mind of God" tittēn libbĕkā kĕlēb ʾĕlōhîm). Such a statement immediately brings to mind the issues surrounding the disobedient consumption of the fruit in Genesis 3. These are, to be specific, the rationale of the serpent ("you will be like God, knowing good and evil"), the immediate effect of their having consumed the fruit ("their eyes were opened"), and the response of God ("see, the man has become like us, knowing good and evil").[10]

Finally, ancient commentators considered Ezek 28:11-19 a reflection of the primal man tradition. The Targum's reading of the phrase corresponding to MT hôtēm toknît suggests "the sculptural pattern" or "sculptural mold," highlighting Adam as the first human, the mold for all subsequent generations. Likewise, rabbinic sources explicitly speak of Ezek 28:11-19 as a reference to Adam. Thus, b. B.B. 75a makes reference to Adam in Ezek 28:13 in the following manner:

> "The Holy One, blessed be He, made ten canopies for Adam in the garden of Eden; for it is said: Thou was in Eden, the garden of God; every precious stone was thy covering..."

Likewise Adam is perceived in the background of Ezek 28:11–19 in Eccl. R. 7:36:

> "another interpretation of 'who is as the wise man?' This alludes to Adam of whom it is written, 'Thou seal most

---

[10] M. Pope understood this oracle to be an expression of an Ugaritic myth pertaining specifically to the god El. See El in the Ugaritic Texts, (Leiden: Brill, 1955) 97–98. The thematic closeness of this oracle with the Eden narrative of Genesis 3, however, makes it difficult to conclude that the Israelite audience restricted the reference to only Ugaritic ideas without understanding some direct connection to its own tradition.

accurate, full of wisdom...thou was in Eden the garden of God.[11]

At the turn of the century, modern commentators continued to consider Ezek 28:11–19 a variant of the Eden narrative of Gen 2–3. H. Gunkel, for example, understood Gen 2–3 and Ezek 28:11-19 to be essentially the same story. For Gunkel, the essential difference between the two traditions was that the Ezekiel oracle was more "mythological," evident in his interpretation of the protagonist in Ezekiel as something of a "demigod."[12]

III

Having established the background of the oracle, we may turn now more specifically to the phrase in question, beginning with MT *ḥôtēm*. It is evident that the reading *ḥôtām* "seal" most likely represents the earlier text. First, both the LXX ἀποσφράγισμα and Vulgate *signaculum* render "seal."[13] On this basis alone, the emendation to *ḥôtam* "seal" has been widely adopted. The central idea is that of a cylinder or stamp seal used by a person to impress his or her "signature" (as it were) on a document or similar item.[14]

Secondly, such an emendation is supported by the fact that in three places in the Hebrew Bible, a person is referred to metaphorically as a seal. The notion of a seal symbolizing the king as Yahweh's vice regent is found in Jer 22:24:

> "As I live, declares the Lord, if Coniah the son of Jehoiakim, king of Judah, is a signet (*ḥôtām*) on my right hand, then from there shall I tear you; and I will place

---

[11] Cf. Pes. R. 14:10.

[12] For discussion and additional references, see Gunkel, *Genesis*, 37.

[13] *ḥôtam* is in the construct state, reflecting the genetive construction in LXX and Vulgate.

[14] Commentators have been divided whether to understand "seal" as the signet ring or the impression it leaves. ἀποσφράγισμα regularly signifies the impression of a seal, and *signaculum* is used in general to convey a "mark" or "sign," and in particular a seal or a signet (see LSJ for examples of ἀποσφράγισμα signifying the impression of a seal).

> you into the hand of those who seek your life...even into the hand of Nebuchadrezzar king of Babylon"[15]

In a similar fashion, the prophet Haggai relates in 2:23:

> "on that day, declares the Lord of hosts, I will take you Zerubbabel my servant, the son of Shealtiel, says the Lord, and I will make you like the signet (*kaḥôtām*); for I have chosen you, says the Lord of hosts."

One other passage in which a person is referred to as a seal is Song of Songs 8:6 "place me as the seal upon your heart (*śîmēnî kaḥôtām ʿal libbekā*); as the seal upon your arm (*kaḥôtām ʿal zĕrôʿekā*)." It is difficult to discern the precise meaning of this verse; still, the words that follow ("for love is as strong as death; jealousy is as harsh as the grave") make clear that it is to be regarded as a statement of considerable force.[16]

Thirdly, the examples of Jehoiachin and Zerubbabel in Jer 22:24 and Hag 2:23 further corroborate the metaphorical use of "seal" in Ezekiel 28 insofar as both passages apply the imagery specifically within a royal context. Following the statement that Jehoiachin will be torn off of the hand of Yahweh, we are told that he would be placed in the hand of "those who seek [his] life." To be "given into the hand (*bĕyad*)" of the enemy is a common idiom. Here, *ʿal yad* suggests a double-entendre, signifying that the seal is torn from the hand of YHWH and placed upon the hand of Nebuchuchadnezzar. This may also refer to a disowning of the Davidic king as Yahweh's representative (cf. v. 30). It may signify that the very symbol of his

---

[15] There is some question about the syntax of the verse. This statement uses an anomalous construction to coordinate the two clauses. כִּי אִם with the oath formula conventionally expresses an asseverative, but it is not attested with a subsequent clause introduced by כִּי; hence, "Coniah is indeed a signet...surely I will tear him from there." If taken as a conditional sentence, it is probably better understood as expressing a real condition as opposed to unreal (contra NRSV "Even if...even from there" and NJB "even if...still I would")

[16] On the interpretation of this verse, see M. Pope, *Song of Songs* (AB; Garden City, NY: Doubleday, 1964) 666-69. According to Hallo, the beloved's desire for "physical intimacy" and "the status-symbol seal function assumed by the seal in burials" is the key to the text: "even as the latter perpetuates the owner's standing in death, so the beloved declares that her lover's role with regard to her will outlive him." W. W. Hallo, "'As a Seal upon Thine Arm': Glyptic Metaphors in the Biblical World," *Ancient Seals and the Bible* (ed. L. Gorelick and E. Williams-Forte; Malibu, CA: Undena, 1983) 12-13.

presence and authority would be given over for desecration, an idea akin to what is expressed elsewhere in Ezekiel 24:21[17] It does seem to make clear that the exile of Jehoiachin is interpreted as the once vice regent and representative of Yahweh being lowered to the status of subservience to a foreign ruler.[18] In Hag 2:21-23 the prophet proclaims the impending overthrow of the earth's ruling nations and the establishment of Yahweh's kingdom. In the new age, Zerubbabel will be elevated to a new status on the world stage. Making Zerubbabel "like the signet" strongly suggests that Zerubbabel, Yahweh's servant, and *choice*, and who is called governor of Judah (2:4), will reign in the new kingdom as Yahweh's representative and vice regent over the nations.[19] The examples in Jeremiah and in Haggai demonstrate that the seal as an image of royal authority was in use prior to and after the exile; hence, Ezekiel's use is by no means unusual.

A passage in the Joseph narrative demonstrates this significance of the seal with respect to the royal office. In Gen 42:39-45, Pharaoh makes Joseph his major domo and vice regent through the official act of investing Joseph with his seal:

> "you shall be over my house, and all my people shall order themselves as you command; only as regards the throne will I be greater than you." And Pharaoh said to Joseph, "Behold, I have set you over all the land of Egypt." Then Pharaoh took his signet ring from his hand and put it on Joseph's hand, and arrayed him in garments of fine linen, and put a gold chain about his neck; and he made him to ride in his second chariot; and they cried before him, "Bow the knee!" Thus he set him over all the land of Egypt. Moreover Pharaoh said to Joseph, "I am Pharaoh, and without your consent no man shall lift up hand or foot in all the land of Egypt."

---

[17]"Behold, I will profane my sanctuary, the pride of your power, the delight of your eyes, and the desire of your soul; and your sons and your daughters whom you left behind shall fall by the sword." Cf. Ezek 7:22, Ps 89:38–45.

[18]Cf. 2 Kings 24:12-15.

[19] The language of "choice" here invokes the notion of kingship; cf. Deut 17:15; 1 Chron 29:1. See also discussion of H. Seebass in *TDOT* (Grand Rapids: Eerdmans, 1975) 5:76–78.

In this narrative, Joseph becomes for all intents and purposes the essence of Pharaoh as the bearer of his seal.[20] He is the virtual ruler of Egypt. Nevertheless, the people did not bow to Joseph for Joseph's sake; they in effect bowed *in recognition of the seal* now *in Joseph's possession*, the embodiment and representation of Pharaoh himself.[21] Through bearing the seal, Joseph has become, for all intents and purposes, Pharaoh—an idea made explicit in the statement "*I* am Pharaoh, and without *your* consent...."[22]

In the cases of Coniah (Jehoiachin) and Zerubbabel, the seal imagery was an expression of their role as vice-regent. In Mesopotamia, the practice of kings considering themselves the vice-regent of a god is well known. In Assyrian royal inscriptions, the kings referred to themselves with terms such as "governor of Enlil" (*šakin* ^{d}*Enlil*) and "vice-regent of Aššur" (*iššâk* ^{d}*Aššur*).[23] It is significant for our purposes to note the observation that the epithet "vice-regent of Aššur" alluded specifically to the king as "intermediary between the god and the community."[24] In this respect, Coniah and Zerubbabel were expected to execute the divine will.

---

[20]The word for seal here is *ṭabbaʾat*. Both *ḥôtām* and *ṭabbaʾat* are most likely Egyptian in origin; see T.O. Lambdin "Egyptian Loan Words in the Old Testament," *JAOS* 73:145-55).

[21]By this I do not wish to imply any sense of "mystical" embodiment. The import is ideological and practical. Whoever had been granted the seal presumably would have been the (virtual) object of such actions.

[22]The same situation occurs in the book of Esther with regard to Haman (3:10), where we read "the king took his signet ring from his hand and gave it to Haman," who then is told to "do with [the people] as it seems good to you" (v. 11). This scenario is repeated in chapter 8 "The king took off his signet ring...and gave it to Mordecai" (v. 2). The king tells Mordecai "You may write as you please...in the name of the king, and seal it with the king's ring; for an edict written in the name of the king and is sealed with the king's ring cannot be revoked" (8:2, 8). The word in each case is *ṭabbaʾat*. On presentation seals in Mesopotamia, see J. A. Franke, "Presentation Seals of the Ur III/Isin-Larsa Period," *Seals and Sealings in the Ancient Near East* (ed. M. Gibson and R. D. Biggs; Bibliotheca Mesopotamica, 6; Malibu: Undena, 1977) 61-66.

[23]See *inter alios* P. Machinist "Literature as Politics: The Tukulti-Ninurta Epic and the Bible," *CBQ* 38 (1976) p. 465 and references.

[24]M. T. Larsen, *The Old Assyrian City State and Its Colonies* (Copenhagen: Akademisk Forlag, 1976) p. 119. Cited by S. Parpola "The Assyrian Tree of Life: Tracing the Origins of Jewish Monotheism and Greek Philosophy," *JNES* 52 (1993) 167 n. 28.

If the reading is correct here, it is not difficult to find explanation for expressing vice regency through the imagery of a seal. The significance of the seal lies in the realm of representation and authority—it represents the owner and signifies the owner's authority. The original significance of the seal is thought to be legal, having emerged along with capital formation as a mark of ownership or contractual obligation by an individual and a symbolic representation of the individual.[25] In this sense, the seal represents the "essence" of a person.[26]

The understanding of the seal as representing the owner may be observed in a different sense in the phenomenon of Mesopotamian votive seals. These seals inscribed with petitions concerning the life of the donor were deposited, just like votive statues, in the sanctuary "to convey that prayer to the deity in place of the donor himself or his statue."[27] That a seal could serve in the same capacity as a statue suggests a close connection of the ideas associated with the two. Thus a connection becomes evident between seal and statue in royal contexts in which the ruler is understood to be the representative of God. Gen 1:26 reflects this connection in the following terms:

> Then God said, "Let us make humankind in our image (bĕṣalmēnû), according to our likeness (kidmûtēnû); and let them have dominion over the fish of the sea, and over the birds of the air, and over the cattle, and over all the wild animals of the earth, and over every creeping thing that creeps upon the earth."

---

[25]See Hallo, "'As a Seal upon Thine Arm,'" 8. See also J. Renger, "Legal Aspects of Sealing in Ancient Mesopotamia," *Seals and Sealing in the Ancient Near East* (ed. M. Gibson and R. D. Biggs; Bibliotheca Mesopotamica, 6; Malibu: Undena, 1977) 75-88.

[26]The case in Genesis 38 according to which Judah's seal is used to identify him illustrates this (and at the same time draws attention to how items "owned" by an individual can likewise represent that person's essence). Here, Judah established his identity and has legally bound himself to a pledge by leaving his seal. Hallo interprets the cord and "staff" as the cord on which the seal is worn (around the neck) and the pin with which the seal is connected to the cord (Hallo, "'As a Seal upon Thine Arm,'" 8, 14).

[27]Hallo, "'As a Seal upon Thine Arm,'" 9. Cf. the Egyptian funerary practice of placing shawabti figurines in burial chambers to do the labor of the deceased.

H. Wildberger and W.H. Schmidt have gathered considerable evidence to demonstrate the notion of "image" as representative.[28] Wildberger argued that Gen 1:26 is based on the same royal language which describes the king as the *ṣalmu* or *muššulu* (image, likeness) of his god in Mesopotamia. And as P. Bird, among others, has correctly observed:

> Akkadian *ṣalmu* exhibits the same range of meaning as its Hebrew cognate, designating in its basic use a statue (in the round), a likeness or representation, usually of a deity or king, especially as set up in a temple as a visible sign and manifestation of the living god or person. It may also describe a relief or drawing, again usually of a king or deity. In transferred uses the basic idea of a likeness is maintained, with emphasis on resemblance, correspondence and representation.[29]

The imagery in Gen 1:26 is suggestive of royal statuary, taken figuratively, of course. Such an understanding has been strengthened by the Aramaic Tell el-Fakhariyeh inscription. Both Aramaic cognate words (*ṣlm* and *dmwt*) occur in the text, and both ultimately make reference to a "statue."

> ...*ṣlm:hdysᶜy*
> *mlk:gwzn:wzy:skn:wzy:ʾzrn:lʾrmwddt:krsʾh*
> *wlmʾrk:ḥywh:wlmᶜn:ʾmrt:pmh:ʾl:ʾlhn:wʾl:ʾnšn*
> *tyṭb:dmwtʾ:zʾt:ᶜbd:ʾl:zy:qdm:ḥwtr:qdm:hdd*
> *ysb:skn:mrʾ:ḥbwr:ṣlmh:šm*[30]

Image of Hadd-yis·y
King of Guzan and of Sikan and of Azran
for exalting and [?] his throne

---

[28] H. Wildberger "Das Abbild Gottes," *TZ* 21 (1965) 245-59, 481-501; see especially pp. 251-55. See also W. H. Schmidt, *Die Schöpfungsgeschichte der Priesterschrift* (WMANT 17; Neukirchen-Vluyn: Neukirchener Verlag, 1964).

[29] P. A. Bird "Male and Female He Created Them: Gen 1:27b in the Context of the Priestly Account of Creation," *HTR* 74 (1981) 142. "The image stands for the original, which it reproduces and shows forth. The term is basically concrete. It does not refer to an idea, nor does it describe a model, pattern or prototype."

[30] Lines 12, 15, 16. For text, see A. R. Millard and P. Bordreuil "A Statue from Syria with Assyrian and Aramaic Inscriptions," *BA* 45 (1982) 135-41. For *dmwt* see also line one.

and for lengthening his life,
and that the word of his mouth be good before the gods
and the people.
This *likeness* he made bigger than any before;
Before Hadad, who dwells at Sikan, Lord of Habur, his
image he has erected.

In simple terms, what has been erected is a statue *in the likeness* of
the king. The physical likeness of the king to the gods is expressed in
the Tukulti Ninurta Epic:

> *ina* (AŠ) *ši-mat* dNu-dím-mud ma-ni it-ti *šīr* (UZU)
> *ilāni* (DINGIRmeš) *mi-na-a-šu*

> *ina* (AŠ) *purussû* (EŠ.BAR) *bēl mātāti* (EN KUR.KUR)
> *ina* (AŠ) *ra-a-aṭ šas / turri* (ŠÀ.TÙR) *ilāni* (DINGIRmeš)
> *ši-pi-ik-šu i-te-eš-ra*

> *šu-û-ma ṣa-lam* dIllil (BE) *da-ru-ú še-e-mu pi-i nišē*
> (UK Umeš) *mi-lik māti* (KUR)

> *ú-šar-bi-šu-ma* dIllil (BE) *ki-ma a-bi a-li-di ar-ki*
> *mār(i)* (DUMU) *bu-uk-ri-šu*

By the fate (determined by) Nudimmud (Ea) his
(=Tukulti-Ninurta's) form is reckoned with the flesh of
the gods (*šēr ilāni*).

By the decision of the lord of the lands he was successfully
cast into/poured through the channel of the womb of the
gods.[31]

He alone is the eternal image (*ṣalam*) of Enlil, attentive
to the voice of the people, to the counsel of the land.

Enlil raised him like a natural father, after his first-born
son (=Ninurta).[32]

---

[31]The filial imagery of the formation of the king and the divine womb is
not insignificant and recalls the Judaean doctrine of divine adoption (Ps
89:26–27 [Heb. 27–28]), 2 Sam 7:14.

[32]Translation: P. Machinist, "Literature as Politics: The Tukulti-Ninurta
Epic and the Bible," *CBQ* 38 (1976) 455-82, esp. 456-66.

Here, to be the image of the deity, understood in terms of statuary, is a statement of royal status. The metaphorical equating of Jehoiachin and Zerubbabel with the seal may be considered related imagery. The use of the term "seal" to describe the protagonist in Ezek 28:11 thus makes sense as an expression of royal imagery that reflects what is articulated about the primal man in Gen 1:26. The picture is that of an authoritative representative of YHWH.

IV

We move now to a discussion of the second of the two words under consideration, *toknît*. The best available evidence for constructing an understanding to account for MT *toknît* comes once again from the LXX and Vulgate, each of which preserves a reading belonging to the same general semantic sphere of *toknît* and *tabnît*. These render ὁμοίωσις "likeness, resemblance" and *similitūdō* "resemblance, likeness," respectively.[33] Several reasons may be given in support of the reading "likeness."

First, such a translation on the part of the Versions is in accord with the semantic range suggested by MT *toknît*. The reading *toknît* is certainly the more vexing of the two words in question. Unlike the relatively ubiquitous *hôtām*, the word *toknît* appears elsewhere in the biblical record only in Ezek 43:10, an apparently corrupt text. Despite the obvious textual problems, *toknît* in Ezek 43:10 seems to signify a pattern or model.[34] The word *toknît* is conjectured to be based on the root *tkn*, thought to mean "to regulate, measure, estimate," and in Ezek 43:10 it is used as the object of the verb *mdd* "measure."[35] As a result, *toknît* is commonly rendered "measurement, proportion" or "example."

Zimmerli is accurate, I believe, in characterizing the general semantic range of the root *tkn* as containing the idea of "correctness." But although he too accepts the emendation "seal" (in

---

[33] See LSJ, 1225 and *The Oxford Latin Dictionary* (New York: Oxford University Press, 1982) 1764, respectively.

[34] The correct reading may be תכונתו, "its arrangement," which appears in 43:11.

[35] BDB 1067. There is some ambiguity with this instance as well, and in view of the textual variations, the verse throws little direct light on the meaning in Ezekiel 28.

the construct form *ḥôtam*), his translation "completed signet" defies explanation. This he acknowledges openly in his reticence to suggest what the phrase might mean.[36] Similarly, NRSV renders *toknît* in 28:12 "perfection" and translates the phrase "signet of perfection," while pointing out to the reader in a textual note that "the meaning of the Hebrew is uncertain." The problem here is that although the idea of a "perfect" or "completed" seal makes sense semantically, in context it holds little meaning. Is a "perfect" seal here being juxtaposed with an imperfect? What would that imply? Or is a "completed" juxtaposed with an "incomplete?" Although one could conjecture on this at length, the lack of analogous language or ideas in the Hebrew Bible rob such translations of any real meaning. Nevertheless, there is a great deal to be said for the ideas "correctness," "completion," and "perfection" insofar as all are suggestive of *conformance* to an exemplar or ideal. The answer is within the realm of these ideas.

Secondly, the Versions' "likeness" reflects even more closely what is the most likely emendation of *toknît*. Given that *toknît* is a virtual *hapax legomenon*, appearing in only two possibly corrupt texts, it is reasonable to seek an emendation. If an emendation is to be made here, the first candidate should certainly be *tabnît* "image." The probability of misreading *tabnît* for *toknît* in the consonantal Hebrew text is quite high on the grounds of a graphic confusion of *k* and *b*. *tabnît* is fairly common in the biblical text and is found elsewhere in the book of Ezekiel. It is used in Ezek 8:3 with the meaning "form" or "image" referring to the hand of God, and again in 8:10, in reference to painted images of animals on the wall of the sanctuary court. The Greek text of Aquila gives the reading ὁμοίωσις for MT *tabnît*, further indicating the plausibility of reading *tabnît* in the Hebrew text.[37] It bears noting that the probability of a misreading is even higher, given that *tabnît* and the root *tkn* appear to lie within the same general semantic sphere of conformance to an exemplar. Although the text-critical principle of *lectio difficilior* recommends the less common reading *toknît*, I believe there is sufficient warrant for accepting *tabnît*.

---

[36]Zimmerli cites the following as examples reflecting the underlying notion of "correctness": "to be right" (*niphal*) in 18:25, 29; "to put right" (*piel*) in Isa 40:13; "to determine the measure" in Isa 40:12; Job 28:25; and "to test" (*qal*) in Prov 16:27; 21:2; 24:12. (*Ezekiel*, 2.81, 91-2).

[37] Other LXX witnesses preserve ὁμοίωμα.

Finally, the readings of LXX and Vulgate, make immediate sense within the context of the oracle, by alluding to the primal man through language identical to that found in the Priestly account of the creation of man in Genesis. The use of the terms ὁμοίωσις and *similitudo*, "likeness," in a context so generally suggestive of the primal man establishes a connection with Genesis 1:26, in which the LXX and Vulgate use ὁμοίωσις and *similitudo*, respectively, to express what MT preserves as *děmût*, "likeness." In two other places in the LXX text of Ezekiel, ὁμοίωσις translates *děmût*. In 1:10 the text describes the "likeness" of the faces of four living creatures." In 10:22, Ezekiel again describes the likeness of those same faces, seen on a different occasion. A survey of the LXX text reveals that ὁμοίωσις almost always translates *děmût*.[38] And as already mentioned, in the only other place where ὁμοίωσις appears in the book of Ezekiel (that is, other than 1:10; 10:22; and 28:12), the Greek text of Aquila renders ὁμοίωσις for MT *tabnît*.[39] Thus, it is difficult to imagine that the translators, working on a passage with such strong primal man overtones, did not have Gen 1:26 in mind.

If we accept such an understanding, how then is the phrase best translated? One option is to follow the genitive construction suggested by LXX ἀποσφράγισμα ὁμοιώσεος and Vulgate *signaculum similitudinis*, which reflect the Hebrew construct relation *hôtam tabnît*. It might then be rendered "seal of likeness," "seal of resemblance," or perhaps "resembling seal." This makes for somewhat of an awkward English translation, not to mention the fact that the phrase is no more immediately meaningful than translations we have considered above, such as "seal of perfection." Thus, I am inclined to accept another option: to construe *tabnît* as being in simple apposition (or parallel, in a sense) to *hôtām* (Heb. absolute state). Hence, "You were a seal, a likeness."[40] Each word now stands on its own, and directs the attention of the audience more readily to the ideas expressed in the pair *ṣelem* and *děmût* in

---

[38] In Dan 7:5 ὁμοίωσις translates Aramaic *děmāh*.

[39] It should also be noted, that the LXX of Ezekiel represents the work of more than one translator. See *inter alia* McGregor, *The Greek Text of Ezekiel* (Atlanta: Scholars Press, 1986).

[40] Cant 2:1 provides an example of a comparable construction, though slightly longer and more obviously written in verse: *ʾănî hăvaṣélet haššārôn, šôšanat hāᶜămāqîm*, "I am a rose of Sharon, a lily of the valleys" (NRSV).

Gen 1:26. The pairs *ṣélem* and *dĕmût*, and *ḥôtām* and *tabnît* are semantically congruent, insofar as each expresses the idea of form and conformance. They are also "ideologically" (for lack of a better word) congruent insofar as each pair may be seen as an expression of royal imagery. They are two different, but related ways of expressing the same general idea: that of a royally conceived primal man.[41] Beyond this, such a translation provides two distinct grammatical members to balance the two statements that follow in the text: "full of wisdom and perfect in beauty."

V

Ezekiel's use of the imagery of seal and likeness, homologous to that of *ṣélem* and *dĕmût* of Gen 1:26, can be explained in part by the fact that Ezekiel, as is widely held, made extensive use of Israelite traditional material and perhaps proto-scripture. He drew upon, as did other prophets, the popular traditions concerning slavery in Egypt, exodus, and conquest (ch. 20). But he made use of many other Israelite traditions as well; for instance he alludes to Exod 24:9 and to the sin of Korah in Numbers 16 in recounting his vision of seventy elders "each with a censer in his hand." It has long been recognized that the book of Ezekiel draws upon traditional creation imagery by its use of the chaos monster (chs. 29, 32) and Eden (chs. 31, 36). The oracle against the king of Tyre is but one more example of this tendency within the Ezekielian tradition.

It is also true that the book of Ezekiel displays a marked interest in priestly matters, which is consistent with the identification of the prophet as a "priest" in Ezek 1:3. As such, the book reflects language and ideas similar to the priestly material of the Pentateuch. The closest examples have been observed in the book of Leviticus, and the most clearly demonstrable ties exist between material in Leviticus 26 and that found in Ezekiel 4—7 and 34—37.

Although most of the common allusions between Leviticus 26 and Ezekiel are found in 4–7 and 34–37, chapter 28 shows signs of the presence of allusions found in Lev 26 as well. The statement in

---

[41] cf. Psalm 8. See H. G. May's general summary of the evidence, "The King in the Garden of Eden," *Israel's Prophetic Heritage* (ed. Bernard Anderson and Walter Harrelson; New York: Harper, 1962) 166–76.

Lev 26:19, "I will break your proud glory (gě'ôn ʿuzzěkem)," reflects similar imagery in Ezek 28:17, "your heart was proud (gābah libbekā) because of your beauty" (cf. Ezek 28:2).[42] Likewise, the curse in Lev 26:32, "I will devastate the land so that your enemies who come to settle in it shall be appalled (šāměmû)," is reflected in Ezek 28:19, "all who know you among the peoples were appalled (šāměmû) at you". The correspondences between Ezekiel 28 and Leviticus 26 in all likelihood derive from a situation whereby each draws from a common stream of tradition, although it is not certain that one did not adapt material borrowed from the other.

Leviticus 26 also represents a potential point of contact between the creation traditions in Ezek 28:11-19 and the creation traditions of Genesis 1–3, insofar as Leviticus 26 appears to preserve references to material in both the P and J creation accounts. Lev 26:9 presents a classic P statement when God affirms "I will look with favor upon you and make you fruitful and multiply you." Within the same context (v. 12), is an allusion to J's tradition when he continues "And I will walk among you" (hithallaktî betôkěkem), reminiscent of God "walking about" in the Garden of Eden in the presence of the first couple (Gen 3:8). Likewise, it is seems evident that the original situation of Eden is alluded to in the statement that "the land shall yield its produce, and the trees of the field shall yield their fruit" (26:4).

The interpretation of seal and likeness proposed in this paper renders the oracle in Ezekiel 28:11–19 more clearly homologous with the composite image of the primal man as presented in Gen 1–3. In each case, the protagonist moves from the status of exalted regent to that of cursed transgressor.

VI

In this paper I have argued that the MT term ḥôtēm toknît should be emended to ḥôtām tabnît and that it may be considered equivalent to the terms ṣélem and děmût in Genesis 1:26.

Ezekiel's use of this metaphor for the king of Tyre might be explained in several ways. R. Wilson argues that it was an "oblique"

---

[42] Note that the root gbh is frequently construed to be synonymous with g'h (e.g. Zeph 3:11; Jer 48:29; Prov 16:18, etc.).

oracle directed against Israel itself and that it represented an indictment of the Israelite priesthood.[43] It may have been based on the close relationship between Israel and Tyre, particularly under the United Monarchy. The ties between the two nations resulted in the involvement of Tyre with the construction of the temple at Jerusalem. The application to Tyre may be purely incidental, and as such might have been applied to any other nation. Or, it may have been a combination of these factors: Tyre was a particularly appropriate vehicle to express ideas that had a much more general application. This is certainly true in the sense that the oracles against foreign nations repeat similar themes, such as death and destruction wrought by invading powers. But such themes are found in oracles directed against Israel as well. Although oracles against the nations likely functioned more as instruments of the cult for catharsis than as actual messages to be delivered to their named recipients, they were at once reminders and warnings of undesirable conduct, providing an opportunity for Israel to reflect on the gravity of such actions and their consequences. This certainly explains their preservation and ultimate inclusion in Israel's canon of scripture.

---

[43] "The Death of the King of Tyre: The Editorial History of Ezekiel 28," *Love & Death in the Ancient Near East: Essays in Honor of Marvin H. Pope* (ed. J.H. Marks and R.M. Good; Guilford, CT: Four Quarters Publishing, 1986) 211–18.

Genre and Persona in Ezekiel 24:15-24[1]

Margaret S. Odell, St. Olaf College

When the members of the steering committee decided to include a session on anthropology in Ezekiel, we considered calling it the "absence of humanity." Though we later discarded the phrase as unwieldy and ambiguous, some of us were struck by the manner in which the book diminished humanity almost to the point of invisibility or inconsequence. In light of that concern, I highlighted two questions which have often been asked about the characterization of Ezekiel. The first question concerns the ironical presentation of Ezekiel's persona: although the autobiographical voice keeps the prophet in the foreground, nevertheless he is overshadowed by the presence of Yahweh throughout the book.[2] The second question addresses the rather stark emotional character of the prophet and his actions, especially when compared with the expressiveness of the so-called laments of Jeremiah.

This essay addresses both questions through an analysis of the pivotal account of Ezek 24:15-24, in which Ezekiel's symbolic act of not mourning the death of his wife prefigures the exiles' response to the destruction of Jerusalem. This text is often cited as an instance of the problematic portrayal of human beings, in that it apparently denies both Ezekiel and the exiles a normal response to profound loss.[3] However, I will argue that the text signifies something else entirely--that God has chosen the exilic community over Jerusalem, and that Ezekiel's actions are a sign of this election. I will base this argument on a consideration of the genres of the unit and the book of Ezekiel as a whole. The implications of this interpretation will, I hope, become clear in the course of the essay.

---

[1] I wish to thank Gary Stansell for his helpful criticism of an earlier draft of this essay.

In order to differentiate between the prophet Ezekiel and the the book, I will use italics when referring to the latter. When I refer to the author of the book as Ezekiel, I do not mean to imply a simplistic view of authorship. I am not, however, convinced that the book could not have been written within the time frame implied by the dates in the book. See M. Greenberg, *Ezekiel* (2 vols; AB; Garden City, New York: Doubleday, 1983, 1997) 1.15.

[2] Others have noted this paradox; see J. Rosenberg, "Jeremiah and Ezekiel," in *The Literary Guide to the Bible,* ed. R. Alter and F. Kermode (Cambridge: Belknap Press of Harvard University, 1987), 196.

[3] Rosenberg, "Jeremiah and Ezekiel," 200.

Genre and Ezekiel

The underlying assumption of recent genre studies is that genres constitute a form of communication, a system of shared meanings between author and readers.[4] A text can thus only be properly understood if its linguistic cues are properly decoded by its readers. This is no small feat, as it requires the recognition of a "complex of elements" which may or may not all be present.[5] Moreover, the recognition of genres requires some attention to their historical growth and change, as well as to the possibility that different genres have been combined. As A. Fowler notes,

> . . . meaning is genre-bound, and genres are themselves in a continual state of transmutation . . . . Hence recognitive interpretation--that is, re-cognition of the author's meaning--demands recovery of appropriate phases of the genre concerned. Indeed, for distant historical periods it may necessitate reconstructing the then literary model.[6]

According to this theory, then, an adequate comprehension of the meaning of a literary work requires the identification of its genre, which in turn involves a rather sophisticated process of identifying cues which are themselves in a state of flux and recombination.

For the book of Ezekiel as a whole, very little of that work has yet been attempted. Although a working assumption of Ezekiel scholarship is that it is a prophetic book, that is, a collection of the oracles and accounts of the visions and symbolic acts of the prophet Ezekiel,[7] I would argue that

---

[4] For a discussion of genre and methods of biblical interpretation, see J. Barton, *Reading the Old Testament: Method in Biblical Study* (Philadelphia: Westminster, 1984), chap. 1.

[5] A. Fowler, "Life and Death of Literary Forms," *New Literary History* 2 (1971) 202.

[6] Fowler, "Literary Forms," 205; cf. B. O. Long, *1 Kings, with an Introduction to Historical Literature* (FOTL 9; Grand Rapids: Eerdmans, 1984), 4.

[7] W. Zimmerli, *Ezekiel: A Commentary on the Book of the Prophet Ezekiel* (2 vols.; trans. R. E. Clements; Hermeneia; Philadelphia: Fortress, 1979, 1983), 1.68-74; M. Greenberg, *Ezekiel*, 1.1-6; L. C. Allen, *Ezekiel* (2 vols.; WBC; Waco: Word, 1990, 1994), 1.xxv-xxvi.

The one specific treatment of the genre of the book of Ezekiel as a whole is that of R. Hals, in *Ezekiel* (FOTL 19; Grand Rapids: Eerdmans, 1988), 4-5, who argues, on the basis of similarities between Isaiah 1-39, Jeremiah, and Ezekiel, that the latter still reflects the phenomenon of judgment in history and thus should be classified as a "prophetic book of rather typical structure." In his definition of the prophetic book, he notes a considerable degree of flexibility in ordering collections of prophetic oracles (352-53).

this classification is only a partial identification of its genre. The inadequacy of the classification is indicated by the fact that it does little to explain how this particular collection works. Not only do the individual prophetic elements not explain the unprecedented, pervasively autobiographical character of the book, they also do not account for the final vision of restoration, in which prophetic motifs are minimal.[8] Indeed, when it is argued, as Zimmerli does, that chapters 40-48 were added to the book in the final stage of redaction, in a sense at the farthest remove from the collection of prophetic oracles,[9] then it becomes clear that the genre designation, "prophetic book," is at best applicable for chapters 1-39 but not for the book as a whole.

Moreover, the identification of the book as a collection of prophetic oracles may not have fully captured the role played by the character of Ezekiel within the book. The question here is not whether there is an actual Ezekiel behind the text but rather, whether prophetic genres are a sufficient explanation for the shaping of the persona of Ezekiel.[10] This persona is presented almost entirely in terms of Ezekiel's reception of the divine word, his experience of visions, and his performance of symbolic acts--all of which do have antecedents in the prophetic tradition.[11] However, as Carroll has noted, the prophetic persona was relatively insignificant in prophetic

---

Though he concedes that the individual oracles are more easily classified than the book as a whole and that the high number of priestly elements in Ezekiel might call for a modification of the genre classification, he nevertheless he asserts, "it is entirely adequate to say of Ezekiel the priest that his words have been compiled into a prophetic book" (5).

For further discussion of the "prophetic book" as a genre category, see M. Sweeney, *Isaiah 1-39, with an Introduction to Prophetic Lterature* (FOTL 16; Grand Rapids: Eerdmans, 1996), 16-18.

[8] Instructions to the prophet, 43:10-12, 18ff; 44:5ff (note, however, that this instruction to speak does not indicate that Ezekiel is to "prophesy," 44:6); oracles: 44:9ff; 46:1ff. 16ff; 47:13ff.

[9] Zimmerli, *Ezekiel*, 1.74.

[10] By adopting the term persona as a designation of the figure of Ezekiel as he is portrayed in the book, I am following the lead of B. N. Porter, who uses it extensively in her discussion of the persona of Esarhaddon in his Babylonian inscriptions (B. N. Porter, *Images, Power, and Politics: Figurative Aspects of Esarhaddon's Babylonian Policy* [Philadelphia: American Philosophical Society, 1993]).

[11] See W. E. March, "Prophecy," in *Old Testament Form Criticism* (ed. J. H. Hayes, Trinity University Monograph Series in Religion 2; San Antonio: Trinity University Press, 1974), 170-73; Sweeney, *Isaiah 1-39*, 18-22.

collections until the exile.[12]   The question I would like to ask, then, is whether these antecedent prophetic genres adequately explain the development of this sustained interest in the prophetic persona. To put the question in Fowler's terms, does the persona of Ezekiel represent the introduction of new genres not available until the exile?

Ezekiel 24:15-24 illustrates well the problems we face in interpreting the persona of Ezekiel. The account is the report of a symbolic act and thus would appear to be adequately interpreted as a prophetic genre. The Lord Yahweh informs Ezekiel that he is about to take away his wife, the delight of his eyes, in a single blow. Yet, when this happens, Ezekiel is not to mourn but is instead to don his turban and put on his sandals. When his wife dies the next day, he does as the Lord commands, and the people ask him what his actions mean. He announces that they also will do as he has done when God profanes the sanctuary, the delight of *their* eyes.

Even though the narrative contains all the expected features of a report of a symbolic act, the identification of these formal features does not exhaust the problems inherent in this particular narrative.[13]   Much of the critical work has revolved around the use of this narrative as a biographical source; consequently other generic elements have been overlooked. Zimmerli's discussion of the unit is typical. He notes that this is one of only two symbolic acts in Ezekiel which appear to derive from the prophet's actual experience (the other is 12:17-20).[14]   In these accounts, he says, "we gain the impression that the prophet, quite outside his own willing them, must become a 'preacher' by events which overtake him and which make him appear to be overpowered by these experiences."[15]   Along with other commentators, Zimmerli thus assumes that the symbolic act in Ezek 24:15-24 originates in Ezekiel's own direct experience. Where the other symbolic acts are clearly preaching undertaken in obedience to the command of God, this is an instance in which Ezekiel's preaching emerges from the painful experience of the death of his wife.

---

[12] R. P. Carroll, *Jeremiah, A Commentary* (OTL; Philadelphia: Westminster, 1986), 58.

[13] G. Fohrer still provides the basis for studies of symbolic acts (*Die symbolischen Handlungen der Propheten* [ATANT, 25; Zurich: Zwingli, 1953]); see, e.g., Zimmerli, *Ezekiel,* 1.156-57; Greenberg, *Ezekiel,* 1.122-25; March, "Prophecy," 172-73; and Sweeney, *Isaiah 1-39,* 19-20.

[14] Zimmerli, *Ezekiel,* 1.29.

[15] Zimmerli, *Ezekiel,* 1.29.

Critical discussion has therefore revolved around the extent to which this narrative can be used as a source for constructing a biography of the prophet. Critical treatments range from the horror of Hals, that God would cause the death of Ezekiel's wife in order make a point about Jerusalem,[16] to the restraint of Zimmerli, who cautions against treating this account as a transparent historical report.[17] Since, says Zimmerli, the narrative includes only what is necessary for the proclamation of the divine word, it cannot be used as a full and complete description of Ezekiel's experience. He refrains, for example, from saying that the expression "delight of your eyes" means that Ezekiel was happily married.[18] Nevertheless, Zimmerli joins other contemporary critics in assuming that the prohibition against mourning signifies Ezekiel's incapacity to mourn: Ezekiel is "stunned by the tragic loss of his wife and is no longer capable of mourning."[19] Thus despite his restraint, Zimmerli joins other critics in assuming that Ezekiel's experience of emotional paralysis was the basis of his symbolic act.

Largely on the assumption that the symbolic act is based on actual experience, critics have thus failed to examine the literary function of the motifs embedded within the account. In terms of Fowler's discussion of the combination and recombination of genres, one might observe that Ezek 24:15-24 is not only a report of a symbolic act, it is also a story about the curtailment or prohibition of mourning. Thus it is reasonable to ask whether there are comparable stories about mourning in the Hebrew Bible, whether these stories reflect the social and symbolic functions of mourning rituals and, by extension, what it might mean to prohibit public mourning.

Several such stories are found in the narratives about David and are implicitly associated with questions of his succession. David publicly mourns Saul's death (1 Sam 25:1; 2 Sam 1:12). Again, when Joab kills Abner, David explicitly absolves himself of guilt and assumes the role of chief mourner by following the bier (2 Sam 3:31; cf. 3:28). Neither narrative focuses on the emotional desirability of David's expressing grief; rather, each employs mourning to establish David's integrity with respect to the deaths of Saul and Abner. Though David benefits from their deaths, his

---

[16] Hals, *Ezekiel,* 175-76; see also Allen, *Ezekiel,* 1.60-61.

[17] Zimmerli, *Ezekiel,* 1.156-57, 505. See also W. Eichrodt, *Ezekiel, A Commentary* (trans. C. Quin; OTL; Philadelphia: Westminster, 1970), 342; D. I. Block, *The Book of Ezekiel* (2 vols.; NICOT; Grand Rapids: Eerdmans, 1997) 788, 794.

[18] Zimmerli, *Ezekiel,* 1.505-6.

[19] Zimmerli, *Ezekiel,* 1.29.

mourning indicates his innocence and also implies a bond of loyalty between himself and the deceased. Indeed, in the episode in which David expresses his grief over the death of his son Absalom, apparently as a spontaneous outpouring of emotion, Joab rebukes him, since David's indulgence insults those warriors who had defended him against Absalom's treason (2 Sam 19:1, 5-6).

These narratives suggest that the prohibition against mourning in Ezek 24:15-24 has little to do with emotional processes; indeed, the narrative itself notes that both Ezekiel and the people will continue to experience conflicted feelings (24:17, 23). Rather, the symbolic act is concerned with defining political relationships. Ezekiel and the exiles are to sever completely any remaining ties with Jerusalem. The loss is admittedly extreme. Not only does Ezekiel lose his wife, the exiles are forced to consider the fate of the sons and daughters they had left behind. Moreover, since the verb in this latter phrase is ' *zb*, abandon, the implication is that the exiles must acknowledge their culpability in consigning their children to this fate (24:21; cf. 18:2).[20] Though the exiles may continue to pine away in their iniquities and groan to one another, the prohibition against mourning forces a complete separation from the objects of their love. [21]

---

[20] Only Eichrodt has drawn attention to the poignant reference to abandoned sons and daughters (Eichrodt, *Ezekiel,* 344).

In the discussion of Ezek 18, most critics interpret the proverb, "The fathers have eaten sour grapes, and the children's teeth are set on edge," as a criticism of the ancestors, especially from the time of Manasseh and Amon (Greenberg, *Ezekiel*, 1.339; Allen, *Ezekiel*, 1.270-71; Zimmerli argues against a precise identification of the generations, *Ezekiel*, 1.377). However, in light of the reference to sons and daughters in Ezek 24:21, it is also possible that the proverb reflects the generational differences between the exiles and the remaining inhabitants of Jerusalem. The oracle puts both groups on equal footing. Not only does the oracle give each group a chance to repent, it also gives the succeeding generation of both exiles and Jerusalemites--presumably the generation for whom the book was published in the twenty-fifth year of the exile--an opportunity to turn to God.

[21] By drawing attention to David's cessation of mourning on the death of the child born to Bathsheba, K. W. Carley draws a different conclusion about the prohibition of mourning in Ezek 24: "the meaning of the prophecy is that grief for what is lost is not to dominate the future (cp. 2 Sam. 12:22f). Desire for former relationships and old securities, however deep, is not to bring the exiles themselves to the grave in mourning. Despite the bitterness of their loss, the people are, like Ezekiel, to be prepared for a future of new activity." K. W. Carley, *The Book of the Prophet Ezekiel* (Cambridge Bible Commentary on the NEB; Cambridge: Cambridge University Press, 1974), 166.

The inattention to genre in the interpretation of Ezek 24:15-24 has also led to the assumption that all of the actions described in Ezekiel's symbolic act represent a reversal of mourning rituals. Though that is the case for some of the actions described, such as the prohibition against crying and eating mourners' bread, it is not so clear that the action of donning the turban indicates a reversal of mourning.[22] The motif of donning the turban usually appears in other literary contexts, for example, in the description of the clothing worn by priests,[23] or in accounts of election or restoration to high office,[24] or in wedding imagery.[25] These references suggest that turbans signify high status. There is no indication that a turban is ordinary headgear worn in the normal course of events and that it would be taken off to signify mourning. Rather, accounts of mourning begin with a bare head, which is then shaved or covered with ashes or dirt.[26]

Taking off a turban or putting one on has little to do with mourning; but it has everything to do with status transformation.[27] Kings take off their turbans when they are deposed (Ezek 21:25-26; cf. Isa 3:20) and put them on when they assume power (2 Sam 12:30).[28] Similarly, priests don special

---

[22] R. DeVaux cites only Ezek 24:17 as evidence that turbans were removed as part of mourning rituals; yet he also notes that in other contexts of mourning the head may be veiled (2 Sam 19:5; 15:30; R. DeVaux, *Ancient Israel* [2 vols.; New York: McGraw-Hill, 1965], 1.59).

In his discussion of Isa 61:3, G. A. Anderson argues that the donning of the turban signfies the *end* of mourning. However, he also notes that such usage is rare in the ancient near east and in the Hebrew Bible. He notes, furthermore, that the use of the term *p'r* in Isa 61:3 may have been influenced by a wordplay with the word ashes (*'ēper*). Thus, even though he cites Ezek 24:17 as a supporting example for his claim that donning a turban signifies the end of mourning, it is likely that literary and not ritual considerations have contributed to the use of *p'r* in Isa 61:3. In any case, one cannot infer from Isa 61:3 that Ezek 24:17 reverses ritual actions signifying the *onset* of mourning. G. A. Anderson, *A Time to Mourn, A Time to Dance: The Expression of Grief and Joy in Israelite Religion* (University Park, PA: Pennsylvania State Unversity Press, 1991), 47.

[23] Ezek 44:18; Exod 39:28.

[24] Zech 3:5.

[25] Isa 61:10.

[26] Critics have not compared the actions described in Ezek 24:15-24 to mourning rituals described elsewhere in *Ezekiel* (Ezek 7:18; 27:30-31; cf. DeVaux, *Ancient Israel*, 1.59). Though these texts do involve shaving and putting ashes on the head, neither features the removal of a turban.

[27] For clothing and headgear as symbols of status transformation, see V. Turner, *The Ritual Process: Structure and Anti-Structure* (Chicago: Aldine, 1969), 170-71.

[28] This connotation survives into the first century of the common era; cf.

clothing and headgear when they are initiated into the priesthood (Lev 8:6-9; cf. Zech 3:5). In Ezek 24:15-24, then, the turban signifies that, on the death of Jerusalem, the exiles have acquired a new status. This is made explicit in Ezek 24:25-27, where the term "beauty," (*tpʾrh*), employed to describe the sanctuary, establishes a word play with the term used in 24:17, 24 for turban (*pʾr*). The explicit use of these etymologically related terms suggests that Jerusalem's loss is the exiles' gain. That is further underscored in the promise that Ezekiel's mouth will be opened on the day he hears the news of the temple's destruction (Ezek 24:27).

As my discussion of the motifs of the turban and the prohibition of mourning might suggest, the critics' assumption that this episode has a basis in Ezekiel's personal experience has resulted in an inattention to other generic dimensions of the text. It is insufficient to say that Ezek 24:15-24 is record of Ezekiel's experience, or even that it is preaching based on experience. Because it is a story about mourning, it needs to be interpreted in light of other stories about mourning. Moreover, attention to genre would highlight the fact that the motif of the turban is not typically associated with accounts of mourning. Ezekiel's actions are not the reversal of mourning; rather, they belong to an entirely different social and literary context. When Ezekiel's audience asks him what his actions mean, they are truly confused. Donning a turban is not simply the reversal of their expectations, it is a non sequitur.

Moreover, it has been assumed that the meaning of the act revolves around the events of the deaths of Ezekiel's wife and the destruction of Jerusalem. But the narrative directs our attention elsewhere. The exiles ask Ezekiel, "Will you not tell us what these things that you are doing mean for us?" (24:19). Their question draws attention to the significance *for them* of Ezekiel's actions. The focus of the symbolic action is thus not so much on death and destruction as on what happens afterward. Despite their loss, and even despite their culpability in the abandonment of their children, the exiles will nevertheless be honored with divine favor. The symbolic act thus embraces the paradox of life in death and grace in sin: even while they know sorrow and guilt over the death of Jerusalem, they also know unmerited divine grace.

Josephus, *Antiquities,* 17.273, 280, who uses the motif of donning the diadem to indicate a presumption to power. I am grateful to K. C. Hanson for these references.

The critics' focus on Ezekiel's personal experience has also obscured the way in which Ezekiel's actions model the new identity of the gola community. In other symbolic acts, the performative element of Ezekiel's actions are directed outward, toward events in history. By contrast, in Ezek 24:15-24, the focus of the symbolic act is not so much on the historical event as on the subsequent transformation of the exiles. Ezekiel's actions provide a model for their own response to the destruction of Jerusalem. When the time comes, they also will refrain from mourning and don their turbans--not out of emotional paralysis, but as a paradoxical acceptance of their new status as the elect of God.

The use of the turban at this particular point in the book of Ezekiel raises an interesting question about the persona of Ezekiel as a symbolic representative of the people. As I have suggested in the above discussion, Ezekiel's donning the turban is explicitly used as a model for the exilic community. In this sense, the genre of the report of the symbolic act has incorporated a novel element; in fact, one could even go so far as to say that Ezekiel's adaptation of the genre of the report of a symbolic action has created an entirely different literary type. In this narrative, Ezekiel is not simply enacting the prophetic word, he is taking on new significance as a representative of the people. While it is certainly possible that this development of the prophetic persona could have occurred within the prophetic tradition, I think that it is also possible, even likely, that other generic influences are at work. In another essay, I have argued that priestly elements have contributed to the idea of Ezekiel's identification with the people in their suffering.[29] In the second part of this essay, I'd like to consider yet another influence that not only may help to explain Ezekiel's actions in Ezek 24, but which may also eventually contribute to our understanding of his persona in the book as a whole.

Ancient Autobiography

Are there any ancient genres that can explain the unusual prominence of the persona of Ezekiel in his book? One critic who has addressed the centrality of the figure of Ezekiel is K. von Rabenau, who had suggested that Ezekiel had been structured as an autobiography.[30] The main difficulty with von Rabenau's statement, however, is that he did not explain how

---

[29] M. S. Odell, "You Are What You Eat: Ezekiel and the Scroll," *JBL* 117 (1998), 229-48.

[30] K. von Rabenau, "Die Entstehung des Buches Ezechiel in formgeschichtlicher Sicht," *WZ* (1955/56) 659-94.

"autobiography" would have been understood in Ezekiel's context. Autobiography as such did not exist in the ancient world. The term first gained currency in the early nineteenth century and is best used to describe a first person narrative account of one's life, either with respect to one's inner personal development or to one's involvement in larger historical events.[31] Although a wide variety of ancient near eastern literary texts and inscriptions do include first person narrative accounts, these are not, properly speaking, autobiography. In these ancient near eastern texts, the use of the first person is a scribal device, not an indication of authorship. In recognition of the fact that all of these compositions were written by scribes and not by the personages represented therein, Longman has suggested that they be called "fictional autobiographies."[32] But even this designation falls short of capturing the complexity of these compositions, which are by no means restricted to an account of a person's life. In nearly all cases, the central persona is a royal figure, and the purpose of the first person narrative is to introduce a larger work. The focus is not so much on that person's life as on what that person has done in behalf of his gods and subjects. So, for example, Hammurabi's account of how he came to rule justifies the promulgation of his law code.[33] The persona of the royal figure is inseparable from the law code, and vice versa. Given this use of first-person narrative accounts in the ancient world, the term "autobiography" is

---

[31] G. Misch, *A History of Autobiography in Antiquity* (2 vols.; trans. E. W. Dickes; Cambridge: Harvard University Press, 1951), 5-6.

[32] T. Longman III, *Fictional Akkadian Autobiography: A Generic and Comparative Study* (Winona Lake, IN: Eisenbrauns, 1991), 39-48.

Longman notes that there is a good bit of terminological variety in studies of ancient near eastern first-person literature (48). Texts and inscriptions which appear to have a valid claim to the classification "autobiography" because they focus on the life and deeds of an individual are from western Asia; see E. L. Greenstein, "Autobiographies in Ancient Western Asia," in *Civilizations of the Ancient Near East* (ed. J. M. Sasson et al; 4 vols.; New York: Scribner's), 4.2421-23; W. W. Hallo and K. Lawson Younger, Jr., *The Context of Scripture: Canonical Comparisons from the Biblical World* (Leiden: Brill, 1997), 477-82. Inscriptions from Mesopotamia are both more composite and fragmentary; hence genre classifications remain uncertain. See A. K. Grayson, "Assyria and Babylonia," *Orientalia* 49 (1980) 140-94, esp. 187-88; H. G. Güterbock, "Die historische Tradition und ihre Literarische Gestaltung bei Babyloniern und Hethitern bis 1200," *ZA* 42 (1934) 1-91; 44 (1938) 45-149; E. Reiner, "Die akkadische Literatur," in *AltorientalischeLiteraturen* (ed. W. Rollig; *Neues Handbuch der Literaturwissenschaft 1*; Wiesbaden: Athenaion, 1981), 1.151-210, esp. 177-80.

[33] Greenstein, "Autobiographies," in *Civilizations of the Ancient Near East*, 4.2422.

person narrative accounts in the ancient world, the term "autobiography" is inadequate as a genre description not only for Ezekiel, but also for other contemporaneous first-person accounts. It puts too much focus on the presentation of the central figure and fails to articulate the very close relationship that is established between that figure and rest of the composition.[34]

However, once it is recognized that "autobiography" is an inadequate classification both for *Ezekiel* and the near eastern examples of first-person literature, the general resemblance between *Ezekiel* and this literature becomes even clearer. The overall structure of *Ezekiel* resembles the composite works described above, in that it begins as autobiography but ends in a detailed account of rebuilding and restoration. In this respect, the book fits Longman's typological structure by conforming to a three-part pattern which includes 1) a first-person introduction; 2) narrative history; and 3) a variable third section which indicates the purpose of the narrative.[35] Since the third section of Ezekiel focuses on the building of the temple, Ezekiel most closely resembles the genre of building inscriptions.[36]

One question to consider is how Ezekiel would have appropriated the genre. Fowler's discussion of the historical development of literary genres provides a useful theoretical framework for considering the possibilities. According to Fowler, genres are appropriated in one of two ways. The first is by way of a natural, organic development, wherein successive instances of a genre's usage depend for their meaning and intelligibility on past uses. What a genre can mean, then, is the sum total of all previous examples of the genre.[37] There is also a more scholastic, second-order appropriation of the genre. In such cases, an author makes the genre

---

[34] Another difficulty with Longman's designation, "*fictional* autobiography," is that it implies that the inscriptions do not contain biographically accurate information. However, Porter notes that the variations in the presentations of Esarhaddon and Asshurbanipal quite likely reflect the respective interests of these two kings and are thus likely to be biographically accurate, even if stylized (Porter, *Images, Power, Politics*, 109 n. 236).

[35] Longman, *Fictional Akkadian Autobiography*, 55; cf. also Greenstein, "Autobiographies," in *Civilizations of the Ancient Near East*, 4.2423.

[36] For a discussion of the building inscription genre and related building stories, see V. Hurowitz, *I have built you an exalted house. Temple Building in the Bible in Light of Mesopotamian and Northwest Semitic Writings* (JSOTSup, 115; Sheffield: JSOT, 1992), esp. chaps. 2-4.

[37] Fowler, "Literary Forms," 204.

an object of sophisticated imitation, in the Renaissance sense, varying its themes and motifs, perhaps adapting it to slightly different purposes, but retaining all its main features, including those of formal structure." [38]

As an illustration of this secondary development, Fowler notes the differences between the epics of Homer and Virgil. As Fowler notes, the former is heroic, festal, public, the latter literary, private in delivery, and stylistically elevated.[39]

Of the two possibilities, *Ezekiel* is more like a studied, literate, imitative appropriation of the building inscription genre than that of an internal development.[40] The most significant departure from the inscriptional genre, of course, is that the composition is a scroll, not a monument. Ezekiel has appropriated a public style but developed it in a private, literary mode. Another significant adaptation is in the book's presentation of the central figure. The builder is no human king but Yahweh, who reveals his universal lordship in the opening chapter, who narrates history by means of prophetic oracles, and who reveals to his prophet a temple not made of human hands. The degree of imitation becomes that much clearer when the book is compared against one particular instance of the genre, the Babylonian inscriptions of Esarhaddon.[41] Extant in Assyrian and Babylonian versions, these inscriptions set forth Esarhaddon's conciliatory policy toward the Babylonians. Where his father Sennacherib had treated the Babylonians ruthlessly, Esarhaddon secured their support for his rule by rebuilding their temples.[42]

Esarhaddon's Babylonian inscriptions illustrate the first type of genre development described by Fowler. First, where most Assyrian inscriptions

---

[38] Fowler, "Literary Forms," 212.

[39] Fowler, "Literary Forms," 212.

[40] Although building stories are extant in Israelite literature before the exile, it is not likely that *Ezekiel* represents an internal development of this genre. What is distinctive about *Ezekiel*, as opposed to these pre-exilic works, is its consistent use of the first-person narrative voice.

[41] R. Borger, *Die Inschriften Asarhaddons Königs von Assyrien.* (*AfO* Beih 9; Graz, 1956) 11; D. D. Luckenbill, *Ancient Records of Assyria and Babylonia* (2 vols.; New York: Greenwood, 1968; repr. 1927 edition), 2.639-687.

[42] For a critical assessment of Esarhaddon's political strategies as they are reflected in these inscriptions, see J. A. Brinkman, "Through a Glass Darkly: Esarhaddon's Retrospects on the Downfall of Babylon," *JAOS* 103 (1983) 35-42; and B. N. Porter, *Images, Power, and Politics.*

give a summary of a king's military campaigns before describing a particular building project,[43] these inscriptions focus solely on Babylon's destruction and rebuilding. The inscription is thus adapted to focus on Esarhaddon's affairs with respect to this particular city. Second, where inscriptions usually state that a king undertakes a rebuilding project because a building has fallen into disrepair,[44] Esarhaddon more directly links the condition of the city to the abuses of its inhabitants. These adaptations thus rather adroitly allow the king both to account for the city's destruction and to make an elaborate display of his own beneficence.[45]

Because several versions of this inscription are extant, they help to clarify the processes of writing. Porter has noted that the variations between the Assyrian and Babylonian inscriptions reflect conscious attempts to justify Esarhaddon's policies in cultural and political terms that would be understood by his respective audiences. For his Babylonian audience, Esarhaddon omits his genealogy and any reference to Assyrian kingship while emphasizing Babylonian motifs of kingship as well as the role of the Babylonian god Marduk in his rise to power.[46] By contrast, inscriptions composed for his Assyrian audience employ traditional royal Assyrian titles and invoke Assyrian gods. This conscious appropriation of specific motifs for a specific audience would suggest that these inscriptions played a public role in Esarhaddon's announcement of his political strategies both in Babylon and at home.[47]

---

[43] See, e.g., *ARAB* 2.499-524, 689-700B.

[44] *ARAB* 2.702, 706.

[45] Porter, *Images, Power, and Politics*, 26.

[46] Porter, *Images, Power, and Politics*, 93-94.

[47] The question of the intended audience for building inscriptions is open to debate. Since they were buried in the foundations of the buildings to which they refer, Oppenheim had argued that they were not intended to be dissemenated (A. L. Oppenheim, *Ancient Mesopotamia: Portrait of a Dead Civilization* [Chicago: University of Chicago Press, 1964], 147-49). That position has been re-evaluated in recent years. H. Tadmor has argued that these texts served an apologetic function at the time of their publication ("Autobiographical Apology in the Royal Assyrian Literature," in *History, Historiography, and Interpretation: Studies in Biblical and Cuneiform Literatures* (eds. H. Tadmor and M. Weinfeld [Jerusalem: Magnes Press, 1986], 36-57). Liverani has suggested possible avenues for the communication of these inscriptions to literate audiences (M. Liverani, "The Deeds of the Ancient Mesopotamian Kings," in *Civilizations of the Ancient Near East* [4 vols; ed. J. Sasson; New York: Scribner's, 1995], 4.2353-2366, esp. 2354-55). T. Schneider has examined the different contexts and therefore different functions of inscriptional texts (T. J. Schneider, *Form and Context in*

Another variation in the recensions indicates that individual episodes could be expanded or condensed, again in view of audience expectations or of the progress of Esarhaddon's rebuilding. In Episodes 3-4, for example, in which the Babylonians' abuses are recounted, the Assyrian recensions considerably expand the catalogue of offenses.[48] Where the Babylonian version simply says that the Babylonians could not be trusted, the Assyrian version elaborates by declaring that this perfidy exists among all ranks of the people.[49] In addition, it appears that inscriptions were expanded as the restoration progressed. On this latter point, Porter has noted that several Babylonian versions contain a greater degree of detail than others. She conjectures that these more detailed inscriptions reflect later stages of the building.[50]

This flexibility in individual episodes suggests that the inscriptions were basic outlines which could be expanded or condensed according to the needs of the author and the audience. It is this variability and expandability, I believe, which makes it possible for the inscription to provide the basic model for the book of Ezekiel. As Hurowitz notes,

> The 'building account' not only served the Mesopotamian scribes as an independent literary form, but was also the common literary skeleton or vehicle for types of historical writings (royal inscriptions in particular), and was also a literary topos in hymns, myths, and epics.[51]

Others have noted the similarity between *Ezekiel* and the inscriptions' use of the motif of the departure and return of the deity;[52] however, I think that the resemblance is much more pervasive. The imitation is not limited simply to the appropriation of a single motif; rather, the imitation is of the entire structure of Esarhaddon's Babylonian inscriptions,[53] which provide a

---

the Royal Inscriptions of Shalmaneser III [Claremont: Institute for Antiquity and Christianity, 1993]). For a helpful overview of this discussion, see Porter, *Images, Power, and Politics*, 106-13.

[48] M. Cogan, "Omens and Ideology in the Babylonian Inscription of Esarhaddon," in *History, Historiography, and Interpretation,* 76-87.

[49] Cf. Porter, *Images Power, and Politics,* 100-103.

[50] Porter, *Images, Power, and Politics,* 104.

[51] Hurowitz, *I have built you a sure house,* 312.

[52] D. I. Block, "The Absence of God in the Book of Ezekiel," presented to the SBL Ezekiel Seminar, November 1997; J. F. Kutsko, "The Presence and Absence of God in the Book of Ezekiel," (Ph.D. diss., Harvard University, 1997).

[53] For a detailed comparison of Ezekiel and Esarhaddon's Babylonian inscriptions,

general framework for the structuring, not of inscriptional elements, but of Israelite prophetic and priestly materials. Though the general outline of *Ezekiel* resembles that of Esarhaddon's inscription, its individual units remain, for the most part, thoroughly immersed in Judaean prophetic and priestly traditions.

Although this essay does not permit an exhaustive analysis of the parallels, I would like to draw attention to the way in which Ezekiel's donning the turban in chapter 24 parallels the re-introduction of the figure of Esarhaddon in the inscription. At the beginning of the inscription, Esarhaddon had introduced himself by means of a series of titles and then had turned his attention to an historical account of the destruction of Babylon. Midway through the inscription, his persona reappears. What is striking about his reappearance is that it includes an account of his election to kingship, even though he has already presented himself as king in the beginning of the inscription. Alluding briefly to his conflict with his brothers over his succession, he declares that Marduk has chosen him to rule. In some versions, he assumes his kingship by sitting on the royal throne; however, in at least one account, he indicates his royal status by donning the royal tiara.[54]

---

see the appendix.

A related question is whether Ezekiel would have been acquainted with Assyrian literary traditions, and thus in a position to be acquainted with Esarhaddon's Babylonian inscriptions. Although the comparison in the appendix speaks for itself, it is corroborated by other evidence of Assyrian influence on Ezekiel. Though a detailed discussion is outside the scope of this essay, there is sufficient evidence to suggest that Ezekiel was well acquainted with Assyrian culture. This is reflected in his knowledge of political policy (Ezek 17; cf. M. Tsevat, "The Neo-Assyrian and Neo-Babylonian Vassal Oaths and the Prophet Ezekiel," *JBL* 78 [1959] 199-204); iconographical and representational art (Ezek 1, 23:14-15; and historiographical traditions (Ezek 38-39). Certainly, if Ezekiel was thirty years old in the fifth year of the deportation, his education would have begun while Assyria was still the dominant world power. Assyria's ongoing cultural influence cannot have been insignificant. See P. Machinist, "The Fall of Assyria in Comparative Ancient Perspective," in *Assyria 1995: Proceedings of the 10th Anniversary Symposium of the Neo-Assyrian Text Corpus Project* (eds. S. Parpola and R. M. Whiting; Helsinki: Neo-Assyrian Text Corpus Project, 1997) 179-95; and J. Reade, "Neo-Assyrian Monuments in their Historical Context," in *Assyrian Royal Inscriptions: New Horizons in Literary, Ideological, and Historical Analysis* (Rome: Oriental Institute, 1981), 167.

[54] *a-ge-a be-lu-ti a-pi-ru-um-[m]a*, Ba 22; in Borger, *Inschriften Asarhaddons*, 17; *ARAB* 2.659C. In a parallel version in K 2801, the royal tiara is a gift to Esarhaddon from the god Anu; *ARAB* 2.669. For parallel expressions indicating that the donning of

Ezekiel 24:15-24 parallels Esarhaddon's account in at least three respects. First, it occurs at the book's midpoint and, like the account of Esarhaddon's accession, it signifies a turning point in the account of the city's fortunes. Second, it reflects a concern over succession, in this case, between the Jerusalemites and the exiles. Through the motif of donning the turban, it indicates that God has chosen Ezekiel and the exiles over Jerusalem. Third, the question of succession is linked to the restoration of the city. Especially with the promise that Ezekiel's mouth will be opened on when he hears of Jerusalem's destruction, the unit anticipates the involvement of Ezekiel and the exiles in the city's renewal. Where it differs, of course, is that neither Ezekiel nor the exiles are kings. I turn now to consider what that variation might mean in Ezekiel's appropriation of a clearly royal motif.

The Anti-royal Persona of Ezekiel

In Esarhaddon's Babylonian inscription, humanity is defined in terms of one's relationship to the gods. There are only two modes of existence-- obedient subjection or rebellion. Where the inhabitants of the city illustrate the latter, Esarhaddon models the former. He is especially well-equipped for carrying out the will of Marduk, who has elevated him above his brothers to the kingship. Esarhaddon has not grasped at kingship but rather has humbly accepted this responsibility. He continues to reveal his pious attentiveness to the divine will by waiting for confirmation that he is to rebuild Babylon. Only after receiving dual confirmation--first through astrological signs and then through confirmed, written prophecy--does he begin the work (Eps. 12-17).

In the inscription, the king models proper human behavior. The inscription shows no interest in the inhabitants as persons--whether they learn by imitating the model of Esarhaddon, or rebel again. But then, the

---

headgear marks accession to kingship, see under *agû* (tiara) and *apāru* (to provide with a headdress) in CAD. I am tempted to wonder whether the phonetic resemblance between the Hebrew *p'r* and the Akk. *apāru*, especially in some of its conjugations, has influenced the choice of terms in Ezek 24:17, 23.

Though both Borger and Luckenbill translate the noun *agû* as "crown," CAD notes that the translations "crown" and "tiara" "denote only the functional aspect of *agû*" and that consideration must also be given to geographical and historical variations in the types of headdresses used to signify divinity and royalty (CAD 1.I.157). In view of the parallelism of turban (*miṣěnepet*) and crown (*ʿatarâ*) in Ezek 21:31, it is likely that a similar situation existed for Judaean headgear--that is, different types of headdresses might signify different degrees of status, but that all headdresses are status indicators.

building inscription genre focuses on the king and his piety, not that of the city's inhabitants. The king does what the inhabitants appear incapable of doing: by his pious attentiveness to the god Marduk, he undoes the effect of their rebellion, renders the city fit for habitation, and restores their privileges of citizenship.

In Ezekiel's appropriation of the motif of the royal persona holding together the entire work, Ezekiel has split the role of the central figure of the narrative. In *Ezekiel*, the royal figure is, of course, Yahweh. It is Yahweh who reveals himself enthroned in the heavens and ruling over the four corners of the earth; who gives an account of the rebellion of his subjects through the oracles uttered by his prophet; and who describes what he has done to restore the city and rehabilitate his people. One reason for the apparent "absence of humanity" in the book, then, is that, Ezekiel has appropriated a genre which extolls the deeds of human kings but has used it to assert the opposite: the task of ruling humankind (or in any case, the House of Israel) is reserved for God alone.

As Yahweh's prophet, Ezekiel shares this central position in the book. One indication of this is the fact that the recognition formula, normally reserved for the acknowledgment that Yahweh has been disclosed in the events reported in the book, is also used of Ezekiel: "And they will know that a prophet has been among them" (Ezek 2:5; 33:33).[55] Ezekiel's role is by no means royal. By contrast with Lord Yahweh, he is *ben 'ādām*, son of man, a term which designates not only Ezekiel's humanness, but also the proper status of subjection before the divine king.[56] His role as ideal subject

---

[55] Cf. Zimmerli, *Ezekiel,* 1.133-34.

[56] For the connotation of *'ādām* as "subject" or "commoner" and the implied contrast between *melek* and *'ādām*, see especially V. P. Hamilton, *'dm, NIDOTTE* 1.262-66.

The expression *ben 'ādām* is used in such a formulaic manner in *Ezekiel* that critics may well have overlooked its significance. The term is by no means evenly distributed throughout the Old Testament. As C. Westermann notes, the highest concentrations are in Ezekiel (132x, 93x in the phrase *ben 'ādām),* Genesis 1-11 (46x, but nowhere else in Genesis), and Ecclesiastes (49x), with secondary concentrations in Proverbs (45x) and Psalms (62x). Though several lexicographers observe that the distribution of the word is noteworthy, none treats the book of Ezekiel as a significant contribution to the development of the term's theological significance. If, however, one regards Genesis 1-11 in its final form as a post-exilic composition, then it can be argued that Ezekiel is the first to make any significant use of the term. In addition to Hamilton, see also C. Westermann, "*'ādam* Mensch" *THAT* 1.41-57; and V. Maass, *'adham," TDOT* 1.75-87.

is further clarified in Yahweh's command that he is not to be rebellious like the House of Israel (Ezek 2:8).

That a prophet, and not a king, should be the model for humanity, is consistent not only with Yahweh's central role, but also with the generally negative assessment of kingship in the book.[57] Perhaps it is no coincidence that the Judaean king takes off his turban in 21:31 and Ezekiel as *ben'ādām* puts his on in 24:17. In the oracles against the nations, the king of Tyre becomes a further lesson in the humanity of kings: even though he claims to be god, yet the Lord Yahweh declares, "you are *'ādām*, and not *'el*" (Ezek 28:9). As the restoration proceeds, there is a concern both to limit royal power[58] and to ensure that God's subjects learn that they are *'ādām*. At the end of Ezekiel 34, for example, in a passage which is generally understood to be corrupt because the term *'ādām* appears to be redundant,[59] the relationship between Yahweh and people is clearly defined. Indeed, in what is arguably an adaptation of the covenantal formula, Israel's relation to God is defined and delimited by their status as *adam*: "You are my flock, the flock of my pasture; you are *'ādām*; I am your God" (*'ādām 'attem 'anî 'elohêkem;* Ezek 34:31).

If the persona of Ezekiel has been influenced by the royal persona in the Babylonian inscriptions of Esarhaddon, it has not been by means of a simple borrowing. Ezekiel has appropriated the motif but has adapted it in order to define the proper relationship between God and his people. First, because only Yahweh is king, the central human persona is merely *'ādām*. As *ben 'ādām*, Ezekiel does not assume an exalted position above the exiles; rather, he models for them what it means to be *'ādām*. By contrast with Esarhaddon, who alone wears the turban, Ezekiel is first among equals; the exiles will do as Ezekiel has done. Second, far from diminishing human responsibility, Ezekiel enhances it. As I have noted above, the Babylonian inscriptions do not ascribe moral responsibility to the inhabitants of Babylon. They are culpable but not responsible: they can destroy the city through their rebellion, but they are passively dependent on Esarhaddon's actions to

---

[57] I.M. Duguid, *Ezekiel and the Leaders of Israel* (VTSup, 56; Leiden, New York: Brill, 1994) 10-57; J. D. Levenson, *Theology of the Program of Restoration of Ezekiel 40-48* (HSM, 10; Missoula, Mont: Scholars, 1976) 57-69.

[58] See especially Levenson: "Messianic theology does not entail an endorsement of imperial power in Ezekiel's theology but has been severed from its politico-mythological matrix" (*Theology of the Program of Restoration,* 67).

[59] Zimmerli, *Ezekiel,* 2.211; Allen, *Ezekiel,* 2.158; Greenberg, *Ezekiel* 2.704.

make things right again. In Ezekiel, by contrast, individual responsibility is required, even demanded (Ezek 18; 36; 40-48). This responsibility is defined in two ways: first, in recognition that humans are *'ādām* and thus subject to God (Ezek 34:35); and second, as a consequence of this fact, they act in obedience to the laws and commandments of their Great King (cf. Ezek 20:11, 13, 21).

Conclusion

This essay has examined the contribution of genre to the presentation of the persona of Ezekiel. Two ongoing issues in the consideration of this question have been the extent to which the character of Ezekiel has been overshadowed by the voice of Yahweh, and the extent to which Ezekiel's emotional response to clearly traumatic events seems strangely muted. It is my hope that this analysis of genre will contribute to the critical discussion in two ways.

First, the comparison of the book of Ezekiel with the Babylonian inscriptions of Esarhaddon should shed new light on the way in which the figures of Ezekiel and Yahweh divide up features reserved only for the human king in the inscriptions. Critics have asked why the character of Ezekiel has been so completely obscured by the voice of God; but a comparison of *Ezekiel* with Esarhaddon's Babylonian inscriptions would rather indicate that the real surprise of *Ezekiel* is that any human figure is allowed to emerge at all. In this light, it would be interesting to raise further questions about the role of Ezekiel as a sign (Ezek 24). In Esarhaddon's inscriptions, signs and portents are suprahuman;[60] by contrast, in *Ezekiel,* the prophet himself is the sign; he is the one whose mouth is opened (Ezek 24:25-27; 29:17-21; 33:22); and he is the one through whom God's spirit moves to bring the exiles back to life (Ezek 37). Far from diminishing humanity, this dimension of Ezekiel's involvement suggests that divine activity must be incarnate.

Second, my analysis of genres with respect to mourning should suggest that Ezek 24:15-24 does not revolve around the suppression of emotion. To compare the prophets Ezekiel and Jeremiah on this point is to confuse genres. Where the persona of Jeremiah rests on the genre of the complaint psalms, that of Ezekiel is derived from the autobiographical conventions of Mesopotamian building inscriptions. What is astonishing about *Ezekiel's* use of these inscriptions is not its consequent suppression of

---

[60] See Appendix.

emotion but its democratization. Particularly in the motif of Ezekiel and the exiles' donning turbans, the actions are stylized representations of status, a transfer of power from Jerusalem to the exiles. To assume that this passage is concerned with the expression of emotion is to miss this point. Turbans are indicators of high status; that all of the exiles should do as Ezekiel has done is to suggest that all of them share in the transition to this honored status.

**Appendix: A Comparison of the Structure of
The Book of Ezekiel
and
The Babylonian Inscriptions of Esarhaddon[1]**

Esarhaddon's Inscription	*Ezekiel*
Self-identification of Esarhaddon (1)	Self-identification of Yahweh, in vision (1)
Evil omens (signs) (2)	Yahweh appoints Ezekiel as *nābî*, who acts as "sign" (2:1-5:4)
Babylonian civil and cultic abuses (3-5)	Jerusalemite civil and cultic abuses (5:5-8:18)
Flood destroys the city (7)	Fire from altar destroys the city (9:1-10:17)
Gods abandon the city, flee heavenward (8)	Yahweh abandons the city (10:20-22)
People flee to another land (9)	Expulsion from the land is decreed (11:7, 14-21; 12:1-16)
Marduk reverses his decree of destruction (10)	Yahweh does not spare Jerusalem or its inhabitants (12:1-24:14)
Marduk appoints Esarhaddon as restorer of Babylon, elects him as king over his brothers; Esarhaddon dons the tiara (11)[2]	Yahweh elects exiles; Ezekiel dons the turban as insignia of their election (24:15-25)
Good omens for restoring the city (12-15)	Oracles against the nations (25-32)
Fearful of beginning the work, Esarhaddon prays, receives encouraging oracles which are written down, and in which Esarhaddon trusts (15-17)	Ezekiel's mouth is "opened" (33)

Preparations for rebuilding: Esarhaddon gathers the builders, makes the plans (18-24)	Preparations for rebuilding: Yahweh judges leaders, cleanses people, brings them back to life; people cleanse land (34-39)
In a good month, on a favorable day, Esarhaddon lays the foundation of Esagila, measures the temple precincts, and describes the building materials (26-31)	*In the twenty-fifth year,* Ezekiel is transported by vision to Jerusalem; an angel measures the temple precincts, rooms, recesses, doors (40-42)
Esarhaddon refurbishes the divine images and returns them to Esagila (32)	Yahweh's glory returns to the temple (43:1-5)
Esarhaddon provides sacred vessels, reinstates the religious ordinances and rituals, and reinstates the priesthood (33, recension C)	Yahweh establishes the dimensions of the altar, reinstates its ordinances and personnel; makes provisions for a holy district (43:13-45:30)
Esarhaddon rebuilds the tower of Etemenanki (34, recension C)	
Esarhaddon measures and rebuilds Imgur-Enki (35)	
Esarhaddon returns gods which had been abducted to Assyria and Elam (36, recension C)	
Esarhaddon reinstates the *anduraru, kidinnu,* and *subaru* rights of the people, regathers those who had been sold into slavery, gives back stolen property, clothes the naked, restores *zakatu,* and establishes entrances to city on all four sides, so that Babylon's inhabitants may return (37)	Yahweh restores rights of the people: laws for the *nāsí* establish justice for the people (45:7-12); sacral laws establish guidelines for popular worship (46); river for food and healing (47:1-12); restoring the land as inheritance (47:13-48:29); exits on all four sides of the city (48:30-34)

Esarhaddon invokes blessings on his
kingship (39)

Esarhaddon commands that a stele be built
and honored by all future generations
(40-41)

The name of the city is its memorial (48:35)

---

[1] Different recensions of this inscription have been
found in Nineveh and Babylon. Only those of
Babylonian provenience have been used in this
comparison. Except where noted, all episodes are
that of Recension A. In only two instances have I left
a gap in the sequence of episodes: episode 6 is
attested only in a Nineveh recension, and episode 38
is illegible. The classification of the recensions and
the enumeration of the episodes follow the edition of
R. Borger, *Die Inschriften Asarhaddons Königs von
Assyrien* (*Afo* Beih 9; 1956).
[2] This motif is in recension B, which was found in
Nineveh.

FINDING DATA IN UNEXPECTED PLACES
(OR: FROM TEXT LINGUISTICS TO SOCIO-RHETORIC).
A SOCIO-RHETORICAL READING OF JOHN'S GOSPEL.

Gerhard van den Heever
University of South Africa

ABSTRACT

Vernon Robbins in his *Tapestry of early Christian discourse* and in *Exploring the texture of texts* has argued that socio-rhetorical analysis is an interpretation of the interplay between various arenas of texture. For this, such an analysis makes use of data from various fields, be it linguistic (inner texture), literary comparative (intertexture), social and historical (social and cultural texture) and the ideology of the text (ideological texture). While as a general statement of the method this is adequate, it has to be recognised that 'data' is by no means a static entity with an objective existence. The reader's understanding of the interplay of the various textures and the reader's imaginative construction of the text's rhetorical situation can radically alter the way the 'data' for such a socio-rhetorical analysis is conceptualised, and dramatically change the inferences made from the text. This is illustrated with reference to the Gospel of John. It is shown how the language of imperium (language of the imperial cult) pervades the text and its projection of the image of Jesus. This is done by re-imagining the connections of the various textures as well as the networks of significations surrounding the text.

INTRODUCTION: RHETORICAL READING IS ALL ABOUT WEBS OF DATA

The work of Vernon Robbins on the method of socio-rhetorical analysis of Scripture, especially his monographs *Tapestry of early Christian discourse* and *Exploring the texture of texts*, will remain for many years the benchmarks against which all applications of rhetorical method to biblical texts will be measured.

Following Robbins' approach, the rhetoric of the text as the persuasive strategy can be identified from the interplay of the various arenas of textures. A rhetorical analysis is then the interpretation of how the interplay of textures aids or 'constructs' the persuasive strategy. A rhetorical analysis makes use of data from various fields, be it linguistic (inner texture), literary comparative (intertexture), social and historical (social and cultural texture) and the ideology of the text (ideological texture) (Robbins 1996: 1—17, 237—240).

New Testament texts are not simply historical, theological or linguistic treatises. Rather, their written discourse is a highly interactive and complex environment. Interpreting a biblical text is an act of entering a world where body and mind, interacting with one another, create and evoke highly complex patterns and configurations of meanings in historical, social, cultural and ideological contexts of religious belief. Rhetorical argument, social act and religious belief intertwine in them like threads and yarn in a richly textured tapestry (Robbins 1996: 14).

On the most immediate level, from the perspective of the reader, the text is the interweaving of words, phrases, expressions, motifs and themes, and references to an 'outside' world which as an ensemble give material voice to the vision of reality and the world espoused by the author and projected to the audience as an invitation to share in the vision (level 1). On another level the text is the nexus of rhetorical situation, audience and the complex world in which the communication event took place (level 2). On yet a third level, the text is also a nexus of all the above and the present reader, him/herself immersed in social settings and ideologies at a remove from the world in which the textual communication originated (level 3). Textual communication implies a simultaneous movement — and interplay — of connotation and denotation. Thus a socio-rhetorical reading is a 'conscious strategy of reading and rereading a text from different angles' (Robbins 1996: 3) or a challenge to interpreters 'to explore human reality and religious belief and practice through multiple approaches to written discourse in texts' (Robbins: 13). One has to keep in mind, however, that the 'interplay of connotation and denotation' is a 'simul-play', simultaneously mutually determining, and furthermore that the 'different angles' or 'multiple approaches' do not describe successive stages in the reading process as in consecutive steps to be followed in the application of a method. Rather, the concerns of present-day readers informed and determined by their social location and ideology or vision of the world (level 3), determine how we imagine the rhetorical situation in which the textual communication had its place (level 2) and determine our selection of textual data to construct the rhetorical situation and communicative aim (level 1). All this happens simultaneously in the reading process.

While as a general statement of the method the introduction to socio-rhetorical method by Robbins (:1—17, 237—240) is adequate, it has to be recognised that 'data' is by no means a static entity with an objective existence. This is because it is much more difficult in the case of a complex narrative text (such as John's Gospel, which enjoys a reputation of being a notoriously dense text) to determine the relationship between textures such as recurring word or motif-patterns, intertextual 'reminiscences' of other/earlier texts, the social and historical context implied by the text and the perspective adopted by/in the text.

THE PROBLEM OF NARRATIVES

Presented the way it is, a socio-rhetorical method works well when the examples used are taken from argumentative material (the method is illustrated in *The tapestry of early Christian discourse* with reference to 1 Corinthians 9). In an argumentative text the aim of the author, the rhetoric, is verbalised explicitly. It explicitly engages the obtaining situation, gives explicit instructions and comments explicitly on its own use of symbols (for example, relating the Christian epic, the narratives about Jesus Christ and other early Christian symbols, as well as the Hebrew epic, the narratives and symbols from the past to the present situation of the author-and-audience and thus showing up their relevance to the situation). Being much more direct communication, argumentative material is more readily recognised as being rhetorical in character (witness the many studies on the rhetorical figures and tropes employed in, for example, New Testament letters).

A complex narrative on the other hand, only gives away its ideology and rhetorical aim very reluctantly ('... it is embedded in the totality of the text and ... is only verbalised in bits and pieces.' Van Tilborg 1989: 27). This is because of the unique characteristics of the communicative genre of narrative. Since Gérard Genette it has become commonplace to distinguish three aspects of narrative reality (Genette 1980: 27). On the one hand one has the narrative content (*story*), then the narrative text itself as the story facts-as-presented (*narrative* or *narrative text*), and finally the act that produces the narrative including the situation in which the narrative action took place (*narrating* or *narration*).[1] To understand what a narrative text tries to convey is to understand also the relationship between these three aspects.[2] What complicates the matter further is that we only have access to the story facts-as-presented, the narrative text, to ideologically 'distorted history'.[3] The text is the material remains of the act of communication and the historical situation of author-and-audience, of the act of narration. But it is the situation (now gone) that would furnish the clues as to what was 'distorted' and how are we to take the 'facts' of the story to be 'true', representative of 'how things really were'? Are we, in other words, to take an author at his word?[4]

Consider the Gospel of John: on the surface it is about what happened in Palestine 60 years before (if one accepts the conventional dating), the history, the words and actions of Jesus of Nazareth and the public around him. And yet it is conceded in the introduction to all commentaries on the gospel that it had a purpose relevant to its original place of composition, whether that be Western Asia Minor — Ephesus , Syria, even Egypt, or Palestina, in any case a purpose aimed at a situation different in time and place to the events narrated in the gospel. And now the question, how does one determine the narrative's address to a situation when it is not explicitly *about* that situation? What counts as data is determined by the reader's understanding of the interplay of the various textures and the reader's imaginative construction of the text's rhetorical situation and that, in turn, can radically alter the way the 'data' for such a socio-rhetorical analysis is conceptualised, and dramatically changes the inferences made from the text.

How do we imagine the relation between biblical texts and the world of which they were part and to which they refer? And how do we imagine the 'message' of the biblical text, that is, what it tries to accomplish as an act of communication in a certain, specific context? These questions touch on some of the most fundamental assumptions governing our interaction with biblical texts, assumptions that will determine fundamentally the way we construe the 'meaning' of the texts.

All along it is implied that, regardless of the claims made in a text of itself or by others (claims, for example, that characterise the text under discussion as of a revelatory nature), all texts are 'texts in contexts, specific acts of communication between specified individuals, at specific points in time and space, about specifiable subjects' (Smith J Z 1982:xiii). In the context Jonathan Smith referred to 'myth or other religious materials' which, after Kenneth Burke's definition of a proverb, should be understood as 'strategies for dealing with situations'. With these words the programmatic starting point of the present study is formulated. Religious texts have to do with human life-worlds, human contexts, human social contexts — somewhere at some point in time — and because of their nature as acts of communication they essentially imply a relationship between partners in communication, but a relationship which is not static, rather it is a two-way interaction structured by input, cybernetic feedback, revised input, et cetera. Furthermore, communicative interaction is much more than the transfer of idea content. It entails communication of world-view as well as guidelines on how to live according to the world-view... but in the act of communicating religion and world-view are themselves 'created' or 'conserved' depending on the communication situation. While the ancient world and its lived experiences have disappeared in the ongoing march of history, things — 'stuff', artifacts — have remained. The challenge is to interpret these artifacts in order to imagine the ancient world as well as the inner workings of the ancient world and world-view. Ancient texts, like the biblical documents, are special kinds of artifacts. Unlike other artifacts, ancient texts (from literary works to inscriptions) quite consciously speak about the world of which they were part. And in the case of the biblical texts the Christian religious tradition has kept them alive and in use as a canonised source of spirituality, that is as a source of present-day world-view construction (or religious life, if you wish). Ancient texts, then, need to be interpreted. One aspect of interpretation is to enter into the world projected by the text and to imagine the fit between the text and the world-view contemporaneous to it. This 'fit' between text-as-artifact and world-view has to be imagined and constructed and one does so by linking the text and what it says to as many other texts and artifactual remains as possible, in so doing, constructing the web of meaning giving relations of which the text was part. Another important element of this 'ancient world construction' is the use of appropriate and relevant methods of inquiry (fields of study such as cultural anthropology, sociology, and so on, and to this we may add text linguistics and socio-rhetorical analysis, for the use of the text as a 'window' on how a group visualised its place and preferred way of living in the ancient world is explored here). Since our focus here is on a text, the Gospel of John, we will have to ask ourselves 'in what way does this text reflect the world of the partners in communication?' 'How does it speak about the world?' 'What type of world is projected and constructed?' The answers we give to questions such as these allow us to make inferences as to the communicative situation or historical context in which the text was produced as act of communication between the historical partners of that communication event.[5]

DIFFERENT KINDS OF DATA

This means that we have two kinds of data to work with in our reconstruction of the life world of the persons involved in the production (i.e. the author) and reception (i.e. the reader) of the text. First, we have explicit data. The text mentions places, names of characters or historical figures, or refers to historical events. We can correlate this with other texts or inscriptions which also refer to the same personae, customs or events, or with archaeological remains like buildings, temples or iconographic depictions such as mural paintings or coins. Second, we also deal with implicit data. The values espoused by the author, the outlook on life propagated, how the inner workings of their world were conceived, all this is rarely spelled out explicitly in a text, at least not in complex narratives such as the Gospel of John. Much of it has to be inferred from the way the text manipulates historical references to project its world. It is thus from the rhetoric or the art or patterns of persuasion in a text, that is from the way it 'distorts' reality in order to create a new perspective on the world for the readers (as if to say 'this is how you should think the world works'), that we can infer somewhat about the historical situation and this in turn creates historical data to use in our reconstruction of the ancient life-world and endeavour to understand the ancient world-view.

It is in this context that aspects of text linguistics (such as text pragmatics, but more specifically, script or frame theories) can enrich our understanding of the rhetoric of a complex narrative (as I have indicated in note 5 above). Not only should the focus be on the 'base story' (Genette's *histoire/story*, Bal's *geschiedenis/fabula* or Rimmon-Kenan's *story*) but also on the discourse, or the way the story is told (Genette's *récit/narrative*, Bal's *verhaal/story*, or Rimmon-Kenan's *text*). This distinction makes it possible to see the juxtaposition of other 'languages' on to a base story through which evocations of other meanings are transported into the narrative as subtle guides provided by the author to steer the readers' reaction to the narrative.

There is one last complicating factor to be considered and this has to do with the special character of the Gospel of John. The narrative is shot through with metaphors.[6] From expressions which are out and out metaphorical (like the 'I am' sayings and the imagery connected to the discourse in which the sayings appear, and the root metaphor of life around which all the other metaphors are organised), to all the other expressions which in such a text organisation *become* metaphorical (that is, which come to say more and something differently from what is explicitly stated, see Weinrich 1976: 328—341 for a description of the movement from micro-metaphorics to macro- or text metaphorics to the text-as-metaphor) the focus should shift to how the text itself as text-in-function becomes a metaphor in the widest sense: 'a metaphor is a text in a counter-determining situation' (Weinrich 1976: 341. My translation). Words receive their meanings from the context of use. This is an elementary linguistic insight. The same goes for texts as larger configurations of catenae of words. They too receive their meaning from the situation, the situation being the context in which the text is communicated. This is where the 'Streit um Metaphern' (Weinrich) becomes relevant: no two readers will imagine the counter-determining situation in exactly the same way, therefore the meaning of the text will not be constructed identically. No matter how explicit a text is, the counter-determining context is not a given in the material sense.

IMAGINED SITUATION AND IMAGINED PURPOSE.

None of the above is possible without a presupposition on the part of the interpreter as to the rhetorical situation (or context) which gave rise to the Gospel of John. Indeed, the very term 'socio-rhetoric' implies an intimate and indispensable relation between the text as communicative act and its historical context.

It is time to proceed to a few examples. I discuss three examples.[7] The first example is derived from a 'traditional', theological reading of the gospel and I refer here to the introductory sections to some commentaries on John's gospel where the 'theology' or 'purpose' is set out and I want to draw attention to how the specific construction of the 'theology' or 'purpose' is constructed and justified with reference to text phenomena.

In the past three decades it has become somewhat of a communio opinis that the Gospel of John evidences the separation of church and synagogue (one can point to the seminal works of Wayne Meeks 'The man from heaven in Johannine sectarianism' [1972], J Louis Martyn *History and theology in the Fourth Gospel* [1968/1979] and Jerome Neyrey's *An ideology of revolt. John's Christology in social-science perspective* [1988]). In this second example I will discuss the arguments of Meeks ('Breaking away: three New Testament pictures of Christianity's separation from the Jewish communities' [1985]) and Richard Cassidy (*John's Gospel in new perspective. Christology and the realities of Roman power* [1992]).

Finally, I will present my own reading of the gospel. In identifying in John a utopian 'language of the anti-imperium' I do not wish to give the impression that this is the totality of the ideology or rhetoric of the narrative.

The narrative is far too complex for that, but at least, and that is my contention, gives direction to a plausible reading of the narrative in its supposed context.

Traditional theological readings of John's purpose

In his recent commentary Leon Morris discusses without going into much detail a few possible aims of the gospel: a supplement to the Synoptic Gospels, a polemic against Gnosticism, polemic against docetism[8], against unbelieving Jews[9], opposing the continuing following of John the Baptist, opposing Christian teachers who lay either too much or too little stress on the sacraments[10], and as a presentation to the world of a kind of 'Hellenised Christianity'[11]. Finally, Morris elects (as most commentators on the purpose of John's Gospel do) to be led by the author's own verbalisation of his purpose, namely John 20: 30,31. John shows to his audience that Jesus is the Christ, the son of God. Through this showing they are brought into the sphere of belief and new life and in telling this story, the audience is confronted with a challenge to accept the message and so enter the domain of light or remain in darkness if they should not commit themselves to this message and the person who is the content of the message (Morris 1995: 30—34).

According to George Beasley-Murray John writes to 'provide an authoritative interpretation of the traditions concerning Jesus current in his own communities ... in so doing he is concerned above all to impart an adequate understanding of the person, words and deeds of Jesus the Christ and Son of God' (1987: lxxxviii). This again proceeds from a consideration of John 20: 30,31. Taking the cue from text critical considerations regarding the tense of the verb (Aorist or Imperfect) 'to believe' in John 20: 30, 31, Beasley-Murray takes the gospel to be both catechetical *and* missionary in nature. In so far as the narrative instructs believers it also combats false and inadequate beliefs. So the gospel has both an evangelistic and didactic aim. The perceived polemics in the narrative combat the 'new winds of doctrine' challenged by the author of the gospel, albeit it not the main aim of the gospel. Some of these include a polemic against the views of John the Baptist and his movement[12], a polemic against the 'Jews'[13], and finally an anti-Gnostic and anti-docetic polemic.[14]

The last example in this group is taken from Raymond Brown's commentary (1966: LXVII—LXXIX). Because he understands the gospel to be a heavily redacted text, Brown allows for the possibility that text parts supporting or suggesting certain aims may actually be indicative of the aim of the text at a certain stage of its dissemination and redaction. However, the 'main' aim of the gospel is to strengthen the faith of Christian believers, thus taking 20: 31 not to indicate a missionary purpose.[15] All the theological emphases are 'directed to crises in the believing Church' (:LXXVIII). The believing Church encompasses both Jew and Gentile.[16] Further apologetic aims of the gospel include a polemic against the sectarians of John the Baptist, a polemic against the Jews (with a justification of Christian claims against Jewish unbelief as well an appeal to Jewish Christians in the diaspora), and it may contain a polemic against Christian heretics (such as Gnostics, Ebionites and Docetics).

The presupposition chiefly responsible for this line of interpretation is a theological presupposition which causes early Christian writings to be seen as unique and early Christianity as a revealed, unique movement growing out of Second Temple Judaism over against which the Graeco-Roman world and its 'religious languages' are collapsed into 'background'. This is seen clearly in the way both Beasley-Murray and Brown list the other possible languages echoed in the language of John (following Dodd in referring to Gnosticism, Mandaism, Hellenistic thought — Greek philosophy, Philo and Hermeticism, Qumran, Palestinian Judaism and Rabbinic Judaism). After listing the parallels, they remain just parallels since the gospel is insulated from the wider contemporary world.

Another presupposition deals with the place of the Old Testament and the overtly (anti-) Jewish polemics in the text. The many references to the Old Testament in the context of Jewish polemics cause scholars to construe the rhetorical situation of John's Gospel as one of the separation of church and synagogue.

Readings with a view to John's context

Meeks ('Breaking away') and Cassidy (*New perspective*) both take the gospel to express social realities pertaining to the gospel's place of communication first and foremost. This is the value of these approaches, namely to read the text as a way of engaging in social realities and struggles.

According to Cassidy 'John was concerned to present elements and themes that were especially significant for Christian readers facing Roman imperial claims and for any who faced Roman persecution ... [with reference to the variously identified backgrounds to the gospel — GvdH] may it not be the case that the gospel consciously responds to significant developments within the Roman world?' (: 1). The realities to which Cassidy refers are the Jewish temple tax and the cult of the Roman emperor with its attendant denouncements and persecution. The reality of the temple tax instituted by Vespasian as punishment for the Jewish War and rigorously brought to bear by Domitian forced the issue of deciding who are Jews. This created the conditions under which many Christians could eventually expect to be denounced and led to trial. The aim of these treason trials was to enforce loyalty to the emperor. According to Cassidy this situation is reflected in the way the gospel portrays Jesus as sovereign with titles such as 'saviour of the world', 'Lord' and 'Lord and God', all titles also used for the emperors in their cult. Even the trial narrative becomes an opportunity to portray the trial and crucifixion as manifestation of Jesus' sovereignty. In the farewell discourses these contemporary issues and the situation of the readers are thematised in the many warnings about persecution, warnings against apostasy (which we know from Pliny's letters to Trajan did happen), encouragement of the faithful to stay closely bonded to his name, to mutually encourage and support each other in this time of persecution, and finally to accept and live in the light of Jesus' assurances that he has final sovereignty over the world.

Meeks argues that the gospel text is the material remains of a schism within Judaism.[17] The party or sect of Samaritans and Galileans is defined over against the 'Jews' and the narrative is produced from their perspective. Samaritans and Galileans occupy a special and positive place in the gospel narrative. Several aspects of the way the narrative is represented lead to this reading. First, the importance of locale in the narrative and the presence of local traditions in the gospel would suggest that it assumes a situation where Samaritans, Galileans and 'Jews' (= Jewish leaders) are interacting (possibly Galilee —Meeks). Second, the many references to *aposynagogoi* etc attest to the fact that the Johannine community is no longer part of the Jewish communities centred in synagogues. Third, the many references to Jewish traditions, feasts, religion and so on, would suggest a polis setting ('urbanized and hellenized' — so Meeks 1985: 101) with a relatively large population of Jews, Samaritans and Galilean immigrants, and among them the Johannine community. At any rate, this section of the population of such a city setting would be dominated by the Jews and Jewish leaders. John's 'world' (in the negative sense) is this world from which the community conceptually dissociates itself. The trauma of the divorce from the synagogue forces the emerging Johannine Christian community to organise itself in a new social structure (so well known from the organisation of other migratory cults, namely the household) just like Jews and Samaritans had done in diasporic centres where they had a presence. The implication of this for an understanding of the gospel is that we see here more that just the history of Jesus of Nazareth. We also read in the narrative the history of the Johannine group's separation from the dominant form of Judaism as well as the laying down of the ground rules for the future existence of the new household community.

John and the language of imperium.[18]

I should state at the outset that my own reading (which is here only represented in bits and parts) has much in common with those of Meeks and Cassidy. My focus is wider than that of Meeks, and here I am inclined to agree with Cassidy in reading John in the setting of a large Graeco-Roman city and then in Western Asia Minor. I do not attempt to prove that John originated in Ephesus, although I do believe its language use makes eminently sense in such a setting. The form in which we have the narrative now (the latest edition?) shows definite similarities to the language of religious and political reality in the world of a city like Ephesus. Since I have argued all along that identifying the rhetorical situation and the rhetorical reading of the text mutually determines each other, one should still pay attention to the early church tradition which identified a bond between the Johannine tradition and the city of Ephesus (in any case, with the Roman province of Asia) as an important indicator of how Johannine language was appropriated by and resonated in the minds of an Ephesian audience. Shifting the perspective to a more religio-historical approach, an attempt is made here to read the Gospel of John as a Graeco-Roman (Ephesian) narrative, embedded in the life of urban Ephesus.[19] Within this perspective the Johannine appropriation of 'other languages' is considered, specifically the language of imperium (the language of the imperial cult). It is shown how John's Gospel narrates key episodes *in the very terms* of the imperial cult.

The triumphal entry

It has already been argued that the portrayal of Jesus' triumphal entry in the gospel tradition corresponds with the Roman triumphus or adventus.[20] The adventus as acclamatory and honour ritual would involve the city's population who would, in decorated and festive procession, hail the dignitary into the city with songs and praises. In the case of the emperors, there often was a meeting between the emperor and the local senate, during which requests were made and granted, and here, in a very real sense, the emperor could be the benefactor and saviour of his subjects (MacCormack:723).

In a short cameo scene John narrates Jesus' adventus thus: when it was announced that Jesus was coming to the city, the crowds went out to meet him carrying palm branches, acclaiming him as 'the king of Israel' (12:12—19). In this account John uses the technical term for the reception of a ruler — *hypantesis* — which regularly appears in Hellenistic sources describing an adventus. 'The use of this term indicates that Christ's arrival in Jerusalem can be considered in the context of arrivals of Hellenistic rulers and their successors' (MacCormack:725). I want to add another consideration, namely that the point of an imperial triumphal entry would not have been lost on an

Ephesian audience. Given the origins of the ritual in the cult of Dionysus (as conquering god), an imperial triumphal entry would very definitely carry religious overtones, ever since the first entry (for the period I am interested in) of Mark Antony as 'New Dionysus' in 38 BCE (an event which was of momentous significance for Ephesus, since they had backed the wrong horse — one could surmise that the later clamour for a neokorate was not only an attempt to curry favour with the emperor but also to undo the damage of an earlier wrong alliance) and the adventus of Hadrian again as 'New Dionysus' in 129 CE. In John's narrative it is also clear that a god is entering the city.

This line taken up again in 18:28ff with the passion narrative. The scenes following from 19:1ff have a significance that derives from their interference with the reality of the Roman imperium. One could label the trial scenes an installation of an imperial pretender for these scenes described by John are situations that typically occurred with each usurpation of power by an imperial pretender (cf Van Tilborg 1992: 110—111).

John portrays this in the following fashion: 19:1—3: the soldiers make Jesus emperor. They give him a crown and purple toga, 'greet' and 'acclaim' him.

19:4—7: the epiphany before the people. Pilate shows him to the assembled people. Pilate is Jesus' herald who goes out before him to let the people hear who Jesus is.

19:8—12: the discussion about power with a member of the senate. God is the source of power and Jesus as Son of God has a unique relation to the source of power. The people, Pilate and even the emperor are subject to it.

And now one can interpret the significance of these scenes. Jesus is received into the city as 'King of Israel'. He is acclaimed by the citizens but the leaders are absent — for them he is not their king. For this reason he is delivered over to the Roman governor by the Jewish leaders on the charge that he started a sedition vying to be king in the emperor's place. Jesus' defence is that he is not that type of king (18:36). Nevertheless the Romans make him king (see the inscription on the cross 19: 19—22), but the Jews refuse to have him foisted on them, instead they demand his execution for he made himself a son of God which is tantamount to saying the designated person is emperor, for they shout that they have no king except Caesar.

The narrated, represented short career of Jesus as king in the narrative is symptomatic of Rome's dealings with its client kings and Jewish reactions to this phenomenon is well illustrated by the episode on the deliberations of the Council in 11:45—53. The relationship with Rome determines the relative freedom they would enjoy. While this is true for other situations as well, it was especially true for client kingdoms. Perceived loyalty to Rome could bring many benefits, a typical benefit regularly praised in inscriptions is 'restored freedom and independence', alleviation of tax burdens and so forth. It is this context that the phrase 'being a friend of Caesar' becomes relevant. The Romans made kings and deposed kings. According to the perspective of the text the Jews buy into the Roman imperial ideology. They opt for loyalty to the Roman emperor.

Benefactions, benefactors and saviours

From this point one can now approach the narrative from back to front, from the end to the beginning. One nexus between the reality of the imperium and public life in Ephesus (and thus the Johannine narrative) can be seen in the phenomenon of public benefactions.[21] In an inscription from Kyme (not too far from Ephesus) a Kleanax is honoured for his generous dispensing of food and wine (cf note 21 above). Apart from public building works, funding games and so on, feasting counted as one of the important expressions of euergetism. The Romans, and especially since Augustus, the emperors took this clamour for honour to new levels. Thus one finds returning with chronic regularity honorific titles such as 'Benefactor', 'Saviour' and the combination 'Saviour and benefactor', and also (in a slightly different semantic domain) 'Founder'. The narratives in John 2 and 6 not only evoke the political reality of benefactions, but also other associations: the combination of the episodes of dispensing wine and bread finds its counterpart in the combination of the cultic associations of Dionysus and Demeter in Ephesus. Again the language of political reality is interwoven into 'religious language'. It is, however, important to note how the 'eucharistic' discourse of chapter 6 is narrated.

Accounts of the cultic meals of religious associations in the Graeco-Roman world show that the usual fare consists of bread and fish (as in John 6), which accords with the earliest pictorial depictions of the eucharist. The narrative effect of this is to place the divine benefaction not in the public sphere but in the 'private' domain where the Christian (Johannine) cult community gathers withdrawn from participating in civic life.

In the context of the culture of benefaction we find honorific titles heaped on benefactors. Thus we have Augustus labelled 'the one and only', 'first and foremost' — this is the language of panegyric and exaggeration. But functionally it is not too far removed from epithets for Jesus in John like *monogenes*, unique, the one and only, an appellation that concords with the description of the bread as divine food, the wine of the Cana miracle as unsurpassed wine.

The names of Jesus

A very important feature of John's narrative is the portrayal of Jesus via nomenclature. It has often been remarked that the identity of Jesus is of paramount importance in the gospel. This is borne out by the many epithets for Jesus[22]. The narrative starts with the question of identity (1: 19—23). With the Andrew/Simon and Nathaniel scene the first pole of the programmatic naming closure occurs (Jesus identified as Messiah = Christ, Son of God and King of Israel). The other pole of the naming closure occurs at the (original) end of the narrative (20: 30, 31) with Jesus again named Son of God and Christ (=Messiah). In between Jesus dies as King of Israel/King of the Jews and is acclaimed Lord and God. The net effect of this naming system is to portray the main character of the narrative as someone embodying political ideals and as having a special relationship with God. This practice of relating emperors/kings with gods was of course not new.[23] In the Roman province of Asia (Western Asia Minor) this had special significance for the first century CE. Arguably, the cult of the emperor took off here in the Greek-speaking Eastern provinces of the empire and was promoted here to levels previously unknown as a way (so Price) of dealing with the new phenomenon (for the

Greeks) of Roman imperial power. As a first century papyrus says: 'What is a god? *Ti kratoun* — that which exercises power.' From the first tentative appropriations of the title 'god' its recipients grew bolder and more and more uninhibited so that by the end of the century Domitian could insist on being addressed as *dominus et deus*, lord and god. From Nero onwards the use of the title kyrios escalates (from 43 times with reference to Nero, to 115 with reference to Domitian, 280 with reference to Trajan and 492 with reference to Hadrian, counting the papyrus evidence). 'Lord' thus becomes an important indication of the divine character of the emperor (Van Tilborg 1996: 47). The apotheosis, or divinisation, of the emperor was an important religious and political issue in Ephesus. The main altar of the Antonines in Ephesus depicts in a frieze the apotheosis of Trajan and his wife Plotina (described in Van Tilborg 1996: 41). In a world where emperors became gods, is there an implicit criticism of this practice in John's narrative of a god-king who descended and ascended again?

That we have in this terminology not only 'political' reality is demonstrated by the fact that at least two Graeco-Roman deities were known as conquering gods. I have already referred to Dionysus, who according to myth trekked across Asia Minor into Greece in a mythical anabasis, an ideology which served as the basis and origin of the Roman ritual of the triumph (Versnel 1974). The other deity was the hellenised Egyptian goddess Isis (for a detailed discussion of the line I am following here, cf. Versnel 1990: 35—95). In the most complete Isis aretalogy, that is self-advertising in I am-saying format, namely, that found in Kyme, Asia Minor, first century BCE to first century CE, we read:

l.1: I am Isis, tyrant of every land...

l.25: I broke down the governments of tyrants...

l.40: I am the Queen of war...

l.48: I set free those in bonds...[24]

Isis is portrayed as a conquering as well as a liberating goddess. In this she embodies an old Greek idea of the gods as destroyers of tyrants. However, Isis is simultaneously 'tyrant of every land' and it is this double play on Isis as tyrant and destroyer of tyrants which reflect accurately the double role of

Rome as conquering empire and its self-promotion as upholder and restorer of early freedoms and constitutions (cf. Magie I). After an inauspicious start to her career as deity in the Roman empire (her cult being proscribed at Rome several times in the course of the second and first centuries BCE), by a strange reversal of fate she endeared herself to the Flavians to eventually become the representation of Roman power at the borders of the empire in Europe from the second century onward (cf. Takacs).

The significant point about both Dionysus and Isis is that, as conquering deities, they demand complete loyalty. Regularly occurring acclamations like *heis Dionysos* (Dionysus is one!) or Isis, una quae es omnia (Isis, you are the one and only) provide an insight into the mentality in operation in the Roman imperial ideology. Total allegiance is what is at issue.

John against the 'Jews'.

Slowly a pattern becomes visible in John's narrative. John uses the same language of uniqueness of the emperors and the gods Dionysus and Isis to achieve the opposite, namely to dissociate from the symbolic universe evoked by this language. The gospel is a narrative of the coming into the world of a God as Logos, who does what emperors do, who is enthroned in a way as king and is acclaimed with the same metaphysical epithets as was used to express the divine character of the emperors. But he is unique, *monogenes*, one of a kind (1: 18). No-one else has had the contact with God he had, he is the only image of God and the only way into contact and mutual indwelling between humans and God (14: 6—14; 15: 1—10). Even the metaphors in John point to this polemic which is nothing less than a total reorientation of life (Van den Heever 1992).

But there is no denying that there is also a polemic against the Jews. How should this be understood in the light of the foregoing? If one may summarise very broadly, the polemic in chapters 7 to 11 centre on two issues, namely: Who represents the true Jewish/Israelite tradition? And, are the Jews really free? Concerning the first question, it can be said that there were groups roughly contemporaneous to the writing of John's gospel who saw themselves as the 'true Israel'. This is the sense I make of inscriptions found at the synagogue of the Samaritans at Delos, who consistently called themselves 'Israelites' (Llewelyn 1997: 148—151). Given the positive evaluation of the term Israel in the gospel as well as the fact that Samaritan interests were known in Ephesus[25] and the interest in Samaria as locale in the narrative, might one not surmise that the Johannine community stood in close relationship with Samaritans (while possibly not Samaritans by religious affiliation)?

The second question touches on the place or at-home-ness of Jews in the Graeco-Roman world. In the narrated debate between Jesus and his Jewish opponents, their retort to his accusation that they are slaves is that they have never been slaves, being children of Abraham. This could not have been true for Jews in Palestine. However, it is not far off the mark with regard to first century Asia Minor. David Magie (I: 478—479) describes the role Herod (later 'the Great')[26] played in Asia Minor in securing favours for the Jews (and especially for Ephesus) from the emperor when he accompanied Agrippa, the son-in-law of Augustus, on a 'triumphal tour' of the eastern Roman provinces. The Herodian clan had a presence in the Roman world which extended far beyond the boundaries of Palestine (for the following, cf Hengel & Schwemer: 229ff). A large clan of Herodians were living in Rome as well as in Antioch. But even more, the Herodian family was linked by blood to all the client kingdoms in the region, from Armenia, Pontus, Commagene, Emesa, Galatia and Parthia, to minor aristocratic houses in Arabia and west to Pergamon and Ephesus (Hengel & Schwemer: 454 n 1178). The Herodians as an extensive clan were thus politically open towards Roman rule and the Gentile client princes of the East (Hengel & Schwemer: 229 n 1184). They viewed the rule of Rome as ordained by God's will, just as Josephus too considered the Roman power God-given. The polemic against the Jews, when read against this counter-determining context, is aimed at values such as these portrayed above.

Conclusion

Read in this way, John's gospel is a narrative that creates a new utopia in opposition to the utopia implied by the language of the imperium. One can read it as a text that resists totalising language and at-home-ness in totalitarian utopias and forges a new community on the margins of society.

Such a construal of the interplay between the various textures makes it possible to understand the rhetoric of John's Gospel as the construction of an 'anti-Caesar' with the main character of the narrative (Jesus) as the foundation for a small(-ish) group opting out of civil society, but the narrative simultaneously serves as critique of the at-home-ness in contemporary civil society of other adherents of the hellenistic Judaic tradition. This interpretation is made possible by 'reifying' subtle evocations, wordings and terminologies into 'soft artifacts' (inferences as 'objects') over against 'hard artifacts' which are objects, words or other texts.

Such a reading also makes it possible to apply the Gospel of John to similar present day situations where adherents of Christianity are faced with totalising claims to ultimate loyalty.

NOTES

[1.] I made use of the terms from the English translation of Genette's work. The corresponding terms from Mieke Bal (*Narratology: introduction to the theory of narrative.* 1985) and Shlomith Rimmon-Kenan (*Narrative fiction: contemporary poetics.* 1983) are:

Genette:	Bal:	Rimmon-Kenan:
histoire/story	fabula	story
récit/narrative	story	text
narration/ narrating	text	narration

[2.] In line with this view of the threefold distinction of aspects to narrative, one should locate the rhetorical situation *outside* the text, in the act of narration and not at the level of the narrative text. In a narrative the words and actions of actors are not themselves the rhetoric of the text but are imbedded, as narrative, in the encompassing act of narration, being selected and manipulated to be useful in the act of communication between author and audience, much like a present-day minister would select the parts of the Scripture reading to highlight, expound and apply in a sermon. But of course, the whole process is guided and determined by the way the preacher constructs in his or her own mind what the situation of the audience, the congregation, is and what should be of use to them to hear in that situation. An interesting example of such a double reading of a biblical text in terms of the rhetorical situation outside it can be found in Craig Loscalzo's contribution, 'A rhetorical model' (a reading of Luke 24:13—35, the Emmaus episode) in Bailey, R 1992: 105—134. Loscalzo also provides a brief but good characterisation of Burkeian rhetorical criticism (pp 105—107;114—123).

[3.] Behind the term 'distorted history' lies the distinction between story and discourse, between story facts and how they are presented, imbued with value, interpreted through metaphorical juxtapositions and so on. The distinction is derived from Seymore Chatman: *Story and discourse*, 1978. See also the discussion of this twofold distinction with regard to literary readings of the gospels and its relation to rhetorical criticism of narrative in Stephen Moore: *Literary criticism and the gospels. The theoretical challenge*, 1989, pp 56—68.

[4.] In the case of modern literary works we have the advantage of large corpuses of texts extraneous to a narrative which can be used to measure the mimetic faithfulness of a work (which in turn could help determine the genre, and thereby aids the decoding process — what we as readers should do with the text), texts about the world the narrative purports to describe (histories, travelogues, etc), biographical and autobiographical texts about the author and his/her social location, situation of writing and even about the process of writing itself. Very inconveniently all this is absent in the case of the gospel narratives. How trustworthy are the later identifications of authorship and situation of writing (for example, the Papias fragments, the Muratorian canon and the like)? That's anybody's guess.

[5.] All along I have assumed an identity between rhetoric and communication. Historically rhetoric is synonymous with communication events, after all rhetoric had its place in dialogue and public, interpersonal oratory: 'how to speak well and move the audience'. In many modern text theories there is again a confluence between the two strands of rhetoric and communication. Many studies in the Burkeian tradition of rhetorical criticism appeared in journals such as *Quarterly Journal of Speech*, *Communication Quarterly*, *Central States Speech Journal*, *Western Speech*, *Southern Speech Communication Journal*, *The Journal of Communication* to name really but a few. See for an extended discussion Brock, B L, Scott, R L & Chesebro, J W (eds). *Methods of rhetorical criticism. A twentieth century perspective*

(1989). Another 'school' of text linguistics that has to be mentioned is C-I-T-Linguistics: communication-instruction-text linguistics. A very full and clear discussion of the theory is to be found in Harald Weinrich, *Sprache in Texten* (1976). In the field of discourse analysis the primary interest lies in the use of forms of language in communication (for an overview of discourse analysis and its constituent disciplines of text linguistics, socio-linguistics and literary linguistics, see A H Snyman, A semantic discourse analysis of the Letter to Philemon, in Hartin, P J & Petzer, J H (eds). *Text and interpretation. New approaches in the criticism of the New Testament* (1991). See also the many works by Teun van Dijk. Related to this is text pragmatics. Again, at the confluence of text linguistics, discourse analysis and text pragmatics one finds studies that focus simultaneously on text planning or text production (= the deliberate organisation of language use and text parts in order to convey the desired message) and text comprehension. See for example Ruth Wodak, Strategies in text production and text comprehension: a new perspective, in Dieter Stein (ed), *Cooperating with written texts. The pragmatics and comprehension of written texts* (1992) in the series Studies in Anthropological Linguistics (!). It is shown how, for example, 'cognitional schemata' or frames of cognition or scripts, that is cultural knowledge in the long-term memory together with context in its aspect of socio-psychological influence, steer the process of the production of textual meaning as well as the process of interpreting the textual meaning. Applied to gospel texts this would mean that we should be on the outlook for the schemata or frames that conditioned the author's (in our case, John's) reception of prior tradition (or representation of tradition in his own mind) and production of a new text (thus giving evidence of an author's understanding of the meaning possibilities on offer in the prior text and the deliberate fit between intended communication and intended addressed context). The 'deliberate fit between intended communication and intended addressed context' is achieved inter alia through the selection of terminology, narratable episodes, metaphorical juxtaposition of fixed expression onto new contexts of meaning, what to say and how to say it to make sense in the context. In short, moulding language to suit the context! Of course, readers do the same. Their representation of the text (as decoded or interpreted, how they 'summarise' what the text means) is not the same as the original text. They too are conditioned by their frames or schemata. While we cannot, of course, have empirical data on the representation of the text by the original readers, we can at least imagine from the frames or schemata employed by the author how he envisaged them and their context to be. In literary theoretical parlance: implied readers. In the case our reading of the Gospel of John, it would mean determining which are the correct frames or schemata to fit to the text-as-communication. Cognitional frames form the implicit text base without which the explicit text base (the material text) would not be intelligible in its context. For a fuller exposition of frame theory, see Dieter Metzing (ed), *Frame conceptions and text understanding*(1980), in the series Research in text theory; Hans-Jürgen Eikmeyer & Hannes Rieser (eds), *Words, worlds and contexts. New approaches in word semantics* (1981) also in the series Research in text theory, and Annely Rothkegel & Barbara Sandig (eds), *Text-Textsorten-Semantik. Linguistische Modellen und maschinelle Verfahren* (19..). An application of text pragmatics to biblical exegesis can be found in Hubert Frankemölle, *Biblische Handlungsanweisungen. Beispiele pragmatischer Exegese* (1983) with many references to literature in the field of *Textwissenschaft*. Literature on the subject is vast and inexhaustible. Only a few representative examples must suffice. Different theories and approaches focus on different aspects of the complex phenomenon of communication. Recently, Bruce Malina applied insights from socio-linguistics (speech accommodation theory, antilanguage perspectives and the socio-linguistics of intimacy) to a reading of John's Gospel and through John's use of language concluded that the Johannine community was 'a maverick Christian group' (John's: The maverick Christian group. The evidence of sociolinguistics, *BTB* 24 [1996] :167—182). On the relation between rhetorical criticism and modern text theories, see the overview of Wilhelm Wuellner, Rhetorical criticism and its theory in culture-critical perspective: the narrative rhetoric of John 11, in Hartin & Petzer (eds): 171—185. According to Wuellner, one of the senses in which the term 'rhetorical criticism' has come to be used is 'the rhetoric *of* a given biblical text, where rhetoric stands for the aspect of the text as a whole, or text as an integral act of communication and appeal to action. In the latter sense, rhetoricity becomes synonymous with textuality' (p 176).

What has become clear is the convergence of different theoretical approaches. Broadly speaking, all tend to focus on the relationships between a) the act of communication in its context, b) the agent of the act of communication, c) the addressees of the communication, d) the medium of the act of communication (how language is used) and e) the purpose of the communication. This coheres with the Burkeian pentad of act (what happens, or what is being done), scene (where it happens, the context in time and place), agent (who acts), agency (the medium through which is acted) and purpose (what is the intended result or achievement). One should, however, keep in mind that while the pentad creates the impression of unilinear communication, there very definitely exists a cybernetic feedback relation between the process of text planning and production and the process of text reception, between what an author wants to convey and the audience as he/she imagines them to be, which determines how the message is clothed and the language moulded to suit their situation.

The Burkeian dramaturgical perspective on rhetorical criticism seems to me most suited to a description of the rhetoric of a narrative as it consistently keeps within the purview other and extratextual levels in the communication process. It focuses the attention to text acts as vehicles of interaction between people connected in some way or another in time and place. In a way this is how we should see (even) religious texts, as dissolved into the process of interacting. For too long theology as an exegetical enterprise saw its purpose in the extraction of doctrinal statements from the material text. And so sight was lost of the fact that religion is also world creation, rhetorical vision — a verb, not a noun. God-talk is a discursive practice, a battle for a way of seeing the world (how else does one explain the fight for the position of truth, the stress on church discipline and the drawing of boundaries between orthodoxy and heresy in early Christian literature? And note, the mere mention of boundaries between orthodox and heterodox positions implies social realities, those who are inside and those who are outside, boundaries created by speech acts.).

Within the Burkeian dramaturgical perspective I followed two more specific approaches, namely a dramatistic approach (see Brock, B L 1989:183—195) and fantasy theme approach (Bormann, E G 1989:210—222). Broadly speaking, Brock thematises the use of the pentad to illustrate how a conceptualisation of the 'ratio' between the pentadic elements serves to interpret the rhetorical tendencies of an utterance or text. Bormann illustrates with the fantasy theme approach how small groups build up through communication a shared vision of the world (a 'fantasy'), how this vision is legitimated when members of the group lock into it ('fantasy chain') and how this becomes a larger rhetorical vision when more groups lock into this shared vision of how things are, 'how the world is'. One need hardly point out the relevance of these approaches to an understanding of a gospel narrative text. The dramatistic approach furnishes the conceptual tools with which to imagine the interrelatedness of 'John'-as-author-and-Ephesian audience, the gospel text as deliberate configuration of text elements, selected and manipulated to fit the imagined context, and the possible aim of this narrative text-as-communication. In my view, a fantasy theme analysis expands the view to an outlook on the wider effects of the process. What comes into view is how a singular communicative event (the gospel narrative as communication in a specific time and place) broadened out to become a rhetorical vision encapsulating an early Christian utopian vision as against the Roman imperium (or imperial ideology) as a utopian vision. The early distribution and circulation of the Gospel of John (see the manuscript evidence) attests to its power to involve readers/audiences in its alternative view of the world.

One should constantly be aware that we do not deal with an exact science in such a rhetorical reading. Birdsell (1989) sounds a few cautionary statements in this regard: 'The implication for the practice of pentadic criticism is that a critic must consciously choose among the charts available, and pursue the implications of that chart in mapping the motives in a text. No one chart is intrinsically more "objective" than another; each is valuable in the context of a given critics needs (204) ... Failure to consider actively and adjust to the variety of possibilities within a text can produce problems between the pentad as a device and a text as an expression of motive. Whatever term the critic decides to use will influence the nature of the criticism as surely as the pentadic alignment characterizes the subject under study. To produce conclusions that are unique to a rooted pentadic perspective, a pentadic analysis must conform to its own logic. Since in large part that logic is evolved by the critic, this requires that the critic arrive at the most complete and consistent explanation for a text, and then lay the logic out for inspection (205) ... A great deal of the pentad's explanatory power rests upon the assumption that the terms in fact are ambiguous, that there is no consistent rule for applying the terms across situations, and that there is not necessarily a single, "correct" rule for applying the terms in any particular situation (208) ... This means that the critic who would make the fullest use of the pentad must experiment with the ratios between the terms in order to find the most consistent or the most illuminating explanation for a given text or event (209).' In essence, different readers will imagine the interplay of textures and components of the rhetorical act differently.

At any rate, by way of a lengthy conclusion, given that the keyword is 'relationships' or 'interrelatedness', a rhetorical reading cannot be built solely on a consideration of the explicit text base. But once the implicit text base (imagined or constructed by the reader) is juxtaposed on to the explicit text base in the reading process, and once the pentadic elements are imagined in their interrelatedness, and once the gospel narrative is read as 'distorted history', then the way is paved for different configurations of meanings to emerge from readings of the same text. The significance of the same text elements within the overall ideology of the text will not be the same for every reader. More pointedly, the text elements, the structure of the text as meaning-being-built-up will not be the same for every reader. But is part of the adventure of reading.

6. I have discussed the metaphorical nature of the gospel in greater detail elsewhere (Van den Heever 1992).

7. Time and space constraints do not allow me a full, detailed and in-depth discussion of all the possible readings of the Gospel of John. That will have to wait for a later opportunity.

8. Hence the references to the Word coming in the flesh (e g 1:14).

9. Referring to the (mainly) negative use of the term 'Jews' in the gospel.

10. Depending on whether one accepts chapters 3 and 6 to be veiled references to baptism and the eucharist respectively. This illustrates the problem with regard to the reading of

narratives. The spirits will always be divided, especially if a text is not resolutely read in terms of its communicative context and not as disembodied theological treatises. Symptomatic is Morris' judgement on the issue: 'Since precisely opposite conclusions have been drawn from this evidence, *the argument clearly rests on no certain basis*' (pp 33; my emphasis).

[11.] With reference to the occurrence of philosophical terms such as Logos. However, Morris argues that the gospel is to be understood as stemming from a thoroughly Jewish and not Hellenistic way of thinking. Compare also the many Aramaisms in the language of the text.

[12.] References to Jesus and his movement and teaching replacing that of John the Baptist, e g 1: 8, 1: 19—23, 29—31; 3: 25—30; with Acts 19: 1—7 providing the context.

[13.] The term 'the Jews' is used mainly in a pejorative sense and refers to the Jewish leaders. The Johannine narrative serves to encourage Christians persecuted by Jewish leaders as well to call on Jews to heed to witness to Jesus from their own tradition (e g 5: 19—47).

[14.] Of importance are the references to the Word becoming flesh, and the stress on incarnation in the narrative, for example chapter 6 especially 6: 51—58 and 19:34 the water and blood coming from Jesus' pierced body.

[15.] In this view, chapters 10 and 13 to 17 have the life of the Christian believer within the community in focus.

[16.] See the universalist perspective of the author with his emphasis on the world: 1: 9; 1: 29; 3: 17; 12: 32 — the 'Greeks' in the latter episode should be taken to mean Gentiles, not Greek-speaking Jews, according to Brown.

[17.] 'The rupture between the followers of Jesus and "the Jews" is as the centre of attention; it has manifestly shaped the Johannine groups' language and their perception of the world' (: 94). Also '[T]here is a broad consensus that many aspects of the confrontation between Jesus and the Jewish authorities are projections into the narrative from the experience of the Johannine community ... Consequently, we can use the dialogues and stories in John to learn something about the separation sometime in the last quarter of the first century between these particular Christian groups and the Jewish communities' (:95).

[18.] What follows is a short summary of a thesis worked out in more detail elsewhere. See my 'John and the language of imperium' (forthcoming).

[19.] I have been fundamentally influenced by the work of Sjef van Tilborg. In this regard, see his *Reading John in Ephesus* (1995). In this monograph, which is not a systematic interpretation of John's gospel, but rather an imbedding of the narrative in the social reality of the city, much detail is unearthed to give an idea of the possible relationship between the reality imagined in the text and the social reality of the city that can be historically constructed.

[20.] See MacCormack; Kinman — with some reservations; see also Schmidt with reference to the gospel of Mark; for the history of the ritual, cf. Versnel 1974.

[21.] This has been studied exhaustively, cf Danker. See also the study by Kearsley in *New Documents illustrating early Christianity* 7: 233—241.

[22.] One finds: Lamb of God (and if one accepts that this refers to the apocalyptic ram, then one should place in the same domain: Son of Man), God's chosen One, Rabbi, Messiah (= Christ), Son of God, King of Israel/King of the Jews, Prophet, Lord, Teacher and Lord, Lord and God, God's Holy One. In the course of the narrative all of these titles at some point overlap and/or are connected as mutually illuminating terms.

[23.] I do not concern myself here with a discussion of the emperor cult per se. There are excellent discussions in Van Tilborg 1996: 36—57; Fishwick 1993; Klauck 1996; Versnel

1988 and Price 1984.

[24.] It is to these 'I am' sayings of the Isis aretalogies that we should look to as parallels for the 'I am' sayings of the Gospel of John.

[25.] Witness the inscription erected ±129 CE in honour of the proconsul Falco by Samaritans from Neapolis (Sebaste) (Van Tilborg 1992: 105).

[26.] Note that Herod is called 'King of the Jews' by Josephus Ant 16.311, the same form as the accusation against Jesus.

BIBLIOGRAPHY

Castelli, E A & Taussig, H (eds) 1996. *Reimagining Christian origins: a colloquium honoring Burton L Mack.* Valley Forge: Trinity Press International.

Chestnut, G F 1978. The ruler and the logos in Neopythagorean, Middle Platonic, and late Stoic political philosophy. In Haase, W (Hrsg). *Aufstieg und Niedergang der römischen Welt* II.16.2. Berlin: De Gruyter: 1310—1332.

Danker, F W 1982. *Benefactor. Epigraphic study of a Graeco-Roman and New Testament semantic field.* St Louis: Clayton Publishing House.

Fishwick, D 1993. *The imperial cult in the Latin West. Studies in the ruler cult of the western provinces of the Roman empire.* I,1. Leiden: Brill. (EPRO 108)

Grabbe, L L 1995. Hellenistic Judaism. In Neusner, J (ed). *Judaism in late Antiquity. Part Two: Historical syntheses.* Leiden: Brill. (HdO 1.17.2)

Hendrix, H 1986. Beyond 'imperial cult' and 'cult of magistrates'. *SBL Seminar papers.* Chico: Scholars Press: 301—308.

Hengel, M & Schwemer, A M 1997. *Paul between Damascus and Antioch. The unknown years.* London: SCM Press.

Horstmanhoff, H F J & Pleket, H W 1988. De macht van de monarch in de romeinse wereld tijdens het principaat. *Lampas* 21/3: 185—205.

Kearsley, R A 1994. New Testament and other studies. §10: A civic benefactor of the first century in Asia Minor. In Llewelyn, S R & Kearsley, R A. *New documents illustrating Early Christianity* Vol 7. The Ancient History Documentary Research Centre Macquarrie University.

Kinman, B 1995. *Jesus' entry into Jerusalem. In the context of Lukan theology and the politics of his day*. Leiden: Brill. (AGAJU 28)

Klauck, H-J 1996. *Die religiöse Umwelt des Urchristentums II. Herrscher- und Kaiserkult, Philosophie, Gnosis*. Stuttgart: Kohlhammer.

Knibbe, D 1978. Ephesos — nicht nur die Stadt der Artemis. Die 'anderen' ephesischen Götter. In Sahin, S, Schwertheim, E & Wagner, J (Hrsg). *Studien zur Religion und Kultur Kleinasiens*. Bd 2. Leiden: Brill.

Koester, H (ed) 1995. *Ephesos metropolis of Asia: an interdisciplinary approach to its archaeology, religion and culture*. Valley Forge: Trinity Press International. (Harvard Theological Studies 41)

Llewelyn, S R 1997. §12 An association of Samaritans at Delos. In Llewelyn, S R (ed). *New documents illustrating Early Christianity* Vol. 8. Grand Rapids: Eerdmans.

MacCormack, S 1972. Change and continuity in late Antiquity: the ceremony of *adventus*. *Historia* 21: 721—752.

Magie, D 1950. *Roman rule in Asia Minor I & II*. Princeton: Princeton University Press.

Meeks, W A 1985. Breaking away: three New Testament pictures of Christianity's separation of the Jewish communities. In Neusner, J & Frerichs, E S (eds). *"To see ourselves as others see us"*. *Christians, Jews, "Others" in late Antiquity*. Chico: Scholars Press: 93—115.

Pleket, H W 1965. An aspect of the emperor cult: imperial mysteries. *Harvard Theological Review* 58/4: 331—347.

Price, S R F 1984. *Rituals and power. The roman imperial cult in Asia Minor*. Cambridge: Cambridge University Press.

Robbins, V K 1996. *The tapestry of early Christian discourse. Rhetoric, society and ideology*. London: Routledge.

Schmidt, T E 1995. Mark 15.16—32: The crucifixion narrative and the Roman triumphal procession. *New Testament Studies* 41/1: 1—18.

Singor, H W 1988. Imperator. De romeinse keizer als opperbevelhebber van het leger in de eerste twee eeuwen van het principaat. *Lampas* 21/3: 206—232.

Smelik, K A D 1989. Tussen tolerantie en vervolging. Reacties op het Jodendom in de hellenistisch-Romeinse periode. *Lampas* 22/3:168—187.

Smith, J Z 1982. Imagining religion. From Babylon to Jonestown. Chicago: Chicago University Press.

Strubbe, J H M 1989. Joden en Grieken. Onverzoenlijke vijanden? De integratie van Joden in Kleinaziatische steden in de keizertijd. *Lampas* 22/3: 188—204.

Takacs, S A 1995. *Isis and Sarapis in the Roman world.* Leiden: Brill. (RGRW 124)

Van den Heever, G A 1992. Theological metaphorics and the metaphors of John's Gospel. *Neotestamentica* 26/1: 89—100.

Van Henten, J W 1989. Jodendom versus hellenisme: een valse tegenstelling. *Lampas* 22/3: 149—167.

Van Tilborg, S 1989. The Gospel of John: communicative processes in a narrative text. *Neotestamentica* 23/1: 19—32.

Van Tilborg, S 1992. Efese en het Johannesevangelie. *Schrift* 141 (July): 79—111.

Van Tilborg, S 1996. *Reading John in Ephesus.* Leiden: Brill. (Supplements to Novum Testamentum 83)

Versnel, H S 1970. *Triumphus. An enquiry into the origin, development and meaning of the Roman triumph.* Leiden: Brill.

Versnel, H S 1988. Geef de keizer wat des keizers is en Gode wat Gods is. Een essay over een utopisch conflict. *Lampas* 21/3: 233—256.

Versnel, H S 1990. *Ter Unus. Isis, Dionysos, Hermes. Three studies in henotheism. (Inconsistencies in Greek and Roman religion 1.)* Leiden: Brill. (SGRR 6)

Witt, R E 1971. *Isis in the Graeco-Roman world.* Ithaca: Cornell University Press.

The Terminology of the Cross and the Rhetoric of Paul

Demetrius K. Williams

Tulane University

It was upon the preaching of the Crucified Savior that Paul established Gentile churches (cf. 1 Cor 1:17, 23). The preaching and narrative about the cross was central to his message and a characteristic mark of Pauline communities.[1] The preaching of the cross revealed that the purpose of the eschatological event, i.e., the decisive action of God through Jesus Christ, exemplified in the death, burial and resurrection that inaugurated the "last days" (cf. 2 Cor 5:19), was the establishment of a new community.[2] This understanding of the cross was crucial for Paul's calling and orientation as an apostle (1 Cor 2:1-5; 3:10-17; cf. 1 Thess 1:5-7). The terminology of the cross[3] (any form of the words σταυρός ["cross"] or σταυρόω ["crucify"]) was also essential in Paul's appeals to his communities and in his polemical rhetoric against the personal attacks of his religious opponents, who competed for influence over the communities he established.

To be sure, Paul does not use cross terminology necessarily in reaction to some overt abuse or neglect of the cross by his opponents, but he rather employs it as the rhetorical *terminology of argumentation*. Ernst Käsemann has argued that the "theology of the cross is a polemical theology."[4] His assertion is correct but it needs to be nuanced. I would only add that the "terminology of the cross" functions as a *rhetorical tool of argumentation*. Therefore, cross terminology for Paul is primarily the terminology of contestation.[5] Paul employs it to articulate his own position

---

[1] The *kerygma* of the cross expressed in the eschatological ritual (eucharist) and recited in the passion narrative was the basis of Pauline communities. See Helmut Koester, "The Historical Jesus and the Cult of Kyrios Christos," *HDB* 24/3 (1995): 13-18.

[2] The eschatological community, the church, composed of both Jew and Gentile on the basis of faith in Jesus Christ (cf. Rom 3: 12-31).

[3] J. Christiaan Beker, *Paul the Apostle: The Triumph of God in Life and Thought* (Philadelphia: Fortress Press, 1980), 199, uses the term "cross terminology." Both "terminology of the cross" and "cross terminology" will be used with no change in meaning.

[4] *Perspectives on Paul* (Philadelphia: Fortress Press, 1971), p. 36.

[5] Käsemann, 35-36. Cf. 1 Cor 1:13, 17, 18; 2:2, 8; 2 Cor 13:4, Gal 2:20, 3:1, 13, 5:11, 6:12, 14, and Phil 2:8, 3:18. The only arguably non-polemical place is in Rom 6:6.

in any given situation against opposition. Hence, the terminology of the cross while having great theological presuppositions,[6] was for Paul a *rhetorical device.* As such cross terminology in Paul's polemical discourses could be used to address a wide range of personal, theological, ethical, and ecclesiastical concerns.

This study seeks to explore the rhetorical function of cross terminology in the context of Paul's *discourse of the cross.*[7] The *discourse of the cross* describes the units of discourse or argumentation in which any cross terminology appears. In addition, it refers to the range of meaning the terminology of the cross embraces in a given unit of discourse. It will be proposed, then, that in Paul's debates with his competitors and in his appeal to his communities he employed cross terminology as an essential element of his rhetorical strategy.

The Terminology of the Cross in Paul

J. Christiaan Beker has observed that while it has been argued that the "cross" is central to Paul's theology, a "theology of the cross" is indeed rare in the New Testament.[8] The term itself will never be found there. It made its way into Pauline studies through reformation scholarship. The term "theology of the cross" was coined by Martin Luther as a theological hermeneutic to combat the scholastic theologians of his day, who represented a "theology of glory" in Luther's terms because they believed that knowledge of God could be gained through philosophy and natural theology. For Luther a "theology of the cross" means that the knowledge and the will of God is revealed only through the Crucified One. Hence, his theology of the cross represented a particular theological system.[9] In modern Pauline studies it has come to mean "the hub of theology, in the

---

6 Duane Litfin, *St. Paul's Theology of Proclamation: 1 Corinthians 1-4 and Greco-Roman Rhetoric* (Cambridge: UK: Cambridge University Press, 1994), 1. "Presuppositions and practice go hand in hand."

7 This is one way to translate Λόγος τοῦ σταυροῦ (1 Cor 1:18). The translation is intended to emphasize the discursive or rhetorical element of the phrase.

8 Beker, *Paul*, 208.

9 Charles B. Cousar, *A Theology of the Cross: The Death of Jesus in the Pauline Letters* (Minneapolis: Fortress Press, 1990), 7-9; cf. *Luther's Works*, ed. Jaroslav Pelikan and Helmut T. Lehmann (Philadelphia: Muhlenberg Press, 1957): 31:40; Walther von Loewenich, *Luther's Theology of the Cross*, tr. by Herbert J.A. Bouman (Minneapolis: Augsburg, 1976); and Alister E. McGrath, *Luther's Theology of the Cross: Martin Luther's Theological Breakthrough* (Oxford: Basil Blackwell, 1985), 7.

sense that from it statements of anthropology, views of history, ecclesiology, ethics, etc., radiate."[10] Like Luther's view, it represents a theological system.

The closest Paul comes to any "system" for understanding the significance of the death of Jesus in terms of cross terminology can be found, perhaps, in the phrase he uses in 1 Corinthians 1:18, λόγος τοῦ σταυροῦ. This can be translated as "message," "word," or "discourse of the cross." Paul employed this *message* of the cross in his mission and preaching among the Gentiles. But the *discursive* or rhetorical element of cross terminology has not been given adequate attention. The theological implications have taken such precedent over the rhetorical that a "theology of the cross" has been argued as the center of Paul's theology.[11]

While scholars have argued for and against a "theology of the cross" as the single guiding principle of Pauline thought, Paul assigns no single role to the death of Jesus nor does he employ any fixed terms to describe it.[12] In many places where Paul discusses the death of Jesus the terminology of the cross is missing. In Paul's letters Jesus' death can be viewed as self-giving[13] or at other times it is God who gives.[14] Sometimes the death imparts significance to the individual.[15] The death of Jesus can also be linked to the resurrection,[16] or it can be affirmed as the event by which God effects atonement for human sinfulness.[17] Therefore, Paul was also able to utilize language from the early Christian tradition expressing both specialized and general terms; "expiation" and "blood" (ἱλαστήριον,

---

[10] Ulrich Luz, "*Theologia crucis* als Mitte der Theology im Neuen Testament, "*EvTh* 34 (1974): 116-141; 116.

[11] Martin Kähler, "Das Kreuz: Grund und Mass fur die Christologie" *BFCT* 15 (1911): 10-19. Wolfgang Schrage, "Das Verständnis des Todes Jesu Christi im Neuen Testament," in *Das Kreuz Jesu Christi als Grund des Heils,* Fritz Viering ed.,(Gütersloh: Gerd Mohn, 1967), 67-68; H.W. Kuhn, "Jesus als Gekreuzigter in der früchristlichen Verkündigung bis zur Mitte des 2. Jahrhunderts," *ZThK* 72 (1975): 1-46; Lutz, 116-141.

[12] Cousar, 21.

[13] Gal 2:20; παραδόντος ἑαυτὸν ὑπὲρ ἐμοῦ ("he gave himself for me").

[14] Rom 8:32; ἀλλὰ ὑπὲρ ἡμῶν πάντων παρέδωκεν [Θεὸς] αὐτόν ("But God gave him over for us all").

[15] 1 Cor 8:11; ὁ ἀδελφὸς δι᾽ ὃν Χριστὸς ἀπέθανεν ("The brother for whom Christ died").

[16] Rom 4:25; ὃς παρεδόθη διὰ τὰ παραπτώματα ἡμῶν καὶ ἠγέρθη διὰ τὴν δικαίωσιν ἡμῶν ("who was handed over for our trespasses and was raised for our justification").

[17] Rom 3:25; ὃν προέθετο ὁ Θεὸς ἱλαστήριον ("whom God put forth as an atonement").

αἷμα; Rom 3:25) and very simple language such as "die" (θάνατος; 1 Cor 15:3).[18]

Beker notes, again, that the terminology of the "cross" does not appear in the traditional sequence of "he died and rose again [or was raised]" (cf. 1 Cor 15:3ff).[19] He observes also that "the cross" is never associated with the sacrificial formulas "hyper" and "peri" (ὑπέρ, περί, "on behalf of"). Whereas "death" and "dying" (θάνατος, ἀποθνῄσκειν) are regularly connected with the resurrection and frequently with the sacrificial motif of Jesus' death, the latter motif [resurrection] is absent in the discourse of the cross.[20] This leads Beker to conclude that the focus on the death of Christ in the terminology of the cross is often so exclusive that in most contexts no explicit "life" terminology relieves its darkness and judgment.[21] Yet, in only three contexts in Paul's letters does cross terminology appear in relation to the death of Jesus (and this out of 14 occurrences![22]). And of these three contexts, only in one place is cross terminology linked in a sequence with the death of Jesus, but in a non-formulaic manner.[23]

In the Christ-Hymn of Philippians 2:8 cross terminology is associated very closely with the death of Jesus: "[who] was obedient unto death, even death of a cross" (ὑπήκοος μέχρι θανάτου, θανάτου δέ σταυροῦ).[24] The word "death" appears twice to emphasize and introduce Paul's addition of the word "cross." In Philippians 3:18 cross terminology appears in the same unit of discourse (3:1-4:1) as the death of Jesus (3:10), but there is no syntactical or formulaic relationship. Finally, the same

---

[18] 2 Cor 5: 14; εἷς ὑπὲρ πάντων ἀπέθανεν ("one died on behalf of all"). See Cousar, 21ff., for further discussion on the range of concepts and terminology used for understanding and interpreting the death of Jesus in Paul.

[19] Although Beker (198) notes that the statement "Christ died for you" probably lurks behind the query "Was Paul crucified for you?" (1 Cor. 1:13), it is the only time that Paul interprets the "death" formula in terms of the cross.

[20] Beker, 199; but cf. Gal. 6: 14: "But far be it from me to glory except in the cross of our Lord Jesus Christ, by which [δι οὗ] the world has been crucified to me, and I to the world." Here is one possible instance of a sacrificial formula being used in connection with cross terminology.

[21] Beker, 198.

[22] See footnote 5.

[23] E.g., a formulaic sequence as in the death and resurrection ("died and was raised"). The word death (θάνατος) occurs six times in Philippians (1:20; 2:8 (twice), 27, 30; 3:10) but it is associated with the death of Jesus only twice at 2:8 and 3:10. The other occurrences are related to Paul (1:20) and Epaphroditus (2:27 and 30).

[24] The second part of the phrase is considered a deliberate Pauline addition; Joachim Jeremias, "Zu Phil. ii 7: ΕΑΥΤΟΝ ΕΚΕΝΩΣΕΝ," NovT 6 (1963): 182-88.

situation obtains in Romans 6:1-11, where the death of Jesus embraces believers as a community who are considered participants in Jesus' death through baptism: "We have been baptized into his death" (εἰς τὸν θάνατον αὐτοῦ ἐβαπτίσθημεν [v. 3]). Cross terminology is employed at v. 6 to express the symbolic crucifixion of the old humanity of the believer together with Christ: "Our old humanity has been crucified together with him" (ὁ παλαιὸς ἡμῶν ἄνθρωπος συνεσταυρώθη). But the use of cross terminology here too has no formulaic relationship with Jesus' death. Therefore, since the terminology of the cross is so infrequently linked with the death of Jesus, it is most likely a distinctively Pauline term which has particular function depending on the context. Thus if the theology of the cross is Paul's distinctive understanding for expressing the meaning of the death of Jesus and the axis upon which his theological thought rotates, only a few passages in Paul's letters (and in the NT in general[25]) use cross terminology.[26]

It is interesting that in Romans, for example, where Paul has much to say about the significance of the death and resurrection of Jesus Christ, he uses cross terminology only once (Rom 6:6). It must certainly come as a surprise that this letter, which is considered Paul's crowning theological achievement, speaking as frequently as it does of God's justification of humanity, contains no further reference to the death of Jesus Christ in terms of crucifixion language. One is compelled to take note of Cousar's statement: "If Paul's characteristic understanding of the death of Jesus is to be located *exclusively* in crucifixion language, then one has to say it is missing from Romans."[27] It may be better then to suggest that Paul has a theology of the death and resurrection of Jesus and could use a variety of terms to express it, including the terminology of the cross. But since the terminology of the cross occurs infrequently in Paul to express the death of Jesus theologically, it must have a different function. This function has profound meaning for Paul in polemical contexts.[28]

The Contexts of the Cross Terminology

---

[25] Cross terminology appears in the Gospels primarily in the passion narratives, or in verses pointing toward the passion.
[26] About 15 times in Paul. This is relatively modest usage in comparison to its significance in modern interpretation. Cf. Cousar, p. 21.
[27] Cousar, 21, [emphasis mine].
[28] Beker, 199.

The New Testament has been described in recent years as a "bad tempered" book.[29] The reason for this less than favorable assessment is that most of the 27 documents in the New Testament are steeped in polemics. The opponents, some real or others imagined, who were the targets of such tense and heated discourse were perceived as a threat to the particular writer's community. While almost all of the authors of the New Testament engage in polemics of one sort or another, Paul is perhaps "the most belligerent of them all."[30] It is primarily in these "belligerent" acts of discourse that the terminology of the cross appears. In all of its occurrences (except for Romans), cross terminology occurs in polemical or contestational contexts; that is, the apostle seems to be in debate with his community or some opposing group or ideological/theological position or ethical/religious practice. In this regard, Käsemann makes two indispensable observations about Paul's use of cross terminology as opposed to other terms for Jesus' death. First, the use of "the theology of the cross" is from beginning to end a polemical theology.[31] Paul's proclamation of the cross brought about great hostility. For Paul his own ministry was an example of what living under the shadow of the cross entails. He mentions afflictions, perplexities, and persecutions as examples and "proof" of what one encounters when the example of the crucified Lord is taken seriously. He acknowledges that the cross will even evoke rejection (Gal 5:11). One could say that these conflicts expanded and deepened his affinity with and use of the cross in his polemical contests. In fact, Käsemann argues that it loses its force and vitality when employed in non-polemical contexts. He states,

> [T]he catchword about the "theology of the cross" loses its
> original meaning if it is used non-polemically. It was always
> a critical attack on the dominating traditional interpretation
> of the Christian message, and it was not by chance that it
> characterized Protestant beginnings.[32]

---

[29] John Barclay, "Mirror Reading," *JSNT* 31 (1987): 73-93. He quotes Christopher Evans who assessed the NT in this way. Barclay goes on to say "one has only to think of Matthean attacks on the Pharisees, Johannine polemic against 'the Jews' or the schismatics, and Petrine abuse of 'the dogs who turn back to their own vomit' to realize the extent of the New Testament's 'bad temper.'"

[30] Barclay, 73.

[31] Käsemann, 36.

[32] Ibid. Käsemann argues further: "Since Paul, all theological controversy has

Peter Stuhlmacher concurs that the context of cross terminology in the Pauline letters is polemical. He states, however, that this does not mean that Paul used the proclamation of the cross and cross terminology only in polemical contexts.[33] There is, nevertheless, only one use of cross terminology outside of a situation of conflict. Thus, the function of cross terminology in these polemical and contestational contexts calls for some brief explanation.

The Function of Cross Terminology in Polemical Contexts

Cross terminology appears in the polemical contexts of 1 Corinthians 1-4, 2 Corinthians 10-13, Galatians and Philippians 2-3. To be sure, Paul does not employ cross terminology in his conflicts so that he may express his theology, rather he employs it to exploit its rhetorical and evocative power.[34] The means by which Paul exploits the rhetorical power of cross terminology is through the use of three modes of proof, ἔθος, πάθος, and λόγος. Paul uses these three modes of proof in a calculated and effective way to challenge disturbing perceptions, answer his opponents, validate his apostolic credentials, and to re-establish his leadership.[35]

It is to Aristotle that we must look for a definition of the three modes of Proof.[36] Ethos (ἦθος) is proof which is exhibited through the character and moral appeal of the speaker himself. To be persuasive the

---

radiated ultimately from one central point and can hence only be decided at that point: *crux sola nostra theologia.*" Ibid., 59

[33] Peter Stuhlmacher, "Eighteen Theses on Paul's Theology of the Cross," *Reconciliation, Law and Righteousness* (Philadelphia: Fortress Press, 1986), 155-168; "It is unmistakable that the apostle shapes the central assertions of his proclamation about the cross in controversy with the Corinthian enthusiasts, intent on Christian wisdom and pneumatic power (cf. 1 Cor. 1:13, 17; 1:18ff., 23ff., 30; 2:2, 8; 2 Cor. 4:7ff.; 12:7ff.; 13:4), and with the Christian nomism threatening in Galatia (cf. Gal. 2: 19-20; 3:1ff., 13 ; 5:11; 5:22ff. ; 6:12, 14, 17)." (156) I would add Philippians, especially, chapter 3 to the polemical context of the cross.

[34] Litfin, 220; Stephen M. Pogoloff, *Logos and Sophia: The Rhetorical Situation of 1 Corinthians* (Atlanta: Scholars Press, 1992), 99.

[35] Mario M. DiCicco, *Paul's use of Ethos, Pathos, and Logos in 2 Corinthians 10-13* (Lewiston: Mellen Biblical Press, 1995), 12. He focuses on these three modes of proof that are necessary for a persuasive rhetorical response. While his work is not concerned with particular issues related to cross terminology, it was extremely helpful for providing an understanding of the importance of ethos in Paul's conflict with his opponents.

[36] Litfin, 76-78, for a discussion of proof in Aristotle and his contributions to rhetoric.

speaker needs something more than enthymenes and examples (usually related to the *logos* [λόγος] of a speech) to persuade and move an audience.[37] The "something more" can be found in the speakers ability to gain a favorable disposition from the audience. Aristotle writes that an orator can persuade by moral character when the speech is delivered in such a manner as to render the speaker worthy of confidence.[38] The ἦθος of a speaker established in his presentation helps to determine the outcome of his argument.[39]

Pathos (πάθος) is concerned with the speaker putting the hearer into a certain frame of mind.[40] According to Aristotle, this is important because people are not convinced by logical argument alone, because "the judgments we deliver are not the same when we are influenced by joy or sorrow, love or hate."[41] The speaker must be able to rouse the emotions of his hearers against his enemies but toward his favor.

The logos (λόγος) of a speech is concerned with logical presentation or rhetorical reasoning. "Persuasion is produced by the speech itself, in so far as it proves or seems to prove."[42] This type of reasoning is based on probable proofs and makes use of two important instruments of all logical thinking, namely syllogism (enthymene) and induction (examples).[43] The λόγος of a speech can be a crucial method of proof because the speech must "make sense."

But herein is a problem for Paul. Paul's message about the cross did not make "logical sense" in the Greco-Roman world (1 Cor 1:23-25). Paul, therefore, found it difficult to use certain aspects of the Greco-Roman rhetorical tradition. There developed, then, a conflict between Greco-Roman rhetoric and Christian preaching.[44] Paul is credited as the first

---

[37] Deliberative rhetoric chiefly depends on ethos and examples and comparison of examples. Duane F. Watson, *Invention, Arrangement, and Style: Rhetorical Criticism of Jude and 2 Peter.* (Atlanta: Scholars Press, 1988), 19.

[38] Ar. Rh. 1.2.4.

[39] DiCicco, 104; cf., 37-38.

[40] Ar. Rh. 1.2.3; 1.2.5; cf. DiCicco, 113.

[41] Ar. Rh. 1.2.5.; cf. DiCicco, 113.

[42] Ar. Rh. 1.2.5; DiCicco, 188.

[43] DiCicco, 188, "Rhetorical reasoning is not a strict science. It is a δύναμις, a faculty or art of demonstrating the true or apparently true on any given subject."

[44] The early church fathers also had to address the issue (Augustine and Lactantius). Michael A. Bullmore, *St. Paul's Theology of Rhetorical Style: An Examination of 1 Corinthians 2:1-5 in Light of First Century Greco-Roman Rhetorical Culture* (San Francisco: International Scholars Publication, 1995), 1-2; The dialectic between homiletics and rhetoric, 20.

person to effectively introduce Christian preaching into the cultural and intellectual market of the Roman Empire. He is also the earliest self-conscious theoretician of Christian preaching whose theoretical contributions are extant.[45] For Paul the gospel must be presented without recourse to "persuasive words of wisdom," i.e., rhetorical ornamentation (1 Cor 2:1-5). This meant that the success of the preaching of the cross would not depend on the rhetorical skill of the preacher. But "the genius of the rhetorical dynamic was its emphasis upon adaptation with a view to engineering πίστις, the emphasis to proclamation was precisely the opposite. The herald was one who carried the message of another. It was not the herald's task to persuade, but to announce."[46] That which engineered πίστις became increasingly associated with style. According to Michael Bullmore, "it is clear that [Paul] considers rhetorical style an illegitimate means of persuasion and an illegitimate basis for the kind of belief he was hoping to see engendered."[47] It becomes clear that Paul could use discourse of the cross because it did not conform to nor validate classical Greco-Roman styles of persuasion.

To understand better the function of cross terminology, it must be explored in the context of a complete unit of argumentation or discourse. The primary place to begin an exploration Paul's rhetorical use of cross terminology is 1 Cor 1-4. The bulk of our analysis will be concentrated on this text because it is in this unit of argumentation that Paul provides the presuppositions for preaching and he advances the terminology of the cross into a situation of conflict. This provides an opportunity to understand Paul's preaching, rhetorical strategy and the presuppositions which undergirds them both. It will be possible, then, after a more brief examination of the remaining texts, to view the range of meaning the terminology of the cross can embrace in a given unit of discourse. That is, "the discourse of the cross" - the modifying terms and concepts Paul can employ to expand or enlarge the function of his cross terminology. Only Paul's use of the cross to establish his ethos will be explored in each text for brevity.

---

[45]Bullmore, 3; 1 Cor 1-2, especially 2:1-5 (cf. 2 Cor 2:17, 4:25, 5:11-12, 10:1-18, 11:6-7, 2 Thess 1:5, 2:3-9). Litfin (2) agrees that only in 1 Cor 1-4 do we have some reasoned exploration of how Paul operated as a preacher and why (1:17-2:5 in particular).

[46] Litfin, 248; Bullmore, 13.

[47] Bullmore, 17.

1 Corinthians 1 - 4

The situation Paul encountered in 1 Corinthians chapters 1-4 has invited much speculation. There are primarily three approaches to understanding its situation. It has been argued that Paul is combating either Gnostics,[48] wisdom speculation,[49] or the Greco-Roman rhetorical tradition.[50] The term which gives rise to these approaches is the phrase σοφία λόγου.[51] What does it mean in the context of 1 Corinthians 1-4? A theological perspective has prevailed in the past in many interpretations and commentaries. But a theological approach has begun to change due to the resurgence of rhetorical approaches to interpreting the New Testament.[52] It is suspected that Paul is most likely responding to the Greco-Roman rhetorical tradition.[53] Duane Litfin has argued convincingly that according to the rhetorical view, Paul was criticized by some in Corinth because his preaching did not meet the expected standards of Greco-Roman culture profoundly influenced by an unparalleled rhetorical heritage. Paul defends himself in 1 Corinthians 1-4 (esp. 1:17-2:5) against this criticism, because speaking (indeed preaching!) in the public arena was essential to his apostolic mission and calling. Thus, the most appropriate background against which to see σοφία λόγου and "[P]aul's statements about his *modus operandi* as a preacher is the broad and persuasive rhetorical tradition which played such an important role in first century society."[54]

Bullmore seeks to identify a "specific and well-known kind" of rhetoric. He argues that the proposal of Litfin is too broad and should be seen against a narrower backdrop on a specific practice or theoretical construct strain in classical rhetoric.[55] Bullmore's proposal is that it was

---

[48] Cf. R. Mcl. Wilson, "How Gnostic were the Corinthians?" *NTS* 19 (9172-73): 65-74.

[49] Richard Horsley, "Wisdom of Words and Words of Wisdom in Corinth," *CBQ* 39 (1977) 224-39. Cf. Hans Conzelmann, *A Commentary on the First Epistle to the Corinthians* (Philadelphia: Fortress Press, 1975), 34, 45. According to this teaching the faithful were to take their example from the exalted Lord.

[50] Litfin, 3 n. 8.

[51] Litfin, 3-4.

[52] Paul is not battling Jewish wisdom speculation, Judaizers, or Gnostics. Cf. Bullmore, 6-9, n. 13. Paul's argument is not theological for there is no theological debate. Cf. Pogoloff, 104. There is no theological problem. Cf. Litfin, 202, n. 70.

[53] Paul is most likely reflecting on the Greek rhetorical tradition. Litfin, 14ff.

[54] Litfin, 3-4, 244.

[55] Bullmore, 13-15.

against the Corinthian's love affair with *rhetorical style* [emphasis mine] that Paul presented his own rhetorical theory, a theory which focused the incompatibility between his preaching and a certain kind of rhetoric which Paul saw as a threat to his own rhetorical enterprise. In this way, the emergence of style as the leading rhetorical concern and as the ground of persuasion is the most appropriate backdrop and reference point for Paul's argument in 1 Cor 1-4 (esp., 2:1-5).[56] Paul's response to the σοφία λόγου calls forth the λόγος τοῦ σταυροῦ ("the message or discourse of the cross").

How does Paul use the terminology of the cross to establish his character (ἦθος)? Cross terminology is concentrated in chapters one and two (at 1:13, 17, 18, 23; 2:2 and 8). Paul advances "the discourse of the cross" against an exigence of division in the Corinthian community[57] which is related to rhetoric, i.e., cultural wisdom, wherein the perceptions of one's rhetorical and cultural wisdom is an important cultural determinate of status. Thus, the divisions within the Corinthian community were examples of rivalries for the status of having the wisest teacher.[58] This made Paul one among many teachers and, perhaps, not even the wisest.[59] Paul used the λόγος τοῦ σταυροῦ to undermine the Corinthian's socio-linguistic world, defend his preaching style and perhaps his message about the cross. Paul attempted to accomplish these things most effectively by establishing his ethos (ἦθος) in association with the terminology of the cross.

In 1 Corinthians 1:13 Paul immediately identifies himself with the language of the cross: "Is Christ divided? Was Paul crucified for you? Or

---

[56] Bullmore, 17; But Pogoloff, 120-21, argues against Timothy Lim ("Not in Persuasive Words of Wisdom, but in the Demonstration of the Spirit and Power." *NovTest* 29 (1987): 137-49; 146, 149) that there is a special kind of rhetoric Paul attacks, and against Peter Marshall (*Enmity in Corinth: Social Conventions in Paul's Relations with the Corinthians* (WUNT, 2; Tübingen: J.C.B. Mohr (Paul Siebeck), 1987), 388-93) that Paul employed "grand style" when speaking but turned it off when writing. However, Bullmore is probably correct.

[57] Pogoloff, 73, states that traditionally contests in verbal wisdom could cause divisions.

[58] The Corinthian rivalries for boasts of status were a normal part of Hellenistic culture in which individuals strove for status and political influence through persuasive rhetoric. If one did not have a genteel birth, education or political power, association with one who did was an important cultural benefit. Cf. Pogoloff, 237.

[59] Many scholars have suggest that the claim of most eloquent speaker and teacher in the Corinthian church might belong to Apollos (Acts 18:24-28; cf. 1 Cor 1: 12; 3:1-9, 21-23).

were you baptized in the name of Paul?" This is an important rhetorical strategy for Paul and the most important means by which he seeks to establish his ethos. After an apparent digression related to his practice of baptism, Paul returns to the topic of the cross in 1:17, which serves as a transition into the exposition of the true meaning of the λόγος τοῦ σταυροῦ in 1:18-31. Verse 17 sets up Paul's strategy by contrasting the cross of Christ (σταυρὸς τοῦ Χριστοῦ) with the eloquence of words (σοφία λόγου). Paul says: "Christ did not send me to baptize but to proclaim (εὐαγγελίζεσθαι[60]) the gospel, and not with eloquent wisdom (σοφία λόγου) , so that the cross of Christ might not be emptied of its power." It appears from this verse that Paul has three constraints or exigencies upon him: his preaching, wisdom speech, and the cross of Christ.[61] These three constraints are related by the issue of σοφία λόγου. Paul begins his response with "the cross of Christ."

Paul employs he terminology of the cross in 1:18-31 as a counter argument against the wisdom (eloquence) of speech, using the rhetorical strategy of *reversal*. Paul's concern here is to *reverse the values* of the Corinthians with respect to wisdom. He seeks to establish his ethos as one who is trustworthy and faithful because the message of the cross which he preaches might appear foolish, but it is the very means by which God's power and human salvation are conveyed. Hence, Paul's ethos is established by his association with the cross (1:18-25). The preaching of the cross may not conform to human wisdom (which the Corinthian's valued) for it cannot be discerned by "those who are perishing" (1:18, 22-24). But for "those who are being saved" it is the "power of God." Thus God's true wisdom and power conveyed through the cross is advanced to reverse the fraudulent notions of wisdom and power held by the Corinthian's. By gaining a divine perspective Paul shows that his message is really powerful because it represents God's perspective. The Corinthian's perspective, on the other hand, which they thought was powerful, is really weak (1:25). To add to his appeal Paul presents an *ad hominem* argument in 1:26-31. He says, "for consider your own calling, brothers, that not many of you were wise according to the flesh, not many powerful, not many of noble birth,

---

[60] Paul uses terms to describe his preaching activity (εὐαγγελίζω, κηρύσσω, καταγγέλλω, μαρτυρέω) that avoid association with Greco-Roman rhetorical practices (except for πείθω). Litfin, 195.

[61] Pogoloff, 108-09.

when called. But God has chosen what is foolish in the world to shame the wise; God chose what is weak to shame the wise (1:27). With this one statement Paul has cut to the heart of the Corinthian's search for worldly wisdom and status. While the Corinthians were seeking association with the eloquent rhetorical wisdom of the wise and cultured leaders, a striving which tended to exalt the individual and ignite false aspirations for status, Paul reminds them that if they considered their own situation, they would truly understand the meaning of the message of the cross. While the preaching of the cross of Christ appears weak, foolish and powerless, from God's perspective it is strong, wise and powerful - true wisdom. The first step in establishing his ethos and reversal through the cross is complete.

In 2:1-16 Paul seeks to *reverse their perception* of him as preacher of the gospel. This section is important for supplying Paul's presuppositions as a preacher of the gospel and for establishing his *modus operandi*.[62] Paul reminds the Corinthians of his preaching style when he arrived. His message was not in "lofty words or wisdom" (ὑπεροχὴν λόγου ἢ σοφίας) when he proclaimed (καταγγέλλων) the mystery of God (v. 1). But he decided to know nothing among them except Christ and him crucified (Χριστὸν καὶ τοῦτον ἐσταυρωμένον, v. 2). Paul attempts to establish his ethos in this section by appropriating for himself terms λόγος, σοφία, and the mystery (μυστήριον) of God through the terminology of the cross (Χριστὸν ἐσταυρωμένον).

In 2:1-5 Paul develops the topic he began in 1:17, namely, his unconventional mode of proclamation. The content and topic of Paul's message ("Christ and him crucified") did not conform to traditional rhetorical standards of wise speech. His style of delivery was also unconventional. Paul's delivery of his message to the community was "in weakness, fear and much trembling" (2:3).[63] In 2:4-5 Paul reiterates what he said in 2:1-3 but adds three important elements: his proclamation was not in "the persuasive (πειθοῖς) words of wisdom, but in the demonstration (ἀποδείξει) of the spirit and power (δύναμις), so that the Corinthians faith (πίστις) would not rest in human wisdom but in the wisdom of God. Paul did not proclaim the message of the cross in persuasive words and human wisdom like the influential and eloquent

---

[62] Litfin, 2; Bullmore, 3.

[63] Paul's appearance as a preacher was the opposite of the cultural rhetor. Paul's delivery was with "fear and trembling." Pogoloff, 143.

rhetors of his day. He did not want the gospel of the cross to depend on rhetorical style to determine the outcome if its persuasiveness, "lest the cross of Christ be emptied of its power" (1:17). If the gospel depended on individual ability to engender faith (πίστις), it would rest in human power and not the power of God. Therefore, Paul presents himself as a herald because the herald is not responsible for the content nor the persuasiveness of the message he carries. The herald's job is simply to announce the message of another. His ethos is established here as a herald who proclaims the message of the cross faithfully, regardless of its incompatibility with human wisdom, i.e., the pervasive and persuasive rhetorical style of ancient rhetoric. However there is a wisdom of words and a wisdom of God to be seen in the mystery of the cross of Christ.

It is possible that 2:6-16 is the most important section for understanding how Paul establishes his ethos through the terminology of the cross. Paul admits in 2:6 that after all he has said to disavow the wisdom of words, he does possess the ability for wisdom speech (σοφίαν δὲ λαλοῦμεν)[64] but it is only understood by the mature (τελείοις).[65] He makes clear, however, that it is not a wisdom of the present age.

> But we speak God's wisdom in a mystery, secret and hidden
> .... None of the rulers of this age understood this; for if they
> had, they would not have crucified (ἐσταύρωσαν) the
> Lord of glory" (2:7-8).

With this brief statement Paul shows that he is the one who is truly wise because he understands the hidden mystery and wisdom of God. Paul is able to exploit his association with the wisdom of the cross by the subtle use of entymene (syllogism). The syllogism might go something like this: The mind of God can only be known by the Spirit (2:11). Paul has received the Spirit (2:10, 12). Thus, Paul has the mind of God (Christ, 2:16). In this way Paul establishes his ethos as the one true teacher and proclaimer of the powerful words of God's wisdom, which God has made known to him by the spirit. This wisdom is to be found in the mystery of the cross.

---

[64] Paul's speech is not in "words taught by human wisdom" (the opposite is "words taught by the spirit" [2:13]). He may be referring to rhetorical training in various schools of rhetoric. Pogoloff, 140.

[65] Speech was the way in which the wise were to be appraised in Greco-Roman rhetorical culture. Litfin, 69, 96.

It is clearer now to see the benefit Paul gains through the terminology of the cross. It is not necessary to propose that his proclamation of the cross was under attack. There is no indication in the text that this is necessarily the case. The problem is with the Corinthians use and understanding of the term wisdom (σοφία), and Paul advances the cross to reverse the wisdom claim of the Corinthians.[66] Paul's language, then, is much more persuasive if the cross is the one point that he and "those who cause divisions" agree upon. For it is by means of the cross that Paul is also able to "prove" himself (establish his ethos!) among the Corinthians as the one true leader and teacher of wisdom, a wisdom hidden in the cross! A very brief overview of chapters 3 and 4 will help to show how Paul attempts to elaborate upon the theme of his wise leadership based upon the ethos he has established in chapters 1 and 2.

In 3:1-9 Paul explains to the Corinthians how their division and attachment to various leaders is a sign of their lack of spirituality and the reason why they do not understand the wisdom of God hidden in the cross (3:1-3). Paul then attempts to explain the proper role of a leader by appeal to Apollos and himself. Both he and Apollos are laborers who work together on "God's building" (3:5-9). The difference is that Paul is the "wise (σοφός) builder" who has laid the foundation and others must be careful how they build upon it. That foundation is Jesus Christ (the only leader worthy of unconditional allegiance, and Paul is his faithful representative, 3:10-17). Here, again, Paul distances himself from any other rivals by establishing himself as the true and wisest leader. In the final verses (3:18-23) Paul admonishes the Corinthians to become "fools" (the perception they have of him) so that they might be truly wise (like himself).

In 4:1-6 Paul identifies himself as a servant and steward of the mysteries of God. He chides the Corinthians for improper judgment of himself and admonishes them to "judge nothing before its time."[67] In 4:8-13 Paul presents the basis of their faulty judgment of him. It has to do with the present nature of his apostleship, which is characterized by weakness,

---

[66] Both Paul and the Corinthians are committed to σοφία but their views are diametrically opposed. Σοφία does not play a large role in Paul's ministry but he will exploit it to advance his cause. Cf. Litfin, 2-3.

[67] In Greco-Roman rhetorical culture the audience were the judges of the orator to appraise his speech. Litfin, 100, 105-06.

trials, hunger, persecution, homelessness and dishonor. This makes Paul appear as a "fool for Christ" but the Corinthians wise, him weak but the Corinthians strong. But this is only a surface view. In reality he is wise and strong and they are weak and foolish. In 4:14-21 Paul makes a direct appeal to the Corinthians to follow his example (4:16) because he has become their spiritual father through the gospel (4:15). In the final analysis, he is not only the wisest leader, but one who counsels with the love and care of a wise father.

Paul's rhetorical strategy in 1 Corinthians contrasts the wisdom of God hidden in the cross with the human wisdom of wise speech valued by the Corinthians. Paul employs cross terminology to establish his ethos as truly the wisest leader and founder of the Corinthian community and to show that true wisdom, the wisdom he proclaims, is to be found in the cross of Christ. This explains how he can at once attack rhetoric and yet employ it in his attack.[68] While the preaching of the cross did not confer worldly status, the reversal of his status in the world through the cross gave him access to the true wisdom of God.[69] Things, then, will be in order in the community once the significance of Christ as crucified is understood anew.

2 Corinthians 10 -13

In 2 Corinthians 10-13 the terminology of the cross is used only once, at 13:4, but its influence on Paul's impassioned response to his opponents is seen throughout chapters 10-13.[70] In this passage Paul has to defend his apostleship and praxis against a fierce attack by eloquent and charismatic "super-apostles" who claim that he lacks confidence (ταπεινός, 10:1), walks according to the flesh (κατὰ σάρκα, 10:2), is bold (θάρρος) from the safe distance of letters (10:2), does not belong to Christ ([οὐ] Χριστοῦ εἶναι, 10:7), is weak (ἀσθενής) and his speech contemptible (λόγος ἐξουθενημένος, 10:10), is lacking powerful

---

[68] Because Paul rejects the cultural values wedded to rhetoric. Pogoloff, 121.

[69] Pogoloff, 119-20.

[70] Who the opponents were, their theology, tradition, rhetorical training and purpose see Victor P. Furnish, *II Corinthians* (Garden City; NY: Doubleday, 1984), Dieter Georgi, *The Opponents of Paul in Second Corinthians* (Philadelphia: Fortress Press, 1986) and Jerry L. Sumney, *Identifying Paul's Opponents: The Question of Method in 2 Corinthians* (Sheffield: Sheffield Academic Press, 1990)..

physical presence (παρουσία τοῦ σώματος ἀσθενὴς, 10:10), is untrained in speech (ἰδιώτης τῷ λόγω, 11:6), not exhibiting the signs, wonders and mighty works of an apostle (τὰ σημεῖα [καὶ τέπρατα καὶ δυνάμις] τοῦ ἀποστόλου, 12:12), is crafty (πανοῦγος, 12:16), inferior to the super apostles (ὑστερηκέναι τῶν ὑπερλίαν ἀποστόλων, 11:5), and does not exhibit the evidence of Christ speaking to him (δοκιμή...τοῦ ἐν [αὐτῷ] λαλοῦντος Χριστοῦ, 13:3).[71] These missionaries, whose activities Paul sought to counter aggressively, held that apostolic mission and praxis should exhibit the transcendent power of the exalted Christ.[72] In order to clear his name against such charges, he sought to establish his ethos in 2 Cor 10-13 and to dispose his audience to accept him as a legitimate apostle.[73] Paul advances two claims for the quality of his ethos his περιστάσεις, the catalogue of hardships on behalf of the gospel (11:23-33), and the example of his rapture into the third heaven where he enjoyed extraordinary revelations (12:1-6).[74]

In his catalogue of trials (11:23-33) Paul recounts his sufferings as an apostle. Here and throughout his discourse Paul accepts the "super-apostles'" characterization of him as weak and powerless. This is an important rhetorical strategy for Paul because by emphasizing his own shortcomings, he can interpret his apostolic life through defense of the cross.[75] The opponents, however, did not accept Paul or the "weak" Jesus he represented. So Paul wants to show that the Jesus he preaches is the one who is really powerful (11:4; 13:4). Paul uses his understanding of suffering and their accusation of weakness to designate himself as a follower of the Crucified One and at the same time to show-up the "super-apostles." They seem powerful and influential, but they are really "false apostles and deceitful workers who transform themselves into apostles of Christ," as does Satan who "transforms himself into an angel of light"

---

[71] DiCicco, 78, 82.

[72] Jewett, Robert. "Conflicting Movements in the Early Church as Reflected in Philippians," *NovT* 12 (1970): 362-90; 368.

[73] Before addressing the opponent's claim, he had to establish his ἦθος as a man of θρόνησις, ἀρετή, and εὔνοια, the sources from which ἦθος arose. (Ar. Rh. 2.1.5) DiCicco, 78.

[74] DiCicco, 84.

[75] The *peristasis* catalogue was a respectable technique in the ancient world to reveal character and to win the confidence of an audience. DiCicco, 87. Cf. J. Fitzgerald, *Cracks in an Earthen Vessel: An Examination of the Catalogues of Hardship in the Corinthian Correspondence* (Atlanta: Scholars Press, 1988), 203. Paul employs it as proof of his calling and reality of virtue. DiCicco, 91.

(11:12-15). The Corinthians are now confronted with a choice, to follow Paul or the super-apostles. For Paul the choice is clear: "[t]o follow the false apostles is...to follow an illusion (11:14). These false apostles will end up with the same destiny as the Evil One whose ministers they are (11:15)."[76]

In 12:1-10 Paul continues his defense and the theme of weakness by turning to the topic of spiritual visions. He wants to show that Christ speaks in him, but most profoundly through his suffering. Even after experiencing an exalted spiritual vision and hearing things ineffable, Paul receives a "thorn in the flesh" (12:1-10). He requests its removal but is told by Christ: "My grace is sufficient for you, for my strength is made complete (τελεῖται) in weakness" (12:9).[77] Then Paul realizes "when I am weak, then am I strong" (12:10). True power is in the very qualities the opponents claim defines Paul and his apostleship - weakness, suffering and humility. Paul's rhetorical "punchline" which links his ethos with cross terminology arrives at the end of his long defense at 13:4. Paul says, "He [Jesus] was crucified (ἐσταυρώθη) in weakness (ἀσθενείας), but lives (ζῇ) by the power (δυνάμεως) of God." The first part of this verse could even be translated, "He was crucified a weakling..."[78]

In the final analysis the "super-apostles" are found to be inadequate servants of Christ because they do not follow the example of the cross as exemplified in weakness and humility. The rhetorical punchline coming at the end of his response has significant meaning for the way in which Paul shaped his discourse.[79] He combined cross terminology with the idea of

---

[76] DiCicco, 170. Paul's example equals service to God. The opponent's, on the other hand, equals service to Satan. This is a use of enthymenes to make an argument from the more or less or the *a fortiori* argument to claim contrasts. Ibid., 246.

[77] In the Greco-Roman world hardships were a sign of God's love, as well as a sign of God's approval and esteem. Fitzgerald, 76-82. DiCicco, 88.

[78] Cousar (1), following Rudolph Bultmann, *The Second Letter to the Corinthians,* trans. Roy A. Harrisville (Minneapolis: Augsburg Press, 1985), p. 243.

[79] "The argument syllogistically would go something like this: The weakness of the crucified Jesus is the source of Jesus' power from God (13:4). I, Paul, have experienced weakness in the same spirit and 'willingly boast of my weakness' instead of boasting in my accomplishments. Therefore, "the power of Christ rests upon me." (12:9) This is the validating stamp of approval of my gospel and ministry. Paul subtly offers this latest syllogism to the Corinthians as one which paradoxically supersedes the original argument intended to convince the Corinthians. He comes at this indirectly since he needs first to entertain the original universal proposition already accepted by the Corinthians, namely, that signs and wonders are the legitimating marks of a true apostle....It is the subtle transposition of major premises which in either form establishes the fact of his delegated power from God and the motive for the allegiance of the Corinthians." DiCicco, 243-44.

weakness and suffering to enlarge the semantic field and rhetorical function of cross terminology. The terminology of the cross supports Paul's own example of weakness and humility against the claims of the "super-apostles." Both Jesus and Paul might be perceived as weak by some, but this is a misconception according to Paul: "For we are weak in him [Jesus Christ], but in dealing with you we shall live with him by the power of God" (the remainder of v. 4). Paul has, in effect, polarized his opponent's example from his own by his identification with suffering and the cross.[80] Paul's ethos is established through the concepts of weakness, suffering, and humility, all of which fall under the shadow and influence of cross terminology.

Galatians

In Galatians Paul uses cross terminology seven times.[81] The brief examination of 2 Corinthians has shown that this does not necessarily indicate the intensity of the debate, but the strategy Paul perceives is necessary to establish his ethos. The Galatians accepted Paul initially despite a physical infirmity (ἀσθένεια τῆς σαρκὸς, 4:13-14).[82] But the intimate relationship deteriorated quickly. Paul views the Galatian's departure from his gospel as so serious that he dispenses with his customary thanksgiving and launches directly into the issue at hand: "I am astonished that you are so quickly deserting him who called you in the grace of Christ and turning to a different gospel..." (1:6). The problem is related to the entrance of opponents who drew the Galatian's allegiance away from Paul (1:17). They accuse Paul of trying to please people (1:10), so he cannot be trusted. They also preached a different gospel (1:6-9). Their position was that Paul's gospel was incomplete because it did not

---

[80] Synkrisis (συγκρίσις) is a means of amplifying one's virtues and achievements and depreciating those of another. Marshall, 325. For Paul this has the effect of creating "polar opposites". See Elizabeth A. Castelli, *Imitating Paul: A Discourse of Power* (Atlanta: Westminster Press, 1991), 134-35 (who is followed by Timothy C. Geoffrion, *The Rhetorical Purpose and the Political and Military Character of Philippians: A call to Stand Firm* (Lewiston, NJ: Mellen Biblical Press, 1993), 152-57) who argues that Paul uses his example against his opponents' to create "polar opposites."

[81] συσταυρόω, 2:20, σταυρός, 5:11; 6:12; 14; and σταυρόω, 3:1; 5:24; 6:14. It is possible that 3:13 ("hang on a tree") and 6:17 ("I bear in my body the marks of the Lord") are circumlocutions for cross terms.

[82] Paul's weakness (ἀσθενεία) may have ben related to Paul's status. In other words, it may reflect a social judgment. Marshall, 153.

include the commandment of circumcision which was a prerequisite for full membership as the people of God (5:3-4; 6;12-13).[83] The Galatian's defection was so complete (3:1-5)[84] that it left Paul astonished (1:6), disappointed (4:11) and perplexed (4:20).[85] Establishing his ethos was an important task because it was necessary for him to win back their allegiance. In this effort the terminology of the cross was advanced.

Within Galatians the terminology of the cross is used to contrast the law and circumcision (2:15-21) and establish Paul's ethos. In effect, Paul employs cross terminology to *polarize* his opponent's and their position, and to defend his apostleship and the validity of his gospel. This *strategy of polarization* can be seen in several places. After discussing the origin of his gospel coming through direct revelation (1:11-12; 15-16), Paul argues that he was faithful to the gospel and a trustworthy apostle before the Galatians (1:1-24), the false brethren (2:4-5), and amongst the other apostles (even Peter, 2:11ff).[86] Then he states that he has been "crucified with Christ" (2:21). This establishes he ethos with cross terminology. The gospel of the cross which he preaches is the foundation of his argument on justification (2:15-21), but this also sets him and his gospel apart from those who teach justification by means of the law. This use of cross terminology allows him to *polarize* his opponents and their perspective. Paul's preaching of the cross initiated the Galatian's faith (3:1-5), but it also invites persecution upon him (5:11). His opponents preach circumcision in order that they might avoid persecution (6:12). Nevertheless, Paul will not forsake his preaching of the cross for in this is his glory and boasting (6:14). These few examples underscore the *polarizing* function of Paul's cross discourse in Galatians.

Philippians

---

[83] Johan S. Vos, "Paul's Argumentation in Galatians 1-2," *HTR* 87:1 (1994): 1-6; 2.

[84] For Paul, something irrational must have happened to them because he cannot explain why they would so quickly abandon the gospel he preached and in which they so quickly came to believe. Hans D. Bets, *Galatians* (Philadelphia: Fortress Press, 1970), 132.

[85] Marshall, 154; Paul is now their enemy because of the sudden withdrawal of affection and support, and the tranferral of their allegiance.

[86] Vos, 14.

The terminology of the cross appears twice in Philippians.[87] In 2:8 the terminology of the cross is used to inspire community cohesion, and in 3:18 to combat opponents who pose a potential threat to the Philippian community.[88] In Phil 2:18 Paul uses a hymn (2:6-11) to encourage unity among the Philippian community. It seems as though the hymn was missing Paul's important emphasis of the cross, so he added cross terminology in v. 8 ("even death on a cross").[89] This indicates that the use of cross terminology at v. 8 has a larger function in Paul's construction of his argument for unity among the Philippian church. This terminology of the cross is not used to establish Paul's ethos here but to serve as the basis for the Philippian's unity and selflessness like the Savior "who was obedient unto death, even death on a cross" (2:8).

In 3:1-4:1 Paul uses cross terminology once at 3:18: "there are many who live as enemies of the cross of Christ; whose end is destruction..." Paul is not under personal attack here but cross terminology is used to anchor his authority and to exhort the Philippians. While Paul's discourse of the cross in this passage is pregnant with meaning, I will concentrate on two functions of cross discourse. The function of polarization is clear from the language, but the cross terminology in this passage allows Paul to establish his ethos by using his personal example of *the pattern of a cruciform* existence.[90] This also allows him to articulate the eternal destiny of the eschatological community which patterns itself on the same cruciform model.

Paul's personal example in 3:4-11 is cast in terms of the paradoxical pattern of the privilege-loss-exaltation of the redeemer who suffered death, "even death on a cross" in the Christ-hymn of 2:6-11.[91] Paul begins his own example by discussing the privileges he was accorded on the basis of birth,

---

[87] Nicholas D. Gould, " 'Servants of the Cross': Cross Theology in Philippians," *RQ* 18 (1975): 93-101 is interested in the theology of the cross, but he does not incorporate Phil 3 into his discussion. He explores only the theological significance of the Christ Hymn in 2:6-11. This study argues that Philippians 3 is equally important not only for understanding the theology of the cross, but also the rhetorical function of cross discourse.

[88] George B. Caird, *Paul's Letters from Prison* (Oxford: Oxford Univeristy Press, 1976). John J. Gunther, *St. Paul's Opponents and their Background: A Study of Apocalyptic and Jewish Sectarian Teachings* (Leiden: E. J. Brill), 2-4 for a chart of no less than 18 proposals as to the identiy of the opponents.

[89] See note 24.

[90] Gordon Fee, *Paul's Letter to the Philippians* (Grand Rapids: Eerdmans, 1995), 104.

[91] Wayne Meeks, The First Urban Christians: The Social World of the Apostle Paul (New Haven: Yale Univerisy Press, 1983), 81.

ethnicity, religion, and personal accomplishments (3:5-6). After his encounter with Christ, he counted all of his former privileges as loss (3:7-8b) because of the gain he found in Christ (3:8c-9). Paul portrays his abandonment of his Jewish heritage to "know Christ" and to find a righteousness based on faith, as an abandonment of a position of "earthly" status for one of present humiliation.[92] In short, the preaching of the cross effected a status reversal. Now he awaits the resurrection (exaltation), which will be gained through his participation in the sufferings of Christ (3:10-11). The sequence of privilege-loss-hope of resurrection in Paul's life suggests such a connection with the Christ-hymn and is also to be rhetorically expressive of a cruciform existence.

One who lives in the cruciform manner exhibited in Paul's example is an ally of the cross and can be assured of ultimate transformation. Philippians 3 shows that in Paul's concern for the life and safety of his communities, his example of cruciform existence is used to reinforce group identity (3:3, 15-17) and the future goal of the eschatological community (vv. 20-21). Instead of following the example of the "enemies of the cross whose end is destruction," the Philippians are encouraged instead to "walk" in Paul's example, which models the pattern of the cross and to "take notice" (σκοπεῖτε) of those who walk in his example (3:17). This becomes a way to emphasize his association with Christ and the pattern of the cross, and to express God's ultimate goal (τέλος) for those who remain faithful. Paul wants to show that the destiny (τέλος) of those who walk in the pattern of the cross is to reach the ultimate eschatological goal of completion/ perfection (τελειόω, vv. 20-21). But the end (τέλος) of "the enemies of the cross," who refuse to walk in the example of the cross, is destruction (vv. 18-19).

The Discourse of the Cross in Paul's Argumentation

In assessing the features of the "discourse of the cross" in Paul's rhetoric it must be remembered that it has two meanings. First, the units of discouse or argumentation in which cross terminology occurs. Second, the range of terms and concepts Paul uses to enlarge the semantic field and

---

[92] Joachim Gnilka, *Der Philipperbrief* (Freiburg: Herder, 1976), 186-89.

conceptual range of cross terminology. The former has already been explored, it is the second meaning that will be examined briefly here.

From the above analysis of Paul's use of cross terminology several themes and concepts appear in association with his discourse of the cross.

1. Paul always associates himself with cross terminology
2. Paul accepts a self designation as weak, humble, suffering
3. The cross effects low status in the world
4. The cross effects a reveral of values, opinions, perceptions
5. The cross polarizes Paul's position from his opponents
6. Direct appeal to the audience (to imitation - directly or indirectly; to the "wise," "spiritual")

These features occur in varying degrees of frequency in Paul's discourse of the cross. These features serve as a source of topics and themes to which Paul can refer depending on the context of the debate. Thus in Paul's conflicts with his opponents he could access a range of terms and concepts with which to defend himself, his mission, communities and praxis.

Conclusion

This study has attempted to show that Paul's cross terminology has just as much to do with rhetoric, as it does with a theology of suffering and death. The function of cross terminology is missed if it is viewed as having only to do with death and suffering. The cross of Christ constituted the theological framework for establishing the new eschatological community. But introducing the terminology of the cross into his polemical discourse was a rhetorical stratagem which could accomplish several ends for Paul. The terminology of the cross could serve as a rhetorical weapon against his opponents to critique their praxis and their claims or it could function to promote group identity and nurture in the believers an identification of themselves as people of the cross; people who bear in their life and praxis the meaning and example of the cross of Christ. Finally it could be used to instruct the churches about their unity, destiny, calling, and witness in the world. This brief analysis shows that there is a rich perspective for exploring the use and function of cross terminology in Paul's rhetoric.

Biblical Quotations as Rhetorical Devices
in Paul's Letter to the Galatians

Christopher D. Stanley
McKendree College

The last few years have seen a growing interest in the way Jews and Christians interpreted Scripture in the Greco-Roman period. Much of the research in this area has revolved around hermeneutical questions about the way ancient authors understood and interpreted the biblical text. Relatively little has been said about the rhetorical effects of these explicit appeals to the Jewish Scriptures. While there are clearly places in the literature where a Jewish or Christian author seeks to understand the biblical text for its own sake, most often the text is quoted as part of a broader argument designed to convince others to believe or act in a certain way. This is a rhetorical act, and it should be investigated as such.

The apostle Paul in particular shows a pattern of appealing to the Jewish Scriptures in order to shape the thoughts and actions of his intended audience. As a devout and educated Jew, Paul remained deeply engaged with the Jewish Scriptures throughout his life, so that his thinking and mode of expression were shaped and reshaped by the symbolic universe of the Bible and the language of specific passages.[1] But when Paul wrote to his churches, his purpose was

---

[1]Dietrich-Alex Koch in particular has called attention to the evidence for Paul's intensive studies in the Jewish Scriptures: "Je stärker Paulus sich veranlaßt sieht, seine eigene Position theologisch zu klären, desto intensiver

not simply to lay out his theological beliefs, but to motivate specific first-century Christians to believe and/or act (or stop believing or acting) in particular ways. Quoting the words of Scripture was one of the strategies that Paul used to achieve this goal.[2] Yet rhetorical studies of Paul's appeals to Scripture are hard to find.

A rhetorical analysis of Paul's biblical quotations will examine how quotations "work" within the surface structure of his letters, not how Paul himself read and understood the biblical text. The focus will be on the way the quotations advance (or fail to advance) Paul's rhetorical aims in a given passage. Questions will be raised about why Paul introduced a biblical citation at this particular point in his argument, what he hoped to accomplish by it, and how a first-century audience from diverse social and religious backgrounds might have regarded this sudden intrusion of material from a Jewish religious text. Attention will be given to the affective and poetic as well as the intellectual aspects of such an encounter with the holy

---

wird zugleich auch die Beschäftigung mit der Schrift und ihre Verwendung in seinen Briefen" (*Die Schrift als Zeuge des Evangeliums* [Tübingen: Mohr, 1986] 101; cf. 98-9). Richard Hays makes a similar point (*Echoes of Scripture in the Letters of Paul* [New Haven: Yale U. Press, 1989] 16): "The vocabulary and cadences of Scripture—particularly of the LXX—are imprinted deeply on Paul's mind, and the great stories of Israel continue to serve for him as a fund of symbols and metaphors that condition his perception of the world, of God's promised deliverance of his people, and of his own identity and calling. His faith, in short, is one whose articulation is inevitably intertextual in character."

[2]The importance of biblical quotations for Paul's argumentation is sometimes overestimated. Paul quotes directly from Scripture in only four of his assured letters (Galatians, 1 and 2 Corinthians, and Romans), and he often addresses weighty issues of belief and practice without adducing specific verses in support of his arguments (e. g., Gal 3:19-4:7, 5:16-26, 1 Cor 7:1-8:13, 2 Cor 3:7-18, 5:1-21, Rom 1:18-32, 5:1-8:30, 12:1-16; cf. Phil 3:1-21, 1 Thess 4:1-12, 2 Thess 2:1-12). On the other hand, many of his quotations appear in contexts that bear little relation to those "central issues of the faith" that are said to have motivated Paul's studies in the Jewish Scriptures (e. g., 1 Cor 2:16, 9:9, 14:21, 2 Cor 4:13, 8:15, 9:9, Rom 14:11, 15:21).

Scriptures of Israel. The primary evaluative question will not be "How effectively does Paul integrate the biblical text into his own theology?" but "How well do Paul's quotations cohere with his own rhetorical aims and the needs and capabilities of his first-century audience?" In short, a rhetorical study will focus on what quotations <u>do</u> as part of a developing argument, not just what they <u>say</u>.

This article offers some initial soundings in the development of a rhetorical approach to the study of biblical quotations in antiquity. After a discussion of some of the theoretical issues underlying this approach, the paper will examine a key passage from Paul's letter to the Galatians to highlight some of the issues that might arise from a rhetorical analysis of Paul's quotations.

The Rhetoric of Quotations

Quotations are the orphaned stepchild of modern rhetorical studies. Speakers and writers have used quotations to enhance the rhetorical quality of their works for centuries, but textbooks on rhetoric and speech communication have little to say about their functions in speeches and other rhetorical works.[3] The subject is

---

[3]The same is true for the ancient rhetorical handbooks. Aristotle does refer briefly to the practice of citing "ancient witnesses" (defined as "the poets and all other notable persons whose judgments are known to all," *Rhetoric* 1.15) to support an argument, but he limits their usefulness to providing analogies that can be applied to a contemporary legal case (2.23). The use of proverbs and maxims (arguably a special form of quotation) is restricted here to elderly men whose long experience gives them the credibility to cite traditional wisdom (2.21). In the right hands, says Aristotle, maxims can prove helpful to the orator "due to the want of intelligence in his hearers, who love to hear him succeed in expressing as a universal truth the opinions which they hold themselves about particular cases" (2.21). Quintilian offers similar observations in a brief section where he recommends the use of quotations to lend authority to the orator's pronouncements (*Inst. Orat.* 5.36-44).

normally treated rather briefly (if at all) in a section dealing with the use of evidence or testimony to lend credibility to an argument.[4] According to Chaim Perelman, such an "argument from authority" is typically used to anticipate and/or close off debate regarding a statement made by the speaker/author in direct speech: "One resorts to it when agreement on the question is in danger of being debated."[5] The argument is therefore heavily "power-coded," especially when accompanied by power imbalances between speaker and audience. Such power imbalances can affect the way an authoritative source is interpreted: "The superior participant will often choose to mask his or her own position by exploiting the ambiguities available in the language" of the source.[6] The effectiveness of appeals to authority (including quotations) will depend in large part on the audience's perception of the authority and/or credibility of the original source, though the credibility of the speaker/author can also affect the reception of evidence.[7] In most cases, the argument from authority

---

Pronouncements from the past are valuable because "they form a sort of testimony, which is rendered all the more impressive by the fact that it was not given to suit special cases, but was the utterance... of minds swayed neither by prejudice or influence, simply because it seemed the most honourable or honest thing to say" (5.37). Maxims can also be useful because they have "carried conviction of their truth to all mankind" (5.41). This is as far as the ancient sources take us.

[4]For example, the index of the classic work by Chaim Perelman and L. Olbrechts-Tyteca, *The New Rhetoric: A Treatise on Argumentation* (Notre Dame, IN: U. of Notre Dame Press, 1969), lists four references (in 514 pages!) to the subject of "quotations," all of them quite brief.

[5]*New Rhetoric*, 308.

[6]Dick Leith and George Myerson, *The Power of Address: Explorations in Rhetoric* (London: Routledge, 1989) 124.

[7]In his book *Persuasion* (Englewood Cliffs, NJ: Prentice-Hall, 1983), Robert Bostrom describes the detailed experiments of James McCroskey, who demonstrated that appeals to evidence could be quite effective for speakers who were perceived as having low- to medium-credibility by the audience, but were of minimal help for a high-credibility speaker (146-50).

plays only a secondary role for the speaker; as Chaim Perelman notes, "More often than not, the argument from authority will not constitute the only proof, but will round off well-developed argumentation."[8]

Occasionally a rhetorician will recognize that quotations do more than appeal to authority. Quotations can also be used to illustrate or exemplify a point made by a speaker using ordinary language. The effect here is less direct, and therefore less predictable. According to one popular text, "The value and power of any literary material quoted in a speech depends upon its relevance to the point of the message and upon its strength in saying something—with grace, felicity, and a sense of the poetic or the dramatic—that could not be said as aptly in the speaker's own words."[9] Here we see an acknowledgment of the poetic dimension of the quotation process. The "value and power" of a quotation can depend as much on the manner of expression as on the content or source of the statement.

Quotations also serve to create a sense of communion between speaker and audience.[10] In cases where the speaker is already viewed favorably by the audience, quotations from a source deemed reliable by both parties can serve to highlight the bond between them, thus enhancing the audience's receptivity to the speaker's message.

"Effectiveness" is defined here as the production of lasting changes in the beliefs and/or attitudes of the immediate audience (150-52).

[8] *New Rhetoric*, 307.

[9] Kenneth G. Hance, David C. Ralph, and Milton J. Wiksell, *Principles of Speaking* (3d ed.; Belmont, CA: Wadsworth, 1989) 88.

[10] Perelman, *New Rhetoric*, 177-78. Perelman also includes allusions, maxims, and proverbs in his list of "figures that relate to communion." Inexplicably, Perelman limits this "communion-building" function to times when the act of quotation "is not fulfilling its normal role of backing up a statement with the weight of authority" (177).

In cases where the audience is uncertain or hostile toward the speaker, "a well-chosen quotation will suffice to create a feeling of confidence, by showing that the speaker and his audience have common values."[11] In both cases the quotation appeals to the emotions of the audience, "the emotion created by memories, or community pride."[12]

In broad terms, then, rhetorical studies tell us that a direct quotation from a recognized authority can serve to increase an audience's receptivity to a speaker's message. But when we attempt to apply these insights to a study of Paul's quotations, we discover additional questions that are not addressed in these studies. Why did Paul introduce an explicit quotation from the Jewish Scriptures at this or that point in his argument? What was he trying to accomplish? How did he expect his audience to respond? Was his audience able and willing to offer the desired response? In sum, was the use of explicit biblical quotations an effective strategy for influencing the beliefs and/or conduct of Paul's first-century congregations? Or might Paul have misjudged the ability (or willingness) of his largely Gentile Christian audience to respond to this particular method of argumentation? To answer all of these questions would require more time and space than is available in the present volume.[13] But we can identify certain criteria that any piece

---

[11]Perelman, *New Rhetoric*, 496. In other words, quotations can serve to enhance the speaker's *ethos*, a key concern of rhetoricians at least since Aristotle.

[12]Perelman, *New Rhetoric*, 177. In classical terms, this is an appeal to *pathos*, Aristotle's second mode of persuasion.

[13]A full response to these questions will appear in a book-length study that is currently in progress. Some of the methodological questions are discussed in Christopher D. Stanley, "The Rhetoric of Quotations: An Essay on Method," *Early Christian Interpretation of the Scriptures of Israel: Investigation and Proposals* (eds. Craig A. Evans and James A. Sanders; Sheffield: Sheffield

of rhetoric must meet in order to be effective. This in turn will give us a theoretical basis for evaluating the effectiveness of Paul's rhetorical appeals to Scripture.

Effective Rhetorical Communication

One of the chief tasks of a rhetorical critic is to evaluate the effectiveness of a speaker/author's argumentation. But various theorists have different ideas about what constitutes "effective argumentation." The form of analysis to be followed here is rooted in the "New Rhetoric" of Chaim Perelman and his followers, as developed especially in the work of Eugene E. White.[14] According to White (and Perelman before him), all rhetorical acts are situational, in that they are rooted in what White calls a "provoking rhetorical urgency."[15] By "provoking rhetorical urgency," White means "a structured perception of ongoing events" that a speaker/author

---

Academic Press, 1997) 44-58. On the audience's ability to respond to Paul's quotations, see Christopher D. Stanley, "'Pearls Before Swine': Did Paul's Audiences Understand His Biblical Quotations?" (forthcoming in *Novum Testamentum*).

[14]See especially Eugene E. White, *The Context of Human Discourse: A Configurational Criticism of Rhetoric* (Columbia, SC: U. of South Carolina Press, 1992).

[15]White's idea of "provoking rhetorical urgency" is quite close to the concept of "rhetorical situation" developed by Lloyd Bitzer in his classic essay, "The Rhetorical Situation," *Philosophy and Rhetoric* 1 (1968) 1-14. Bitzer defines "rhetorical situation" as "a complex of persons, events, objects, and relations presenting an actual or potential exigence which can be completely or partially removed if discourse, introduced into the situation, can so constrain human decision or action as to bring about the significant modification of the exigence." Bitzer offers a significant refinement of his ideas in "Functional Communication: A Situational Perspective," *Rhetoric in Transition: Studies in the Nature and Uses of Rhetoric* (ed. Eugene E. White; University Park, PA: Pennsylvania State U. Press, 1980) 21-38.

constructs out of his or her knowledge of a particular situation.[16] The presence and nature of a "rhetorical urgency" depends entirely on the perceptions of the speaker/author; as White puts it, "Rhetorical urgencies are not really 'out there' as sequences of objective events; they are patterns of thought and feeling in people's heads."[17] What makes such a situation "rhetorical" is the perception by a speaker/author that (a) things are not as they should be, and (b) language can be used to induce an audience to bring about a change in the situation.[18] By addressing a group of people in terms meant to win their adherence, the speaker/author hopes to induce the audience to think or act in such a way as to eliminate the rhetorical urgency that provoked the address.[19] Rhetorical speech is thus

---

[16]*Context*, 105. This insistence on the "socially constructed" nature of "rhetorical urgencies" is what makes White's approach preferable to that of Bitzer, who has been criticized for the "Platonic idealism" inherent in his concept of "rhetorical situation." See Robert L. Scott, "Intentionality in the Rhetorical Process," in White, ed., *Rhetoric in Transition*, 56-58.

[17]*Context*, 105. The speaker/author's perception of a situation as a "rhetorical urgency" is shaped by a broad array of factors, including the nature of the information available to the speaker/author, the speaker/author's relation to the audience, the personal beliefs and values of the speaker/author, and the broader pattern of societal influences (*Context*, 110-11, 146-47). As with estimates of a speaker/author's intentions (see below), the critic's judgment about a speaker/author's perception of a situation will never be more than probable (*Context*, 119).

[18]This way of conceiving the rhetorical process is clearly better suited to persuasive than to epideictic rhetoric, a fact that White seems to overlook. But even epideictic speech can be viewed as a response to a "provoking rhetorical urgency" within a particular social system: in our own society, a death requires a funeral oration, a wedding reception calls forth a toast, a graduation ceremony evokes a final charge to the graduates, etc. Chaim Perelman, whose influence can be seen throughout White's study, goes so far as to argue that "the epideictic genre is central to discourse because its role is to intensify adherence to values without which discourses that aim at provoking action cannot find the lever to move or inspire their listeners" (*The Realm of Rhetoric* [Notre Dame, IN: U. of Notre Dame Press, 1982] 19).

[19]As White observes, "The ultimate purpose of talk is *not* to induce change in readers or listeners. That is an intermediate step toward the ultimate goal

audience-centered speech; its purpose is to promote action on the part of the audience, not merely to communicate the ideas of the speaker/author.

White does not believe that the critic can establish with certainty the intentions behind a rhetorical work. But experience tells him that "with careful digging, one can usually form reasoned conclusions about persuaders' purposes."[20] White identifies five aspects of the message that can shed light on the speaker/author's intentions: the basic thesis of the communication; the substance of what is said; the arrangement of the ideas; the language with which the ideas are clothed; and the paralinguistic characteristics that accompany the formal language.[21] Information about the historical and social setting of the rhetorical act can also illuminate the "internalized self-systems" that influenced the speaker/author's rhetorical choices.[22]

The primary criterion by which the effectiveness of a rhetorical act should be judged, according to White, is the degree of

---

of applying pressure on the urgency" (*Context*, 39). Yet even this is not the end of the matter. As White recognizes, "It is quite possible—even likely—that the changed state of the original urgency will, in turn, constitute new provoking urgencies that give rise to later rhetorical efforts toward modification" (*Context*, 35). We see this clearly in Paul's correspondence with the Corinthians.

[20]*Context*, 53.

[21]*Context*, 64. Because of his situational view of rhetoric, White insists that "in estimating rhetorical intent, it is neither necessary nor desirable to use psychoanalytical approaches" (73).

[22]*Context*, 74-75. Exploring the speaker/author's "self-system" can be helpful because "self-systems (individual or collective) condition the way persuaders view urgencies, audiences, and occasions, and the ways persuaders conceptualize their relationships to these forces. Persuaders' self-systems determine their rhetorical choices, including their choices of purpose" (*Context*, 74-75). This recalls White's insistence on the importance of the speaker/author's *perception* of the audience's situation.

"congruence" between the speaker/author's use of language and the various circumstantial forces that influence the rhetorical process.23 As White notes, "A communication can be based on 'good reasons,' be eloquent in style, be expressive of high moral principles, have sound documentation and helpful internal summaries, and still be incongruent with other forces that help to shape the configuration in which the communication occurs."24 Such a communication can hardly be labeled "effective." White list six constraints that impinge upon the effectiveness of a rhetorical communication:

1. The potential for modification of the urgency;
2. The capacity of the readers/listeners to alter the urgency;
3. The readiness of the readers/listeners to be influenced;
4. The occasion—the immediate circumstances in which the communication takes place;
5. Relevant aspects of the persuader's self-system; and
6. The persuader's real and apparent purposes in communicating.

Chief among these rhetorical constraints, in White's view, is the audience. The success of a rhetorical communication depends in

---

23This criterion flows naturally out of what White calls the "master concept" of his work: "To the degree that rhetorical constraints are matched by appropriate rhetorical responses, persuasion can take place" (*Context*, 36). According to White (14-15), the degree of "congruence" among rhetorical forces is a better barometer of effectiveness than the actual "effects" of a rhetorical act, since "effects" are notoriously difficult to trace to a single cause, and even an exemplary rhetorical effort can lead to limited results due to other forces in the configuration (cf. Demosthenes). Moreover, "congruence" can be evaluated in terms of "degrees," whereas "effects" are an all-or-nothing enterprise.
24*Context*, 17.

large part on the willingness of the audience to allow themselves to be influenced by the words and ideas of the speaker/author.[25] To induce a positive response, the speaker/author must be able to create a sense of coherence between the beliefs and values commended in the message and the prior convictions of the audience.[26] The recipients' opinions about the character of the speaker/author and their perception of the degree of "fit" between the message and their situation will also influence their response to the message.[27]

In some cases, the audience may be either unable or unwilling to provide the response that the speaker/author desires. They might harbor negative feelings about the character and/or the beliefs or values of the person who addresses them; they might view the situation in different terms than the speaker/author; they might be

---

[25]As White puts it, "Persuaders do not unilaterally determine the standards for judgments.... Readers and listeners determine *for themselves* whether they will attend to what persuaders say and what changes, if any, they will make in the ways they think and feel" (*Context*, 208-9). The importance of the audience's disposition is stressed throughout White's study: "How ready the readers and listeners are to be influenced by a message conditions the way they respond to what is said and, derivatively, the way they eventually influence the urgency. Successful persuaders accept that the potential responsiveness of audiences constrains what they can successfully do and say" (*Context*, 63).

[26]White uses the term "identification" to describe both the speaker/author's efforts to appeal to the beliefs and values of the audience and the audience's response to those appeals (*Context*, 17-18, 210-19). He explains the process as follows: "To begin persuading, an advocate must meet readers and listeners where they are at the outset of the communication. He or she must provide them with language and ideas that will enable them to perceive analogies between what is being said and some aspect of their own relevant knowledge, beliefs, values, attitudes, and behaviors. Without some initial identification, persuasion cannot begin. To promote further movement toward closure, the persuader must enable his or her readers/listeners to enlarge and reinforce the initial beachheads of identification and to perceive fresh areas of identification. The persuadees must continue to recognize analogies between themselves and what is being said as communication develops" (216).

[27]*Context*, 252-63.

incapable of understanding the ideas and/or language used by the author; they might be divided among (or within) themselves over the issue; or they might simply be disinterested in the subject of the discourse. If the speaker/author fails to recognize and counter these potentially damaging influences, the practical effectiveness of the rhetorical act will be diminished. The effective communicator is one who takes full account of the capabilities and likely responses of the audience within a particular rhetorical context.

Evaluating Paul's Quotations

So how did Paul's predominantly Gentile churches view his practice of quoting from the Jewish Scriptures? Did they find his biblical argumentation persuasive? Or did they simply ignore it as obscure and/or irrelevant? Did they share Paul's high regard for the Jewish Scriptures, including his drive to ground Christian belief and practice in its words? Or did they view his biblical quotations as a distraction, a means of obscuring the real issues under discussion?

Questions such as these highlight how little we really know about the way Paul's letters were received by his first-century audiences. The fact that the letters were preserved indicates that at least some of the recipients found them valuable. Presumably these people also found his arguments persuasive. But how common was this response? The simple answer is that we do not know. We can guess that those whom we commonly style Paul's "opponents" were less than enthusiastic in their response. Most likely they brought forward additional arguments to counter those raised in Paul's letters, perhaps including new arguments from Scripture.[28] We can likewise assume that those who already agreed with Paul's positions (Prisca and Aquila, Chloe, the anti-law Galatians, etc.) found his argumentation convincing. For the bulk of Paul's audience, we simply have no information.

On the purely historical level, then, we can know very little about the way Paul's biblical argumentation was received in his churches. But careful investigation can lead us toward a reasonable estimation of their response. Using White's model as our guide, we can (a) examine Paul's rhetoric to determine how quotations fit into his broader discursive strategy, and then (b) compare this with what we know about Paul's audience to determine whether they were capable of responding in the way Paul expected. From this process we can develop reasoned historical judgments about the likely effectiveness of Paul's use of biblical quotations as a rhetorical strategy.

Paul's Use of Quotations

A careful exmination of the way Paul used biblical quotations in his argumentation yields the following broad observations.[29]

---

[28]Over against static and/or unidirectional interpretations of the rhetorical process, White describes rhetoric as a dynamic process in which the speaker/author, the audience, and the message are shaped and reshaped by the changing configuration of their relationship. We see this clearly in the Corinthian correspondence. As White puts it, "Any persuasive experience is experience of a dynamic, cyclical flow of antecedents-events-consequences that, in the course of its developing, encompasses not only the particular piece(s) of persuasion that we are interested in but also all other successful and abortive attempts at modification that are relevant to experiencing that rhetoric" (*Context*, 13; cf. 34-36, 208-10).

[29]The evidence for these conclusions will be presented in the book-length

1. In Eugene White's terms, Paul faced a different "provoking rhetorical urgency" when writing to each of his churches. The identification of each situation as a "rhetorical urgency" requiring a written response reflects Paul's own perception of the circumstances, which may or may not have coincided with the perceptions of others in the audience (or the "real" situation). In each case Paul crafted a response that he believed would persuade the audience to (a) see things as he did and (b) follow his advice about eliminating the "rhetorical urgency."

2. In a few of these letters (Galatians, 1 and 2 Corinthians, and Romans), Paul used explicit quotations from the Jewish Scriptures as part of his rhetorical strategy. It is probably no accident that the four letters in which Paul quotes directly from Scripture were written to churches where Paul's integrity and/or apostolic authority had been called into question. Apparently Paul expected that his repeated appeals to Scripture would reinforce his standing with the audience by highlighting the common bond that united them all, Jew and Gentile alike, around the God of Israel. He may also have hoped that his skill in handling the community's holy text would enhance his stature with the audience and thus secure a favorable hearing for his message.

3. From Paul's quotations we can see that he, like other Jews, believed that quoting the words of Scripture should close off all debate on a subject.[30] His appeals to the authoritative text reveal

---

study cited in note 13.

[30]As Chaim Perelman observes concerning arguments from authority, "The greater the authority, the more unquestionable does his pronouncement become. The extreme case is the divine authority which overcomes all the obstacles that reason might raise" (*New Rhetoric*, 308).

his conviction that the words of Israel's God carry a force that transcends all human argumentation. Like many other Jews, he expected his non-Jewish audience to share this view. By citing the words of Scripture, Paul sought to bring his audience face-to-face with the God of Israel, whose authority (he assumed) they could not deny. This subtle appeal to the audience's prior convictions and emotions would have carried great weight with those who shared Paul's high view of Scripture.

4. Though he wrote to predominantly Gentile churches, Paul often left to his audience the task of filling in the background and context of his biblical quotations. In other words, he expected the audience to participate in the construction of his message.[31] To do so, they had to recall not only particular passages of Scripture but also major elements of the belief-system that they had inherited from Judaism. This implicit appeal to a common belief-system served as a bridge between Paul and his audience, allowing him to frame his response to the "provoking rhetorical urgency" in a way that built on these shared beliefs and values.[32]

5. Even in passages where quotations play a key role, Paul rarely grounds his argument on the authority of Scripture alone. His usual practice is to embed his quotations in a series of carefully structured arguments that he believes will speak to the needs and capacities of his audience. Some of these arguments are framed

---

[31]Wolfgang Iser (*The Act of Reading: A Theory of Aesthetic Response* [Baltimore: Johns Hopkins U. Press, 1978]) argues that this process of "filling in the gaps" is central to all experiences of reading, so that every encounter with a text is an interactive process that produces both intellectual and affective responses in the reader.

[32]According to White's analysis, this two-way process of "identification" between speaker and audience is crucial to the success of any rhetorical endeavor--see note 26.

around specific biblical passages, but more often Paul simply follows the normal canons of rhetorical speech, appealing to Scripture as one element in a broader argument. Occasionally Paul quotes a verse of Scripture not to trade on its authority, but for other reasons: to illustrate or exemplify a point, to say something in a particularly apt manner, to provide the premise of an argument, to remind the audience of a biblical character or event, etc.[33] In these cases the rhetorical purpose of the quotation cannot always be determined with confidence.

6. To increase the chances that his audience would understand and respond to these "words of God" in the way he intended, Paul regularly adapted the wording of his quotations so as to highlight the link between the biblical passage and his own argument.[34] He also routinely included introductory and/or exegetical comments that explained how he intended the quotation to be understood. In these cases we have a reasonably clear indication as to the rhetorical strategy that informed Paul's handling of the biblical text, though we cannot always be sure about ancillary aspects of the quotation.

7. Sometimes Paul fails to clarify how a particular quotation fits into his broader argument. In some cases the ambiguity is only temporary, i. e., the audience is left to puzzle about the quotation

---

[33]In an often-cited article ("The Basic Functions of Quotation," *Sign, Language, Culture* (ed. A. J. Greimas et al.; The Hague: Mouton, 1970] 690-705), Stefan Morawski discusses the following common reasons for quotation: (1) the authority function (grounding one's position in the views of another); (2) the erudite function (presenting excerpts from a work under review); (3) the stimulative-amplificatory function (using another's words in place of one's own argument); and (4) the ornamental function (quoting for their aesthetic effect). Obviously this list is too broad and generic to be of much use when applied to the letters of Paul.

[34]For evidence that Paul adapted the wording of quotations to coincide with his own rhetorical agenda, see the study cited in note 13.

until its significance becomes clear from the ensuing discussion. In other cases the quotation takes the place of a direct argument, whether because the wording of the text was deemed particularly apt or because Paul wanted to protect himself against possible challenges to his own words. In still other cases the link remains obscure. While it is possible that these remaining ambiguities are intentional,[35] most rhetoricians would regard them as missteps in a developing argumentative strategy.

8. Paul did not quote Scripture in a vacuum. When writing to the Galatians and Corinthians, Paul assumes that they will remember at least some of his biblical teaching (e. g., the stories of Abraham and Moses) from his earlier visits to their communities. Other people had also taught from the Scriptures in these churches, some of them in ways that Paul believed to be wrong-headed and dangerous. At least some of Paul's quotations from Scripture were designed to counter these "false teachings" and to offer alternative ways of understanding the authoritative biblical text. How much Paul knew about these opposing viewpoints, and whether his "opponents" subsequently cited Scripture to counter the arguments raised in Paul's letters, is unfortunately lost to us. But we can be sure that Paul's letters represent only one stage in a developing rhetorical situation.

---

[35]For example, Paul may have wanted to leave the door open for multiple interpretations, or he may have felt that the text was clear and required no comment.

Quotations and Paul's Audience

Clearly Paul believed that direct quotations from the Jewish Scriptures would be an effective tool for influencing his audience to accept his ideas and follow his recommendations in certain areas. But was he correct in this view? For a piece of rhetoric to be effective, careful crafting alone is not enough; the work must also be appropriate to the audience. This means that the audience must be (a) capable of following the argument sufficiently to grasp the speaker's point, and (b) willing to seriously consider the course of action recommended by the speaker. If problems are anticipated in either of these areas, an effective speaker will take these factors into account and craft the speech accordingly. Was Paul an "effective speaker" in this sense? A review of what we can know about Paul's first-century audience raises serious questions about Paul's practice.[36]

1. In Paul's day, what we call "the Septuagint" (the only text of Scripture that Paul's Greek-speaking audience could understand) was a diverse collection of scrolls that did not exist under a single cover until the invention of the codex no earlier than the late first century CE.[37] In view of the ongoing tensions between the early

---

[36]A more thorough investigation of the capabilities of Paul's audience can be found in the article cited in note 13.

[37]The ambiguity surrounding the term "Septuagint" (or "LXX") in modern scholarship has led many investigators to adopt the designation "Old Greek" to refer to the (theoretical) original translation of individual biblical books. The label "LXX" is then reserved either for the Greek Pentateuch (so Leonard Greenspoon, "The Use and Misuse of the Term 'LXX' and Related Terminology in Recent Scholarship," *BIOSCS* 20 [1987] 21-29) or for the collection of translations represented in the great codices of the fourth and fifth centuries CE (so Emanuel Tov, "The Septuagint," in *Mikra: Text, Translation, Reading and Interpretation of the Hebrew Bible in Ancient*

Christians and many Jewish communities, it seems unlikely that either Paul or the recipients of his letters would have been able to visit the local synagogue regularly to study the Scriptures for themselves. As for private ownership, books (i. e., scrolls) were expensive in antiquity, and few people had the resources to purchase even a single book from the Jewish Scriptures, much less an entire collection.[38] While it remains possible that some of the wealthy patrons of Paul's churches owned copies of a few key biblical scrolls, we have no clear evidence for such a practice in Paul's day.[39] More likely Paul and other educated Christians followed the standard practice of keeping a personal notebook into which they copied key passages from the Jewish Scriptures whenever they gained access to

---

Judaism and Early Christianity [ed. Martin Jan Mulder; Compendia Rerum Iudaicarum II/1; Assen: Van Gorcum, 1988; Philadelphia: Fortress, 1988] 161). On the technology and use of books in the ancient world (including the rise of the codex in the early Christian era), see C. H. Roberts and T. C. Skeat, *The Birth of the Codex* (Oxford: Oxford University Press for the British Academy, 1983); E. G. Turner, *Greek Manuscripts of the Ancient World* (Princeton: Princeton U. Press, 1971) and *The Typology of the Early Codex* (Philadelphia: U. of Pennsylvania Press, 1977); Harry Y. Gamble, *Books and Readers in the Early Church: A History of Early Christian Texts* (New Haven: Yale U. Press, 1995); and the various entries under "Buch" in *Reallexicon für Antike und Christentum* (1954).

[38]On the costliness and relative scarcity of books in antiquity, see William Harris, *Ancient Literacy* (Cambridge: Harvard U. Press, 1989) 193-6, 224-5; Gamble, *Books*, 83-93. As Gamble notes, "The Scriptures of Judaism comprised not a single book but a collection of scrolls, five of the Torah and more of the prophetic books. These books were relatively costly, and their availability even to all synagogues cannot be taken for granted" (214).

[39]The possibility that local Christian leaders might have owned biblical scrolls for use within their congregations is heightened by recent sociological studies that highlight the patronal role and high social status of house-church leaders in the Pauline congregations. See Gerd Theissen, *The Social Setting of Pauline Christianity* (Philadelphia: Fortress, 1982); Wayne Meeks, *The First Urban Christians* (New Haven: Yale U. Press, 1983); Abraham Malherbe, *Social Aspects of Early Christianity* (2d ed.; Philadelphia: Fortress, 1983). For more on private libraries among aristocratic Greeks, Jews, and Christians in antiquity, see Gamble, *Books*, 188-202.

a scroll.[40] For the ordinary members of Paul's churches, a first-hand encounter with a biblical scroll was probably an unusual event.

2. Even if biblical scrolls had been available in Paul's churches, most people would have been unable to read them. In his acclaimed study of ancient literacy, William Harris concluded that no more than 10 to 20% of the populace could read or write at any level throughout the classical, Hellenistic, and Roman imperial periods.[41] In a subsequent investigation of early Christian literacy, Harry Gamble concluded that even if the early church had a disproportionate number of craftspeople and small business workers among its members, the literacy level in the earliest churches would not have exceeded the upper end of the range specified by Harris.[42] We have no reason to think that Paul's churches were any different. Thus it seems probable that not more than a handful of people in a given church, those recruited from the educated elite, would have been able to read and study the Jewish Scriptures for themselves.[43]

---

[40]For evidence concerning the common practice of note-taking in antiquity and its significance for the apostle Paul, see Stanley, *Paul*, 73-8. Several techniques were available: to copy the texts directly onto a papyrus scroll, to use one of the sturdier parchment notebooks that were already becoming available by this time, or to take notes onto a wax tablet and transfer them later to a more permanent repository. According to William Harris (*Literacy*, 194), codices of up to ten wax tablets were common, with each tablet able to hold fifty or more words per side. For more on the technology of note-taking, see Gamble, *Books*, 50-53; Roberts and Skeat, *Codex*, 18-29; B. M. W. Knox and P. E. Easterling, "Books and Readers in the Ancient World," in *Cambridge History of Ancient Literature* (eds. B. M. W. Knox and P. E. Easterling, 2 vols.; Cambridge: Cambridge University Press, 1985) 18; Frederic Kenyon, *Books and Readers in Ancient Greece and Rome* (Oxford: Clarendon, 1932) 91-92.
[41]Harris, *Literacy*, 272, 284, 328-30. Of course, literacy levels were lower for women than for men throughout the ancient world; see Susan Guettel Cole, "Could Greek Women Read and Write?" *Reflections of Women in Antiquity* (ed. Helene P. Foley; New York: Gordon and Breach, 1981) 219-45.
[42]Gamble, *Books*, 2-11.
[43]On the social composition of Paul's churches, see the works cited in note 39.

3. All of Paul's letters (and thus his quotations) were directed to predominantly "Gentile" congregations. Apart from the few who had attended the synagogue as Jewish sympathizers, we can assume that no one in Paul's churches had any significant knowledge of the Jewish Scriptures before they entered the Christian church.[44] If the bulk of these Gentile converts were illiterate, and if biblical scrolls were not readily available in the churches, then the common belief that Paul's audiences engaged in regular personal study of the Jewish Scriptures would appear to be unfounded. Whatever they knew about the content of the Jewish Scriptures would have come to them via oral instruction from the few literate and/or Jewish members of the congregation.[45] When Paul quoted from a passage that they had not previously encountered, their understanding of the verse would have been shaped by the broader rhetorical context in which the quotation was embedded.[46] They had no easy means of

---

[44]Of course, non-Jews were familiar with Jewish beliefs and practices, including their reverence for a collection of holy texts, but they did not (so far as we know) read the Jewish Scriptures for themselves. Even the literati of Greco-Roman society had wild ideas about the content of the Jewish Scriptures; see the citations in Menahem Stern, ed., *Greek and Latin Authors on Jews and Judaism* (3 vols.; Jerusalem: Israel Academy of Sciences and Humanities, 1974-84), and the discussion in Louis H. Feldman, *Jew and Gentile in the Ancient World* (Princeton, NJ: Princeton U. Press, 1993). The earliest non-Jewish source that reveals a familiarity with the content of the Jewish Scriptures is a quotation by Pseudo-Longinus in *On the Sublime* toward the end of the first century.

[45]Harry Gamble makes a strong argument that literacy would have been a key factor in determining who would be recognized as leaders in the early Christian community. In Gamble's words, "Given that texts were important to Christianity from the beginning, though only the Jewish Scriptures at first, it is difficult to imagine any Christian community where either no one could read or no authority accrued to those who could. In a community in which texts had a constitutive importance and only a few persons were literate, it was inevitable that those who were able to explicate texts would acquire authority for that reason alone" (*Books*, 9-10).

[46]For more on the way interpretational comments affect the audience's

checking Paul's usage against the original context of the quotation, nor of supplying any context that might have been missing.

4. Of course, illiteracy did not prevent the Gentiles in Paul's audience from learning something about the Jewish Scriptures. The Christian gospel was accompanied by biblical prooftexts from its earliest days, and Christian moral instruction was likewise grounded in part on biblical injunctions. Certain key biblical passages (e. g., the Ten Commandments) and stories about important biblical figures (Abraham, Moses, Elijah, David) were no doubt passed on orally in every Christian congregation. The same was probably true for texts that could assist the members in defending their faith before a hostile world. But this is a far cry from the kind of biblical knowledge that would be required to grasp the significance of the many quotations that Paul offers, for example, in Romans 9-11, especially when the letter was being read aloud before a gathered congregation. The inevitable conclusion is that only the handful of literate members who had time to study and discuss what Paul had said would have come close to understanding the full import of Paul's biblical quotations.

The Power of Quotations

So why did Paul quote so freely from the Jewish Scriptures in his letters to illiterate Gentile churches? Part of the reason can be traced to his subject matter, which at times required him to grapple seriously with traditional Jewish interpretations of the biblical text. This was especially true in cases where people were quoting

---

understanding of a quotation, see Meir Sternberg, "Proteus in Quotation-Land: Mimesis and the From of Reported Discourse," *Poetics Today* 3 (1982) 107-56, and Stanley, "Rhetoric" (note 13).

Scripture in support of ideas that Paul felt compelled to reject, as in Galatians. Another factor was his own deep grounding in the Jewish Scriptures, which seems to have brought many quotations unbidden to his mind. But the primary reason was no doubt the rhetorical effectiveness of biblical quotations within the early Christian community. Paul knew that his audiences revered the Jewish Scriptures, even if most of them were unable to read the text for themselves. In this context, biblical quotations carried weight regardless of whether the recipients understood the reference, since the quotation showed the God of Israel standing firmly on the side of the speaker. The ability to quote and interpret Scripture can be a potent weapon within a religious community, especially when the skill is limited to a handful of practitioners, and Paul did not hesitate to use this weapon in his letters. Neither literacy nor familiarity with the original context is required for people to be moved by a citation from a text deemed authoritative by their community. As long as the recipients of Paul's letters acknowledged the authority of the Jewish Scriptures, quotations from the holy text would be greeted with respect and (Paul hoped) submission. Who would dare to argue with the mouthpiece of God?

Conclusions

If the rhetorical effectiveness of a biblical quotation depends on the recipients being able to understand and approve the author's handling of the biblical text, then Paul must be judged ineffective in many of his appeals to Scripture. But if we situate Paul's practice within the social context of early Christian veneration of the Jewish

Scriptures, we see a more effective rhetorician at work. Even if the audience did not fully understand Paul's quotations, their high regard for the source text would have insured a fair hearing for the arguments in which they were embedded. And the fact that Paul could quote and interpret such a holy text would have reinforced his status in the eyes of those to whom his letters were directed, thus enhancing the success of his rhetoric. While one could argue that Paul might have done better to avoid biblical argumentation altogether in view of the limited capabilities of his audience, we can hardly fault him for playing on the authority of Scripture to gain (or sustain) adherence to what he believed was the will of the God who stood behind the Scriptures.

Quotations in Galatians: A Case Study

According to most commentators, quotations from the Jewish Scriptures play a key role in the argumentation of Paul's letter to the Galatians. Yet the letter contains only nine or ten explicit quotations in 146 verses of text, all but one of which can be found in two passages, Gal 3:6-16 and Gal 4:27-30.[47]

So why do we have the impression that biblical quotations are so important in this letter? Most of us would probably say that it is because the quotations appear at crucial points in Paul's developing argument. But what makes these passages more crucial than 2:15-21, 3:1-5, 3:19-25, or 4:1-11? All of these passages could be said to be crucial to Paul's argument in Galatians, yet none of them contains any explicit quotations from Scripture. More to the point is the

---

[47]The exception is Gal 5:14, which quotes Lev 19:18.

observation that much of Paul's argumentation in Galatians is framed around references to the Jewish Scriptures, even where no specific verses are quoted (e. g., Gal 3:6-29, 4:21-31). But there remain vast stretches of text where Paul apparently felt no need to refer to the Jewish Scriptures to uphold his argument. So why does Paul quote when he does? Why does he choose to reproduce the wording of an outside text at this or that point in his developing argument? Unfortunately, Paul's true motives are forever lost to us. But we can examine his argumentation to see how it seeks to move the audience to adopt a particular point of view. Fortunately, Paul's use of quotations in Galatians is consistent enough to allow for a reasonably confident assessment of his rhetorical purposes.

From Paul's argument we can surmise that (a) someone in the Galatian churches had appealed to the story of Abraham (most likely Genesis 17) to argue for the circumcision of male Gentile Christians, and (b) many of the Galatians had found this argument convincing. For Paul, this was a "provoking rhetorical urgency" that forced him to develop a far-ranging counterargument from Scripture. Included in this argument was a detailed counterexposition of the story of Abraham. Explicit quotations were used when it appeared that they would add weight to the argument, but they remain only one element in a broader rhetorical presentation.

Most modern interpreters would agree with this overview of Paul's biblical argumentation in Galatians. But when we ask how a particular quotation helps to advance the rhetorical purposes of the letter, interpreters invariably talk instead about Paul's personal engagement with Scripture. A review of recent commentaries on Gal 3:10-16, for example, reveals several common topics of discussion: (a) how the quotation in v. 10 relates to contemporary Jewish interpretations of classical Deuteronomic theology; (b) how Paul might have read Habakkuk and Leviticus (quoted in vv. 11 and 12) as foreshadowing his own theology of "justification by faith"; (c) how the verse cited in v. 13 (from Deut 21:23) might have influenced Paul's thinking about the meaning of Jesus' death; and (d) how Paul's rather bizarre interpretation of Genesis in v. 16 could be said to make sense within the context of Paul's own theology and contemporary Jewish exegetical practice. These are all valid concerns, but they do not address the question of how the quotations in these verses help to advance the argument of the letter. Apart from the references to Abraham, Paul's theological engagement with the text of Scripture was largely hidden from the Galatians, who encountered Paul's quotations only in the context of his own argumentation. It is this context-of-quotation, not the original context of Scripture, that determined how the Galatians understood and responded to Paul's quotations.[48]

A full rhetorical analysis of Paul's quotations in Galatians is beyond the scope of the present study.[49] But a few comments on Gal 3:6-13 will illustrate some of the issues that might be raised by such an approach. In the first two chapters of Galatians (including 3:1-5), Paul uses a variety of rhetorical techniques to challenge the idea (accepted by some of the Galatians) that Gentile followers of Jesus must obey Torah in order to be rightly related to the God of the Jews. Throughout these chapters, Paul presents himself as a divinely-commissioned authority figure who deserves the Galatians' respect

---

[48]For more on this point, see Sternberg, "Proteus" (note 46).
[49]A fuller exposition will appear in the book-length study cited in note 13.

and obedience. By stressing the divine origins of his ministry and message, Paul hopes to shame and/or frighten the Galatians into turning away from the teaching of his "opponents," which he rejects as inconsistent with his own God-given message of "justification by faith." Nowhere in these chapters does he discuss the merits of the opposing argument. The fact that it runs counter to his own teaching is reason enough to reject it.

When we come to Gal 3:6, however, we see a turning point in Paul's rhetorical strategy. Here for the first time Paul begins to lay out a reasoned response to the biblical arguments raised by his "opponents" (whom he never explicitly mentions in this section). On first glance, it appears that Paul has abandoned his earlier strategy of intimidating the Galatians with his authority in favor of reasoning with them from the Scriptures. But the first two chapters have not been forgotten; the carefully reasoned argument of Gal 3:6-4:7 is still the teaching of an authoritative apostle who received his message "by revelation from Jesus Christ" (1:12). The earlier assertions of authority continue to hover in the background, influencing the audience's reception of the message despite the more reasonable tone.

In vv. 6-9, Paul commences his biblical argument with a rather cryptic commentary on the story of Abraham, the outlines of which he assumes the Galatians already know.[50] His treatment of these

---

[50]The matter-of-fact way in which Paul introduces the figure of Abraham seems to imply that he may have taught the Galatians the story of Abraham at an earlier date. If not, one might question whether he assumed too much at this point, since he had no sure way of knowing what parts of the Abraham story had been passed on by his "opponents." For evidence that Paul had only limited knowledge about the situation in Galatia, see Christopher D. Stanley, "'Under a Curse': A Fresh Reading of Gal 3.10-14," *NTS* 36 (1990) 488-90.

verse seems designed to achieve at least three ends: (a) to recall and reinforce the bond that his earlier teaching had forged between himself and the Galatians; (b) to demonstrate his commitment to the authoritative Scriptures, which had been at least implicitly challenged by his "opponents"; and (c) to wean the Galatians away from the views of his "opponents" by offering an alternative interpretation of the texts that they had used to support their position.[51] The two quotations from Genesis (vv. 6 and 8) serve to highlight the divine activity in the story. By embedding them in a carefully worded interpretive framework, Paul guides the Galatians toward an understanding of the story that supports his own position, i. e., that God planned all along to extend "righteousness by faith" to the Gentiles (v. 8). Thus Paul meets the challenge of his "opponents" in the only way he could—by arguing that the story of Abraham (as presented in the authoritative Scriptures) actually supports his position, not theirs.

In vv. 10-13, however, Paul moves the biblical argument to a new level. Leaving behind the story of Abraham (which his audience seems to have known already), he proceeds to lay out new arguments from Scripture that he believes will reinforce his point.[52] Paul gives no indication that he expects his audience to be familiar with the verses cited in this passage. The interpretive comments that he uses to introduce each quotation serve as before to guide the Galatians toward his own interpretation of the verses, without

---

[51]These three effects correspond broadly to the appeals to *pathos, ethos,* and *logos* as described by Aristotle.

[52]This is of course only a hiatus in the argument: v. 14 links the ideas of vv. 10-13 back to the "blessing" pronounced in vv. 8-9, and v. 15 resumes the reinterpretation of the Abraham story, including a quotation in v. 16 that clearly assumes prior knowledge of the text.

regard for their "original sense." In fact, a reader who knew the original wording and context of his quotations might well have been bothered rather than helped by some of the biblical interpretation presupposed in these verses.[53] The highly condensed nature of the argument suggests that Paul has found these same verses useful on other occasions, so that he can introduce them here as a set piece of argumentation. Unfortunately, the argument of these verses is so condensed that the precise link between Paul's own assertions and the verses cited to support them is unclear even to contemporary interpreters.[54]

Does this mean that Paul's rhetoric in these verses must be judged defective? Only if we assume that he meant for his audience to figure out and approve the implied links between his own assertions and the biblical text. When we recall that Paul's letters were written to be read aloud to a group of mostly illiterate Gentile Christians, this seems quite unlikely. Paul would have been aware of the limitations of his audience as a result of his long experience as both a Diaspora Jew and a Christian missionary. But he also knew that his Christian audience would respond more favorably to his arguments about law and faith if he could quote the Jewish Scriptures in support of his position. If the law/faith issue had already been raised by his "opponents," then a biblical counterargument would have been necessary for Paul to convince the Galatians of his beliefs.[55]

---

[53]Problems include uncertainty about the way Paul understood some of the passages he quotes and the fact that he leaves some of his premises unstated. For more on Paul's treatment of the biblical text in these verses, see Stanley, "Under a Curse," 497-507.

[54]For a review of the literature on v. 10, see Stanley, "Under a Curse," 481-86.

[55]While it is possible that Paul's "opponents" had already framed the relation

At the rhetorical level, the simple fact that Paul could quote the Jewish Scriptures in support of his views was more important than the precise verses that he chose to quote. Presumably there were people in the audience who, given time, could have inquired into Paul's handling of the biblical text in order to either refute it or explain it to the others in the congregation. But Paul was writing to shape the beliefs and actions of the entire audience, not to give the literate members of his churches something to study. By making his own statements as clear as possible (vv. 10a, 11a, 12a, 13a) and then quoting Scripture in support of his assertions (vv. 10b, 11b, 12b, 13b), Paul left the Galatians with a fairly clear presentation of his own ideas and the general impression that his views were firmly grounded in the Jewish Scriptures. What more could a first-century rhetor ask?

This cursory review has left much unsaid about about the way the quotations in vv. 10-13 work to advance the argument of Paul's letter to the Galatians. But the material presented thus far should give us a fairly good sense of the rhetorical power of these verses. We could of course follow Plato (or Socrates) in raising questions about the logical and moral value of using rhetorical arguments that cannot be rationally substantiated by the audience, as Paul appears to do in vv. 10-13. But Paul, like most of his contemporaries, shows no sign of being troubled by these concerns. Paul's rhetorical goal

---

between law and faith in a way that Paul deemed objectionable (e. g., that followers of Jesus should exhibit their faith by obeying God's laws), there is no evidence that they had used any of the verses that Paul cites in support of his position. On the other hand, it is equally possible that Paul himself first called attention to the law/faith issue as a fundamental problem with their position. It certainly would not be unusual for Paul to attack a concrete problem by underlining what he sees as the fundamental principle at stake—see Gal 1:6-9, 2:14-21, 5:2-4.

was to win the Galatians back from what he called "another gospel" (1:6), a set of ideas that in his view threatened to lead them back into slavery to the demonic forces they had once served. His letter shows that he was willing to use every rhetorical tool at his disposal to fulfill this God-given commission.

Apocalyptic *Ethos*

Greg Carey, Winthrop University

Stephen O'Leary has demonstrated that authority is an essential *topos* of apocalyptic argumentation.[1] Though based upon careful exegetical work on the Book of Revelation, the Millerite movement, and Hal Lindsey, this conclusion appears a logical necessity. Claims about the end of the world, the nature of heavenly and hellish realms, or the ultimate fate of human beings necessarily rely on revelatory experience or downright speculation; most hearers respond with skepticism. To a claim concerning "the things that must happen shortly" (Rev 1:1), the audience responds, "Who says so?" or, "How do you know?"[2] The answer can be an appeal to the speaker's character and experience.[3] "I was in the Spirit on the Lord's day" (Rev 1:10)," or "I saw, and behold, a door had opened in heaven" (Rev 4:1). Even apocalyptic interpretations of sacred texts depend upon the authoritative revelation behind the texts themselves.

Given the revolutionary potential of O'Leary's insights, it is appropriate to apply them to the larger body of early Jewish and Christian apocalyptic discourse. How did apocalyptic writers (and presumably, speakers) ground their claims? How did they construct their authority? These questions call for a comparative study of a wide variety of ancient texts. Such an investigation also demands an appropriate model for assessing authority in a diverse body of ancient and largely narrative texts, what I will call *"narrative ethos."*

---

[1] Stephen D. O'Leary, *Arguing the Apocalypse: A Theory of Millennial Rhetoric* (Oxford: Oxford University, 1994).

[2] Ibid., 203.

[3] At a secondary level, it may involve claims to a singularly valid interpretation of revealed texts.

Narrative *Ethos*

We may define *ethos* (ἦθος) as a speaker or author's self-representation in the attempt to earn an audience's trust and goodwill. *Ethos*, then, is an attempt to grasp power, the authority to represent oneself and the world in a given rhetorical situation.

The model of narrative *ethos* derives from three sources: the Greek and Latin rhetorical tradition and its modern interpreters, contemporary literary criticism, especially as it relates to point of view, and theories of postcolonial and resistance literature. The ancient rhetorical tradition carefully examined the persuasive power of a speaker's character, or *ethos*. Its insights would appear to be an appropriate starting point for a study of Greek apocalyptic literature, like the New Testament apocalyptic literature, *Hermas*, the *Apocalypse of Peter*, and the Christian *Sibyllines*. Helpful as it is, classical ethical theory has its limitations for a study of ancient apocalyptic discourse. A large body of apocalyptic literature would have little if any connection with the classical tradition, and even the Greek apocalypses are not speeches but narratives.[4] Contemporary literary theory addresses this problem through sophisticated analysis of how authors represent themselves and their experiences through narration. At the same time, postcolonial and resistance criticisms both enable cross-cultural awareness and heighten our awareness of the relationship between narration and authority, or power.

Greek and Latin Ethical Practice

Greek and Latin rhetorical theorists recognized that *ethos* was an essential element of persuasive speech.[5] While one may trace the development

---

[4] For this reason, the groundbreaking work by Bruce J. Malina and Jerome H. Neyrey (*Portraits of Paul: An Archaeology of Ancient Personality* [Louisville: Westminster John Knox, 1996]) has not been particularly helpful to this study. Apocalyptic discourse is rarely as direct about *ethos* as are the *encomia* and public defense speeches.

[5] Aristotle, *Rhet.* 1.2.3-4; 1.3.1; Cicero, *De. Or.* 2.114-15, 178-84; Quintilian, *Inst. Or.* 4.1.5-35; 6.2.8-19; 12.1.1-3; *Rhetorica ad Herennium* 1.5.8.

of *ethos* in ancient theory and practice,[6] for our purposes a synchronic approach may be more useful: How did speakers' characters contribute to their arguments in antiquity?

The following discussion of classical *ethos* draws upon two resources. The rhetorical handbooks offer systematic ethical theories, while Cicero's speeches exemplify actual practice. Few apocalyptic writers — much less their audiences — had ever heard of Aristotle's *Rhetoric* (edited about 341 BCE), Cicero's *De Oratore* (54 BCE), the *Rhetorica ad Herennium* (around 84 BCE), or Quintilian's *Institutio Oratoria* (around 94 CE).[7] But these texts reveal more than abstract theory produced by Greek and Roman elites. Occasions for public speech were part of daily life in the ancient Mediterranean. The handbooks represent what was commonly practiced in the public assemblies of the day.[8] To complement the handbooks, I have chosen one example of *ethos* in action: Cicero's political speeches, in which these techniques are clearly at work.[9] Cicero so well represents Latin oratory that Quintilian cited his name "not as the name of a man, but as the name of eloquence itself" (*Inst. Or.* 12.1.112).[10]

The handbooks agree that *ethos* performs an essential function in any speech act. Aristotle laid the groundwork for this view by naming *ethos* along with *logos*, an argument's rational force, and *pathos*, its emotional effect upon the audience, as the three categories of argumentative proof (πίστεις; *Rhet.*

---

[6] As does Jakob Wisse, *Ethos and Pathos from Aristotle to Cicero* (Amsterdam: Adolf M. Hakkert, 1989).

[7] Dates taken from George A. Kennedy, *Classical Rhetoric and Its Christian and Secular Tradition from Ancient to Modern Times* (Chapel Hill: University of North Carolina, 1980).

[8] *Rhet.* 1.1.1; *De Or.*, 1.32.46; *Inst. Or.* 1.10; *ad Her.* 1.1.1-1.2.2). Cf. Brian Vickers, *In Defence of Rhetoric* (Oxford: Clarendon, 1988) 1.

[9] From Cicero's huge body of work (twenty-eight volumes in the LCL) I have chosen to examine *Selected Political Speeches of Cicero* (ed. and trans. Michael Grant; rev. ed.; New York: Penguin, 1973). Citations include page numbers in Grant's edition.

[10] Cited in Kennedy, *Classical Rhetoric*, 102; cf. Vickers, *In Defence of Rhetoric*, 76-77.

1.2.3). Aristotle goes so far as to call *ethos* "the most effective means of proof" (1.2.4). Cicero agreed, saying not only that winning over the audience was one of the three sources of persuasion (*De Or.* 2.114-115), but also that it could be more compelling, "when agreeably and feelingly handled. . . , than the merits of the case" (2.184).

> Now nothing in oratory . . . is more important than to win for the orator the favor of his hearer, and to have the latter so affected as to be swayed by something resembling a mental impulse or emotion, rather than by judgement or deliberation. (*De Or.* 2.178)

Likewise, Quintilian subordinated logical proof as less effective than *ethos* and *pathos* as a means of convincing an audience.[11] Quintilian maintains that *ethos* (and here he uses the word) is most effective in "making it seem that all that we say derives directly from the nature of the facts and persons concerned and in the revelation of the character[12] of the orator in such a way that all may recognise it" (6.2.13). In Quintilian's system, an appeal to *ethos* is absolutely necessary when moral character[13] is at issue (6.2.17).

Our synchronic approach to *ethos* should acknowledge an important conceptual shift that occurred between Greek and Latin understandings of *ethos*.[14] While Greek *ethos* emphasizes the content of the speech itself, Latin *ethos* is more concerned with the broader rhetorical situation.[15] Factors such

---

[11] Cited (but with an incorrect reference to *Inst. Or.* 5.19.29-31) in Vickers, *Defence of Rhetoric*, 77. The correct reference is 5.14.29-31.

[12] *Mores*, the word which, according to Quintilian, usually translates ἦθως (6.2.8-9).

[13] *Mores* again.

[14] The distinction between Greek and Latin approaches to *ethos* is by no means neat or absolute. Latin rhetoric was heavily influenced by Aristotle, Isocrates, and other Greek figures, and the Greek tradition was by no means univocal. Still, the distinction does provide heuristic value for understanding how ethical theory developed over time.

[15] Wisse, *Ethos and Pathos*; Richard Leo Enos and Karen Rossi Schnakenberg, "Cicero Latinizes Hellenic *Ethos*," in **Ethos: *New Essays in Rhetorical and Critical Theory*** (SMU Studies in Composition and Rhetoric; ed. James S. Baumlin and Tita French Baumlin;

as the speaker's reputation and the mood of the audience become increasingly important. This theoretical distinction has practical implications for how we read apocalyptic literature. Aristotle's more intratextual approach will be appropriate for most of the apocalypses, which are pseudonymous, while Paul's apocalyptic *ethos* is more clearly linked to an elusive word of extratextual relationships.

Despite the distinction between Greek and Latin ethical theory, several common motifs run throughout ancient rhetorical practice. These themes provide the background against which to assess ancient apocalyptic discourse.

1. Speakers sought to identify themselves as persons of *virtue, knowledge, and pure motives*. These values, modified from Aristotle's trilogy of good sense, virtue, and goodwill (*Rhet.* 2.1.5), may be variously expressed but are common among all the handbooks. Virtue and pure motives are most prominent in the tradition, as Aristotle argued that the moral purpose of a speech should be clear in order to establish the speaker's character (*Rhet.* 2.21.16; 3.16.8). The Latin handbooks share a concern that speakers ought to remind audiences of their meritorious service in the past (*Ad Her.* 1.8; 3.6.10-12; *De Or.* 2.182; *Inst. Or.* 4.1.7; 6.2.13). At the same time, they argue that speakers do well who demonstrate that they are speaking not out of greed or hope of glory but due to duty, friendship, patriotism, or some other altruistic motivation. It is even desirable that speakers should express their own reluctance to take the floor in the first place (*Ad Her.* 3.6.10-12; *De Or.* 2.182; *Inst. Or.* 4.1.7-10). Virtue and proper motives come together when one speaks from a sense of moral obligation:

> For as everything treated by the orator may be regarded from the ethical standpoint, we may apply the word *ethos* whenever he speaks of what is honourable and expedient or of what ought or ought not to be done. (*Inst. Or.* 6.2.11)

By linking them to religious rhetoric, Cicero exemplifies the importance of pure motives. Not only does he frequently praise the gods, he often identifies himself with their favor and authority. The gods direct Cicero (108;

Dallas: Southern Methodist University, 1994) 191-209.

119); he appeals to them frequently (69; 93; 109; 126); his efforts cooperate with their love for Rome (110; 120-21); and his opponents are their enemies (121-22). Such a pious man must surely be working from pure motivations. He thinks of Rome before he thinks of himself (142). He represents peace rather than war (108), seeking reconciliation for his enemies (102). He holds pity for his enemies rather than hate (84), and though he is fearful he remains faithful to his duty (85; 135; 217; 318). He serves Rome even at the risk of his own life (87, 99, 136-39, 144), but he turns down opportunities for glory and power (69). All he asks is that the people keep his memory (144).

Cicero confirms his virtuous intentions through crisis rhetoric. Like the apocalyptic visionaries, Cicero portrayed himself as intervening at critical moments, envisioning grand destruction and wrapping it in the rhetoric of ultimacy.

> And yet I also have a vision of this city, the light of the world and the stronghold of every nation, suddenly plunged into all-engulfing flames. I see, in my mind's eye, our country reduced to a graveyard. I see the corpses of unburied citizens lying in miserable heaps. . . . I shudder at the wails of mothers, the panic flight of girls and boys, the rape of Vestal Virgins. (137)

As Ch. Perelman and L. Olbrechts-Tyteca point out, the urgent — the unique, the precarious, and the irremediable — is a rhetorical commonplace (*topos*) sure to get attention.[16] While the primary effects of crisis rhetoric relate to *pathos*, there is also an ethical dimension: The speaker is represented as someone who is speaking from pure motives, someone who must be heard because she or he is addressing important issues.

Among virtue, knowledge, and pure motives, the least discussed of these is knowledge, though the handbooks agree that speakers ought to be broadly educated (cf. *Ad Her.* 1.2; *Inst. Or.* 12.2.1-10). The need for knowledge among orators may be the primary concern in Cicero's *De Oratore*:

---

[16] *The New Rhetoric: A Treatise on Argumentation* (Notre Dame: University of Notre Dame, 1969) 91-92. Aristotle would call this the *topos* of magnitude (*Rhet.* 2.19.26-27).

> No man can be an orator complete in all points of merit, who has not
> obtained a knowledge of all important subjects and arts. For it is from
> knowledge that oratory must derive its beauty and fullness, and unless
> there is such knowledge, well-grasped and comprehended by the
> speaker, there must be something empty and almost childish in the
> utterance. (*De Or.* 1.20)

Speakers in the hellenistic world sought to present themselves as persons who
could be trusted because of their exemplary character, command over the
subject matter, and blameless motivation.

    2. Ancient rhetorical theorists approached *ethos* with *caution*. They
advised speakers to construct *ethos* with great care; after all, boasting would
be a sign of ὕβρις, one of the most despised personality traits in the hellenistic
world. This caution is related to the issue of proper motivation as well, since
judicial and deliberative speeches were not primarily meant to glorify the
speaker. So Cicero advocates a gentle style as an indication of goodwill (*De
Or.* 2.129) and modesty in approach (2.182).[17] And in *De Partitione Oratoria*
Cicero suggests that both praise and blame are achieved through narrative
rather than propositional argument, thus "gently influencing the emotions"
(71). As the *Rhetorica ad Herennium* demands self-praise without arrogance
(1.8) and Quintilian forgoes pride and elevated rhetoric (*Inst. Or.* 6.2.19), we
see the dilemma the ancient speaker faced: How does one praise oneself
without sounding boastful? Aristotle hints that building *ethos* is actually a sly
operation:

> And you should at once introduce yourself and your adversary as being
> of a certain character, that the hearers may regard you or him as such;
> *but do not let it be seen.* (Λανθάνων δὲ ποίει; *Rhet.* 3.16.10, emphasis
> mine)

As an indirect means of building *ethos*, Aristotle suggests mentioning
witnesses. If by speaking too well of oneself the speaker may incite envy —

---

[17] As we shall see below, in practice Cicero's "modesty" is often what we might call
audacity.

or even outright contradiction! — perhaps "we must make another speak in our place" (*Rhet.* 3.17.16).

Sure enough, Cicero avoids being overly arrogant by appealing to witnesses.[18] The city held a special day in recognition of his suppression of Catalina. These honors he did not confer upon himself; instead, they were granted by others, even the very audience he is addressing.

> In the first place, you expressed gratitude to myself in superlative terms, and declared that it was my courage and energy which enabled the machinations of these traitors to be revealed. . . . And above all you decreed a thanksgiving in my name, an honour which no man acting in a civil capacity had ever been awarded before.[19]

3. The handbooks all agree: *ethos* applies to speakers as well as their *opponents* (*Rhet.* 3.19.1; 3.17.16; *Ad Her.* 1.8; *De Or.* 2.182;).[20] Speakers are to discuss their opponents' past conduct, habits, character traits, and motivations, simply using the same techniques they would employ in praising themselves (*Inst. Or.* 4.1.14-15).

4. Complementing the emphasis on opponents, *vivid characterization* was a prominent feature of ancient stylistics. Though this characteristic stands in some tension with the tentative nature of ancient ethical theory, speakers and writers desired εναργείας, the vivid sort of description that places things "before the eyes," and which was especially useful against one's enemies. A characteristic of ancient literary theory in general (Pseudo-Demetrius, *On Style* 208-22; Aristotle, *Poet.* 17.1; Longinus, *On the Sublime* 15.1), it was effectively appropriated by the rhetorical tradition (*Rhet.* 1.9-10; 3.16.10; *Inst.*

---

[18] This claim runs the risk of oversimplification, as Cicero could also characterize himself as a person of superhuman vigilance and skill. To Catalina he says, "No single thing you do, nothing you attempt or even contemplate, escapes my notice" *(Political Speeches*, 79).

[19] *Political Speeches*, 132. In an earlier speech Cicero reminds the audience of what the thanksgiving said: "because I had saved the city from the flames, the citizens from massacre and Italy from war" (118).

[20] According to *Ad Her.* (1.8) and Quintilian (*Inst. Or.* 4.1.16), goodwill may also be obtained through discussing one's audience (1.8).

Or. 4.1.15).[21] Cicero advised speakers to "paint their characters in words" (*De Or.* 2.184; cf. 3.202), and even Quintilian approved of exaggeration in characterization (*Inst. Or.* 4.1.15).

In the *Rhetorica ad Herennium* we find lengthy discussions of Portrayal, representing a person's bodily form, Character Delineation,[22] the depiction of someone's distinctive traits, Dialogue, imitation of a person's speech, and Personification,[23] which among other things is "representing an absent person as present" (4.63-66). Ancient characterization tended to identify a subject with a single attribute,[24] making Character Delineation especially valuable as a means of exposing a person's ruling passion in the public light:

> Character Delineations of this kind which describe the qualities proper to each man's nature carry very great charm, for they set before our eyes a person's whole character . . . in short, by such delineation any one's ruling passion can be brought into the open. (*Ad Her.* 4.65)

Though much of what Cicero does would offend modern rhetorical tastes, these speeches reveal how *ethos* served polemic purposes. Most striking is the contrast between contemporary standards of restraint and the intensity characteristic of ancient polemics, particularly among philosophers

---

[21] Beth Innocenti ("Towards a Theory of Vivid Description as Practiced in Cicero's *Verrine* Orations," *Rhetorica* 12 [1994]) argues that vivid description does not receive full theoretical treatment in the Latin handbooks, then goes on to fill in the gaps by connecting the references from the handbooks themselves. In my opinion, the treatment in *Ad Her.* is indeed systematic.

[22] ἠθοποιία in the Greek tradition according to Harry Caplan, the translator of the LCL edition of *Ad Her.* Cf. *De Or.* 3.204.

[23] According to Caplan, προσοποιία in the Greek tradition.

[24] The most famous examples might be Theophrastus' *Character Sketches* and Homer's Achilles (cf. Robert Scholes and Robert Kellogg, *The Nature of Narrative* [Oxford: Oxford University, 1966] 88, 161-65). Aristotle argues for the persuasive power of drawing upon "what is specially characteristic of yourself or of the adversary" (*Rhet.* 3.16.10).

and religionists.[25] Though Luke T. Johnson generalizes that, "Abuse tends to gain in volume when it is powerless,"[26] Cicero could be extremely vicious in states of relative power as well as weakness.

Cicero could adapt a mild tone when speaking of his opponents (302), but his vivid characterization often takes the form of demonization and debasement.[27] He freely sketches his opponent's motives, often associating them with debauchery. His characterization of Catalina provides one example:

> For imagine every type of criminality and wickedness that you can think of; he is behind them all. In the whole of Italy there is not one single poisoner, gladiator, robber, assassin, parricide, will-forger, cheat, glutton, wastrel, adulterer, prostitute, corrupter of youth, or youth who has been corrupted, indeed any nasty individual of any kind whatever, who would not be obliged to admit he has been Catalina's intimate. (97)

The ultimate result of such characterization is a kind of dualism: Cicero represents the side of good against absolute evil (e.g., *Political Speeches*, 234). Cicero goes on, recounting Catalina's sexual offenses:

> Not one single act of filthy lechery has been committed without him being its guiding spirit. For no one has had such a talent for seducing young men. He himself became the lover of a number of them, in the

---

[25] Luke Timothy Johnson, "The New Testament's Anti-Jewish Slander and the Conventions of Ancient Polemic," *JBL* 108 (1989) 430-41; cf. Peder Borgen, "Polemic in the Book of Revelation," in *Anti-Semitism and Early Christianity* (ed. Craig A. Evans and Donald A. Hagner; Minneapolis: Fortress, 1993) 199-211; and Sean Freyne, "Vilifying the Other and Defining the Self: Matthew's and John's Anti-Jewish Polemic in Focus," in *"To See Ourselves as Others See Us": Christians, Jews, "Others" in Late Antiquity* (ed. Jacob Neusner and Ernest S. Frerichs; Scholars Press Studies in the Humanities; Chico, CA: Scholars Press, 1985) 117-143. It is evident from Cicero's speeches that at least in the Rome of the late Republic extremely serious charges were a comm on means of rhetorical and legal attack.

[26] Johnson, "Anti-Jewish Slander," 424.

[27] I have adapted debasement as a rhetorical category from David Spurr, *The Rhetoric of Empire: Colonial Discourse in Journalism, Travel Writing, and Imperial Administration* (Post-Contemporary Interventions; Durham, NC: Duke University, 1993).

most repulsive fashion; and he disgustingly allowed others to make love to himself. (97)[28]

Such simplicity combined with vividness is the mark of ancient characterization, a feature we should expect to find applied to speakers and especially to their opponents.

5. Though Cicero argued that *ethos* should be constructed throughout the speech (*De Or.* 2.184), most theorists especially identified *ethos* with the *beginning and end* of speeches.[29] (We will note below that Cicero's own speeches concentrate *ethos* heavily in the *exordium*, narration, and epilogue.) Sometimes *ethos* is covered in discussions of arrangement, as is the case for Aristotle (*Rhet.* 3.14.7; 3.19.1) and the *Rhetorica ad Herennium* (1.8; 2.50). Quintilian exemplifies this tension between *ethos* as it works throughout an address and *ethos* concentrated in beginnings and endings. Though he locates *ethos* in his discourse on the exordium (*Inst. Or.* 4.1.7-29), he acknowledges that *ethos* is continuous, relevant whenever one speaks of what is right or expedient (6.2.10-11). While *ethos* is embedded in the entire text, we should be particularly alert to beginnings and endings.

Narrators in Literary Theory

Ancient apocalyptic discourse occurs in narrative form or presupposes narratives concerning revelatory experiences. Sophisticated as ancient ethical theory was, it lacked systematic attention to the ethical dimension of narration. Fortunately, the movement of literary criticism toward more rhetorical

---

[28] To desire sexual penetration by a social inferior was regarded as dishonorable in the Greek world (John J. Winkler, *The Constraints of Desire: The Anthropology of Sex and Gender in Ancient Greece* [New Ancient World Series; New York: Routledge, 1990] 46-54) and probably among Romans as well (Dale B. Martin, "Heterosexism and the Interpretation of Romans 1:18-32," *BibInt* 3 [1995] 344-46).

[29] Edward P. J. Corbett maintains that though *ethos* must be sustained throughout a speech, the introduction and conclusion are especially important (*Classical Rhetoric for the Modern Student* [2nd ed.; New York: Oxford University, 1971] 95).

concerns over the past three decades[30] has renewed interest in the narrating voice. Who tells a story? How does this narrator establish relationships to the story being told and to its characters, as well as to the audience?

These questions have often been assigned to the literary-critical category of point of view. But they need not be restricted to the formalist context with which they are often associated, a setting in which texts are detached from their historical contexts and audiences.[31] Instead, point of view may serve as a rhetorical category, a means of analyzing a narrative's *ethos* through the voices which present it. Particular attention should be devoted to the formal

---

[30] Wayne C. Booth's *The Rhetoric of Fiction* (2nd ed.; Chicago: University of Chicago, 1983 [1961]) may have been the catalyst for the revival of rhetorical modes of literary criticism. For general announcements and retrospectives on this trend, see Susan R. Suleiman, "Introduction: Varieties of Audience-Oriented Criticism," in *The Reader in the Text: Essays on Audience and Interpretation* (ed. Susan R. Suleiman and Inge Crosman; Princeton: Princeton University, 1980) 7-11; Jane P. Tompkins, "The Reader in History: The Changing Shape of Literary Response," in *Reader-Response Criticism: From Formalism to Post-Structuralism* (ed. Jane P. Tompkins; Baltimore: Johns Hopkins University, 1980) 201-26; Terry Eagleton, *Literary Theory: An Introduction* (Minneapolis: University of Minnesota, 1983) 203-12; and Bryan C. Short, "Literary *Ethos*: Dispersion, Resistance, Mystification," in ***Ethos***: *New Essays in Rhetorical and Literary Theory* (SMU Studies in Composition and Rhetoric; ed. James S. Baumlin and Tita French Baumlin; Dallas: Southern Methodist University, 1994) 367.

[31] The Bible and Culture Collective (*The Postmodern Bible* [New Haven: Yale University, 1995] 84-85) associates point of view and critics such as Wayne C. Booth with formalism, neglecting Booth's own self-identification with ethical (in the sense of values and morals) and rhetorical criticism. They do not mention the use of point of view as a category for feminist and ideological criticisms, as in the case of Susan Snaider Lanser, whose works do not appear in their impressive bibliography. Booth and Lanser are critical figures for my own approach to *ethos* through narrative criticism. It is ironic that the Collective neglects this category's potential for postmodern and liberating practice, since Michel Foucault's work on the power of looking and writing is a prominent feature of much postmodern criticism (cf. Edward W. Said, *Orientalism* [New York: Random House, 1978]; Spurr, *Rhetoric of Empire*, 11).

apocalypses, which authorize their messages through the *ethoi* of their visionary narrators.

Wayne C. Booth's *The Rhetoric of Fiction* renewed interest in narration in the 1960s and provided a systematic analysis of point of view.[32] Booth contends that novels are produced for certain rhetorical ends. The narrator is the agent employed by the implied author (direct access to the real author being impossible) to carry out the story's tasks.[33] The reader, then, depends upon the narrator for his or her experience of the story. In general, he or she learns only what the narrator reveals and perceives characters and events as mediated by the narrator's point of view. Booth is not so naive as to overlook the possibility of and need for resisting readers; nevertheless, even those readers begin with their experience of the text as narrated.[34]

Booth's project implies a thorough study of the various modes of narration. The categories he provides include: (a) person; (b) dramatized or undramatized narration; (c) narrators as observers or as agents; (d) scene or summary narration; (e) commentary; (f) self-consciousness in narrating or the lack thereof; (g) distance (intellectual, moral, spatial, or temporal) between the narrator and the author, reader, or the characters, a category which encompasses reliability and unreliability; (h) isolation (being unsupported or uncorrected by other narrators) or its opposite; (i) privilege or limitation in knowledge; and (j) depth and axis of inside views of characters.[35]

---

[32] *The Rhetoric of Fiction* (2nd ed.; Chicago: University of Chicago, 1983 [1961]).

[33] The distinction between implied author and narrator is not entirely appropriate to Revelation, since the two figures amount to almost the same character.

[34] Booth calls this process surrendering to the text (*The Company We Keep: An Ethics of Fiction* [Berkeley: University of California, 1989] 32), a task which must be performed even in the act of resisting it (257). For example, according to Jonathan Culler: "The practicioner of deconstruction works within the terms of the system in order to breach it" (*On Deconstruction: Theory and Criticism after Structuralism* [Ithaca: Cornell University, 1982] 86).

[35] "Distance and Point-of-View: An Essay in Classification," *Essays in Criticism* 11 (1961) 60-79. This article is an expanded version of Chapter Six of *Rhetoric of Fiction*.

For our purposes, the critical thing is not so much where apocalyptic narrators might fit into all these fields, but how these categories might enlighten our reconstruction of apocalyptic *ethos*. Most apocalyptic visionaries are first-person, dramatized narrator-agents who: use scene more than summary; are frequently self-conscious; maintain various degrees of moral and intellectual distance from their audience and characters; are sometimes corrected and frequently supported by other voices; are extremely privileged; and almost never provide deep views of their characters. Each of these factors provides insight into how apocalypses win their audiences' trust.

Distance between narrator and audience is a critical factor in apocalyptic discourse, and it lies at the heart of Kenneth Burke's *A Rhetoric of Motives*. Burke argues that identification is a common factor in all attempts to form attitudes or induce actions.[36] By identifying themselves with their audiences' prejudices, writers and speakers may enlist them in a "partnership" of interest. Speakers may invite audiences to identify with their goals and values, or they may identify their opponents with symbols which will repulse their audiences. Quoting Augustine's *De Doctrina Christiana*, Burke suggests that a person is persuaded who:

> likes what you promise, fears what you say is imminent, hates what you censure, embraces what you commend, regrets whatever you built up as regrettable, rejoices at what you say is cause for rejoicing, sympathizes with those whose wretchedness your words bring before his very eyes, shuns those whom you admonish him to shun . . . and in whatever other ways your high eloquence can affect the minds of your hearers, bringing them not merely to know what should be done, but to do what they know should be done.[37]

Susan Snaider Lanser's project is similar to Booth's in that she works to identify how narrative techniques serve rhetorical ends. But she develops a more complex multi-dimensional scheme for assessing the possibilities for

---

[36] *A Rhetoric of Motives* (Berkeley: University of California, 1969 [1950]).

[37] Ibid., 50, quoting Augustine, *On Christian Doctrine*, 4.12.

narration, a framework couched less in alternative terms (e.g., dramatized versus undramatized narrators) than in positions on relative poles (e.g., degree of privilege). And Lanser is more engaged in a specific mode of ideological analysis: she wants to know how gender interacts with authorial authority.[38]

Lanser employs speech act theory as a means of assessing narration: fictions seek to perform specific actions.[39] This reading strategy tends to close the distance between author and audience, as every aspect of a text is the author's ideological product.[40] Unless a text indicates otherwise, the narrator is directly identified with the implied author.[41] The goal is to assess ideology at work in various levels and kinds of narration, "the act of using language . . . defined, constrained and conventionalized according to a system of values, norms, and perceptions of the world."[42]

Lanser divides the modalities of narration into three categories: status, contact, and stance. Each of these fields includes many more sub-groups, too many to be summarized here. *Status* pertains to the narrator's qualifications: his or her identity, credibility, sincerity, and skill. This category somewhat resembles Aristotelian *ethos*, and it addresses the narrator's representation as a person who knows what she or he is talking about. The difference is that Lanser is describing fiction rather than prescribing rhetoric: she does not judge more knowledge or skill as necessarily better than less. *Contact* involves the narrator's relationship to an audience, a concern similar to that of the Latin tradition. Is the narrator self-conscious, confident, formal? Does she address the audience directly and show respect for them? *Stance* reflects the narrator's perspective toward the message, including her or his ideological and

---

[38] *The Narrative Act: Point of View in Prose Fiction* (Princeton: Princeton University, 1981); *Fictions of Authority: Women Writers and Narrative Voice* (Ithaca: Cornell University, 1992).

[39] *Narrative Act*, 67-73.

[40] Cf. ibid., 18, 32, 64.

[41] Ibid., 151; *Fictions of Authority*, 16.

[42] *Narrative Act*, 64.

psychological point of view. Of course, narrators may employ the points at which their stance coincides with the audiences' as a step toward transforming the audiences' view on other matters.[43] On the other hand, narrators who seem particularly concerned with their audiences' response, or who go out of their way to defend themselves, may lack confidence that their messages will be well-received.[44]

Booth and Lanser enable us to make careful discriminations concerning how apocalyptic narrators construct *ethos*. What do they know, and what do they tell? How do they align their perceptions with those of God and their audiences? How do their angles of vision manipulate their audiences' perception of them and their opponents? When we ask questions like these, we enhance our understanding of apocalyptic *ethos*.

Narrative Authority in Theories of Resistance Literature

A large body of apocalyptic literature reflects concerns with imperial domination. Relationships of domination and resistance lie at the heart of postcolonial and resistance literature and theory. Such discourses share an assumption with the rhetorical tradition and the literary theorists we have reviewed above: Textual strategies reflect and affect social and political conditions and behaviors. "Worlds exist by means of languages," according to one team of postcolonial critics,[45] and the textual construction of worlds is a site of struggle.[46] Resistance literatures tend to reject aesthetic understandings of literature,[47] arguing that technology is politics, technique is ideology in action. "Postcolonial criticism bears witness to the unequal and

---

[43] Ibid., 216-17. Cf. Burke, *Rhetoric of Motives*, 46; Perelman and Olbrechts-Tyteca, *New Rhetoric*, 320.

[44] *Narrative Act*, 178. Cf. Booth, *Rhetoric of Fiction*, 179.

[45] Bill Ashcroft, Gareth Griffiths, and Helen Tiffin, *The Empire Writes Back: Theory and Practice in Post-Colonial Literatures* (New Accents; New York: Routledge, 1989) 44.

[46] Barbara Harlow, *Resistance Literature* (New York: Methuen, 1987) 2.

[47] Ibid., 40.

uneven forces of cultural representation involved in the contest for political and social authority within the modern world order."[48]

The practice of narration is especially important to postcolonial critics like the Nigerian author/critic Chinua Achebe. In his reading of *Heart of Darkness*, Achebe holds Joseph Conrad responsible for his first-person narrator, Marlow, who is a vehicle for "the dehumanization of Africa and Africans."[49]

But if Conrad's intention is to draw a *cordon sanitaire* between himself and the moral and psychological malaise of his narrator, his care seems to me totally wasted because he neglects to hint however subtly or tentatively at an alternative frame of reference by which we may judge the actions or opinions of his characters. It would not have been beyond Conrad's power to make that provision if he had found it necessary.[50]

By contrast, Achebe's own novels employ narration as a liberating practice. Achebe, like other postcolonial writers, uses fiction as a means of critique toward relations of domination.[51] His novel *Things Fall Apart*, the first of four novels which represent Nigeria in successive stages of colonialism and independence,[52] presents a complex but coherent portrait of an Ibo culture before contact with European colonizers as well as a representation of the Europeans themselves. He often uses inside views of characters to demonstrate African ambivalence toward Europeans and vice versa. For example, a first encounter with white missionary preaching leads one village

---

[48] Homi K. Bhabha, "Postcolonial Criticism," in *Redrawing the Boundaries: The Transformation of English and American Literary Studies* (ed. Stephen Greenblatt and Giles Gunn; New York: Modern Language Association of America, 1992) 437.

[49] "An Image of Africa," *Massachusetts Review* 18 (1977) 788.

[50] Ibid., 787.

[51] Cf. Harlow, *Resistance Literature*, 36-37; Ashcroft, Griffiths, and Tiffin, *The Empire Writes Back*, 32-33.

[52] *Things Fall Apart* (African Writers Series 1; Postmouth, NH: Heinemann, 1962 [1958]).

leader to conclude that the Europeans are crazy, while his son sits captivated.[53] These inside views are a rich resource for parody and irony; many of Achebe's Europeans believe they embody liberal or progressive values even though they actually slander Ibo culture. While one European administrator reflects on his bringing civilization to Africa, he plans a book: *The Pacification of the Primitive Tribes of the Lower Niger.*[54] His plan provides the novel's last words just as it expresses Achebe's salient conviction: Books function within and contribute to relations of domination and resistance. Narration, the power to represent oneself and the world, is always an act of power; the relationship between writing about and being written about is one of domination.[55] Moreover, given enough emphasis and time, representation becomes "reality."[56]

Because resistance theorists take seriously the power of representation, they work to destabilize the apparent monolithic authority of narrators, reporters, and so forth. Gayatri Chakravorty Spivak uses deconstruction to identify "traces" left over in what seem to be self-contained descriptions. The idea is that when one group characterizes itself as superior to another, it is often avoiding its own vulnerability.[57] And David Spurr's rhetoric of colonial journalism and travel writing reveals that their representation of colonial subjects represents an attempt to cover European insecurity.[58] Booth and Lanser share this sentiment: When narrators go to great lengths to demonstrate

---

[53] Ibid., 101-04.

[54] Ibid., 148.

[55] Cf. Edward Said, *Orientalism* (New York: Random House, 1978) 32, 308; "The World, the Text, and the Critic," in *Critical Theory Since Plato* (ed. Hazard Adams; rev. ed.; Fort Worth: Harcourt Brace Jovanovich, 1992) 1218. Both Said and David Spurr (*Rhetoric of Empire*) rely heavily upon Michel Foucault for their perspectives.

[56] Cf. Edward Said, "Orientalism Reconsidered," *Cultural Critique* 1 (1985) 92.

[57] *In Other Worlds: Essays in Cultural Politics* (New York: Routledge, 1988) 46.

[58] *Rhetoric of Empire.*

control over the subject matter, they likely betray anxiety for their own authority.[59]

Counter-discourses such as postcolonial and resistance literatures struggle against appropriating the *ethos* of the imperial center.[60] Though asserting difference from the center may be an effective rhetorical device,[61] difference always defines itself by what it excludes.[62] The danger is "counter-determination," the symmetry between a resistance discourse and that which it seeks to decenter.[63] When some apocalyptic discourses demonize political powers, they replicate the imperial *ethos*.

Results

Ancient ethical theory, literary criticism on narration, and postcolonial and resistance theories contribute to a multidimensional model of narrative *ethos*. Greek and Roman ethical conventions provide a primary context against which to read apocalyptic *ethos*. To my knowledge, however, ancient Greek and Latin critics did not discuss narrative voice much, and not at all in terms of authority. Contemporary literary critics do, and some of them connect what would seem to be stylistic insights on point of view with acute ethical and ideological analysis. Moreover, postcolonial and resistance discourses identify

---

[59] Lanser, *Narrative Act*, 178; Booth, *Rhetoric of Fiction*, 179.

[60] This theme permeates Ashcroft, Griffiths, and Tiffin, *Empire Writes Back*. Cf. Linda Hutcheon, *The Politics of Postmodernism* (New Accents; New York: Routledge, 1989), for the thesis that one is always implicated in the object of criticism, what she calls "complicitous critique." Richard Terdiman argues that "counter-discourses are always interlocked with the domination they contest" (*Discourse/Counter-Discourse: The Theory and Practice of Symbolic Resistance in Nineteenth-Century France* [Ithaca: Cornell University, 1985] 16).

[61] Cf. Harlow, *Resistance Literature*, 29; Neil ten Kortenaar, "Beyond Authenticity and Creolization: Reading Achebe Writing Culture," *PMLA* 110 (1995) 41.

[62] Terdiman, *Discourse/Counter-Discourse*, 278.

[63] Ashcroft, Griffiths, and Tiffin, *Empire Writes Back*, 170.

narrative voice with power, and they question whether and how representation can be liberative. These resources lead to a model of narrative *ethos*, a vehicle for examining how apocalyptic writers constructed their authority to be heard. Their works are assertions of power, attempts to reconfigure themselves, their audiences, and the world.

Ethos in Apocalyptic Discourse

Apocalyptic literature and motifs thrived among Jews and Christians. The literature ranges from revelations of historical salvation to tours of otherworldly realms, and it emerges from concerns as varied as apostasy, oppression, theodicy, and dissent. Despite the variety within the literature, with complex lines of dependence and innovation, certain consistent *topoi* emerge.[64] The question is not literary dependence but the conventions available to apocalyptic writers and their audiences. Specifically, how do the Jewish apocalyptic texts construct *ethos*? And how did first century Christians employ apocalyptic to authorize their own messages?

1. The most prominent and universal means of achieving apocalyptic *ethos* was *pseudonymity*, "a constant feature of Jewish apocalypses."[65] Almost all apocalypses (those defined as members of the genre) claim to report visions of venerable figures of the distant past, especially persons with mystical associations like Enoch, Moses, Baruch, Isaiah, Daniel, Peter, and Paul. That "Enoch walked with God — and then he was not, for God took him" (Gen 5:24) was ample cause for mystical and even eschatological speculation. And Moses, an authoritative figure through the Exodus and his reception of the Torah, had other apocalyptic credentials. Not only had he heard God's voice, he had even seen God (Exod 34:6-9). In addition, God had once ambushed Moses with the intent to kill him (Exod 4:24). God had promised safety to Baruch "wherever you might go," even in the midst of worldwide judgment

---

[64] The *ethos* of the Jewish and Christian *Sibylline Oracles* differs greatly from the vast majority of apocalyptic texts.

[65] John J. Collins, *The Apocalyptic Imagination: An Introduction to the Jewish Matrix of Christianity* (New York: Crossroad, 1984) 211.

(Jer 45:5). But the book of Jeremiah does not tell us where Baruch finally settled, thus making him a fitting object of mystical speculation. Daniel appears to have been a legendary figure associated with wisdom and righteousness, as in Ezekiel (14:14; 28:3) and the Ugaritic tale of Aqhat.[66] Within the Christian literature, Isaiah had received the vision of God's throne, Peter had been present during Jesus' transfiguration and apocalyptic discourses, and Paul had traveled to the third heaven. Other figures who had mystical associations and became "authors" of apocalyptic literature include Adam, Shem, Abraham, and Elijah.

We can only guess whether the first audiences of *1 Enoch* or Daniel considered the names on their title pages to represent their authentic authorship. We can conclude, however, that pseudonymity played a necessary role in these texts' self-representation. Pseudonymity is so universal among ancient apocalypses as to be listed among their defining characteristics.[67] Yet despite its widespread occurence, little has been done to identify the role of pseudonymity toward the rhetorical effect of ancient apocalypses.

Kenneth Burke's rhetoric of identification may provide a clue as to pseudonymity's contribution to apocalyptic rhetoric.[68] By identifying apocalypses with legendary figures, their authors sought instant identification with authoritative mystical traditions. In some cases, pseudonymity automatically offers the audience a sense of the author's character. By the time *1 Enoch* had approached its present form, Enoch, never a developed character

---

[66] Ibid., 69.

[67] Philipp Vielhauer and Georg Strecker list pseudonymity first among the fixed features of Jewish apocalypses ("Apocalypses and Related Subjects: Introduction," in *New Testament Apocrypha. Volume Two: Writings Related to the Apostles; Apocalypses and Related Subjects* [rev. ed.; ed. Wilhelm Schneemelcher; trans. R. McL. Wilson; Louisville: Westminster/John Knox, 1994] 545), while Klaus Koch listed it among the six typical features of apocalypses (*The Rediscovery of Apocalyptic* [SBT 22; Naperville, IL: Alec R. Allenson, 1972] 26).

[68] *Rhetoric of Motives*, 46. For Lanser, this device would enable more intimate contact with the audience.

in the Hebrew Bible, had become a *topos* of speculation: "Enoch pleased the Lord, and was transformed, as an example of repentance to the nations" (Sir 44:16). And, "No one has been created upon the earth the like of Enoch, for he was taken up from the earth" (Sir 49:14).

2. *Legends* concerning an apocalypse's implied author or the origin of its revelation provided a second standard apocalyptic ethical technique. The case of Daniel is the best-known example, but many other apocalypses narrate how pious persons receive supernatural revelation. Several apocalypses, including *2 Baruch*, *3 Baruch*, and *4 Ezra*, depict how sincerely their protagonists mourn Jerusalem's fate. Fasting and prayer mark their preparation for the mystical experience, as it does for Daniel (6:10-13; 9:3-21) and for Enoch (*1 Enoch* 12-13; 39:9-14; 84).[69]

As a result of their prayer and fasting, visionaries often receive words of divine commendation. After Daniel's prayer of confession, he learns his special vocation:

> Daniel, I have now come forth to instruct you in wisdom. At the beginning of your prayer a word came forth, so I came to announce it to you; for you are the chosen person (Dan 9:22-23, LXX; cf. 10:11, 19).[70]

Likewise, Hermas, who is continually fasting and confessing his sins, receives commendation for his piety (e.g., 2:4; 7:2; 9:1-9; 22:4; 112:2).

Particularly flattering to the protagonists is the narration of their intercession on behalf of the people. This device demonstrates their intimacy with God and access to divine knowledge. *Fourth Ezra* is perhaps the finest example of this process, though we may observe similar devices in *1 Enoch*,

---

[69] Christopher Rowland (*The Open Heaven: A Study of Apocalyptic in Judaism and Early Christianity* [New York: Crossroad, 1982] 215-31) argues that apocalyptic visions probably did follow preparation by meditation and fasting.

[70] Both Theodotian's Greek (ἀνήρ ἐπιθυμιῶν σὺ εἶ) and the Hebrew (ητ) τωδωμξ) are syntactically problematic. Cf. Paul Joüon, *A Grammar of Biblical Hebrew* [Subsidia Biblica 14; 2 vols.; trans. and rev. T. Muraoka; Rome: Editrice Pontificio Istituto Biblico, 1991] §136e); and BDF §165.

Daniel, *2 Baruch*, and *3 Baruch*.[71] Much of *Fourth Ezra* is structured as a dialogue: Ezra intercedes with God on Israel's behalf.

> I was troubled as I lay on my bed, and my thoughts welled up in my heart, because I saw the desolation of Zion and the wealth of those who lived in Babylon. My spirit was greatly agitated, and I began to speak anxious words to the Most High . . . (3:1-3).[72]

In reply, God sends Uriel as an angelic mediator of the revelation.[73] But Ezra is still dissatisfied: Why have God's people been handed over to Gentiles (4:22-25)?

From these dialogues Ezra emerges as a pious person who is at once humble before the divine but tenacious regarding Israel. Ezra resembles other great characters like Abraham (Gen 18:16-33) and Moses (Exod 33:12-23) who step between God and the people. These characters are specially favored, even chosen, by God and mediate knowledge of God's purposes which would otherwise be inaccessible to their communities. Their compassion moves them to risk their own welfare in an effort to address God.

Occasionally a prophetic call might precede the apocalyptic vision. In the *Apocalypse of Abraham* (9:1-10), *4 Ezra* (1:4-11), and Revelation (1:12-20), these calls echo canonical models. When Abraham hears a voice calling his name twice, his response echoes that of Samuel: "Here I am" (9:1; cf. 1 Sam 3). In Ezra's case the word of the Lord commands, "Go and declare to my people their evil deeds" (1:4), vaguely echoing Isaiah 58:1. And in Revelation the risen Christ commands John to write down the things he sees (1:19; cf. 21:5; 22:16), a motif with several prophetic parallels (e.g., Isa 8:1; Jer 30:2; 36:2, 28; Ezek 43:11; Hab 2:2).

---

[71] Note especially *1 Enoch* 12:1-6; 13:6-7; 84:5-6; Dan 9; *2 Baruch* 6:2; 21:1-26; *3 Baruch* 1.

[72] Quotations from the Pseudepigrapha follow those in *OTP*.

[73] One of the curious things about apocalyptic literature is the confusion among levels of discourse. The reader is often unsure whether God is speaking directly or through an intermediary, nor is one sure whether God is being addressed directly. In *4 Ezra*, the word of the Lord comes to Ezra (1:4), Ezra responds by consulting an angel (2:44), Ezra addresses the Most High (3:3), and is answered by the angel Uriel (4:1).

Prophetic calls and divine commendations are ethical devices. They use multiple levels of narration and heavenly witnesses to attest to the visionaries' character. By setting them apart as persons especially meriting divine revelation and by aligning their knowledge and point of view with that of God, these methods certify their character and access to hidden knowledge.

3. *Modes of revelation* through which the visionary gains access to knowledge and the *nature of that knowledge* provide another cluster of ethical devices, especially in the formal apocalypses. The types of knowledge vary, including dreams, dialogues with heavenly figures, tours of heavenly regions, and esoteric knowledge concerning primeval history or the fundamental elements of the universe. What does not vary is that the knowledge is otherwise inaccessible. Christopher Rowland's shorthand definition of apocalyptic as "knowledge of the divine mysteries through revelation"[74] may appear reductionist, but it emphasizes the power of apocalyptic rhetoric to represent itself through the absolute certainty of eyewitness accounts.

Knowledge is crucial to any speaker's credibility. Paul's three most impassioned defenses of his ministry all reflect apocalyptic *ethos*. In defending his apostolic message of the resurrection, Paul asserts that Jesus "was revealed (ὤφθη) also to me" (1 Cor 15:8). And his opposition to what he considers to be "different" or "other" gospels in 2 Cor 11-12 and Gal 1-2[75] rests upon his "apocalypse of Jesus Christ" (ἀποκαλύψεως Ἰησοῦ Χριστοῦ, Gal 1:12) and "visions and apocalypses (ὀπτασίας καὶ ἀποκαλύψεως) of the Lord" (2 Cor 12:1). Only in his most desperate struggles does Paul invoke his revelatory experiences.[76]

---

[74] *Open Heaven*, 9.

[75] Only here does Paul use such strong language: ἄλλον Ἰησουν and εὐαγγέλιον ἕτερον (2 Cor 11:4); ἕτερον εὐαγγέλιον (Gal 1:6); and ἄλλο εὐαγγέλιον (Gal 1:7).

[76] See Alan F. Segal, *Paul the Convert: The Apostolate and Apostasy of Saul the Pharisee* (New Haven: Yale University, 1990) 36-37, for the possibility that both Gal 1:12 and 2 Cor 12 refer to Paul's conversion experience as well as bibliographic notes on the scholarly debate of this problem. J. Christiaan Beker (*Paul the Apostle: The Triumph of God in Life and Thought* [Philadelphia: Fortress, 1980] 42-47) associates Gal 1 with 2 Cor 10-13 on the

Apocalyptic knowledge often follows a complicated path. In *3 Baruch*, Baruch passes through four heavens and stands at the gate of the fifth, where God dwells. In the first four heavens, Baruch sees things that other mortals cannot see. What he does not understand an angel interprets for him. But there are secrets even Baruch cannot know. When he arrives at the fifth heaven, Baruch cannot see what is going on. Baruch's relation to his audience, then, is that of an especially privileged human being. He shares what he has learned about the most holy of realities, but the limits to his knowledge strengthen his contact with the audience.

Such knowledge rarely comes easily. Almost always visionaries need help in understanding their revelations. Daniel, for example, struggles to understand a vision, so God sends Gabriel (8:16) to explain things. In another case, Daniel hears ambiguous references to the amount of time for the eschatological tribulation. When Daniel asks for specifics, they are not available: "Go, Daniel, for the words are sealed up tight (ἐμπεφραγμένοι καὶ ἐσφραγισμένοι) until the end time" (12:9).[77]

Fourth Ezra may present the most compelling struggle for heavenly insight in apocalyptic literature. Ezra confesses that Israel has indeed been sinful, but he questions why Babylon should prosper while Zion is desolate. Surely Babylon is no less sinful than Jerusalem? But the angel Uriel challenges Ezra.

> Uriel: Your understanding has utterly failed regarding this world, and do you think you can comprehend the way of the Most High?
>
> Ezra (always humble): Yes, my lord.

---

same grounds that I do — that Paul is fighting for his authority — and argues that Gal 1:12-17 relates Paul's "conversion story" (6). My point here is that in defending his authority Paul sometimes appeals to his revelatory experiences.

[77] Paul (2 Cor 12:4) and the narrator of Revelation (10:4) also receive knowledge they cannot repeat (Jean-Pierre Ruiz, "Hearing and Seeing but Not Saying: A Look at Revelation 10:4 and 2 Corinthians 12:4," *SBLSP* 33 [1994] 192).

> Uriel: I have been sent to show you three problems. If you can solve
> one of them for me, I also will show you the way you desire to see, and
> will teach you why the heart is evil. (4:1-4)

Confronted by his inability to pass the tests or to understand the divine ways
(4:10-11), Ezra falls on his face and says, "It would be better for us not to be
here than to come here and live in ungodliness, and to suffer and not
understand why" (4:12). This, then, is the plot of *4 Ezra*: Ezra seeks
understanding, and he receives revelations, but the process is a constant
negotiation between Ezra and the Most High. Finally, almost as a necessary
conclusion, Ezra is given a drink which instills in him (and five accomplices)
the wisdom necessary to restore the Bible and to draft sevently books fit only
for the wisest of the people.

Sometimes the revelation overcomes the visionary physically.[78] As Ezra
awakens after the conclusion of one vision, his "body shuddered violently, and
my soul was so troubled that it fainted" (*4 Ezra* 5:14). What happens then is
common for those points when a visionary is overwhelmed: the angel holds
him, strengthens him, and sets him on his feet (5:15). Daniel is likewise
overcome by his visionary experiences. After the vision in ch. 7, his face pales
but he discusses the experience with no one (7:28). A similar pattern occurs
in 10:7-10, in which Daniel loses his strength and becomes extremely pale
before entering a trance. When the angel touches him, all Daniel can do is rise
to his hands and knees. And when Daniel hears the heavenly voice addressing
Gabriel, he is frightened and falls on his face. The angel comforts him, puts
him into a deep sleep, and causes him to stand (8:16-18). The effects become
even more severe after the vision when Daniel becomes exhausted and remains
ill for several days (8:27).

Such palpable effects confirm the authenticity of the revelatory event.
The angel usually intervenes so as to preserve the visionary from
overwhelming fear or severe physical harm, revealing the narrator's divine
approval. Moreover, the visionary's response echoes that of biblical characters

---

[78] For a discussion of the similar physical effects of *merkabah* experiences, see Rowland,
Open Heaven, 229-36. Similar effects occur in *1 Enoch* 14:14, 24; Rev ; and *Herm.* 9:5.

who have encounted the divine glory,[79] lending verisimilitude to his character. Again preserved is the delicate balance between extraordinary privilege and human limitation.

What are we to make of apocalyptic modes and levels of knowledge in terms of *ethos*? Commissioned by God to perceive secrets, visionaries stand out as persons of extraordinary knowledge as well as virtue and pure motives. But visionaries are limited in terms of their knowledge, and their bodies experience exhaustion in the face of divine mysteries. While visionaries' knowledge marks them as different from the rest of humanity, their limitations invite a sense of identification from their audiences. Enhancing this contact, visionaries always respond to their experiences in ways their audiences will approve.

4. Allusion to ancient *myths* also enhances apocalyptic *ethos*. Paul D. Hanson's study of early apocalyptic eschatology in the Hebrew Bible emphasizes how the Divine Warrior myth contributed to the rise of Jewish apocalyptic eschatology,[80] an insight Norman Cohn makes the guiding principle for understanding "apocalyptic faith." According to Cohn, the cosmic struggle between the forces of order and those of chaos is the mythological thread which runs throughout Near Eastern history and energizes both early Judaism and Christianity.[81]

Combat between chaos monsters and YHWH figures prominently in Hebrew Bible mythology.[82] John employs this tradition to identify the imperial cult, represented by the Beast from the Sea and the Other Beast, with the ultimate powers of evil. The Other Beast promotes worship of the First Beast

---

[79] E.g., Ezek 1:28-2:2; Gen 32:18; and Isa 6:5. And cf. Exod 33:20, in which God warns that "a person shall not see my face and live."

[80] *The Dawn of Apocalyptic: The Historical and Sociological Roots of Jewish Apocalyptic Eschatology* (rev. ed.; Philadelphia: Fortress, 1979) 404-05.

[81] *Cosmos, Chaos and the World to Come: The Ancient Roots of Apocalyptic Faith* (New Haven: Yale University, 1993).

[82] E.g., Ps 74:13-14; 89:9-10; Job 9:13; 26:12-13; Isa 27:1; 30:7; 51:9-11; Ezek 32:2-8).

as it exercises authority over the earth (Rev 13).[83] As part of a much larger network of negative allusions in Revelation, they contribute to John's *ethos* by attacking his opponents and demonstrating his continuity with the biblical tradition.[84]

To be sure, ancient myths of primordial events, cosmic conflict, and the afterlife occur frequently in apocalyptic literature. A certain conservative effect marks these allusions. Narrators who appeal to ancient visions of order demonstrate their own awareness of a culture's roots, establishing their credibility as persons who identify with order and peace. While this appeal suggests conservative ideals, it need not preclude revolutionary functions.[85] The appeal to foundational cultural myths provides an audience a point of identification that can legitimate or subvert the existing order.

5. The narrative framework of the apocalypses enables various modes of *address to the audience*. Sometimes the audience "overhears" discourse about itself; in other cases intermediate characters within the narrative sit in the implied audience's place.

---

[83] Detailed studies include Adela Yarbro Collins, *The Combat Myth in the Book of Revelation* (HDR 9; Missoula: Scholars Press, 1976); John M. Court, *Myth and History in the Book of Revelation* (Atlanta: John Knox, 1979); and Jan Willem van Henten, "Dragon Myth and Imperial Ideology in Revelation 12-13," *SBLSP* 33 (1994) 496-515.

[84] Sophie Laws, *In the Light of the Lamb: Imagery, Parody, and Theology in the Apocalypse of John* (GNS 31; Wilmington: Michael Glazier, 1988).

[85] For the debate concerning the social contexts and functions of apocalyptic discourse, see Hanson, *Dawn of Apocalyptic*, esp. 228-79; Stephen L. Cook, *Prophecy and Apocalypticism: The Postexilic Social Setting* (Minneapolis: Fortress, 1995); Jonathan Z. Smith, "Wisdom and Apocalyptic," in *Map Is not Territory: Studies in the History of Religions* (SJLA 23; Leiden: Brill, 1978) 67-87; and Wayne A. Meeks, "Social Functions of Apocalyptic Language in Pauline Christianity," in *Apocalypticism in the Mediterranean World and the Near East: Proceedings of the International Colloquium on Apocalypticism, Uppsala, August 12-17, 1979* (ed. David Hellholm; Tübingen: Mohr, 1983] 687-705. Though taken somewhat out of context, John J. Collins' assessment is also appropriate here: "Apocalyptic thought allows for considerable fluidity in its mythological conceptions" (*Apocalyptic Imagination*, 85).

We may observe both methods at work in *2 Baruch*. First, Baruch mentions that there are two groups among God's people — those moving away from the Law and those returning to it — and asks God about their fates. God answers that evil will come to the apostates but good to those who have believed (42:1-2). Another example of this device occurs in chs. 44-47, in which Baruch calls his son along with some of the elders and tells them how to admonish the people. In both cases the audience hears about itself through Baruch's conversations with other characters in the narrative.

Second, the audience sits in the place of the people in chs. 31-34. Baruch speaks in future terms of what is for the historical audience a past event: the Temple's destruction. But the audience also hears a message which applies in its own time:

> We should not . . . be so sad regarding the evil which has come now, but much more (distressed) regarding that which is in the future. For greater than the two evils will be the trial when the Mighty One will renew his creation. (32:5-7)

2 Baruch ends with an extended hortatory letter from Baruch to the scattered nine and a half tribes. But Baruch ties the letter around an eagle's neck and sends it away. Again the intended audience hears the letter as if it were addressed to them: they are told to read it in their assemblies and to meditate upon it during feasts (86:1).

This indirect approach of addressing an audience, though properly related to *pathos*, is also an ethical device. By gaining fictional distance from the intended audience, it avoids direct confrontation. In doing so, it "mystifies" the relationship between the historical author and the intended audience. The actual author is enabled to engage the audience without facing possible challenges to his or her authority; instead, the audience overhears authoritative figures such as God, Baruch, or Enoch. Even if the audience remains unconvinced that these persons are in fact the ones who have spoken, the person ultimately accountable still manages to linger in concealment.

6. *Crisis* rhetoric also contributes to apocalyptic *ethos*. As we have seen in Cicero's speeches and the rhetorical tradition, crisis rhetoric implies that the

speaker is working from pure motives. So prominent is this crisis rhetoric in apocalyptic literature that until recently it was common to locate apocalyptic as a discourse of the oppressed. One scholar, David Hellholm, has taken this feature of apocalyptic discourse to be the distinguishing function of apocalypses in general.[86]

We may observe crisis rhetoric at work in *4 Ezra*. Ezra is lying in bed disturbed by Jerusalem's destruction, and he questions God: Why destroy Jerusalem and let Babylon (Rome) continue to prosper (3:1-3, 28-36)? Ezra learns that he is living near the end of the age, when the evil which has been sown in the world will bring forth its harvest (4:26-28). A day is coming which will feature terror and iniquity with cosmic disturbances (5:1-13). Near the end of *4 Ezra* is a warning. The last days are near, complete with multiplied evils. It is time to put away mortal concerns and dwell on heavenly things (14:10-18).

Crisis rhetoric also empowers the Book of Revelation. John's vision applies to "the things which must happen soon" (1:1; 22:6). Distress, imprisonment, and martyrdom define the present (1:9; 2:10, 13; 5:9). The letters to the seven churches (chs. 2-3) all promise that whoever conquers the present age will receive eschatological rewards.

Crisis rhetoric identifies with an audience's sense that it is living in particularly difficult times. At the same time, crisis serves *ethos*. Crisis rhetors demonstrate their pure motivations by affirming the epochal significance of the present.

Conclusion

Apocalyptic discourse provides powerful resources for building *ethos*. The *topoi* discussed here are provide a starting point for further investigation. Authors almost always write in the names of prominent or enigmatic figures from Israel's past, often contributing legends that characterized them as persons of extraordinary virtue and privilege. Through dreams, dialogues with heavenly figures, tours of heavenly regions, and lessons about primeval history

---

[86] "The Problem of Apocalyptic Genre and the Apocalypse of John," *Semeia* 36 (1986) 27.

or the fundamental elements of the cosmos visionaries demonstrate their exclusive knowledge. These experiences often leave them terrified or exhausted, reminding the audience of their humanity. The apocalypses identify with the audience's cultural heritage and desire for stability by alluding to ancient myths in which order overcomes chaos. Using direct address, they invite the audience to share their construction of reality, which is marked by crisis. Crisis rhetoric demonstrates the visionary's goodwill while affirming the audience's sense that its struggles are of cosmic significance. From a rhetorical perspective, apocalyptic discourse is an especially effective means for establishing authority.

The Lamb in the Rhetorical Program of the Apocalypse of John

LOREN L. JOHNS
BLUFFTON COLLEGE
BLUFFTON, OHIO

INTRODUCTION

The Apocalypse of John is rich in its potential for being studied via rhetorical criticism. The author is eager to "persuade"[1] his audience and he uses a sophisticated rhetorical style to do so. The goal of his persuasion cannot be defined in narrow, deliberative terms, such as might be used in identifying a clear set of desired actions. The goal of his persuasion is nothing less than a realignment of allegiances and a radical revolution in his audience's world view. The apocalyptic vision in this book represents an imaginative relocation of the community's self-understanding that will have significant social consequences. That is why definition, redefinition, and parody are central to his rhetoric.[2]

---

[1] I am using *persuade* here in the broader, more encompassing sense characteristic of rhetorical criticism generally, not in the narrower, logocentric sense. The persuasion of the Apocalypse is primarily a persuasion to see the universe through different lenses, to effect a world view that fits with the understanding of Jesus' slaughter as the key to victory over evil.

[2] On redefinition and parody as central characteristics in the rhetoric of the Apocalypse, see esp. James H. Charlesworth, "The Apocalypse of John: Its Theology and Impact on Subsequent Apocalypses," pt. 2 in *The New Testament Apocrypha and Pseudepigrapha: A Guide to Publications, with Excursuses on Apocalypses*, edited by James H. Charlesworth (Metuchen and London: The American Theological Library Association and Scarecrow Press, 1987), pp. 19–51; and Sophie Laws, *In the Light of the Lamb: Imagery, Parody, and Theology in the Apocalypse of John* (Wilmington, Del.: M. Glazier, 1988).

In her essay, "A Rhetorical Analysis of Revelation,"[3] Elisabeth Schüssler Fiorenza has called for a paradigm shift in the interpretation of Revelation—a shift "from an allegorical-spiritual, predictive-literalist, or historical-factual paradigm to a rhetorical-evocative paradigm that can do justice to the sociohistorical matrix as well as to the literary-dramatic character of the book." Fiorenza has helpfully emphasized the ethical and political potential of a hermeneutic that privileges a rhetorical approach to this book.

This paper confirms the identification of the Apocalypse as an example primarily of epideictic rhetoric emphasizing πάθος, and then shows how the lamb Christology works rhetorically to inform and sustain a stance of nonviolent resistance over against the forces of compromise in first-century Asia.

THE RHETORIC OF THE APOCALYPSE

It is not necessary to suppose that either the author or his audience were highly familiar with the study of rhetoric. This essay does not suggest that the author self-consciously used Greek rhetorical conventions or that his audience identified the conventions he used—at least on the conscious level.[4] Rather, this essay suggests that rhetorical criticism is a tool that can help the reader—whether ancient or modern—to apprehend how this book communicates and to appreciate what it "does" to the reader and why.

Although Robert Royalty has emphasized the epideictic nature of the book's rhetoric, Elisabeth Schüssler Fiorenza warns against identifying any one of the three modes of rhetoric—epideictic, deliberative, and judicial—as central at the expense of the rest.[5] She main-

---

[3] Elisabeth Schüssler Fiorenza, "A Rhetorical Analysis of Revelation," in the Introduction to *Revelation: Vision of a Just World* (Proclamation Commentaries; Minneapolis: Fortress Press, 1991), pp. 20–37.

[4] Cf. Robert M. Royalty, Jr., "The Rhetoric of Revelation," *Society of Biblical Literature 1997 Seminar Papers* (No. 36; Atlanta: Scholars Press, 1997), pp. 596–617; esp. 600–602. Adding "at least on the conscious level" recognizes the fact that all communication depends upon conventions learned at the subconscious level.

[5] Fiorenza, "Rhetorical Analysis," p. 26.

tains that all three have shaped parts of the Apocalypse. The oracles of Revelation 2–3, with their appeal to decision and their emphasis on the requisite deeds of the seven churches in the immediate future, have a clear deliberative edge to them. And there are signs of judicial rhetoric in the bitter denunciation of Rome, the condemnation of the author's opponents in Rev 2–3, and the calls for the reader to judge the claims of those who call themselves one thing, but are not.[6] But, Fiorenza concludes, "to decide for one [mode of rhetoric] over and against the other would not enhance but diminish our readings."[7]

Royalty nevertheless claims that, for several reasons, epideictic rhetoric predominates:

> First, epideictic tries to affect an audience's view, opinions, or values. ... Second, epideictic rhetoric includes speeches of praise (encomium, panegyric, *laudatio*) and blame (ψόγος, *vituperatio*) of persons and cities. ... Third, epideictic rhetoric is distinguished by its amplification (ἐργασία, *amplificatio*) of topics and imagery; vivid description (ἔκφρασις); and compassion (σύγκρισις). All three of these characteristics are prominent features in Revelation.[8]

The phenomenon of naming in the Apocalypse supports the identification of this book's rhetoric as epideictic.[9] The author uses

---

[6] The examples of *self*-naming are all positive claims to authority or privilege that are challenged by the author: those who call themselves apostles and are not (2:2); those who call themselves Jews and are not (2:9; 3:9); and the woman Jezebel, who [falsely?] calls herself a prophet (2:20).

The examples of judicial rhetoric could be multiplied if one expands the definition of judicial rhetoric to include in it forms of argumentation that were developed by apocalypticists and other ancient Jewish and Christian writers, as Robert G. Hall argues we should. See Robert G. Hall, "Arguing Like an Apocalypse: Galatians and an Ancient *Topos* Outside the Greco-Roman Rhetorical Tradition," *NTS* 42 (1996), pp. 434–53.

[7] Fiorenza, "Rhetorical Analysis," p. 26.

[8] Royalty, "The Rhetoric of Revelation," pp. 601–2.

[9] On naming, see the excellent paper by Edith M. Humphrey, "On Visions, Arguments and Naming: The Rhetoric of Specificity and Mystery in the Apocalypse," a presentation at the annual meeting of the Society of Biblical Literature,

names, epithets, and sobriquets to reshape the perceptions and world view of his audience and to make subtle normative claims on reality. Epideictic rhetoric is the rhetorical mode that privileges blame and praise. "Naming" in the Apocalypse is one of the more effective ways in which the author blames and praises. This naming evokes stories and images, and places value—both positive and negative—on the individuals, groups, or deities thus named. The author employs all three of the traditional modes of proof in the Apocalypse—ἦθος, πάθος, and λόγος—but not in equal proportion: pathetical proofs (πάθος) pervade this book.

Despite Royalty's correction of Fiorenza, we should be cautious about under-appreciating the deliberative edge to the epideictic rhetoric of the Apocalypse. Epideictic is "the most difficult to define"[10] of the three universal species of rhetoric. Nevertheless, epideictic and deliberative rhetoric clearly overlap.[11] George Kennedy warns that "a great deal of what is commonly called epideictic is deliberative, written in an epideictic style."[12]

A good example of the overlap in these categories can be found in the "macarisms" of Revelation. The author pronounces macarisms, or blessings, in the first and last chapters of the Apocalypse book on those who respond to or "keep" what John writes. Although macarisms are a medium of praise that formally fit well with epideictic rhetoric, the macarisms of the Apocalypse highlight and evoke the readers' *praxis*, their *response* to the words of this book:

San Francisco, November 1997. (The present author gained access to this paper at http://www.wright.edu/academics/faculty/dbarr/ humphrey.htm).

[10] George A. Kennedy, *New Testament Interpretation Through Rhetorical Criticism* (Studies in Religion; Chapel Hill, N.C.: University of North Carolina Press, 1984), p. 73.

[11] Cf. Aristotle, *Rhetoric* 1.9.35-37; cf. also George A. Kennedy, *Classical Rhetoric and Its Christian and Secular Tradition from Ancient Times to Modern Times* (Chapel Hill, N.C.: University of North Carolina Press, 1980), pp. 73-75; and Kennedy, *New Testament Interpretation*, pp. 73-74.

[12] Kennedy, *Classical Rhetoric*, p. 74.

1:3   Blessed is the one who reads aloud and those who hear the words of the prophecy *and who keep what is written in it,* for the time is near.

14:13   Blessed are the dead who die in the Lord from now on.[13]

16:15   Blessed is the one who stays awake and who keeps his or her clothes on.[14]

19:9   Blessed are those who have been invited to the lamb's wedding reception.

20:6   Blessed and holy is the one who has a part in the first resurrection.

22:7   Blessed is the one who keeps the words of the prophecy of this book.

22:14   Blessed are those who wash their robes.[15]

All of the "blessings" in the book relate in some way to the resistance ethic of the book. The occasional editorial address to the implied reader underscores this deliberative agenda: "Here is a call for the endurance of the saints, those who keep the commandments of God and hold fast to the faith of Jesus" (14:12). Thus, whatever else we conclude about the purpose of this book, a central part of its purpose was to effect a faithful response on the part of its hearers/readers—a rhetorical function normally associated with the deliberative.

Since deliberative rhetoric emerges more clearly in the prophetic oracles of Revelation 2–3, it is not surprising that John T. Kirby

---

[13] Those who die in the Apocalypse are those who maintain "faithful witness."

[14] Clothing in the Apocalypse represents the righteous deeds of the saints; cf. 19:8.

[15] Despite Stephen Goranson's efforts to argue to the contrary (Stephen Goranson, "The Text of Revelation 22.14," *NTS* 43 [1997]: 154-57), the reading, πλύνοντες τὰς στολὰς αὐτῶν (those who wash their robes) in 22:14 has better external witnesses and is the more difficult reading, compared to ποιοῦντες τὰς ἐντολὰς αὐτοῦ (those who do his commandments). While "doing his commandments" is certainly an important concern for the author, it is more likely that a later scribe was perplexed by a blessing on those who washed their robes (which is nevertheless in keeping with 7:14; cf. also 3:4-5,18; 6:11; 15:6; 16:15; 19:8,14) than by a blessing on those who do his commandments. In practical terms, there is little difference between the two readings.

identifies deliberative as the primary rhetorical mode of the Apocalypse.[16] Royalty rejects Kirby's identification and charges that Kirby has inadequately appreciated the rhetorical purposes of the Apocalypse.[17]

The rhetoric of the Apocalypse is more negative than positive in its expression. It is primarily dissuasive, rather than hortatory,[18] insofar as its burden is that of resistance—resistance to moral compromise, to false allegiances, and to false world views. The Apocalypse has much more to say about what generally is wrong in the readers' world than what generally is right—about what *not* to do, than what *to* do positively.

Nevertheless, the actions encouraged by the author are vague or immaterial to the central rhetorical force of the book, suggesting that epideictic rhetoric is central to the book after all. Kennedy notes that even "funeral orations and panegyrics [as prime examples of epideictic rhetoric] were intended to be persuasive and often imply some need for actions, though in a more general way than does deliberative oratory."[19] If he is right, then the category of rhetoric that best fits the Apocalypse is epideictic. At the heart of the Apocalypse is a concern to reform, even revolutionize, the values and world view of the readers.

Thus, while epideictic rhetoric predominates in the book, deliberative concerns are not far behind. The sort of proper world view and values envisioned by the author are those that will lead to proper *action*, which necessarily entails a concern for how the community of the faithful should therefore live. In Kennedy's words, even epideictic rhetoric can "take on a more or less subtle deliberative purpose,"[20]

---

[16] John T. Kirby, "The Rhetorical Situations of Revelation 1–3," *NTS* 34 (1988), 197–207.

[17] Royalty, "The Rhetoric of Revelation," p. 602, note 22.

[18] On the categorization of deliberative rhetoric as hortatory and dissuasive, see Aristotle, *Rhetoric* 1.3.3; and Kennedy, *New Testament Interpretation*, p. 20.

[19] Kennedy, *New Testament Interpretation*, p. 73.

[20] Kennedy, *New Testament Interpretation*, p. 74.

and we see this happening in the Apocalypse. It is not just vision or imagination with which the Apocalypse is concerned, but with will and intentionality.[21]

Furthermore, recent students of rhetoric have affirmed the power of epideictic rhetoric to shape the social sphere. Depending on the view of the author, epideictic rhetoric can shore up the *status quo*, reaffirming traditional values in a nonthreatening way, or it can have sweeping social implications. In either case, the inculcation of values is not politically neutral or inherently conservative; rather, by focusing on values, epideictic rhetoric not only "messes with the mind" of the readers, both individually and collectively; it also represents a socially significant act.[22] John used the tools this sort of rhetoric provided not only to criticize the prevailing values of the seven churches, but also to suggest the sorts of values that were in keeping with the new order being revealed by God. With this in mind, we are now prepared to examine more directly the role of the lamb in the rhetorical program of the Apocalypse.

The Lamb in the Apocalypse

Some commentators have made the mistake of analyzing the image of the lamb through a narrowly conceived symbol analysis, without adequate attention to how the book's lamb Christology fits with other key elements in the rhetoric of the Apocalypse. These key elements include, among other things, its understanding of "conquering" (2:7, 11, 17, 26; 3:5, 12; 5:5; 6:2; 11:7; 12:11; 13:7; 15:2; 17:14; 21:7), its emphasis on being a faithful witness (1:2, 5, 9; 2:13; 3:14; 6:9; 11:3, 7; 12:11, 17; 15:5; 17:6; 19:10; 20:4; 22:16, 18, 20), and the power of the Apocalypse to shape one's world view through naming (in both praise and blame). One of the key studies of the Apocalypse is that of the "naming" of Christ in this book.

---

[21] Cf. Amos N. Wilder, "The Rhetoric of Ancient and Modern Apocalyptic," *Interpretation* 25 (1971), pp. 436–53, esp. p. 453.

[22] For a helpful and insightful analysis of epideictic rhetoric's propensity to shape the social sphere, see Takis Poulakos, "Towards a Cultural Understanding of Classical Epideictic Oratory," in *Pre/Text* 9 (1988), pp. 147–166.

The Christology of the Apocalypse is dynamic rather than static. While there is an obvious interest in names and titles, there is little interest in arguing for one title as over against another or for establishing the implications of any particular title. Titular approaches to the study of the Christologies of the New Testament tend to be reductionistic in assuming that the weight of an author's Christology can be and is carried in the titles used by that author. If we understand *title* in its narrower sense, then most of the "titles" that appear in the book are not really titles at all, and none is the key to the Christology of the Apocalypse.

The author applies many images to Christ in the Apocalypse as part of his strategy of naming. While names for God and for Christ abound, so do names for Satan, for the beast—indeed for anyone, mythological or historical, who opposes the will of God. The preponderance of participial constructions indicates that the author has a dynamic understanding of Christ and of his work. Even traditionally weighty "titles," such as "Son of God" and "son of man," are used so infrequently and inconsequentially as to suggest their relative unimportance.[23] The key to appropriating the author's Christology lies in responding to the prophetic word, in recognizing the power of Christ's presence in the worshiping community, and in understanding both the power and the ethical relevance of his death and resurrection for lives of faith in the first century C.E.

Names and epithets used of Christ include Jesus Christ (1:1, 2, 5); the faithful witness (1:5; cf. 3:14); the firstborn from the dead (1:5); the ruler of the kings of the earth (1:5; cf. 17:18); the one who continually loves us (1:5; cf. 3:9); the one who has freed us from our sins with his blood (1:5); Jesus (1:9 [*bis*]; 12:17; 14:12; 17:6; 19:10 [*bis*]; 20:4; 22:16); the voice (1:12); one like a son of man (1:13; 14:14), the first and the last (1:17; 2:8; 22:13); the living one (1:18); the one who holds

---

[23] For a careful investigation of the "Son of Man" "title" in the Apocalypse, see A[dela] Yarbro Collins, "The 'Son of Man' Tradition and the Book of Revelation," in *The Messiah: Developments in Earliest Judaism and Christianity*, edited by James H. Charlesworth, in collaboration with J. Brownson, M. T. Davis, S. J. Kraftchick, and A. F. Segal (Minneapolis: Fortress Press, 1992), 536–68. See esp. p. 568: "The use of the quasi-titular definite form of the phrase is apparently unknown to the author of Revelation."

the seven stars in his right hand (2:1; cf. 3:1); the one who walks in the midst of the seven golden lampstands (2:1); the one who has the sharp, two-edged sword (2:12); the Son of God (2:18); the one who has eyes like a flame of fire (2:18); the one whose feet are like burnished bronze (2:18); the one who searches mind and heart (2:23); the one who has the seven spirits of God and the seven stars (3:1; cf. 2:1); the holy one (3:7); the true one (3:7); the one who has the key of David (3:7); the one who opens and no one will shut (3:7); the one who shuts and no one opens (3:7); the Amen (3:14); the faithful and true witness (3:14; cf. 1:5; 19:11); the beginning of God's creation (3:14); the lion from the tribe of Judah (5:5); the root of David (5:5; cf. 22:16); the lamb (5:6, 8, 12, 13; 6:1, 16; 7:9, 10, 14, 17; 12:11; 13:8; 14:1, 4 [bis], 10; 15:3; 17:14 [bis]; 19:7, 9; 21:9, 14, 22, 23, 27; 22:1, 3; cf. 13:11; lamb is modified by ἐσφαγμένον [slaughtered] in 5:12 and 13:8); messiah (11:15; 12:10; 20:4, 6; cf. 1:1, 2, 5); child (12:5); male son (12:5); the one who is about to rule all the nations (12:5; cf. 7:17); lord of lords (17:14; 19:16); king of kings (17:14; 19:16); lord (11:8; 14:13; 22:20); the one who sits on the cloud (14:15, 16; cf. 14:14); the word of God (19:13); the one who sits on the horse (19:19, 21); the alpha and the omega (22:13; cf. 1:8 and 21:6, where this phrase refers to God); the beginning and the end (22:13; cf. 1:8mar and 21:6, where this phrase refers to God); the bright morning star (22:16; cf. 2:28); and Lord Jesus (22:20, 21).[24]

The one name that is used more than any other is *lamb*. The Greek word here is ἀρνίον, one of eight words used for lamb in the Septuagint. This particular word appears in Ps. 114(113):4, 6, where it "translates" בְּנֵי־צֹאן; in Isaiah 40:11Aq, where it "translates" טָלֶה; in Jeremiah 11:19, where it "translates" כֶּבֶשׂ; and in Jeremiah 50(27):45, where it "translates" צְעִירֵי הַצֹּאן. It also appears in Psalms of Solomon 8:23, where there is no Hebrew equivalent.

The variety of Hebrew words behind the term suggests that there is more than mere translation going on here. In each of these contexts, the *lamb* in question is not a literal, flesh-and-blood lamb,

---

[24] For a fuller description of these titles, see Appendix II of my dissertation: Loren L. Johns, *The Origins and Rhetorical Force of the Lamb Christology of the Apocalypse of John*, Ph.D. dissertation (Princeton, N.J.: Princeton Theological Seminary, 1998).

but rather a *symbol* for something. Furthermore, in each case, ἀρνίον is used symbolically to signify vulnerability.

ἀρνίον is never used in the Septuagint with reference to the Passover victim, the sacrificial lamb, or the Suffering Servant of Isaiah. The word is not used of rams in the extant Greek literature. This observation suggests that the theme of vulnerability be investigated in the Apocalypse to determine the appropriateness of this symbolic association.

From a rhetorical-critical perspective, it is not enough simply to identify a symbol's linguistic background or its tradition history, nor to define its role within literature by reducing it to an "essence," nor simply to identify its referent. The exegete of the Apocalypse is not one who strives to crack a code. Rather, one must, in Elisabeth Schüssler Fiorenza's words,

> trace [a symbol's] position within the overall form-content configuration (Gestalt) of Rev. and see its relationships to other images and within the 'strategic' positions of the composition. ... Only a 'proportional' analysis of its images can determine what they are about within the structure of the work determining the phase of action in which they are invoked.[25]

Thus, even if the seven lampstands "are" the seven churches (1:20), simply *identifying* them as such reveals only a part of the image's capacity to communicate. And to say that the lamb in Revelation "is" Jesus does little justice to its capacity to communicate, as it is with identifying the λόγος of the prologue of the Fourth Gospel as Jesus. These identifications may be accurate, but they do not fully mine the meaning capacity of the symbols. Rhetorical criticism moves beyond mere "identification" and/or source criticism to ask about the nature, function, power, imaginative force, and effect of the symbolic system being constructed in the text.

The semantic value or overall cultural Gestalt attributed to animals in the Graeco-Roman world was significant. Although the "meaning" of the ram varied from region to region and from one era to the next in the Graeco-Roman world, there was at least a more sig-

---

[25] Elisabeth Schüssler Fiorenza, *The Book of Revelation: Justice and Judgment* (Philadelphia: Fortress, 1985), p. 188.

nificant and well-formed cultural Gestalt for the ram than there was for the lamb. Rams were generally considered more valuable than lambs in sacrifice. With few exceptions, lambs were not considered particularly valuable or desirable as sacrificial victims, comparatively speaking. In Egypt, rams were associated with creation, an association Philo knew.[26] In some localities rams symbolized fertility, while in others, protection. While the lion was the preeminent symbol of aggressive violence in sculpture, iconography, and the Homeric epic, the wolf was the preeminent symbol of aggressive violence in most Classical Greek literature. The ram was the preeminent symbol of defensive violence in Egypt. Although the association of the ram with fertility and violence did not extend to the lamb, both rams and lambs were widely associated with divination and the consultation of oracles in Greece, even though rams predominated in Egypt.

Symbolic values reflected in the Aesopic traditions clearly attribute to sheep—and especially to lambs—the value of vulnerability.[27] They were not necessarily *victims*, but they were *vulnerable*. In the Aesopic traditions, lambs often appear in relation to wolves, their mortal enemy. The vulnerability of the lamb is also central to the animal's semantic value in Homer, though its archetypal enemy there seems to be the lion. What emerges most significantly in relation to the Apocalypse is the fact that lambs in the Graeco-Roman world were most often and most directly associated with divination, with the consulting and interpretation of oracles, and with vulnerability.

But vulnerability hardly seems to fit the rhetoric of the Apocalypse! The lamb of the Apocalypse is a strong and victorious charac-

---

[26] Philo, *The Works of Philo: Complete and Unabridged*, translated by C. D. Yonge, with an introduction by David M. Scholer (Peabody, Mass.: Hendrickson Publishers, 1993), 842–43. This particular work, "Questions and Answers on Genesis," is not extant in Greek and does not appear in the Loeb editions.

[27] The symbolism most consistently associated with lambs in these fables revolves around the vulnerability of the lambs (cf. Babrius 51; 89; 93; 113; 128; 132; Phaedrus 1.1; 1.17; Perotti's Appendix, Fable 26; Other Aesopic Fables, nos. 160, 209, 234, 342, 366, 451, 595, 596, 636, 655, and 705). In some of these cases the vulnerability of the sheep is not the fable's main concern, but is part of the fable's set-up for another point, revealing that the vulnerability of the sheep or lamb is part of the deep structure of the symbolic language in the Aesopic tradition.

ter. In Revelation 6 the kings of the earth and the magnates, the generals, the rich and the powerful—indeed, everyone, both slave and free, called to the mountains and rocks, "Fall on us and hide us from the presence of the One seated on the throne and from the wrath of the lamb" (6:15-16)! This is no sweet lambkin, but a powerful and victorious hero!

It was apparently the inappropriateness of this conception of the lamb as a cute, dear lambkin that propelled Friedrich Spitta to translate ἀρνίον as "ram" and to look for a militant conquering ram tradition in Early Judaism.[28] If vulnerability *is* in view in the Apocalypse, it can only be a gutsy, costly, and effective kind of vulnerability and an apocalyptic challenge to the usual meaning and value of vulnerability.

Unfortunately, despite the fact that many Bible dictionaries and commentaries on the Apocalypse appeal to a supposed militaristic lamb-redeemer figure in Early Judaism, there is little evidence to support such a tradition. Joachim Jeremias,[29] Traugott Holtz,[30] and Sophie Laws[31] have denied that such a tradition existed. At the same time, other commentators have spoken confidently about the warrior lamb figure in Early Judaism and have appealed to traditions about that figure in explaining the origins and function of John's lamb Christology. Scholars who appeal to some version of the lamb-redeemer figure in Early Judaism as a key to understanding the symbolism of the lamb in the Apocalypse include such scholars as

---

[28] Friedrich Spitta, "Christus das Lamm," in *Streitfragen der Geschichte Jesu* (Göttingen: Vandenhoeck und Ruprecht, 1907), pp. 172–223.

[29] Joachim Jeremias, "ἀμνός, ἀρήν, ἀρνίον," in *Theological Dictionary of the New Testament*, edited by Gerhard Kittel, translated and edited by Geoffrey W. Bromiley (Grand Rapids: Wm. B. Eerdmans Publishing Company, 1964), 1.338–41.

[30] Traugott Holtz, *Die Christologie der Apokalypse des Johannes*, 2nd ed. (Texte und Untersuchungen, vol. 85; Berlin: Akademie, 1971), pp. 48–50.

[31] Sophie Laws, *In the Light of the Lamb: Imagery, Parody, and Theology in the Apocalypse of John* (Wilmington, Del.: M. Glazier, 1988), pp. 27–28.

Raymond Brown,[32] George Wesley Buchanan,[33] R. H. Charles,[34] Jacques M. Chevalier,[35] C. H. Dodd,[36] Ernst Lohmeyer,[37] Josephine Massyngberde-Ford,[38] Leon Morris,[39] Robert H. Mounce,[40] Charles H. Talbert,[41] and Etienne Trocmé.[42]

---

[32] Raymond E. Brown, *The Gospel According to John, I-XII: A New Translation with Introduction and Commentary*, 2d ed. (The Anchor Bible, vol. 29; Garden City, N.Y.: Doubleday & Co., 1981), pp. 58–60.

[33] George Wesley Buchanan, *The Book of Revelation: Its Introduction and Prophecy* (New Testament Series, vol. 22; Lewston/Queenston/Lampeter: Mellen Biblical Press, 1993), pp. 149–50.

[34] R. H. Charles, *A Critical and Exegetical Commentary on the Revelation of St. John*, Vol. 1 (The International Critical Commentary; Edinburgh: T. & T. Clark, 1920), p. 141.

[35] Jacques M. Chevalier, *A Postmodern Revelation: Signs of Astrology and the Apocalypse* (Toronto: Toronto University Press, 1997), p. 250.

[36] C. H. Dodd, *The Interpretation of the Fourth Gospel* (Cambridge, England: Cambridge University Press, 1953), p. 236.

[37] Ernst Lohmeyer, *Die Offenbarung des Johannes*, 6th ed. (Handbuch zum Neuen Testament, no. 16; Tübingen: J.C.B. Mohr, 1953), pp. 51–55.

[38] J. Massyngberde Ford, *Revelation* (The Anchor Bible, vol. 38; Garden City, N.Y.: Doubleday & Company, 1975), pp. 88–89.

[39] Leon Morris, *The Gospel According to John*, 2nd ed. (Grand Rapids, Mich.: Eerdmans, 1995), p. 129.

[40] Robert H. Mounce, *The Book of Revelation* (New International Commentary on the New Testament; Grand Rapids, Mich.: Eerdmans, 1977), p. 145; cf. also Robert H. Mounce, "Christology of the Apocalypse," *Foundations* 11 (January-March 1968): 42–51.

[41] Charles H. Talbert, *The Apocalypse: A Reading of the Revelation of John* (Louisville: Westminster John Knox Press, 1994), p. 29.

[42] Etienne Trocmé, "Lamb of God," in *The Oxford Companion to the Bible*, edited by Bruce M. Metzger and Michael D. Coogan (New York and Oxford: Oxford University Press, 1993), pp. 418–19.

From a rhetorical-critical point of view, the stakes in this debate are high. If these scholars are right in positing a traditional militaristic lamb-redeemer figure in Early Judaism, then this could easily clarify how and why John chose to portray Christ as a lamb, and what force it carries in the book. The image of Christ as ἀρνίον would then be a continuation or extension of military might suggested in the titles ὁ λέων ὁ ἐκ τῆς φυλῆς Ἰουδα (the lion from the tribe of Judah), and ἡ ῥίζα Δαυίδ (the root [or shoot] of David) from Rev 5:5. On the other hand, if the lamb is a symbol of vulnerability, as suggested by the linguistic evidence in the Septuagint and the cultural associations in the Graeco-Roman world, then it could serve to turn the old ideas of power upside down.

So is the lamb a symbol of vulnerability or of force? If Bruce Malina is right, it is the latter. According to Malina, the purpose of portraying Christ as a cosmic lamb becomes apparent when one realizes that the cosmic lamb is really the powerful and violent ram of Aries. "All the imagery associated with the lamb is that of power, force, control, and conquest."[43] It was his power that was significant to John, and "power means the ability to control others based on an implied sanction of force."[44] Although the readers of the Apocalypse were suffering no persecution, according to Malina,[45] such a message

---

[43] Bruce J. Malina, *On the Genre and Message of Revelation: Star Visions and Sky Journeys* (Peabody, Mass: Hendrickson Publishers, 1995), p. 101.

[44] Malina, *Genre and Message*, p. 263.

[45] On the issue of the social situation of the seven churches—especially with regard to persecution as a central factor in the occasion of the writing—I agree with Bruce Malina, Robert Royalty (cf. Royalty, "Rhetoric of Revelation," p. 599–600), Leonard Thompson (Leonard Thompson, *The Book of Revelation: Apocalypse and Empire* (New York: Oxford University Press), p. 175 *et passim*), and others that there was no systematic, full-scale persecution of the church under Domitian. I do take Rev 1:9 as evidence of some persecution because of John's Christian witness, and Rev 2:13 as evidence of a martyrdom in the distant past, but the primary implied problem in Rev 2–3 is that of spiritual dullness and assimilation, not a crisis due to oppression from without. In Royalty's words, "the text does not *reflect* a situation of crisis or oppression so much as it tries to *create* a crisis in the social world of its original audience" ("Rhetoric of Revelation," p. 599).

would have been welcome "in a culture that submitted to nature and its forces" and would have provided a "renewed zest for living."[46]

Although it is the *use* of the lamb Christology within the Apocalypse that is ultimately crucial for determining the rhetorical force of that Christology, a brief review of the supposed evidence for a militaristic lamb-redeemer figure in the traditions of Early Judaism may be helpful here.[47] There are primarily three texts that have been used to posit such a symbolic-theological tradition: Testament of Joseph 19:8, Testament of Benjamin 3:8, and the Animal Apocalypse of 1 Enoch (1 Enoch 89–90).[48] The first two of these are either Christian

---

[46] Malina, *Genre and Message*, p. 263. A variation on this misinterpretation is that of the dispensationalists, who, despite the lack of any support in the book of Revelation, treat Jesus' *first* coming as one characterized by the lamb, and his *second* coming as one characterized by the lion. This interpretation is typical among Fundamentalist Evangelicals in North America. For instance, Hal Lindsey says, "When Jesus came to earth the first time He came in humility to offer Himself as the Lamb of God to die for the sins of men [*sic*]. But when He comes again He'll return in the strength and supremacy of a lion" (*There's a New World Coming: A Prophetic Odyssey* [Santa Ana, Cal.: Vision House Publishers, 1973], p. 94); cf. also George Eldon Ladd: "[The] Messiah has a twofold role to fulfill. First, he must come in humility and meekness to suffer and die; then at the end of the age he must return in power and glory to put all his enemies under his feet. ... The reigning King must be first a crucified Savior" (*A Commentary on the Revelation of John* [Grand Rapids: William B. Eerdmans Publishing Company, 1972], pp. 86–87). Note also the subtitle of the Fisherman Bible Studyguide to John's Apocalypse: *Revelation: The Lamb Who Is the Lion*, Gladys Hunt, rev. ed. (Wheaton, Ill.: Harold Shaw Publishers, 1994 [orig. pub. 1973]).

[47] For more on the history of this discussion, see chap. 4 of Johns, *Origins and Rhetorical Force*.

[48] In addition to these, some have appealed to the Targum Pseudo-Jonathan on Exodus 1:15 (e.g., Klaus Koch, "Das Lamm, das Ägypten vernichtet. Ein Fragment aus Jannes und Jambres und sein Geschichtlicher Hintergrund," *Zeitschrift für die Neutestamentliche Wissenschaft* 57 [1966]: 79-93) or to the Tosephta Targum on 1 Samuel 17:43 (J. C. de Moor and E. van Staalduine-Sulman, "The Aramaic Song of the Lamb," *Journal for the Study of Judaism* 24:2 [1993]: 266-79). But the traditions in these targums cannot confidently be dated to the first century and the appeals cannot be sustained.

compositions indebted to the Apocalypse of John or have Christian interpolations that are so indebted.[49]

In the Animal Apocalypse, David and others, such as those who suffered persecution under Antiochus IV Epiphanes, are portrayed as defenseless lambs, which then become rams and enter into conflict with the ravens (i.e., the Seleucids). Numerous commentators on the Apocalypse have attempted to explain its lamb Christology by pointing out that the Maccabeans are represented as horned lambs in this passage.[50] This statement, however, is misleading at best, since the lambs must become something else, like rams, in order to function as leaders and rulers. The bleating lambs whose cries are not heard (1 Enoch 90:6-12) probably refer to the Maccabeans (and other faithful Jews) who experienced the violent persecution of Antiochus Epiphanes before the one lamb grew a great horn and became a ram (i.e., before Judas Maccabeus began to exercise his leadership).[51]

The image of one animal "becoming" another animal is not just a passing observation or minor point here. The Animal Apocalypse reflects a keen interest in a strict hierarchy of beings, with each metamorphosis significant.[52] The lamb who grew "one great horn" (90:9;

---

[49] The attempts by B. Murmelstein ("Das Lamm in Test. Jos. 19:8," *Zeitschrift für die Neutestamentliche Wissenschaft* 59 [1968] 273-74) and by J. C. O'Neill ("The Lamb of God in the Testaments of the Twelve Patriarchs," in *New Testament Backgrounds: A Sheffield Reader*, edited by Craig A. Evans and Stanley E. Porter [The Biblical Seminar, vol. 43; Sheffield: Sheffield Academic Press, 1997], pp. 46–66, a reprint of the article by the same title in *Journal for the Study of the New Testament* 2 [1979]: 2-30) to recover the precise wording of a pre-Christian *Vorlage* in these texts that would bear witness to a militaristic lamb-redeemer figure in Early Judaism have not been successful.

[50] See, e.g., Robert Mounce: "In I Enoch 90:9 the Maccabees are symbolized as 'horned lambs'"; Mounce, *The Book of Revelation*, p. 145.

[51] For the identification of the "great horn" in 90:9 as Judas Maccabeus, see, *inter alia*, James C. VanderKam, *Enoch and the Growth of an Apocalyptic Tradition* (The Catholic Biblical Quarterly Monograph Series, no. 16; Washington, D.C.: The Catholic Biblical Association of America, 1984), pp. 161–62; and Patrick A. Tiller, *A Commentary on the Animal Apocalypse of I Enoch* (Early Judaism and Its Literature, no. 4; Atlanta, Ga.: Scholars Press, 1993), pp. 62–63.

[52] For a discussion of the metamorphoses through the various levels in the Animal Apocalypse, see David Bryan, *Cosmos, Chaos and Kosher Mentality* (Jour-

Judas Maccabeus) is, from 90:13 on, called a "ram" (κριός in the Greek). Thus, the text itself implies that "lamb" is not an appropriate symbol for a leader or a ruler, unless it be for a ruler who is temporarily suffering persecution. The lamb in the Apocalypse never "becomes" any other animal—not a ram, a lion, or any other creature. It remains a lamb from beginning to end.

But the method by which the lamb is introduced is significant. As a narrative, the Apocalypse of John has both characterization and plot.[53] The rhetorical fulcrum of the Apocalypse is the scene in heaven in chapters 4 and 5. According to Schüssler Fiorenza, "chapters 4–5 lay the rhetorical foundation and provide the key symbolic images for all that follows."[54] It is here that many of the important themes in the Apocalypse are introduced for the first time: the throne (though see 1:4; 3:21), the One sitting on the throne, the four living creatures, the twenty-four elders, and the Book (or scroll). Though this scene is a unity, it is not independent from the rest of the book.[55]

While the throne vision of chapter 4 is the necessary context, the climax of this scene comes in the fifth chapter. The scene revolves around the question, "Who is worthy to take the scroll?" It is announced that the lion conqueror is worthy. But what does the seer see? "A lamb standing as slaughtered" (5:6). This scene, with its shocking switch[56] of images, lies at the theological heart of the Apoc-

---

nal for the Study of the Pseudepigrapha Supplement Series, no. 12; England: Sheffield Academic Press, 1995), pp. 47-52.

[53] Cf. Thomas Harding, "Take Back the Apocalypse," *Touchstone* 3:1 (January 1985): 29-35; David E. Aune, "The Apocalypse of John and the Problem of Genre," *Semeia* 36 (1986): 65-96; David L. Barr, "Using Plot to Discern Structure in John's Apocalypse," in *Proceedings of the Eastern Great Lakes and Mid-West Biblical Societies* (1995), pp. 23-33.

[54] Fiorenza, *Revelation*, p. 58.

[55] Cf. Nikola Hohnjec, "*Das Lamm, τὸ ἀρνίον*" in der Offenbarung des Johannes: Eine Exegetisch-Theologische Untersuchung (Roma: Herder, 1980), p. 36.

[56] I prefer to speak of the "switch" of images here, rather than the "juxtaposition" of images, since *juxtaposition* could imply a continuing relationship based on proximity. In this case, however, Jesus is never again referred to as a lion. *Lamb* takes over as the controlling metaphor.

alypse. From here on, the image of Christ as lamb serves as the dominant image for Christ.[57]

Eugene Boring rightly calls this "one of the most mind-
wrenching and theologically pregnant transformations of imagery in
literature."[58] David Barr says, "A more complete reversal of value
would be hard to imagine."[59] In Donald Guthrie's words, "there
could hardly be a more striking or unexpected contrast."[60] By the
time we finally catch sight of the lamb for the first time in chapter 5,
we have already seen most of the titles or names used for Christ. This
mid-stream switch of images seems designed specifically to communicate the shock and irony of the author's message—that God's
messiah conquers by being a slain lamb, not a devouring lion. The
Seer introduces the lamb in Revelation 5 in such a way as to underscore a central reversal in his apocalypse. At the heart of this reversal
is a redefinition of power as perceived in John's theology of the cross.

Of course, this interpretation holds only if the lamb turns out
really to be a symbol of vulnerability rather than a symbol of the
power of violence. Is there corroborating evidence of some kind to
enable one to confirm the integrity of such a reading?

There is, though space considerations preclude anything more
than an outline of such corroborating evidence. First, as we have
already seen, the linguistic evidence supports the connection with
vulnerability. If John had intended to communicate Jesus' power and
unmitigated force, he could not have chosen a more inappropriate
animal with which to symbolize him. And within the semantic

---

[57] Appearing 28 times with reference to Christ, ἀρνίον appears in fully
half of the 22 chapters of the Apocalypse, and his presence is implied in others
(e.g., 8:1). More importantly, the image of Christ as lamb serves to control and
interpret other themes in the book. Cf. Laws, *In the Light of the Lamb*, pp. 24–31.

[58] M. Eugene Boring, "Narrative Christology in the Apocalypse," *The
Catholic Biblical Quarterly* 54 (1992): 708.

[59] David L. Barr, "The Apocalypse as a Symbolic Transformation of the
World: A Literary Analysis," *Interpretation* 38 (January 1984): 41.

[60] Donald Guthrie, "The Lamb in the Structure of the Book of Revelation,"
Vox Evangelica 12 (1987): 64.

domain, he could not have chosen a more inappropriate word for lamb than ἀρνίον.

Second, ancillary details in the presentation of the lamb make it clear that vulnerability, not militaristic force is in view. This lamb has been "slaughtered." The first time John sees this lamb, it is standing, even though it bears the marks of its slaughter (5:6). The lamb is declared worthy precisely because it was slaughtered (5:9), and its having been slaughtered is an essential part of its identity (5:12; 13:8). The reference cannot be to the lamb as a sacrifice for sin in the sacrificial cult, for the language used is that of butchery and murder, not ritual sacrifice.[61] And there is no interest in the act of sacrifice itself in the Apocalypse. Whatever else was a concern of this author, expiation for sin was not central to it.[62]

Third, many of the other "names" for Christ fall into two inter-related categories: terms that emphasize the overcoming of death[63]

---

[61] The New Revised Standard Version correctly translates ἐσφαγμένον as "slaughtered" rather than "sacrificed" or "slain." "Murdered" would have been another acceptable choice here. Σφάζω is the language of the slaughterhouse, while θύω, which does not appear in the Apocalypse, is the language of sacrifice. Apart from 5:6, 9, 12; 13:8, σφάζω refers to the murder of humans in 6:4, 9; 13:3; 18:24. For more on σφάζω as slaughterhouse language, see Laws, *In the Light of the Lamb*, p. 30.

[62] The only hymn in which expiation of sins is inferred is the one hymn the author did not compose himself, but which he drew from traditional material (1:5b-6). Cf. David R. Carnegie, "Worthy is the Lamb: The Hymns in Revelation," in *Christ the Lord: Studies in Christology Presented to Donald Guthrie*, edited by Harold H. Rowdon (Downers Grove, Ill.: InterVarsity Press, 1982), pp. 246–47.

[63] These include "the firstborn from the dead" (ὁ πρωτότοκος τῶν νεκρῶν; 1:5), "the one who has freed us from our sins with his blood" (τῷ ... λύσαντι ἡμᾶς ἐκ τῶν ἁμαρτιῶν ἡμῶν ἐν τῷ αἵματι αὐτοῦ; 1:5), "the first and the last" (ὁ πρῶτος καὶ ὁ ἔσχατος; 1:17; 2:8; 22:13), "the living one" (ὁ ζῶν; 1:18; cf. 2:8); "the faithful and true witness" (ὁ μάρτυς ὁ πιστός; 3:14; cf. 1:5; 19:11); "the alpha and the omega" (τὸ ἄλφα καὶ τὸ ὦ; 22:13); "the beginning and the end" (ἡ ἀρχὴ καὶ τὸ τέλος; 22:13). In context, these turn out to have strong political implications as well.

and terms that have strong political overtones.[64] The political critique of kingship and the relativizing of royal authority inherent in these titles draw on well-established Jewish traditions, such as the critique of kingship preserved by the Deuteronomist in 1 Samuel 8 and the critique of kingship in the composite known as 1 Enoch.[65]

The implication for the Apocalypse is that the lordship of Christ proclaimed in this book represented a challenge to the contemporary political powers—a challenge that the author maintains cannot be met through the threat of the death penalty, since Christ has overcome death. Despite the success Constantinian Christianity has enjoyed in schooling Christian readers to see this language as "spiritual" rather than "political," the political critique could hardly have been missed by first-century readers. The challenge to the Roman emperor and to the emperor cult in Asia inherent in such language would have been obvious.[66] The reader is encouraged to see in the christological language of the Apocalypse a political critique that cannot be repressed by means of state murder.

Fourth, the author makes a clear connection between the character, work, and fate of the lamb and the character, work, and fate of the believers to whom he is writing. We see this, for instance,

---

[64] The latter include "the ruler of the kings of the earth" (ὁ ἄρχων τῶν βασιλέων τῆς γῆς; 1:5), "messiah" (Χριστός; 11:15, 12:10, 20:4, 6), "the one who is about to rule all the nations" (ὃς μέλλει ποιμαίνειν πάντα τὰ ἔθνη; 12:5), "lord" (κύριος; 11:8; 14:13; 22:20), "lord of lords and king of kings" (κύριος κυρίων ... καὶ βασιλεὺς βασιλέων; 17:14; 19:16), "the lion from the tribe of Judah" (ὁ λέων ὁ ἐκ τῆς φυλῆς Ἰούδα; 5:5), the root of David (ἡ ῥίζα Δαυίδ; 5:5; 22:16), "the one who has the key of David" (ὁ ἔχων τὴν κλεῖν Δαυίδ; 3:7), "the one who sits on the horse" (ὁ καθήμενος ἐπὶ τοῦ ἵππου; 19:19, 21); cf. also 6:2, 4, 5, 8; 9:17; 19:18 where we have other riders of other horses).

[65] See 1 Enoch 9:4; 12:3; 25:3, 5, 7; 27:3 [Book I]; 38:4-5; 46:3-5; 53:5; 54:2; 55:3-4; 63:2, 4, 7 [Book II]; 81:3 [Book III]; 84:2-5 [Book IV]; 91:13 [Book V]).

[66] The widely acknowledged critique of the emperor cult in Revelation 13 is even more direct. Even though expressed somewhat obliquely, by means of epideictic rhetoric rather than judicial rhetoric, the intent is clear.

in the insistence that the holy warriors[67] in 14:4 "follow the lamb wherever he goes." The repeated promise of reward to the one who conquers in Rev 2–3 is specifically linked to Christ's own conquering (i.e., through his death): "I will grant the conqueror to sit with me on my throne, just as I conquered and sat with my father on his throne" (3:21).

Fifth, the lamb does not do battle in any conventional way. There is war in the Apocalypse, but it is strangely unconventional. Just when one appears to be on the verge of seeing a real battle, it turns out that it is already over. In the "holy war" of Revelation 7, the 144,000 appear to be soldiers mustered for war. But they are robed in white (7:13-14), and have made their robes white in the blood of the Lamb (7:14), suggesting that their victory comes by way of their own deaths. In Rev 2:16, Christ warns the people of Pergamum about the Nicolaitans among them. He says he will make war with them with the sword of his mouth. In 12:7 there is war in heaven as Michael and his angels fight the dragon and his angels. In 13:4 the whole earth worships the beast and questions whether anyone can resist (i.e., "make war on") the beast. In 17:14 the ten kings make war on the lamb, but the lamb conquers them "because he is lord of lords and king of kings and the ones with him are called and chosen and faithful." Thus the Lamb and his followers apparently gain the victory because of their righteous deeds off the battlefield, not because of their skill in physical combat.

The closest we get to a battle scene in the Apocalypse is in chapter 19. There we read that John saw heaven opened and, behold, a white horse, and the one seated on it was faithful, called, and true (cf. 1:5; 3:14), and he judges and "makes war" (πολεμεῖ) in righteousness. The rider approaches the battle dressed in a robe dipped in blood (19:13) — his own blood of witness/martyrdom. In

---

[67] These followers "have not defiled themselves with women" (14:4), suggesting that their "victory" is won in a holy war. Refraint from sexual intercourse is a traditional element in the holy war motif. See 1 Samuel 21:4-5; cf. also Deuteronomy 20:1-9; 23:9-10; Philo, *De Cherubim* 49-50. See esp. the comments of Charles Homer Giblin, "The Cohesive Thematic of God's Holy War of Liberation," appendix in *The Book of Revelation: The Open Book of Prophecy*, Good News Studies, no. 34 (Collegeville, Minn.: Liturgical Press, 1991), pp. 222-31.

keeping with the pivotal scene in Revelation 5 and the message of the book as a whole (cf. esp. the references to blood in 1:5; 7:14; 12:11), the blood here is the blood of martyrdom, in contrast to Isaiah 63:1-3, the source of this imagery, where the blood is the blood of the enemies of the divine warrior.[68] John is, in fact, challenging the reader to look more carefully at his language and to reinterpret Isaiah 63 in the light of the lamb. The warrior himself is called "the word of God" (19:13) and his only weapon is the sword that comes out of his mouth (19:15; cf. 1:16; 2:12).

Thus, even here, no real battle scene is narrated. No story is possible, since the decisive battle is long over.[69] That is also why he can already ride the white horse. His victory is consistently portrayed in terms of his death and resurrection. The ones with him are not human warriors eager to take vengeance on the nations, but "armies of heaven, wearing fine linen, white and pure" (19:14). And we have just been informed that the wearing of fine linen is granted by God and that it refers to τὰ δικαιώματα τῶν ἁγίων (the righteous deeds of the saints; 19:8).

Paradoxically, the lamb conquers not by victory through the strength of force or domination, but by victory through faithful witness — a faithful witness the author is convinced will lead to both per-

---

[68] Cf. esp. M. Eugene Boring, *Revelation*, 196–97; and Wilfrid J. Harrington, *Revelation* (Sacra Pagina, vol. 16; Wilmington, Del.: Michael Glazier, 1993), pp. 192–94; cf. also John Sweet, *Revelation* (Philadelphia: Trinity Press International, 1990), pp. 282–83; Pablo Richard, *Apocalypse: A People's Commentary on the Book of Revelation* (The Bible & Liberation Series; Maryknoll, N.Y.: Orbis Books, 1995), p. 147; Gerhard A. Krodel, *Revelation* (Augsburg Commentary on the New Testament; Minneapolis: Augsburg Publishing House, 1989), p. 323. G. B. Caird, however, argues that the blood on the rider's garments is neither his own nor that of his enemies, but that of the martyr saints (George B. Caird, The Revelation of St. John the Divine (Black's New Testament Commentaries; London: Adam & Charles Black, 1984), p. 243.

[69] Cf. Ted Grimsrud, "Peace Theology and the Justice of God in the Book of Revelation," in *Essays on Peace Theology and Witness*, edited by Willard M. Swartley (Occasional Papers, no. 12; Elkhart, Ind.: Institute of Mennonite Studies, 1988), p. 145; Vernard Eller, *The Most Revealing Book of the Bible: Making Sense Out of Revelation* (Grand Rapids, Mich.: William B. Eerdmans Publishing Company, 1974), pp. 176–79.

secution and martyrdom. This is why the battle scenes in the book are never narrated satisfactorily: the key battle has already been won on the cross despite the ongoing nature of the conflict and the ever-present need for consistent resistance.[70]

CONCLUSION

The most significant battle in the Apocalypse is thus a battle for perception fought on the rhetorical battlefield. At stake were the hearts, minds, perceptions, and allegiances of the Asian believers. Were they to define their reality and values in terms that were readily available to them as residents of the province of Asia? Would a good, long look out of their windows provide the data necessary for determining what was really going on in the world? Or did they need a revelation of Jesus Christ from God (through John, by way of God's messenger angel) to know what was really going on?

The message of the Apocalypse was that whether or not they recognized it,[71] the Asian believers were facing a life-and-death struggle—a struggle they were being invited to embrace and join. This struggle would necessarily be characterized by real conflict. But the primary weapon by which this conflict would be engaged was the weapon of faithful witness—a witness that the author fully expected would lead to their martyrdom. But instead of arguing logocentrically by means of a judicial rhetoric why such an embrace of the struggle was the only faithful response, or exhorting them directly by means of a deliberative rhetoric to engage in the struggle, he uses an epideictic rhetoric of praise to the lamb and invective against the beasts and the whore of Rome to move his readers to embrace his values.

---

[70] "Consistent resistance" is Elisabeth Schüssler Fiorenza's apt translation of ὑπομονή; Fiorenza, *The Book of Revelation*, pp. 4, 182.

[71] The implied problem in Revelation 2-3 is that most of them did *not* recognize the crisis in their situation for what it really was.

THE PERSUASIVE STRATEGY OF THE APOCALYPSE: A SOCIO-RHETORICAL INVESTIGATION OF REVELATION 14:6-13

David A. deSilva
Ashland Theological Seminary

Aristotle assigns an important place to narration in forensic and epideictic speeches, but holds that "in deliberative oratory narrative is very rare, because no one can narrate things to come" (*Rh.* 3.16.11). Most apocalypses, however, claim to be able to do precisely what Aristotle presents as impossible. The narration of events yet to come using vivid imagery and symbolism and the report of occurrences in the realms usually inaccessible to human beings (e.g., heaven or the abyss) set an apocalypse apart from the typical attempt to persuade (e.g., a sermon or a letter) to which the tools of rhetorical criticism may be applied with ease and immediacy.

Nevertheless, scholars rightly sense that an apocalypse is no less an instrument of persuasion than one of Epictetus' dissertations or Paul's letters, and that it should be possible to analyze how an apocalypse effects persuasion — how it wins over its hearers to its view of the world and its assessment of a correct response to that world.[1] Classical rhetorical criticism is not entirely helpless before the Revelation of John. For example, familiarity with the rhetorical handbooks can help the student discern topics which John uses to motivate the hearers to adopt or maintain the response to the dominant culture which he advocates. We are able, on the strength of the *Rhetorica ad Alexandrum* or *Rhetorica ad Herennium*, to discern when John is using topics of the just, expedient, and honorable, or when he is depicting one behavior or commitment as right or safe and another as dishonorable or dangerous.[2] We may discern appeals to *pathos*, armed with the discussion in Aristotle (*Rh.* 2.2.1-11). We may also discern pieces of argumentation in the occasional enthymemes embedded in the hymns or angelic pronouncements, as well as

---

[1] The dedication of both sessions of this year's Rhetoric and the New Testament Section as well as the production of a collection of essays edited by Gregory L. Bloomquist and W. Gregory Carey (*Apocalyptic Rhetoric* [St. Louis, MO: Chalice Press, 1999]) attest to growing interest and scholarly collaboration in this area.

[2] Cf. *Rhet. Alex.* 1421b21-1423a13; *Rhet. Her.* 3.2.3-3.4.8.

elements of praise and censure in the depiction, lauding, or indicting of certain figures. And, of course, much of Revelation works by considering the consequences of a course of action (cf. Aristotle, *Rh.* 3.17.4).

The student of the rhetoric of Revelation, therefore, may certainly begin to discover the persuasive strategy of this, or another, apocalypse by any of these entrees afforded by rhetorical criticism. It is clear, however, that as John participated in the stage of "invention" of his "arguments" he went far beyond the topics treated in the schools of oratory. He uses a wealth of intertextual resources, weaving in phrases, resonances, and echoes of Jewish Scriptures and Jesus traditions throughout his text. He chooses labels and engages in characterization carefully and strategically. He uses repetition of words and phrases to guide his audiences' perception of their world, their choices, and the consequences of those choices. He brings the hearers into contact with voices beyond the realm of human experience, which affirm certain values and denounce other behaviors.

In order to grasp the multidimensional strategy employed by John to promote a group-sustaining response among his hearers, one must reach beyond (although certainly not ignore) what rhetorical criticism has to offer. It is here that socio-rhetorical interpretation offers an abundance of helpful resources for the investigation of how an apocalypse persuades.[3] This "interpretive analytic" leads the student to consider how John has structured and patterned his own text and interacted with other available texts (broadly conceived to include cultural knowledge and social codes as well as individual, written texts), how he orients his hearers to the groups and cultures around them, how he attempts to locate Christian discourse within the discourse of other cultures, and finally how he engages and overturns opposing ideologies in order to promote his own. Socio-rhetorical interpretation shows us that persuasion is allusive and associative as well as argumentative, and it is especially in this regard that it well equips the student to investigate a document as allusive as Revelation.

What follows is not an attempt at a comprehensive socio-rhetorical analysis of Revelation 14:6-13.[4] Rather, I will attempt a reading of this

---

[3] Vernon K. Robbins, *Exploring the Texture of Texts* (Valley Forge, PA: Trinity Press International, 1996); *The Tapestry of Early Christian Discourse* (London: Routledge, 1996).

[4] A "comprehensive" deployment of socio-rhetorical resources in the interpretation of this passage will appear in *BBR* 9 (1999).

passage which exhibits the principle strategies which John employs and orchestrates in order to motivate his audiences to see their world and construe their choices as he would have them, and to choose the path of maintaining the distinctive culture of the Christian group, which he promotes as the truly advantageous course.

THE RHETORICAL SITUATION

John writes to seven different Christian communities, each facing distinctive challenges.[5] Part of the genius of Revelation is its ability to speak to each of these different situations while also articulating what John hopes will be adopted as the universal ethos for the Christian culture. Chapters 2-3 present seven oracles spoken by the Glorified Christ to each of the seven churches, praising certain commitments and behaviors, censuring others, and calling the audiences to adopt certain courses of action for their future well-being. The language is overtly deliberative, urging particular courses of action for the sake of gaining advantages (the rewards) and avoiding disadvantages (the threatened punishments or consequences), supported by epideictic topics concerning what is praiseworthy and what is dishonorable within each congregation. These oracles give us the clearest picture of the rhetorical situations addressed by Revelation, a sense of what John wishes to see happen in each congregation.

Some of the hearers are given encouragement to continue in their present course. John hopes that his visions will embolden believers in Smyrna and Philadelphia to continue to choose loyalty to the values of the Christian group even at the cost of ongoing and escalated hostility from the dominant culture or other, more powerful groups (like the Jewish community). Many in Pergamum and Thyatira, and a few in Sardis, have also shown exceptional

---

[5] I agree with those who place the composition of Revelation near the end of Domitian's reign: cf. A. Y. Collins, "Dating the Apocalypse of John," *Biblical Research* 26 (1981) 33-45; *idem.*, *Crisis and Catharsis: The Power of the Apocalypse* (Philadelphia, PA: Westminster, 1984), 25-83; D. E. Aune, "The Social Matrix of the Apocalypse of John," *Biblical Research* 26 (1981) 16-32; R. H. Mounce, *The Book of Revelation* (rev. ed.; Grand Rapids, MI: Eerdmans, 1998) 15-21; L. L. Thompson, *The Book of Revelation: Apocalypse and Empire* (Oxford: Oxford University, 1990) 12-17. For a fuller discussion of the setting of Revelation, see D. A. deSilva, "The Social Setting of the Apocalypse of John: Conflicts Within, Fears Without," *WTJ* 54 (1992) 273-302.

loyalty to God and Jesus (those who "have not denied my name," 2:13, and who have refused to accept the Nicolaitan teaching, 2:24-25), or have remained adequately uninvested in the dominant culture (the few in Sardis who "have not soiled their garments," 3:4). Such Christians are also encouraged to persevere in their commitment to their current course of action as the way to eternal advantage.

The congregations at Ephesus, Pergamum and Thyatira have been exposed to the influence of an alternative interpretation of Christian values and behavior. The Nicolaitans and Jezebel represent an interpretation of the group's central values which would make room for participation in activities like idol worship, which represents values central to the dominant culture. They contend that worship of God and participation in the rites which assure their non-Christian neighbors of their goodwill, reliability, and solidarity are not contradictory.[6] They represent a voice which calls for lessening tension between the Christian group and the dominant culture, seeking the security of the group through peaceful co-existence.[7] John seeks to demonstrate that the worship of God and the worship of idols is fundamentally incompatible, and that the person who engages in the latter cannot escape punishment for sharing God's honor with God's enemies. He regards these other voices as especially great dangers to the churches, and dedicates much of his vision to rendering their position untenable.

Still other congregations, like the majority of believers at Sardis or the church at Laodicea, labor under such self-deception that John sees his task to be to "wake them up" to the dangerous position they occupy. Laodicean Christians profit along with their non-Christian neighbors, drinking in the wealth that the "peace of Rome" makes possible, without knowing their poverty — and the partner with whom they are unwittingly sleeping! By their

---

[6] For discussion of the social and economic dangers facing those who abstained from all idolatrous expressions of worship, running the risk of being regarded as impious or atheistic, see Ford, *Revelation*, 406; R. H. Charles, *A Critical and Exegetical Commentary on the Revelation of St. John* (Edinburgh: T. & T. Clark, 1920), 1.69-70; Mounce, *Revelation*, 85-86; D. A. deSilva, *Despising Shame: Honor Discourse and Community Maintenance in the Epistle to the Hebrews* (Atlanta, GA: Scholars Press, 1995) 146-151.

[7] Thus C. H. Talbert, *The Apocalypse: A Reading of the Revelation of John* (Louisville, KY: Westminster/ John Knox Press, 1994) 19; J. M. Ford, *Revelation* (New York: Doubleday, 1975) 291; Mounce, *Revelation*, 81; A. LeGrys, "Conflict and Vengeance in the Book of Revelation" (*Expository Times* 104 [1992] 76-80); G. B. Caird, *The Revelation of St. John* (London: A. & C. Black, 1966) 39.

attitudes toward wealth, and toward the present time as an opportunity to become enriched, they show themselves to have accepted the ideology of Rome itself. John seeks to topple this ideology through his visions, showing believers the "true" nature of Rome and her emperors, warning them against accepting any share in or partnership with a system built on the violence, injustice, and arrogance which calls down God's vengeance.

The visions of chapters 4-22 support the rhetorical goal of each oracle, providing the larger context of space and time which demonstrates the courses urged in the oracles to be truly advantageous and the objects of censure or warning ultimately disadvantageous. Each audience will continue to "deepen" its reading of its own situation and options in light of those visions. As we look at one short passage from these visions, we should keep in mind the different situations of the hearers and the courses of action to which John calls them. How does John orient the hearers to the realities of their situations? How does he color their perception of that world and undermine opposing ideologies? How does he present topics of advantage and disadvantage to motivate the hearers to follow his prescriptions? How does he persuade them to accept his interpretation of their situations and of the advantageous?

REV 14:6-7: THE CALL TO RESPOND JUSTLY TO THE DIVINE PATRON

> And I saw another angel flying in midheaven, having an eternal gospel to proclaim to those sitting on the earth, even to every nation and tribe and language and people, saying in a loud voice: "Fear God and give him honor, for the hour of his judgment came, and bow down to the one who made heaven and earth and sea and springs of water."

The passage opens with the words "I saw another angel" (εἶδον ἄλλον ἄγγελον, 14:6). This angel becomes the speaker of the first message (λέγων ἐν φωνῇ μεγάλῃ, 14:7). John's own voice intrudes into the passage only here and at 14:13, where he says "I heard a voice speaking from heaven" commanding him to write down what is spoken (ἤκουσα φωνῆς ἐκ τοῦ οὐρανοῦ λεγούσης, Γράψον, 14:13). John presents himself merely as the vehicle and not the source of the message. He enters the text only as a means of reminding the hearers of the explicated source of the content of the visions, namely angels, Christ, the Spirit, or God's own self (cf. 1:1, which already establishes the "real" author of the text). In terms derived from Max

Weber's taxonomy of legitimate authority, Rev 14:6-13 continues to promote acceptance of John's authority to define the audience's situation and to prescribe direction for their future on the basis of charismatic legitimation (rather than traditional or functional).[8]

Every "I saw" or "I heard" in Revelation, then, functions as an appeal to *ethos*, supporting the reliability and credibility of the message by placing it on the lips of figures whose authority is unassailable. This is a powerful means by which John promotes his view of the world and the courses of action he seeks to move the audiences to take. To refuse John's message is to refuse not one itinerant prophet (perhaps in favor of another, like "Jezebel") but to refuse God's own word. John does not merely embed his *ethos* in that of God and supernatural beings. By acting as the spokesperson for justice and piety in 14:6-13, calling for the pursuit of virtue and avoidance of vice, he also shows his commitment to these virtues (Aristotle, *Rh.* 1.9.1).

This angel declares his message to "every nation and tribe and language and people" (ἐπὶ πᾶν ἔθνος καὶ φυλὴν καὶ γλῶσσαν καὶ λαόν, 14:6). Attention to the repetitive texture of Revelation as a whole shows that the hearer will have been exposed to this, or a very similar, phrase five time prior to its occurrence at 14:6 and one time thereafter (5:9; 7:9; 10:11; 11:9; 13:7; 17:15). These repetitions construct a web of echoes which itself carries a message to the hearers which is essential to John's success — the Lamb and the beast are in competition, and the prize for which they compete is humanity thus described. The beast and the whore have power "over every tribe and people and language and nation" (ἐδόθη αὐτῷ ἐξουσία ἐπὶ πᾶσαν φυλὴν καὶ λαὸν καὶ γλῶσσαν καὶ ἔθνος, 13:7; cf. 17:15), but the Lamb ransoms a holy people from out of these groups (5:9; 7:9). The message of God's judgement is displayed before these people groups (10:11; 11:9; 14:6) as part of that competition — those who respond to the call of God's servants are separated out for God, while those who fail to respond share in the fate of the beast and the whore. There can therefore be no cooperation between those who belong to the Lamb and those who worship the beast, for they belong essentially to two different kingdoms. Through such repetitive patterns, John subtly leads his audiences away from the position which Jezebel and the Nicolaitans would persuade them to adopt, creating divisions and positing

---

[8] For a fine application of Weber's model to Paul's attempts to legitimate his authority in Corinth, see Bengt Holmberg, *Paul and Power* (Philadelphia: Fortress, 1978).

incompatible alternatives where other voices in the seven churches do not see such stark separations.

The message itself is a call to respond to God, the Creator and Judge of all, with the honor which is God's due: "Fear God and give God honor" (Φοβήθητε τὸν θεὸν καὶ δότε αὐτῷ δόξαν, 14:7). The angel provides two rationales supporting this course of action as "advantageous." The first reason is that "the hour of God's judgement arrived" (ἦλθεν ἡ ὥρα τῆς κρίσεως αὐτοῦ) John has been interested in creating a sense of "crisis" (pun intended) since 1:7, and this is an important element of his strategy for defusing the appeal of rival prophets and motivating certain elements of the churches to "shape up." It represents, in effect, part of the "means" by which John achieves his goals for the hearers.[9] The announcement of this certain, future event, which is a prominent element in both Jewish and Christian cultural knowledge, calls for a strategy to encounter and survive the judgement. The author is here introducing the topic of "safety" or "security," a subtopic of "advantage" in the scheme of the *Rhetorica ad Herennium* (3.2.3), proposing "some plan or other for ensuring the avoidance of a present or iminent danger." Since God will judge the world, and the factuality of that judgement is beyond question, it will be advantageous to be found among God's faithful clients (God's allies, as it were) rather than among God's enemies upon whom he will enact judgement. The ability of an apocalypse to "narrate" events yet to come allows John to show God's judgements being in fact poured out upon all who refuse this call to "repent," "fear God," and "glorify God" (16:9, 11).

The command is reduplicated in the remainder of the announcement: "worship the one who made heaven and earth and sea and springs of water" (προσκυνήσατε τῷ ποιήσαντι τὸν οὐρανὸν καὶ τὴν γῆν, 14:7). In this reiteration of the basic call to honor God (here specifically in the physical replication of that honor, the "bowing down" of the vassals to the regent), a second rationale is articulated implicitly as attention is drawn to God's creative activity. As giver of all life and creator of all things, God merits gratitude from those whom God has benefitted. The human being owes to

---

[9] The positing of God's judgement, as well as all-out culture wars, as "events shortly to come to pass" belongs to the arena of ideological texture, as John "creates" the needs to which he also provides the solutions. What Robbins (*Tapestry*, 224) says about 1 Corinthians 9 is no less applicable, *mutatis mutandis*, to Revelation: "In the context of creating the need, the discourse offers the answer.... this ideology creates a need for the very kind of thinking and clarification the discourse in the letter presents."

God a debt similar to that owed by a client to his or her patron. Those who were given "favor" were obliged to show "gratitude" to the giver, the first element of which was the duty to show respect to, and increase the honor of, the giver. When the gift was life itself, the obligation was immeasurable. In the words of Aristotle, "no one could ever render the gods the honor they deserve, and a person is deemed virtuous if he or she pays them all the honor he or she can" (*Eth. Nic.* 8.14.4).

The summons to honor God is bolstered by the use of terms and phrases found in the Jewish Scriptures to promote not merely the worship of the God of Israel, but the exclusive worship of this God. God is frequently identified as the "maker of heaven and earth" (Isa 37:16; 2 Kgs 19:15; cf. Gen 1:1; Isa 45:18; Bel 1:5) or the "maker of heaven and earth and sea" (LXX Ps 145:6; cf. Exod 20:11; Neh 9:6; Acts 4:24). In many of these texts, however, God is thus identified to distinguish him from other gods or to emphasize that he alone is God (2 Kgs 19:15; Neh 9:6; Isa 37:16; Exod 20:11, given the proximity of 20:2-5; Bel 1:5), sometimes specifically God "alone over all the kingdoms of the inhabited world (Isa 37:16; 2 Kgs 19:15).

"Fearing God" also carries a prominent evocations in Jewish texts. Most frequently, "fearing God" means "keeping God's commandments," the covenant stipulations of the Torah (whether as a means of reinforcing regulations governing "horizontal" relationships, as in Lev 19:14, 32; 25:17, 36; 25:43; or as a general synonym for keeping the just decrees or commandments of God, as in Deut 6:2, 24; 10:12; 17:18; 31:12-13; 2 Kgs 17:35-38; LXX Esth 2:20; Tob 4:21). When the first angel, then, bids all people "fear God," he calls them to honor God's commandments, the first of which is to have no other gods beside the One God.[10] Making room for idolatry violates the unique claim God has to such displays of honor, and would result in the dreadful experience of God's satisfaction of God's honor through the punishment of the offender. Exclusive worship of the One God is thus promoted as the proper enactment of "the just" (*Rhet. Alex.* 1421b37-

---

[10] Mounce (*Revelation*, 271) says succinctly that "to fear God is to reverence him," but this hardly helps the reader understand the evocative power of the first angel's message (and, of course, begs the question of what constitutes reverence). Exploration of intertexture (whether oral-scribal or cultural) and social texture (the responsibilities of gratitude) offer helpful resources for fleshing out for the modern reader — indeed, for the person seeking to apply the text in a community of faith — to discover the evocations of "fearing" and "revering" one who is identified as a "Creator" in ways that older, inner-disciplinary modes of interpretation do not.

1422a2; *Rhet. Her.* 3.3.4; it is therefore "right" and "advantageous") and ultimately "safe" course of action.

This message is presented as an "eternal gospel," a description which has led many commentators to think that John has here in view a universal proclamation of "the gospel of the kingdom" (Matt 24:14) which precedes the "end."[11] It is more likely, however, that we should allow the actual message of the angel — the announcement of the "hour of judgement" which signals God's final enactment of God's accession to the "kingdom of this world" (Rev 11:15)[12] — to inform our understanding of the term "gospel" here. As a message about the accession of a regent, "gospel" here has strong resonances with Greco-Roman cultural knowledge, specifically the "good news" announced to the world in Augustus' birth (cf. the Priene Inscription) or Vespasian's accession (see Josephus, *BJ* 4.656).[13] The importance of the Priene inscription as an intertextual resource for Luke's infancy narrative interacts should push the interpreter to consider possible ramifications of John's conversation with this cultural allusion. Within dominant cultural discourse, the accession of Augustus was "good news," the temporal proof of divine favor. After the civil wars of 68-69 AD, the accession of Vespasian was also "good news" which signaled the healing and rebirth of the empire. The first angel puts these lesser accessions into perspective by claiming that God's rule was "eternal," replacing the rule of all human regents — especially

---

[11] Caird (*Revelation*, 182-183), for example, forcefully supports this view, asserting that the hearers would fill it the term and supplement the content of the angel's actual message with "the full rich content of the apostolic preaching." We should always beware of importing meanings into the text which are not supported or reinforced by elements within the text itself. Moreover, "gospel" may have other cultural resonances for the hearers which Caird ignores (or of which does not know) — resonances from the hearers' primary socialization in the dominant culture. Acts 14:15, moreover, would argue against Caird's assumption, since there we find a second example of "gospel" being essentially a call to abandon idol worship and to "turn to a living God who made heaven and earth and sea and all that is in them" (the parallel to Rev 14:7 is striking)..

[12] Thus, rightly, Ford, *Revelation*, 247; Mounce, *Revelation*, 270.

[13] Ford (*Revelation*, 247) includes an excellent discussion of the resonances here with the Roman imperial overtones of "gospel." She understands the angel's proclamation to signify the eternal sovereignty of God, as opposed to "the transitory nature of the emperor's rule." Her suggestion, which both does justice to the Greco-Roman (dominant cultural) resonances of the term and to the given content of the angel's message in 14:7, is the strongest among the commentators surveyed.

those who usurped the cultic honors which were God's prerogative alone. In light of this eternal accession, and God's forthcoming visitation to hold all the inhabitants of the earth responsible for their failures to act justly toward God, the honorable and safe course was exclusive worship of the One God, maintaining that alliance inviolate.

14:8: CENSURE OF ROME AND OF PARTNERSHIP WITH ROME

> And another angel, a second, followed, saying: "She fell, she fell —
> Babylon the great who made all nations drink of the wine of the
> violent passion of her fornication."

Plutarch writes thus about Rome's significance: "Time, who, with God's help, laid her foundations, yoked Fortune and Virtue together, so as to use the special powers of both in creating for all mankind a hearth truly 'holy and wealth-giving', a secure 'mooring-cable', an abiding element, an 'anchor in the surge and drift' of this shifting world, as Democritus has it" (*Mor.* 317A).[14] In one paragraph, Plutarch unites the essential elements of Roman imperial ideology: Rome's founding by the will of Jupiter (cf. Virgil, *Aen.* 1.234-237), the role of Rome as bringer of stability, rule of law, and peace (cf. Virgil, *Aen.* 4.231-2), and the fruits of divine favor manifested in temporal prosperity.

It is precisely this ideology which Revelation (particularly 16:18-19:4) seeks to overturn, holding up instead Rome's violence, economic exploitation, and self-glorifying arrogance. The second angel's message provides in summary fashion what the remainder of Revelation will explicate at greater length. This message does not explicitly call for a course of action, but rather works in an epideictic mode to present the figure of Babylon as a censurable one — debauched and vice-ridden, shamefully spreading her vices among the nations. Repetition of the label "Babylon" together with the charges of fornication, pollution, and deception throughout Rev 16:18-19:4 reinforces the particular image John wants his audiences to have of Rome.

John's choice of the label "Babylon" for Rome (shared among several Jewish and Christian communities, as 4 Ezra, 2 Baruch, and 1 Peter attest) enables him to harness the resources of the denunciations of Babylon in Isaiah

---

[14] Plutarch, *Selected Essays and Dialogues*, tr. Donald Russell (Oxford: OUP, 1993).

and Jeremiah for his deconstruction of Roman imperial ideology (particularly in chapters 17-18). The second angel's message in 14:8 combines and recontextualizes (that is, incorporates without citing) phrases from Isa 21:9 and Jer 25:7-8, and virtually every phrase in chapter 18 is derived from these earlier prophets. Why does John weave so many pieces of "authoritative" texts into his vision while at the same time refusing to refer to them as such (thus scores of recontextualizations but few if any recitations)? By recontextualizing the content of authoritative "prophecy," John lends considerable authority for his own visions. He is, in effect, reinterpreting numerous portions of Isaiah and Jeremiah (and Ezekiel as well) as applicable to Rome, setting up a typological construction which sees Rome as the antitype of Babylon (shared by 4 Ezra and 2 Baruch), and which makes Isaiah's and Jeremiah's prophecies about the type applicable to the antitype. Rome, guilty of the same crimes as Babylon in the eyes of John (as of the authors of 4 Ezra and 2 Baruch), will most assuredly fall under the judgement of the same God. This is an unusual, but strikingly effective, way of considering an historical precedent to predict the outcome of a new venture. His close association (indeed, virtual identification) of Babylon and Rome achieve the same end as the example in deliberative rhetoric (Aristotle, *Rh.* 1.2.8; 1.4.9; 1.9.40; 2.20.8; *Rhet. Alex.* 1428b12-17; 1429a25-28), although more potently as John continues to "narrate" events yet to transpire.

By labeling Rome as Βαβυλὼν, John asserts that Rome replicates Babylon's character — a character marked by arrogance, violence, and oppression through imperialism. John replaces the dominant culture's discourse about the character and destiny of Rome (exemplified by the excerpt from Plutarch above) with the Jewish scriptural discourse about the character and fate of Babylon.[15] 14:8 does not yet explicate this, but rather lays the foundations for this ideological *coup d'etat*. Labeling Rome's administration and rule as πορνεία is also calculated to present Rome in an ideologically colored light — one which obscures any benefits Roman rule has brought in order to highlight the negative consequences of Roman rule. It replaces any appreciation of connection with Rome as a path to lasting peace, order, and prosperity with a picture of such connection as "fornication," a debased and

---

[15] Jurgen Roloff (*The Revelation of John* [Minneapolis, MN: Fortress, 1993] 175) recognizes this as he writes that "Babylon is naturally used as a synonym for Rome, not so much to disguise what is truly meant but to reveal its true meaning." The label allows John to overlay a set of meanings onto "Rome."

debasing relationship (and a counterfeit relationship as well). Labels and broader associations are thus a potent part of John's persuasive strategy.

The angel declares Babylon to have fallen, affirming that vice comes to a bad end. The cause for Rome's fall will be fully explicated in chapters 17-18 — it results from God' riposte to her challenge to God's honor (her arrogant disregard for God's authority over earthly kingdoms, her hostility specifically toward God's faithful clients, her insolent disregard for the honor of all people). The vice for which Babylon is specifically censured when she is first introduced at 14:8 involved "making all the nations to drink the wine of the wrath of her fornication" (ἐκ τοῦ οἴνου τοῦ θυμοῦ τῆς πορνείας αὐτῆς πεπότικεν πάντα τὰ ἔθνη). Attention to repetitive texture at this point reveals two elements of John's persuasive strategy. First, describing the wine she offers as "her fornication" (τῆς πορνείας αὐτῆς, 14:8) John is able to associate Jezebel the prophetess, previously censured for not repenting from "her fornication" (τῆς πορνείας αὐτῆς, 2:21) and for deceiving God's servant through leading them into "fornication," with this figure of Babylon who is already condemned before God and ready to fall. Through these verbal associations, John depicts his rival's ministry as leading believers to enter into the webs of fornication spun by Babylon. He paints this rival prophet in the same colors that he paints the godless city which stands under judgement, making a strong attack on her authority and on the appeal of her message.[16]

Second, repetitive patterning within the passage reinforces the impression that association with Rome is disadvantageous. This emerges from the juxtaposition of the "wine of the violent passion" of Babylon (14:8) and of God (14:10).

ἐκ τοῦ οἴνου τοῦ θυμοῦ τῆς πορνείας αὐτῆς πεπότικεν (14:8)
ἐκ τοῦ οἴνου τοῦ θυμοῦ τοῦ θεοῦ   [πίεται] (14:10).

This pair connects the cup which Babylon gives to delude the nations with the cup that God gives to punish the worshiper of the beast and its image. The effect of this repetition seems to be to suggest that if one "drinks in" the

---

[16] P. E. Hughes (*The Book of the Revelation* [Grand Rapids, MI: Wm. B. Eerdmans, 1990] 171), falls into the trap of reading the references to "fornication" as indications of "sexual licentiousness of every kind." The difficulty with this sort of mirror-reading is that it takes language which belongs properly to John's ideological coloration of the world of the hearers and reads it as an actual, accurate representation of that world.

ideology of Rome as benefactress of the world and engages in the cultic expressions of gratitude to that benefactress and her representatives, the emperors (the topic of the third angel's message), one will also "drink in" the wrath of God as a sort of chaser. The movement here from fornication to idolatry to God's wrath may well recall the episode recorded in Num 25:1-3, where the Midianite women led the Israelite men into idolatry and assimilation with their people by way of fornication, an episode already clearly evoked in Rev 2:14, 20.

The second angel's message begins to lead John's audiences, contrary to the public discourse, to regard association and partnership with Rome as ultimately disadvantageous on two counts. First, connection with Rome would be a source of disgrace, since Rome is herself dishonorable, leading her partners into activities which are censurable before God's court. Second, since Rome's destruction has already been decreed, partnership with Rome offers not security but rather the danger of incurring the wrath of God as Rome's clients are led to participate in Rome's sins against God. The characterization of Rome's activity as spreading pollution and depicting her imperialism as fornication may also serve to arouse indignation against Rome — the feeling that the good fortune she now enjoys is contrary to all merit and the longing for Rome to receive what is truly her due. While 14:8 is not sufficient to do this on its own, it serves as a prelude to 16:18-19:4, a lengthy treatment which certainly has the arousal of emotions in view as part of its rhetorical strategy. 14:8 begins to plant the suggestions which will make the explicit exhortation of 18:5 — "come out from her, my people, in order that you not become participants in her sins and receive her punishments" — all the more "logical," expedient and persuasive.

14:9-12: GOD'S RESPONSE TO THE IDOLATER'S CHALLENGE

And another angel, a third, followed them, saying in a loud voice: "If any bow down to the beast and its image and receive a mark on their foreheads or on their hands, they will also themselves drink the wine of God's wrath, poured out undiluted into the cup of his anger, and they will be tormented by means of fire and sulfur in the sight of the holy angels and in the sight of the Lamb. And the smoke of their torment ascends up forever and ever, and they do not have rest day or night, those who bow down to the beast and its image and if anyone receives the mark of its name." Here is the endurance of the

holy ones, who are keeping the commandments of God and keeping
faith with Jesus.

While the second angel's message looks forward to an episode of detailed
ideological warfare, the third angel's message looks backward to John's
deconstruction of the first pillar of Roman imperial ideology, namely the
emperor (12:1-13:18). The third angel's message, therefore, capitalizes on
the impact of that treatment.

The imperial cult was, for the majority who participated in it, an
expression of gratitude and loyalty toward the patron of the Mediterranean
world, the *pater patriae*.[17] Participation in this institution, as in the cults of
the traditional gods, showed one's *pietas* or εὐσεβεία — one's reliability
with regard to the fulfillment of all one's social and civic obligations. It
reflected one's solidarity with one's fellow citizens, one's commitment to the
ongoing stability and well-being of the city that depended on maintaining the
favor of those over. The cult was one engine among many which promoted
a certain picture of the emperor as the mediator of divine blessings, as the
beneficent patron of a vastly extended household, and as the protector of
peace. In short, the dominant culture in Asia Minor regarded participation in
the imperial cult as a "just" action. Withdrawing from cultic expressions of
solidarity with the citizenry and loyalty and gratitude toward those who
secured the well-being of the city would be considered "unjust" and
"ungrateful." Gentile Christians especially were held in suspicion and stood
at risk of being viewed as subversive, unreliable, and even dangerous
elements of society.[18]

---

[17] Cf. S. R. F. Price, *Rituals and Power: The Roman imperial cult in Asia Minor*
(Cambridge: Cambridge University, 1984); G. W. Bowersock, "The Imperial Cult:
Perceptions and Persistence," in B. F. Meyer and E. P. Sanders (eds.), *Jewish and Christian
Self-Definition* (Philadelphia: Fortress, 1982) 3.170-182; D. Earl, *The Age of Augustus* (New
York: Exeter, 1968) 166-76; L. L. Thompson, *The Book of Revelation*, 95-170. These
developments are summarized, and John's counter-propaganda explored, in D. A. deSilva,
"The `Image of the Beast' and the Christians in Asia Minor: Escalation of Sectarian Tension
in Revelation 13," *TrinJ* 12NS (1991) 185-208.

[18] The author of 1 Peter, for example, speaks of the origin of the society's hostility
in the unbelievers' surprise that their former colleagues no longer join them in their
accustomed rituals and practices (4:3-5). While 1 Peter censures these activities as "excesses
of dissipation," these activities included the "lawless idolatry" (4:3) which was the
foundation of civic loyalty and solidarity. A view from the "other side" comes from Pliny

John inverts the public discourse about Rome's emperors. The very choice of label — "beast" (14:9) — effectively obscures the humanness of the emperor and any legitimate claims he could make on the gratitude and loyalty of John's audiences. In chapters 12 and 13, John had depicted this beast as the appointee of Satan, God's primal enemy. It is the beast and his supporters who enact Satan's next stage of antagonism against God and God's holy ones (12:14 — 13:4). The emperor's authority comes not from the beneficent gods but from a malevolent enemy; his character is not piety but impiety, as he stands at the head of an idolatrous priesthood (*pontifex maximus*); the cultic honors offered to him constitute an insidious tool of forcing legitimation of his illegitimate rule and pose a clear and present danger to those who know true piety (13:15-18).[19] It remains now for the third angel to show the ultimate disadvantage of participating in the dominant culture's machine for self-legitimation.

Rev 14:9-11 returns to the more overtly deliberative mode established in 14:6-7 but set aside in 14:8. Specifically, it seeks to dissuade hearers from a course of action which represents the alternative to the course urged in 14:6-7 (the exclusive worship of the One God) by discussing its consequences (a frequent topic in exhortation and dissuasion; cf. Aristotle, *Rh.* 2.23.21; 3.17.4). If honor and safety were the chief components of deliberation (*Rhet. Her.* 3.2.3), engagement with the cult of the beast would be the most disadvantageous path for any believer to take. Participation there would mean exposure to everlasting torment at God's judgement (thus one's safety would be utterly lost), as well as public degradation and loss of honor as the angels and Lamb bear witness to one's punishment (βασανισθήσεται ἐν πυρὶ καὶ θείῳ ἐνώπιον ἀγγέλων ἁγίων καὶ ἐνώπιον τοῦ ἀρνίου, 14:10).

John has already acknowledged that non-participation could carry a heavy cost (13:15-18), but here introduces topics of "relative expediency" (Aristotle, *Rh.* 1.7.1-2). "Those things are greater evils," and therefore more

---

the Younger (*Ep.* X.96), who sees the renewed interest in traditional religious activity as the healthy result of his investigation of the deviant Christians, many of whom are now returning to fulfill their social and civic obligations.

[19] John's treatment of the imperial cult as the focus for the society's assaults on the Christians (at a time when no such official enforcement of the cult appears to have been taking place) is an ingenious way of escalating the sense of crisis and the mutual incompatibility of the Christian group's values and the dominant culture's values. This would present an especially poignant challenge to those voices which affirm the compatibility of Christian worship and participation in idolatrous rituals.

to be avoided, "the punishment for which is greater" (*Rh.* 1.7.30). While the Christian who remains committed to the exclusive worship of One God might lose economic enfranchisement or even his or her life (like Antipas), those who do not maintain that display of piety inviolate will suffer an eternal punishment, with the holy angels and the Lamb as witnesses of their dishonor. As the concluding verse of this passage will quickly affirm, however, those who choose piety with temporary disadvantage will also enjoy eternal honor. Setting temporary disadvantage against "eternal" advantage is a technique common to subcultures and countercultures, whose members must frequently accept some degree of disadvantage as the price of maintaining their alternative culture. This requires, of course, that members accept the counter-definitions of reality which allow for such a contrast.

Other textures of this passage support the argumentative texture. Repetition of words again reinforces the incompatibility of piety and idolatry, subtly moving the audience to see bipolar oppositions where rival prophets and the dominant culture would have them see compatible choices. A striking example of this centers on the word "rest":

οὐκ ἔχουσιν ἀνάπαυσιν ἡμέρας καὶ νυκτός (14:11)
ἵνα   ἀναπαήσονται ἐκ τῶν κόπων αὐτῶν (14:13)

The grim picture of public torment without rest or reprieve for those who worship the beast or receive its mark is juxtaposed with the rest enjoyed by those who have died "favored" or "blessed" by God (Μακάριοι οἱ νεκροὶ). The repetition of "rest" reinforces the message that those who die rather than submit to participation in the emperor cult have chosen wisely, since they will enjoy what is eternally denied those who worship the beast. A second, and more impressive, repetition connects 14:11 with 4:8:

οὐκ ἔχουσιν ἀνάπαυσιν ἡμέρας καὶ νυκτός (14:11)
ἀνάπαυσιν οὐκ ἔχουσιν ἡμέρας καὶ νυκτὸς (4:8)

The phrase appears almost verbatim in the earlier context of the angelic liturgy, where the four cherubim "do not rest day and night saying 'Holy, holy, holy is the Lord God Almighty'." This parody again reinforces the alternatives facing all creatures — worship God without lapse, or suffer God's vengeance without pause.

Another prominent repetition involves the word "worship." Within the passage, this highlights the contrast between worshiping God and worshiping the beast and its image:

> προσκυνήσατε τῷ ποιήσαντι τὸν οὐρανὸν καὶ τὴν γῆν (14:7)
> Εἴ τις προσκυνεῖ   τὸ θηρίον καὶ τὴν εἰκόνα αὐτοῦ (14:9)
> οἱ   προσκυνοῦντες τὸ θηρίον καὶ τὴν εἰκόνα αὐτοῦ (14:11)

The incompatibility of these acts of adoration is reinforced by the broader reverberations of "worship" throughout Revelation (cf. especially 4:10; 5:14; 9:20-21; 13:4; 19:10, 20; 20:4; 22:8-9), but also by the intertextual resonances of the term. The Hexateuch, for example, is replete with injunctions to "fear" or "serve" the One God and to avoid the "worship" of other gods, those gods of the non-Jewish peoples (οὐ γὰρ μὴ προσκυνήσητε θεῷ ἑτέρῳ, Exod 23:34; cf. 20:3-5; 34:13; Lev 26:1; Deut 5:9; 8:19; 11:16; 30:17; Josh 23:16), particularly their idols.[20] John's use of the word "worship" in the context of declaring what is due God and what is not due recontextualizes a pervasive and prominent Jewish discourse on the topic of proper worship versus impious worship. John brings the weight of this core Jewish and Christian value to bear on the particular phenomenon of Roman imperial cult (occasionally extended to the idolatry which accompanies Greco-Roman piety, cf. 9:20-21; 13:4).

The third angel's message contains several other potent echoes of phrases used elsewhere in Revelation. One cluster of these repetitions lead the audience to conclude that the one who participates in activities which legitimate the rule of the beast and the whore will also share in the judgements which God has decreed for those figures. Both the worshiper of the beast and Babylon herself drink from the "wine of the wrath of God" and the "cup of God's anger":

> αὐτὸς πίεται ἐκ τοῦ οἴνου τοῦ θυμοῦ τοῦ θεοῦ ... ἐν τῷ ποτηρίῳ τῆς ὀργῆς αὐτοῦ (14:10)
> δοῦναι αὐτῇ τὸ ποτήριον τοῦ οἴνου τοῦ θυμοῦ τῆς ὀργῆς αὐτοῦ (16:19)

The smoke of the torment of the idolater "goes up into the ages of ages," as does the smoke of Babylon's burning:

---

[20] Cf. Ford, *Revelation*, 248.

καὶ ὁ καπνὸς ... αὐτῶν εἰς αἰῶνας αἰώνων ἀναβαίνει, 14:11)
καὶ ὁ καπνὸς αὐτῆς ἀναβαίνει εἰς τοὺς αἰῶνας τῶν αἰώνων (19:3)

Finally, those who wish to be seen as grateful clients of the beast will be seen by God as enemies to be punished along with Satan, the beast, and the false prophet. Repetitions of "torment" (14:10; 20:10), "fire and sulfur" (14:10; 19:20; 20:10), and "day and night" (14:11; 20:10) associate their fates.

In this third message, John reminds the believer of the consequences of idolatry, presenting it as an act of injustice against God. Idolatrous worship provokes God's "anger" (τῆς ὀργῆς αὐτοῦ, 14:10), since it violates God's determination to "share God's glory" with no other figure. In giving such honors to a lesser benefactor, or, rather, to an anti-Patron who serves God's enemy (Rev 13:1-8), the worshiper of the beast challenges God's honor and should expect to suffer God's punishment. Aristotle (*Rh.* 2.2.1, 8) shows that anger is an expected response to an affront to one's honor, particularly when the affront comes from those whom one has benefitted (as God has benefitted all). God's anger is the anger of a slighted benefactor, whose favor meets not with gratitude (such as the first angel calls for) but with disobedience of his commands — the refusal to render the Patron the service he requires of the client.[21] In the perpetual punishment of the idolater, God reasserts his honor.[22] What the dominant culture defines as the just and secure path, John redefines as unjust and dangerous.

Discussion of the inexpedient consequences which attend the violation of monolatry gives way without transition to a pronouncement (14:12). Perhaps the words are the angel's, or perhaps it will be heard as John's gloss on the angel's message (cf. 13:10). The assurance that worshipers of other gods will be punished is offered as the ground for the "endurance of the holy

---

[21] On the obligations of clients, see F. W. Danker, *Benefactor: An Epigraphic Study of a Graeco-Roman and New Testament Semantic Field* (St. Louis, MO: Clayton House Publishing, 1982; D. A. deSilva, "Exchanging Favor for Wrath: Apostasy in Hebrews and Patron-Client Relations," *JBL* 115 (1996) 91-116.

[22] Aulus Gellius (*Attic Nights* 7.14.2-4) shows that "punishment" is itself closely related to the social code of honor. One term for punishment, τιμωρία, refers to punishment inflicted "when the dignity and prestige of the one who is sinned against must be maintained, lest the omission of punishment bring him into contempt and diminish the esteem in which he is held; and therefore they think that was given a name derived from the preservation of honour (τιμή)."

ones" (ἡ ὑπομονὴ τῶν ἁγίων). John does not specify precisely how the third angel's message should engender endurance, but one may surmise that this word will have a different effect on different audiences. For those who are experiencing loss of some kind for their commitment to the One God, this will encourage them to persevere in the assurance of reversal. Their jeopardized honor will be restored by God as their detractors are punished. For those wavering in their commitment to monolatry, the third angel's declaration may urge them to persevere out of a desire to avoid the consequences.

"Holiness" is a strong, positive value in Jewish and Christian culture. The "holy ones" are defined as "those who keep God's commandments and keep faith with Jesus" (οἱ τηροῦντες τὰς ἐντολὰς τοῦ θεοῦ καὶ τὴν πίστιν Ἰησοῦ).[23] This statement reaffirms central values of the Christian culture. They are "holy," "set apart" for God from a society which is throughout Revelation portrayed as a source of pollution (3:4-5; 17:4-6; 18:2-3). John thus affirms through his use of this term a sectarian posture toward the host society. This holiness is defined as giving God the obedience which is God's due (service to their Patron in form of keeping the commandments) and remaining loyal to the Lamb who ransomed them to be holy to God, who acted as their mediator or broker. In elevating these values, John moves back into an epideictic mode in support of his objectives, namely urging the audiences to hold onto their distinctive cultural values and to maintain a social identity of separateness from the dominant culture.

14:13: REDEFINING THE HONORABLE DEATH

> And I heard a voice saying from heaven: "Write: honored are the dead who die in the Lord from now on." "Yes," says the Spirit, "in order that they may rest from their labors, for their works follow after them."

The final pronouncement within this passage moves fully into an epideictic mode, describing the qualities of those who are "honored" and "favored"

---

[23] Mounce (*Revelation*, 275) also favors a translation of this genitive as an objective genitive.

(Μακάριοι, 14:13).[24] John draws special attention to the fact that the source of this pronouncement and its accompanying rationale are voices from heaven, one of which is identified as the "Spirit," emphasizing thus the reliability of the evaluation being made. These statements are calculated to rouse emulation among the hearers, moving them to seek to embody those values which receive approbation and bring honor. John's strategy involves leading the hearers to believe that their honor lies in maintaining precisely those commitments which also serve to maintain the boundaries and distinctive values of the Christian group.

This "makarism" is one of seven which punctuate Revelation (1:3; 14:13; 16:15; 19:9; 20:6; 22:7, 14). What characterizes the person who is "honored" or "favored" in God's sight is thus developed and reinforced through the repetitive texture of the larger work. Here it is particularly the "dead who die in the Lord" who are "blessed" as the recipients of divine favor. In light of the foregoing messages, the hearers will understand those who "die in the Lord" to be those who have "kept God's commandments and kept faith with Jesus," who have remained committed to monolatry in a world which promoted idolatry as pious and just. These enter the "rest" which is forever denied the worshiper of the beast (14:11), and their works will bear them favorable testimony before God's court (cf. 20:12-13). The makarism applies not only to those who are violently killed, but to all who "die in the Lord."[25] The use of the more general ἀποθνῄσκω rather than a passive form of ἀποκτείνω strongly supports this observation. Nevertheless, the related makarism of 20:6 will especially highlight the positive value of being executed for the sake of one's loyalty to God and the Lamb. Moreover, John has been leading the audiences to expect violence from the non-Christian world, such that they would themselves participate in the completion of the number of the martyrs (6:9-11).

While it elevates the value of dying loyal to God, whatever the form of death, it also helps to redefine the ultimate experience of disapproval and censure at the hands of society (namely execution) as the experience of entering into eternal honor before God. Society's attempts to reform the deviant become, in John's hands, the occasion for the one who "endures"

---

[24] On the translation of this term, see K. C. Hanson, "How Honorable! How Shameful! A Cultural Analysis of Matthew's Makarisms and Reproaches," *Semeia* 68 (1996) 81-111.

[25] Thus W. J. Harrington, *Revelation* (Collegeville, MN: Michael Glazier, 1993) 152.

(14:12) to win honor where that honor will be preserved forever, where his or her "works" of obedience to God and loyalty to Jesus and the fellow-believers will become the cause of renown. What the dominant culture would intend as a dishonorable death, John depicts the voice from heaven and the Spirit (known elsewhere in Johannine Christianity as the reliable witness; John 16:12-15; 1 John 5:7-9) affirming as a noble death.

We must again guard against reading John's forecasts of hostility as a reflection of the audiences' general situation. The dominant culture has not yet been engaged in the systematic execution of Christians. John's discussions of martyrdom, on the one hand, prepare the believers for that possibility, but they also serve John's ideological agenda, namely painting the relationship between church and society as one under great tension. He guides his audiences to "see" the outside world in such a way that the partnership or peaceful co-existence with it urged by John's rivals becomes impossible.

CONCLUSION

John seeks to effect persuasion by means of a number of different strategies operating concurrently, and the tools of socio-rhetorical interpretation are especially suited to teasing out the persuasive effects of these various strategies. First, John does indeed present arguments readily discernible as elements of argumentative texture. He promotes certain actions and cautions against others using topics of advantage and disadvantage (the just, praiseworthy, and the safe, and their opposites), and uses topics of praise and blame to reinforce his exhortations. As would any orator, John also appeals to *ethos* and *pathos*, although sometimes these appeals take on forms distinctive to the genre of apocalypse.

But John also persuades through means which are not so conventional in the halls of oratory. He employs consciously repetitive language to create webs of associations throughout his visions which subtly guide the audiences to divide their world, calculate their choices, and evaluate options in ways which John can control. These repetitive patterns can serve a wide variety of ends, from deconstructing the *ethos* of his opponents to reinforcing the disadvantageous consequences of refusing to hold to the course John urges.

Moreover, John's discourse is teeming with intersections between his text and older texts, most notably the Jewish Scriptures. An important aspect of the persuasive power of Revelation is its ability to set the hearers' present situation and their present world in the interpretive context of authoritative Scriptures, for example exploring the character and projecting the fate of Rome using the oracles against Babylon in Isaiah, Jeremiah, and Ezekiel. Similarly, dissuasion from participating in idolatrous Greco-Roman cults is supported by means of John's invocation of the rich scriptural resonances of "worship" and "fearing" the God "who made heaven and earth and sea," reminding the hearers of what has always been a cardinal feature of Jewish and Christian culture — monolatry.

Socio-rhetorical investigation, moreover, does not merely invite us to probe the rhetorical strategy of the text, but also its social effects and cultural location. A full socio-rhetorical analysis would also require that one probe more fully the ways in which John orients his audiences toward the world (does Revelation nurture revolutionist, introversionist, reformist, or other responses to the world?) and the cultural relationship of John's discourse to the discourse of other groups (e.g., the dominant culture, the Jewish ethnic subculture). We have already seen how ideologically motivated John's visions are: he takes on the pillars of Roman imperial ideology and replacing it with a rather subversive view of the origins, character, purpose, and destiny of what the dominant culture holds dear; he creates the sense of crisis and the sets of bipolar oppositions which will motivate and guide the audiences to choose his recommended courses of action over those proposed by rival prophets. Again, socio-rhetorical interpretation provides the essential questions and language for investigating this aspect of John's rhetorical agenda.

Analysis of the rhetoric of Revelation is indeed possible, but will require the use of more tools than rhetorical criticism provides. Indeed, study of Revelation from this perspective also helps the student understand more about the process of persuasion itself — how a speaker brings various resources to bear to make others "see" things differently, inviting them into a world constructed by a speech in which certain choices actually become advantageous or honorable, regardless of how they appear in the world outside, or prior to, the speech. John asks his readers to continue to live from the world inside Revelation, even as they move about in the world outside the text. If they "keep" the words of his prophecy (1:3) — and this is the main point of which he must convince them — they will indeed be honored and secure.

Offspring and Parent: A Lucan Prolegomena to Ethics

Robert L. Brawley
McCormick Theological Seminary

Richard Hays formulates five ways biblical materials inform ethics: moral law, principles, analogies to contemporary situations, understanding of the world and human beings, and understanding of God.[1] But in Luke-Acts, these categories lead toward prolegomena more than ethics. (1) Luke-Acts is weak in appeals to moral law for ethics. The law informs εὐσέβεια more than ethics (Luke 1:6; 2:22, 27; Acts 22:3). (2) The lawyer in Luke 10:25-37 epitomizes the law as love of God and neighbor, indelibly inscribed on each other. But his subsequent question shows that the principles as such do not eventuate in ethics. (3) If readers make analogies between themselves and Jesus' followers, they discover characters with whom they can identify in their deficiencies and in whom they can witness concrete cases of the realization of God's rule, but whom they can hardly emulate. The disciples' opposition to the bringing of infants to Jesus is a case in point (18:15). (4) The understanding of the world and human beings and (5) the understanding of God invade each other. In Luke-Acts, Satan may drive human beings. By contrast, the ideological perspective is that it is of the essence of humans to be in a relationship with God. Thus anthropology is simultaneously theology.[2] This is not ethics, however, but prolegomena. Accordingly, this paper examines relationships underlying behavior as a prolegomena to ethics. Though foreshadowing and retrospection come into play, I basically read Luke-Acts sequentially for motifs that point toward the source(s) of behavior with emphasis on the image of parent and child.

As if anticipating anti-foundationalism, Luke-Acts begins not with universality but particularity. The narrativization (διήγησις) itself is a

---

[1] R. Hays, "Relations Natural and Unnatural: A Response to John Boswell's Exegesis of Romans 1," *JRE* 14, 1 (1986) 206-07.

[2] R. Bultmann, *Theology of the New Testament* (2 vols.; New York: Scribner's, 1951-55) 1. 191.

particular emplotment and troping.[3] The Temple tempts readers to presume global significance.[4] The locus, however, is not only the *axis mundi* but the hearts of a couple who are childless and shamed--socially and religiously (Luke 1:25).[5] Their shame provokes a δέησις[6] (1:13). The δέησις plays figuratively with the rising incense that Zechariah offers: "Let my prayer be counted as incense before you" (Ps 141:2). Hardly a prayer of faith (Zechariah disbelieves), it is a cry over an ideal marriage[7] that has born no fruit of the womb. This cry annuls anti-foundationalism, because God heeds the stigmatized couple's cry.

But this is macrocosm in microcosm. A second level has to do with parents and children, not in a nuclear family but in Israel's family. Luke 1:17 anticipates John's role as a solution to a problem: "To turn the hearts of parents to children." But what is the problem? The solution may imply: (1) Parents have neglected their children.[8] (2) Children have forsaken the sentiments of their forebears' hearts, particularly if the πατέρες are the patriarchs.[9] (3) Adults may turn again as if they were children.[10] Progressive discovery of what is true in the narrative world brings some clarification. For the moment, John's birth is God's response to Israel's family just as to the family of Zechariah and Elizabeth. God hears a couple's δέησις. Does God also hear a δέησις from Israel?

---

[3]L. Johnson, *The Gospel of Luke* (Sacra Pagina 3; Collegeville, Minn.: Glazier, 1991) 4.

[4]On the Temple as a model of the universe and the *axis mundi* see Josephus *Ant.* 3.6.4 §123; 3.7.7 §180-87; Philo *Special Laws* 1.66-67; *Noah's Work* 126; *Moses* 2.88; *b Yoma* 54b; *b Sanh.* 37a.

[5]On childlessness as a social and theological problem see T. Naumann, *Ismael: Theologische und erzählanalytische Studien zu einem biblischen Konzept der Selbstwahrnehmung Israels im Kreis der Völker aus der Nachkommenschaft Abrahams* (Habilitationsschrift, Universität Bern, 1996) 25.

[6]On δέησις as "entreaty," "want," "need," "asking," "seeking," see LSJ; H. Greeven, "δέομαι, δέησις," *TDNT* 2. 40-41.

[7]Ancestry and piety establish Zechariah and Elizabeth as ideal. See D. Bock, *Luke* (2 vols.; Baker Exegetical Commentary on the NT; Grand Rapids: Baker, 1994) 1. 76-78.

[8]Johnson, *Luke*, 33; R. Brown, *The Birth of the Messiah* (Doubleday, 1977) 278.

[9]A. Loisy, *L'Évangile selon Luc* (Paris: Nourry, 1924) 81-82.

[10]A. Leaney, *The Gospel According to St. Luke* (HNTC; New York: Harper, 1958) 80.

Apparently. God hears a cry over the demise of Israel's kingdom. Readers hear this δέησις in Simeon's expectation of Israel's consolation and in Anna's anticipation of Jerusalem's redemption (2:25, 38). God heeds. This too is macrocosm in microcosm. Born in particularity to a virgin in Nazareth (1:26-27), Jesus will reign universally (1:32-33). How? The same way that aged Elizabeth can have a child--"anything is not impossible with God" (1:37).

But if Zechariah, Elizabeth, and Israel have a δέησις, Mary has not asked. In fact, news that God is with her perplexes her.[11] God's grace (1:28, 30) allows Mary no vote as if Luke-Acts never heard of women's suffrage much less freedom of choice. Moreover, causing a pregnancy for a woman without her consent is most unethical. God's removes reproach from Elizabeth in the microcosm and from Israel in the macrocosm. But Mary's pregnancy puts her in ambiguous light. From then on generations may call her blessed, but under eyebrows raised by pregnancy outside of wedlock.[12] However, Mary has a δέησις in retrospect: "I am the devoted child [δούλη] of the Lord. May it be for me according to your word" (1:38).[13] Mary thus becomes a child who reflects the heart of her parent God. Further, she prophetically[14] connects her narrative to a meta-narrative of a perpetual promise and memory--God's memory of a promise to Abraham and his seed (1:54-55).

The incident in the Temple when Jesus was twelve is hardly his transformation into adulthood.[15] Mary still calls him τέκνον (2:48). Rather he identifies himself as a child who reflects the heart of his parent God: "It is

---

[11]The "greeting" that perplexes Mary is the entire announcement in 1:28, not merely χαῖρε. A. Strobel, "Der Gruss an Maria (Lc 1,28): Eine philologische Betrachtung zu seinem Sinngehalt," *ZNW* 53 (1962) 91-92, 108.

[12]J. Schaberg, *The Illegitimacy of Jesus: A Feminist Theological Interpretation of the Infancy Narratives* (San Francisco: Harper & Row, 1987). D. Landry argues compellingly that the preferable narrative logic is virginal conception rather than conception outside marriage ("Narrative Logic in the Annunciation to Mary [Luke 1:26-38]," *JBL* 114 [1995] 65-79). But the social stigma still holds.

[13]On Mary's response as a prayer for God's will to be accomplished, see R. Fuller, "A Note on Luke 1:28 and 38," *The New Testament Age: Essays in Honor of Bo Reicke*, vol. 1 (ed. W. Weinrich; Macon, GA: Mercer University Press, 1984) 202. Mary also asserts her place in God's household. See Johnson, *Luke*, 38; Green, *Luke*, 92.

[14]On Mary's prophetic role see B. Gaventa, *Mary: Glimpses of the Mother of Jesus* (Columbia, SC: University of South Carolina Press, 1995) 56-59.

[15]As Johnson suggests, *Luke*, 58.

necessary for me to be in my father's things" (2:49).

Parentage is significant because for the Baptizer it is the source of behavior (3:1-22). John's warning against claiming Abraham as parent is multivocal. First, the offspring of vipers may be *identified with* Abraham's children. Abraham and Sarah might as well have given birth to stones. Second, fruits of repentance are criteria for an authentic Abrahamic heritage, so that the offspring of vipers may be *contrasted with* Abraham's children. In this case, the God with whom anything is not impossible, can make stones (even offspring of vipers?) into Abraham's children. The foreshadowing of John's story in 1:17 means that John's preaching is about children, including his audience, reflecting what is at the hearts of parents, including Abraham.

Jesus' baptism shows that John is hardly finished with parents and children.[16] The heavenly voice that names Jesus God's offspring places him in contrast with the offspring of vipers. Moreover, God is well pleased with Jesus. He is a child reflecting what is at the heart of his parent.

Jesus' mission in 4:18-21 is unburdening people who implicitly lift up a δέησις.[17] The programmatic character of 4:18 makes all of Jesus' exorcisms and healings derivative of being anointed by the spirit, which as the parallelism in his baptism shows, is equivalent to being God's υἱός. The summary of 4:41 develops the motif of parent and child where demons declare (iterative) Jesus to be God's child when he unfetters people.

In 4:43 Jesus announces his mission to proclaim God's kingdom. This forms an inclusion with 4:18-21, and shows that Jesus' spirit-anointed mission is synonymous with proclaiming God's kingdom. Luke 4:43 is also programmatic in that Jesus declares the proclamation of God's kingdom to be

---

[16]Against Conzelmann's separation of Jesus' baptism from John see M. Bachmann, "Johannes der Täufer bei Lukas: Nachzüger oder Vorläufer?" *Wort in der Zeit: Festschrift K. H. Rengstorf* (ed. W. Hanbeck & M. Bachmann; Leiden: Brill, 1980) 123-55; U. Busse, "Das 'Evangelium' des Lukas: Die Funktion der Vorgeschichte im lukanischen Doppelwerk," *Der Treue Gottes trauen: Beiträge zum Werk des Lukas: Für Gerhard Schneider* [ed. C. Bussmann & W. Radl; Freiburg: Herder, 1991] 166-69).

[17]S. Roth, *The Blind, the Lame, and the Poor: Character Types in Luke-Acts* (JSNTSup 144; Sheffield: Sheffield Academic Press, 1997) 97-141, 152-64.

his purpose henceforth.[18] "Kingdom" introduces a political image of ruler and citizen that is distinct from but compatible with the familial figure of parent and child.

God's kingdom, inversions, and God's children are conspicuous in the sermon on the plain. Given the programmatic weight of God's kingdom in 4:43, the first beatitude is not merely first in a series but thematic: "Yours is the kingdom of God." The second and third beatitudes promise inversions, and the fourth implies inversions, which are grounded in God's kingdom.[19] The poor, without a δέησις except to God, are blessed because God's rule inverts their tragedy (6:20-23).

In contrast to the inversions in the beatitudes, the first woe is not a reversal at all (6:24). That is just the issue. The woe is that the rich remain as they are: "You are receiving your succor in full." Similarly, the last woe entails no inversion except that the false social affirmation, with its warped parentage (πατέρες αὐτῶν), is already an inversion. But the second and third woes are harsh reversals--from plenty to hunger, from laughing to mourning. Can God make children of vipers into children of Abraham? Does the God who inverts the woes of the poor and for whom anything is not impossible invert the woes of the rich?

Two aspects of Luke's sermon on the plain imply possible inversions also for those who suffer the woes. First, little suggests eschatological finality in either blessings or woes. True, 6:23 speaks of a reward in heaven. But "in that day" is the day when people revile Jesus' followers, and it corresponds to the false social affirmation of the rich in 6:26.[20] As with the joy in heaven in the parable of the lost sheep (15:7; see 15:10), the reward in heaven expresses divine approval.

Second, the sermon itself attempts to invert the woes by tensive focal

---

[18]On the programmatic character of 4:43 see M. Wolter, "'Reich Gottes' bei Lukas," *NTS* 41 (1995) 541, 549; Johnson, *Luke*, 84.

[19]On the grounding of future promises in God's present kingdom, see J. Herr, "Freut euch, ihr Armen . . . : Herausforderung zum Glaubenshumor durch Jesus," *Die Freude an Gott--unsere Kraft: Festschrift für Otto Bernhard Knoch* (ed. J. Dagenhardt; Stuttgart: Katholisches Bibelwerk, 1991) 433-36.

[20]In proximate agreement see Bock, *Luke*, 1. 580-81.

instances that deconstruct. Walter Wink has made a case for 6:29-30 as strategies of the historical Jesus for the oppressed to take initiative from oppressors.[21] But the Lucan context does not determine that the address is to the oppressed. The admonitions following the woes challenge those to whom the woes are addressed ("to you who hear" 6:27). Jesus apparently admonishes the rich to give to beggars. One who takes the goods of another probably pilfers from the rich. Lending (6:34-35) fits the rich. Ultimately, the enemies and the abusers of 6:27-28 can be defined only from the perspective of one who considers them to be enemies and abusers. Finally, Jesus declares that God is kind to the ungrateful and evil--the types to whom Jesus addresses the woes.[22]

Two major images imprint 6:27-45. One is a merciful father--back to parent and child.[23] On its own Jesus' admonition to "be merciful as your father is merciful" (6:36) may sound like an imitation ethic.[24] But the reward of 6:35 is in synonymous parallelism with being children of the Most High. The reward is nothing other than being God's children.[25] Being God's children also *is* the macarism of "yours is the kingdom of God" (6:20). So for disciples to be like the teacher (6:40) is to be children who reflect God's heart. The second image is a tree bearing fruit (6:43-44)--virtually plagiarized from the Baptizer (3:9). It also appears to make ethics a matter of ethical energy. Each tree produces it own fruit--good from good, bad from bad. But the tree is a variation on and thus a reiteration of the parent-child image. In fact, the tree turns into a heart: "Out of the good treasure of the heart the good person bears good [fruit]" (6:45)--the child's heart turned toward the heart of the parent God.

The blessing of possessing God's kingdom is reiterated in a parent-child image in 7:28. Contrary to Conzelmann's thesis, contrasting belonging to the

---

[21] W. Wink, "Neither Passivity nor Violence: Jesus' Third Way (Matt 5:38//Luke 6:29-30)," *Forum* 7 (1991) 5-28.

[22] D. Catchpole takes Q 6:27-35 as anthropocentric ("Jesus and the Community of Israel--The Inaugural Discourse in Q," *BJRL* 68 [1986] 304). But Luke 6:36 in the context makes it theocentric.

[23] "Luke unmistakably roots all expected behavior in the character of God [as merciful parent]" (Green, *Luke*, 271, see 274-75).

[24] So Catchpole, "Jesus and the Community," 309-10.

[25] So also R. Gluelich, *The Sermon on the Mount* (Waco: Word, 1982) 230.

kingdom with the birth of John does not split John from the kingdom.[26] In fact, Jesus' allusion to John's birth drives readers back to Elizabeth, so that John's greatness recapitulates his mission "to turn the hearts of parents to children." John's birth to Elizabeth in all its importance hyperbolically sets off children whose parent is God to greater advantage. The people of "this generation" (γενεά) of 7:31, then, are not the Judean people but those who are born of women.[27] In contrast to children of God, they are like children in the market, because they have rejected John's mission,"to turn the hearts of parents to children," and likewise the mission of Jesus, a child who reflects the heart of his parent God. Wisdom and her children, then, correspond to God and God's children (7:35).[28]

The good heart beats again in the explanation of the parable of the sower. For readers, the secrets of the kingdom (8:10) are no secret. God's kingdom is about bearing fruit. The seed plays dual roles. First, the word is the seed. But those who hear are also the seed. At one extreme of this agricultural enterprise lies the relationship of the heart to the devil. Feasting birds in 8:5 slide into a chthonic demon consuming human hearts in 8:12. At the other extreme lies the relationship of the doubly good heart (καλὴ καὶ ἀγαθή, 8:15) to--but here we are quite metaphorically stuck in mother earth. The explanation of the parable is no explanation but parable. The good heart is stuck in mother earth, which nurtures the seed and can only be a kind of ground of being.

But the behavior of the naked wild man in Gerasa shows that he is like seed stuck in earth that is not good (8:26-39). Jesus' mission is to invert such tragedy. "Therefore, there is nothing hidden that will not become visible nor anything concealed that will not be known and come to be obvious" (8:17). Thus, when Jesus exorcizes this man's demons, the people come out to *see* (8:35). Further, when a woman hemorrhaging for twelve years violates social barriers in order to invert her tragedy, she cannot *hide* (8:47). Jesus calls her a

---

[26]H. Conzelmann, *The Theology of St Luke* (New York: Harper & Row, 1961) 18-27
[27]On γενεά as "offspring" see LSJ.
[28]Johnson, *Luke*, 124; Green, *Luke*, 304. W. Cotter advances the intriguing thesis that the children ἐν ἀγορᾷ parody a court ("The Parable of the Children in the Market-Place, Q [Lk] 7:31-35: An Examination of the Parable's Image and Significance," *NovT* 29 [1987] 289-304; "Children Sitting in the Agora: Q (Luke) 7:31-35," *Forum* 5,2 [1989] 63-82).

daughter and commends her faith.[29] Whose daughter? Not Jesus'. He is about thirty (3:23), she at least twenty-four. But if faith is a relationship between human beings and God, this woman, in violating social barriers in order to invert her tragedy, is a daughter who reflects the heart of her parent God.

The transfiguration reaffirms Jesus as God's child. The voice that identifies Jesus as God's child enjoins listening to Jesus (9:35). Listening to what? Although the enjoinder may apply to all Jesus says, immediately before and after the transfiguration he predicts his passion, and in the middle he discusses his ἔξοδος (9:22; 9:44).[30] But the next incident is not a saying but an exorcism. Do actions speak louder than words?

But words interpret exorcisms. Grounding his disciples in God's rule, Jesus doubly empowers (δύναμις and ἐξουσία) the twelve to invert tragedy without him (9:1-2). When they are with him again, they narrate what they have done without him (9:10). During the transfiguration, they are again without him. But when they are with him again, a man who has a δέησις (9:38, 40), tells Jesus what they *did not do* without him (9:40). Jesus' exasperation about a faithless and twisted γενεά can hardly mean an entire generation, but "offspring" of deficient faith now doubly impotent, seed stuck in earth that bears no fruit. By contrast, Jesus inverts tragedy because as God's son (9:35) he is seed nurtured in the ground of being.

The disciples' struggle over their hierarchy reveals a similar deficiency. Jesus subverts both the hierarchy and the struggle by associating himself not with the most prominent among them but with a child (9:46-48). This child has no δέησις. But Jesus gives the child the δέησις to be accepted. This is derivative ethics. To accept the child in Jesus' name is to become a child of the parent whose heart Jesus as God's child reflects.

An anonymous exorcist does in Jesus' absence what his disciples could not do without him (9:49-50). John's attempt to stop the exorcist shows that he

---

[29]Jesus "embraces her in the family of God by referring to her as 'daughter'" (Green, *Luke*, 349). Faith characterizes the woman toward whom Jesus deflects praise from himself (V. Robbins, "The Woman Who Touched Jesus' Garments: Socio-Rhetorical Analysis of the Synoptic Accounts," *NTS* 33 [1987] 512-13).

[30]Conzelmann, *Theology*, 57-59.

is slow to comprehend derivative ethics. Like opposing receiving a child in Jesus' name, John opposes one who inverts tragedy in Jesus' name. Immediately, a Samaritan village does not receive Jesus. Jesus rebukes James and John for wanting to call down fire on them, leaving readers to wonder if such a Samaritan village might accept a child in Jesus' name--perhaps Philip in Acts 8.

The mission of the seventy revises the figure of fruit--not sowing but harvesting. The mission to invert the tragedies of the ἀσθενεῖς and to interpret the inversion as God's rule (Luke 10:9) derives from God, who sends laborers into the harvest. God reaps a harvest when the recipients of the mission become children whose hearts reflect their parent God. In mixed metaphors Jesus' disciples are herbivores who not only harvest but are subject to being harvested by carnivores. The logion of 10:16 shows the derivative nature of both lambs and wolves: "The one who listens to you listens to me, and the one who repudiates you repudiates me, and the one who repudiates me repudiates the one who sent me."

When the seventy return, Jesus names the one who sent him, who conceals and reveals, "father" (10:21-22). But what is concealed is to be made known. What is made known is that God is the parent of God's infants and that Jesus as God's child derives everything from his parent God. What is concealed is no longer hidden for readers unless they remain wise and sagacious. Readers who see what the disciples see (10:23) see that Jesus is a child who reflects the heart of his parent God, and that they also are God's children. Against its literary frame, the parable of the good Samaritan dramatizes one who in loving neighbor loves God (10:25-37). Does the lawyer who hears the parable remain wise and sagacious or become an infant?[31]

According to 9:48, in welcoming Jesus into her home (10:38) Martha welcomes the one who sent him[32] and corresponds to an infant who sees God's hidden things. In listening to Jesus, Mary also is an infant seeing and hearing

---

[31]On the open ending see Green, *Luke*, 432.

[32]A. Reinhartz, "From Narrative to History: The Resurrection of Mary and Martha," *"Women Like This": New Perspectives on Jewish Women in the Greco-Roman World* (SBLEJL 1; ed. A.-J. Levine; Atlanta: Scholars Press, 1991) 169-70. For Reinhartz, the pericope is less androcentric than christocentric.

what prophets and kings wanted to see and hear (10:23-24). However, Jesus identifies a deficiency in Martha's attempt to dislodge Mary from listening. Martha's anxiety interferes with her own διακονία, and she subordinates Mary's choice to hers.[33] So Martha hovers on the threshold between remaining an infant or becoming wise and sagacious. Does Jesus persuade her to remain an infant?

One disciple has a δέησις that the disciples be taught how to have a δέησις (11:1). More than recommending a formula, Jesus' response is a matter of infants appealing to a parent (πάτερ) with a δέησις.[34] The notice that anyone who asks receives is not carte blanche but poetic confidence that the one who has a δέησις also has an inimitable parent (11:10).[35] Having a δέησις as God's child means tautologically that one is God's child (11:13).

Inverting the image of God's child, opponents derive Jesus' exorcisms from Beelzebul (11:14-20)--identifying him as an offspring of vipers in John's imagery. Jesus' riposte derives his exorcisms from God as instances of God's rule (11:20). Reminiscent of Jesus' beatitudes, a woman preaches a macarism about the womb that bore Jesus and the breasts that suckled him. Though she reiterates Elizabeth's exclamation in 1:42, she derives blessedness from the fruit of belly and breasts.[36] Jesus rather derives blessedness from a divine parent, which is the lot of all who derive their living from God, potentially including this woman (11:27-28).

The woes against stereotyped Pharisees and lawyers paint them out of the picture of God and God's children in 11:1-36. Luke 11:42 plays their tithing off against ethics deriving from God (τοῦ θεοῦ), so that their parentage (πατέρες ὑμῶν, 11:47) contrasts with the divine parent. Again, "this generation" is not the Judean populace as such but offspring of defective parentage (11:50, 51). The key of knowledge, in which lawyers are deficient (11:52), is to know who

---

[33]F. Breydon, "A temps nouveau, nouvelles questions: Luc 10,38-42," *Foi et vie* 88,5 (1989) 27.

[34]On the relation of 11:1-4 to 10:21-22 see Green, *Luke*, 438, 440-41.

[35]On prayer as a metonym for reliance on a beneficent God see Green, *Luke*, 639.

[36]L. Schottroff, *Let the Oppressed Go Free: Feminist Perspectives on the New Testament* (Gender and the Biblical Tradition; Louisville: Westminster John Knox, 1993) 115-16. The woman's words are clearly metonymy.

is a child and who a parent (10:21-22). Here stereotyped Pharisees and lawyers remain wise and sagacious in terms of 10:21. Are they beyond becoming infants?

Parentage is problematic for stereotyped Pharisees. But 12:8-12 equates the situation of disciples (12:1), who face apostasy, with theirs. A replication of 8:17 fits both Pharisees and disciples, "Nothing is veiled that will not be uncovered and hidden that will not become known" (12:2). First, what becomes known is hypocrisy/apostasy (12:3, 9-10). But then what becomes known is God's character as judge and guardian. The judge can throw people into agony (12:5, 46; 13:28). But the guardian cares as "your parent" (12:6-7, 30). "Your parent is happy to give you the kingdom" (12:32), which is to have God as parent. To jump forward, this contrasts with human parents in 21:16 who betray their children as if Luke knows Ps 26:10 LXX: "Because my father and mother have forsaken me, the Lord has taken me up." Moreover, having God as parent means that the child's heart reflects the parent's heart: "For where your treasure is, there also will be your heart " (Luke 12:34).

The child's heart that reflects the parent's heart corresponds also to the fruit that the planter and gardener seek in 13:6-9.[37] This imagery combines motifs of fruit trees from the Baptizer and of mother earth from Jesus' parable of the sower. The problem is the relationship of the fig tree to mother earth--the ground of being. The case of the woman bent double presents a double challenge (13:10-17). (1) Jesus liberates her like the gardener who cultivates the fig tree.[38] As a daughter of Abraham, she embodies fulfillment of God's

---

[37]Some interpret the fig tree as stock imagery for Israel. L. Schottroff, "Von den Bäumen lernen, dass Gott nahe ist," *Abschied vom Männergott: Schöpfungsverantwort für Frauen und Männer* (ed. J. Jäger-Sommer; Luzern: Exodus, 1995)262-71. Nevertheless, Schottroff emphasizes God's initiative for repentance, hope, and redemption. But the incidents in Luke 13:1-5 focus on individual sin and repentance. In relationship with 13:1-5, 13:6-9 focuses on the bearing of fruit in individual lives. Further, the gardener takes initiative to enable the tree to bear fruit. See M. Gourges, "Regroupement littéraire et équilibrage théologique. Le cas de Lc 13,1-9," *The Four Gospels 1992: Festschrift Frans Neirynck* (BETL; ed. F. Segbroech *et al.*; Leuven: Leuven University Press, 1992) 1597-99.

[38]E. Schüssler Fiorenza, "Liberation, Unity and Equality in Community: a New Testament Case Study," *Beyond Unity-in-Tension: Unity, Renewal and the Community of Women and Men* (ed. T. Best; Geneva: WCC Publications, 1988) 59. R. O'Toole views the woman as a model for imitation ("Some Exegetical Reflections on Luke 13, 10-17," *Bib* 73

promise of blessing to Abraham (Acts 3:25). (2) The synagogue ruler precipitates a challenge by objecting to the liberation of the woman on the Sabbath. But Jesus' counter charge of hypocrisy is in the plural, and all those opposing him are put to shame. Is Jesus a gardener who also cultivates opponents as fig trees that might bear fruit? Might they grow in mother earth like a mustard seed? (13:18-20).[39]

The parable in 15:11-32 functions as a *mise en abyme*,[40] an explanatory variant that mirrors in miniature larger stories of children who turn to the heart of their parent. The parable replicates two levels of the diegetic story: (1) the story of God in relation to Israel, and (2) Jesus' relationship with toll collectors and sinners to which stereotyped Pharisees and scribes object.[41] The narrator explicitly links the parable to Jesus' debate with his contemporaries. The replicated conclusions to the lost sheep and lost coin explicitly link the parable with God's story. Further, (1) "father" and "son" are metadiegetic replications of characters on the diegetic level. (2) Jesus as the author of the parable, who welcomes sinners and eats with them, replicates himself on one level as the father who welcomes back the younger son and eats with him. (3) On another level the parable replicates God as the father who welcomes sinners, especially in light of the conclusions to the lost sheep and lost coin. (4) Conflict among characters in the parable evokes the setting in 15:1-2. The younger son evokes identification with the toll collectors and sinners. The angry brother who confronts his father evokes the setting of controversy between Jesus and stereotyped Pharisees and scribes. (5) As narrator of the parable, Jesus has a similar relationship to his metadiegetic narrative as the narrator to the diegetic

---

[1992] 94-95). But Jesus' actions are the focus rather than the woman's.

[39]E. Schüssler Fiorenza claims that readers know that Jesus' call to repentance will meet rejection (*But She Said: Feminist Practices of Biblical Interpretation* [Boston: Beacon, 1992] 207). But readers who differentiate among Jesus' opponents to the extent that Luke-Acts differentiates cannot identify these opponents with those who ultimately reject.

[40]The *relationship* between the parable and the larger narrative is itself figurative. See P. Verelst, "Texte et iconographie: une curieuse mise en abyme dans un 'Rebaut de Mantauban' inédit (XVe s.)," *Onze études sur la mise en abyme* (Tomanica Bandensia 17; ed. F. Hallyn; Blandijnberg: George Michiels, 1980) 151.

[41]On ways in which a *mise en abyme* replicates the larger narrative see L. Dällenbach, *The Mirror in the Text* (Chicago: University of Chicago Press, 1989) 24, 35.

narrative. Thus Jesus speaks reliably in the name of the narrator, and vice versa.[42]

The younger son not only distances himself from his father but also from his heritage. Squandering his οὐσία has significance both for his possessions and his Judaism. Relinquishing the legacy that the family traced back to Abraham through the allocation of the land shows his abdication of Jewish identity as much as feeding swine. But upon his return, he experiences being a child of his parent beyond what he had known before. The older brother's hostility distances him from reflecting the heart of his parent, though not from his parent's heart. The parent with his older son is like the gardener cultivating the fig tree. The story suspends on the older brother's decision.[43] Does he become a child who reflects his parent's heart?

The context implies that older brothers may change. The parable of the dishonest steward continues the thematic development of children who derive what they do from their parentage. The steward, like the prodigal son,[44] squanders property acquired from someone else (16:1, 5-7). Jesus characterizes him not as ἄδικος but as τῆς ἀδικίας (genitive of origin, BDF §162) in close synonymity with calling him a child of this age (16:8).[45] This child of this age

---

[42]On identifying the microcosm and macrocosm see Dällenbach, *Mirror in the Text*, 18, 46-47, 52. M. Bal critiques Dällenbach for being too analytical and emphasizes any aspect of the microcosm that is pertinent and continuous with the macrocosm but also stresses direct references to resemblance and (para)synonyms ("Mise en abyme et iconicité," *Littérature* 29 [1978] 121-24). See also M. Ron, "The Restricted Abyss: Nine Problems in the Theory of *Mise en Abyme*," *Poetics Today* 8 (1987) 426-27; J. Richardou, "La population des mirrors: Problèmes de la similitude à partir d'un texte d'Alain Robbe-Grillet," *Poétique* 22 (1975) 218; J. Lértora, "La estructura de la 'mise en abyme' en *Fragmentos de Apocalipsis*," *Semiosis* 4 (1980) 83.

[43]On the ending as a call to repentance rather than a polemic, see P. Pokorný, "Lukas 15,11-32 und die lukanische Soteriologie," *Christus bezeugen: Festschrift für Wolfgang Trilling* (ed. K. Kertelge et al.; Leipzig: St. Benno, 1987) 192. On the contrast with V. Propp's expected transformation of the older brother into a villain see P. Pokorný, "Saint Luke's Message about the Christian Relationship towards Israel," *Explorations* 11, 2 (1997) 4.

[44]On parallels between the prodigal and the dishonest steward see M. Austin, "The Hypocritical Son," *EQ* 57 (1985) 310-14.

[45]See H. Kosmala, "The Parable of the Unjust Steward in the Light of Qumran," *ASTI* 3 (1964) 114-15. The manager's actions (16:1, 5-7) proceed from ἀδικία--unrecognized by W. Loader in his critique of Kosmala ("Jesus and the Rogue in Luke 16,1-8a: The Parable

deals with children of this age *including the rich patron who commends him*, and Jesus contrasts *all of them* with children of light. The criterion of serving God subverts the rich patron's commendation. He is a child of this age who serves mammon.

Making friends by action that derives from the mammon of unrighteousness clashes with the ideological perspective in Luke-Acts and constitutes what Michel Riffaterre labels an "ungrammaticality," an incongruity that drives readers beyond the literal level.[46] Consequently, readers may take 16:9 as irony.[47] The subversion of the wise and sagacious in 10:21 predisposes readers to take φρονίμως, and therefore also the oxymoronic "eternal tents," as ironic.[48] Is Jesus saying, "Make friends with mammon and see how 'eternal' they and their dwellings are"? Further, the explanatory comments in 16:11-13 keep the steward from being an example to emulate.[49]

---

of the Unjust Steward," *RB* 96 [1989] 526). H. Drexler takes the genitive as a genitive of quality where the genitive replaces an adjective ("Zu Lukas 16:1-7," *ZNW* 58 [1967] 288 n. 8). But this misses the parentage implied by the υἱοί in the second half of Luke 16:8.

[46]M. Riffaterre, *Semiotics of Poetry* (Bloomington: Indiana University Press, 1978) 2-8, 42, 63, 109-10, 115-24, *passim*; *Text Production* (New York: Columbia University Press, 1983) 51, 88, 118, 200, 317 n. 57; "La trace d l'intertext," *La pensée* 215 (Oct. 1980) 6-18; "The Intertextual Unconscious," *Critical Inquiry* 13 (1987) 371-81. C. Torrey's attempt to view 16:8-9 as a mistranslation of Aramaic (*Our Translated Gospel* [New York: Harper & Row, 1936] 59) is indicative of the ungrammaticalities.

[47]For the conventional focus on shrewdness see C. Blomberg, "'Your Faith Has Made You Whole': The Evangelical Liberation Theology of Jesus," *Jesus of Nazareth: Lord and Christ--Essays on the Historical Jesus and New Testament Theology: In Honor of I. Howard Marshall* (Grand Rapids: Eerdmans, 1994) 90-91 nn. 81-85. Johnson takes the third person plural as equivalent to a divine passive (*Luke*, 245). But this ignores the antecedent φίλοι.

[48]I. du Plessis, "Philanthropy or Sarcasm?--Another Look at the Parable of the Dishonest Manager (Luke 16:1-13)," *Neot* 24 (1990) 10-13; D. Fletcher, "The Riddle of the Unjust Steward: Is Irony the Key?" *JBL* 82 (1963) 29; S. Porter, "The Parable of the Unjust Steward (Luke 16:1-13): Irony Is the Key," *The Bible in Three Dimensions: Essays in Celebration of Forty Years of Biblical Studies in the University of Sheffield* (ed. D. Clines *et al*; JSOTSup 87; Sheffield: Sheffield Academic Press, 1990) 127-53, esp. 148-53. Porter catches irony in light of the prodigal son and the rich man in 16:19-31 in attempts to make friends by money.

[49]W. Oesterly, *The Gospel Parables in the Light of Their Jewish Background* (New York: Macmillan, 1936) 195-203; Fletcher, "Riddle of the Unjust Steward," 20-21; Porter, "Parable of the Unjust Steward," 130. For J. Kloppenborg, the parable challenges social codes of honor and shame ("The Dishonored Master [Luke 16,1-8a]," *Bib* 70 [1989] 474-95). But this implies the rehabilitation of the manager who remains characterized pejoratively.

Some stereotyped Pharisees, who love money and ridicule Jesus (16:14), recall the preceding parable. Like the steward, they derive what they do from mammon. Like the rich man, they rationalize what they derive from mammon. The heart of the matter is the heart: "God knows your hearts" (16:15).

The parable of the rich man and Lazarus presents an unusual case of sibling non-rivalry. Spatially--and metaphorically--Lazarus winds up close to Abraham's heart (16:22-23). Though the rich man is still Abraham's τέκνον, and Abraham his parent (16:25, 27, 30), he is distanced from Abraham's heart. In the parabolic world, the one rising from the dead is not Jesus (though readers will hardly overlook the *mise en abyme*) but Lazarus, whose name and suffering imply a δέησις.[50] The rich man also has a δέησις. On one level, there is no Abrahamic mercy to cool his tongue. But he has another δέησις for his siblings. On this level, there is mercy in Moses and the prophets, not to exclude Abraham. The parable suspends on the five siblings as the prodigal son suspends on the older brother.[51] Moreover, stereotyped Pharisees and scribes, who correspond to the older brother, correspond also to stereotyped Pharisees who derive what they do from mammon in 16:14, who in turn correspond to the five siblings on whom repentance suspends. Do they listen so that their hearts reflect God's heart?[52]

The problem in Jesus' warning against causing scandals is again parentage (17:1-4). Strikingly, however, Jesus' admonishes *disciples* that they not beget falling little ones. The disciples potentially replicate the stereotyped lawyers in 11:52, whereas the little ones replicate the infants of 10:21 who know who is a father and who a child. But Jesus' warning has positive potential.

---

[50]J. Jeremias finds the name Lazarus significant on the level of the historical Jesus (*The Parables of Jesus* [New York: Scribner's, 1972] 183-86). Greek readers might not infer "God helps" from the name.

[51]See Bock, *Luke*, 2. 1377. Johnson overlooks the conditional form in 16:31 to "seal their [the five siblings'] rejection" (*Luke*, 256).

[52]On openness to change in Pharisees see Green, *Luke*, 611. The suspended ending undermines O. Glombitza's interpretation that it is too late for the synagogue that has overlooked Jesus ("Der reiche Mann und der arme Lazarus: Luk. Xvi 19-31: Zur Frage nach der Botschaft des Textes," *NovT* 12 [1970] 173-79) and V. Tanghe's view that the parable opposes Jewish refusal to repent ("Abraham, son fils et son envoyé [Luc 16,19-31] *RB* 91 [1984] 577).

Disciples have opportunity to be surrogate parents of their siblings by evoking repentance, reprising the rich man's role in the previous parable with respect to his siblings.

In 18:1-30 five portraits contrast those bereft of divine parentage with God's children. Two incidents that juxtapose these portraits come before Jesus' blessing of children and two follow. Thus, a symmetrical structure centers on Jesus' blessing of children (18:16-17). (A) A resolute woman has two opponents--one who has wronged her and a judge who is wrong (τῆς ἀδικίας, 18:6, genitive of origin). But the woman has a δέησις like those who cry to God (18:7). (B) A parable compares a stereotyped Pharisee, whose prayer is not a δέησις, with a toll collector, who like the woman, does have a δέησις. After Jesus' blessing of children, (B') a grieving rich ruler is a focal instance of one whose parentage is mammon, (A') then the disciples are focal instances of those whose parent is God.

Jesus addresses the parable of the stereotyped Pharisee and the toll collector to those whose dependence on themselves makes them their own parents. (The image stops short of implying that they had intercourse with themselves.) Are they permanently their own parents? Or does the hinge in the symmetrical structure matter? Disciples, who replicate the role of stereotyped lawyers in 11:52, and who are perilously close to having millstones around their necks (17:2), hinder those who bring children to Jesus (18:15-17). Children are infants on whom Jesus places his hands; they are adults whose hearts may turn again as if they were children of their parent God. Thus, readers can hardly abandon those who are their own parents any more than they can the disciples, because with God anything is not impossible (1:37), or in a new variation, "Impossibilities in human hands are mighty deeds in God's hands" (18:27).

Readers soon see an impossibility in human hands become a mighty deed in God's. Zacchaeus is another rich man (19:1-10). "It is easier for a camel to go through the eye of a needle than for a rich person to go into the kingdom of God" (18:25). In contrast to his sorrowful counterpart in 18:23, Zacchaeus rejoices as he receives Jesus. "The one who receives me, receives the one who sent me" (9:48). According to Zacchaeus's pledge, he stops deriving his living from mammon and begins to derive it from his parent God, which is to say that instead of an offspring of vipers, he is a child of Abraham.

Luke 19:41-45 personifies Jerusalem as a parent from whom the things that make for peace are hidden. In 10:22 what is hidden is who is a parent and who a child. In one sense Jerusalem does not recognize that Jesus is God's child.[53] But derivatively Jerusalem also does not recognize itself as God's child. In retrospect readers may recall such a derivative childhood in Jesus' δέησις in 13:34: "How often have I desired to gather your children the way a hen gathers her own brood under her wings."

After Jesus' claim on the Temple, temple operatives ask Jesus to name the power in which he acts (20:2). Jesus' rejoinder shows that, as with John's baptism, parentage is at stake: Is it from God or human beings? The answer remains problematic for the temple operatives, but for readers who remember 10:21-22, what is hidden from the wise and sagacious is who is a parent and who a child.

Not only does a flashback to 10:21-22 evoke such correlations, so does the parable of the wicked tenants that follows. Another *mise en abyme*, it replicates the narrative that contains it. Paradoxically, as a replication of salvation history of which Luke-Acts is a part,[54] the parable contains the narrative that contains it. The parable's auditors clearly link the metadiegetic and the diegetic levels.[55] Temple operatives also perceive themselves in the parable. In addition, (1) the "beloved son" mirrors Jesus on the diegetic level. (2) Jesus as the author of the parable replicates himself in the son of the parable.[56] (3) The encounter between the son and the tenants replicates Jesus' encounter with temple operatives in the setting. When the temple operatives recognize themselves in the story, they are both characters in the parable and its audience.[57] (4) The fruit of the vineyard replicates motifs of bearing fruit in the

---

[53]On ambiguity in the syntax of 19:42 see Johnson, *Luke*, 298.

[54]Fitzmyer, *Luke*, 2. 1281.

[55]On identifying the microcosm and macrocosm see n. 42.

[56]This is a case of a hero becoming a virtual narrator. W. Smekens, "Proust en diagonale," *Onze études sur la mise en abyme* (Romanica Gandensia 17; ed. F. Hallyn; Blandijnberg: Beorge Michiels, 1980) 102-05; Ron, "Restricted Abyss," 419-20.

[57]See R. Vandenbrande, "'Les acteurs de bonne foi' de Marivaux ou la comédie au bord de l'abîme, *Onze études sur la mise en abyme* (Romanica Gandensia 17; ed. F. Hallyn; Blandijnberg: Beorge Michiels, 1980) 141.

diegetic narrative. (5) Jesus' voice coheres with the narrator's so that he offers reliable commentary on the macrocosmic narrative.[58]

Bernard Scott contends that the parable manifests no interest in fruits of the vineyard.[59] However, the owner of the vineyard repeatedly attempts to acquire fruit. Moreover, the vineyard recalls trees that bear fruit, seed stuck in mother earth, and a cultivated fig tree. It is also reminiscent of the unproductive vineyard of Isa 5:1-7. But against interpretations of the parable as a rejection of Israel, the vineyard, unlike the one in Isaiah, is not destroyed. Rather, the tenants are destroyed, and giving the vineyard to others presumes that it will render fruit. In the narrative world, Jesus' promise to the twelve that they will judge the tribes of Israel (Luke 22:30) implicates them as the "other tenants." The narrative anticipates that the twelve will not replicate the stereotyped lawyers of 11:52, as the disciples did when they hindered children from coming to Jesus in 18:15. They will rather replicate the gardener of 13:8 who cultivates for fruit from the ground of being.

The controversy on paying taxes to Caesar suspends on an enigma. Readers must decide what belongs to Caesar and what to God (20:25). But Jesus' saying replicates "you cannot serve God and mammon" and serves as a call to repentance.[60] Next, against some stereotyped Sadducees, Jesus claims that in the world of the resurrection, people live as siblings (υἱοί εἰσιν θεοῦ) who draw their living from their divine parent (20:27-38).[61] Is Jesus persuasive? At least some scribes agree with him (20:39).

Context and motif help to resolve the puzzle of the messiah as David's son (20:41-44). In the thematic development, Jesus is David's σπέρμα who will rule over the house of Jacob forever. Acts 2:34-35 uses the same text that Jesus quotes here from Ps 110:1 clearly with reference to the risen Jesus whose

---

[58]Dällenbach, *Mirror in the Text*, 18, 52.

[59]B. Scott, *Hear Then the Parable: A Commentary on the Parables of Jesus* (Minneapolis: Fortress, 1989) 251.

[60]On Jesus' saying as a call to repentance see M. Bünker, "'Gebt dem Kaiser, was des Kaisers ist!'--Aber: Was ist des Kaisers? Überlegungen zur Perikope von der Kaisersteuer," *Kairos* 29 (1987) 95.

[61]On those who have a place in the resurrection age as children of God see J. Kilgallen, "The Sadducees and the Resurrection from the Dead: Luke 20,27-40," *Bib* 67 (1986) 485-86.

regency derives from God. Readers who know Acts 2:34-35 can understand in retrospect that the messiah's status in Luke 20:41 derives not from being a child of David but from being a child of God, namely, the status of Abraham, Isaac, Jacob (20:37), and implicitly also of David.

Jesus' anticipation of the fulfillment of Passover in God's kingdom (22:16) finds a correlate in his claim that his divine parent has assigned him a kingdom (22:29). As Jesus' passion is being fulfilled, he has a δέησις that his destiny will derive from his divine parent: "Πάτερ, . . . not my will but yours be done" (22:42). Further, Jesus aligns himself with God's power in synonymity with being God's child (22:69-70).

In the sermon on the plain Jesus admonishes: "Pray for those who abuse you" (6:28). In its context, as I suggest above, such behavior derives from God's rule--from a child who reflects the parent's heart. Variant ᴍs traditions aside, Jesus' prayer for those who crucify him arises similarly from his relationship with his parent God (πάτερ, 23:34).

At the beginning of Jesus' venture God names him God's child (3:22). At the end Jesus names God his parent. In his final extremity on the cross, Jesus has a δέησις: "Πάτερ, into your hands I commend my πνεῦμα" (23:46). Πνεῦμα here is likely the totality of Jesus' existence.[62] As a child, Jesus murmurs a prayer reminiscent of "I pray thee Lord my soul to keep," in which he declares his dependence upon his parent.[63]

When Jesus walks with Cleopas and his companion to Emmaus, they

---

[62]Ps 30:11 LXX has a reference to ζωή that is apparently synonymous with πνεῦμα. W. Bieder, F. Baumgärtel, H. Kleinknecht, "πνεῦμα," *TDNT* 6.334-35; 360-61, 364; 368-69; W. Grundmann, *Das Evangelium nach Lukas* (THKNT 3; Berlin: Evangelische Verlag, 1961) 435; J. Ernst, *Das Evangelium nach Lukas: Übersetzt und erklärt* (RNT; Regensberg: Pustet, 1977) 639; D. Senior, *The Passion of Jesus in the Gospel of Luke* (Wilmington, DE: Glazier, 1989) 168; F. Untergassmair, *Kreuzweg und Kreuzigung Jesu: Ein Beitrag zur lukanischen Redactionsgeschichte und zur Frage nach der lukanische "Kreuzestheologie"* (Paderborner theologische Studien 10; Paderborn: Schömomogh, 1980) 88-89; J. Neyrey, *The Passion According to Luke: A Redactional Study of Luke's Soteriology* (Mahwah, NJ: Paulist, 1985) 146-54; E. Bons, "Das Sterbewort Jesu nach Lk 23,46 und sein alttestamentlicher Hintergrund," *BZ* 38 (1994) 93-101.

[63]Perhaps Jesus dies with a conventional Jewish bedtime prayer on his lips (Ps 31:5). Dating the traditions to the time of Jesus is impossible, but see *b. Ber.* 4b-5a; *Midr. Rabbah* Num 20:20; and *Midr. Tanh* B VII.23 on Numbers.

reprise the role of the five siblings in the parable of the rich man and Lazarus. They are not persuaded even though someone is raised from the dead. But they have an ironic δέησις: "Stay with us" (24:29).[64]   It is not merely in the breaking of bread that their eyes are opened, but as the inclusion of 24:27 and 24:32 shows, they also listen to Moses and the prophets.[65]

The final words of the risen Jesus in Luke characterize God simultaneously as Jesus' parent and as the one who sends what this parent has promised (24:49). In the narrative world, the parent promises to give the holy spirit to those who ask as children (11:13).[66] Apparently Jesus' followers have such a δέησις.

Early in Acts, Jesus' followers, like mute Zechariah, are suspended between promise and fulfillment. Jesus reiterates the promise but characterizes God as ὁ πατήρ (1:4; see also 2:33) rather than as ὁ πατήρ μου (Luke 24:49). The repetition with variation shows that Jesus' parent is not his exclusively. Jesus' followers express explicitly their δέησις over the demise of Israel's kingdom (Acts 1:6) as do Simeon, Anna, Joseph of Arimathea, and the two on the road to Emmaus. The restoration of the kingdom in their δέησις is never in question. Rather the issue is timing, and the waiting for the spirit and the consequent witness to the ends of the earth is associated with the restoration of the kingdom to Israel.[67]

In using Joel to explain Pentecost, Peter derives the prophesying of sons and daughters from God (2:17-18). In contrast to Joel 3:2 LXX, in Peter's

---

[64]H. Betz, "The Origin and Nature of Christian Faith According to the Emmaus Legend (Luke 24:13-32)," *Int* 23 (1969) 37.

[65]H. Merkel, "Israel im lukanischen Werk," *NTS* 40 (1994) 383; Betz, "Origin and Nature," 38, 40-41.

[66]R. Tannehill, *The Narrative Unity of Luke-Acts* (2 vols.; FFNT; Philadelphia and Minneapolis: Fortress, 1986-90) 1. 239; R. Pesch, *Die Apostelgeschichte* (2 vols.; EKK 5; Zürich: Benzinger, 1986) 1. 66.

[67]This is before the ascension so that the parousia is not at issue. *Pace* E. Haenchen, *The Acts of the Apostles: A Commentary* (Philadelphia: Westminster, 1971) 142-43. In at least partial support see R. Tannehill, "Israel in Luke-Acts: A Tragic Story," *JBL* 104 (1985) 76; C. Barrett, *A Critical and Exegetical Commentary on the Acts of the Apostles* (Edinburgh: T & T Clark, 1994) 77-78; L. Johnson, *The Acts of the Apostles* (Sacra Pagina 5; Collegeville, Minn.: Liturgical, 1992) 38-39; G. Schneider, *Die Apostelgeschichte* (2 vols.; HTKNT 5; Freiburg: Herder, 1980-82) 1. 201; Merkel, "Israel im lukanischen Werk," 397.

version these are God's δοῦλοι and δοῦλαι--reminiscent of Mary (Luke 1:38). The parable of the rich man and Lazarus anticipates the futility of convincing siblings by someone who has been raised from the dead. But this is what Peter attempts (Acts 2:29-37, note ἀδεφοί). However, in keeping with the parable, Peter proclaims Jesus' resurrection as a matter of listening to Moses and the prophets. The next incident repeats Peter's attempt to persuade siblings by proclaiming someone who has been raised from the dead (3:17), and again this is a matter of listening to Moses and the prophets (3:18, 21, 24).

Characterizing the God who raised Jesus as the God of Abraham, Isaac, and Jacob (3:13) implies that to reject Jesus is to have hearts that do not reflect the πατέρες. Significantly, these are the πατέρες to whom God gave the Abrahamic covenant: "And in your seed all the πατριαί of the earth shall be blessed" (3:25). The πατριαί are derivative, more than linguistically, from the πατέρες. If God can raise up children to Abraham from stones (Luke 3:8), who might the πατριαί of the πατέρες be? One answer is that the Abrahamic blessing is available to Peter's listeners (Acts 3:26). On the other hand, it is the continuation of God's blessing to the πατέρες.[68] Further, the healing of a lame man at the Temple is a focal instance of blessing "in Abraham's seed."[69]

There are two kinds of πατέρες in Stephen's speech. On the one hand, there are the patriarchs, Abraham, Isaac, and Jacob. On the other, there are the forebears of Stephen's audience whose hearts did not reflect the hearts of Abraham, Isaac, and Jacob. That these are only some of the forebears is indicated by a neutral use of πατέρες for the forebears who had the tent of testimony (7:44-45). Stephen's charge against his opponents is that their behavior derives from faulty parentage (7:51).

Cornelius has a δέησις (Acts 10:2, 4, 31). But readers find it difficult to deduce problems from solutions. The solutions, focalized through Peter, are that

---

[68]Haenchen, *Acts*, 205; H. Conzelmann, *Acts of the Apostles: A Commentary on the Acts of the Apostles* (Hermeneia; Philadelphia: Fortress, 1987) 28; Barrett, *Acts*, 188; Johnson, *Acts*, 67.

[69]Against Barrett (*Acts*, 212), there is no new covenant or covenant renewal. Against Johnson (*Acts*, 70), "seed" may play ambiguously on the singular ("Jesus") and the collective. Barrett, *Acts*, 191; Roloff, *Apostelgeschichte*, 78; Pesch, *Apostelgeschichte*, 157-58.

Cornelius counts among those δεκτός to God (10:35) and his sins are forgiven (10:43). But when the same situation is focalized through the narrator, an angel, and Cornelius, Cornelius is already δεκτός to God (10:4, 31). So the nature of his δέησις is unclear. At first, Peter has a δέησις of protest: "I have never eaten anything profane and unclean" (10:14). The distress of his δέησις is masked under a culturally exclusive heart allegedly reflecting God's heart. Initially, Peter is unaware of his distress--a socially shared unawareness as Acts 11:3 and 15:2, 5 show. His vision (10:11; 11:5) perplexes him until he associates with Gentiles and interprets the vision not in terms of food but of human beings (10:28). After his interpretation, δεκτός to God means δεκτός to Peter. Peter interprets what happens to the Gentiles in 15:8-9 as a matter of the heart, whereas he sublimates the demand of the circumcision party as a matter of the neck (15:10). Against the veiled distress of ethnic preference, divine obligation happens.

In Pisidian Antioch, Paul also plays the role anticipated by the parable of the rich man and Lazarus--attempting to persuade siblings (13:16, 26) by someone who is raised from the dead. But like Peter, he too proclaims Jesus' resurrection as a matter of listening to Moses and the prophets. Paul's survey of the story of Israel's πατέρες (13:17) peaks in one sense at David, in another at God, because the speech is theocentric. David also is a πατήρ, because he has a descendant, Jesus, whom God has sent. But deriving Jesus from David is more than lineage (Luke 3:31). It is also a matter of the heart. David reflected God's heart (Acts 13:22). Jesus is derivative of David in that sense as well. In addition, Paul and his hearers are also derivative of their parentage (πατέρες ἡμῶν, 13:17; children of Abraham's family, 13:26). As such they are also in the line of promises to the πατέρες.

According to Paul's speech in Athens, one human is the universal ancestor (17:26). But in keeping with popular poetry and Adam's genesis from God in Luke 3:38, all humans are God's offspring (17:28). Similarly, Musonius Rufus considered Zeus to be the common πατήρ of all humans. Humans are therefore the likeness (μίμημα) of Zeus, and for Musonius Rufus ethics is a matter of living in accord with this likeness as an emulator of Zeus (ὁμοίως ἔχειν; ζηλωτός).[70] But in Paul's speech, likeness has to do with what the deity is not. The deity is not like (ὅμοιον) metal or stone or an artistic image. Paul's deduction from divine parentage suspends on a cognitive level--ignorance on the one hand, conventional thinking on the other (17:29-30). But the object is not, as with Musonius, to imitate God. It is to find God (17:27). In one sense, human beings already live and move and have their being in God. When, however, humans find God, whose offspring they are, living, moving, and having being rise to the level of the sublime.

After Paul's arrest in Jerusalem, his defense speeches accentuate that his commission derives from the God of the πατέρες (22:14; 24:14). In 22:3 and 23:6, Paul claims to be a Judean who serves the God of the forebears according to "the way." His adherence to the way comes through an encounter with the risen Jesus. But true to the parable of the rich man and Lazarus, Moses and the prophets interpret his encounter with the risen one (24:14; 26:6-7; see 28:20). In 3:25 God's promise is the blessing of all the families of the earth, and synonymity in the promise in 26:6-7 means that the resurrection, a specific case already having occurred, is a way God blesses all the families of the earth.

Paul claims to have an eyeopening commission from the God of the promises. But what if Paul's eyeopening commission does not open eyes? In Rome, Paul characterizes his unbelieving Judean guests as offspring of the resistant πατέρες of Isa 6:9-10. In the face of closed eyes, does Isaiah's commission to open eyes cease? Does Paul's? The use of Isa 6:9-10 indicates a grave situation. But at the end there stands a promise of God to heal the people: καὶ ἰάσομαι αὐτούς (Acts 28:27). Modern versions almost invariably translate ἰάσομαι as if it were subjunctive.[71] But in the LXX, ἰάσομαι expresses God's promise to reestablish the people in the land. Whereas Isaiah

---

[70]C. Lutz, *Musonius Rufus: "The Roman Socrates"* (Yale Classical Studies 10; New Haven: Yale University Press, 1947) 104, 108. I translate ζηλωτός as "emulator" rather than "enviable" as Lutz translates.

[71]Schneider takes the future as replacing the subjunctive (*Apostelgeschichte* 2. 419 n. 85). See BDF § 369 (3). But even BDF notes that the future consequence has a kind of independence. L. Johnson translates ἰάσομαι as future but comments only that it is odd (*Acts*, 468, 472). F. Bovon agrees that ἐπιστρέψωσιν and ἰάσομαι are independent from μήποτε ("'Schon hat der heilige Geist durch den Propheten Jesaja zu euren Vätern gesprochen' [Act 28:5]." *ZNW* 75 [1984] 230).

6 in Hebrew predicts utter emptiness in the land and devastation like burning the stump of a tree that has already been cut down, the LXX says that a remnant will multiple in the land, "And one-tenth shall still be in it, and it will once again be for foraging like a terebinth[72] and like a nut when it falls from its husk" (Isa 6:13 LXX). Paul cites Isa 6:9-10 in a setting where his believing guests are like a remnant among those who disbelieved, and at the end there stands a promise of God to heal: "And should they turn, I will heal them" (Acts 28:27). Even with ears hardly hearing and eyes that are closed, the turning of these people is a matter of the heart--hearts that should they turn will reflect God's heart. As in Isaiah so in Luke-Acts God's judgment is penultimate rather than ultimate.

Thus, Paul proclaims openly God's rule to all who come to him--contextually, Gentiles, Judeans who believe, and Judeans who do not believe.[73] Is Paul wasting his breath? It would be fatally contradictory if Luke-Acts were to end with people who don't have a δέησις.

---

[72]On the terebinth kernel as a source for food see I. Löw, *Die Flor der Juden*, 4 vols. (Hildesheim: Georg Olms, 1967) 1. 199.

[73]See D. Marguerat, "'Et quand nous somes entré dans Rome': L'Énigme de la fin du Livre des Actes (28,16-31)," *RHPR* 73 (1993) 15-21.

The Character of God in the Book of the Twelve

Much of the work of the Seminar on the Book of the Twelve has been devoted to trying to understand the redactional layers behind the text, the literary unity of the Twelve, and the way separate segments of the Twelve are linked into a whole.[1] There has also been serious discussion about whether it is advisable to treat the twelve prophecies as one book, or whether it is more reasonable to examine each in its separate context. Time has been spent discussing the merits of the Septuagint over against the Masoretic text, and vice versa.[2] Qumran texts have not been neglected altogether. Hermeneutical matters, such as the value of using words such as "unity" and "coherence," have at least been broached. One of the newer areas of exploration, however, is the theological coherence of the Twelve (or lack thereof). Rolf Rendtorff offered the first treatment of the Twelve's theology in 1997, and this paper seeks to follow in his large footsteps.

One seeking to analyze the Twelve's theology runs many of the same risks as those who attempt to examine the book's redaction, literary unity, or historical background. The fact remains that twelve separate prophecies must be treated as a single corpus. It is still true that there are two possible canonical traditions that may be considered. The Twelve's thematic unity and diversity has not miraculously disappeared. These facts should not dissuade the theologian from pressing forward, but they should make that theologian be humble in his or her assertions. Hopefully this paper will strike some balance between the need to make assertions and the necessity of exercising caution while doing so.

An analysis of the Twelve's theology, even a brief one such as this effort, ought to consist of three very basic parts: an explanation of methodology, a treatment of relevant texts, and a unifying summary of common ideas, or themes.[3] Each of these components is necessary for an informed discussion of the Twelve's theology to proceed, for each one addresses a major concern of Old Testament studies in general and of Old Testament theology in particular. Old Testament

---

[1] Several of the earlier papers have been adapted and published in J. W. Watts and P.R. House, *Forming Prophetic Literature: Essays on Isaiah and the Twelve in Honor of John D.W. Watts*, JSOTS 205 (Sheffield: Sheffield Academic Press, 1996).

[2] On this subject see Barry Jones, *The Formation of the Book of the Twelve: A Study in Text and Canon*, SBLDS 149 (Atlanta: Scholars Press, 1995).

[3] My own approach to Old Testament theology and a more lengthy treatment of the Twelve's theology see P.R. House, *Old Testament Theology* (Downers Grove, IL: InterVarsity Press, 1998).

theology, like its counterparts New Testament theology and Systematic theology, is currently involved in methodological debates. Therefore, exegetical and theological reflection are often held in abeyance. Theoretical discussions are not inconsequential, but it is also appropriate for Old Testament theologians to state their chosen methodology, offer their analyses, and defend their work as the need arises.

At its heart, Old Testament theology is a study of what the biblical text says about God. In other words, it is God's character that is the object of study. As is true in all compelling literature, the nature of a character in an Old Testament book is revealed through that character's actions, thoughts, statements, etc. The person's character may also be revealed through what other individuals in the text think or say about the person in question. It is also true that a character's nature is developed by an author in tandem with the text's major themes and events. When these elements are taken into consideration God's character in the book of the Twelve unfolds alongside the book's main emphases. This fact means that warning characterization techniques dominate the depiction of God in Hosea-Micah, judgment terminology marks Nahum-Zephaniah, and renewal metaphors take precedence in Haggai-Zechariah.

Methodology

Though it is an overstatement to say that there have been nearly as many methodologies for Old Testament theology as there have been Old Testament theologians, this comment is not far from true. Scholars have employed Systematic theology categories, utilized a single theme as an organizing principle, sought ancient kerygmatic statements around which the whole of Old Testament theology can be gathered, and attempted to use the canon as an organizing principle for theological reflection. More recently, there have been theological analyses written from a variety of reader response perspectives and from pluralistic viewpoints. Clearly, there is no shortage of ways to approach the task.[4]

Because of the challenges involved in analyzing the book of the Twelve, it is important to adopt a methodology that can take unity within diversity into account. Historical matters should not be neglected altogether, but it must be remembered

---

[4] For an summary of these viewpoints see J. H. Hayes and F.C. Prussner, *Old Testament Theology: Its History and Development* (Atlanta: John Knox, 1985); G.F. Hasel, *Old Testament Theology: Basic Issues in the Current Debate*, 4th ed. (Grand Rapids: Eerdmans, 1991); and L.G. Perdue, *The Collapse of History: Reconstructing Old Testament Theology* (Minneapolis: Fortress, 1994).

that it is the claims of the text itself that matter most. Redactional issues are not unimportant, yet by definition they cannot be taken as the final point from which to make theological observations. Therefore it is appropriate to utilize a canonical approach to the Twelve's theology, since this methodology allows for a reading of the text as a coherent whole without losing a sense of each separate book's origins.

Of course, it is necessary to define what is meant by "canonical approach." This methodology has been rightly associated with the program set forth by Brevard Childs, though it has benefitted from insights by such thinkers as Christopher Seitz, James Sanders, and John Sailhamer.[5] By "canonical" I mean analysis that is God-centered, intertextually oriented, authority-conscious, historically-sensitive, and devoted to the pursuit of the wholeness of the Old Testament message. It means theological reflection that deals carefully with the Twelve in a manner that will make its influence on subsequent biblical texts more evident.

This type of canonical study also acknowledges that it is appropriate to note the individual prophecies' historical setting, structural details, and thematic emphases as they build together what becomes finally the book of the Twelve. Each of these elements aid an understanding of how the individual books supplement the earlier and succeeding prophecies. There is no doubt that the first readers of the book of the Twelve knew that the books placed together did not unfold in specific chronological order. Thus, familiar themes and descriptions of God, Israel, and the nations probably took precedence in their minds as they read. It makes sense, then, to examine how historical context and literary concepts help create the theology of this one book.

Alongside this broad methodology must stand a more specific principle, which is that the book of the Twelve describes only one God. A variety of perspectives on God's character are offered, but the authors all believe they are writing about the same deity. There is no sense that they think they are depicting rival gods. Rather, they all claim to speak for and with the God who has been uniquely revealed to Israel in the events and texts that mark their people's history. Therefore, it is appropriate to describe their theology as a whole, not as a group of unrelated parts, or as set of competing voices.

---

[5] Cf. B.S. Childs, *Old Testament Theology in a Canonical Context* (Philadelphia: Fortress, 1986); J.A. Sanders, *Torah and Canon* (Philadelphia: Fortress, 1972); J.H. Sailhamer, *Introduction to Old Testament Theology: A Canonical Approach* (Grand Rapids: Zondervan, 1995); and C.R. Seitz, *Word Without End: The Old Testament as Abiding Theological Witness* (Grand Rapids: Eerdmans, 1998).

In practice, this canonical methodology gathers the primary statements about God in the Twelve. It collates these statements with previous and/or subsequent passages. It determines ways to state the text's common confessions about God as well as the unique contributions a prophecy or grouping of prophecies may make to Old Testament theology. In other words, this approach gathers exegetical data, draws together similar ideas from other contextually relevant texts, states propositions about what the texts claim about God, and attempts to present conclusions in a way that makes the data accessible to interested parties. Of course, such goals are beyond my ability to achieve them even in a longer work, so the attempt to do so more briefly here is a worthy challenge.

Textual Analysis

Before noting some of the specific aspects of the Twelve's theology, perhaps it will be helpful to outline the book's general thematic emphases.[6] When one reads the Twelve as a canonical partner with Isaiah, Jeremiah, and Ezekiel, several common prophetic notions are readily apparent. These ideas help order an effective analysis of the book's theology. For instance, the fundamental sin of covenant breaking receives significant treatment in all the prophetic books, and the Twelve is no exception. In the Twelve, however, this theme has particular significance in Hosea-Micah. This segment focuses upon the specific and general ways that Israel suffered for their covenant infidelity. These prophecies define, describe, and denounce these infidelities. They threaten punishment for the transgressions, and they anticipate coming judgment for what has been done. They do the same for gentile nations as well. As a group, these six prophecies stress the God who warns of coming punishment for sin. The warning includes descriptions of devastating judgment and promises of ultimate renewal beyond the chastisement, but warning is the main notion nonetheless.

Nahum, Habakkuk, and Zephaniah move beyond the description of sin and threats of punishment to specific threats about the coming day of the Lord. Here the Lord is depicted as a judge even more surely than in Hosea-Micah. All nations will be destroyed because of their sins, regardless of the people's size or current influence. Covenant and non-covenant countries alike are included in the

---

[6] For a more detailed discussion of the Twelve's literary unity see P.R. House, *The Unity of the Twelve*, JSOTS 97 (Sheffield: Almond Press, 1990). If I were to write this book again one of the significant changes I would make would be to change the title to *Literary Unity in the Twelve* to reflect the fact that literary unity is but one type of unity the Twelve exhibits. The book's conclusion makes this point (pp. 243-245), but the title does not.

destruction, for they are all accountable to the one God, who is their creator. All creation is swept away by the end of Zephaniah; all, that is, but a multi-national remnant of faithful persons. The Lord remains the God who spares a remnant to serve the creator and inherit blessings.

Just as parts of Isaiah, Jeremiah, and Ezekiel look beyond judgment to a brighter future based on God's presence and the existence of a believing remnant, so Haggai, Zechariah, and Malachi point towards God's eventual transformation of judgment to glory. Temple, city, and people are all devastated by Israel's enemies. But God promises to restore all these aspects of Israelite life. The renewal will someday be as complete as the devastation, a fact that has been hinted at throughout the earlier portions of the Twelve. God's determination to forgive and restore reinforces the canon's insistence that punishment is meted out in order to effect cleansing and restoration. When Malachi closes the Twelve has spanned three centuries of history and the full range of prophetic theology. Prophecy and reality are kept tightly woven together.

The God Who Warns and Loves: Hosea

Perhaps no prophet pays a higher price for his or her calling than Hosea. Like other prophets he preaches the covenant truths already stated in the canon. Like other prophets he embodies his message. Unlike other prophets, however, he suffers profound personal agony through his wife's marital infidelity. By loving this woman despite her failure to remain faithful to him, Hosea demonstrates for Israel the persevering love of God for a constantly straying chosen people.

This love is portrayed in two basic ways in the two major sections of the prophecy. First, Hosea 1-3 expresses the love God has for an idolatrous/adulterous nation. Second, Hosea 4-14 describes the warnings a loving God extends to the corrupted people. All of the nation's sins are treated as a breach of faith akin to adultery in the first section, while the imagery expands to include judicial and parental metaphors in the second part.

Hosea's marriage to a compromised woman in chs. 1-3 fits other canonical depictions of God as a mistreated spouse. After all, Ezekiel 20 considers Israel idolatrous even before the exodus, a view reflected in Joshua 24:2, and in Amos 2:4, which says Judah follows lies their fathers pursued. Exodus 32-34 may also at least imply that the people had some prior knowledge of idolatry before leaving Egypt. Given these passages, it is certainly plausible that Gomer engaged in pre-marital sexual deviancy and that from the start Hosea's marriage to her demonstrates the immeasurable, grace-oriented love God has for Israel.

Hosea's children's names indicate that the God who loves is also the God who warns. Each name, whether Jezreel, Not Pitied, or Bastard, reveal God's anger at the Israelite monarchy and people. These names speak of terrible pain in Hosea's household and in God's heart. They also prefigure tremendous agony to come for a disobedient nation. The warnings have begun in earnest.

The spousal terminology is supplemented in Hosea 4-14, yet the prophecy's tone changes little. Judicial language is used to describe the Lord in 4:1-3. Here God "contends" with Israel for ongoing transgression. The prophet declares a divinely-initiated lawsuit against law breakers, a procedure that also occurs in 2:4-17, 4:4-6, and 5:3-15, as well as in Isaiah 1:18-20, Jeremiah 2:5-29, Micah 6:1-5, and Malachi 3:5.[7] The reason for the suit is the breach of the Sinai covenant (4:1-2), and the result is that the land mourns (4:3). Clearly, rejecting God for other gods leads to corrupt behavior. Israel's spouse is also Israel's judge, so the nation is forewarned of future punishment.

Parental imagery marks 11:1-11, a passage that surveys Israel's past and argues that the Lord has done more for Israel than the covenant demands. First, God chose Israel and delivered them from Egypt (11:1). Nowhere does any Old Testament text so much as imply that this election was anything other than the Lord's unmerited mercy towards Israel. Second, the Lord called Israel despite the people's constant descent into Baalism and other forms of idolatry (11:2). Third, God established the northern kingdom because of Solomon's idolatry (cf. 1 Kgs 11:1-40), yet the people turned from their healer, God (11:3). Fourth, God has sustained the nation. Fifth, the Lord will punish the people in the future (11:5-7). Sixth, after punishing the "son," God will again have compassion on the straying child (11:9-11).

Israel's history is presented as the story of a loving parent faced with raising a rebellious child. God called Israel, taught them how to walk, fed them, and guided them (11:1-5). This love has been spurned, yet the Lord cannot give them up completely. Judgment must give way--indeed must create--renewal (11:8-11). Ultimately, God will heal the people's infidelity, ingratitude, ignorance, and rebellion.

Hosea has been examined in more detail than subsequent prophecies because it sets the stage for the Twelve's characterization of the Lord. It portrays God as a loving-yet- betrayed spouse, dishonored parent, and mighty judge. It warns that unless faithfulness to God's kindness results the nation can expect the reluctant punishing judge to act.

Subsequent prophecies in the Twelve operate in a similar manner. A variety of characterization techniques appear, all designed to discuss the nature and acts of

---

[7] Claus Westermann, *Basic Forms of Prophetic Speech*, trans. H.C. White (Philadelphia: Westminster, 1967) 199-200.

the covenant God. Each technique reveals God's patience, yet at the same time stresses the limits of that patience. Threats, comfort, and promise co-exist side-by-side to demonstrate the magnitude of the Lord's person.

The God Who Warns and Promises: Joel

Joel has been and will continue to be an enigma in the Twelve. Historical and redaction critics have debated the prophecy's authorship, date, and original audience. Interesting theories about how Joel fits into the Twelve have been forwarded by Jim Nogalski.[8] This diversity of opinion has affected theological analysis as well, since Old Testament theology does not exist in a vacuum. What is apparent, however, is that Joel shares Hosea's concern to warn Israel to repent. It is also evident that Joel states that judgment will come, but that beyond the punishment lies great renewal. Thus, the prophecy's emphasis on the God who warns and promises is in keeping with Hosea's themes and those in the rest of the Twelve.

Joel's chief means of warning is through the description of the day of the Lord. Having warned the people to fast and mourn in 1:1-14, the "day" is announced in 1:15. This proclamation closely parallels earlier canonical passages. The language echoes Isaiah 13:6 and Ezekiel 30:23, and brings to mind the terrible scenes depicted in Deuteronomy 27-28 and 32, where God sends military defeat and plagues for persistent covenant breaking.[9] In all there are at least sixteen passages that discuss judgement as the day of the Lord.[10] Joel launches the Twelve's treatment of the subject. In each of the sixteen texts a quick, decisive return to the Lord is the only prudent response to the warnings.

Judgment is not God's final word, for the Lord promises to renew the people's fortunes in 2:18-3:21. God's love here mirrors Ezekiel 16 and Hosea 11:1-9. God refuses to release the beloved nation. Why? As in Isaiah 45:5, 45:21, and 49:23, the answer is plain: to demonstrate that the Lord is God and there is no other

---

[8] James Nogalski, *Literary Precursors to the Book of the Twelve*, BZAW 217 (Berlin: Walter de Gruyter, 1993) and *Redactional Processes in the Book of the Twelve*, BZAW 218 (Berlin: Walter de Gruyter, 1993).

[9] For a comparison of these texts consult S.R. Driver, *The Books of Joel and Amos*, CB (Cambridge: Cambridge Univ. Press, 1901) 19; H.W. Wolff, *Joel and Amos*, trans. S.D. McBride, Jr., et al, Herm (Philadelphia: Fortress, 1977) 10; and D.S. Stuart, *Hosea-Jonah*, WBC 31 (Waco, TX: Word, 1987) 228.

[10] Cf. Gerhard von Rad, *Old Testament Theology: Volume II*, trans. D.M.G. Stalker (New York: Harper and Row, 1965) 199-225.

(2:27). Devotion to this monotheistic principle will eliminate the transgressions that lead to judgment.

God's spirit will effect the promised renewal (2:28-32). All God's people will receive the spirit of the Lord, an infusion Ezekiel 36:24-32 expects to turn the people's hearts from stone to flesh and create a restored land. Scott Hafemann concludes correctly that "it is the future bestowal of this life-giving (divine) Spirit which forms the core of the prophetic expectation for restoration."[11]

Significant for the issue of God's sovereignty is the fact that the Lord will judge sinners both inside and outside Israel (3:1-15). All nations should hear the Lord's warnings as if God were a roaring lion about to devour them (3:16). The description of God as a roaring lion exercising universal jurisdiction appears in Amos 1:2, thereby serving as a linking image between prophecies.

Clearly, God's promises are two-edged in Joel. The Lord pledges good or ill depending upon the peoples' level of repentance. Warning and hope co-exist as time and the Twelve press forward. So far God has warned and promised as a spouse, parent, judge, and healer--all to no avail.

The God Who Roars Against Sin: Amos

Amos 1:2 picks up the Joel 3:16 image of a leonine Lord roaring against the people. God's anger is directed at Israel and Judah, as well as at six other nations. The covenant people have broken faith with God in a manner similar to that described in Hosea and Joel. For their part, the nations have shown excessive cruelty in war, sold captives into slavery, cast off normal human compassion, and broken treaties made in good faith (1:3-2:16). God's roaring serves as a grave warning of imminent international punishment. It also prefigures a new way for the Twelve to describe the Lord's person and work.

God commands attention in this section by demanding that the people "listen" (3:1; 4:1; 5:1) to a stunning summary of their sins. By rejecting God they have rebelled against the creator of all the earth (4:13; 5:8). As the creator it is God's prerogative to turn the light to darkness or send the waters from their boundaries into the land. Israel and the nations must both bow before their maker. God deserves and demands exclusive worship. Having received neither, the creator will become the destroyer (5:18-27).

Amos 7:1-9:15 includes several images of God that coincide with emphases in Hosea and Joel. For example, God promises extraordinary punishment in 7:1-

---

[11] S.J. Hafemann, *Paul, Moses, and the History of Israel*, WUNT 31 (Tubingen: Mohr/Siebeck, 1995) 182. Hafemann's painstaking analysis of Paul's use of "the letter and the spirit" demonstrates that the New Testament interprets Joel 2:28-29 contextually and canonically.

8:3, yet allows compassion to stay execution just as in Hosea 1-3 and 11:1-9. Likewise, the hopeful statements about the Lord's desire to renew the covenant people matches the bright future pledged in Joel 2:28-3:21. Further, the day of the Lord passages in Joel 3:1-21 and Amos 1:3-2:16 emphasize the universal scope of divine power. These examples are not cited to attempt to diminish Amos's theological achievement in its own specific historical context. Rather, it is just that a paper like this one collects ongoing theological statements in the Twelve. It does not try to pit one prophecy's achievement against the other.

In the context of the Twelve, Amos continues the book's emphasis on God's loving, kind, familial, and faithful character. At the same time it stresses that the Lord is ruler and judge of all the earth. In mercy God sends prophets such as Amos to deliver the divine word, and in righteousness the Lord pledges to punish the earth's wicked and bless those who obey the covenant.

The prophecy also works with new characterizations of the Lord. God is portrayed as a terrible lion about to devour the wicked. Amos stresses God's sovereignty over the whole earth, a theme that adds texture to the Twelve's reasoning for God's power over the gentiles. Amos' creation metaphors begin a trend that reoccurs later in the Twelve and links the prophecy to texts that span the Law, Prophets, and Writings.

The God Who Warns Against Pride: Obadiah

Pride is an attitude that has been denounced in both the Twelve and earlier prophecies (cf. Hos 9:1; 10:1; Jo 3:1-3; Am 6:1-7; Isa 14:12-16; Eze 28:17; etc). Thus, it is no surprise that pride is singled out in Obadiah as the main reason for Edom's judgment. God's displeasure unfolds in three parts. First, Obadiah 1-9 announces Edom's impending doom for its pride and hateful attitude towards Israel. Second, Obadiah 10-14 denounces Edom's glee over Jerusalem's demise. Third, Obadiah 15-21 contrasts the fall of Edom with the blessing of the righteous remnant on the day of the Lord. As in Amos, it is the day of the Lord that will make sinners pay for what they have done, and that will vindicate the faithful by blessing them.

Without question, Obadiah furthers the Twelve's emphasis on the gentiles' sin and on the Lord's right to judge the entire earth. Edom's activities demonstrate that only God's direct intervention can halt sin outside Israel's borders. Clearly, the day of the Lord is as necessary beyond Israel as it is within it, since repentance is not forthcoming from either group. It is this direct action against the sin of pride and hatefulness that also provides the backdrop for Jonah.

The God Who Warns the Gentiles: Jonah

Jonah eases fears that God does not care for the gentiles that may have arisen due to statements in Joel, Amos, and Obadiah. Jonah shows that the Lord loves even the Assyrians, the most powerful and vicious of Israel's ancient foes. Of course, Isaiah 19:19-25 has already made this point canonically. God sends a prophet to alert the Assyrians so that they, too, can come to know the God who created the heavens and the earth. Jonah's reluctance to undertake this task continues the Twelve's emphasis on the hatred Israel and the nations have for one another, a situation that makes it unlikely that these enemies will be reconciled before the day of the Lord.

The contents of Jonah's clean narrative illustrate God's persistent warning and redemption of the Assyrians. First, Jonah 1:1-16 recounts God's call to Jonah and the prophet's desire to flee from the Lord. The God who calls is the God who cares for Nineveh. Second, Jonah 1:17-2:10 covers the prophet's time in the fish and his subsequent decision to undertake the preaching mission to Nineveh. Here the Lord is the creator of the great fish, the one who coerces the prophet, and the one who preserves the prophet's life. Third, Jonah 3:1-10 discloses Jonah's "ministry" to the Assyrians. Jonah's halfhearted effort highlights God's grace when his hearers repent. Fourth, Jonah 4:1-11 reveals the prophet's anger at the Lord's mercy. Again the point is that God loves all people. Their sins are God's concern. In contrast, Jonah complains about God's kindness, despite the fact that he himself has been a beneficiary of the Lord's mercy.

The opening segment underscores the Lord's direct action in the saving of human beings. Just as God intervened in the lives of Abraham, Isaac, and Jacob, so the Lord now moves on behalf of gentiles. Sadly, the prophet does not accept the Lord's vision, nor does he resonate with texts such as Isaiah 19:19-25 or grasp the implications of his own confession that the Lord created the world. His view of God remains landlocked and culture bound.

Jonah's time in and deliverance from the belly of the fish re-emphasizes Amos's creation motifs. At the same time the experience allows Jonah to comment that the Lord alone is a living, hearing, acting, saving God. The issue that remains unresolved is whether or not the prophet will translate this stated theology into active ministry.

Upon hearing Jonah's sermon, the people of Nineveh hope that the Lord is a merciful God, and they are not disappointed. God "relents," just as, for example, in the golden calf incident, where the Lord relents from destroying Israel and beginning anew with Moses (Ex 32:12). God's forgiveness in this instance is hardly a failure of prophecy. Rather, it fulfills the intent of prophecy in the whole canon. After all, Hosea 6:1-3 counsels the people to repent and be forgiven, yet no change occurs. Joel 2:12-14 encourages repentance and hopes for renewal in language very close to that of Jonah 3:9. Amos 4:6-13 mourns the nation's refusal to repent and thereby avoid judgment.

Prophecy is not offered simply to relieve God of the responsibility to warn before punishing. It intends to effect change in hearers and make them part of God's faithful remnant. If Jonah believes he has failed because the city survives, then he does not grasp the purpose of prophecy any more than he understands the practical implications of creation theology.

The final scene captures the essence of the canon's description of God's nature. The same God creates, calls, reveals, judges, and forgives. There is no other deity able to do these things. In fact, there are no other gods who have ontological existence at all. Thus, God's character remains intact in Jonah. Sadly, it appears, however, that even an Israelite prophet intends to do little to alleviate the animosity between Israel and the nations. Sin continues to distort and impair international relationships even as the Lord continues to warn against such activities.

The God Who Testifies Against Sin: Micah

Micah completes the first half of the Twelve's discussion of worldwide sin and its consequences by summarizing and expanding concepts already introduced in Hosea-Jonah. Set in the latter half of the eighth-century BCE (1:1), this prophecy rehearses the tragic fact that the punishment depicted in the next three prophecies of the Twelve need never have occurred. Repentance could have staved off judgment, as Jonah proves, but the covenant people fail to change, a trait they share with the gentiles here. Therefore, as Obadiah has already shown, punishment will overtake them.

Micah portrays God as testifying against the earth for its inhabitants' refusal to heed divine warnings. Micah 1-3 highlights God testifying against the present sins of Israel and the gentiles. This testimony constitutes a warning to change while change and forgiveness are yet possible. Micah 4-5 finds God testifying to the righteousness and future blessing of the remnant. Here the Lord guarantees a blessed future by sending an ideal Davidic ruler. Micah 6-7 describes the Lord as one who testifies to the eternal nature of the Abrahamic covenant. In this section God removes sin for Abraham's sake. Therefore, in Micah the Lord speaks against sin in the present and future by emphasizing past promises.

Micah 1-3 pronounces "woe" on the wicked by cataloguing contemporary sins in ways reminiscent of earlier canonical texts. God's vehement anger over worldwide iniquity in 1:2-4 sounds very much like the powerful statements in Isaiah 1-6 and Amos 1-2, to name just two passages. Likewise, the cause of the divine anger, idolatry (1:5-7), revisits the complaints of Isaiah, Jeremiah, Ezekiel, Hosea, and Amos, and calling idolatry "harlotry" (1:7) reminds readers of Hosea. Though quite creative in its own right,[12] the list of towns to be destroyed in 1:10-16 is not unlike Amos 1:2-2:3 or even Isaiah 13-23 or Jeremiah 46-51 in strategy or intent.

Though they are not objects of God's wrath, Micah 4-5 makes it clear that the remnant will suffer before being redeemed (4:1-7). They must endure exile, as well as political and personal travail (4:8-10). Their hope lies in God, whose plans cannot be thwarted (4:11-13). More specifically, Micah 5:1-15 concludes, much as Isaiah 7-12 has already stated, that renewal can only come through the emergence and ministry of a unique Davidic ruler. From Bethlehem will come one "whose origin is from old days, from everlasting days" (5:2). This king's realm will extend throughout the earth. His origins mark him as a supernatural figure, much as the description of the king in Isaiah 9:6 as a "mighty God" and "everlasting father" does there. This king will provide rest, sustenance, and peace for the harried people of God (5:3-6). Idols will be removed from the earth (5:10-15), a sure sign of God's triumph.

Having staked out the future, Micah 6-7 returns to the present, and also reaches back into the distant past. It is significant that Micah concludes with a statement on the removal of sin as it relates to the Abrahamic covenant. By closing this way, Micah conceives of a history that spans from the patriarchal era to the final judgment at the end of time. By Micah's day God's promises to the patriarchs had resulted in exodus, conquest, Davidic dynasty, national division, and impending destruction. Micah envisions an accompanying new exodus, new David, and new city of God. These promises mean that each successive generation has historically-relevant pledges to sustain their present and give hope to their future. Clearly, Micah neither neglects the realities of the present nor the possibilities of the future.

As Micah closes, a host of warning images have been applied to God in keeping with the Twelve's overall thematic emphasis. God is spouse, parent, judge, healer, witness, lion, creator, deliverer, and only deity. God is merciful, loving, patient, and yet also holy, good, righteous, and firm. Each characterization undergirds the Twelve's belief to this point that judgment is not and never will be inevitable. The God who warns is the God who stands ready to heal and forgive.

---

[12] For an excellent translation of this section, consult H.W. Wolff, *Micah the Prophet*, trans. R.D. Gehrke (Philadelphia: Westminster, 1981) 14-16.

The God Who Destroys Assyria : Nahum

Though the first six prophecies in the Twelve stress the reality of judgment repeatedly, their general place in history means that this punishment is either potential or lies mainly in the future. Obadiah is an exception to this rule, of course, but even there Edom's sins have yet to be addressed. In Nahum, Habakkuk, and Zephaniah the Twelve turns to treating punishment as if it is a near certainty. Israel and the nations will indeed feel the sting of the Lord's justifiable wrath. Warnings have been spurned, so the consequences of rejecting mercy will now unfold.

Nahum begins this emphasis on the God who judges by stating that the end has come for Assyria, the very nation to whom Jonah had preached. From the outset the prophecy establishes the Lord's character as the basis for the announced punishment of Nineveh. In fact, 1:2-11 summarizes the divine qualities found in the Twelve and earlier canonical texts. God is jealous for good reason (1:2), as the explanation for the prohibitions against idolatry in Exodus 20:4-5 have demonstrated. This jealousy amounts to zeal for righteousness. At the same time, the Lord is patient and just (1:3), points made in Exodus 20:1-6, Exodus 34:6-7, and elsewhere. As creator, God rules nature (1:3-5), as Amos has emphasized. God is good (1:7), and the wicked cannot endure the Lord's presence (1:6-8). Assyria's plotting against other nations amounts to scheming against God (1:9-11), so such activities will result in death. Pride and viciousness will bring down even the mightiest country.

It is also important to note that Nahum 1:1-15 indicates that the repentance described in Jonah either did not spread or did not last. God sent Jonah to warn the Assyrians of punishment, so Nineveh cannot argue that God is patient with the Jews but not with them. The problem is that God's mercy has not been met with long-term commitment.

Nahum 2-3 reveals that God opposes and will humiliate Nineveh. These statements could appear vindictive had the previous prophecies and Nahum 1:1-15 not set forth God's case against the nations. It will not surprise readers of Amos 1-2 to discover that judgment falls because Nineveh is filled with lies, violence, and oppression (3:1), or because Nineveh enslaves others (3:4) and is cruel (3:19). God may rightly expose their nakedness (3:5), make them an object of contempt (3:6), and render them powerless (3:8-9) because of their overwhelming cruelty.

There is no question that Nahum's depiction of God and Nineveh is plainspoken. God no longer roars. Now God devours. God is the universal Lord who saves and punishes. God's power and justice dictate the flow of history. God has been patient, yet has begun to move against evil in an evident and telling fashion. What is lacking here are the parental and spousal metaphors that have dotted the earlier texts. Judge characterization techniques dominate the scene now.

The God Who Inspires Faith in Crisis: Habakkuk

Through the use of a creative, dramatic structure, Habakkuk reworks a number of theological ideas already prominent among its predecessors. For example, the book announces national and international iniquity. It depicts God using a powerful nation, this time Babylon, to punish sinners in Israel, and highlights the prophet's relationship to the Lord. In Habakkuk God acts as revealer, judge, comforter, instructor, deliverer, and sovereign Lord of history. These common notions are mixed with an uncommon depiction of a prophet to make a strong theological statement about how God inspires faith in the faithful even as crises unfold.

Habakkuk 1:2-11 reminds readers that God reveals the future to special messengers. When Habakkuk asks how long Israel's wicked will continue, the Lord responds by divulging that Babylon will destroy Israel's wicked. The prophet can be certain that sin will not remain unchecked forever. Just as Assyria receives its just rewards, so the covenant people will as well.

God's answer only partly satisfies Habakkuk. He is interested in the complete triumph of good over evil, so one wicked nation defeating another does not seem a proper solution to him (1:12-2:1). God's next reply helps clarify matters. Habakkuk may count upon the fact that though final judgment seems to come slowly, it will indeed come and it will devastate the wicked (2:2-3, 5). The current posture Habakkuk and all those who call upon the Lord is that of faith. In fact, the just person lives by faith, just as the covenant person lives by every word that comes from God (Dt 8:3). Such faith, and such faith alone, can sustain the prophet and those like him. God will bring woe upon Babylon (2:5-11). Habakkuk need not fear that God's character has somehow been diminished. Idolaters such as Babylon will be crushed (2:12-20).

Habakkuk concludes with a psalm of trust, which underscores God's ability to engender faith in the remnant. The psalm longs for God to redeem the faithful by removing the wicked. This act would mean mercy for the oppressed, and the prophet longs to see this work that only God can do. Habakkuk asks God to repeat the exodus deliverance, when God freed Israel from Egypt (3:3-15). Such would mean a renewal of divine, revelatory activity; it would constitute grace for the righteous who live by faith. For this sort of miracle the prophet is willing to wait (3:16). By faith he will wait, though everything around him seems bleak (3:17-19). He will live by faith despite the fact that Israel and Babylon must fall before his faith will be vindicated. God's word alone is enough to fuel this belief.

Nahum and Habakkuk leave readers with no question that the day of the Lord is coming soon upon Assyria, Israel, and Babylon. Obadiah depicts Jerusalem's fall, and also pledges the destruction of Edom. The only comfort that appears in these books is for the faithful, and even they can expect tremendous difficulties that may cause searching, Habakkuk-like questions about God's nature.

The God Who Punishes to Create a Remnant: Zephaniah

Zephaniah leaves no doubt that God will not limit judgment to the wicked in Israel, Assyria, and Babylon. All creation will suffer for their transgressions (1:2-3). Assyria and Babylon will be joined in judgment by other countries who have offended the Lord (2:4-12). Though God's just anger continues to be a main theme, the fact that this wrath falls in order to forge a multi-national remnant also receives major attention (3:6-20). The goal of God's judgment, then, is not simply punitive. Rather, it is ultimately redemptive.

Zephaniah 1:1-17a stresses that old sins such as idolatry will cause the Lord to sweep away everything created in Genesis 1:1-26 (1:2-3). While creation is the setting for the wrath, the objects of God's anger are the wicked of the earth (1:3). God will reverse creation as in the days of the flood,[13] which will remove violence and fraud (1:8-9), apathy (1:12-13), and polytheism. This day of the Lord will be as fearsome as Joel and Amos predicted.

Next, Zephaniah 1:17b-3:5 indicates that every wicked nation will be devastated on the day of the Lord. But one group will survive the conflagration. The "humble of the land" who seek the Lord, the law, righteousness, and humility (2:3) will become the remnant that will possess the land (2:7, 9). Those mentioned in 2:3, 7, and 9 are clearly Israelites, but 2:11 offers the possibility of extending the identity of the remnant to people from other lands.

This potential is realized in Zephaniah 3:6-20. God states that divine indignation (3:8) will "change the speech of the peoples to pure speech" (3:9) and cause worshipers to come from "beyond the rivers of Ethiopia" (3:10). While 3:10 may refer specifically to exiled Israelites, the plural word "peoples" indicates that the remnant has a multi-national identity. Given the presence of 2:11, the prophecy's overall context argues for this definition of "the remnant." And it is to this remnant that all the creator's blessings are promised (3:11-20).

Zephaniah concludes the emphasis on judgment begun in Nahum. At this point in the Twelve all polytheists stand under divine condemnation. The sins chronicled in Hosea-Micah will be eradicated. Still, renewal is the goal beyond

---

[13] Michael De Roche, "Zephaniah 1:2-3: The 'Sweeping of Creation,'" *VT* 30 (1980) 104-109.

devastation, so hope for the future is hardly gone. The creator/deliverer who reaches out to Nineveh remains concerned with all peoples. This hope rests unexplained, but the next three books address the matter of how the God who warns and judges is also the God who forgives and renews.

The God Who Renews the Temple: Haggai

Zephaniah concludes without stating exactly how renewal will occur in history. Haggai, Zechariah, and Malachi discuss this matter and offer a consistent pattern for how complete restoration will unfold. Each one written after the Jews' initial return from exile, the prophecies are perfectly honest about how preliminary and preparatory to total restoration their era is, but they are hopeful and confident that the foundations that have been laid will be vital for the future.

Haggai contends that full national renewal cannot take place until the temple destroyed by Babylon is rebuilt. Ezra 3:8-4:24 indicates that earlier efforts to rebuild took place, but were stopped by political enemies. Haggai believes the time has come to try again, and offers four messages that motivate the people to build. First, 1:1-15 argues that God deserves honor, so the people should construct a temple that demonstrates their commitment to the Lord. Indeed they will suffer hardship until they obey. Second, 2:1-9 presents God as the one who promises greater glory for the new temple. Though it is humble in size and origins, the people must not underestimate the importance of their fresh start. Their captivity is over. Their lives have begun anew. Greater days lie ahead. Third, 2:10-19 states that God purifies the people so that they can be a worthy remnant. Fourth, 2:20-23 claims that God renews the covenant with David. With the people back in the land, the temple in place, and the Davidic covenant reaffirmed, Haggai declares that full renewal is not only possible, but already under way.

Israel has persevered in exile because their God has remained constant. Unwilling to give up the people (Hos 11:1-9), the Lord has brought them home and given them a humble new beginning. There is no question in Haggai's mind that the same God operates in his day as in earlier eras. God continues to warn, explain, reveal, and heal. Now, however, the focus is upon healing, and the people themselves seem more obedient to these divine overtures.

The God Who Renews Jerusalem: Zechariah

Zechariah is a magnificent and difficult prophecy. It has been divided in many ways by scholars through the years, and strong debates over issues such as authorship, date, and original audience have marked its history of interpretation. This paper cannot address these issues, nor can it do justice to Zechariah's multi-faceted theological depth. Still, even a brief treatment must mention two specific ways the prophecy depicts God: as the one who is jealous for Zion, and as the shepherd of Israel.

Having begun with a defense of God's dealings with Israel in 1:1-6, the prophecy proceeds to stress that the people's recent repentance (1:6) signals a new era in Israelite history. God is once again jealous, or protective, of Jerusalem (1:14), which means the city's enemies will be scattered and impediments to its rebuilding removed rather than the Jews being scattered and destroyed. Eight visions follow, which taken together demonstrate that every important element of Israelite life damaged by defeat and exile will be mended (1:7-6:15).

A vital key to this renewal and a proof of God's interest in Israel is the emergence of a person God calls "my servant the branch" (3:8, 10). This individual will remove Israel's sin and allow them to live in peace. He is a Davidic heir and one who will make the temple glorious again (6:12-13). There is little doubt that this individual is the same as the one promised in Isaiah 4:2, Isaiah 11:1, and Jeremiah 23:1-8, passages which also utilize branch/root imagery for the coming ideal Davidic ruler.

Thus, 3:8-10 and 6:12-13 combine royal and priestly metaphors to describe one who can rebuild the temple, destroy sin, and serve God and the people. As a result of the Lord's kindness, the branch's labors, and their repentance the covenant people will be forgiven. God's jealousy for Jerusalem and Israel will make it so (cf. 7:1-8:23).

Zechariah 9-14 continues the picture of future glory begun in the previous chapters. Zechariah 9:1 begins a "burden," or oracle, that continues through 11:17. Another "burden" stretches from 12:1-14:21. This recurring term helps bond Zechariah and Malachi, which begins with a "burden of its own. In its present context Zechariah's first "burden" explains that all Israel's oppressors and ancient foes will be defeated by the Lord (9:1-8; cf. 9:4). Coupled with 8:20-23, Zechariah 9:1-8 demonstrates God's sovereignty beyond Israel. All the earth belongs to the Lord (9:1), God watches the whole earth to make certain Israel is safe, and the Lord has determined to give the nations to the chosen people (9:7-8).

All these wonders will occur because of the coming king (9:9-10) and because God shepherds Israel like a flock (9:16-17). The Jews suffer under poor shepherds (10:1-2), a common prophetic image for wicked rulers (cf. Jer 25:34-38; Eze 34:7-10). But now God will be their shepherd, which means Israel will prevail over the shepherd/leaders of other lands (10:3-11:3). No one is capable of frustrating the sovereign shepherd's purposes, a fact Ezekiel 34:11-31 declares in an earlier passage that connects the Lord's shepherding of Israel, the Davidic ruler, and Israel's ultimate restoration. Worthless human shepherds will be driven from the land as a prelude to that day (11:4-17).

Jerusalem's restoration will be complete only when God dwells in Zion and all sin is eradicated. This action will drive wickedness from the chosen city, priesthood, and throne. Then the nations will consider Jerusalem, Zion, the dwelling place of God, their capital city. Then the city will be entirely "holy to the Lord" (14:16-21). Before that time, the God who created the heavens, the earth, and the human race (12:1) will strengthen Jerusalem. All who oppose God's purposes will be destroyed "on that day" (12:9), which is an obvious reference to the judgment day imagery found in previous prophecies.

Clearly, Zechariah's characterization of God is much more like that of Hosea than it is of, say, Zephaniah. God is once again a benevolent, though not irresponsible, figure. The Lord is shepherd, healer, and the one who sends the Davidic ruler to restore people and city. Restoration themes require a change in the way the Lord is described, and these changes take the text back to its warning mode.

The God Who Loves and Renews Israel: Malachi

Malachi expresses the cost of renewal and explains how barriers to restoration may be removed. It does so in a creative style that utilizes questions, answers, exhortations, oracles, and narrative-like description of activity while presenting its message. In particular, questions form six distinct segments that isolate the sins that God will overcome in achieving the people's renewal. To effect renewal, the Lord is presented as the God who loves Israel (1:1-5), the God who instructs and corrects priests (1:6-2:9), the God who denounces infidelity (2:10-16), the God who establishes justice (2:17-3:5), the God who never changes (3:6-12), and the God who exposes arrogance (3:13-15). Following these foundational sections, 3:16-4:6 presents the Lord as creator of the remnant. The emergence of the remnant at the end of the book highlights the people's ultimate renewal. As in the earlier prophecies, however, only the Lord's direct intervention in history through the day of the Lord makes this renewal possible.

Malachi 1:1-5 emphasizes that it is God's love that undergirds the coming renewal. In this way the last book of the Twelve connects with the first. It was God's electing, patient love that made it possible for remnant persons like Hosea to exist, and possible for straying persons like Gomer to repent and come back to God. Here it is God's love that keeps the people. All future hope is based upon the belief that the God who remains loving and faithful for three centuries will maintain that loyalty indefinitely. God's love cannot be in question. Any pain the nation encounters must of necessity originate elsewhere. Renewal, on the other hand, cannot originate anywhere but with the Lord.

Summary of Characterization of God in the Twelve

Malachi brings both the Twelve and the Prophets to a close. As the last segment of the Twelve, the prophecy completes the book's charting of Israel and the nations' sins, the just and inevitable punishment of that sin, and the renewal the judgment is sent to effect. Set near 450 BCE, Malachi finishes the Twelve's historical odyssey from before Assyria's defeat of Samaria, through Babylon's destruction of Jerusalem, to Persia's dominance over the chosen people and the promised land. Thus, the Twelve covers three centuries of decline, defeat, and initial recovery. Malachi also emphasizes the future envisioned by the rest of the Twelve, which focuses on God's intervention in history on behalf of the believing remnant.

To sustain these thematic threads the Twelve has had to employ a fully-developed portrait of the Lord. The warning texts require God to be both benevolent and menacing, depending on the needs of the particular messages. The judgment passages dictate an emphasis on imagery that allows the Lord to act decisively in a punishing manner. Similarly, the renewal texts need characterizations that underscore the just and forgiving aspects of the Lord's nature. Thus, a full-orbed portrait of God includes images of God as spouse, parent, judge, healer, creator, sovereign ruler, shepherd, deliverer, and refiner of a sinful world.

Are these descriptions simply competing voices? No, for the writers depict what they deem to be the same God. Further, texts that summarize the Lord's person, such as Nahum 1:2-8, include all these aspects of personality, or at least a majority of them. The writers of the Twelve do not consider it odd that a fully-developed person may have several characteristics. Finally, the depiction of God in the Twelve does not differ significantly from that of earlier books, nor of earlier summary texts such as Exodus 34:6-7. It seems reasonable, then, to conclude that a single character can have this many characteristics and remain consistent, and that the canon as a whole accepts the notion that God is one, yet not limited in personality. In this way the Twelve keeps faith with the rest of the canon by linking God's character to specific texts and events, and by using characterization techniques relevant to the action it conveys.

"Israel" and "Jacob" in the Book of Micah:
Micah in the Context of the Twelve

Mark E. Biddle
Baptist Theological Seminary at Richmond

Within the first several verses of the book of Micah, the reader encounters an array of phenomena that raise questions to linger throughout the book. The clearly "deuteronomistic" heading (1:1)[1] identifies the book as the words of a certain Micah, a Judean, roughly contemporary with Isaiah, who preached concerning Samaria and Jerusalem. The expectation that the book will address the fates of the capital cities of the Northern and Southern kingdoms, perhaps in a fashion similar to the way 2 Kings 17; Jeremiah 3:6-11; and Ezekiel 23 employ the catastrophe befallen Samaria as an object lesson for Judah and Jerusalem,[2] is immediately met by a brief unit (1:2-4) describing YHWH's theophany in universal terms. Employing language related on some intertextual level to the description of YHWH's judgment against the nations, especially Edom, found in Isaiah 34,[3] this theophany description recalls similar announcements of YHWH's world-wide judgment throughout the Dodekapropheton (Am 1:2; Nah 1:5; Zeph 1:2; cf. Zeph 3:8).

---

[1] For a recent discussion of these "deuteronomistic" superscriptions, see A. Schart, *Die Entstehung des Zwölfprophetenbuchs: Neubearbeitungen von Amos im Rahmen schriftenübergreifender Redaktionsprozesse* (BZAW 260; New York: de Gruyter, 1998), 31-49.

[2] J. Nogalski (*Literary Precursors to the Book of the Twelve* [BZAW 217; New York: de Gruyter, 1993) argues that Micah once constituted the third of four books (Hosea, Amos, Micah, and Zephaniah) in a corpus older than the Twelve. In this "deuteronomistic" corpus," Hosea and Amos record God's prophetic word to the Northern Kingdom while Micah and Zephaniah functioned as Southern counterparts...Broadly stated, Hosea alternates between YHWH's pronouncements of judgment and salvation for Israel. Amos presumes Israel's recalcitrance in Hosea, and announces judgment on Israel. Micah assumes Samaria's destruction from Amos as a warning to Judah of a similar fate if it does not change...Zephaniah centers its message on YHWH's judgment, like Amos, but that message is directed to Judah and Jerusalem" (Nogalski, *Redactional Processes in the Book of the Twelve* [BZAW 218; New York: de Gruyter, 1993], 274).

[3] M. Biddle, "Intertextuality, Micah, and the Book of the Twelve: A Question of Method" (unpublished paper presented to the Seminar on the Formation of the Book of the Twelve at the 1996 SBL Annual Meeting in New Orleans, LA).

Abruptly, a lengthy lament turns attention, as might have been anticipated from the heading to the book, to the manner in which the sins of Samaria have reached and infected Judah (1:9). The introduction (1:5) to this lament, however, surprisingly refers to "Jacob," confusing the matter of the precise identity of the addressees. If Jacob's transgression is Samaria, are the "sins of the house of Israel" and the "high place of Judah" (= Jerusalem!!) parallel? This confusion of addressees continues throughout the subsequent lament. Why are the "sins of Israel" associated with Judean Lachish (1:13) and what possible benefit could the "kings of Israel" have hoped to derive from the southern village of Achzib (1:14)? Did Micah employ "Israel" as a synonym for "Judah" and reserve "Jacob" for the Northern Kingdom?[4]

In fact, the entire book of Micah manifests a very curious tendency with respect to names of the people of God, a tendency characteristic of the Dodekapropheton, as well. The book refers to "Judah," Micah's presumptive addressee, only four times, only three times excluding the deuteronomistic chronological information in the superscription (1:1, 5, 9; 5:1). Instead of this expected designation, references to "Israel" (12x's) and "Jacob" (11x's) predominate. Notably, this preference pertains both to sections of the book generally regarded to be "authentic" (i.e. 3:1, 8, 9) and to those widely held to be redactional expansions (i.e. 2:12; 4:14; 5:6, 7). Were it not for the superscription, one might easily conclude that Micah was a northern prophet who addressed a northern audience. Instead, and governed no doubt by an

---

[4]Interpreters adopt every possible position with respect to the referents of these terms in Micah. For example, T. Lescow (*Worte und Wirkungen des Propheten Micha: Ein kompositionsgeschichtlicher Kommentar* [Arbeiten zur Theologie 84; Stuttgart: Calwer, 1997], 39-47, 96) argues that Micah employs both "Jacob" and "Israel" to refer to Judah. In support of this position he appeals, with respect to "Jacob," to parallels in Isaiah (48:1), and with respect to "Israel," to parallels in Jeremiah (2:4-6; 4:1-4; 5:15-17, 20-31; 18:1-6, 13-170. In contrast, W. D. Whitt ("The Jacob Traditions in Hosea and their Relation to Genesis," *ZAW* 103 [1991]: 21) argues that "Israel" refers to both kingdoms in Mic 1:14-16 and that "Jacob" consistently denotes Judah, adducing yet other Jeremiah texts in support (10:25; 30:7, 10; 31:11; 46:27, 28). W. McKane ("Micah 1,2-7," *ZAW* 107 [1995]: 434) employs historical criteria to draw the source-critical conclusion that "Micah was a Judean prophet and vv. 5a, 6-7 are not his work." I. Willi-Plein (*Vorformen der Schriftexegese innerhalb des Alten Testaments: Untersuchungen zum literarischen Werden der auf Amos, Hosea, und Micha zurückgehender Bücher im hebräischen Zwölfprophetenbuch* [BZAW 123; New York: de Gruyter, 1971], 70-71) resolves the problem text-critically, arguing that Mic 1:5b is a gloss..

acceptance of the historical setting for Micah's ministry provided by this superscription, scholarship assumes, for the most part, that Micah employed the terms Judah, Israel, and Jacob interchangeably.[5]

Admittedly, these terms manifest a surprising fluidity in the Hebrew Bible. The general consensus of scholarship holds that authors or speakers prior to the fall of Samaria usually reserved the name "Israel" for the Northern kingdom,[6] whereas authors or speakers after the fall of Samaria, and especially after the Exile, could appropriate the name for southerners as the surviving claimants to the patriarchal heritage.[7] Similarly, prior to the fall of Samaria, Jacob was often employed as a synonym for Israel,[8] while Judeans in the exilic and post-exilic period seem to have favored Jacob as a designation permitting them to lay claim to the earliest tradition and still avoid the negative political and historical connotations of "Israel."[9] Micah's usage, then, seems to conform to exilic and post-exilic practice rather than to that of the 8th century. Does this circumstance reflect the preferences of Micah the prophet or the program of the tradents and redactors of the book?

If the explicit claim of the superscription and the evidence of the southern place names in the lament (1:8-16) confirm not only the notion that Micah was a Judean, but, more significantly, that the editors and tradents of the book considered him so, this peculiarity deserves exploration and explanation. Two aspects of the phenomenon suggest that it represents a

---

[5] H. W. Wolff (*Dodekapropheton 4: Micha* [BKAT XIV/4; Neukirchen: Neukirchener Verlag, 1982], 15-16) can argue, for example, that "Micah thinks in 3:8 with reference to `Jacob' and `Israel' exclusively of Judah and Jerusalem (cf. 3:1, 9)" and can conclude that the same is true of 1:5a. Mic 1:5b he then labels as an insertion designed to link the superscription with the existing material.

[6] For example, Hos 1:6; 4:1; and often; Amos 2:6; 3:14; and often; Isa 7:1; 9:8, 14.

[7] For example, Isa 40:27; 41:8, 14; 43:1, 22, 28; 44:1, and often in Isaiah; Zech 12:1; Mal 1:1; Ezra 3:1; 7:7, 10; etc; Neh 9:2; 12:47.

[8] For example, Isa 8:17; 9:7; 10:20, 21; 17:4; Am 3:13; 6:8; 7:2, 5; 8:7; 9:8; Hos 10:11; 12:3, 13.

[9] For "Jacob" as a designation for southern exiles, see especially Isa 43:1; 44:1; 46:3; Jer 10:25; 30:7, 10; 31:11; 46:27, 28. For a helpful summaries of the situation, see H.-J. Zobel, "יעקׂ(ו)ב," *TWAT* III, 771-778; W. D. Whitt, "Jacob Traditions," 20-21; and W. Maier, *The Book of Nahum: A Commentary* (St. Louis: Concordia, 1959), 228. It must be stressed that each occurrence of the terms must be evaluated very careful. As Micah 1 demonstrates, the twin dangers of circular reasoning and easy assumptions may lead one to overlook the complexity of a given instance of an address.

redactional program, not only the redactional program that produced the book of Micah, itself, but also that produced the Book of the Twelve. First, Jacob and Israel dominate all sections of Micah, from the very confusing, and supposedly "authentic" opening chapter, to the equally ambiguous core chapter 3, and including the surely redactional expansions to chapter 2 (vv 12-13) and the eschatological "Zion" oracles of chapters 4-5.

Secondly, a similar preference for the names "Jacob" and "Israel" characterizes the Book of the Twelve up to Nahum 2:3. The distribution of these two names manifests an intriguing concentration at the front of the corpus. Of only twenty-eight instances of "Jacob," twenty-one appear in the four contiguous books of Amos (6x's), Obadiah (3x's), Micah (11x's), and Nahum (1x). Hosea (3x's) and Malachi (4x's) account for the remaining seven usages. Interestingly, key references to "Jacob" in Hosea (12:3-4), the first book in the Twelve, and in Malachi (1:2-5), the last, focus on the patriarch's relationship with his brother, Esau/Edom. Nahum marks a similar dividing point in the distribution of "Israel" (Hos - Nah, 91x's; Hab - Mal, 14x's). By contrast, the sixty-three instances of the name "Judah" divide rather equally (Hos - Nah, 31x's; Hab - Mal 32x's).

The substance and scope of this paper is thereby sharply circumscribed. What are the details of the usage pattern for these names in the book of Micah, itself? And, does this pattern participate in some scheme extending beyond the pages of Micah and reaching into the books surrounding Micah in the Minor Prophets corpus? For heuristic purposes, instances of the names Jacob and Israel as they appear in each of the three major literary divisions of Micah, namely Micah 1-3 (the "core" collection), Micah 4-5 (the eschatological "Zion" expansion), and Micah 6-7 (a divine law-suit and prophetic liturgy composition), will be examined as distinct groups. As will be seen, not coincidentally, certain characteristic formulae and phrases involving the names in these sections confirm the standard literary analysis and suggest parameters for an understanding of "Israel" and "Jacob" in the book of Micah and beyond.

"(House of) Jacob and (House of) Israel"
In the Core Collection

On the face of it, the expression "house of Jacob and house of Israel" and its variants[10] would appear to be the common merism encompassing both kingdoms (Jacob would then be a reference to Judah). Several structural elements establish a framework or inclusio around Micah 1:5-3:12* and set the parameters for understanding the connotations of its use of "Jacob" and "Israel." The section opens with the announcement that "all this" is or will be "because of the rebellion (בְּפֶשַׁע) of Jacob" and "because of the sins (וּבְחַטֹּאות) of the house of Israel" (1:5), phrases echoed at the end in the prophet's description of his mission "to declare to Jacob his rebellion (פִּשְׁעוֹ) and to Israel his sin (חַטָּאתוֹ)" (3:8). The jarring reference to Jerusalem as the "high place of Judah" (בָּמוֹת יְהוּדָה)" (1:5) not only relates back to the theophany of 1:2-4 (v 3), but also prefigures the announcement that Zion will become a "ploughed field (שָׂדֶה תֵחָרֵשׁ)," Jerusalem a "ruin" (עִיִּין),"[11] and the temple mount a "high place of the forest (לְבָמוֹת יָעַר)" (3:12). This framework, then, likens the fate of Jerusalem (3:10-12), the "high place of Judah," with that of Samaria (1:6-7) and, by virtue of the redactional linkage to the theophany description opening the book, sets the fates of both in the context of the destruction of the "high places" and mountains of the world (1:2-4).

The unexpected reference to Jerusalem as a "high place" suggests the dependence of 1:5, where the term connotes the pejorative sense of the Canaanite cultic site, on 3:10-12, where the term emphasizes the aftermath of destruction. Provisionally, then, Mic 1:5, which sits very loosely in its

---

[10]"House of Jacob. . . and house of Israel" appears in 3:9; "Jacob. . . and the house of Israel" in 1:5; 3:1; "Jacob. . . and Israel" in 3:8. "Israel" appears unaccompanied in 1:13,14,15 and "the house of Jacob" in 2:7. Since these uses appear in material that belong, for the most part, to the same redactional layer as the binary expression, or more appropriately, since their current position nestled among the binary expressions influences a homogenous reading, they can be provisionally understood as synonymous with their occurrences in the binary forms. "Jacob, all of you. . . and remnant of Israel" in 2:12 will be treated separately below.

[11]Compare 1:6, "I will make Samaria a ruin of the field (לְעִי הַשָּׂדֶה)."

context,[12] seems to have been composed specifically further to link the Samaria (1:6-7) and Jerusalem (3:10-12) inclusio to the opening section of the book. These three distinct uses of the term "high place" (the world's heights, 1:3; a pejorative reference to Jerusalem as a cult site, 1:5; a description of the Jerusalem as a barren hill, 3:12), then, while serving to bind this section as a compositional unit, also betray something of the redactional history of Micah.

In fact, this theme of the fate of the "high places" plays a role in anchoring Micah in the book of the Twelve. Hos 10:8; Amos 4:13; 7:9; and Hab 3:19 also discuss "high places" in a ways that suggest some literary relationship to the texts in Micah. A. Schart[13] has already called attention to the close parallels between Mic 3:12 and Hos 10:8, but the Hosea text and Mic 1:5 exhibit an even stronger resemblance. Hos 10:8 identifies the "high place of Awen" appositionally as the "sin of Israel." The parallelism of Mic 1:5 similarly equates the "sins of the house of Israel" with "the high place of Judah." Amos 7:9 forms the third member in this chain of inter-prophetic allusions. J. Jeremias has already called attention to aspects of this brief pronouncement that seem foreign to the book of Amos, while at the same time demonstrating unmistakable affinities with the book of Hosea, and especially Hos 10:8.[14] It remains only to note the unusual relationship between Amos' condemnation of the "high places of Isaac," itself a peculiar reference to the northern kingdom,[15] and Micah's condemnation of the "high places of Judah."[16]

---

[12]It can hardly be read as the logical continuation of vv 2-4, which speak of a world-wide cataclysm in association with YHWH's appearance. "All this" must refer to what follows. Concerning the problem of the discontinuity between vv 2-4 and v 5, see W. Rudolph, *Micha – Nahum – Habakuk – Zephanja* (KAT 13/3; Gütersloh: Gerd Mohn, 1975), 39-41; Wolff, 14-16; T. Lescow, "Redaktionsgeschichtliche Analyse von Micha 1-5," *ZAW* 84 (1972): 55-61; Nogalski, *Literary Precursors*, 129-137; Lescow, *Worte und Wirkungen*, 28-30; B. Zapff, *Redaktionsgeschichtliche Studien zum Michabuch im Kontext des Dodekapropheton* (BZAW 256; New York: de Gruyter, 1997), 262-268.

[13]*Entstehung*, 190.

[14]*Der Prophet Amos: Übersetzt und Erklärt* (ATD 24/2; Göttingen, Vandenhoeck & Ruprecht, 1995), 111-112.

[15]Jeremias (111, n. 13) remarks that, "The use of the term 'Isaac,' that besides Am 7:9,16 never parallels Israel in the OT and is never used in reference to the northern

The Samaria/Jerusalem framework of Micah 1-3 employs Jacob and Israel as references to the North and the South, respectively. Do references within this framework conform to this pattern? "Israel" occurs three times unaccompanied in the lament of Mic 1:8-16. H. W. Wolff suggests that the phrase "glory of Israel" (1:15), usually a divine epithet,[17] should be understood here as a parallel to the "king of Israel" (1:14). In his view, it recalls David's flight to Adullam at the "low point" of his life (2 Sam 23:13).[18] Since all the place names that serve as the basis for the word-plays in the lament indicate locations in the Judean Shephelah, "Israel" must refer to Judah. Only Mic 1:13b falls outside this pattern. Although it employs the familiar pair rebellion/sin (1:5; 3:8), they occur here in reverse order. It disrupts the terse rhythm of the word-plays. Furthermore, it interprets Samaria's wound which has reached Judah (1:9) in relation to Israel's rebellion found in Lachish: the sole instance in Micah 1-3 in which Israel refers unmistakably to the northern kingdom.[19]

The remaining three instances of the Jacob/Israel pair (3:1, 8, 9; disregarding 2:12 for the moment) along with the sole instance of "house of Jacob" alone (2:7) in Micah 1-3 present another profile altogether. A. Schart rightly calls attention to a "summons to hear" series stretching across the books of Hosea (4:1; 5:1), Amos (3:1; 4:1; 5:1; 8:4), and Micah, and culminating in Mic 3:1, 9 and 6:2.[20] In his view, several intertextual connections suggest some literary relationship between the three books involved: Mic 3:1 (הלוא לכם לדעת את־המשפט) picks up on the charge to

---

kingdom, remains unexplained." He considers it likely that "Isaac" here is somehow related to the unusual double reference to Beersheba (Am 5:5; 8:14).

[16]The picture in Amos 4:13 (one of three late doxological acknowledgements of the justice of YHWH's dealings with Israel/Judah) of YHWH, the creator God who "bestrides the high places of the earth," on the other hand, more closely parallels Mic 1:3. The relationship between these two texts belongs, therefore, to a later phase in the growth of the Twelve. The enigmatic conclusion to Habakkuk's prayer celebrating YHWH's theophany (3:19) may also be related to this "theophany" layer of material. See the helpful discussion and summary of research on Amos 4:13; 5:8-9; and 9:5-6 in D. U. Rottzoll, *Studien zur Redaktion und Komposition des Amosbuchs* (BZAW 243; New York: de Gruyter, 1996), 242-250.

[17]Isa 17:3, 4; Ezek 10:19; 11:22.
[18]*Micha*, 33.
[19]So also Schart, 182-183.
[20]186-189.

the leadership responsible for justice voiced in Hos 5:1 (כי לכם המשפט);
Mic 6:2, the last in the series, cites Hos 4:1, the first in the series, almost
verbatim (כי ריב ליהוה עם); like Amos 5:19 and 9:3, Mic 3:5 refers to the
snake's bite; both Hos 4:2 and Mic 3:10 refer to "bloody deeds"; and, the
reference to threat posed by the fact that "YHWH is in the [people's] midst"
in Mic 3:11 can only be understood against the background of Amos 5:17
and 7:8, 10. Schart's observations can be expanded: (1) The citation of
Micah's opponents who call for him to cease "preaching" (נטף) recalls Amos
7:16;[21] (2) Mic 3:2 (שנאי טוב ואהבי רעה) describes the wicked behaviors
of Micah's audience in terms reversed precisely in the call to repentance
issued in Am 5:15 (שנאו־רע ואהבו טוב); (3) In general terms, Micah and
Amos adopt a very similar stance on the theme of social and economic
justice (note especially Mic 3:9||Amos 5:10 [תעב]; editors supplied Hosea
with this theme, as well, see Hos 5:10).

The question of the direction and nature of the relationship between
these "summons to hear" (and their contexts) in Micah, on the one hand, and
in Hosea and Amos, on the other, is inseparable from the question of the
meaning of "Jacob...and...Israel" in Mic 3:1, 8, and 9. Schart recognizes two
possible interpretations of the significance of the "summons to hear" series
and other intertextualities between Micah, Hosea, and Amos: either the
hand responsible for Mic 3:1-12 knew a more-or-less final form of the
Hosea-Amos "book of the Two"[22] or the editors responsible for combining
Hosea and Amos on one scroll were themselves also responsible for the final
form of Mic 3:1-12, i.e. they included Micah along with Hosea and Amos
from the outset (a "book of the Three"). For Schart, who opts for the first
explanation, the referent of "Israel" in Micah 3 provides the key. As he

---

[21]The second instance of the peculiar "house of Isaac" in Amos 7. It clearly refers
to the North. Is "house of Jacob" in Mic 2:7 meant as a counterpart? Is the reader of the
Twelve to understand that, just as Amos' opponent called upon him not to preach to the
"house of Isaac" (= the North), Micah's opponent, the "house of Jacob" (= Judah), called
upon him stop proclaiming his message publicly?

[22] J. Jeremias, "Die Anfänge des Dodekapropheton: Hosea und Amos," in
Congress Volume Paris 1992, J. Emerton, ed. (VTSup 61; Leiden: Brill, 1995), 87-106
(= *Hosea und Amos: Studien zu den Anfängen des Dodekapropheton* [FAT 13;
Tübingen: J.C.B. Mohr, 1996], 34-54).

observes, "if one has this [summons] series before one's eyes, then it becomes problematical to relate the expression 'house of Israel' in Mic 3:1, 9 to Judah."[23] Conversely, he concludes that, since, in Micah, "Israel" refers to Judah, the tradents responsible for the summons texts in Hosea and Amos could not have authored the Micah texts. He reasons that, should "Israel" here refer to the North, one would be forced "to envision the scene as though the northern kingdom were an uninvolved spectator."[24]

In response to Schart, however, one might object that the superscription of the book, the enigmatic redactional unit in 1:5, and the address to Samaria in 1:6-7 all presume precisely that the northern kingdom is involved, *at least from the perspective of the fictive reality created by the book itself*. Grounds other than "historical" realities, namely the (literary) contexts of these address forms, must be adduced to resolve the question of the referents of Mic 3:1, 8, and 9. In respect to these contexts, however, the two axes to which these "summons" texts relate, namely Micah 1, on the one hand, and the other "summons" texts in Hosea and Amos, on the other, are in conflict. In the context of Micah, these summons call upon the leadership of both North (Jacob = Samaria, Mic 1:5) and South (Israel = Judah, Mic 1:5, 14, 15); in the context of the Twelve Jacob and Israel would be synonymous references to the North only. In neither case does a contextual reading justify understanding both terms as designations for Judah alone. The editor responsible for the superscription worked with a text that could be understood as having reference to both North and South. If Mic 3:1-12 constituted part of that book, the editor, given the affinities with Hosea and Amos already outlined above, will have likely understood it as a blanket condemnation of both kingdoms, culminating, of course, in harsh words for Jerusalem (just as the body of the book begins with equally harsh words for Samaria).

---

[23]186, n. 100.
[24]188, n. 111.

"Remnant of Israel" and "Remnant of Jacob" in the Eschatological/Zion Composition Micah 4-5

As already anticipated in the oddly placed oracle in Mic 2:12-13, the book of Micah turns from theological interpretation of history (Mic 1:2-3:12*) to eschatological promises for Jerusalem (Mic 4:1-5:14). These Jerusalem promises attract particular interest in relation to the topic at hand for several reasons. First, if reconstructions of the growth of the Dodekapropheton such as those offered by J. Nogalski[25] prove accurate with regard to the "eschatologizing," or even "apocalypticizing," function of the book of Joel in the Twelve, Micah 4-5 will either represent the earliest *concentration* of such eschatological material in the "Deuteronomistic" corpus or will manifest evidence of having been incorporated into Micah at some point after Micah's inclusion in the proto-scroll. Second, even a cursory reading of Micah 4-5 suggests that the material preserved here originated in a variety of settings and reflects a variety of ideologies. It can be expected that the manifold connotations of the names "Jacob" and "Israel" may serve as a diagnostic criterion. Third, despite evidence of a history of growth, Micah 4-5 displays a beautifully symmetrical structure, marred only at a few points (Mic 4:6-7; 5:4-8) which, significantly, include unique references to the "remnant of Jacob" (Mic 5:6, 7). This high degree of literary structure and the location of the composition in the middle of the book must be considered in relation to the question of whether it comprised part of the book when Micah joined the proto-collection. Finally, individual units in the composition resemble isolated redactional insertions in others of the Minor Prophets. A taxonomy of these eschatological units in the Dodekapropheton will provide additional data for reconstructing Micah's role in the growth of the Twelve.

Before grouping and examining individual occurrences of the names "Israel" and "Jacob" in this eschatological composition, it will be helpful first to analyze its structure and second to suggest an initial taxonomy of eschatological texts in the Twelve. Against this background of the two

---

[25] *Redactional Processes*, 275-278.

primary contexts for Israel/Jacob in the book of Micah, the profiles of these figures should emerge with greater clarity.

The Macro-Structure of Micah 4-5

Two features of Micah 4-5 lend it remarkable coherence. First, with few exceptions (5:3-8; 9-14 and, perhaps, 4:6-8), all of the units deal explicitly with the future of Jerusalem. Second, it exhibits a very sophisticated literary skeleton. Four types of introductory phrases clearly demarcate the constitutive units of Micah's eschatological Jerusalem composition: "eschatological" formulae ("and it will be in the latter days [והיה באחרית הימים]," 4:1; "in that day [ביום ההוא]," 4:6; and "and it will be in that day [והיה ביום־ההוא]," 5:9), vocative 2nd masculine singular pronouns addressed directly to personifications of architectural features of cities or cities themselves ("and you, O...stronghold of daughter of Zion/Bethlehem [ואתה . . . בת־ציון/בית־לחם]," Mic 4:8; 5:1 [5:2 Eng]), a temporal adverb contrasting the current state with the future predicted in the "eschatological" units ("now [ועתה/עתה]," 4:9, 11, 14; the nearly homonymous pairing of the pronoun and the adverb is a masterfully poetic touch), and a series of "to be" verbs with the simple copula ("and...will be, [והיה]," 5:4, 6, 7). As the following chart demonstrates: (1) Chiasm accentuates the contrast between the present and the future which dominates the structure overall; and, (2) in its current state, the structure is imbalanced at precisely those points which do not deal explicitly with the fact of Jerusalem, the theme of the composition.

והיה באחרית הימים

ביום ההוא

ואתה

עתה

ועתה

עתה

ואתה

והיה

והיה

והיה

והיה ביום־ההוא

For the moment, the fact that four units (4:6-8; 5:4-5, 6, 7 [5:5-6, 7, 8, Eng]) disrupt this balanced chiasm will only be noted. The latter two of them will become the focus of attention below.

A Taxonomy of "Eschatological" Texts in the Minor Prophets

Several themes that figure prominently in sections of Mic 2:12-13; 4:1-5:15 (the nations' pilgrimage to/siege against Jerusalem/the fate of the nations;   YHWH's reign on Mt. Zion/the restoration of the Davidic monarchy; the gathering and return of the Diaspora) resurface elsewhere in the Minor Prophets (Hos 2:1-2; Joel 4:1-3, 16-21; Amos 9:11-15; Ob 8-10, 15-21; Zeph 2:7; 3:8-20; Zech 8:1-18, 9-15; 12:1-6; Mal 1:2-5). Although these texts manifest considerable lexical similarity (i.e. the vocabulary for "gathering [קבץ]" the Diaspora; Hos 2:2; Joel 4:2; Mic 2:12), the specific treatments made of these themes vary widely. The relationship between these texts may elucidate the relationship between the redaction history of Micah and the growth of the Twelve. Did Micah assume more-or-less its current form *before* joining the Minor Prophets scroll or *during* the formation of the corpus?

Micah 4:1-4, 11-13; 5:1, 14; Joel 4:2, 9-17; Zeph 3:8; Zech 12:2, 3-5, 6, 8, 9; 14:1-3, 12-15, 16-19 all deal with the topic of "the nations gathered in/against Jerusalem." In general, these texts can be divided into two major categories:[26] in one view, the nations assemble against Jerusalem to lay siege, but, since they do not understand YHWH's plan for history, they will be surprised by the day of YHWH (Mic 4:11-13; 5:1; Joel 4:9-17; Zeph 3:8; Zech 12:2, 3-5, 6, 9; 14:1-3, 12-15); in another, the nations pilgrimage to Zion to worship YHWH or submit to his lordship (Mic 4:1-4; Zech 14:16-19; cf. Zech 2:11; 8:22-23; 9:10). While none of the pertinent Micah texts employ the names "Jacob" or Israel," and thus are not specifically germane to this study, several background observations regarding the interrelationships evidenced among texts dealing with this broad topic may illuminate the redaction history of Micah 4-5. First, the two viewpoints clearly conflict with one another, and may even represent competing ideologies. Second, a complicated system of interdependency links these texts across the bounds of the limits of the books constitutive of the Twelve.[27] Third, and perhaps most importantly at this point, the conflict manifests itself within Micah (4:1-5 contra 4:12-13; 5:14).

Similar circumstances prevail with respect to the theme of kingship in Jerusalem: One group of texts rather simplistically expect the

---

[26]Joel 4:2 is eccentric. According to it, YHWH will assemble the nations in the "Valley of Jehosophat" in order to plead with them to release the Jews of the Diaspora.

[27]For example, either Joel 4:10 or Mic 4:3 cites, and reverses, the other. The direction of the dependency is far from clear (for the priority of Joel, see Zapff, 261, n. 84; in support of the contrary, see, E. Bosshard, "Beobachtungen zum Zwölfprophetenbuch," *BN* 40 (1987): 42; Schart, 268-269). Similarly, Joel 4:12 and Mic 4:3 also allude to one another (YHWH judging the nations) and Joel 4:13 and Mic 4:13 seem to be related in some way. While at present, no clear criterion for determining the direction of dependence between Joel 4:10 and Mic 4:3 seems to have been established, the fact that Mic 4:1-5 and Zech 14:16-19 stand out in the Twelve for their utopian vision deserves full consideration. It is tempting to hypothesize a development in post-exilic thought from a bitter expectation of revenge on the nations to a more humanitarian hope for universal peace. The two ideas could well have arisen and existed alongside one another, however. At any rate, Zech 14:16-19 makes a unique and valiant attempt to reconcile the two perspectives on the fates of the nations. It envisions a time after YHWH exercises worldwide vengeance on Israel's enemies when the survivors of that judgment will come annually to Zion to worship the Lord during Succoth. See J. Rubenstein, *The History of Sukkot in the Second Temple and Rabbinic Periods* (Brown Judaic Studies 302; Atlanta: Scholars, 1995), 45-50.

reestablishment of the Davidic monarchy (Hos 2:1-2; Amos 9:11-15; Mic 5:1-3; Zech 3:8; 6:12-13), while another focuses rather on the reign of YHWH (Joel 4:9-16 [implicitly]; Obad 21; Mic 4:1-5; Zeph 3:8-20; Zech 8:1-9; Zech 14:9, 16-17). Presumably, the focus on YHWH's reign reflects the embarrassment of the community at the delayed restoration of the Davidic monarchy, an embarrassment which may explain the strange attitude toward the house of David expressed in Zech 12:7.[28] Once again, Micah 4-5 manifests ties with other sections of the Twelve;[29] once again, individual texts within Micah 4-5 adopt contradictory stances.

The theme of the return of the Exiles or the Diaspora, a theme in which the use of the names "Israel" and "Jacob" plays a significant role, may provide criteria that will help to clarify the intricacies of these intertextual relationships. The texts in question may be classified as follows:

1) Hos 2:1-2 (1:10-11 Eng) focuses rather simplistically on the numerical growth of "Israel" (the North), the reestablishment of a single (Davidic) ruler over both houses of Israel, "the sons of Judah and the sons of Israel, together," and the return from Exile.[30] These emphases suggest that the text stems from the period before the Samaritan schism, when the hope

---

[28]It should be noted once again that Zecharaiah 12-14 seems interested in balancing certain tensions in the Twelve. These observations concerning the commentary character of certain texts in Zechariah 9-14 is consistent with a growing body of scholarship that views Zechariah 9-14 as an anthology of extrapolations of earlier prophecy. See, for example, Magne Saebø, *Sacharja 9-14* (WMANT 34; Neukirchen-Vluyn: Neukirchener Verlag, 1969); P. L. Reditt, "Israel's Shepherds: Hope and Pessimism in Zechariah 9-14," *CBQ* 51 (1989): 631-42; O. H. Steck, *Der Abschluß der Prophetie im Alten Testament: Ein Versuch zur Frage der Vorgeschichte des Kanons* (Biblisch-Theologische Studien 17; Neukirchnen: Neukirchener, 1991); N. Tai, *Prophetie als Schriftauslegung in Sacharja 9-14: Traditions- und kompositions-geschichtliche Studien* (Calwer Theologische Monographien 17; Stuttgart: Calwer, 1996); K. Larkin, *The Eschatology of Second Zechariah: A Study of the Formation of a Mantological Wisdom Anthology* (Contributions to Biblical Exegesis & Theology 6; Kampen: Kok Paros, 1994); Nogalski, *Redactional Processes*, 213-47; and R. F. Person, *Second Zechariah and the Deuteronomic School* (JSOTSup 167; Sheffield: Sheffield, 1993).

[29]Mic 4:6-8 and Zeph 3:14-20 bear a particularly strong resemblance to one another. Both focus on Zion/Daughter Jerusalem's wondrous restoration; both describe YHWH as king; and both refer to the gathering and return of the "lame (הצלעה)" and the "driven out (הנדחה)."

[30]See J. Jeremias, *Der Prophet Hosea: Übersetzt und Erklärt* (ATD 24/1; Göttingen: Vandenhoeck & Ruprecht), 34-36.

for a reunited Israel would require only the return of the Exiles and the establishment of Davidic rule extending even over the north. The reestablishment of Davidic rule and the return of the "captivity (שְׁבוּת)" of Israel (the northern Diaspora?) also characterizes the two units combined in Amos 9:11-15. Together these two texts may have once served as a linking framework around the early Hosea/Amos corpus.

2) Like Hosea 2:1-2; Amos 9:11-15; and Joel 4:1-3, Obad 10, 15-21 (v 18) distinguishes between northerners ("the house of Joseph") and southerners ("the house of Jacob"), suggesting a historical setting prior to the Samaritan schism. Like Amos 9:11-15 and Joel 4:16-21, it expresses anger toward Edom. It differs from its kindred texts, however, in three key regards. First of all, it seems less interested in the restoration and reunification of the nation, which it seems to presume, than in vengeance against Israel's enemies. Second, although Obadiah targets Edom for its most severe disdain, its tone of universal revenge (v 15) and climactic announcement of YHWH's sovereignty lends it an air of the apocalyptic. Third, the avoidance of the straightforward terms "Israel" and "Judah" may betray a sensitivity toward them such as characterizes certain late exilic and early post-exilic texts.[31]

Mic 2:12-13 employs the terms "Jacob" and "remnant of Israel" in a rather unique fashion. This passage, one of the more ambiguous in the book of Micah,[32] contrasts "all" of Jacob with "the remnant of Israel" in a way that clearly suggests a distinction between the two. Apparently, the author considered "all" of Jacob (= the Judean Exiles) worthy of return, while only a few of the survivors of the northern kingdom will be involved in the restoration. Zapff has recently called attention to a possible solution to the text-critical problems of vv 12b and 13a and to the passage's rich

---

[31]Note especially the care taken to establish the "proper" referents of these terms in Isa 48:1, for example.

[32]Partly because it appears in the midst of Micah 2-3, the "accusation" section of the book of Micah, and partly because of the linguistic difficulty presented by vv 12b-13, interpreters disagree as to the basic question of whether this saying offers hope (return from Exile) or judgment (going into Exile). Zapff surveys the positions taken in the literature (16-17). The distinction between "all" of Jacob and "the remnant" of Israel provides a clue as to the interpretation of the passage, as does the parallelism between "their king before them" and "YHWH at their head."

intertextualities and argued that it bears a strong relationship to a number of texts (including Amos 9:11-15, Joel 4:16-21; Mal 1:2-5; see especially Isa 34-35; 63:1-6) that, as O.H. Steck has argued,[33] demonize Edom. Zapff argues, quite convincingly, for accepting the MT reading "Bozrah" and repointing "from man/men" to "from Edom." Two allusions recall patriarchal promises (תהימנה alludes to the promise of offspring made to Abraham, Gen 17:4-5; פרץ likewise recalls the promise to Jacob, Gen 28:14).[34] In the eschatological schema outlined by these texts, Edom will be the staging area for the entry of the final return of the exiles. Edom's destruction will usher in the universal judgment upon the nations and the returning Exiles will then pass through Edom's territory unhindered. Mic 1:2-4, which, as mentioned above, fits very awkwardly in its current context and manifests every indication of being a late insertion, shares with Mic 2:12-13 an interesting syntactical feature. Mic 1:2 begins with a summons to hear addressed to the nations that includes an awkward third personal pronominal suffix: "Hear O nations, all of them (כֻּלָּם), draw near, O earth and all its fullness." Similarly, Mic 2:12, in which YHWH promises to "assemble Jacob," includes the incongruous second personal pronominal suffix, "all of you (כֻּלָּךְ)." Unless emended, for which there is little manuscript support, the two suffixes can best be understood *as asides to the reader* and testify to the work of a common hand in the two texts.

If Zapff is correct that Mic 2:12-13 resonates with Steck's anti-Edom schema, it comes as no surprise that Mic 1:2-4 also demonstrates a number of intertextualities with Isaiah 34, a key text in this anti-Edom eschatological schema.[35] A late redactional layer of the book of Micah, then, sought to

---

[33]*Bereitete Heimkehr: Jesaja 35 als redaktionelle Brücke zwischen dem Ersten und dem Zweiten Jesaja* (SBS 121; Stuttgart: Katholisches Bibelwerk, 1985), 42-44, 49-50.

[34]Zapff, 23-30.

[35]Only these two texts summon (קרב and שמע) the nations along with "the earth and its fullness (ארץ ומלאה) to hear a pronouncement of YHWH's judgment on all the nations of the earth. Both introduce descriptions of YHWH's intervention with affinities to theophany traditions. In both, the sins of a single people have prompted the universal day of YHWH. Both contexts refer to the "jackal" and the "ostrich." In addition, certain themes and phrases in Isaiah 34 parallel other passages in Micah and further suggest some intentional relationship. The nations stand under YHWH's חֶרֶם (Isa 34:2; Mic

relate the book of the Amos/Joel/Obadiah/Malachi discussion of Edom's role in universal history. The text's apparent partiality to "all" of Jacob is an additional indicator of this redactional layer's relationship to the book of Isaiah, especially.[36]

3) Joel 4:1-3 (3:1-3 Eng), on the other hand, distinguishes between the "captivity of Judah and Jerusalem" and the "Israelites who are dispersed among the nations." It envisions a period when YHWH will have restored (שׁוּב) the "captivity," but the "dispersion" remains among the nations, and may well reflect the circumstances of the Persian period, after the rebuilding of the temple.

4) Joel 4:16-21 (3:16-21 Eng) employs the terms "Judah" and "Israel" in yet a third sense, identifying "sons of Israel" (v 16; the Zion reference in the context of a theophany establishes the Jerusalem orientation of this text) with "Judah" (v 20; Zion is YHWH's dwelling place). The book of Zechariah also consistently treats Israel and Judah as synonyms (see 12:1-6). These texts reflect a period remote enough from the 8th century crisis, on the one hand, and also from the Samaritan schism, on the other,[37] so that the name Israel has no negative connotations.

This synonymous usage also characterizes Mic 4:14 (5:1 Eng); 5:1-2. Mic 4:14 belongs to oldest core of Micah 4-5,[38] and may even preserve a

4:13); YHWH has a day of vengeance (נָקָם) on Edom/the nations (Isa 34:8; Mic 5:14 [5:15 Eng]). Cities under YHWH's judgment become overgrown wastelands (Isa 34:13; Mic 3:12; 5:11). The unusual legitimating expression, "for the mouth [of YHWH] has commanded/spoken (כִּי פִי וַיהוה צוּה/רבר)" is very intriguing. Isa 34:17 speaks of YHWH "casting the lot (גורל hiph. נפל)" and "apportioning by the line (חלק בקו)" when assigning Edomite territory to the wild animals and desert demons. Mic 2:5 speaks of YHWH disinheriting the greedy in Israel leaving them with no one "to cast the line (חבל hiph. שׁלךּ) by lot (בגורל)."

[36]On the relationship between the redactional history of the book of Isaiah and the formation history of the Twelve, see Bosshard, 30-62; Bosshard and R. G. Kratz, "Maleachi im Zwölfprophetenbuch," *BN* 52 (1990): 27-46; Steck, *Abschluß*.

[37]It reflects, not a tension between Jew and Samaritan, but conflict between Jerusalem and Judah. Cf. Larkin, 40-41, 140-145, 147-158.

[38]Wolff, 108; Rudolph (93-94) associates Mic 4:14 with the Assyrian siege of Jerusalem described in 2 Kgs 18:17ff. 19:8; T. Lescow, "Redaktionsgeschichtliche Analyse von Micha 1-5," *ZAW* 84 (1972): 65-74; Lescow, *Worte und Wirkungen*, 140-148; Zapff (125) comments that, "...none of the texts in Mic 4-5 is to be attributed ot the prophet Micah himself. Instead, the oldest components of these chapters are to be dated, in any case, to the late pre-exilic period, more precisely in the period of the neo-

historical memory of the treatment of some Judean (Zion references) king at the hands of a foreign invader (the Babylonians? even the oldest portion of Micah 4-5, then, would date no earlier than the exilic period; cf. esp. Lam 3:30). Mic 5:1, on the other hand, while still employing Israel and Judah synonymously, reflects a period when expectations for the restoration of the Davidic monarchy run high. Several allusions to other passages in the Twelve, esp. Amos 9:11 and several "messianic" texts in Zechariah, establish the late exilic period as the intellectual milieu of Mic 5:1. The expression, "as in the olden days" (Mic 5:1 [5:2 Eng]), does not refer to the eternity of the Davidic line, but, synonymous with the usage in Amos 9:11, looks forward to the reestablishment of the throne. Avoidance of the term "king" characterizes late exilic/early Persian period texts, written as they were in a period of heightened sensitivity to rebellion on the part of the Imperial powers (for מושל see, for example, Zech 6:13). On the other hand, Mic 5:2, which refers to the exilic inhabitants of Eretz Israel as the "sons of Israel," seems to be motivated by a different source of embarrassment altogether, namely the delay in the restoration of the Davidic house. Micah's insistence on the insignificance of the Davidic house (which is never named) recalls Zech 12:6-14, which is also concerned with establishing that, despite the importance of the Davidites, the tribe of Judah (אלפי יהודה) is even more significant (Zech 12:4-6), and evidences, then, the common intellectual milieu of Mic 5:1-2 and portions of the book of Zechariah.

It should be noted here that this use of "Israel" as a synonym for "Judeans" substantially coincides with usage in Mic 1, but not Micah 2-3. Given the composite nature of Micah 1, this resemblance suggests that the redaction that produced the core of Mic 4-5 may also have given Mic 1:6-16 substantially its current shape.

5) The precise connotation of "remnant of Jacob" in Mic 5:6, 7 depends entirely on: (a) the significance of the metaphors of dew and rain in 5:6 , (b) relatedly, whether v 6 and v 7 are to be understood synonymously, (c) whether v 8 summarizes both vv 6 and 7, v 7 only, or is a later comment,

Babylonian threat to Judah. That is, an original collection of the words of Micah, which is probably to be sought primarily in Mic 1-3, was actualized in the late pre-exilic period through references to the 8th century threat (for example, by Mic 4:9, 10a, b, cα, 14)...."

and (d) what the phrase, repeated in both units, "in the midst of many nations," signifies. Metaphorically, "dew" can represent several notions in the Hebrew bible: Because of its mysterious appearance, it can be likened to an ambush (2 Sam 17:12). In the arid Levant, it can symbolize fecundity (Gen 27:27-29; Deut 32:2; 33:13; Hos 14:6; Psa 133:3). Scholarly opinions range from Wolff's conclusion that "the first saying asks, then, not about what the 'remnant of Jacob' means for the nations, but about the wondrous origin of its future existence in the midst of the nations"[39] to Zapff's that "the promise of blessing given Jacob will be transferred, as it were, via the personified 'remnant of Jacob' to all the nations who...adopt a positive attitude toward the remnant of Jacob."[40]

Both vv 6 and 7 supply the metaphors with an interpretive clause calling attention to the likeness. The remnant of Jacob will be like a lion in that it will "tread down and tear in pieces so that none can deliver." The similarity between the remnant and the dew and rain, on the other hand, hinges around the indifference of the dew and the rain to those whom it benefits. People hope for dew and rainfall; dew and rainfall "do not look for man, nor await the sons of man." They simply fall where they fall. The implication, then, seems to be that the remnant among the nations is indifferent to its impact upon them - certainly an unusual sentiment in the Hebrew Bible!

How does this sentiment relate to that expressed in v 7? It may be significant that the explanatory clause in v 7c is conditional: "if he (the lion) should pass through...." Vv 6-7 can be understood then as something of a warning not to disturb the remnant that wishes simply to be left alone. Should the nations disturb Jacob, the lion may well "tear, with none to deliver."

This sayings couplet concludes with a summary statement addressed to an unspecified masculine figure, presumably Jacob. Grammatically, if the conclusion means to continue vv 6-7, it should address "the remnant," a

---

[39]*Micha*, 129.
[40]Zapff, 100-102. He considers it especially significant that the imagery of "dew" and of the "lion" both appear in the context of patriarchal promise (dew, Gen 27:27-9) and blessing (lion, Gen 49:9-10).

feminine noun. Metaphors give way to idiomatic expression. Therefore, although v 8 understands vv 6-7 unambiguously, it can best be taken as the earliest commentary on these two units.

Finally, the phrase "in the midst of many nations (עמים רבים)" may be understood diametrically to mean either "in the midst of (each of) many nations" (i.e. the Diaspora; the image of the remnant spread abroad as the dew supports this interpretation) or "(as a group gathered in one place [presumably Eretz Israel], which place is) in the midst of the many nations." The seemingly redundant "among the peoples (בגוים)," likely a variant reading preserved in the text of MT, points to the former understanding.

Israel and Jacob in the Prophetic Liturgy: Micah 6-7

Only one occurrence each of "Israel" and "Jacob" appear in the final section of the book. In both instances, the appeal to traditions common to the twelve tribes (Exodus, Balaam, Abraham) obscure any political connotations for these terms. In fact, the universally-Israelite tone of this material, probably the intentional result of the canonical redaction of the book, points to the danger of over reliance on the presumed historical setting of the prophet's career as an interpretive key. These books have been consciously edited for use by later generations of any who call themselves "Israel."

Conclusions

In the book of Micah, as often elsewhere in the Hebrew Bible, the terms "Jacob" and "Israel" may be seen as variables. The reader of Micah who seeks to establish their value confronts a bewildering situation. Read synchronously, the book sets the values of these terms in Mic 1:5 such that "Jacob = the Northern Kingdom" and "Israel = Judah." This equation, however, cannot be sustained throughout the book, and, since Mic 1:5 is clearly redactional, the critical reader may appeal to another basis for establishing the values of the key terms. Usually, interpreters privilege the prophet's assumed historical setting (established by the superscription to the book) and stipulated kerygmatic purpose (usually identified with the message of Mic 2-3). Read in this fashion, the book sets the values of the terms in question in Mic 3:1 such that "Jacob = Israel = Judah." This equation, however, seems ridiculous on its face and can be applied nowhere else in the book. Apparently, the ambiguity and variability of the terms "Jacob" and "Israel" in the book of Micah point to its redactional history and give evidence of the relationship between the book of Micah and the Minor Prophets corpus.

The preliminary observations offered above yield at least five (also preliminary) conclusions. First, the deuteronomistic heading assumes a book concerned with the fates of the capital cities of Israel and Judah. Now, in fact, a significant portion of the book addresses these cities directly, often personifying them (Mic 1:6-16; 3:10-12; 4:1-14; 7:8-13). Notably, these passages do not employ the term "Jacob"[41] and use "Israel" in its broadest sense to include Judah. Consequently, the deuteronomistic heading provides little data for understanding the terms as employed in Micah, except to establish that the deuteronomistic editor(s) worked with a book which could be considered to have joint addressees.

Second, Mic 1:5, which equates Jacob with the North and Israel with the South, gives every appearance of being a late addition, itself concerned with clarifying the confusion in addressees in a pre-existing book of Micah. It is particularly striking in terms of its negative attitude toward Jerusalem, an attitude not otherwise attested in the Minor Prophets (cf. Isa 57).

Third, setting aside the question of "authentic" Mican usage since the earliest form of the book possible to reconstruct will have been the form incorporated into a corpus, probably by the "deuteronomistic" editors responsible for the heading, the vexing summons to hear formulae in Mic 3:1, 8, 9 must be interpreted in the *literary* context of the book of Micah and the Twelve. In other words, the fact that the prophet may have been a southerner who would surely have addressed his message to his compatriots

---

[41]Disregarding the cultic phrase "God of Jacob" in 4:2.

is of no consequence. In the context of the book, and certainly in the context of the Twelve, nothing prevents, and a great deal encourages, understanding the Micah 3 as an accusation leveled at the leadership of both houses of Israel, whether "Jacob" and "Israel" are understood as a merism or as synonyms for all Israel.

Fourth, much of Micah 4-5 (excluding perhaps those portions of Mic 4:9-14 which may have figured in the accusation against Jerusalem in the earliest form of the book) displays significant affinity, lexically and theologically, with Zechariah 12-14. This material focuses on the Remnant, whether designated "Jacob" or "Israel." Typical of late eschatological/early apocalyptic, these texts describe the nebulous situation in which the Remnant finds itself: amidst the nations, at enmity with them, hopeful of restoration, but unsure of the traditional foundations for that hope.

Fifth, Mic 2:12-13 (and Mic 1:2-4) also participate in a much broader program within the Twelve, indeed within the prophetic corpus, as a whole. Like Isaiah 34-35 and 63, and commenting on texts in Amos, Joel, Obadiah, and Malachi, these two interrelated passages in Micah portray the role of Edom as the first to suffer in the coming universal judgment against YHWH's enemies.

Finally, then, this analysis of the names "Israel" and "Jacob" in Micah suggests that the book of Micah contains materials related to its broader context in the Book of the Twelve on at least three levels (representing perhaps three distinct redactional phases): a) Mic 1:16-3:12*; 4:9-14*, together with the "deuteronomistic" superscription seem to function, as Nogalski and others have argued, as a continuation and broadening of the accusations of Hosea and Amos (especially) to include Judah. b) Mic 1:2-4; 2:12-13 link the book to the Edom-polemic which stretches across the Twelve, adding to Micah an interest in universal judgment. C) The final form of Micah 4-5 seems to be an "anthology"[42] of late post-exilic reflections on the fate of the remnant somehow related to Zechariah 12-14.

---

[42]On "anthologizing" as a late technique for extrapolating/exegeting existing prophecies, see Larkin, 32, 35-37.

The Daughter of Zion Oracles and the Appendices to Malachi: Evidence on the Latter Redactors and Redactions of the Book of the Twelve

by Byron G. Curtis
Assistant Professor of Biblical Studies
Geneva College, Beaver Falls, Pennsylvania

> *"Words differently arranged have a different meaning,*
> *and meanings differently arranged have a different effect."*
> —Blaise Pascal (1623-1662), *Les Pensées*, #23.

1. Introduction

The final form of the Book of the Twelve (=B12) presents the books of Haggai, Zechariah and Malachi as the closing portions of a large and substantial work comprised of a dozen brief prophetic books. How did this placement come about, and by whom was it accomplished? In a 1993 SBL paper entitled "Social Location and Redaction History in the Haggai-Zechariah-Malachi Corpus," I presented a theory of a multi-staged redaction history of the B12, building in part on R.E. Wolfe's 1935 article on the editing of the B12, D.A. Schneider's 1979 dissertation on the unity of the B12, and D.N. Freedman's 1987 article entitled "Headings in the Books of the Eighth-Century Prophets."[1] There I defended a new proposal which in part claimed the following:

> By the end of the exile, then, a set of at least six, but likely seven, books already existed, promulgated in two groups of three, a Hezekian-era set [=Hosea-Amos-Micah] and a Josianic era set [=Nahum-Habakkuk-Zephaniah], along with the insertion of Obadiah, composed just after Jerusalem's destruction and linked programmatically and intertextually with Amos, which it immediately follows. Whether Joel or Jonah yet appeared within this collection is

---

[1] R.E. Wolfe, "The editing of the book of the twelve." *ZAW* 53 (1935): 90-129; D.A. Schneider, *The unity of the book of the twelve.* (Ph.D. Dissertation, Yale University, 1979); D.N. Freedman's article now conveniently appears in *Divine Commitment and Human Obligation: Selected Writings of David Noel Freedman.* Volume One: *History and Religion.* Edited by John R. Huddleston. Grand Rapids; Eerdmans, 1997: 367-82.

doubtful: post-exilic origins for these two books seem reasonably assured.[2]

My 1993 paper also identified a social location for the final stages of this redaction, namely, within a prophetic traditio-circle which was heir to the restorationist prophetic movement begun by the historical Haggai and Zechariah.

1.1 My proposal ran counter to the statement by P.D. Hanson, among others, that an early form of the Book of the Twelve once ended with Zechariah 8.[3] Rather, I proposed that the books of Haggai-Zechariah-Malachi comprised a single prophetic corpus at an early stage in their history and were added *as a group* to the preexisting collection that became the B12, a collection that ended with Zephaniah.

1.2 Like J. Nogalski, whose Zurich dissertation also appeared in 1993,[4] but which I had not even heard of yet, I argued for several discrete literary precursors to the B12. Nogalski identified these as a Deuteronomistic group containing Hosea, Amos, Micah and Zephaniah; and a Haggai-Zechariah corpus ending with Zech 8. Also, as Nogalski did, I discerned a major redactional seam connecting Zephaniah 3 with the Haggai-Zechariah corpus. Like Nogalski, I was convinced (following Meyers and Meyers) that Haggai-Zechariah 1-8 once circulated independently.[5] Unlike Nogalski, I believed that this latter corpus was likely not attached to the body of the B12 until it came to include Zechariah 9-14 and Malachi as well.

1.3 This paper seeks to augment my earlier proposal by examining the concluding portion of Zephaniah, the Daughter of Zion oracle of Zeph 3.14-20, and to relate this oracle to two later redactional seams

---

[2] B.G. Curtis, "Social Location and Redaction History in the Haggai-Zechariah-Malachi Corpus." Unpublished seminar paper, SBL, 1993: 4.

[3] *The Dawn of Apocalyptic*, revised edition. Philadelphia: Fortress Press, 1979: 386, note 68.

[4] *Literary Precursors to the Book of the Twelve*. BZAW 217. Berlin: Walter de Gruyter, 1993. Part two is separately entitled: *Redactional Processes in the Book of the Twelve*. BZAW 218. Berlin: Walter de Gruyter, 1993.

[5] E.M. Meyers and C.L. Meyers. *Haggai—Zechariah 1-8*. Volume 25B *in The Anchor Bible Commentary*. Edited by D.N. Freedman. Garden City, NY: Doubleday, 1987.

in the Book of the Twelve, the new unit that begins in Zech 9, and the concluding "hem" in Mal 3.22-24. I wish to argue that the Daughter of Zion oracle of Zeph 3.14-20 bears clear marks of redactional linking to the Haggai-Zechariah-Malachi corpus, and that this redactional work shows us something about the ideology and social location of these late redactors.

1.4 My paper proceeds in this manner: first, an interaction with some of the scholarship on the late redactions of the B12, especially a fresh look at Roland E. Wolfe's foundational 1935 paper on the subject;[6] second, a detailed examination of the Daughter of Zion oracle in Zephaniah 3.14-20; third, a tentative proposal that this redactional work is closely and intentionally related to the similar Daughter of Zion oracles in the B12, especially Zech 9:9-10; fourth, that the Zion ideology of this material comports well with the ideology and socio-literary ethos of the appendices to Malachi in 3.22-24 (ET 4.5-6); and fifth, that we perhaps may best look to the Daughter of Zion oracles and to the appendices of Malachi, taken together, as our clearest light on the latter redactors of the B12.

2. Review of the Scholarship
Modern discussion of the redaction history of the Twelve hearkens back to the important but unacceptably speculative work of Roland E. Wolfe. Prior to the publication of Wolfe's 1935 article, most discussion proceeded along the lines of an individual accumulation of scrolls.[7]

2.1 Wolfe proposed that there were two distinct processes at work in the formation of the Twelve as a single composite scroll. First he proposed a source-critical analysis that divided the books into strands, with a separate redaction to incorporate each strand. The dozen strands he identified included an "anti-idol polemicist," a "doxologist," a group of "eschatologists," a "messianist," a "nationalist school," a "Judaistic editor of Hosea," and a "late exilic editor," among others, each assigned to a particular time and setting.

---

[6] "The editing of the Book of the Twelve." *ZAW* 53 (1935): 90-129. Wolfe's article is a condensation of the author's 1935 Harvard dissertation.
[7] So K. Budde, *Eine folgenschwere Redaktion des Zwölfprophetenbuchs.* *ZAW* 39 (1921): 218-29.

2.2 Secondly he discerned a process of collection of books in stages. Thus the books of Hosea and Amos formed an original nucleus, a book of two. This was later expanded to form a "Book of the Six" comprised of Hosea, Amos, Micah, Nahum, Habakkuk and Zephaniah. Later still, according to Wolfe, a single editor inserted Joel, Jonah and Obadiah "at inopportune places," thus forming a "Book of the Nine." The final stage of adding whole books came with an alleged third-century scribal school that appended Haggai, Zechariah and Malachi to form the B12. Supplementation and revision, he says, continued at least until the time of Ben Sira.[8]

2.3 Wolfe succeeded in giving a new direction to scholarly research on the collection of the Twelve, but his documentary approach, modeled closely upon the Graf-Wellhausen hypothesis proved to be "too sweeping to be convincing."[9] Wolfe had merely identified common themes, phrasings and genres within the prophetic collection and attributed each to a common source, in a mirror-image of the Graf-Wellhausen hypothesis.

2.4 R.E. Wolfe also undermined the traditions of attribution within the B12, where the origins of the individual books are carefully preserved by the attribution of author's names. In the B12 Hosea, Amos, Micah, Haggai and Zechariah, etc., are presented as real individuals and authors of portions of the whole. This point says nothing decisive against the common view that Malachi is an anonym, or that the prophet Joel, as Nogalski now hints, is merely a literary construct; though it does stand in tension with E. Ben-Zvi's view that the prophet Zephaniah is at best a shadowy figure only but loosely attached to the pre-compositional stage of the book that now bears his name.[10] But, after all the historical, literary and redactional analyses of the last hundred years are sifted, this tradition of named attributions remains our most powerful set of evidences about the origins of the B12. We should be loathe to give it up. At the same time, the widespread realization that the B12 has its own composite unity must surely alter the way we view the total production of the individual books as we now possess them.

---

[8] R.E. Wolfe, ibid., pp. 93, 95, 107 and 118-122.
[9] E. Dyck, "Jonah among the Prophets: A Study in Canonical Context." *JETS* 33:63-73.
[10] *A Historical-Critical Study of the Book of Zephaniah. BZAW* 198. Berlin, Walter de Gruyter, 1991.

2.5 Wolfe himself may have been less than persuaded by his own proposal: although he claims to discern the redactional layering of the B12 "almost as accurately as the various geological strata on a hillside slope," the concluding paragraph of his article calls it "merely a hypothetical reconstruction of an obscure chapter in the history of prophecy," a point ironically noted in W. Rudolph's critical response.[11]

2.6 Thankfully, few have followed R.E. Wolfe in discerning so many redactional stratifications common to the books of the B12. Despite serious weaknesses, Wolfe asked many of the right questions and shed light upon the path. For my purposes it is sufficient to point out a few of his proposals regarding redactions of Zephaniah, and their relationship to Zechariah.

2.7 Wolfe believed, perhaps in spite of himself, that Zephaniah was an authentic seventh century Judean prophet whose collected oracles—though much altered by many redactors—once concluded "the Book of the Six," and later "the Book of the Nine," to which Haggai-Zechariah-Malachi was then added. I think there is merit to this supposition.

2.8 He also believed, as have many both before and after, that Zeph 3 had undergone considerable redactional change over the generations. Zeph 3.5's paeon to the righteous Yahweh who "does no wrong" and whose justice is goes forth "morning by morning," accordingly, is ascribed to the psalm-loving eleventh editor, working between 275 and 250 BCE.[12] Yahweh's announcement of doom to the nations in Zeph 3.8, when he stands to testify against them on the day of his "burning anger," is attributed to the inspired redactor of protest, editor seven, the "Day of Yahweh" redactor who also penned the parallel "Day of Yahweh" passages in Amos, Obadiah, Joel, and Zephaniah 1-2, around 325 BCE. The remaining interpolations in Zeph 3, Wolfe says, are all attributable to an editorial school of "eschatologists," eighth in historical order, who worked around 300 BCE. These writers were also responsible for

---

[11] R.E. Wolfe 1935: 125, 129; W. Rudolph, *Haggai—Sacharja 1-8—Sacharja 9-14—Maleachi*. Band 13/14 in *Kommentar zum alten Testament*. Gütersloh: Gütersloher Verlagshaus Mohn, 1976: 299.

[12] R.E. Wolfe, *Ibid*, 1935: 114.

Zech 9.16-17's announcement that "on that day" Yahweh will "save his people like a flock." They also wrote virtually all of Zech 12-14, as well as many other passages from Hosea 1 onwards. It is to these prophets of eschatological salvation that Wolfe also attributes two portions of our Daughter of Zion oracle: Zeph 3.15cd, and 3.18-20.

2.9 Several others members of this Seminar on the Formation of the Book of the Twelve have turned their attention to the difficult problems in the history of the Twelve, and with some similar results. J. Nogalski, for example, agrees that the Book of Zephaniah once concluded what he has identified as one of two major "multi-volume corpora" which he usefully labels as "precursors" to the Twelve.[13] In 1996 Aaron Schart carried the case of the superscriptions a little further than D.N. Freedman had, by arguing that the unifying system of superscriptions found in Hos 1.1, Am 1.1, Mic 1.1 and Zeph 1.1 is matched by other unifying features such as the summons "Hear...!" found in three of them and the "futility curses" found in all four, and thus the four books should be viewed as having been copied on one scroll.[14] Schart's view would seemingly support Freedman's generally early dating of the prophetic books. E. Ben-Zvi, on the other hand, pushes the "compositional stage" of the Book of Zephaniah into the post-monarchical era, and, with it, probably most of the B12.[15] Ben-Zvi's distinctively new approach is received with appreciation, even if without full endorsement, by A. Berlin in her 1994 Zephaniah commentary, who leaves the dating issue unresolved.[16]

2.10 In my own view, I think it is significant that two of the presumably seventh-century books do not share the dated superscription form of the other books surrounding them. Instead, "oracle" מַשָּׂא (massa) headings introduce the books of Nahum and Habakkuk. This incipit form does not persist in Zephaniah, which, in the order of reading, returns to the formulae of the books dated to the eighth-century kings, though, of course, updated to the late seventh century reign of King Josiah (1.1). No other book among the

---

[13] J. Nogalski, *ibid.*
[14] A. Schart, "The Combination of Hosea, Amos, Micah and Zephaniah on a Single Scroll: Unifying Devices and Redactional Intentions." Unpublished SBL Paper, 1996.
[15] Ben-Zvi, ibid, 347-52.
[16] Berlin, ibid, 33-42.

Twelve except for Zephaniah returns to employ the eighth-century superscription form.

2.11 In this regard, then, if we posit with Hans Walter Wolff an exilic-era Deuteronomistic redaction for the body of the Twelve ending with Zephaniah,[17] we then have no adequate way to account for the *Rezeptionsgeschichte* of Nahum and Habbakkuk. Instead, I posit with Andersen and Freedman a Hezekian-era collection of three, and with Schneider a Josianic-era collection of three, which were then combined. In this way we may account for a greater number of the books within the Twelve.

2.12 Accordingly, I propose that an early version the Twelve, containing two pre-exilic collections of three books each (minus Isaiah) once circulated independently, a collection whose order was Hosea, Amos, and Micah followed by Nahum, Habakkuk and Zephaniah. If this hypothesis is true, then Zephaniah's heading once would have formed an *inclusio* with the earliest headings in the collection. Nogalski calls this grouping of four headings a "framing device," and surely this is correct.[18] Such a literary linkage may provide further occasion for the relative clause's lengthy geneology in Zeph 1.1. This clause, which links the prophet to an ancestral Hezekiah, also links this incipit to the eighth-century collection, whose incipits also contain the name Hezekiah (Hos 1.1; Mic 1.1). Presumably, since Hezekiah is an unusual name, the prophet is of the royal house, although, of course, this cannot be proved.[19]

2.13 Zephaniah's oracles of stern judgment and reform provide a fitting conclusion to the body of the Twelve in its late pre-exilic form. Since no allusion to Jerusalem's fall appears in these three books, and since their concern is, in Gottwald's words, with "the international power shift" from Neo-Assyria to Neo-Babylonia,[20] I think their first promulgation probably took place before 587. For

---

[17] H.W. Wolff, *Joel and Amos. Hermeneia*. Philadelphia: Fortress Press, 1977.
[18] "Intertextuality and the Twelve." *Forming Prophetic Literature (John D.W.Watts festschrift)*, edited by J.W. Watts and P, R. House. JSOTSS 235. Sheffield: Sheffield Academic Press, 1996: 118-19.
[19] J. Blenkinsopp. *A History of Prophecy in Israel*. Revised edition. Louisville: Westminster/John Knox, 1996: 113. O. Eissfeldt. *The Old Testament: An Introduction*. New York: Harper & Row, 1965: 425.
[20] N.K. Gottwald. *The Hebrew Bible: A Socio-Literary Introduction*. Philadelphia: Fortress Press, 1985: 390.

these prophets and their early promulgators, Jerusalem may be threatened, but it is not yet destroyed.

3. Zephaniah 3.14-20

Scholars have proposed many further expansions, supplementations and redactions in the individual books of the Twelve. Most of these proposals proceed without particular regard for the scope of the whole collection, but only in light of the individual book or unit (see the summaries in J. Blenkinsopp's *History of Prophecy in Israel*). However, several passages evidence such substantial redactional shaping as to provide significant clues to the character of the redactional groups that lies behind them, and therefore have significant bearing upon the social-location and social-historical questions at hand.

3.1 I propose then to discuss Zeph 3.14-20, with some reference to Zech 9 and Mal 3.22-24 [ET 4.4-6]. The first and third of these stand as *codae* to the books that contain them; the second appears as the opening unit of Zechariah 9-14, which is (at least) a major compositional unit in its own right. All three units, therefore, stand at significant points in the overall compositional structure of the B12.

3.2 It has long been thought that the ending of the Daughter of Zion oracle in Zeph 3 contains exilic or post-exilic supplementation. I think the coda of Zeph 3 provides evidence of supplementation that may supply a substantial clue to the identity of the final or near-final promulgators. In 1987 R.J. Coggins proposed a linkage between the close of Zeph 3 and the prophet Haggai:

> In our present study we have seen links between Haggai and Zechariah and between Zechariah and Malachi, and it is surely also legitimate to see Haggai's concern for the proper ordering of the temple as owing something to the hymnic passage in Zephaniah which immediately precedes it, promising a great festival in the temple on Zion when God himself would be in the midst of his people (Zeph. 3.17f.). In just the same way Haggai's community could look forward to God's presence with them when all his commands had been carried out (Hag. 2.5).[21]

---

[21] R.J. Coggins. *Haggai, Zechariah, Malachi.* Old Testament Guides. Sheffield: JSOT Press, 1987: 85.

3.3 I would like to suggest the specific manner in which such a linkage took place. As we shall explore below, Zeph 3.14-20 may serve as a linchpin in the latter phases of the growth of the Twelve. The text with poetic delineation and prose particle analysis is reproduced below. Prose particle analysis is also briefly explained below.

Zephaniah 3.14-20

poetic accent count	prose particle count	poetic delineation	
2+2		הָרִיעוּ יִשְׂרָאֵל	רָנִּי בַּת־צִיּוֹן ¹⁴
3+1		בַּת יְרוּשָׁלָ͏ִם׃	שִׂמְחִי וְעָלְזִי בְּכָל־לֵב
3+2		פִּנָּה אֹיְבֵךְ	הֵסִיר יְהוָה מִשְׁפָּטַיִךְ ¹⁵
3+3		לֹא־תִירְאִי רָע עוֹד׃	מֶלֶךְ יִשְׂרָאֵל ׀ יְהוָה בְּקִרְבֵּךְ
2+2	ה=1	יֵאָמֵר לִירוּשָׁלַ͏ִם	בַּיּוֹם הַהוּא ¹⁶
2+2		אַל־יִרְפּוּ יָדָיִךְ׃	אַל־תִּירְאִי צִיּוֹן
3+2		גִּבּוֹר יוֹשִׁיעַ	יְהוָה אֱלֹהַיִךְ בְּקִרְבֵּךְ ¹⁷
		יַחֲרִישׁ בְּאַהֲבָתוֹ	יָשִׂישׂ עָלַיִךְ בְּשִׂמְחָה
3+2+3			יָגִיל עָלַיִךְ בְּרִנָּה׃
		מִמֵּךְ הָיוּ	נוּגֵי מִמּוֹעֵד אָסַפְתִּי ¹⁸
2+2+3			מַשְׂאֵת עָלֶיהָ חֶרְפָּה׃
prose accent count	**prose particle count**	**delineation as oracular prose**	
5	את+ה=2	הִנְנִי עֹשֶׂה אֶת־כָּל־מְעַנַּיִךְ בָּעֵת הַהִיא ¹⁹	
4	את+ה+ה=3	וְהוֹשַׁעְתִּי אֶת־הַצֹּלֵעָה וְהַנִּדָּחָה אֲקַבֵּץ	
5	ה=1	וְשַׂמְתִּים לִתְהִלָּה וּלְשֵׁם בְּכָל־הָאָרֶץ בָּשְׁתָּם׃	
7	ה+את+את=3	בָּעֵת הַהִיא אָבִיא אֶתְכֶם וּבָעֵת קַבְּצִי אֶתְכֶם ²⁰	
5	את+ה=2	כִּי־אֶתֵּן אֶתְכֶם לְשֵׁם וְלִתְהִלָּה בְּכֹל עַמֵּי הָאָרֶץ	
5	את=1	בְּשׁוּבִי אֶת־שְׁבוּתֵיכֶם לְעֵינֵיכֶם אָמַר יְהוָה׃	

Zephaniah 3.14-20: Translation

poetry

14   Shout for joy, O Zion-Daughter!
                    Raise the triumph-call, O Israel!
              Be glad and exult with all your heart,
                    O Jerusalem-Daughter!

15   Yahweh has cleared away your punishment,
                    Swept away your enemies!
              As King, O Israel, Yahweh lives among you;
                    You shall fear disaster no more!

16   On that Day
                    It will be proclaimed to Jerusalem:
              "Fear not!" — and to Zion:
                    "Be not discouraged!"

17   "Yahweh your God lives among you,
                    A Hero who rescues!"
              He delights over you with gladness;
                    He is quiet in his love;
                    He rejoices over you with singing.

18   Those who were afflicted   [?]
transition   because of the appointed feasts
to oracular   —I have gathered [them].
prose??   They came from you;   [?]
              [But such] reproach [was] a burden on her. [?]

oracular prose

19   "I will surely deal with all your oppressors at that Time!
       I shall rescue the lame; and the scattered I shall gather.
       I shall turn their shame into Praise and Fame in all the earth!

20   At that Time I will bring you [home];
       at [that] Time I will gather you.
       For I shall make you Fame and Praise
       among all the peoples of the earth,
       when I restore your fortunes before your very eyes!"
              —says Yahweh.

3.4 The method of prose particle analysis, though still in some respects experimental, produces significant results in distinguishing Hebrew poetry from Hebrew prose. This method was developed around 1980 by F.I. Andersen and D.N. Freedman, and based on massive computerized analyses of the Hebrew text.[22] The prose particles are the relative particle אֲשֶׁר, the definite direct object marker אֵת, and the definite article ה. It has long been noted that these particles are common in prose, but rare in poetry. The method measures the frequency of these three prose particles within any given text, and yields a percentage figure which represents the prose particle density (PPD) of that text.

3.5 Freedman concludes after a close comparison of the statistics with passages generally accepted as poetry and those generally accepted as prose, that "practically everything with a reading of 5% or less will be poetry," and "practically everything with a reading above 15% will be prose."[23] My own testing of the data confirms this thesis sufficiently to sustain the proposal as a good working hypothesis in adjudicating disputed texts and in discerning more precisely the boundaries between poetry and prose. I note that Andrew E. Hill, who made his name as a scholar in the historical linguistic analysis of the book of Malachi, makes rich use of this method in determining the literary genre of that book in his commentary, published earlier this year.[24]

3.6 Most oracular material happens to fall between these two limits, into a category many now call "oracular prose," a form of exalted prose speech that owes much to the line structure and ornamentation techniques employed in poetry.[25] On the other hand, M. O'Connor

---

[22] "'Prose particle' counts of the Hebrew Bible." *The Word of the Lord Shall Go Forth*, edited by C.L. Meyers and M. O'Connor. Winona Lake, IN: Eisenbrauns/ASOR, 165-183.

[23] "Another look at Biblical Hebrew poetry" [1987]. *Divine Commitment and Human Obligation: Selected Writing of David Noel Freedman*. Volume Two: *Poetry and Orthography*, edited by J.R. Huddlestun. Grand Rapids: Eerdmans, 1997: 215.

[24] A.E. Hill, *Malachi, The Anchor Bible* 25D. Edited by D.N. Freedman. Garden City, NY: Doubleday, 1998. See the bibliography for Hill's published articles on the historical linguistics of Malachi and Zechariah 9-14.

[25] So C.L. Meyers and E.M. Meyers, *Haggai, Zechariah 1-8. The Anchor Bible Commentary* 25B. Edited by D.N. Freedman. Garden City, NY: Doubleday, 1987: lxiv; and most recently, A.E. Hill, *ibid*, p. 26.

considers the book of Zephaniah to exemplify what he calls "prophetic verse," a style that A. Berlin calls "not formally metrical," but containing many poetic rhythms and tropes, enough for the book to qualify. Thus for O'Connor and Berlin, Zephaniah *is* verse, but of the prophetic variety .[26]

3.7 I shall not attempt to resolve the apparent incongruity between the two positions and their preferred terms, "oracular prose" and "prophetic verse." It is sufficient for this paper simply to note that regardless of the term, prophetic speech is dissimilar in some important respects from both the Hebrew of prose narrative, and the Hebrew of the books universally recognized as poetry such as the Psalms, Job and Lamentations.

3.8 Freedman also suggests that prose particle counts (PPC's) may help us distinguish earlier poetry from later poetry. He writes: "There is some evidence to show that the so-called prose particles are almost entirely absent from the earliest poetry, while they increase in number in late poetry."[27] This tool has limits, however: while no early poetry features high PPC's, some late poems have low PPC's.

3.9 The Masoretic Text of Zephaniah contains 767 words, of which 94 are prose particles. Thus the PPD for Zephaniah 1-3 is 12.3%, which lies within Freedman's designated range for oracular prose. Detailed examination of the individual units of Zephaniah, yields a more complex picture. If we follow the delineation of units presented in BHS, with only a few revisions, the following picture appears:

---

[26] M. O'Conner. *Hebrew Verse Structure*. Winona Lake, IN: Eisenbrauns, 1980: 240-62; A. Berlin, ibid, 11.
[27] ibid, p. 214.

Zephaniah 1-3 Prose Particle Density				
Unit	Descriptor	PPC	Words	PPD
Zeph 1.1	superscription	1	20	0.5%
1.2-3	against all earth	9	27	33.3%
1.4-6	against Judah	19	43	44.2%
1.7	"Hush!.."	0	14	0%
1.8-9	against Judah's princes	7	28	25.0%
1.10-11	against merchants	5	27	18.5%
1.12-13	against the complacent	6	35	17.1%
1.14-16	"Yahweh's great Day..."	7	39	17.9%
1.17-18	"I will bring distress..."	3	36	8.3%
Subtotal for Chapter 1		**57**	**269**	**21.2%**
Zeph 2.1-3	"Gather the nations..."	4	43	9.3%
2.4-7	against Philistia	2	39	5.1%
2.8-11	against Moab & Ammon	5	80	6.3%
2.12	against Cush	0	6	0%
2.13-15	against Assyria	6	54	11.1%
Subtotal for Chapter 2		**17**	**222**	**7.7%**
Zeph 3.1-5	"Woe to the city..."	2	54	3.7%
3.6-8	"I have cut off nations..."	3	58	5.2%
3.9-13	"I will purify..."	2	70	2.9%
3.14-18	"Shout, Zion-Daughter..."	1	55	1.8%
3.19-20	"At that Time..."	12	39	30.8%
Subtotal for Chapter 3		**20**	**276**	**7.2%**
Zephaniah Total		**94**	**767**	**12.3%**

3.10 According to the charted analysis, the Book of Zephaniah's highest PPD occurs in the cluster of units from 1.2 to 1.16. There the PPD ranges as high as 44.2%. One single line, the "Hush..." of verse 7, contains no prose particles, but the remainder is rich with them. The highest densities are found in the oracles of judgment against all the earth (1.2-3 = 33.3%), against Judah (1.4-6 = 44.2%), and against Judah's princes (1.8-9 = 25.0%). This pattern breaks off in 1.17-18, where the PPD is only 8.3%, in a passage which otherwise looks like a continuation of the "Day of Yahweh" oracle of 1.14-16. The high PPD is peculiar for a prophetic book, and more closely matches the PPD of prose narrative books.

3.11 The 8.3% PPD of this last unit of Zeph 1, vss 17-18, comports well with Zeph 2, which averages a PPD of 7.7%, with a plus-or-minus deviation of only 3.4. On these grounds perhaps Zeph 1.17-18 should be associated more closely with the Zeph 2, than with Zeph 1 in future analyses of the book's rhetorical structure.

3.12 Every rhetorical unit of Zeph 2, with the exception of the single-line oracle against Cush in 2.12, falls within Freedman's 5%-15% range for oracular prose, and in this respect its PPD of 7.7% is unremarkable.

3.13 Zeph 3, however, bears a remarkable feature. The whole chapter averages a PPD of 7.2%, very close to the previous chapter's 7.7%. But this percentage masks an important difference. The whole chapter, except for 3.19-20, has a very low PPD. Factoring out the last unit, Zeph 3.1-18 has a PPD of merely 3.4%, with a deviation of a mere plus-or-minus 1.8. Zeph 3.19-20, on the other hand, has no less than 12 prose particles in 39 words, yielding a PPD of 30.8%, a very high figure.

3.14 As Berlin's discussion of the divisions of the text of Zephaniah indicates, the majority of interpreters take Zeph 3.14 to be the beginning of a new rhetorical unit; many consider the unit to extend to the end of the chapter, to 3.20.[28] But the prose particle analysis suggests that 3.19-20 is a prose elaboration of a poetical oracle. To my mind it looks like a commentary upon a previously existing poetical text. Note the PPD figures for Zeph 3.14-20:

---

[28] A. Berlin. *Zephaniah. The Anchor Bible Commentary* 25A. Edited by D.N. Freedman. Garden City, NY: Doubleday, 1994: 18-19.

Unit	Descriptor	PPC	Words	PPD
3.14-18	"Shout, Zion-Daughter"	1	55	1.8%
3.19-20	"At that Time..."	12	39	30.8%

3.15 Ivan J. Ball observes that most of Zephaniah is written with a low density of parallelism and meter, but that twice the book reaches "a high density of parallelism and meter, at the two most significant and climactic points in Zephaniah, breaking into 'pure' poetry." The first occasion appears in what he calls the "great hymn on the 'Day of Wrath'" in 1.15-16; the second appears in the "Zion hymn of YHWH's kingship" in 3.14-17.[29] Ball uses these observations as a rhetorical argument for the strong authorial unity of the book. Such unity is also advocated by O. Palmer Robertson.[30]

3.16 I am reluctant to separate out supposedly "secondary" material embedded within otherwise original prophetic oracles. I think that it is better to err (if it is to err) on the side of caution with the claim that the collections of prophetic oracular and visionary material we now call books were preserved with comparatively little redactional supplementation to the oracles and prophetic speeches themselves. Editorial activity, of course, is abundant in the collection, least obtrusively in the shaping and framing the material. But the newer approach to the B12, reading the book as an editorially constructed composite unity, as exemplified by the members of this SBL Seminar, permits us to see a broader range of redactional activity at work.

3.17 Supplementation, when it does occur, is more likely at the links between groups and collections of oracles, and at the opening and closing points of particular books. Thus we ought to look for supplementation in the penning of editorial superscriptions and introductory marks at the heads of books, in closing appendices, summaries, parting exhortations, or colophons at the ends, and at the seams between the collected portions of whole books, as Mark Biddle argued in this seminar in 1996, and as J. Nogalski's work on

---

[29] I.J. Ball. *A Rhetorical Study of Zephaniah.* Berkeley: BIBAL Press, 1988:12-13.

[30] O.P. Robertson. *The Books of Nahum, Habakkuk, and Zephaniah.* NICOT. Grand Rapids: Eerdmans, 1990; P.R. House argues for a thematic unity to the book. See his *Zephaniah: A Prophetic Drama.* Sheffield: Almond Press, 1989.

Literary Precursors to the Book of the Twelve and *Redactional Processes in the Book of the Twelve* amply displays.[31] This is difficult work, and finding it elsewhere is even more difficult work, as any perusal of J. Nogalski's will show.

3.18 In making this claim, I do not wish to rule out the kind of editorial activity described by R.E. Clements in his insightful essay entitled "The Prophet and His Editors." While emphasizing the role of the redactors as *re*-appropriaters of the prophetic word for new generations, Clements can still write: "Fundamentally, we encounter prophetic literature as a written record based on messages that prophets originally spoke to their contemporaries.[32] I think that—even after Nogalski—this claim is still sustainable.

3.19 Arguments for authorial unity such as Ivan Ball's bear more weight if Zephaniah, Ball's example, is seen as an isolated literary unit. But the Book of the Twelve bears an editorially constructed aspect as a collected and composite work. If, as I have argued, the body of the Twelve probably once concluded with Zephaniah, in a book of six or probably seven prophets, then the closing oracle of Zephaniah is a very likely place to look for a bridge-like editorial link between the pre-exilic/exilic collection and the post-exilic concluding trilogy.

3.20 Many scholars have seen supplementation in the conclusion of Zephaniah, usually arguing it on historical and ideological grounds. A recent proposal along these lines comes from Mária Széles (1987:64-65), who posits a long development of the book, from original pre-exilic sayings to a final post-exilic arrangement and editing. Regarding Zeph 3.14-20 she writes:

> ...finally, in several stages, prophecies on salvation [appear] in 3.14-20. ...The latest sections are to be attributed to a period after the return from exile... the

---

[31] "Intertextuality, Micah, and the Book of the Twelve: A Question of Method." Unpublished seminar paper. SBL, 1996. For a published discussion along similar lines, see D.N. Freedman, "Headings in the Books of the Eighth-Century Prophets." *AUSS* 25 (1987):9-26. J. Nogalski, *ibid.*

[32] R.E. Clements. "The Prophet and his editors." *The Bible in Three Dimensions*. Edited by D.J.A. Clines, *et al. JSOTSS* 87. Sheffield: JSOT Press, 205.

closing declaration being 3.16-20. Here there appear the typical eschatological motifs of the later period—the overcoming of the power of the enemy, the restoration, the gathering together of the diaspora, the promise of a safe and peaceful life, and the enhancement of the chosen people before the eyes of the pagans.[33]

And:

It is probable that verse 17 is a gloss originating from the captivity or from a period after it. On the basis of the influence of the previous verses, the editor has here written down his own witness to the promised future.[34]

Széles attributes vss 18-20 to a late post-exilic editor of the whole book. That such views are commonly held is attested by their presence in the 1973 *New Oxford Annotated Bible's* notes on Zeph 3, which remain unrevised in the 1991 edition. Both editions report that the whole of 3.14-20 is held to be a later addition.

3.21 At the extreme we may take L.P. Smith and E. R. Lacheman. Their professed aim is to consider the book "as a whole" with its "chief emphases", yet find in the process a complex series of layerings, from a single old and original Zephaniah oracle to heavily redacted late apocalyptic material, dating to the crisis of the Jerusalem's Hellenists of 200 BCE.

Luckily the survival of a name (1:1, Zephaniah) in connection with the old oracle (1:4ff.) gave it its place in the Book of the Twelve (1950:141-42).[35]

Smith and Lacheman do not appear to be troubled by Ben Sira's reference to the Twelve ca 180 BCE, comfortably surmising that he refers to quite a recent production, newly enrolled in the collection of sacred books.

---

[33] M Széles. *Wrath and Mercy: A Commentary on the Books of Habakkuk and Zephaniah.* Translated by G.A.F. Knight. *International Theological Commentary.* Grand Rapids: Eerdmans, 1987: 64-65.

[34] Ibid, p. 113.

[35] L. Smith and E.R. Lacheman. "The Authorship of the Book of Zephaniah." *JNES* 9 (1950): 137-42.

3.22 The only prose particle within 3.14-18 is in the formulaic הָהוּא
בַּיּוֹם of vs 16. If the thirty-nine words of 3. 19-20 are analyzed
separately from the fifty-five words of 3. 14-18, the percentage yield
for prose particles for vss 14-18 then equals a mere 1.8%, while it
equals 30.8% for 3.19-20. It is possible that Ball is right in seeing
artful rhetorical work here, an original prose elaboration of an
original poetical oracle. However, another solution seems also
possible. The low percentage for vss 14-18 is generally consistent
with early oracular and poetic material; the high percentage for vss
19-20 is generally consistent with later oracular prose.

3.23 Seen in this light, it is possible to read Zeph 3.14-20 as an early
poetic oracle with its own late prose commentary, suffused with
restorationist ideology. Zeph 3.14-18 contain the generic language of
the victory hymn in which no fixed events can be identified. The
unit's themes of expulsion of the enemy and Yahweh's victorious
habitation of Zion are common eschatological motifs with a long
history in Israel's prophetic literature, as G. Von Rad and many
others have shown. Only in vss 19-20 do the historically-specific
themes of return from exile and Zion's restoration appear.

3.24 In making this observation I do not claim, as many have, that
prophetic sayings of return to the homeland must be late in origin.
The punitive policies of the Neo-Assyrians included population
deportation, and render credible both the threats of deportation and
the promises of return found in even the earliest prophetic books
(Anderson and Freedman 1990:893).[36] The Akkadian "Poem of Erra"
dated to no later than about 750 BCE features the themes of national
remnant and national restoration, including, like those in the
Hebrew prophetic books, promises of renewed fertility, rebuilt
temples and hegemony over enemy peoples.

3.25 Accordingly, as in Zeph 3 and the endings of several of the
individual books, the conclusion of the Erra poem ends with the god
Erra decreeing the restoration of the ravaged country and promising
to the decimated Babylonians a great victory over their enemies.
Erra promises the scattered Babylonian remnant that they shall

---

[36] F.I. Andersen and D.N. Freedman. *Amos. The Anchor Bible* 24A. Garden
City: Doubleday, 1989: 893.

again be great, and receive the tribute of all the surrounding countries.[37]

3.26 Also as H.W. Wolff pointed out, the expression שׁוּב שְׁבוּת, "restore the fortunes," (only in Hos 6.11; Joel 4.1 [= ET 3.1]; Am 9.14; and Zeph 2.7 and 3.20 among the Twelve) so often attributed only to late sources, now has an eighth-century parallel in the Sefire treaty stele (line 3.24) where the cognate phrase הֹשִׁיב שׁבית, "to cause the restoration of," is attested.[38] The concluding *topoi* of return and restoration in Zeph 3.19-20, however, provide an ideal bridge to the restorationist oracles of Haggai, and, indeed, to the whole remaining corpus of the B12: Haggai, Zechariah and Malachi. It thus serves not merely as an appendix to Zephaniah; but as an introduction to the prophets of Zion's restoration.

4. Zeph 3.14-20 and the Book of the Twelve

R.J. Coggins' suggestion has led us to propose a specific manner in which Zeph 3 relates to the subsequent body of restorationist prophecy of the B12. Zeph 3.14-18 stand as an early oracle pointing to the restorationist hope. This was the unit that concluded the body of the Twelve in its exilic and early post-exilic form. I wish to hypothesize, then, that Zeph 3.19-20 is the late, editorial addition *created specifically by the promulgators of the restorationist prophecy now located in the concluding trilogy of the Twelve.* Our holistic and redactional reading makes this conclusion plausible, perhaps probable, though far from certain.

4.1 This reading of the B12 may be pressed still further. The Daughter of Zion oracle of Zephaniah 3 has a literary connection to the Daughter of Zion oracle of Zechariah 9. I suggest that these two

---

[37] G.W. Lambert. "The Poem of Erra." *Iraq* 24 (1962): 119-25.

[38] H.W. Wolff, *Joel and Amos. Hermeneia.* Philadelphia: Fortress press, 1977: 76 n. 19. An impressive collection and discussion of deportation themes in ANE literature, drawn from Egyptian, Hittite, Sumerian, Mari, Nuzi, Babylonian, Assyrian, Neo-Assyrian and Israelite sources can be found in J.B. Diggs, *Implications from Ancient Near Eastern Deportation Practices for an Understanding of the Authorship of* עד־בבל in *Micah 4:10.* Unpublished Ph.D. Dissertation. Fort Worth, TX: Southwestern Baptist Theological Seminary. Some of this material is also surveyed in G. Hasel's *The Remnant. The History and Theology of the Remnant Idea from Genesis to Isaiah.* Berrien Springs, MI: Andrews University Press, 1974.

units are editorially and thematically significant for the redactors responsible for appending Haggai-Zechariah-Malachi to the trunk of the preceding books. The two Daughter of Zion oracles thus appear in strategic redactional points within the Book of the Twelve.[39] The first, Zeph 3.14-20, bridges the gap from the pre-exilic prophets to the restorationist prophets; the second, Zech 9.9-10 bridges the gap from the early restorationists, Haggai and Zechariah, to the later restorationist prophets represented in Zechariah 9-14 and Malachi.

4.2 The prose particle count for this unit, Zech 9, is 3 out of 196 words, yielding a PPD of 1.5%. This count is exceedingly low for post-exilic Hebrew literature. How may one account for this phenomenon?

4.3 The Daughter of Zion oracle tradition, a kind of microcosm within the macrocosm of the whole Zion tradition, plays a key role here.[40] Both oracles represent a relatively early linguistic stratum; both appear in contexts that include much later material. The late prose commentary on the early poetic oracle of Zephaniah 3, matches post-exilic context of the reuse of Zechariah 9. I wish to hypothesize, then, that the oracle in Zeph 3.14-18 is early, roughly matching the original date for the oracle now contained in Zech 9; and that the prosaic material of Zeph 3.19-20 is a late editorial addition to that book, roughly matching the date at which the original and irrecoverable form of Zech 9 found a significant reuse in the post-exilic era, as suggested by C.L. Meyers and E.M. Meyers.[41]

5 Conclusion

---

[39] The expression בַּת־צִיּוֹן ("Daughter of Zion") appears elsewhere within the book of the twelve only at Micah 1.3; 4.8,10,13 and Zechariah 2.7,10. Micah 4 is a loose collection of Zion oracles; 4.9-11 may be seen as the converse side of the בַּת־צִיּוֹן tradition. There the woman-figure, bereft of king and counselor, cries out in agony. In Zech 9.9-10 she cries out for joy when the king appears. In both oracles the verb used is the hiphil of רוּעַ , "cry out, shout," but with opposite rhetorical effect.

[40] Elsewhere in Zechariah, the appeal to the exiles in 2.10f (ET 2.6f) depends upon the בַּת־בָּבֶל / בַּת־צִיּוֹן "Daughter of Babel"/"Daughter of Zion" wordplay of vss 11 and 14.

[41] *Zechariah 9-14. The Anchor Bible Commentary* 25c. Garden City: Doubleday, 1993.

These oracles then may mark the seams of the closure of B12, standing as they do between the seventh and the sixth-century prophets on the one hand, and between the sixth century and the fifth century prophets on the other hand. They therefore provide a clue to the redactional intent in the collection and juxtaposition of these prophetic books: a single group may well have been responsible for this late stage of collection, supplementation and juxtaposition; that group had a particular interest in the restorationist program announced in the Daughter of Zion oracles; the group believed that the prophets Haggai and Zechariah had pioneered in the fulfillment of the restorationist ideal; and the group believed that the restorationist ideal had been betrayed by the later generations. Hence the terrible threat found in the whole collection's editorial conclusion:

> Behold, I will send you Elijah the prophet
> before the great and terrible day of the LORD comes
> And he will turn the hearts of the fathers to their children
> and the hearts of the children to their fathers,
> lest I come and smite the land with a curse.
> —Malachi 3.23-24 (ET 4.5-6)

Redactional Models: Comparisons, Contrasts, Agreements, Disagreements [1]

The *Introduction to the Old Testament as Scripture* by Brevard S. Childs represents an important shift in the research on prophetic books.[2] In the legacy of Hermann Gunkel the main interest had been in the small units which could be perceived as delivered in an oral setting. It was common to imagine the prophet standing somewhere in the streets confronting his hearers with the divinely inspired message. In his commentary on Hosea, for example, Hans W. Wolff considered many texts to be "*Auftrittsskizzen*" written hastily during or immediately after the oral communication.[3] Wolff impressively presented Hosea, Amos and Micah as participants in the social conflicts of their historic societies, trying to make the conflicting parties hear the unambiguous word of God. At the same time, he noted in his commentary on Amos that many passages, including important ones, were written by redactors from different times.[4] Since then, interest in the historical prophet has declined. Instead, the canonical prophetic book has become more and more important.[5] Prophetic books include the original prophetic oracles in such a fashion that it is, in most cases, almost impossible to reconstruct the oral setting.[6] The final text is, for the most part, the result of many different redactional activities, which wanted to focus the prophetic claims upon new generations. Within this new stream of research the fact was registered with fresh insight that the Book of the Twelve Prophets was considered as one book in antiquity. It seems appropriate to

---

[1] I would like to thank Prof. J. Nogalski for improving the English of this paper.

[2] B. S. Childs, *Introduction to the Old Testament as Scripture*. Philadelphia: Fortress Press, 1979.

[3] H. W. Wolff, *Dodekapropheton 1: Hosea*. Biblischer Kommentar Altes Testament, vol. 14,1. Neukirchen: Neukirchener Verlag, 1961, XXV.

[4] Compare H. W. Wolff, *Dodekapropheton 2. Joel und Amos*. Biblischer Kommentar Altes Testament, vol. 14,2. 3 ed. Neukirchen-Vluyn: Neukirchener Verlag, 1985,129-138.

[5] As an example one may quote O. H. Steck, *Die Prophetenbücher und ihr theologisches Zeugnis. Wege der Nachfrage und Fährten zur Antwort*. Tübingen: Mohr, 1996, who states that a "durch die heutige Zeit donnernder Amos ... seine unmittelbare Stunde längst gehabt" habe (p. 124).

[6] Steck, *Prophetenbücher*, 120-123 is very skeptical in this respect.

reserve the word "book" to denote the collection as a whole and to speak of the twelve units ascribed to different prophets as "writings."[7]

The Book of the Twelve as a Redactional Unit

E. Ben Zvi has vehemently denied that the Book of the Twelve was originally meant to be a unit.[8] He conceives the book as a collection of writings, some of which may indeed manifest thematic overlaps, or even allude to one another, but which have no redactional sense as a whole. A reader may impinge a meaning upon the whole, but one should be clear that this is not what the final redactors had in mind. They wanted to preserve the individual writings. Ben Zvi rightly emphasizes the problem regarding how one can discern that the redactors wanted to present the twelve prophets as part of a larger unity. The most unambiguous evidence is lacking: the Book of the Twelve has no superscription. So, what else can be accepted as signal of redactional purpose?

Widely acknowledged is the "*Stichwortverkettung*" (catchword chain) phenomenon. F. Delitzsch noted that the ending of one writing and the beginning of the adjacent one often share significant vocabulary.[9] Most often the following instances were considered to be significant: Hos 14:2 // Joel 2:12; Joel 4:16 // Amos 1:2; Amos 9:12 // Obad 19; Obad 1 // Jonah (as messenger to the nations); Jonah 4:2 // Mic 7:18-19 // Nah 1:2-3; Nah 1:1 // Hab 1:1 (משא); Hab 2:20 // Zef 1:7. Some assumed that redactors grouped writings together that accidentally contained such *Stichwörter*. Others postulated that the Stichwörter were implemented in order to stitch together writings, which the redactors wanted to place after one another. This second hypothesis is strongly supported by J. Nogalski, who has most thoroughly treated the *Stichwort* phenomenon. He even discovered a lot of *Stichwörter* which had been overlooked to that point. For example, the inconspicuous

---

[7] That's the way J. Nogalski has done it.

[8] Ben Zvi, E. "Twelve Prophetic Books or 'The Twelve'? A Few Preliminary Considerations." *Forming Prophetic Literature: Essays on Isaiah and the Twelve in Honor of John D. W. Watts.* Edited by J. W. Watts, and P. R. House. Sheffield: Sheffield Academic Press, 1996, 125-156.

[9] Delitzsch, F. "Wann weissagte Obadja?" *Zeitschrift für die gesammte Lutherische Theologie und Kirche* 12 (1851): 92-93.

word "time" (עת) connects Zeph 3:20 with Hag 1:2,4. The glorious future envisioned in Zeph 3:9-20 is contrasted with the unsatisfactory state of the people living around the ruins of the temple.[10]

B. A. Jones and Ben Zvi doubt that the *Stichwörter* can provide evidence for the redactional linking of the writings. One problem is that shared vocabulary exists between writings that do not stand adjacent to one another. Obadiah, for example, could as easily follow Joel 4:19 (where Edom is mentioned) as Amos 9:12, especially since the decisive term "Edom" in Amos 9:12 is (according to Jones) lacking in the Hebrew *Vorlage* of the Septuagint.[11] Jones and Ben Zvi rightly argue that in many cases the *Stichwörter* are not significant enough to preclude an accidental allusion of the respective passages. However, if additional arguments are found, the *Stichwörter* are still valuable clues to the redactional plan. Most important are source critical observations. If, to use a disputed example of Nogalski, almost all differences between Obadiah and its *Vorlage* in Jer 49 pick up vocabulary and themes present in Amos 9, it is probable that Obadiah was designed to fit into its position after Amos.[12] Jones too easily dismisses the arguments of Nogalski, when he states: "Even if Nogalski's conclusion is correct, however, that Obadiah has been shaped redactionally under the influence of Amos 9, again this may explain but does not *require* the arrangement of Amos and Obadiah in the MT Book of the Twelve. One should not be surprised that a relatively late book such as Obadiah has been influenced by the Book of Amos."[13] However, it is unjustified to require this high degree of probability only from the proponents of the idea of a redactional unity. For too long, the Book of the Twelve as a whole was ignored. One should challenge this commonly held reading by inverting the burden of proof. One should start with the

---

[10] J. D. Nogalski, *Literary Precursors to the Book of the Twelve*. BZAW 217. Berlin / New York: de Gruyter, 1993, 215.

[11] B. A. Jones, *The Formation of the Book of the Twelve: A Study in Text and Canon*. SBL.DS 149. Atlanta, GA: Scholars Press, 1995, 175-191.

[12] J. D. Nogalski, *Redactional Processes in the Book of the Twelve*. BZAW 218. Berlin / New York: de Gruyter, 1993, 61-74.

[13] Jones, 211-212.

assumption that the Book of the Twelve is a unit and only relinquish it if the opposite can be demonstrated.[14]

A further question for detecting redactional intention is whether the reading process is designed in such a way that the small units appear as parts of a global discourse structure. One has to ask for example, if a unit presupposes a thought from a previous text or uses a lexeme that has a specific connotation that was established in an earlier passage in the reading process. Frames are also important. For example, Hosea starts with a *Fremdbericht* (Hos 1) and Amos included one in the final vision cycle (Amos 7:10-17). Likewise, a meaningful superstructure points towards a deliberate ordering, e.g., the historical ordering of the writings with Hosea being first (because it mentions the "House of Jehu" in Hos 1:4) and Malachi being last (because it presupposes an operative second temple).[15]

The Order of the Writings

The manuscript evidence of the Book of the Twelve has been investigated by Jones, Fuller and Steck.[16] So far, three variants are known. In the Hebrew tradition all manuscripts follow the Masoretic order with the exception of one of the oldest scrolls, 4QXII(a), where the most plausible reconstruction is that Jonah followed Malachi.[17] In the Septuagint tradition we find a third option. The first six writings are arranged: Hosea, Amos, Micah, Joel, Obadiah, Jonah. The problem of whether we have enough evidence to reconstruct the goal of the final redactors comes up again. Do the different

---

[14] Steck, *Prophetenbücher*, 30.

[15] Compare A. Nogalski, *Die Entstehung des Zwölfprophetenbuchs. Neubearbeitungen von Amos im Rahmen schriftenübergreifender Redaktionsprozesse.* BZAW 260. Berlin / New York: de Gruyter, 1998, 133-150.

[16] Jones (see footnote 11); R. E. Fuller, "The Form and Formation of the Book of the Twelve: The Evidence From the Judean Desert." *Forming Prophetic Literature: Essays on Isaiah and the Twelve in Honor of John D. W. Watts.* Edited by J. W. Watts, and P. R. House. Sheffield: Sheffield Academic Press, 1996, 86-101; Steck, O. H. "Zur Abfolge Maleachi - Jona in 4Q76 (4QXIIa)." *ZAW* 108 (1996): 249-253.

[17] Russell E. Fuller, The Minor Prophets Manuscripts from Qumran, Cave IV. In: Eugene Ulrich, ed., *Qumran Cave 4,* vol. 10: *The Prophets.* DJD 15. Clarendon Press Oxford, 1997, 221-318 + plates XL-LXIV.

variants signal that the order of the writings was meaningless, or to the contrary, that the sequence was important to express a new understanding of the whole by the redactors and/or translators? The consensus so far was that the Masoretic order was the original one.[18] By contrast, Jones considers the Septuagint order to be older.[19] The aim was to group together writings that were similar in content. This is, for example, the reason why Obadiah immediately follows Joel. The main problem with Jones' hypothesis is that it has no explanation as to how the Masoretic order came into being. Much more convincing is the idea that the Septuagint version placed Amos and Micah immediately after Hosea and left all other writings in the order they had in the Masoretic sequence. The reason probably was the historical setting given by the superscriptions. Since Hosea, Amos and Micah prophesied partly under the same kings, they form a closed group, to which Joel, Obadiah and Jonah do not belong.

More convincing is Jones' hypothesis that the oldest order had Jonah after Malachi, as represented by 4QXII(a). Since Jonah has a different position in each of the three variants, Jones argues that it came into the collection last.[20] It seems to be an imaginable process that this strange writing was first attached to the end of the collection, and in a second step found its place close to the prophets from the 8th century, because Jonah ben Amittai lived under Jerobeam II (2 Kings 14:25).

The Global Structure of the Twelve

If the Book of the Twelve is purposefully arranged, one should expect to find a coherent global structure, which directs the reading process.[21] Most important in that respect are the beginnings of the writings, of which nine

---

[18] Schneider, D. A. *The Unity of the Book of the Twelve.* Ph.D. Yale University, 1979, 224-225; Nogalski, *Precursors*, 2.

[19] Jones, 218-220.

[20] Jones, 129-169; Schart, 290.

[21] T. Collins, *The Mantle of Elijah. The Redaction Criticism of the Prophetical Books.* The Biblical Seminar 20. Sheffield: JSOT Press, 1993, 65; P. R. House, *The Unity of the Twelve.* Bible and Literature Series 27. JSOTSup 97. Sheffield: Almond, 1990, 67-71.

contain superscriptions.[22] Since the dated beginnings follow in a historical sequence, the reader gets the impression that the whole collection intends to unfold a certain part of the history of prophecy. The deepest break is located between Zeph and Hag. At this point the Babylonian exile is presupposed, but not mentioned.

According to P. House the implied picture of the history of Israel follows the scheme, "sin – punishment – restoration."[23] Hosea, Joel, Amos, Obadiah, Jonah, and Micah belong to first topic. These writings are not exclusively but mainly concerned with the sin of Israel and the nations. Nahum, Habakkuk, and Zephaniah describe extensively the punishment of that sin. The writings Haggai, Zechariah, and Malachi envision the restoration of Israel within the nations. Although House's description of the global structure of the Twelve contains many insights into the intertextual relationship of the different writings, his scheme seems to be too imprecise.[24] At first glance, it is obvious that all three topics are regularly part of a single writing. Malachi, for example, contains more numerous and more specific accusations than Joel. As a result, it is difficult to limit the aim of Joel to disclosing the sin of Israel or to limit the aim of Malachi to Israel's restoration.[25]

---

[22] Schart only wants to speak of a superscription, if "die Informationen, die sie enthält, auf einer Metaebene zum restlichen Textkorpus liegen und sie weder grammatisch noch semantisch eine lineare Anknüpfung an den folgenden Text aufweist" (32). This is true only for Hos 1:1; Joel 1:1; Amos 1:1; Obad 1a; Mic 1:1; Nah 1:1; Hab 1:1; Zef 1:1 und Mal 1:1.

[23] House, 63-109.

[24] As examples of observations, which were picked up by others, one may name the following: House perceives the summon to hear in Hos 4:1 as opening of an accusation speech, which comes to an end in Mic 6:2-16. In both passages the lexem *ryb* "lawsuit" plays an important role (House, 87; compare Schart, 191-192). Another observation is that the prominent role, which the "love of God" plays in Malachi, refers back to Hosea (House, 108; compare Collins, 81).

[25] House does implicitly admit the difficulty: "Unlike the recipients of Hosea's condemnation, the sin of God's people in Joel is much more subtle. Judgment is fast approaching, but is not coming because of an obvious rejection of Yahweh and a subsequent embracing of idolatry. Rather, the religion pictured in Joel has lost its vitality. The Lord and His presence are taken for granted" (76).

T. Collins presents a more complex model. He identifies a set of recurring themes. "The principal themes of the whole book are those of covenant-election, fidelity and infidelity, fertility and infertility, turning and returning, the justice of God and the mercy of God, the kingship of God, the place of his dwelling (Temple/Mt. Zion), the nations as enemies, the nations as allies."[26] Every prophet adds a certain aspect to the topics, sometimes in accordance, sometimes in opposition to other writings. Collins tries to find the overall unity which can make sense of all the different aspects. How this works may be illustrated from passages dealing with the temple. Hosea accuses the temple of Northern Israel of idolatry, because a calf is worshipped there. In contrast, Joel's call to repentance makes clear that the true worship of YHWH is taking place at the temple in Jerusalem. It is not until Mic 3:12 that the temple on Mt. Zion is condemned. However, immediately thereafter it is envisioned that Mt. Zion will once again be the center of the world, to which all nations will come spontaneously in order to accept the torah as the way to universal peace. Zeph 3:9-20 further explores this topic. In order to fulfill its eschatological responsibility, Mt. Zion must be cleansed and must be the home of holy community. This thought sets the stage for Haggai, Zechariah, and Malachi. Especially Zech 8, which once formed the end of a smaller collection, reminds the reader of Zeph 3 (cf. Zech 8:3 with Zeph 3:11, 15). Malachi then recognizes that the promised, glorious future of Zion "is still impeded by the unworthy behaviour of the priests in the temple, the very place where God's name should be honored most." (Collins, 81). Collins' model is certainly more complex than House's model, but it does more justice to the variety of topics and the sometimes striking differences between the writings than to the unity.

An outstanding topic of the Twelve is the Day of YHWH. No other prophetic book contains as many passages about this day, which are at the same time so central for the overall structure. In addition, the day of YHWH is the concept, which integrates at least some of the basic topics into one scenario. The writing of Joel impressively introduces the Day of YHWH into the collection and the reader is forced to perceive what follows within this framework. R. Rendtorff gives a good example.[27] The passage Amos 5:18-20 implies that

---

[26] Collins, 65.

[27] R. Rendtorff, "Alas for the Day! The "Day of the LORD" in the Book of the Twelve." In: *Festschrift Brueggemann*, to appear in 1998.

the opponents of Amos are longing for the day of YHWH. Since Amos himself never spoke about this day, the hearers must know about it from elsewhere. From the perspective of the reader of the Twelve, it is obvious that they have already heard Joel's message. From reading in this manner, one gets the impression that the contemporaries of Amos used Joel's prophecy in order to evade the call to turn back to God (Amos 5:4-6, 14-15). How they did it, is not spelled out. Amos restates the severe scenario of Joel: for those who do not repent, the coming day will bring complete darkness. Likewise, this reading sets the stage for understanding the Day of YHWH in Obad 18, where it is announced that the "House of Jacob" will burn the "House of Esau." According to Amos 5 and 9:8-10 this eschatological "House of Jacob" will comprise only those who did not reject the message of Amos and at the same time belong to those persons called by God, as stated in Joel 3:5. Rendtorff rightly observes that the nearness of the day of YHWH inspires a call to repentance (Joel 2:12-14; Amos 5:4-6.14-15; Zeph 2:1-3; Mal 3:24). The reader may also infer that every reference to a decisive day, on which YHWH will punish the sin and restore the true Israel, e.g., "on that day" (Amos 2:16; 8:3); "day of trouble" (Nah 1:7), points toward the one Day of YHWH.

R. C. van Leeuwen observes, how the first six writings make use of Exod 34:6-7, a text that contains "an elaboration of the name YHWH expressing the bipolar attributes of mercy and retributive justice."[28] The first allusion he sees already in Hos 1:6, where it is unambiguously declared that the merciful character of God is no longer operative. However, Hos 14:10 implies that the wise know that God forgives those who repent. The redactors seem to exploit the tension God's between mercy and justice in order to show that different prophets emphasized various attributes of the very same God. Joel 2:12 cites Exod 34:6-7. Jonah cites the same verse in 3:9 and 4:2. Micah cites it in 2:8 (conjectured) and 7:18-20. Finally, Nahum cites Exod 34:6-7 in 1:2-3a. The tensions between the different writings are deeply rooted within God. Only a diverse multiplicity of approaches does justice to the mystery of God's personality.

---

[28] Leeuwen, R. C. v. "Scribal Wisdom and Theodicy in the Book of the Twelve." In: *In Search of Wisdom: Essays in Memory of John G. Gammie*. Edited by L. G. Perdue, B. B. Scott, and W. J. Wiseman. Louisville, KY: Westminster / John Knox, 1993, 32.

The Book of the Twelve shares certain features with the Book of Isaiah. One may note, for example, that the Judean kings listed in Isa 1:1 (Uzziah, Jotham, Ahaz, and Hezekiah) are identical with the ones listed in Hos 1:1. Also, Isa 2:2-4 and Mic 4:1-4 are almost identical. For these and other reasons Bosshard-Nepustil has closely examined the relationship between both books. It is remarkable how many cross-references on different layers he detects. He proposes that the main redactions in the Book of the Twelve, which he calls the "Assur/Babel-Redaktion[XIII]" and the "Babel-Redaktion[XII]," were influenced by similar redactions in the Book of Isaiah.[29] Although he tries to display his results in well-structured tables, the sheer complexity of his reconstructions is overwhelming. Many of his source-critical decisions appear to be problematic, and one often has the feeling that the intertextual allusions cannot be controlled.

Models for the Redaction History of the Book of the Twelve

There is no question that a simple synchronic approach is insufficient. The superscriptions already make it unambiguously clear that the different writings originated in different centuries. All of the redaction critical models proposed so far assume that smaller collections predated the final book. Indeed it is highly unlikely from the outset that twelve independent books were combined for the first time in Hellenistic times.

R. E. Wolfe was the first to propose that the thirteen redactional layers, which he differentiates, worked across the boundaries of the individual writings. This is why he labels his model "strata hypothesis."[30] A notable layer, for example, is the "Day of Jahwe Editor," which contains the following passages: "in Amos 4:12b (from עקב); 5:13, 18c (from הוא), 20; Obad 15a (to הגוים); Joel 1:15; 2:1d (from כי)-2b (to וערפל), 10-11; 3:1-5; 4:1-3.12.14-17; Zeph 1:7-8a (to יהוה).14-16.18c (from ביום); 2:1-3; 3:8b-e (from חכו)" (103). Thus, almost every passage containing the phrase "Day of YHWH" belongs to this layer. Wolfe discerns four steps. First, Amos and Hosea were combined. Second, Micah, Nahum, Habakkuk and Zephaniah

---

[29] E. Bosshard-Nepustil, *Rezeptionen von Jesaia 1-39 im Zwölfprophetenbuch. Untersuchungen zur literarischen Verbindung von Prophetenbüchern in babylonischer und persischer Zeit.* OBO 154. Freiburg (Schweiz) / Göttingen: Universitätsverlag / Vandenhoeck & Ruprecht, 1997, summary on page 408.

[30] R. E. Wolfe, "The Editing of the Book of the Twelve." *ZAW* 53 (1935): 91.

were added, yielding a collection of the six pre-exilic prophecies. Third, a "Book of the Nine" developed by the insertion of Joel, Jonah, and Obadiah. The book became complete with the addition of Hag, Zech, and Mal.

D. A. Schneider thinks along similar lines.[31] The basis was the collection of Hosea, Amos and Micah in the time of Hezekiah. Under Josiah's rule Nahum, Habakkuk, and Zephaniah were attached. During the exile, Joel, Obadiah, and Jonah entered the collection. Finally, Haggai, Zechariah, and Malachi were added in the time of Nehemiah.

Nogalski attributes the most extensive redactional activity to the "Joel-related layer." This redaction combined a pre-existing "Deuteronomistic Corpus" (Hosea-Amos-Micah-Zephaniah) with Nahum, Habakkuk, Haggai, Zechariah 1-8, Joel, Obadiah and Malachi. Subsequently, Jonah and Zechariah 9-14 entered the collection.[32]

Schart assumes some more steps in which the collection continually grew. First, Hosea and Amos were combined. For the next step he agrees with Nogalski that there must have been a Corpus consisting of Hosea-Amos-Micah-Zephaniah. Then Nahum and Habakkuk were inserted. After that Haggai and Zechariah 1-8 were attached. Subsequently, Joel, Obadiah and Zechariah 9-14 were added. Finally, Jonah, as a satirical narrative, and Malachi completed the book.[33]

The main difficulty for all the different models is the problem of establishing controls about what is to be considered as deliberate redactional shaping and what is only accidentally connected. Which features should be construed as important goals of the final text, and which should be viewed as less significant ones? It seems wise to begin the reconstruction of the redaction history with those passages, which most obviously stem from editors: the superscriptions.[34] Given that starting point, it is most plausible that Hosea,

---

[31] Schneider (see footnote 18).

[32] See his summaries: Precursors, 276-282; Processes, 274-280.

[33] See his summary, 304-306.

[34] See already G. M. Tucker, "Prophetic Superscriptions and the Growth of a Canon." In: *Canon and Authority. Essays in OT Religion and Theology.* Edited by G. W. Coats, and

Amos, Micah, and Zephaniah once existed as a separate collection. The superscriptions of these four writings follow the same type and through the names of the kings mentioned, they convey the following scenario: First, Hosea and Amos prophesied simultaneously in the Northern Kingdom, thereafter Hosea and Micah at the same time in Judah.[35] The writing of Hosea was deliberately placed in the first position, although the historical prophet Amos probably delivered his oracles earlier than Hosea. The redactors wanted the reader to perceive the writing of Amos in the light of Hosea, presumably because they were committed to Hosea's theological position. Some have used the concept "deuteronomistic" to characterize those redactors.[36] This seems unwise, since typical Deuteronomistic language can only rarely be identified, e.g., in Amos 3:7 ("his servants the prophets").[37] To be more cautious, one may speak of a redaction which inserted some passages in addition to the superscriptions, passages which come close to Deuteronomistic thoughts.[38] Schart, especially, has pulled together numerous observations concerning this redaction which have already been made in the past.[39] The central topic is that all transgressions were conceived as conducted directly against God. The root of all the evil is the distortion of the personal relationship to YHWH, which was established through the Exodus. In order to underline the last point, the redactors inserted passages referring to the exodus at crucial points of the composition of the collection (Amos 2:10; 3:2; 9:7; Mic 6:4-5). Social, cultic, or juridical degeneration is seen to

---

B. O. Long. Philadelphia: Fortress, 1977, 65: "It is all but self-evident that the superscriptions were not created by the prophets themselves. They refer in the third person, and retrospectively, to the activity of the prophet, and to the books which contain the prophetic words."

[35] D. N. Freedman, "Headings in the Books of the Eighth-Century Prophets." *AUSS* 25 (1987) 16-20; Collins, 62; Nogalski, *Precursors*, 84-89; Schart, 41-46.

[36] Schmidt, W. H. "Die deuteronomistische Redaktion des Amosbuches: Zu den theologischen Unterschieden zwischen dem Prophetenwort und seinem Sammler." *ZAW* 77 (1965): 171; Nogalski, *Precursors*, 86-88.

[37] See the critique of Schmidt by N. Lohfink, "Gab es eine deuteronomistische Bewegung?" In: *Studien zum Deuteronomium und zur deuteronomistischen Literatur III.* Stuttgart: Katholisches Bibelwerk, 1995, 65-142.

[38] Collins, 62; Schart, 46.

[39] See for example Schmidt, 191-192; Schart, 218-233.

be the result of the fundamental corruption of the identity of Israel, which is determined by the exodus. It is remarkable, that the redaction also reflected upon the role of the prophets within God's history with Israel and Judah (Amos 2:11-12; 3:7).

If one asks for precursors to this corpus, it can most convincingly be argued that the writings of Hosea and Amos once formed a single composition. J. Jeremias in particular has proposed this hypothesis.[40] On the one hand, there are additions in the writing of Hosea, which pick up language from Amos. The second half of Hos 4:15 pulls together words from Amos 4:4; 5:5 and 8:14. Hos 8:14 is closely related to Amos 3:9-11 and 6:8. The passages appear at positions where a reader from Judah possibly could perceive the transgressions of Northern Israel as something that would never happen in Judah. However, the aim of the redactional additions is to counteract those reactions. On the other hand, there are verses like Amos 3:2; 7:9; 2:8; 5:25; 6:8; and 1:5, which are heavily loaded with vocabulary and topics from the writing of Hosea. Almost all of these redactional passages are located at important points in the composition of the writing of Amos. This implies that the composition of Amos, even at an early stage, must already have been designed with the ideas of Hosea in mind. Schart has further pursued this insight.[41] In his view, the same redactors edited both writings as a single composition. The overall structure was governed by the summons to hear (Hos 4:1; 5:1; Amos 3:1; 4:1; 5:1). In both writings the prophet first addresses "the Israelites" (Hos 4:1; Amos 3:1) and secondly the "House of Israel" (Hos 5:1; Amos 5:1). The writings were combined in order to convince the reader that these prophecies of doom are truly the word of God. Schart points towards the letters from Mari, which show that the authority of oracle, especially unfavorable oracles, could be strengthened if a second oracle, which was independently uttered by a different speaker, confirmed the message of the first one.

As a redactional stage later than the corpus which comprised Hosea, Amos, Micah, and Zephaniah, there must have been something like a "Joel-related layer," which formed a corpus, at the core of which stood the Day of YHWH

---

[40] Jeremias, J. "Die Anfänge des Dodekapropheton: Hosea und Amos." In: *Hosea und Amos: Studien zu den Anfängen des Dodekapropheton*. Tübingen: Mohr, 1996, 34-54. Compare already Wolfe, 91-93; Schneider, 23; Schmidt, 173.

[41] Schart, 101-155.

passages. After some forerunners, it was Nogalski, who put together strong and fascinating arguments for this stage in the formation of the book.[42] Besides large parts of Joel, this layer probably contained a version of Obadiah. According to Nogalski also little glosses dealing with locusts and the fertility of the land were inserted in older writings in order to recall the vivid picture of Joel 1-2, e. g. Nah 3:15aγ.16b and Hab 3:16b-17. However, it seems difficult to find out exactly how many writings and passages this layer comprised. Although Wolfe, Nogalski, Bosshard, and Schart agree, that there was something like a "Day of YHWH-layer," which contained a large part of Joel, the differences between them are considerable. This problem is closely related to those in the last phase of the redaction history of the Book of the Twelve. Did the collection of the Joel-related layer end with a earlier version of Malachi, which was attached to Zechariah 8, as Nogalski proposes?[43] Or did it conclude with Zech (9-)14, with Malachi entering later, as Schart prefers? In any case, Jonah was likely the last independent writing to be added. In this respect Nogalski and Schart agree with Jones, who argues from the manuscript evidence that because Jonah's position within the sequence of the Twelve is different in all three variants it was probably added last. Over the last decades there has emerged a strong consensus that Mal 3:22-24 was added to the Book of the Twelve as conclusion to the second part of the Hebrew canon "Nebiim."[44]

---

[42] Nogalski, Processes, 275-278. See for example Wolfe with his proposed "Day of YHWH-editor," and E. Bosshard, "Beobachtungen zum Zwölfprophetenbuch." *Biblische Notizen* 40 (1987): 30-62.

[43] E. Bosshard, and R. G. Kratz, "Maleachi im Zwölfprophetenbuch." *Biblische Notizen* 52 (1990) 27-46 and O. H. Steck, *Der Abschluß der Prophetie im Alten Testament: Ein Versuch zur Frage der Vorgeschichte des Kanons.* Biblisch-Theologische Studien 17. Neukirchen-Vluyn: Neukirchener Verlag, 1991 suggest an even more complex connection between Zech and Malachi. They suppose that former versions of Mal originally were designed as immediate extension of former versions of Zech 9-14. The superscription Mal 1:1 came in later and the original cohesion was interrupted.

[44] W. Rudolph, *Haggai, Sacharja, Maleachi.* KAT vol. 13,4. Gütersloh: Gütersloher Verlagshaus, 1976, 291; Nogalski, *Processes,* 185; Steck, *Abschluß,* 134-136; Schart, 302-303.

Hermeneutical Implications

These new insights into the redaction history of the Book of the Twelve change the way in which the meaning of the whole and its parts can be adequately construed.[45]

First, the well-known fact should again be emphasized that the original words of the historical prophets underwent a deep transformation within the literary transmission. Without the different redactors, the first written records would have been left somewhere in an archive. With their adaptation, these records became an unparalleled body of literature which played an important role in the interaction between Israel and its God. The ongoing rewriting of the prophetic heritage certifies that the prophetic collections were successful in mediating the word of God into different historical situations. In this respect the prophetic books pursued the function of the original prophets.

A second well-known fact may also be stressed. The literary remains of the pre-exilic prophets were mostly shaped under the impression of the fulfillment of the original oracles. The exiles of Northern Israel and Judah functioned as the basic proof of truth for a precursor of the Book of the Twelve, which presumably contained at least Hosea, Amos, Micah, and Zeph. However, the prophecies of doom also provoked the confident hope that God will once again bring peace and well-being to Israel within the context of a renewed creation.

Thirdly, from an early stage in the transmission process onward, the oracles of one prophet were perceived in light of the history of prophecy. One may already compare Jer 28:8, where Jeremiah uses the conformity of his message with the prophetic tradition as an argument against his opponent. It was even more so the goal of the redactors to present the prophets as a coherent whole. New prophecy had to demonstrate how it is related to the literary prophetic tradition. This does not mean that the prophetic messages remained unchanged during history, but every new prophecy had to be conceivable as picking up and expanding certain aspects of the tradition under the pressure of new experiences of God.

---

[45] Very extensively Steck, *Prophetenbuecher*, 127-204 has dealt with the hermeneutical implications of the latest redaction critical enterprises; see also Childs, B. S. "Retrospective Reading of the Old Testament Prophets," *ZAW* 108 (1996): 362-77.

Fourthly, the prophetic writings were transmitted as parts of collections. It is very likely, that the redactors did expand and rewrite given prophetic writings in the opinion that they articulate what the historical prophet, under whose name they worked, would have said, if the prophet were confronted with the problems of their own time. However, whenever they were confronted with a new prophecy, which could not be harmoniously integrated within the existing collection, a new writing was designed under a new author's name. Presumably this writing circulated in many cases independently for a while before it was added to the existing group. The inclusion became possible when the redactors could develop a theological position, in which the differences between the older corpus and the new writings could either be integrated or became insignificant.[46] Within a given collection, the writings were combined in such a way that the meaning of the whole overruled the meaning that a certain text had in its original historical setting. The theological position that was held by the last redactors was inferred into every part of the collection. For example, within the Joel-related layer all passages dealing with the Day of YHWH were interpreted as references to the scenario described in Joel, no matter what the original meaning of those passages would had been. Therefore, it is imperative that the interpreter not isolate one prophetic writing against others. Rather, the interpreter should read the prophetic writing as part of a collection which contributes to a consistent meaning of the whole. It is especially important to look for those redactional passages which are especially concerned with developing complex scenarios, in which different concepts can be reconciled.

Fifthly, it is important, however, that the redactors did not produce a flat coherence without deviations, tensions, and even contradictions. It must be born in mind that the final text of the Book of the Twelve does not support the idea of one prophet overlooking the whole history of Israel from one point in time, as for example, occurs in the Book of Isaiah. Instead, the corpus presents twelve different prophets from different times. The overarching unity of this book is much more unsettled than in Isaiah. Whereas former exegetes hesitated to conceive the individual messages as part of a higher unity, postmodern thought is intrigued by that idea. The Book of the Twelve postulates that messages from different times, from persons with special insights, speaking from different backgrounds, when read together, form a complex unity. The reader is forced to proceed from

---

[46] See Schart, 309-314.

one prophecy to the next, each time imagining the hidden theme of the whole, the judging and restoring presence of God in history, from a different perspective. For the postmodern reader, it is not important to get a final coherent vision of what the book is about. Much more important is the arrangement of the prophecies in a way that the single unit presents a distinct but memorable perspective, which at the same time needs to be balanced by the next unit. None of the prophecies needs to be criticized as long as the reader has delight in moving on. The trajectory of this complex process is the canonical guidance with respect to how the reader can achieve his or her own vision of the God of Israel.

The Rich and Poor in James
An Apocalyptic Proclamation

Patrick A. Tiller

Introduction

Only two years ago this consultation devoted a whole session to "Wisdom and Eschatology in the Epistle of James." Patrick Hartin gave us "An analysis of wisdom, eschatology and apocalypticism in the Epistle of James."[1] And Matt Jackson-McCabe wrote about "Wisdom and 'Apocalyptic' Eschatology in the Letter of James."[2]

Jackson-McCabe pointed out the many references to older wisdom literature and "the similarity of James' themes to those characteristic of Wisdom literature"[3] but also found certain differences. He concluded that James is better characterized as "moral exhortation rather than as a 'wisdom writing'." On the other hand he found that James' world view corresponds precisely to an understanding of apocalypticism as "a world view 'distinguished primarily by the increased importance attached to supernatural agents and a world beyond this one, and by the hope for judgment and vindication beyond death'."[4] In this connection, he especially noted the themes of final judgment and dualism of good and evil in terms of the opposition of God and the world (not the wise and the fool) or God and the devil. The addressees of the "letter," "the twelve tribes in the Diaspora" in this context are understood to be the eschatological, restored Israel.

Hartin examined the Wisdom traditions reflected in James and the function of eschatology in the epistle. He found that James shares the concerns of biblical wisdom literature and uses many of its typical forms (wisdom sayings, admonitions, beatitudes, various forms of comparison, including similes, metaphors and parabolic discussions). But the function of these forms in James moves in a new direction. According to Hartin, "At the same time wisdom functions as a strategy that integrates aspects taken from the prophetic and eschatological traditions in order to show how faith must give direction to action."[5] James also describes the nature of wisdom: it

---

[1]   Patrick J. Hartin, "'Who is wise and understanding among you?' (James 3:13). An analysis of wisdom, eschatology and apocalypticism in the Epistle of James." (SBLSP 35; Atlanta: Scholars, 1996) 483-503.

[2]   Matt A. Jackson-McCabe, "A Letter to the Twelve Tribes in the Diaspora: Wisdom and 'Apocalyptic' Eschatology in the Letter of James" (SBLSP 35; Atlanta: Scholars, 1996) 504-517.

[3]   *Ibid.*, 506.

[4]   *Ibid.*, 508, quoting from John J. Collins, "Wisdom, Apocalypticism, and Generic Compatibility," in Leo G. Perdue et al., *In Search of Wisdom: Essays in Memory of John G. Gammie* (Louisville, KY: Westminster/John Knox, 1993), 170.

[5]   Hartin, "'Who is wise and understanding among you?'," 487.

comes from God in response to prayer (not diligent study as in Sirach and other wisdom texts) and it leads to a virtuous life (characterized chiefly by mercy) and rebirth. According to Hartin, this wisdom is presented in the context of a comparatively restrained apocalyptic eschatology that understands the present as the beginning of and preparation for the end-time and as the motivation for ethical behavior. The clearest indication of the apocalyptic imagination of the writer is in 5:1-11 where eschatological judgment serves to threaten the wicked and give hope to the righteous. "However, James tends to distance himself from this imagination for two reasons: First of all the usual apocalyptic signs of the end are missing. ...Secondly, despite the view that the coming age does bring with it judgment, the ethos of the whole epistle is that this coming age is to be approached not with fear and trepidation, but with joy and happiness ...."[6] In the second major section of his paper, Hartin compared the Epistle of Enoch with the Epistle of James in order to "further specify the character of the Epistle of James in so far as it relates to the traditions of wisdom, prophecy, eschatology, and apocalyptic."[7] After cataloging several similarities in content and form and noting the clarity of descriptions of judgment and the idea of revelation that are found in Enoch but are lacking from James, Hartin concludes that James is not pure wisdom but uses both wisdom and prophetic forms and contains apocalyptic patterns of thought, which, however, "do not displace his focus on providing exhortations and advice to the readers about how they are to lead their lives in the present."[8]

My purpose is to deal with the same sort of questions as they,[9] but with a more narrow focus on the question of the rich and the poor and social status in general. The presence in James[10] of some of the motifs and ideas that are characteristic of both wisdom and apocalyptic literature is unmistakable. James appropriates forms that are at home in both older Hebrew wisdom and prophetic literature and more recent Hellenistic moral literature.[11] The application of this scholarly vocabulary to James, however, does not advance our understanding of the epistle very far. It is my intent to move the discussion further by asking how and with what effect James has combined

---

[6]   *Ibid.*, 495.

[7]   *Ibid.*, 495.

[8]   *Ibid.*, 499.

[9]   Other writers have treated James with similar interests and observations. E.g., Todd C. Penner, *The Epistle of James and Eschatology: Re-reading and Ancient Christian Letter* (JSNTS 121; Sheffield Academic Press, 1996).

[10]   The question of the authorship of the letter remains unsolved. None of the proposed solutions (James the Lord's brother, some lesser known James, or a pseudonymous author) is entirely persuasive.

[11]   See, for example, the discussion of Luke Timothy Johnson, *The Letter of James: A New Translation with Introduction and Commentary* (AB 37A; New York, London, Toronto, Sydney, Auckland: Doubleday, 1995) 16-24, 27-9.

these apparently disparate forms and themes. By focusing on the question of James's treatment of the rich and poor I will try to uncover something of James's interpretation of the social situation in which he found himself and his audience.

Studies of James have long suffered from James's unfortunate use of Pauline terminology of "faith," "works" and "righteousness" (2:14-26) and the tendency in (especially Protestant) scholarship to privilege Pauline theology at the expense of the rest of the New Testament canon. More recently it seems that the "Jewishness" of James may have contributed to its disrepute in some circles. According to Dibelius, for example, it is precisely in the passages concerning the rich and poor (2:1-12 and 5:1-6) that one finds a "sub-Christian element" that is historically connected "with the small Jewish families of the Diaspora."[12] The present study pays attention to these passages, not because they may be used to locate James (to his disadvantage) within some more normative theology or less offensive social construct, but because in them it is possible to discern what drives James's appropriation and use of earlier traditions.

James' appropriation of sayings of Jesus

The tradition that informs James's theology most significantly is early Christian proclamation, especially as it is otherwise preserved in the Sermon on the Mount/Plain. The parallels between James and the Synoptic Gospels have often been catalogued and studied.[13] In this study I will examine one such parallel in order to discover how James appropriated the teaching of Jesus.

According to Hans Dieter Betz, "One of the greatest puzzles remains the literary and theological relationship between SM [the Sermon on the Mount] and the Epistle of James."[14] James never attributes any of his traditions to Jesus, and consequently it is not always clear whether a particular tradition comes to him as a saying of Jesus or the parallel is due to common use of a more widespread tradition. The fact that the Epistle of James contains so many close parallels to so many different kinds of Jewish,

---

[12]   Martin Dibelius, *James* (Hermeneia; revised by Heinrich Greeven; trans. by Michael A. Williams; Philadelphia: Fortress, 1976) 49, 50. It is probably significant that in this context Dibelius quotes Friedrich Nietzsche with approval. For Dibelius, in the final analysis this "sub-Christian element" is justified "to the extent to which common people must be permitted to be in the right within the context of a world religion" (p. 50).

[13]   See, for example, Patrick J. Hartin, *James and the Q Sayings of Jesus* (JSNTSup, 47; Sheffield: JSOT Press, 1991). For a convenient table of the parallels, see Peter H. Davids, *The Epistle of James: A Commentary on the Greek Text* (NIGTC; Grand Rapids, MI: Eerdmans, 1982) 47-8. For an intentionally shorter list of parallels, see Helmut Koester, *Ancient Christian Gospels: Their History and Development* (London: SCM Press and Philadelphia: Trinity, 1990) 72-73.

[14]   Hans Dieter Betz, *ABD*, 5: 1111.

Christian, and Hellenistic literature makes it likely that at least some of the parallels between James and the teachings of Jesus are purely coincidental. On the other hand, there are a few indications that James was dependent, at least in part, upon the teachings of Jesus.

The sayings of Jesus circulated in both oral and written form, and many, if not most, circulated independently of the context(s) in which they are now found in the various gospels. The Sermon on the Mount/Plain was wildly popular in early Christianity. It appears in Matthew and Luke and portions of it are alluded to or quoted by *Didache* (1; 3.7, 8.2-3, 9.5, 10.5, 15.3), *1 Clement* (13.2), *2 Clement* (4.2; 6.1), *Ep. of Polycarp to the Philippians* (2.3; 7.2; 12.3), *Shepherd of Hermas* (*Sim* 9.28.5-6) and Justin Martyr (*Dial.* 96.3; *1 Apol.* 16.1-2, 5; 15.1-17). It may also appear in Paul (1 Cor 7:10, on divorce), and many of the sayings of the Sermon on the Mount/Plain appear scattered about in the *Gospel of Thomas*. According to Betz, "All Christian writings of the post-NT period up to and inclusive of Justin Martyr contain numerous references and allusions to SM & SP with most of them textually different from the canonical gospels as we have them."[15] It should be noted, however, that some of these texts (Paul, *Gospel of Thomas*, *1 Clement*, *2 Clement*) may not be taken as evidence for the knowledge of Sermon on the Mount/Plain as a unified collection, but only of the traditions that are also in Sermon on the Mount/Plain. This is true as well for James. Since the Sermon on the Mount/Plain was the most popular collection of Jesus' sayings in antiquity and since most of the possible allusions to the teachings of Jesus in James are to the Sermon on the Mount/Plain, it is *a priori* likely that the writer of James, like most of the other Christian writings of his period, had access to the Sermon on the Mount/Plain.

More important, perhaps, is the fact that the particular saying presupposed by the allusion in James can also be shown to be one of the more popular sayings among those that make up the Sermon on the Mount/Plain.

> οὐχ ὁ θεὸς ἐξελέξατο τοὺς πτωχοὺς τῷ κόσμῳ πλουσίους ἐν πίστει καὶ κληρονόμους τῆς βασιλείας ἧς ἐπηγγείλατο τοῖς ἀγαπῶσιν αὐτόν.
> Has not God chosen those who are poor from the world's point of view to be rich in faith and to be heirs of the kingdom that he has promised to those who love him? (James 2:5b)

As it stands this sentence represents a conflation of at least two traditions: that God has chosen the poor and that it has been promised that the poor will inherit the kingdom. The overlap with the beatitude itself is not extensive, but it includes both of the important words: πτωχοί (poor) and βασιλεία (kingdom).[16] The fact that the kingdom is said to have been *promised*

---

15   Betz, *ABD* 5: 1112.

16   The addition of the phrase τῷ κόσμῳ has a function similar to that of Matthew's

encourages us to look for a particular traditional promise. Four ancient texts preserve this particular beatitude, all of which preserve the words used by James.

Matt 5:3: Μακάριοι οἱ <u>πτωχοὶ</u> τῷ πνεύματι, ὅτι αὐτῶν ἐστιν ἡ <u>βασιλεία</u> τῶν οὐρανῶν.
Blessed are the poor in spirit because the kingdom of heaven is theirs.

Luke 6:20: Μακάριοι οἱ <u>πτωχοί</u>, ὅτι ὑμετέρα ἐστὶν ἡ <u>βασιλεία</u> τοῦ θεοῦ.
Blessed are you poor because the kingdom of God is yours.

Gos. Thom. 54: ΠΕΧΕ ΙC ΧΕ ϨΝΜΑΚΑΡΙΟC ΝΕ ΝϨΗΚΕ ΧΕ ΤΩΤΝ ΤΕ ΤΜΝΤΕΡΟ ΝΜΠΗΥΕ
Jesus said, 'Blessed are you poor because the kingdom of heaven is yours.

Polycarp To the Philippians 2.3d: Μακάριοι οἱ <u>πτωχοὶ</u> καὶ οἱ διωκόμενοι ἕνεκεν δικαιοσύνης, ὅτι αὐτῶν ἐστιν ἡ <u>βασιλεία</u> τοῦ θεοῦ.
Blessed are the poor and those who are persecuted on account of righteousness because the kingdom of God is theirs.[17]

The third important word, κληρονόμοι (heirs), may have been imported from one of the other beatitudes in the Matthean version of the collection: μακάριοι οἱ πραεῖς ὅτι αὐτοὶ κληρονομήσουσιν τὴν γῆν ("Blessed are the meek for they shall inherit the earth," Matt 5:5).[18]

The popularity of the beatitude and of the collection of sayings in which it is found is not, by itself, conclusive evidence that it was in the form of the Sermon on the Mount/Plain that James had access to the beatitude. The mere fact, however, that by far most of the parallels with Jesus' teachings in the Epistle of James are to the demonstrably popular Sermon on the Mount/Plain makes it extremely likely that this sermon was in some form (whether oral or written) the source for most of James's knowledge of Jesus' sayings.

The reference to the "royal law" (or more properly, the "king's law" [νόμον βασιλικὸν]) of 2:8 and the kingdom promised to the poor in 2:5 imply the existence of a kingdom and a king.[19] That the kingdom is promised

τῷ πνεύματι. Both restrict the characterization of "poor" by specifying a particular point of view. James is talking about those who are poor from the world's point of view. This restriction implies the possibility of a different, more correct point of view.

[17] Polycarp's conflation of the beatitudes now found in Matt 5:3 and 5:10 shows that the beatitudes were already collected before their appearance in Matthew and probably in Q. None of these texts is directly dependent on the others, and two are entirely independent of the others.

[18] See also Didache 3.7, ἴσθι δὲ πραΰς ἐπεὶ οἱ πραεῖς κληρονομήσουσι τὴν γῆν ("Be meek because the meek will inherit the earth").

[19] I find the argument of Luke Timothy Johnson that the quotation of Lev 19:18 in

to the poor presupposes one who has made such a promise, and the close, verbal parallel with the beatitude makes it virtually certain that at least in this case there is direct dependence. It is, in fact, possible that it is the Sermon on the Mount/Plain that is referred to as the perfect or royal law of liberty.

Thus, James has taken a beatitude of Jesus, conflated it (slightly) with another from the same collection (that the meek would *inherit* the earth), and applied it to his teaching on the treatment of the poor. The most obvious difference between James's allusion and the older collection of beatitudes is that the traditional pronouncement of blessing has become the basis for a rebuke.[20] If Jesus has pronounced the poor blessed, then one ought not to dishonor the poor (vs. 6), but honor them. This is in marked distinction to the treatment of the poor and rich that might normally be expected in "polite society" and that James has (to his dismay) observed. It is here that we may observe how James's theology controls his ethics.

The implied social setting

The precise social situation that serves as the context for James 2:1-7 is not entirely clear. Dibelius has already shown that one cannot assume that the text refers to any real events. Like other paraenetic literature, James

> exaggerates and generalizes (cf. the second person plural address) individual cases which occur occasionally or which are merely possibilities, and does so in order to show the possible or even necessary consequences of these faults--faults which may very well be present among his readers, since they are universal human shortcomings.[21]

More recently Roy Ward has argued that what is depicted (though not in a historicizing sense) is a judicial assembly before which two members of the community have come for litigation.[22] This interpretation makes sense of the places assigned to the two men, and preserves the usual, judicial context for Jewish and Christian discussions of partiality toward the rich. In any case, what we have in this passage is an exhortation to impartiality using judicial language. The exhortation itself is traditional and parallels may be found throughout Jewish and Christian literature.

It is clear enough that James is talking about material wealth and poverty. The contrast between gold rings and fine clothes on the one hand

---

James 2:8 is but one piece of an elaborate complex of references to Leviticus 19 less than totally convincing ("The Use of Leviticus 19 in the Letter of James," *JBL* 101 (1982) 391-401). Even if the argument is correct, the adjective "royal" must mean that the law is understood by James as the law of the kingdom proclaimed by Jesus.

[20] See Koester, *Ancient Christian Gospels*, 71-75, who thinks only that "It is quite possible that some of these sayings and injunctions were known to James as sayings of Jesus" (p. 75).

[21] Dibelius, *James*, 128-30.

[22] Roy Bowen Ward, "Partiality in the Assembly: James 2:2-4," *HTR* 62 (1969) 87-97.

and dirty clothes on the other is unmistakably a reference both to material wealth and to social status.[23] The significance of the hypothetical places offered to the two men may be differently interpreted,[24] but that they are socially graded places is undisputed. The rich man is invited to sit "well" (καλῶς), and the poor man is asked to sit "under my footstool," an unpleasant place, and possibly meant to recall the biblical association with judgment.[25] It is unlikely, however, that this may be taken as unambiguous evidence for the concrete social setting of James or of his addressees. The situation mentioned here is a hypothetical one, and it was probably occasioned by what James perceived as preferential treatment of the wealthy. The most that can probably be concluded is that the congregations addressed by James included people who possessed different amounts of material wealth and that James was bothered by the preferential treatment paid to those who were more wealthy.[26]

But James thinks of much more than a particularly low level of material wealth and social status when he speaks of the poor or the rich. These are not simply terms that describe a socioeconomic status, but also ethical categories. Indeed, in spite of the fact that James must indirectly admit that there are "rich" people among his "twelve tribes of the dispersion" (1:1), he systematically avoids calling them "brothers."[27] This reluctance may have originated in the social condition of most early Christians, but it has also become a theological conviction.

The theological basis

Part of the reason for James' antipathy toward rich people is undoubtedly based on experience. In 2:6-7 James catalogues three offenses committed by rich people. (1) They oppress the addressees; (2) they "drag" the addressees into court; (3) they blaspheme the name of Jesus.[28] The first

---

23   See François Vouga, *L'Épitre de Saint Jacques* (CNT 13a; Geneva: Labor et Fides, 1984) 72; and Johnson, *The Letter of James*, 220.

24   Even the text is uncertain. The placement of the adverbs "here" and "there" varies in different mss. See Dibelius, *James*, 131-2, for a discussion of some of the possible interpretations.

25   Ward, "Partiality in the Assembly," 92. If Ward is correct, that the "synagogue" is a judicial assembly, then "To allow one of the litigants to sit would be an obvious sign of partiality" (p. 91).

26   In 2:6, both the poor and the rich are distinguished from the addressees: "But you have dishonored the poor. Is it not the rich who oppress you?"

27   This has often been noted and is probably due to the fact that for James πλούσιος ("rich") is a boundary marker that excludes the rich from the Christian community. Vouga notes further the movement from the third person to second person (*Jacques*, 25). Though James' real audience surely included people of relative wealth, his implied audience seems to exclude them.

28   In each case the subject ("the rich," "they," "they") is emphatic, either by position

two have sometimes been understood in terms of persecution of Christians. Dibelius argues that these should be understood not as an actual "Christian persecution," but as economic and legal action taken by the rich against Christians for economic reasons similar to those in Acts 16:19 or Acts 19:24 or because of irritation with Christian propaganda.[29] As Johnson correctly observes, however, there need not be any anti-Christian activity alluded to at all, since "It is universal enough a characteristic of the world's rich to oppress and humiliate the poor by 'legal' means."[30] While the charge of blasphemy is directed against religious opponents, the others are not criticisms of religious competitors, but against social exploitation. This is important because James' theological position is based not on religious competition, but on competition between two very different understandings of social ethics. The exploitative actions of the rich are not offensive because they are directed against Christians in particular, but because they represent the norms of a demonic society.

James has similar criticisms of rich people in the two parallel passages, 4:13-17 and 5:1-6. The passages are held together by their content (criticisms of actions characteristic of rich people) and introductory particles ("Come now" plus vocative). The first is directed against "those who say" that they will travel and make a profit by buying and selling, and it criticizes them for failing to recognize their temporality and for their pretentious, evil boasting. They are advised to change their attitude to one of submission to what "the Lord wills." This advice is in marked contrast with the far more severe advice in the next passage addressed to "the rich" who are advised to weep and wail because of their impending doom. They are condemned because of economic exploitation (they have withheld the rightful wages of their agricultural workers) and because they have condemned and murdered the righteous.[31] If, as was suggested above (fn. 27), πλούσιος ("rich") is a boundary marker, then we may conclude that pretentiousness, while sinful, does not exclude one from the community upon which the name of Jesus is named (2:7). The blatant injustice named in 5:1-6, however, does merit the label "rich" and marks those who practice it as bound for judgment.

James' condemnation of economic exploitation is apparently based on the Deuteronomic obligation to act toward the needy with justice and kindness, based on God's justice and love for the poor. According to Deut 10:18-19, God is one

---

or by the use of the emphatic pronoun. For parallels to "the fair name which is called over you" from the DSS, see 4Q418 81 i 12, (ו)קודש <ו>למ[ש לשמ] הנקרא הנקרא וכול ("And everyone who is called by his name ..."), and 4Q285 1 9-10, על[יכם נקרא קודשו ושם ("And his holy name is called ov[er you ...").

29 Dibelius, *James*, 139-40.

30 Johnson, *James*, 226.

31 Presumably the charge of murder is due to the fact that one who lacks an income runs the risk of starvation (cf. Sir 34:21-22).

> who executes justice for the orphan and the widow, and who loves the strangers, providing them food and clothing. You shall also love the stranger, for you were strangers in the land of Egypt.

A similar ethic is found in the Psalms which occasionally discuss God's care for the poor. According to Ps 72:12-13, for example, "He delivers the needy when they call, the poor and those who have no helper. He has pity on the weak and the needy, and saves the lives of the needy." Job echoes this sentiment in his final defense where he affirms the impropriety of failing to feed and clothe the poor, the orphan, and the widow or of acting unjustly toward them (Job 31:16-23). This is apparently also in imitation of God's treatment of the poor: "But he saves the needy from the sword of their [the wicked] mouth, from the hand of the mighty. So the poor have hope, and injustice shuts its mouth" (Job 5:15-16). Ben Sira's advice to his readers explicitly mentions kindness to the poor as a form of imitation of God.

> My child, do not cheat the poor of their living, and do not keep needy eyes waiting. Do not grieve the hungry, or anger one in need. ... Give a hearing to the poor, and return his greeting with deference. Deliver the oppressed from his oppressors; let not right judgment be repugnant to you. To the fatherless be as a father, help the widows in their husbands' stead; then God will call you a son of his, and he will be more tender to you more than a mother. (Sir 4:1-10, NRSV)

The prophets contain similar criticism for those who oppress the poor. Amos proclaims judgment for those who "trample on the needy, and bring to ruin the poor of the land" (Amos 8.4) along with those who are impatient at not being able to do business on the Sabbath and those who use false weights (vs. 5). Many other examples could be cited.

The Epistle of Enoch contains extremely harsh criticisms of the rich.

> Woe to you, you rich, for you have trusted in your riches, and from your riches you will be parted, because you have not remembered the Most High in the days of your riches. You have committed blasphemy and unrighteousness and have become ready for the day of slaughter and for the day of darkness and for the day of the great judgment (1 Enoch 94.8-9).[32]

The precise nature of their unrighteousness, however, is not always clear. In only one case is it clear that oppression of the poor is one of the crimes of the rich:

> Woe unto you, you sinners, for your riches make you appear righteous, but your hearts convict you of being sinners, and this word shall be a testimony against you for a memorial of your evil deeds. Woe to you who eat the finest of the wheat and drink new wine, the choicest of the wine and tread underfoot the poor in your might (1 Enoch 96.4-5).

---

[32]   All translations of *1 Enoch* are taken from Matthew Black, *The Book of Enoch or 1 Enoch: A New English Edition* (SVTP 7; Leiden: Brill, 1985).

In this passage one of the actions that belies the appearance of righteousness is the oppression of the poor. More often, however, it is the persecution of the righteous for which the rich are condemned (*1 Enoch* 95.7). Thus *1 Enoch* may differ from the other examples cited in that its real concern is not so much with economic exploitation of the poor as with social dominance by those who are deemed unrighteous by the Enochic writer.

James's acceptance of the attitude displayed in these traditions is clear in 5:1-6 where the rich are advised to weep and lament in view of their impending judgment. Their injustice has been noted by God and will be judged. In this passage God is the arbiter of injustice done by the rich; the implication is that God's care for the poor is grounds for the judgment of those who oppress the poor. In the light of this assurance, James advises his readers to be patient "because the Lord's coming is near" (James 5:8).

James has also another theological vantage point for developing his ethics of wealth and poverty. The occasional use of the term עֲנָוִים ("humble pious"?) in some of the Psalms has apparently led to a similar use of the term "poor" in some of the Psalms of Solomon.[33] The term is apparently used as a self-designation in certain of the sectarian Qumran texts, possibly because the writers may have identified their piety with a lack of desired social status. This is especially clear in Pesher Habakkuk and the pesher on Psalm 37.

> The interpretation of the word concerns the Wicked Priest, to pay him the reward for what he did to the poor. ... God will sentence him to destruction, exactly as he intended to destroy the poor (4QpHab 12 2-6).

> And the poor shall inherit the land and enjoy peace in plenty. Its interpretation concerns the congregation of the poor who will tolerate the period of distress and will be rescued from all the snares of Belial (4QpPs37 2 9-11).[34]

What is distinctive about James's exhortation to impartiality is not simply that he adopts the identification of poverty and piety (which he seems to do in part), but that he applies his apocalyptic interpretation of the contours of reality to the problem. The eschatology of James is relatively conventional. He appeals to eschatology in order to encourage the pious and to threaten the wicked. Eschatology, however, does not provide the theological foundation for the statements of chapter 2. That foundation is provided by the apocalyptic division of the cosmos into above and below (3:15), God and this world (4:4), God and the devil (4:7; 3:15); and the contrast between desire

---

[33] For example, "And the devout shall give thanks in the assembly of the people, and God will be merciful to the poor to the joy of Israel" (Pss. Sol. 10.6; see also 15.1 and 18.2). Translations of the Psalms of Solomon are from R. B. Wright, "Psalms of Solomon," *OTP* 2: 639-70.

[34] Translations of the DSS are from Florentino García Martínez, *The Dead Sea Scrolls Translated: The Qumran Texts in English* (trans. Wilfred G. E. Watson; Leiden: Brill, 1994).

which leads to sin and the word of truth which gives "us" birth (1:14-18; cf. 4:1-4). James objects to far more than simple acts of exploitation. He objects to a whole cosmic structure that is in open conflict with God and which determines the false and evil social structure in which humans live.

Dibelius is typical in his explanation of apocalypticism as the reason for Jesus' convictions regarding the poor (which have influenced James).

> If the proclaimer of this message and those who followed him lived in poverty, it was not because of thoroughgoing asceticism or strict proletarian consciousness, for Jesus consents to support from others and to being invited as a guest. The decisive element, again, is the apocalyptic expectation. He lives apart from active involvement in the economic functions of the world because he foresees the end of this world. Thanks to the situation in Galilee and the hospitality of his followers, this life of poverty never becomes penurious and proletarian.[35]

He is correct that apocalypticism has influenced this thinking, but he is not correct in emphasizing the "apocalyptic expectation." It was not merely the expectation of certain future events that influenced these attitudes, but more fundamentally it was the apocalyptic way of understanding the present.

James' appropriation of Jesus' beatitude contains a critical window onto his understanding of the meaning of poverty -- James' addition of the little phrase τῷ κόσμῳ ("in the world's point of view"). Unlike Matthew, whose addition of τῷ πνεύματι ("in spirit") limits the scope of the word "poor" to poverty which cannot be measured in material terms, James adds a modifier that accepts the material sense of the word, but at the same time criticizes it as false. The conventional use of the word "poor" is inauthentic because it assumes the social order of the world in which the rich (those who have social as well as material status) are honored and the poor are dishonored and exploited. The fact that God has chosen the poor and dishonored of this world to be rich in faith and to inherit the kingdom is proof that the conventional criteria for assigning honor are false and in need of reversal. The importance of this view for James is evident also in his exhortation to the "lowly" brother (ὁ ἀδελφὸς ὁ ταπεινός) to boast in his exalted position, while the rich man (not "brother") should "boast" in his humiliation in view of the fact that he is about to perish (1:9-10). These verses are a clear declaration of the reversal of values that James believes is in force within the Christian community. Thus the addition of τῷ κόσμῳ clearly connects James' ethics concerning the poor with his wider conviction of the dualism of heaven and earth with its concomitant ethic of social reversal.

One other passage confirms James' negative evaluation of the world. In 3:13-4:10, James contrasts two kinds of wisdom and the consequences of living by one or the other. According to 3:15, one kind of wisdom is "earthly, unspiritual, and demonic" (ἐπίγειος ψυχικὴ δαιμονιώδης); the other

---

[35] Dibelius, *James*, 43.

"comes down from above" (ἄνωθεν κατερχομένη). The latter characterization should be understood in the context of 1:17 which proclaims that "every good and perfect gift is from above (ἄνωθεν), coming down (καταβαῖνον) from the Father of lights." Commentators have rightly understood this characterization of wisdom in the light of the traditional Jewish understanding of wisdom as a gift of God, the one who created wisdom and who is truly wise.[36] It is possible, however, that "coming down from above" is an allusion to a more concrete tradition of the descent of wisdom from heaven to earth to dwell among those who were to receive her (Sir 24:1-12; denied in *1 Enoch* 42:1-2).

James presses this contrast even more forcefully in the discussion of the opposition of the world to God that follows his characterization of wisdom. In his criticism of those who want to have things that they can squander on their own pleasures (4:3), James says that friendship with the world (κόσμος) is hatred toward God (4:4) and that God resists the proud but exalts the lowly (4:6, 10). The readers are accused of being "double-minded) (δίψυχοι) precisely because of their failed attempt to bring this diabolic cosmos (4:7) into harmony with God.

Conclusions

Moral exhortation (how one ought to live in this world) has probably always been one of the functions of apocalyptic literature. Our fascination with the temporal, eschatological aspects of apocalyptic texts and their outlandish descriptions of future judgment and heavenly journeys may sometimes blind us to the function of these mythical descriptions as symbols for an ethical system that involves the rejection of experienced social realities. The scholarly emphasis on the bizarre elements of apocalyptic may have also helped to obscure the fundamental concern with the "here and now" of all apocalyptic texts in so far as they seek to explain and redefine experienced reality and the moral obligations of those who live in that reality. The literary function of the mythical elements is to create an imaginative interpretation of the structure of the cosmos. Texts, such as James, that de-emphasize the geographic contours of heaven and hell and the details of future judgment, but that adopt the dualistic definition of reality that is characteristic of apocalyptic literature should not be excluded from the category of apocalyptic. Some texts (those that belong to the genre of apocalyptic) are characterized by descriptions of the apocalyptic construction of reality. Others, such as James, adopt that construction but focus on understanding one's rightful place within the apocalyptically defined cosmos. By interpreting Jesus' teachings within the context of an apocalyptic construction of reality, James has created a powerful social critique and a positive foundation for granting honor to those who otherwise lack it.

---

[36] E.g., Dibelius, *James*, 212; Johnson, *James*, 272; Vouga, *Jacques*, 105; and Davids, *James*, 152.

Faith, Knowledge, and the Law;
or Maybe the Jews will be saved:
Clement of Alexandria's Reading of Romans 10-11 in Stromateis 2

by

Michael Joseph Brown

Wabash College

The Alexandrian Church, Clement, and Hellenistic Judaism

It must be admitted that our knowledge of the so-called "roots" of the Alexandrian Church is limited.[1] We have almost no data on the history of the Alexandrian Church before the second century.[2] Yet, we do know that Alexandria was a major center of scholarship in the Roman world. Further, given Alexandria's status as a major intellectual center, it is not surprising that it would be a city in which philosophical and theological "schools" developed. Nevertheless, our knowledge of these "schools" is inadequate. Robert Grant admonishes the scholar on the subject of these "schools" by saying, "It must be admitted that we know less about actual procedures at Alexandria and elsewhere than many of our modern authors suggest."[3]

One source for information regarding "schools" in Alexandria is Philo. He gives—it must be admitted—an idealized presentation of the presence of schools within the Jewish community of Alexandria: "Each seventh day there stand wide open in every city thousands of schools of good sense, temperance, courage, justice and the other virtues in which the scholars sit quietly with ears alert and with full attention... while one of special experience rises and sets forth what is the best and sure to be profitable and will make the whole of life grow to something better."[4]

---

[1] "The obscurity that veils the early history of the Church in Egypt and that does not lift until the beginning of the third century constitutes a conspicuous challenge to the history of primitive Christianity," Colin H. Roberts, *Manuscript, Society and Belief in Early Christian Egypt*, The Schweich Lectures of the British Academy (London: Oxford University Press, 1979), p. 1.

[2] For more information about Alexandria, see Christopher Haas, *Alexandria in Late Antiquity: Topography and Social Conflict* (Baltimore and London: John Hopkins University Press, 1997). Although its primary concern is Alexandria in the third century onward, it gives some helpful insights into the preceding period.

[3] Robert M. Grant, "Theological Education at Alexandria," *The Roots of Egyptian Christianity*, eds. Birger A. Pearson and James E. Goehring, Studies in Antiquity and Christianity (Philadelphia: Fortress Press, 1986), p. 178.

[4] *Spec.* 2.62. Recent scholarship has demonstrated that synagogues were not used solely for the purpose of worship. See Shaye Cohen, *From the Maccabees to the Mishnah*, The Library of Early Christianity, vol. 7, ed. Wayne A. Meeks [Philadelphia: Westminster Press, 1989], p. 111-115, and Lee Levine, "The Nature and Origin of the Palestinian Synagogue Reconsidered," *Journal of Biblical Literature* 115 (1996), pp. 425-448.

What makes this presentation appear idealized is its rather overt and conscious attempt to make the "schools" in Alexandria (as described by Philo) resemble Hellenistic philosophical schools. Grant argues that this model, which he perceives to be something like a synagogue, does not appear to establish the best precedent for the Christian schools in Alexandria. Grant holds that one should think of the Christian schools along the line of the Therapeutae by the Mareotic lake (as opposed to the synagogue), described in Philo's *On the Contemplative Life* (*De vita contemplativa*).[5] This thesis is not thoroughly acceptable because the Therapeutae appear to have more in common with later Christian monastic communities than these "schools." There may be practices described in *On the Contemplative Life* that sound a lot like early Christian schools, but Grant cannot make a solid step from intuition to proof based on evidence. The key part of Grant's analysis seems to be his contention that these "schools" in Alexandria contained the *ideal* theological leader. This leader concentrated on exegesis and the allegorical method of interpretation of sacred writings. Whether this contention is absolutely true or not, the importance of the teacher in the community seems consistent in the Alexandrian environment.

The primary focus, according to Grant, in these early Christian "schools" was the Hebrew Scriptures: "In a Jewish setting, whether Alexandrian or not, the first Christians were devoted to learning about the meaning of their Bible or what we call the Old Testament."[6] This argument appears to converge with the argument made by Robert Wilken that there was a "center" or focal point for the development of Christian thought.[7] Quoting H. E. W. Turner, Wilken argues that "in the early period the 'center' was more a matter of 'instinctive feeling than of fixed and definable doctrinal norms.'"[8] This means that in these Christian "schools," particularly those in Alexandria, the later doctrinal norms of Christianity were being developed around certain practices and beliefs that came to be called catholic Christianity. In fact, one of the best examples for the verification of this thesis may be one of its detractors, Celsus. As Wilken notes, "When [Celsus] wishes to offer substantive criticism of

---

[5] Grant, "Theological Education," p. 180; cf. Walter Bauer: "… no one today would dare to suppose with Eusebius (*H.E.* 2.16-17) that Philo's "Therapeutae" were Christians" (*Orthodoxy and Heresy in Earliest Christianity*, trans. Philadelphia Seminar on Christian Origins, eds. Robert A. Kraft and Gerhard Krodel [Philadelphia: Fortress, 1971], p. 47; along with the notes contained therein).

[6] Grant, "Theological Education," p. 180.

[7] Robert L. Wilken, "Diversity and Unity in Early Christianity," *Second Century: A Journal of Early Christian Studies* 1/1 (1981), p. 101-110.

[8] Wilken, "Diversity and Unity," p. 106.

Christianity, he does not discuss the Gnostics or the Marcionites; Celsus assumes he knows what Christianity is, and he does not identify it with one of those parties."[9]

Catechetical instruction was definitely part of the scholarship conducted at Alexandria. For instance, we know that Origen was invited to take charge of the Alexandrian Catechetical school around the year 203 CE. Eusebius gives us the context of this invitation: "At Alexandria there was no one dedicated to elementary Christian teaching, as everyone had fled the threatened persecution" (*H.E.* 6.3.1).[10] Titus Flavius Clemens is also reported to have taught at one of the Christian schools in Alexandria. Eusebius comments about Clement's teaching and his teacher, Pantaenus.[11] He seems to indicate that Christian scholarship in Alexandria was established some time before Pantaenus: "... it was an established custom that an academy of sacred learning should exist among [the Alexandrian Christians]... we know that Pantaenus was one of the most eminent teachers of his day, being an ornament of the philosophic system known as stoicism" (*H.E.* 5.10.1). Thus, we can deduce from these comments that by the time of Clement there were at least elementary "schools" of Christian learning in Alexandria. This does not give one much indication as to the content of the curriculum in these "schools." As Grant comments, "At Alexandria it was hard to differentiate between gnostic and Christian doctrines."[12] Still, we know from the comments made about Pantaenus that Stoic philosophy was prominent in the Christian "schools." Furthermore, it is known that Platonism—found among other places in the writings of Philo—was on the rise in Alexandrian intellectual circles during the time of Clement and Origen.

Since the publication of Walter Bauer's *Orthodoxy and Heresy in Earliest Christianity* (1934), it has been argued that early Christianity in Egypt was predominantly gnostic and heretical. While this assessment does have some merit, it cannot be recognized as the final world on Egyptian Christianity. Colin Roberts makes a strong case for the Hellenistic Jewish roots of the Alexandrian Church based on manuscript evidence.

---

[9] Wilken, "Diversity and Unity," p. 107.

[10] Eusebius, *The History of the Church*, trans. G. A. Williamson, Penguin Classics (New York: Penguin Books, 1965).

[11] This whole historical scenario is questioned by scholars like David Dawson. See *Allegorical Readers and Cultural Revision in Ancient Alexandria* (Los Angeles: University of California Press, 1992), pp. 219-234, for more details.

[12] Grant, "Theological Education," pp. 181-182.

It was a Jewish habit (as we know from the Dead Sea Scrolls) to preserve manuscripts by placing them in jars.[13] This practice is somewhat outlined in *The Assumption of Moses*: "To preserve the books which I have delivered unto thee thou shalt place them in an earthen vessel."[14] The Jews also had a practice of disposing of defective, worn-out, or heretical scriptures by burying them near a cemetery, not to preserve them, but because anything that might contain the name of God may not be destroyed.[15] This practice was adopted by the early Church. Roberts relates that among the earliest Christian texts found in Egypt (dated between 100-199 CE) one was of the book of Exodus, one of Genesis, one of Deuteronomy, three of the Psalms, one of John, two of Matthew, one of Luke, and one of Titus. Moreover, among the writings later not included in the canon, Roberts cites the presence of the *Shepherd of Hermas*, *logia* from the *Gospel of Thomas*, and Irenaeus' *Adversus Haereses*.[16]

Dismissing the argument that the Alexandrian Church started among gnostic Jews,[17] Roberts tries to explain the lack of evidence surrounding this Church by arguing for a strong relationship with Judaism: "If we are forced to conclude that the Church in Egypt in the first century was numerically weak, if not insignificant, the explanation may be found in its relation with Judaism."[18] The Alexandrian Jewish community was distinctive in the ancient world. According to Strabo, a large part of the city was set aside for the Jews, and an ethnarch ruled over the community as if it were an independent state.[19] In fact, once Roman rule began, their

---

[13] The placing of written material in jars for security was widespread throughout the ancient Near East; cf. R. de Vaux in *Revue Biblique* 56 (1949), pp. 591-592, J. T. Milik in *Biblica* 31 (1950), p. 504, and B. Couroyer in *Revue Biblique* 62 (1955), p. 76.

[14] Cf. also Jeremiah 32.14.

[15] Roberts, *Manuscript*, p. 7.

[16] Roberts, *Manuscript*, pp. 10-14; cf. Bauer's statement: "It may seem remarkable that the name *Gospel of the Egyptians* should arise in Egypt itself and be used by Christians there. They would have had no occasion to speak of their *lone* gospel as the gospel "of the Egyptians." It would simply be *the* gospel. The special designation presupposes a plurality of gospels which makes a distinction necessary" (*Orthodoxy and Heresy*, p. 50).

[17] This thesis is advanced by scholars like Birger Pearson. See, e.g., his "Gnosticism in Early Egyptian Christianity," *Gnosticism, Judaism, and Egyptian Christianity*, Studies in Antiquity and Christianity (Minneapolis: Fortress Press, 1990), pp. 194-213.

[18] Roberts, *Manuscript*, p. 55.

[19] Quoted by Josephus, *Antiquities of the Jews* 17.117; from the abundant literature on the Jewish problem in Egypt in the early Roman period two works may be cited here, both with references to the sources and to recent discussions: P. M. Fraser, *Ptolemaic*

possession of a γερουσία gave the Jews a position superior to that of the Greeks in the city.[20] This did not promote good relations between pagans and Jews. The history of revolts and pogroms in Alexandria serves as the best evidence of this statement.

Given what is perceived of the Jesus movement in environments like the early Jerusalem church and manuscripts like Jude and James, the Church in Alexandria would most likely have been associated with the larger Jewish community. This would have made it difficult for the early Christians to dialogue with their Gentile neighbors, much less to proselytize. Roberts comes to this conclusion:

> In the first age of the Church Christians in Alexandria and consequently throughout Egypt were either unable or unwilling to escape from the Jewish connection, or at any rate to appear to do so in the eyes of non-Christians; the fate of the first church in Alexandria would thus have been involved, willy-nilly, with that of Judaism.[21]

If the early Alexandrian Christian community was virtually indistinguishable from its Jewish predecessor, the turning point came with the reign of the emperor Trajan (98-117 CE). Historians of Egyptian Jewry mark this as the period of the beginning of the end.[22] This is when Alexandrian Judaism faded and Christianity seized the initiative. One begins to hear from an Alexandrian Church defining itself over against

---

Alexandria (Oxford, 1972), pp. i.54ff. and 688ff. with the relevant notes, and the prolegomena by V. Tcherikover to the *Corpus Papyrorum Judaicarum* (Harvard, 1957), p. 48ff., whose survey covers the entire period of the papyri; Fraser remarks that the Jewish element in the population of Alexandria was of ever increasing importance from the middle of the second century BCE down to the early Roman period and he accepts with some reservations Philo's figure (*in Flacc.* 43) of one million for the Jewish population in Egypt.

[20] Roberts, *Manuscript*, p. 55.

[21] Roberts, *Manuscript*, p. 57; Eusebius' statement (*H.E.* 2.16-17) that Christianity spread very rapidly in Alexandria and that the leading men (ἀποστολικοὶ ἄνδρες) were of Jewish stock who observed most of the ancient customs in a strictly Jewish fashion must be discounted since it depends on his identification of the first Christian congregation in Alexandria with the Therapeutae. But that the confusion seemed plausible enough to Eusebius may be regarded as supporting evidence for the strongly Jewish coloring of early Christianity there. Eusebius' statement is reproduced by Jerome (*De vir. ill.* 8) who gives a further twist to the story by describing the first Church in Alexandria as *adhuc judaizantem*, a statement for which there is no independent source; W. H. C. Frend in his essay on "Athanasius in the Early Christian Centuries" (reprinted in his *Religion Popular and Unpopular in the Early Christian Centuries* [London, 1976], p. 25ff.) also comments that "Coptic Christianity was to owe more to [the Jewish-Christian tradition] than to any resurgence of national Egyptian sentiment."

[22] Roberts, *Manuscript*, p. 58.

Judaism. It is also during this period that the Alexandrian Church begins to cleave to the Roman Church—another church with arguably a strong Jewish background.[23] Thus, from the evidence one can conclude that the Bauer thesis regarding Egyptian Christianity, i.e., that it was heretical and gnostic, is not wholly tenable. Roberts raises the same issue, "it would be strange if a strongly intellectual movement [i.e., Gnosticism] had a greater appeal to the native population than orthodoxy, particularly if, as we have seen reason to think, it had not in the third century won a dominant position among the Greeks, surely much more open to its attractions."[24]

What, then, appears as the most probable context in which to place the Alexandrian Church? According to the information above, it is most likely that Alexandrian Christianity developed, if not within the Hellenistic Jewish community of Alexandria, at least in close intellectual proximity to it. This would explain a number of issues involved in the discussion. First, the close relationship of Christianity to Hellenistic Judaism best explains the philosophical tendency in the Alexandrian Church. If Philo's contention that Sabbaths should be devoted to philosophy (*De Opificio* 128) is correct,[25] then it can be argued that at least a portion of Judaism in Alexandria was committed to interpreting scripture by means of Hellenistic philosophy.[26] As Philo says, "The Jews every seventh day occupy themselves with the philosophy of their fathers, dedicating that time to the acquiring of knowledge and the study of the truths of nature. For what are our places of prayer throughout the cities but schools of prudence and courage and temperance and justice and also of piety, holiness and every virtue by which duties to God and men are discerned and rightly performed?" (*Mos.* 2.16). Although what Philo conceives of as a "school" sounds a lot like some sort of synagogue service, this cannot be proved conclusively, although we know that synagogues were used as study houses. However, this hypothesis would explain Grant's thesis that scholarship in early Christian Alexandria was devoted primarily to the Hebrew Bible, and it would also explain the presence of the theological leader (i.e., some sort of rabbinic figure). It would likewise assist in explaining Eusebius' claim (*H.E.* 5.10) that Alexandria had an established "academy of sacred

---

[23] See R. M. Grant in *Gnosticism and Early Christianity* (New York and London, 1966), pp. 122-123, where he emphasizes the Jewish character of the theology and moral teaching of Hermas.

[24] Roberts, *Manuscript*, p. 69.

[25] By "philosophical" Philo means a generally Platonic interpretation of Torah.

[26] For a discussion of this in a larger context, consult Annewies van den Hoek, "The 'Catechetical' School of Early Christian Alexandria and Its Philonic Heritage," *Harvard Theological Review* 90/1 (1997), pp. 59-87.

learning." This academy would most likely have been modeled after the kind of "school" described by Philo.

Second, the close relationship between Christianity and Judaism in Alexandria helps to explain the diverse manuscripts described by Roberts. The specifically Jewish manuscripts found are almost all from the Torah: Genesis, Exodus, and Deuteronomy. The copies of the Psalms (i.e., liturgical materials) found could further validate the Jewish foundation of the Christian "schools."[27] The frequent use of diverse texts by Clement and others within the Alexandrian context could be attributed to a church attempting to define itself in contrast to its Jewish antecedents. Bauer's statements in this regard can be most helpful:

> Everything we know of [Alexandrian] Christianity, apart from what has been mentioned already, clearly has grown up apart from all ecclesiastically structured Christendom until far into the second century... We first catch sight of something like "ecclesiastical" Christianity in Demetrius, the bishop of Alexandria from 189 to 231... when Demetrius assumed his office he was the *only* Egyptian "bishop"... [E]ven into the third century, no separation between orthodoxy and heresy was accomplished in Egypt and the two types of Christianity were not yet at all clearly differentiated from each other... there can be heretics only where orthodox Christians stand in contrast to them or serve as a background for them...[28]

If Alexandrian Christianity originated with the model of the "school" as described by Philo, then it is conceivable that a number of "teachers" could have started their own "schools" devoted to the explicating of the Christian philosophy. These "schools" would not have been "orthodox" in the traditional sense given that orthodoxy (as it came to be defined) did not exist.[29] Distinctions between orthodoxy and heresy did not arise until the episcopate of Demetrius. Prior to that time, the Alexandrian Church sought its own voice in the context of its relationship to Alexandrian

---

[27] Jakob J. Petuchowski points out: "One aspect of the synagogue service, the reading and the expounding of Scripture, is probably as old as the synagogue itself. Pentateuchal pericopes were read as part of the morning service of every Sabbath... The Book of Psalms and other hymnic portions of Scripture figure prominently into various rubrics of the synagogue liturgy..." ("The Liturgy of the Synagogue," *The Lord's Prayer and Jewish Liturgy*, ed. Jakob J. Petuchowski and Michael Brocke, [New York: Seabury Press, 1978], p. 55)

[28] Bauer, *Orthodoxy and Heresy*, pp. 48, 53, 59.

[29] E.g., Elaine Pagels illustrates the difficulty of determining what is orthodox. See *The Gnostic Gospels* (New York: Vintage Books, 1981), p. 38.

Hellenistic Judaism. Thus, Clement of Alexandria stands as a pivotal figure in the development of orthodoxy in Alexandrian Christianity.[30]

If it is true that the Alexandrian Church owed a great debt to Hellenistic Judaism, it is even more plausible to believe that the type of Hellenistic Judaism manifested in Philo of Alexandria was predominant in the Egyptian Church. It is not then entirely surprising to find Clement using many concepts developed initially by Philo.[31] It is well-known that Clement borrowed Philo's allegoric method[32] and some of his elaborate allegories. Furthermore, Clement co-opted Philo's doctrine of the *Logos* as the central concept in his presentation of Christianity.[33] Philo, linking the Hebrew phrase "the word of the Lord" with the Stoic doctrine of the *Spermatikos Logos*[34] and Plato's doctrine of Ideas, found in a resulting conception "a divine, rational, and spiritual principle immanent in man and in the universe, and he also found a divine personality, or quasi-personality, to come between the Absolute and the world."[35] Philo's *Logos*

---

[30] Robert Casey says that Clement was the "founder of Christian Platonism and the father of Christian intellectual mysticism" ("Clement of Alexandria and the Beginnings of Christian Platonism," *Studies in Early Christianity: A Collection of Scholarly Essays*, vol. 8, The Early Church and Greco-Roman Thought, eds. Everett Ferguson, David M. Scholer, and Paul Corby Finney [New York: Garland Publishing Inc., 1993], p. 140).

[31] Justin Martyr was purportedly the first Christian to use Philonic and Middle Platonic philosophy in his own writings.

[32] "By adopting the allegorical method of exegesis [Clement] was dispensed from taking into account many of the Jewish elements in Christianity that were fundamentally irreconcilable with his view of ultimate reality, and he could thus concentrate his attention on aspects of Pauline and Johannine thought which could easily be harmonized with his own system and made to enrich it" (Casey, "Clement of Alexandria," p. 140).

[33] T. B. Glover, *Conflict of Religions in the Early Roman Empire* (Boston: Beacon Hill, 1909), p. 271.

[34] "In *Rev. Div. Her.* 119 the Logos is called, among other things, the *spermatikos*, the divine Logos, which 'implants its seed' within men. All men, therefore, participate to some extent in the life of the Logos. All men are, in one sense at least, God's sons, as the Logos can be called God's Son" (Ronald Williamson, *Jews in the Hellenistic World: Philo*, Cambridge Commentaries on Writings of the Jewish and Christian World, 200 BC to AD 200, vol. 1 pt. 2, eds. P. R. Ackroyd, A. R. C. Leaney, J. W. Packer [Cambridge: Cambridge University Press, 1989], p.).

[35] Glover, *Conflict of Religions*, p. 289; see also Casey, "Clement of Alexandria," p. 88.

mediates between humanity and God.[36]   Clement alters this doctrine of the
Logos by equating Philo's *Logos* with the historic Jesus.[37]

Philo's ideas, which have some affinities to Gnosticism,[38] and which
were employed by Clement include: (1) an emphasis on the complete
transcendence of God, (2) an emanationist conception of the doctrine of
God, and (3) a general disparagement of the sense-perceptible world.
Philo's doctrine of the transcendence of God is based on a combination of
Platonic philosophy with the Hebrew Bible. Philo denies the possibility of
knowing the divine essence, and he tends toward a *theologia negativa*.
However, he does not use the term ἄγνωστος (unknowable) of God.[39]   R.
A. Mortley asserts that in the theology of Clement there "is a silence
concerning God that not even the initiated can penetrate."[40]   Clement argues
for a limited reason that must make room for faith. In fact, it, the lack of
limitless reason, is the "veil" that surrounds God, and which attracts the
human mind.[41] It is Clement's *Logos* which reveals this needed and higher
knowledge of God. This higher knowledge of God is inseparable from
faith. J. C. McLelland summarizes Clement's stance on the doctrine of the
unknowable God (and his alteration of Philo's ideas) by saying:
"Immutability asserts God's trustworthiness, impassability his moral

---

[36] On this matter see Christopher Stead, *Philosophy in Christian Antiquity*
(Cambridge: Cambridge University Press, 1994) and Williamson, *Jews*, p. 107.

[37] "Clement's conception of the incarnation has much in common with the Stoic
notion of the perfect Sage. The substance of this was that the nature of things provided the
possibility that all might truly be wise, but that in practice few, if any, were likely to
become so. The main function of this ideal figure, therefore, was to mark out the far limits
of human moral capacity, and to show men what they might be if only they tried hard
enough" (Casey, "Clement of Alexandria," p. 107); cf. Williamson who comments on
Philo's doctrine of the *Logos*: "The Logos, which is between the unbegotten Father on the
one hand, and the universe and man on the other, is neither made or begotten. It is
logically dependent on God and cannot be conceived as self-existent... " (*Jews*, p. 110).

[38] Many have tried to associate Philo to the gnostic movement. Contrariwise, R.
McL. Wilson argues, "Philo is not a gnostic in the strict sense of the term, although he
does have affinities with Gnosticism" (R. McL. Wilson, "Philo of Alexandria and
Gnosticism," *Kairos* 14 [1972], p. 215). Wilson treats Philo extensively in his book, *The
Gnostic Problem* (London: Mowbray, 1958).

[39] Cf. Williamson, *Jews*, p. 105, and H. S. Versnel, "Religious Mentality in
Ancient Prayer," *Faith, Hope, and Worship: Aspects of Religious Mentality in the Ancient
World*, Studies in Greek and Roman Religion, vol. 2, ed. H. S. Versnel (Leiden: E. J.
Brill, 1981), pp. 13, 15-16.

[40] R. A. Mortley, *La connaissance religieuse et herméneutique chez Clément
d'Alexandrie* (Leiden, 1973), p. 58; cf. Casey, "Clement of Alexandria," pp. 90-91 n. 13;
Stead, *Christian Antiquity*, p. 133.

[41] McL. Wilson, "Philo," p. 223.

transcendence, anonymity his eminence beyond our linguistic and conceptual categories."[42]

Another Philonic idea, also found in Clement of Alexandria, is the repudiation of radical dualism. Philo's intermediaries are not the wicked and rebellious archons of Gnostic myth. Further, even though Philo disparages the sense-perceptible world (a basic feature of Neo-Platonism), his ideas are far removed from the Gnostic myth of a premundane Fall that places the world and the Demiurge in the realm of evil.[43] As Wilson comments, "He was a Jew, and it is difficult to imagine him having any sympathy for the gnostic repudiation of the God of the Old Testament."[44] Clement of Alexandria appears to hold the same doctrine, particularly when one views his soteriology. Thus, it seems prudent to associate the Alexandrian Christian community with the Hellenistic Judaism of Alexandria (as exemplified in thinkers such as Philo) when one considers the "archaeological" evidence—particularly that demonstrated by the manuscripts—and the work of Clement of Alexandria.

The Logos and Faith

Clement says that *gnosis* of God comes through the *Logos*, and is given in measure to a person's ability to understand (*Strom.* 7.1.2).[45] The Son or *Logos* plays a much larger role in Clement's theology than does the Father.[46] Clement's theology moves more toward the Son because of his acceptance of an emanationist doctrine of God, and his use of the *Logos* from Philonic and Stoic philosophy. Besides, Clement's focus on the *Logos*

---

[42] J. C. McLelland, *God the Anonymous* (Cambridge: Harvard, 1976), p. 160. See also A. H. Armstrong's comments on this negative theology in "The Self-Definition of Christianity in Relation to Later Platonism," *Jewish and Christian Self-Definition, I: The Shaping of Christianity in the Second and Third Centuries*, ed. E. P. Sanders (Philadelphia: Fortress, 1980), pp. 92-97. See also S. R. C. Lilla, *Clement of Alexandria: A Study in Christian Platonism and Gnosticism* (Oxford, 1971), pp. 217-226.

[43] Philo is our earliest evidence for the distinction made in Neo-Platonism between the *kosmos noetos* and the *kosmos aisthetos* (see, e.g., *Op. Mund.* 15-17, 24), but it is probably not original with Philo. See, e.g., J. Dillon, *The Middle Platonists* (Ithaca, NY: Cornell University Press, 1977), pp. 158-159, and M. Baltes, *Timaios Lokros. Über die Natur des Kosmos und der Seele* (Leiden: E. J. Brill, 1972), p. 105.

[44] McL. Wilson, "Philo," p. 219. See also Philo's *credo* at the end of his treatise on the creation of the world, *Op. Mund.* 170-172.

[45] Most English translations of Clement's works in this paper come from *The Ante-Nicene Fathers: Fathers of the Second Century: Hermas, Tatian, Athenagoras, Theophilus, and Clement of Alexandria (Entire)*, vol. 2, ed. Alexander Roberts and James Donaldson, rev. ed. (Peabody, MA: Hendrickson, 1994; repr. Christian Literature, 1885), except for those that come from *Stromateis* 7.

[46] Cf. Casey, "Clement of Alexandria," p. 102.

allows him to avoid the problem of personality encountered by the Stoics.[47] The Stoics were unclear about what they meant when they said "God" or "gods," and this lack of clarity evolved into an obscure vision in terms of ethics. That is, without a clear vision of God the Stoics lacked a model which could be imitated. Clement overcame this problem by making the *Logos* the focal point of his theology. So, instead of Epictetus' dictum: "What would Socrates do?" (τί ἂν ἐποίησεν ἐν τούτῳ Σωκράτης),[48] Clement asks the hypothetical question, "What would Jesus do?"

Clement's doctrine of the *Logos* is invested—it appears—with a degree of personality.[49] "The Logos is indeed the Great High Priest... The great and characteristic feature of the Logos is that 'he took the mask (προσωπεῖον) of a man and moulded it for himself in flesh and played a part in the drama of mankind's salvation'"[50] (see *Strom.* 2.5). Clement describes the *Logos*, the Son, as the source of Providence (*Strom.* 7.2.5), and as being "never divided, never dissevered, never passing from place to place..." (*Strom.* 7.2.5; οὐ μεριζόμενος οὐκ ἀποτεμνόμενος, οὐ μεταβαίνων ἐκ τόπου εἰς τόπον).[51] The *Logos* is not only ubiquitous, it is the focal point of contemplation that brings disparate humanity into harmony:

> Let us who are many hasten to be gathered unto one love according to the unity of the monadic essence (μοναδικῆς οὐσίας). Since we do good, let us in like manner pursue unity by seeking the good Monad. But the unity of many arising out of a multitude of separate voices takes on a divine harmony and becomes one concordant sound, following one director and teacher, the Logos, and coming to rest at the Truth itself

---

[47] See the discussion in Glover, *Conflict of Religions*, pp. 71-73.

[48] Epictetus, *Enchiridion* 33.

[49] See *Stromateis* 7.2.6; cf. what Williamson says of Philo's conception of the *Logos*: "The 'Thought of God' is expressed primarily in the rational order visible in the universe. In that respect the Logos is the *eikon* of God. But the Logos is also the Thought of God expressed in such a way that man can apprehend and comprehend it... This Logos is a bridge between God and mankind because it is the divine rationality impressed upon the natural order, in so far as it is capable of receiving it, and yet closely united to God as flowing from his essence. It is perhaps only necessary to add that Philo's habit of personifying the Logos as, for example, a high-priest figure, must not be mistaken for full-blooded personalisation" (*Jews*, p. 108).

[50] Glover, *Conflict of Religions*, p. 297.

[51] "As Philo puts it in *Conf. Ling.* 95-7, those who 'serve the Existent,' led by Moses ('the nature beloved of God'), 'shall behold the place which in fact is the Word, where stands God, the never changing, never swerving' and also 'the world of our senses'" (Williamson, *Jews*, p. 110).

saying, "Abba, Father" (Ἀββά, λέγουσα, ὁ πατήρ; *Protrept.* 9.88.2-3).[52]

This idea of the governance of Christ gives one an interesting insight into how Clement employed the Philonic and Stoic[53] doctrines of the *Logos* in formulating a Christian understanding of the relationship between the Father and the Son: "all activity of the Lord is referred to the Almighty, the Son being, so to speak, a certain activity of the Father" (ὡς εἰπεῖν πατρική τις ἐνέργεια ὁ υἱός, *Strom.* 7.2.7).[54]

In *Stromateis* 2.5, speaking of Christ, the *Logos*, Clement says, "... he gave the law by the mouth of the prophets, enjoining and teaching most distinctly what things are to be done, and what not" (see also *Paed.* 1.7.60). This statement translates into Clement's idea that the righteous life is properly the fulfillment of the purpose of the *Logos*. This purpose involves three areas: (1) habits and customs, (2) voluntary or conscious acts, and (3) doctrinal revelation. In other words, the *Logos* acts in the role of παιδαγωγός or διδάσκαλος[55] in order to bring about the divinization of the human being. This educational process is necessary because the remedy for sin is education.[56] As he says, "Sinning arises from being unable to determine what ought to be done, or being unable to do it..." (*Strom.* 2.15).

In *Stromateis* 2 it is clear that Clement draws his ideas concerning the necessity of education from Plato, particularly the *Laws* (see *Strom.* 2.4 *passim.*). It was Plato's belief that the lawgiver should supervise all the activities of the citizens and should instruct them as to right and wrong. In short, the legislator has an educational role. Clement transforms this lawgiver into the *Logos* (*Strom.* 2.5). The *Logos*, working through the Church, serves an educational role in the life of the believer (see *Strom.* 7.2.6). This educational role is further illuminated through the application of moral norms to the believers' lives, which involves both persuasion and coercion.[57] As the lawgiver, the *Logos'* role is to instruct and educate the children (non-gnostics?) in the Church (see *Laws* 857c-e). This is done by

---

[52] "'Abba, Father,' means that beyond this celestial unity of reason and love are still the lofty heights of God" (Casey, "Clement of Alexandria," p. 119).

[53] For more information see Stead, *Christian Antiquity*, pp. 50-51.

[54] See Williamson, *Jews*, p. 108, quoted in note 49 above.

[55] See Van Den Hoek, "The 'Catechetical' School of Early Christian Alexandria," p. 64 n. 23 for a discussion of the terms διδάσκαλος and παιδαγωγός.

[56] Cf., Plutarch, *Moralia*, 439c-f; Plato, *Lysis* 208c, 223a.

[57] See R. F. Stalley, *An Introduction to Plato's Laws* (Indianapolis, IN: Hackett Publishing Co., 1983), p. 42.

means of preambles which use persuasion rather than threats to produce the required behavior (see *Laws* 722c-723d). Part of training people in the right behavior involves the "correct training of the emotions."[58] More than this, Plato believes "that only a limited number of citizens can come to a fully rational understanding."[59] These two ideas seem to correspond very well with how Clement conceives the role of the *Logos* and the attendant role of the Church.[60]

According to Plato, the divine aspect in the human being (i.e., the soul) and its virtue is to be preferred above all human goods (see *Laws* 631b-c, 697b, 726-728c). Within the soul it is the immortal element of reason (*logos*), not the mortal elements (the passions and desires), which is divine (see *Laws* 644c-645c, 713e).[61] Wisdom has first place among the divine goods and looks to reason (*logos*) as its leader (*Laws* 631c-d). One honors the soul by resisting the blandishments of pleasure and by enduring pain and fear (*Laws* 727c). Thus, the goal of the Platonic life is to struggle against pleasure in order to subordinate one's self to the dictates of reason (*logos*).[62]

According to Clement, everything which is contrary to sound reason (παρὰ τὸν λόγον τὸν ὀρθόν) is sin, and virtue is a disposition of the soul in agreement with reason throughout the whole of life (see *Paed.* 1.13). Sin is the misuse of reason and the instability of the emotions (see *Strom.* 2.15 quoted above). The righteous life is then defined as a system of rational behavior, the continuous fulfillment of the teaching of reason (see *Paed.* 1.13.102.3).[63] In short, the *Logos* uses various means to educate: some listen to persuasion but others must be threatened. This disciplinary action on the part of the *Logos* is not to be seen as dysphoric. God disciplines out of love, argues Clement. God's seeming anger is really a sign of divine

---

[58] Stalley, *Plato's Laws*, p. 43.

[59] Stalley, *Plato's Laws*, p. 43.

[60] E.g., *Strom.* 7.1.3.

[61] Cf. *Timaeus* 42c-44d, 69d-e.

[62] Stalley makes the same point: "By right education the disorderly motions of the lower, mortal soul can be subordinated to those of reason" (*Plato's Laws*, p. 67); cf. *Timaeus* 44c, 87a-b.

[63] καὶ γὰρ ὁ βίος ὁ χριστιανῶν ὃν παιδαγωγούμεθα νῦν, σύστημά τί ἐστι λογικῶν πράξεων, τουτέστιν τῶν ὑπὸ τοῦ διδασκομένων ἀδιάπως ἐνέργεια ἣν δὴ πίστιν κεκλήκαμεν. Casey comments on Clement's understanding here by saying, "'Reason' in this connection is ambiguous, since it may refer either to the mind of man or to the divine Logos, but it is probable that both are intended and the Logos is conceived as guiding men by the natural processes of their thought and by the commandments he has issued in Scripture for them to obey" (Casey, "Clement of Alexandria," p. 105.).

love, and God's so-called wrathful acts are designed to cure humanity of sin. Thus, they are not signs of ill but of good will (see *Paed.* 1.8.70.1).

God has a definite legislation for the cosmos: to bring humans into a state of salvation. In this process God is intimately involved. Clement quotes an old Pythagorean dictum in this regard: "God is one and is not, as some suppose, outside creation but in it, existing wholly in the whole cycle, cause and guardian of all, the blending of the universe and fashioner of his own power of all his works, the giver of light in heaven, and father of the universe, mind and animating principle of the whole cycle, mover of all" (*Protrept.* 6.72.4-5). This does not mean, however, that God compels persons to be saved. No, Clement is careful to avoid such an idea with respect to God. Drawing upon Plato's *Republic* (617e), he says that "the conditions laid down by God are equal for all, and no blame can attach to him; but he who is able will choose, and he who wills prevails" (*Strom.* 7.3.20). God's power draws people to God's self, and through the use of persuasion (in order to uphold the doctrine of free will) God draws persons into a state of salvation (*Strom.* 7.2.10). Clement contends that it is God's constant purpose to save humanity, and if they would only believe and repent, all humans can be saved (*Protrept.* 11.116.1). "This fixed intention on God's part is the sure proof of his friendly concern for man, his φιλανθρωπία."[64] This idea of universalism is derived, also, from Platonic philosophy.

Although sometimes overlooked by scholars, faith plays a prominent role in the soteriology of *Stromateis* 2, just as it does in Romans 10-12. Clement lays down a number of theses with respect to faith (πίστις) that extrapolate his use of the term. I will only deal with one. *Faith is based on choice, which is founded on desire, and is intellectual in nature* (*Strom.* 2.2). This understanding of faith is grounded firmly in the doctrine of free will. This is important because it is only through the process of rational choice that human beings exercise their ability to be like God. Rational choice, or intellectual assent, is the foundation for proper action. As he says, "And since choice is the beginning of action, faith is discovered to be the beginning of action, being the foundation of rational choice in the case of any one who exhibits to himself the previous demonstration through faith" (*Strom.* 2.2).

The goal of the righteous life is to perform deeds conformable to reason. Reasonable deeds are manifest in all cultures (see *Strom.* 2.2). "Voluntarily to follow what is useful, is the first principle of understanding" (*Strom.* 2.2; see also 2.3.11). In short, Clement's primary understanding of faith is grounded in what a contemporary theologian

---

[64] Casey, "Clement of Alexandria," p. 97.

would call "the common faith or experience of all men simply as such."[65] In other words, to be a human being is to practice the art of choice.

Choice is based on a deliberate preconception or anticipation (πρόληψις ἑκούσιος), which is the faith or experience common to all human beings simply as such. For example, Albert Camus writes, "We *choose* to continue existing from the moment we do not let ourselves die, and thus we recognize a value, at least, a relative one, in life."[66] In this instance what Clement is saying is twofold. First, he is acknowledging that all human beings possess a common faith (ἡ κοινὴ πίστις; *Strom.* 5.1) which underlies our most basic rational choices. It is something so basic to existence that we make no initial choice for it nor do we reflect much on it (cf. *Strom.* 2.4.16). This common faith, being common, exists in all cultures. It is our initial contact with the grace of God (see *Strom.* 2.4; cf. Rom. 1.18-20).

Second, there is a "special" faith based on common faith along with instruction and the word of God. This "special" faith is the type Clement is referring to in *Strom.* 2.4.1 when he says, "But we, who have heard by the Scriptures that self-determining choice and refusal have been given by the Lord to men, rest in the infallible criterion of faith, manifesting a willing spirit, since we have chosen life and believe God through his voice." This faith is necessary because knowledge (ἐπιστήμη; *Strom.* 2.17.1) has been submerged in ignorance. It is not until knowledge is properly reconstituted by means of faith that a human being has the opportunity to experience the process of salvation. "[T]eaching is reliable when faith on the part of those who hear, being so to speak, a sort of natural art, contributes to the process of learning" (*Strom.* 2.6). In other words, through the "special" faith offered by the *Logos*, human beings have the opportunity to live a righteous life, a life in conformity with the commandments of God.

---

[65] Schubert Ogden, "The Strange Witness of Unbelief," *The Reality of God and Other Essays* (Dallas, Texas: Southern Methodist University Press, 1992), p. 124.

[66] Albert Camus, "The Riddle," *Atlantic Monthly* (June, 1963), p. 85 (emphasis mine). This also appears to be the understanding of faith expressed in *Strom.* 2.4.12.

One's service to God, which Clement calls θεραπεία θεοῦ,[67] is brought about through a process of self-discipline and cherishing one's divine aspect (*Strom.* 7.1).[68] Self-discipline in this case appears to be obedience to the commandments of God.[69] This obedience, in turn, appears to assist the gnostic in cherishing his or her divine aspect. In a Stoic definition of godliness, Clement says it is "the habit of mind which preserves the fitting attitude toward God" (*Strom.* 7.1.3). This "habit of mind" is knowledge of both the theory and practice of right living, by which the gnostic progresses in the process of becoming divine (*Strom.* 7.1.3).[70]

As noted above, there is an element of universalism in Clement's theology.[71] This appears to have been developed in conversation with groups such as the Valentinian gnostics. In distinction to the Valentinians, Clement shows that all righteous persons are in reality equal and perfected in the sight of God. "The notion of this perfection is one of Clement's subtlest thoughts, for in spite of the assertion that Christians share in the perfection of Christ, the meaning is not that Christ and Christians are exactly alike."[72] Perfection (τελείωσις) is understood by Clement in a relative and not an absolute sense. The Clementine doctrine of salvation does not exclude important differences between the *Logos* and the believers, nor does it obscure important differences among believers themselves; but perfection and equality are posited solely in terms of God's providential purpose, which may vary from case to case. The righteous are perfect, not because they all have the same measure of faith or gifts,

---

[67] Jane Harrison explains the term θεραπεία in the following manner: "θεραπεία, service, tendance, covered a large part, perhaps the largest, area of [the Greek] conception of religion. It was a word expressing, not indeed in the Christian sense a religion whose mainspring was love, but at least a religion based on a rational and quite cheerful mutual confidence" (Jane Ellen Harrison, *Prolegomena to the Study of Greek Religion* [Cambridge: Cambridge University Press, 1903; repr. Oxford: Princeton University Press, 1991], p. 4); cf. what H. W. Pleket says about the term: "θεραπεία could denote both the worship of the suppliant and the service of the domestic servant" ("Religious History as the History of Mentality: The 'Believer' as Servant of the Deity in the Greek World," *Faith, Hope, and Worship*, p. 159). Read further in Pleket for a longer discussion of the term.

[68] Cf. Stead, *Christian Antiquity*, p. 61.

[69] Following Stoic teaching, Clement says, "belief and obedience are in our power" (7.3.16); cf. Williamson, *Jews*, p. 114, where he notes that for Philo the changes brought about by the *Logos* are ethical as well as mystical and intellectual.

[70] See Casey, "Clement of Alexandria," p. 134, where he holds that for Clement the *imitatio Dei* is intellectual.

[71] See *Stromateis* 7.2.6.

[72] Casey, "Clement of Alexandria," p. 111.

but because in knowing God they have equally realized the divine will and can fulfill with equal acceptability God's purpose for them.[73]

The Seed of Abraham, the Israelites, and the Law

So far, I have attempted to use to most wide-ranging language possible when discussing Clement's theology (e.g., righteous life instead of Christian life, or "special" faith instead of Christian faith). The rationale has been not to pigeon-hole the language of Clement unnecessarily. As he says, "[W]isdom is intelligence, but all intelligence is not wisdom" (*Strom.* 2.5). In this sense the historical link between the Alexandrian Christian community and the Alexandrian Jewish community is important, because it forces one to reflect on the radically altered relationship between both groups during the second century. It is quite apparent that Clement has no first-hand experience with Judaism.[74] This separation of Jews and Christians was the byproduct of the revolt of 115-117 CE. Anti-Jewish polemic was rife in Alexandria during Clement's time period,[75] and his portrayal of Judaism appears indebted more to a caricature of Jews than to actual contacts.[76] The upshot of this is that Clement's understanding of Judaism is biased, and he tends to place the Jews in the same polemical category as the gnostics whose theology he attempts to invalidate. "For they did not know and do the will of the law; but what they supposed, what they thought the law wished" (*Strom.* 2.9).

The intellectual connection between Alexandrian Christianity and Alexandrian Judaism is without question. The historical connection between the two groups in Alexandria appears reasonably valid. Yet, by the time of Clement there appears to be little to no contact between Christians and Jews in the city—at least using Clement as a barometer. Now the central issue of this paper can be raised: according to Clement, what will happen to the Jews?

A great deal of *Stromateis* 2 discusses the efficacy of the law as presented in the Hebrew Bible. As pointed out earlier, Clement believed

---

[73] Casey, "Clement of Alexandria," p. 111.

[74] Van Den Hoek, "The 'Catechetical' School of Early Christian Alexandria," pp. 80, 82; cf. Christopher Haas who says, "While Clement seems to have been acquainted with at least one Jew in the city, most of his knowledge of Judaism appears to have been acquired at second or third hand" (*Alexandria in Late Antiquity*, pp. 105-106).

[75] Haas says, "While the image of the Jews improved markedly in literature produced elsewhere, Greco-Egyptian literature in the second and third centuries continues to portray Jews in a bitter and degrading manner" (*Alexandria in Late Antiquity*, p. 108).

[76] Van Den Hoek notes, "Only on a few occasions do the words Ἰουδαῖος or Ἰουδαῖοι [in Clement] seem to refer to living people" ("The 'Catechetical' School of Early Christian Alexandria," p. 80 n. 105).

the law to have been given by the *Logos*. This makes it valid and worthy to be followed. As he says, "God deemed it advantageous that from the law and the prophets men should receive a preparatory discipline by the Lord, the fear of the Lord was called the beginning of wisdom, being given by the Lord, through Moses, to the disobedient and hard of heart" (*Strom.* 2.8). The law is called the paedagogue (παιδαγωγός) to Christ (*Strom.* 2.7; cf., Gal. 3.24). The law is right reason (*Strom.* 2.4). It is just (*Strom.* 2.8), and the work of the Lord (*Strom.* 2.12). The "law given to us enjoins us to shun what are in reality bad things—adultery, uncleanness, paederasty, ignorance, wickedness, soul-disease, death (not that which severs the soul from the body, but that which severs the soul from truth)" (*Strom.* 2.7). In short, the law is the *Logos* -implanted truth in Jewish culture, and is superior even to the philosophy of the Greeks (see *Strom.* 2.18). "For those are in truth impious who separate the useful from that which is right according to the law" (*Strom.* 2.22).

Fear is an integral aspect of obedience to the law. The logic for this position proceeds from Clement's understanding of the divine educational project. It is necessary for God to coerce some to act properly (see *Strom.* 2.6). "For those whom reason convinces not, fear tames" (*Strom.* 2.8). This coercion "does not itself generate faith" (*Strom.* 2.6). Fear is the instrument of faith that leads one to salvation. In this respect, fear should not be seen as something bad—as "an irrational aberration, and perturbation of mind" (*Strom.* 2.7)—but as an entirely rational means to instruct one in righteousness. In fact, Clement says that if the philosophical desire to quibble about what he means by fear, he says "let the philosophers term the fear of the law, cautious fear (εὐλάβεια), which is a shunning agreeable to reason" (*Strom.* 2.7).

There is a definite connection between faith and the law. "Learning, then, is also obedience to the commandments, which is faith in God... the highest demonstration, to which we alluded, produces intelligent faith by the adducing and opening up of the Scriptures to the souls of those who desire to learn; the result of which is knowledge (*gnosis*)" (*Strom.* 2.11). Common faith is the foundation upon which "special" faith is built. "Special" faith is nourished through instruction by the *Logos*. The law, and the fear that accompanies it, is an acceptable divine instrument for leading one to salvation. In other words, the new covenant does not nullify the old. Clement makes this clear when he says, "'Now the just shall live by faith,' which is according to the covenant and the commandments; since these, which are two in name and time, given in accordance with the [divine] economy—being in power one—the old and the new, are dispensed through the Son by one God" (*Strom.* 2.6).

If the Jews have the law, and the law has not been nullified under the new covenant, then is it possible that the Jews who possess faith can be saved? This question raises the issue of Clement's presentation of Jews in this text. It cannot be denied that Clement gives some seemingly disparaging remarks about Jews. At the beginning of the treatise, he speaks of the possibility of a Jew reading the text and being converted: "if perchance the Jew also may listen and be able quietly to turn from what he has believed to him on whom he has not believed" (*Strom.* 2.1). Furthermore, the central critique in the treatise regarding Jews comes directly from Clement's reading of Romans 10.2, 3: "For [the Jews] did not know and do the will of the law; but what they supposed, what they thought the law wished" (*Strom.* 2.9).

As mentioned earlier, this critique places the Jews in the same category with the Greeks and the gnostic heretics, who also misunderstand the teaching of the *Logos*. Central to this critique is the issue of scriptural interpretation. He says, "And [the Jews] did not believe the law as prophesying, but the bare word; and they followed through fear, not through disposition and faith" (*Strom.* 2.9). Clement disparages the Jews for not reading the relevant scriptural texts in the same manner as Christians like himself. That is, Clement's method for reading the text places prophecy at the center of scriptural interpretation. Instead of the Jewish practice of reading the prophets as an interpretation of the law, Clement understands the prophets to be disclosing information that is to be understood in addition to the law. Moreover, Clement understands prophecy to be at work in texts not usually understood to be prophetic (e.g., the idea of the seed of Abraham). In this he follows a tradition laid down by Paul in Romans and Galatians.

The first quotation from Romans 10 comes in 2.6 when, quoting Isaiah, he echoes Paul: "Lord, who has believed our report?" (Rom. 10.16; Isa. 53.1). This is followed by Rom. 10.17: "For 'faith cometh by hearing, and hearing by the word of God,' saith the apostle." Subsequently, Clement quotes Rom. 10.14, 15. This leads him to his conclusion: "You see how he brings faith by hearing, and the preaching of the apostles, up to the word of the Lord, and to the Son of God." That is, faith serves as the basis upon which one builds *gnosis*. Now it is not clear as to whether Clement is referring to common faith here or not. What is clear is that this faith serves as the foundation for further learning. Faith itself is not enough. Faith makes one receptive to the teaching of the *Logos* (*Strom.* 2.6). Yet, receptivity does not exclude the need for rational choice. The believer must still choose to follow: "[T]he divine word cries, calling all together; knowing perfectly well those that will not obey; notwithstanding then since to obey or not is in our own power, provided we have not the excuse of ignorance to adduce" (*Strom.* 2.6).

Leaving the implications of ignorance aside, Clement continues his argument by saying, "[The *Logos*] makes a just call, and demands of each according to his strength" (*Strom.* 2.6). In other words, he is drawing on his doctrine of salvation. He says that some are able to reach the fullness of the righteous state, but others, who are not able, have the will or desire to improve. The linchpin is ignorance, and a person can progress only when (s)he is not ignorant.

Drawing upon Rom. 9.4, Clement says that "[The faithful servants] are entrusted with the utterances respecting God and the divine words, the commands with the execution of the injunctions" (*Strom.* 2.6). Here he has clearly altered the Pauline text. In Romans, the Jews are the ones who possess the covenants and the divine commandments. The intent in *Stromateis* appears to be a desire for greater inclusivity. This thesis, I believe, is confirmed when Clement says, "For we are Israelites, who are convinced not by signs, but by hearing" (*Strom.* 2.6). That is, Israelites (or the seed of Abraham) can be either Jews or Gentiles as long as their faith is founded upon hearing. Drawing upon Rom. 10.12 (ὁ γάρ αὐτὸς [ἐστιν] κύριος πάντων), 9.4, and John 14.2, Clement argues for a greater inclusivity based on the inclusive nature of monotheism: "And if the same mansions are promised by prophecy to us and to the patriarchs, the God of both the covenants is shown to be one" (*Strom.* 2.6).

Clement's next statement is troubling for two reasons. First, because it does not appear in the Romans text. Second, because it could suggest that Christians have supplanted Jews as the people of God. It reads: "Thou hast inherited the covenant of Israel" (*Strom.* 2.6). Given what follows, it appears that the best way to understand this statement is to say that Gentiles have inherited the covenant of Israel along with the Jews. This makes sense given that the next statement involves the inclusion of Gentiles into the plan of salvation, and is followed by a statement (quoted above) that maintains that both covenants are in reality one in the divine economy. Furthermore, Clement appears to take on a salvation history perspective when, quoting Rom. 1.17, he says, "… the one salvation which from prophecy to the Gospel is perfected by one and the same Lord" (*Strom.* 2.6). Thus, it appears reasonable to say that Clement's soteriology takes a salvation history perspective and argues not for the displacing of Judaism by Christianity but for the inclusion of Gentiles into the plan of salvation.

The crucial passage concerning Jews in *Stromateis* 2 comes in 2.9. In this section, Clement quotes Paul's famous statement from Rom. 10.2-3 regarding the zeal of the Jews. He then castigates them for their ignorance: "For they did not know and do the will of the law; but what they supposed, what they thought the law wished." This again raises the issue of ignorance. Earlier, in 2.6, Clement has argued that ignorance disables the individual in that the individual cannot know what is right. This is sin (*Strom.* 2.15). As mentioned earlier, the reason for this sin arises from a misinterpretation of scripture, i.e., the Jews "did not believe the law as prophesying" (*Strom.* 2.9).

Following the argument in Rom. 10.19-21,[77] Clement maintains that the Jews are responsible for their own sin. Their disobedience has cut them off from the truth. Yet, it is also their disobedience that opens up the possibility for the salvation of the Gentiles. This turn of events merits the Jews another opportunity for salvation. He says, "Then the goodness of God is shown also in their case..." (*Strom.* 2.9). The extension of salvation to the Gentiles is meant to provoke the Jews to jealousy and willingness to repent.[78] So, it appears that Clement holds that Jews have not been displaced by Christians in the process of salvation. What they need is education, given that repentance is tardy knowledge. This is made all the more intriguing when read in light of *Stromateis* 6.14:

> So that when we hear, "Thy faith hath saved thee," we do not
> understand him to say absolutely that those who have believed
> in any way whatever shall be saved, unless also works follow.
> But it was to the Jews alone that he spoke this utterance, who
> kept the law and lived blamelessly, who wanted only faith in
> the Lord.

It appears that Clement holds out the strong conviction that Jews will be saved, when they accept the Lord. In this conviction he is clearly following the apostle Paul. "Paul seriously counts on it that the Gentile mission will make Israel jealous and lead to its conversion. This hope can be imagined only if the conversion itself stand beyond any doubt and only the way to it obscure."[79]

This thesis is further validated by the passage that follows. Clement cannot speak on how the salvation of the Jews will be effected in the future, but he can account for how those Jews preceding the Lord are saved. He says,

> And the Shepherd, speaking plainly of those who had fallen
> asleep, recognises certain righteous among Gentiles and Jews,
> not only before the appearance of Christ, but before the law,

---

[77] Except, of course, for the quotation of 10.4 immediately preceding this section.

[78] Clement quotes Rom. 11.11 at this point. Moreover, he has already informed us as to what he means by repentance in 2.6: "For repentance is tardy knowledge, and primitive innocence is knowledge. Repentance, then, is an effect of faith." In other words, in order to be able to repent one must already possess faith.

[79] Ernst Käsemann, *Commentary on Romans*, trans. and ed. Geoffrey W. Bromiley (Grand Rapids: Eerdmans, 1980), p. 304. Daniel Patte makes similar point in his exegesis of the passage. See Patte, *Paul's Faith and the Power of the Gospel: A Structural Introduction to the Pauline Letters* (Philadelphia: Fortress, 1983), pp. 291-293.

in virtue of acceptance before God—as Abel, as Noah, as any other righteous man (*Strom.* 2.9).[80]

God has prepared a means for the righteous dead to receive salvation. They are preached to *post mortem* and receive the "seal"[81] of Christ: "they fell asleep in righteousness and in great purity, but wanted only this seal" (*Strom.* 2.9).[82]

So what will become of the Jews? They will be saved, or at least a portion of them will be saved. Clement is not unambiguously clear on this matter. Still, what is apparent is that Christianity has not displaced Judaism, and that the rejection of the Jewish scriptures by certain gnostic groups represents a misunderstanding of the process of salvation. *Stromateis* 2 thus stands at a significant point in the history of Christian theology and scriptural interpretation. It represents a Christian attempt to define itself over against its Jewish predecessor, but in a way that acknowledges its dependence upon Jewish historical and intellectual roots. Paul's discussion of Jews in Romans 10-11 serves as the perfect tool for the accomplishment of this aim.

---

[80] It is interesting that the image of the shepherd also appears in *Strom.* 6.14.

[81] The seal is the "seal of preaching."

[82] None of this appears in the Romans text, but is derived mainly from Hermas.

Readings of Augustine on Paul: their impact on critical studies of Paul.

John K. Riches
University of Glasgow, Glasgow G12 8QQ

Anti-Lutheran readings of Paul, so readily accepted today, have roots more complex than is perhaps always appreciated. Their progenitor, Albert Schweitzer, in his *Paul and his Interpreters*[1] offered a sustained polemic against Lutheran scholars' refusal to recognise the importance of apocalyptic eschatology in Paul. On the one hand, he argued, traditional Lutheran theologians over-emphasised the juridical aspects of Paul's theology and failed to recognise the importance of the cosmological, dualist aspects of Paul's thought.[2] On the other, the History of Religions school read Paul's 'mysticism' in terms of a (so-called) Hellenistic dualism which simply contrasted the heavenly and the earthly world. Faith was then seen as the entering into a new existence of immortality, a rebirth. By contrast, Schweitzer maintained, Paul's eschatology referred to an existence caught up in profound cosmological change, where both the heavenly and the earthly worlds are being changed. The Messianic world is coming into being; the old earthly world, in bondage to angelic powers is being liberated and transformed as it is brought into the new reality of the Messianic age.[3]

At root Schweitzer's protest is a protest against *any* attempt to read Paul exclusively within an ethical/juridical framework. This is directed both against a Lutheranism which sees salvation as the acquittal of the sinner before God; or against the more

---

[1]German edition: *Die Geschichte der paulinischen Forschung*, Tübingen, 1911.

[2]Writing of Otto Everling's *Die paulinische Angelologie und Dämonologie*, 1888, he says: `From the moment when Paul's statements regarding God, the devil, the angels, and the world are apprehended in their organic connexion, it becomes abundantly evident that for him redemption, in its primary and fundamental sense, consists in a deliverance from the powers which have their abode between heaven and earth. It is therefore essentially a future good, dependent on a cosmic event of universal scope.' *Interpreters*, 57.

romantic/Idealist forms of Protestantism to be found in the History of Religions school[4] which see faith as the assumption of a new form of God-consciousness, through which the Christian spirit transcends its this-worldly limitations. Against these Schweitzer asserts that Paul's theology is cast in terms of a cosmic dualism: it speaks of the overthrow of the angelic powers, which hold men and women in thrall, the invasion of the earthly sphere by the triumphant messiah and the transformation of the earthly into 'supersensual' reality.

More recent anti-Lutheran polemic is not always directly related to Schweitzer's. Krister Stendahl's *Paul among Jews and Gentiles*.[5] goes back to lectures given thirty-five years ago and has its (autobiographical) setting in a United States which is 'the first place in the modern world since Philo's Alexandria where Jews and Christians as people, as religious communities, and as learned communities, live together in a manner and in sufficient numbers to allow for open dialogue.'[6] It is a worthy successor to Schweitzer, witty, sparkling, with a fine sense of where the nerve of those Lutheran/Protestant sensibilities lies, which have so profoundly conditioned our understanding of Paul. Whereas Schweitzer relegated justification by faith to the position of a *'Nebenkrater'* of Pauline thought, whose centre, 'participation in Christ', lay in a wholly different mode of dualistic thinking, Stendahl reads Paul's utterances about justification by faith within the context of what he sees as Paul's fundamental concern: the question of the relation between Jews and Gentiles once the Messiah has come. Paul is not dealing in theological abstractions, but essentially attending to questions about the relation of these two *peoples* in the light of his own call to be apostle to the Gentiles. In making this proposal Stendahl is not, however, totally rejecting the juridical/ethical framework for interpreting Paul; he is merely attacking one particular type of juridical interpretation, one which sees Paul dealing in *universal* problems defined in terms of the radical failure of the human will (sin) and which therefore look more

---

[3]*Interpreters*, 223-4.

[4]Cf. Mark D. Chapman's excellent article: `Religion, Ethics and the History of Religion School', **SJTh** 46 (1993) 43-78: `most of the members of the History of Religion School sought refuge in a primordial mystical experience expressive of non-rational feelings, of emotions, moods and fantasies.' 43-4.

[5]Philadelphia, 1976.

[6]*PaJG*, 37.

closely, *'introspectively'*, at the nature of the will and its opera-
tions. By contrast, Stendahl argues, Paul and Pauline Jewish
Christianity were both *particularist* and *robust*. The questions
which exercised them vigorously were ones about the rights and
duties of Gentiles now that the Messiah had come and Paul had
been called to be apostle to the Gentiles. They are indeed discussed within a juridical frame of discourse; but the answers are
cast in the form of a redefinition of *community* norms, not of
exploring the springs of the human will.

To see this is to see how different is the anti-Lutheran
polemic of E. P. Sanders. For Sanders, the trouble with Lutheran
studies of Paul is two-fold: 1) that they read Lutheran polemics
against a mediaeval, Pelagian 'works-righteousness' back into
Paul's debates with Judaizers; 2) that they construe faith and salvation in fundamentally juridical/ethical terms (faith as obedience,
trust, etc.), whereas at the heart of Paul's religion lies the belief
that Christians 'really are one body and one Spirit with Christ'[7].
Sanders, that is to say, rejects *all* attempts to construe Paul in
juridical/ethical terms. Such terms are readily turned to in
attempts to read Paul for to-day; Paul's actual language of participation in Christ is altogether more elusive to the modern mind.[8]

The enormous influence of such attacks on Lutheran readings
of Paul cannot be gainsaid. They have forced scholars to
reconsider their views of first century Judaism and of Paul's place
within it; they have encouraged a more sustained investigation of
Paul's engagement with Jewish apocalyptic eschatology, however
alien such beliefs may appear to those within the broad cultural
traditions of the West. Within this attempt to re-orientate
Christian/Protestant readings of Paul, readings of Augustine's
Confessions have played a small but not insignificant part. Luther
believed that he could find support in Augustine for his own views
of faith and salvation. If then one could show that Augustine had
misread Paul, that indeed he belonged to a very different world
from Paul, this would clearly cut the support and show Luther as
belonging to a different cultural world. This is what Stendahl

---

[7] *Paul and Palestinian Judaism,* London, 1978, 522.

[8] ' We seem to lack a category of "reality" - real participation in Christ, real
possession of the Spirit - which lies between naive cosmological speculation
and belief in magical transference on the one hand and a revised self-
understanding on the other. I must confess that I do not have a new
category of perception to propose here.' *PPJ*, 522f.

attempts in a short passage in *PaJG*: 'Augustine, who has perhaps rightly been called the first truly Western man, was the first person in Antiquity or Christianity to write something so self-centered as his own spiritual autobiography, his *Confessions*. It was he who applied Paul's doctrine of justification to the problem of the introspective conscience, to the question: "On what basis does a person find salvation?"'(16) It was therefore Augustine who started the whole history of Western introspection, which ran through into the struggles of late mediaeval piety, to which Luther sought an answer. Stendahl's views of the value of this tradition are not in doubt. 'The introspective conscience is a Western development and a Western plague.' (17)

Clearly if all this is true, a major barrier has been erected between Paul and Lutheran interpretations of Paul. Augustine writes the first spiritual autobiography; develops (invents?) the introspective mode of consciousness; asks the question about *personal* salvation (as opposed to questions about communal norms and salvation) and first reads Paul in this mode. In that case, such moods and achievements can no longer be laid at Paul's door. But does Augustine really quite do all this? And what, if anything, follows for the interpretation of Paul and Romans, if some of these claims need qualification?

In what sense, then, did Augustine, write the first spiritual autobiography? Two observations. a) There are clearly earlier autobiographies, of which Josephus' *Vita* is one obvious example, which are self-centred enough. Was it a *spiritual* autobiography? Certainly not of the same kind of sophistication or indeed inwardness as the *Confessions*. It records Josephus' early religious search for a suitable type of religious observance from among those on offer within Judaism, but in the end it is not some inward concern which drives his choice, but concerns about public life and his standing within it.9 Similar concerns lie behind most of what follows, as he seeks to demonstrate his own virtue and valour and honour over against his adversary, Justus.10 There is

---

9*Vita*, 9-13, see S.N. Mason, 'Was Josephus a Pharisee? A Re-examination of *Life* 10-12', *JJS* 40,31-45. See also A.L. Baumgarten, *The Flourishing of Jewish Sects in the Maccabean Era: An Interpretation*, Leiden, 1997, 52: 'there is no doubt that the pattern which Josephus claimed to have followed, *of having tried out several groups before making a final choice*, was typical.'

10*Vita*, 340.

certainly an immense difference of tone and mood between this and the *Confessions*. But what if one then tries to place Paul on a scale of 'spirituality' running from Josephus to Augustine? Certainly Paul is concerned with his standing within the churches, both his 'own' and others, like Rome and Jerusalem. But the deeds of valour which he puts forward are strange catalogues of weakness and trials, where the crucial factor is his own 'imitation' of or participation in Christ's life, death (and resurrection). Of course Paul does not write an autobiography, but there is surely no disputing the confessional nature of Galatians and 2 Corinthians, whatever view one may take of Romans 7.

Are there other earlier works of an indirectly 'spiritual autobiographical' nature? Nancy Shumate in *Crisis and Conversion in Apuleius' Metamorphoses*[11] argues that the *Metamorphoses* belong to a broad genre of conversion narratives which embraces Augustine's *Confessions*, Dante's *Divine Comedy*, even the works of Sartre. It is not just that the novel ends up with a description of Lucius' conversion to the Isis cult, but that the earlier books portray the breakdown of the epistemological and moral foundations of his world, which leads up to his entering the cult.

Thus, for all the differences of genre, there are important links between the *Confessions* and the *Metamorphoses*: 'The basic pattern uniting the *Confessions* and the *Metamorphoses* goes deeper than any conventional act-oriented notion of sin and redemption. It hinges on the idea that the sensible world in all its aspects is characterized by *fallacia* ... Both narrators describe a past when they found themselves entangled in a widely accepted web of false values as an equation involving desire and pleasure: their problems began, each narrator suggests, because virtually all their activities were driven by misguided desires.'[12] Such desire relates not only to food and drink (*voluptaria cupiditatis fallacia*: 10.31.44) but also to intellectual pursuits, such as Augustine's study of rhetoric (4.16.30, speaking of his pursuit of these

---

[11]Ann Arbor, 1996.

[12]Shumate, 203-4. Public spectacle is another matter which is the object of false desire, cf. the description of Alypius' attraction to the public games in Carthage: 'The cesspool of Carthaginian morals had absorbed him with its passion for frivolous shows and had drawn him into a mad obsession with the games in the circus ... but I myself neglected to try to persuade him not to destroy his good character by his blind and headlong desire for empty spectacles (*vanorum ludorum caeco et pracipiti studio*)' *Conf.* 6.7.

'meretricious desires', *meretriciae cupiditates*). Of his teachers he writes: 'They assumed that I would try to satisfy the insatiable desires for the poverty that they call wealth and the infamy that they call glory (*ad satiandas insatiabiles cupiditates copiosae inopiae et ignominosae gloriae'*, 1.12.19). Similar language, linking desire not only to sexual activity but also to envy, jealousy, religious divisions and theological disputes can be found in Gal 5:16-21. Thus, if Shumate is right, Augustine is not without at least one North African precursor, who depicted a man's breakdown and loss of his former world-view and his more or less sudden acquisition of a new one. Again, there are links to be made to the Paul who described his old world as σκύβαλα (*skubala*) and his new mode of life as καινὴ κτίσις (*kaine ktisis*).

The lines of division between Augustine and Paul may then not be so sharp as some of Stendahl's formulations may suggest. Not only was the language available to him give an account of the collapse of an individual's world view and ethos, but there were texts which applied such language to individuals and not just to collectivities.

All this however still leaves undiscussed the question of what is actually happening in the *Confessions*. How far is it true to say that it was Augustine 'who applied Paul's doctrine of justification to the problem of the introspective conscience'(16)? Here I must introduce a further major contribution to the debate, Paula Fredriksen's 1986 article, 'Paul and Augustine: conversion narratives, orthodox traditions, and the retrospective self.'[13] This is based on an enviable specialist knowledge of Augustine's writing and specifically of his scriptural exegesis and is a model of the kind of work that needs to be done in this field. Nevertheless, perhaps even a non-specialist may be allowed to raise a few questions.

Fredriksen presents the matter broadly thus: in the *Confessions* Bk 8, chs. 7-12 in recounting his conversion, Augustine 'recapitulates the theological themes that contour the first seven books...: the weight of sin on man the child of Adam; the weakness of the divided will in the face of carnal custom; man's absolute dependence on the freely given, inexplicable grace of God.' In the garden in Milan, he hears the voice commanding him to read Paul and he turns to Romans 13.13-4 and resolves to embark on a life of celibacy. By contrast, so Fredriksen, the writings of the earlier Cassiciacum period present a 'different person.

---

[13]*JThS* 37 (1986) 3-34.

This Augustine is perplexed by the problem of evil philosophically conceived. He again reports that he seized a book of Paul's letters, but they reveal to him the face, not of continence, but of Philosophy.[14] This is a different conversion, one viewed not as the struggle of the will, sin, and grace, but as progress in philosophy.'[15] Further, she argues, these fundamental differences in approach (philosophical/introspective-theological) correspond to different readings of Paul, notably of Romans. Paul 'scarcely appears in the Cassiciacum dialogues', only in effect where Augustine wishes, as in the *de moribus ecclesiae*, to reclaim him from the Manichees. When he does turn to Paul, in 395, Augustine 'pursue[s] the problem of moral evil through an analysis of the dynamics of love, memory, and human motivation as these express the interplay of grace and free-will. Nevertheless in 395, when he comments on Rom 7.15-16, Augustine 'argues against a deterministic reading...: the sinner under the Law ... can freely choose to respond in faith to God's call...' However in the *ad Simplicianum* (397) 'he argues that faith is not man's work, but

---

[14]*c. Acad.* II.ii.5.

[15]Fredriksen, 20.   Throughout her article she appeals to P. Brown, *Augustine of Hippo*, London, 1969, for support, here to his views that the account which Augustine offers of his conversion in the Cassiciacum period is one which stresses continuity and appears as 'an astonishingly tranquil process', Brown, 113. But Fredriksen ignores Brown's rather more nuanced account of the differences in presentation of the two accounts. Brown suggests that the tranquillity of the Cassiciacum writings 'may have had deep, personal roots' which were 'only revealed ten years later' and that the difference in presentation had a good deal to do with the different audiences for whom Augustine was writing: the Cassiciacum writings are formal works, which he `wrote as one public figure to other public men'.   The `classic scene in the garden is passed over in silence. Yet it is only in this scene that we can glimpse the depth of the reorientation which was taking place in Augustine.... When Augustine retired to Cassiciacum, a change had already taken place in him at that deep level.' 114.   Thus Brown emphasises the fundamental agreement between the two accounts: continuity was in fact a feature of Augustine's `conversion'; the later account brings out aspects which the earlier more formal account glosses over. His later emphasis on the deep `reorientation' which was occurring in him was not occasioned by subsequent pressures of ecclesiastical orthodoxy and the influence of the account of Paul's conversion in Acts 9, as Fredriksen asserts, but was a matter of `deep psychological authenticity', 114.

God's gift, and hence no ground for merit... Not man's will, but solely the absolutely unmerited gift of God's grace, can correctly orient man's love toward the Divine. Augustine makes his case exegetically in the *ad Simplicianum* and autobiographically in the *Confessions*, demonstrating it through his description in Book VIII of the conversion.'[16]

Fredriksen's explanation for the differences between Augustine's two versions of his conversion is two-fold: on the one hand Augustine is reacting to the pressures of his ecclesiastical situation on his return to North Africa in 389/390: '[t]here, before the watching eyes of his own church and its schismatic rival, the Donatists, Augustine had to confront publicly a well-organized Manichaean sect that based much of its deterministic and dualistic doctrine on the Pauline Epistles. To proceed against the Manichees, Augustine had to reclaim Paul.[17] On the other, his later reading of Paul is deeply influenced by the picture of Paul's conversion (itself inspired by ecclesiastical orthodoxy) in Acts 9.

Thus she concludes: 'Augustine's account of his conversion in the *Confessions,* in other words, is a theological reinterpretation of a past event, an attempt to render his past coherent to his present self.'[18]

Clearly this construction of the relationship of the *Confessions* to Augustine's 'philosophical' conversion can serve to draw a very sharp line between 'Augustinian', Western, introspective readings of Paul and Paul 'as he actually was'. It is powerfully argued and wonderfully earthed in Augustine's writings of the time. Nevertheless, in what follows I want to suggest that the developments in Augustine's beliefs about the will and grace throughout the 390's are a logical extension of the philosophical debates which he had conducted with Manichaeism in his Milan and Cassiciacum period, and continue his engagement with Paul which also had its roots in that period.

This can, I think best be done by showing how the philosophical debates continue to play a central role in the argument of the *Confessions*. Shumate, we have seen, portrays the *Confessions*, like the *Metamorphoses*, as a narrative of the breakdown of one set of epistemological and moral conventions and their replacement with another. The exchange of one set of metaphysical

---

[16]Fredriksen, 22-3.
[17]Fredriksen, 22.
[18]Fredriksen, 24.

beliefs for another, that is to say, is an integral part of the story that Augustine tells in the *Confessions*, together with the story of his grappling with his misplaced desires and his struggle to overcome his divided will. Moreover the two aspects of his conversion are related because the outcome of his metaphysical debate is to locate the source of evil precisely in the human will.

Let me then turn to the question of the place of philosophy in the *Confessions*. The first seven books document a many-stranded debate concerned, not only with the question of the will and human sinfulness, Augustine's in particular, but with questions of the unity of God, the nature of his presence in the world, the relation of the eternal, unchanging substance to the universe of finite and transitory existents; the question of God's supposed materiality, and of course the central challenge posed by the Manichees: whence is evil? Moreover it is important to see that the 'theological' questions of the weakness of the divided will in the face of carnal custom do not 'contour' these debates but flow directly from them.[19] For Augustine the prior question is how to conceive of the relation of an uncorruptible God to finite and corrupt existents in such a way as to uphold the unity of God. Platonist metaphysics provided an escape from Manichaean dualism, but raised the question of the nature and source of corruption in the world. If God was good and the only spiritual power, whence was evil, *unde malum* (7.5.1)?

Augustine's answer in Book VII, that it derives from the will, is formulated in the language of philosophy: 'And I enquired what iniquity was, and found it to be no substance, but the perversion of the will, turned aside from Thee, O God, the Supreme substance, towards these lower things...'(7.16.22) Once Augustine has come to the clear conviction that all things owe their being to God, in so far as they participate in him, though he alone is pure substance, then the origin of evil has to be sought in the corruption of dependent being. Things which are dependent on God, the supreme substance, are, since they are derived from God, but also

---

[19] Fredriksen makes, we have seen, makes a sharp distinction between Augustine's account of his conversion in *c. Acad*. II. ii.5 as a philosophical conversion and his account in Book 8 of the *Confessions*: which 'recapitulates the theological themes that contour the first seven books': sin, the divided will and grace, 'Paul and Augustine', 20. Now it is true that the conversion story in Book 8 does emphasise such themes, but not that they 'contour' the first seven books.

are not, because they are not what God is.(7.11.17) Within such a great chain of being, there is room for the corruption of that which is yet derived from God. Augustine sees that even things which are corrupted are still in a measure good, because they still exist and so are still dependent on the good. That is to say, things are corrupted in so far (but only in so far) as they are deprived of good (*omnia quae corrumperetur, privantur bono*). To be wholly corrupt, would therefore be to be wholly deprived of good, and therefore to cease to exist. Hence Augustine comes to his doctrine of evil as *privatio boni*, as a lack of goodness, of reality, which is of course in turn a rejection of cosmic dualism, which affirms the reality of evil, independent of the good. (7.11.18)

With the philosophical doctrine of *privatio boni* Augustine firmly turns his back on any kind of dualist explanation of evil. At the same time, such a move raises fresh questions about the nature of the *liberum arbitrium voluntatis* as the source of evil. What is it for the will to choose evil rather than good? It is here that the Pauline literature enters the debate for two related reasons. One is that it is disputed territory between Augustine and the Manichees; the other is that Augustine uses it (whether in accordance with its original sense or no) to reflect more deeply on this question.[20]

Let me develop this point a little further. The problem for Augustine was this: by identifying the freely acting human will as the source of evil in the world, he could certainly offer an alternative view to the Manichaean one that the source of evil lay in an evil substance independent of God and indeed offer a view which, he could argue with some force, was consistent with belief in a good God, the source of all reality. For this indeed Paul might seem to give him support, and he appeals in his *propositionum ex epistola ad Romanos* 44.3, as Fredriksen points out,[21] to Rom 7.15-6 as proof that the 'sinner under the law can freely choose to respond in faith to God's call.' But he then had to face the Manichaean challenge that men and women's freedom to act seemed to be remarkably constrained; and here not only common sense, but also Paul seemed to be against him. The objection was urged by the Manichee, Fortunatus: 'It is plain from this that the

---

[20]So too Paula Fredriksen Landes, *Augustine on Romans*, Chico, California, 1982, ix.
[21]Fredriksen, 22.

good soul ... is seen to sin, and not of its own accord, but following the way in which the 'flesh lusteth against the spirit and that which you wish not, that you do.' And, as Paul says elsewhere: 'I see another law in my members.'[22] Augustine's answer is two-pronged: it is on the one hand, broadly salvation-historical. Adam exercised free-will, and 'there was absolutely nothing could resist his will, if he had willed to keep the precepts of God. But after he voluntarily sinned, we who have descended into his stock were plunged into necessity.' Augustine then backs this up by an appeal to common experience of how habits ensnare us. 'When by that liberty we have done something and the pernicious sweetness and pleasure of that deed has taken hold of the mind, by its own habit the mind is so implicated that afterwards it cannot conquer what by sinning it has fashioned for itself.'[23] What wars against the soul, as he says in the *Confessions* is *violentia consuetudinis,* which outweighs his delight in the law. 'I in vain delighted in thy law according to the inner man, when another law in my members rebelled against the law of my mind, leading me captive in the law of sin which was in my members. That law of sin now is the violence of custom by which the mind of man is drawn and holden even against its will; deserving to be so holden, for that it so willingly slides into that custom.'[24] Clearly here large theological questions are opened up which will resurface again in the later controversies with the Pelagians. There, as Fredriksen points out, Augustine will claim that Paul speaks of himself under grace;[25] in the *Confessions* he takes it to refer to the bondage to habit from which men and women are to be liberated through grace.

Attributing to the human will that evil which the Manichees had located in an independent spiritual agency has of course profound implications. Rather than being enslaved by 'beggarly spirits', as Paul suggests (I believe) in Galatians, the will is itself the cause of its own enslavement to habit; but as enslaved, it cannot free itself from the consequences of its own actions and can look only to the grace of God for such liberation. The rejection of cosmic dualism leads to a much darker view of the

---

[22]C. Fort.21, see Brown, 149.
[23]*C. Fort.*22
[24]*Conf.* 8.5.12.
[25]'Paul and Augustine', 25, referring to *cxontra ii epistolas Pelagianorum,* I.viii.13-14.

human will, which in turn calls for different accounts of human salvation. The more Augustine ponders these matters, the more he inclines to see God as the cause of aspects of human experience which on a dualist view might have been attributed to the agency of supernatural powers. Doctrines of election and the divine hardening are brought in to explain human malice, as well as human goodness.[26]To describe this as the introduction of introspection into the Christian tradition is to emphasise some of the implications of Augustine's philosophical move, which become clearer in the later writings; there is a risk that such a characterisation may obscure the sense in which by embracing a form of philosophical monism, Augustine has suppressed important, dualist elements in Paul's thought.

If this fails to convince, let me suggest another way of showing the continuity between the metaphysical debates and the moral struggles which Augustine portrays in the *Confessions.* By the end of Book Seven, Augustine has effectively resolved his metaphysical debates with the Manichaeans. He has attained to a new world-view of which he is confident; but it does not yet shape his own attitudes and ethos. His former doubts have gone, but he is still not firmly grounded in this new world view: *nec certior de te, sed stabilior in te esse cupiebam* (8.1.1). The rest of the *Confessions* represents Augustine's struggle to appropriate this world-view, to live out its implications for his own life. Much of that struggle is with his own attachment to his old way of life, and this provides the stuff for his reflection on the bondage of the will to the force of habit and the refusal of the will to delight in the objects of true desire, even when presented with them. Part of the consequence of this struggle is, that is to say, further reflection on the nature of the will and the relation between divine and human agency. The shifting opinions about the nature of the will and its freedom which Fredriksen documents so well in her article bear witness to Augustine's continuing struggle with this question. The process of appropriating this new world view with its heavy emphasis on human choice, of developing a corresponding ethos, in turn leads to modification and further clarification of the world view and not, pace Fredriksen, an ἀνάβασις εἰς ἀλλὸ γένος, from philosophy into theology. The more he becomes aware of the weakness of the will to move the mind to action and choice, the more he is forced to contemplate the role of divine grace in

[26]*Exposition quarundam propositionum,* 61-62.

moving the human will.

As Fredriksen and Brown both argue[27], the decisive development (break?) in Augustine's thought here comes in Augustine's reply to Simplicianus' question, why was it that God said: 'I have hated Esau'? As Brown observes, it is a 'long journey from the contemplation of a Logos, whose existence can be "hinted at by innumerable rational proofs", to this acute posing of the unfathomable nature of individual destinies.'[28] A long way indeed, but one which both the Platonist Simplicianus and the former Manichaean 'hearer' Augustine undertake as part of their coming to terms through Paul with the nature of the will's role in bringing evil into the world. A purely Platonist reading of Paul as the 'exponent of a spiritual ascent, of the renewal of the "inner" man, the decay of the "outer"'[29] would no longer satisfy either of them as they grappled with the realities of the corruption of the human will, which had become pivotal for their defence of the sovereignty of God against Manichaean dualism.

Augustine's answer to Simplicianus is characteristically nuanced. He needs to assert the sovereignty of God's grace, the 'divine overruling' of men and women's wills, over against any suggestion that the evil inclination of the human will is the result of demonic forces and influences. Augustine later says that he 'had previously tried hard to uphold the freedom of choice of the human will; but the Grace of God had the upper hand. There was no way out but to conclude that the Apostle must be understood to have said the most obvious truth, when he said: "Who has made you different? What have you got that you did not first receive? If you have received all this, why glory in it as if you had not been given it?"'(1 Cor 4.7)[30] And this assertion of God's

---

[27]Fredriksen, 23, see too the fuller discussion in her dissertation 'Augustine's Early Interpretation of Paul', Princeton, 1979 (not seen by me) and the discussion of ad Simpl. in Brown, 153-57.

[28]Brown, 153.

[29]Brown, 151, citing de quant. anim. xxviii,55 and de vera relig. lii, 101.

[30]Retract. II,27, quoted in Brown 154. As Fredriksen, 23, has it, 'he argues that man's faith is not man's work, but God's gift, and hence no ground for merit. ..Not man's will, but solely the absolute unmerited gift of God's grace, can correctly orient man's love toward the Divine.'

sovereignty[31] is complemented by a profound analysis of human motivation. Central to this discussion is a consideration of the notion of 'delight' What is it that attracts us to a particular object, and which then motivates our will, so that we act with regard to it? The problem is that there is no direct correlation between the beauty of a particular object and the delight that it arouses within the soul. This is as true in the religious life as else-where. 'The fact that those things that make for successful pro-gress towards God should cause us delight is not acquired by our good intentions, earnestness and the value of our own good will - but is dependent on the inspiration granted us by God...[For] Who can embrace wholeheartedly what gives him no delight? But who can determine for himself that what will delight him should come his way, and, when it comes, that it should, in fact, delight him?'[32]

Augustine's search for an ethos, a 'model for' reality which would correspond to his Platonist world-view is a long and difficult one. He notes at one point how in the church, though it was full, 'one went this way, and another that way.'[33] What sort of way of life is appropriate for those who believe that they as human beings bear the - sole - responsibility for the evil that is within the world? that the human freedom which was the cause of such universal disaster is now in bondage to habit? that salvation can lie only in the (free?) acceptance of divine grace, the empower-ment by God's holy Spirit? What sort of 'long-lasting moods and

---

[31]Cf. the first allusion to this text: *quis habet quicquam non tuum?* in 1.4.4, a great hymn to the majesty and sovereignty of God. The same text returns in 7.21.27 where he compares the writings of the philosophers and Paul: 'So I began and found that whatsoever truth I had there read, to be said here with the praise of thy grace. So he that sees should not so glory as if he had not received, not only that which he doth see, but also the power to see [*non solum quod videt, sed etiam ut videat*]. - for what hath he that he hath not received? [*quid enim habet quod non accipit?*] It makes a final appearance in 13.14.15 where it is linked to the exegesis of Gen 1.2-3, the spirit of God moving on the face of the waters and separating light from darkness; which now refers to the Spirit's indwelling of believers by which they are saved by hope and made children of light; here it has strong predestinarian overtones and is linked with Rom 9.21.

[32]*ad Simpl.*I,qu.ii,21.

[33]*Conf.*8.1.2.

motivations'[34] chime in with such a view of reality? And how will the attempt to embody such beliefs in a Christian spirituality in turn affect the understanding of the beliefs themselves.

The answer lies in a rich and varied history of spirituality of which Lutheran piety forms only a part, though an influential one. Augustine's contribution to this quest in the period up to and including the *Confessions* is (at least) two-fold: first he develops an account of the will which sees it as profoundly in bondage to the power of habit and only able to be liberated through the renewing force of delight-inspired-by-God. This still allows a sense in which the human will is the ultimate source of evil in the world, namely in so far as Adam's disobedience was freely willed. It even allows a sense in which the human will may regain its freedom through divine inspiration prompting it to follow that in which the heart delights. It can encourage a simple and joyful trust in God, as it can profoundly undermine confidence in the human will and inspire moods of profound melancholy, guilt and self-doubt, the kind of introspection which Krister Stendahl has rightly described as a plague.

Such reflections on the bondage and weakness of the will do not however form the whole of the second part of the *Confessions*; nor is such introspection Augustine's sole legacy to the history of Christian spirituality. In the latter books there are themes which point in a different direction. Crucial here is Augustine's use at 10.3.3/10.5.7 and 13.31.46[35] of 1 Cor 2.11-12 with its affirmation both of the unknowability for human beings of the 'thoughts of God' and its affirmation of the gift of the Spirit of God given that believers might understand the gifts of God. While it is true that for Augustine the Christian life is principally to be described in terms of pilgrimage[36], Book 13 nevertheless celebrates the gift of the Spirit to Christians, the 'pouring out of

---

[34]The phrase is taken from 'Religion as a Cultural System' in Clifford Geertz, *The Interpretation of Cultures: selected essays*, London, 1975, p.90 Cf. also the distinction Geertz makes between 'models of' and 'models for' reality', between world-view and ethos.

[35] As James J. O'Donnell, *Augustine. Confessions*, 3 vols., Oxford, 1992, points out, the first part with its assertion of the 'unknowability of humanity and divinity' brackets the meditative books 10-13 and is only completed at its final citation. Nevertheless the fact that the citation is completed at the culmination of the work is of no small significance.

[36]See Brown, 152, 202, 210.

God's love into our hearts through the Holy Spirit' (Rom 5:5). And here world-view and ethos: the description of the new life which Augustine the convert now leads, are linked together through the device of an allegorical interpretation of the Genesis creation narrative. Augustine returns to the very issues which had occupied him all through the first seven books, of cosmology, of the relation of the supreme substance to finite existents, of the nature of God's creative act, and draws out of his exposition of the creation narrative an account of the new creation which believers undergo, of the transformation of their minds by the work of the Spirit.

What bearing might such debates about the interpretation of Augustine's *Confessions* have on our understanding of Paul?

1. Paul: conversion or call?

I have been arguing that the *Confessions,* like the *Metamorphoses,* describe the breakdown of an individual's epistemological and moral universe and his embracing of another. In broad terms this seems to me a most persuasive way of portraying what is happening in both works, despite the entirely different genres and degrees of reflexivity. What is in detail interesting are the differences that emerge between Lucius and Augustine and which shed light on Augustine and from there on his treatment of Paul. Augustine's world does not simply collapse around him in such a way that he no longer knows what to think or what to do. He is himself actively involved in the breaking down of the worldview that he has made his own and in this he is greatly helped by the work of the Platonists. There is a fairly continuous line leading from his engagement with Manichaean views of the nature of the two powers in the world to considerations of the origin of evil in the free judgement of the will and from there to considerations of the bondage of the will to desire and habit. The drama of his story comes precisely from this mixture of on the one hand self-conscious questing and critical scrutiny of his cherished beliefs and desires and on the other his powerlessness to embrace the goals that his good will wants. This is not purely a matter of his inability to control his sexual appetites, but of his struggle to break free from the contemporary ethos of his society and its search for honour and wealth (8.1.2). His encounter with the beggar in Book 6 shows the extent to which by then he has already moved to a position where his worldview and ethos are no longer consonant with each other. This struggle to conform world-view and ethos continues for Augustine beyond the actual moment of his conversion and the later books give some indication of how the two are brought closer together.

All this is of course very different from Lucius' conversion and also from Paul's. Does this mean that we should not speak of Paul's spiritual development in terms of conversion at all, but rather of call? Perhaps some of the grounds for arguing against conversion begin to look a little less clear-cut. Fredriksen argues against such a characterisation on the grounds that the move from Pharisaism to a Jewish group which recognised Jesus as the Messiah would not have constituted a 'movement between religions, from one articulated symbol system to another' but only 'a lateral movement *within* Judaism'[37]. Stendahl makes similar points about Paul's not having changed religion but having received a particular charge which caused him to revise certain views about the Messiah and the place of the Gentiles in relation to the law. He is not a 'Jew who gives up his former faith to become a Christian'.[38]

Now it is true I would judge that the religious group/movement into which Paul moved did not see itself as forming a separate religious movement from other Jews and if 'conversion' is going to be restricted solely to changes of affiliation from one (or no) religion to another, then we should not use it to describe Paul's experience. Nevertheless, the question remains: how far had he moved within Judaism? Pharisees, for example, who entered the community at Qumran would, like the fictional Lucius and the autobiographer Augustine, have experienced a breakdown of past beliefs and ethos (now seen as mendacious and the prompting of the angel of darkness) as they embraced a new set of beliefs and values, even though these still related to the same central symbols. Was Paul's 'conversion' like this?

Stendahl wants to play down the extent of Paul's change of world-view. Paul, he says, did not cast 'doubts as to the worth of his background but point[ed] out that his former values, great though they were, [we]re as nothing in the light of his knowledge and recognition of Christ'.[39] And he cites Phil 3.7-9. But to refer to one's former way of life ('values') and beliefs as excrement, σκύβαλα (*skubala*), seems some way from saying that they 'were

---

[37]Fredriksen, 15.
[38] *Paul among Jews and Gentiles,* 9.
[39]*Paul among Jews and Gentiles,* 8-9.

great'. It actually seems closer to saying that they were 'fallacious' or 'mendacious', but it *clearly* is also not that. That is to say that it is like but unlike (yet not wholly unlike) Augustine's and Lucius' experiences, which were of course also like but unlike each other. What all three do have in common is a sense of having moved out of one world into another. The texts that Augustine singles out to describe the new life that he has entered, whether about the renewal of the mind from Romans 12.2 or the texts about leaven (1 Cor 5.7f.) and the conferring of the gift of the Spirit (1 Cor 2.11-12), talk about a new life which has involved a radical change from that which he had lived before. One great difference between Paul and Augustine in this respect might be that Paul both in his old and his new life had 'served the one and the same God'[40] who was attested by one and the same scriptures. This is true, but the differences can be exaggerated: Augustine's Manichaeism was a Christian heresy which rejected the Old Testament and selected parts of the New, but it still contested the interpretation of the remaining scriptures with the church. Paul is clearly engaged in continuing debate both with Jews and Jewish and Gentile Christians about the meaning of Scripture and this is for him and them a matter of life and death. Evidently his new views and behaviour were sufficiently repugnant to some Jews to call on more than one occasion for the most severe of synagogue punishments.

But would we not then expect clearer evidence of inner turmoil in Paul, such as we certainly find in Luther and, in a measure, in Augustine? Maybe, though it is not easy to know what stress and turmoil Paul may have undergone. Is viewing your past values as σκύβαλα (*skubala*) altogether without stress and strain? Nor should we *over*estimate the element of inner turmoil in Augustine. Fredriksen is right to stress the sense of continuity in Augustine's earlier account of his conversion; I have been wanting to argue that, even in the account in the *Confessions*, the sense of turmoil is qualified by a clear sense of intellectual certainty: *nec certior de te sed stabilior in te esse cupiebam*. We must guard against reading Augustine too much through Luther's eyes and recognise the different psychological manifestations of conversion.

---

[40]Stendahl, 7.

2. Paul, it is said, again by Stendahl, was concerned not with questions about 'on what basis does *a person* find salvation',[41] but with ones about the possibility of Gentiles being included in the Messianic *community*. The contrast here seems to be between two different types of religion, one which is personal (and universal) and which relates to a common human predicament which any person can share; and one which is about the way a particular group articulates its values and behaviour: how it regulates membership of the community: who's in, how you might get in, how you stay in, etc. The one is personal, existential, inward looking; the other is something you just get on with without much soul-searching, where changes of allegiance might at best be effected by reports of miracles,[42] not by the kinds of processes of self-examination and self-criticism which Augustine has blessed us all with.

Such a view of the matter seems to assume that there were very stable ethnic religious communities in the ancient world where world-view and ethos were closely coordinated and where changes to the symbolic system (or to its construal by the group) were relatively rare and accomplished without much soul-searching. Maybe this was indeed so, but it is not the case with Judaism where there was great variety in the ways in which people construed the central Jewish symbols and evidence of considerable change of allegiance between different groups and of

---

[41]'His statements are now to be read as answers to the quest for assurance about man's salvation out of a common human predicament.' Stendahl, 86.

[42]Such views about Paul's lack of inwardness and introspection are also broadly supported by the work of A.D. Nock, *Conversion: The Old and the New in Religion from Alexander to Augustine of Hippo*, Oxford, 1933, who argues that, on the basis of his survey of paganism, there is 'little reason to expect that the adhesion of any individual to a cult would involve any marked spiritual reorientation, any recoil from his moral and religious past, any idea of starting a new life...', 138 and R. Macmullen, *Paganism in the Roman Empire*, New Haven, 1981; 'Two Types of Conversion to Early Christianity' *VigChr* 37 (1983)174-92; *Christianizing the Roman Empire, A.D. 100-400*, New Haven, 1984, who argues that views of conversion in this period have been based too much on the literary accounts of the elite, not enough on brief third person and anecdotal accounts. What these latter suggest overwhelmingly is that it was miracles which were the catalyst for mass conversions: '*That* was what produced converts. Nothing else is attested.'

enmity and rivalry between them. This does not of course mean that first century Judaism in its various manifestations sat light to questions of ethnicity or of shared values and practices, which defined them over against other groups. But it does mean that there was a great deal more scope for personal choice and decision for at least some: there were different ways of upholding group norms, of defining the group, of resolving questions about the fate and future of those outside the group.[43] For Augustine ethnicity played very little part in his religion. This does not mean however that he was not interested in group values of any kind. The questions he asked about group allegiance were not spelled out in terms of physical descent but in terms of the value of wealth and rhetoric and of the kind of life-style and goals which he himself pursued in the course of a successful career. In trying to make up his mind about the right course to follow in such matters, he turns to the Bible, the sacred text of a particular community, as a source of truth and guidance. His search is not just for some personal way, but rather for the right way for the church to which he feels called through the teaching of the Platonists. In all this there are perhaps more lines of similarity between Augustine and Paul than Stendahl suggests.

What is of course striking is the emphasis in the *Confessions* on the dynamics of Augustine's decision, on the mobilisation of his will. Was he wholly wrong to find in Paul someone who could help him address such questions? Was Paul solely concerned with questions about the adjustment of the boundaries of the Jewish people in the light of the coming of the Messiah? Did he not also have a burning concern with human action, motivation and choice? How could the Galatians go back on their earlier course of action? How could they abandon his Gospel? What was the nature of the freedom for which Christ had set them free? And what the nature of the bondage from which they had been delivered? Augustine was surely right to see in Paul someone who grappled with such questions about the nature of the human response to the word of God, about human freedom and bondage. For in redefining humanity in terms which transcended former ethnic definitions (Gal 3:28), in terms, that is, not of Jews and Gentiles but of sonship of God and participation in Christ, Paul

---

[43]For a brief sketch of such diversity, see my *The World of Jesus,* New York, 1990.

was putting an enormous weight on human choice and motivation.

3. But did Augustine read Paul's *answers* to these question aright? Martin de Boer[44] has argued that first century Jewish eschatology was of two kinds: one cosmic dualist, which saw the root of evil as lying in the invasion of the world by demonic forces, which held men and women in bondage and which could be overcome only by a final battle between God and the demonic forces (1 Enoch 1-36); another forensic, which saw the source of evil as lying in the human will, of which the resolution lies in some final assize (2 Baruch). These two views may be found in isolation but more often they are found in some kind of dialogue within the same work. It is not I think too difficult to see how Paul himself engages with and indeed in some sense embraces both these views: Rom 1-3 asserts the accountabilty of all (ἀναπολόγητος, *anapologetos* 2.1) for the sin which is nevertheless seen to be omnipresent in the world; Rom 5.12 asserts the universality of sin as a power which has engulfed the world, while still wanting to attribute responsibility for sin to *all* (ἐφ᾿ ᾧ πάντες ἥμαρτον, *eph ho pantes hemarton*). Romans 7 similarly speaks of the struggle of the will with the power of sin which, as Schweitzer was keen to argue, is portrayed as a personal agent. It is the interplay between these two opposed mythologies which in many ways accounts for the richness and elusiveness of Paul's thought. Without an appeal to some kind of supra-human source of evil, it is hard to make sense of the universality of human sin: explanations in terms of the failure of individual wills break down at this point. On the other hand, without an assertion of the moral accountability of each and every human being, human dignity is undermined.

Augustine, I have been wanting to argue, is engaged in the same debates about the nature of evil and its overcoming as were those who wrote in the traditions stemming from Jewish apocalyptic eschatology. He is battling against dualist accounts of the origin and reality of evil in the world; he struggles in the light of the pervasiveness of corruption and moral infirmity to hold on to some view of the freedom of the will as the moral agent responsible for evil in the world. It seems to me that we might do better in trying to understand both Paul and Augustine if we were

---

[44] `Paul and Jewish Apocalyptic Eschatology' in ed. J. Marcus and M.L. Soardes, *Apocalyptic and The New Testament,* Sheffield, 1989, 169-190.

to see them, *for all their differences*, as addressing certain funda-mental questions which were of wide influence and interest in the ancient world, rather than taking their differences of temperament and affective style as definitive. Of course there is a great deal more reflexivity in Augustine's account of his entry to the Christian community than in Paul's of his entry into the Jesus movement. But it is not the case that Augustine is interested only in questions of personal salvation, of how he can find release from sin and guilt, whereas Paul is interested only in questions about the nature and boundaries of the people of God in the light of the coming of the Messiah (existential theology as against some kind of salvation history). Augustine is engrossed by questions about the nature of being, about creation and the relation of finite exist-ents to the ultimate source(s) of reality; about universal history as well as about questions of the freedom of the will, the divided nature of the will and the operation of desire. He engaged with both the Judaeo-Christian tradition and the tradition of Greek and Latin philosophy, as of course, variously, did Jews like Paul and Philo. That is to say, Augustine's conversation partners are not the same but not so far different from Paul's; and, both Paul and Augustine are attempting to deal with some of the same funda-mental issues. Maybe we could begin to see both the Pauline texts which Augustine picks up to illuminate his own enquiries about the dividedness of the will and those which he adopts to describe the new life in Christ as belonging to the same world of discourse, and not as having been wrenched from their context and distorted out of recognition?

But having said that, then we also need to recognise that Augustine has read Paul in a way which eliminates precisely the cosmic dualist elements in his thought. How indeed, after his struggle with Manichaeism, could he do otherwise? Thus what we have in his readings of Romans 7 and Galatians 5 is a exclu-sively forensic reading of Paul. Paul speaks to him of the weak-ness and bondage of the will, not of some angelic agency but to the force of habit which has enslaved all wills since the time of Adam's fall. And where that fails to satisfy, he speaks of the divine hardening. What in Paul is explained partly in terms of bondage to spiritual forces outwith human control, partly in terms of human weakness and failure, partly too in terms of the divine hardening and punishment, is in Augustine presented exclusively in terms of the psychology of the human will and of the divine action upon it. This indeed opens the way to the 'introspective conscience of the West'. It also lays the whole responsibility for the world's ills at the door of the will.

In conclusion, let me return to my opening remarks about the different strands of contemporary anti-Lutheran polemic in Pauline studies. Does the view of Augustine's *Confessions* I have been arguing for reinforce or modify such polemic?

Stendahl's work drew scholars' attention to the enormous emphasis which Augustine places upon the human will and its predicament in his theology. As I have indicated, I think that this is not purely the result of a change in mood and temperament; that such a focus grows out of the central theological issues which Augustine addresses and that here there is common ground with Paul. Nevertheless, it is important to realise the extent to which in Augustine and his Lutheran successors the focus has shifted away from the issues of ethnicity which occupy Paul in Romans and which reflect indeed concerns of great importance to Paul and his fellow Jews. But here I think some caution is required. If we contrast Augustine's conversion and Paul's calling as apostle to the Gentiles too sharply, if we underplay the sense in which Paul has parted company with his inherited Jewish world-view, we may miss the sense in which the writers of the New Testament are also engaged in recasting religious and ethnic identity. Certainly issues of ethnicity were important for Paul and others in a way that they were not for Augustine. But they were profoundly *problematic* issues, which led to deep changes in world-view and ethos. Whether these are properly described as conversion may be a matter of linguistic convention. I hope to have shown that there are at the least instructive points of comparison with Augustine.

What I have been trying to show about the way Augustine suppresses the dualist elements in Paul, suggests, I think, that Schweitzer was essentially right to argue that the apocalyptic aspects of Paul's thought had not merely been overlooked in the Lutheran tradition, but that they were in some profound sense inimical to it.[45] The concentration on the forensic aspects of Paul's thought, which is given such powerful impetus in

---

[45]Cf. Schweitzer's account of the treatment of Richard Kabisch: 'But for all that theology held to the old way and was determined to cast out anyone who set foot upon the new. That is the explanation of the fate which befel (sic) Richard Kabisch's "Eschatology of Paul".' *Paul and his Interpreters*, 58.

Augustine's writings, creates a cultural, theological tradition which, as Sanders asserts, simply does not have the conceptual tools to make sense of Paul's belief in the believers' participation in Christ.

Schweitzer himself attempted to break out of his cultural bondage by invoking the category of mysticism. He placed Paul's Christ-mysticism on a line between primitive magical mysticism and intellectual mysticism, which latter he found in 'Platonism, Stoicism, in Spinoza, Schopenhauer and Hegel.'[46] Although this move has been widely dismissed by Protestant scholars,[47] it interestingly attempts to read Paul in terms of the wider intellectual tradition to which Augustine belonged. Schweitzer of course recognises the sense in which Pauline mysticism does not conform to the higher forms of 'intellectual mysticism', as he recognises the clearly dualistic elements in Paul's thought which had been emphasised by his heroes, Everling and Kabisch. Nevertheless, the categories which he employs to make sense of Paul's doctrine of participation in Christ are monist, non-dualist categories and so are in principle inimical to the beliefs he is trying to interpret. Moreover he does not sufficiently recognise the sense in which Paul's thought is dialectic, dependent on the interplay between dualistic and forensic modes of thought: for him the forensic modes of thought are no more than a side-show. So what he offers is a monist interpretation of the dualist elements in Paul's thought, to the exclusion (largely) of the forensic. It is not an interpretation which has found many followers, though his work enjoyed some popularity in England in the 1930s.

We are left then with the dilemma that the most fruitful interpretations of Paul in the West are those which, stemming from Augustine and Luther, emphasise the language of obedience, trust and righteouness/justification; but that precisely the success of such interpretations has made it increasingly difficult for us to offer effective contemporary interpretations of Paul's beliefs in liberation from bondage to the powers and participation in Christ. Such Lutheran interpretations are, I would want to insist, indeed interpretations of Paul: they draw on and provide powerful readings of Pauline texts from the context of their own metaphysical and theological debates. But they also suppress, reinterpret,

---

[46]*The Mysticism of Paul the Apostle,* London, 1931, 2.
[47]G. Bornkamm, *Paul,* 1971, 155, speaks of mysticism as 'a blurring of the boundary between God and man'.

demythologise other elements of his thought *and their subsequent readings* and so destroy what some at least would see as the inner dynamic of Paul's thought, the interplay of the dualistic and forensic. Does this mean that Paul is lost to us for ever? Maybe it does. If to find Paul would be to recover the sense of real participation in Christ of which he speaks, then maybe we have to say that from the mainstream of our culture we can discern only the outer shell of such doctrines, nothing of the life inside. But maybe then we need to recover those readings which have been more marginal to the dominant culture of the West: the readings of the radical reformation, of millenarian Christianity, of the Pietists and of liberationist theology, as well as of the mystical groups to which Schweitzer referred. Perhaps then a conversation can develop which will, in its own way and time, recapture something of the inner dynamic of Paul's texts.

Exploring the Inner Conflict:

Augustine's Sermons on Romans 7 and 8

Eugene TeSelle

Does Romans 7 refer to life under the law or to the Christian life? Is it to be understood <u>autobiographically</u>, as referring to Paul himself? Or <u>psychologically</u>, as referring to human experience more generally? or <u>objectively</u>, as describing a real situation which does not necessarily correspond with personal experience? Augustine always understood the chapter experientially. And when he applied it to the Christian life he intensified his awareness of--and expectations of--ongoing conflict and struggle within the Christian.

The exact import of Romans 7 is not readily apparent.[1] There are some classic alternatives, and Augustine changed his mind several times.[2]

In his first expositions of Romans during the years 394-396 he assumed that Paul in Romans 7 refers to life under the law. The law shows human beings that, because of sin, they are unable to achieve what is commanded. This leads them to repent and seek divine grace, which at last enables them to fulfill what the law requires.[3]

But in 397 Augustine becomes convinced that grace plays the initiating role.[4] Texts from Paul--especially Romans 9:13--were crucial in persuading him. But Paul's own conversion (as presented, not by Paul, but by Luke in Acts 9) was also an important factor. If Saul, in the midst of seizing and slaying Christians, could be humbled by a word from on high and be led to faith, it is convincing evidence of the role of grace.[5] This new emphasis on grace does not have any immediate impact, however, on Augustine's interpretation of Romans 7; he still seems to assume that the struggle is prior to conversion, not after it. But there is an intensified interest in the inward dynamics of the human self, and it is not surprising that Augustine wrote his <u>Confessions</u> at this same time.

Two decades later, in the sermons being considered here, Augustine comes to a different interpretation of Romans 7: in this chapter, he now thinks, Paul refers to the Christian life, in which, despite grace--or rather because of it--there is a heightened conflict within the self between obedience and sin. The

---

[1]This essay is reprinted, in a condensed form, from <u>Collectanea Augustiniana</u>, Volume V, <u>Augustine: Biblical Exegete</u>. Reprinted with permission of the Augustinian Historical Institute, Villanova.

clinching argument is that only those who feel God's grace can genuinely "delight in the law" (Rom 7:22) and therefore struggle against sin.[6]

There are other ways of reading Romans 7. Rudolf Bultmann, while he agreed that Paul refers in this chapter to life under the law, opposed the psychological interpretation. Paul knew that, far from failing, he was blameless under the law (Phil 3:6) and able to establish a righteousness of his own (Rom 10:3). In denying that he was a sinner he demonstrated how sin can misuse the law and pervert it into a rival way of salvation. Paul in retrospect condemns his very zeal for the law, for his situation is now one of having been justified--declared righteous by the divine judge--in the last times.[7] Augustine was not unaware of this dimension of Paul's theology; like Bultmann, he saw that when Paul speaks of "flesh" he refers to all forms of human self-reliance and self-assertion, even the highest forms of moral and religious zeal.[8]

Another alternative to the "psychological" interpretation, but quite different from Bultmann's, comes from the "Scandinavian school."[9] For them the framework is the "history of salvation." Life under the law, to be sure, is superseded by life in Christ. But God's purpose in all of this is not primarily to resolve a psychological or moral or religious conflict, but to include both Jews and Gentiles in God's saving purpose. Even Paul's own experience, reported quite differently in Galatians 2 and Acts 9, is to be interpreted not as an individual "conversion" but as a call to apostleship directed toward all the nations.

Augustine was aware of this dimension of Paul. In the sermons to be discussed here, he saw the Old Testament as an anticipation of the New, Israel as an anticipation of the Church[10]; even where there is a contrast between the two, the same Spirit is at work.[11] The narrative of the Canaanite woman is interpreted as prefiguring the Gentile mission that was still to come.[12]

Even more to the point, Augustine thought in terms of four successive "ages" in the spiritual history of the human race: "before the law," when there was ignorance of sin; "under the law," when sin is made known by the law; "under grace," when grace defeats sin, but does not entirely conquer it; and "in peace," when perfect harmony will at last be gained in eternal life.[13]

There is, nonetheless, a fundamental difference between Augustine and the Scandinavian school. The Augustinian emphasis, we might say, sees the broader history of humanity as the life of the self writ large, always retaining its psychological or moral overtones. The Scandinavian school, by contrast, sees Augustine's moral and psychological interests as the wider history of salvation writ small-- but erroneously, through misinterpretation.[14] For them, even the strong language of Romans 7 is to be understood not as a psychological cry for help or an autobiographical reliving of an earlier experience, but as a rhetorical reinforcement of the larger argument of the epistle to the Romans.[15] For Stendahl, Paul is merely observing the obvious difference between what we ought to do and what we actually do. The problem, he says, is this:

> Unfortunately--or fortunately--Paul happened to express this supporting argument so well that what to him and his contemporaries was a common sense observation appeared to later interpreters to be a most penetrating insight into the nature of man and into the nature of sin.[16]

Paula Fredriksen, who is similarly convinced that Augustine's interpretation of Romans 7 was erroneous, suggests at least two ways in which it was a fruitful mistake. Not only did he go beyond the view, typical in the ancient world, that human being is "a soul occupying a body," by appropriating the body and internalizing its inclinations.[17] In addition, by reinterpreting the more cosmic dimensions of Paul's thinking (especially his mention of "creation groaning in travail" in Rom 8:22) he freed himself of "late antiquity's map of the cosmos" and offered a concept of the human person that "could survive Galileo's revolution and so endure, meaningfully, to our own day."[18]

Perhaps even more can be said in Augustine's behalf. He did not isolate human subjectivity from the broader issues of human history. As The City of God abundantly demonstrates, he was responsive to the whole scope of human life as he knew it. His own conviction was that everything in human history is to be understood as the expression of desires and fears and potentialities that we also experience within ourselves.

The Sermons

It has long been recognized that Sermons 151-156 have a unity, even in the manuscript tradition. The sermons were preached in Carthage, in several different basilicas whose names are noted by the stenographers. They go through Romans 7 and 8 more or less sequentially. But Augustine leaps ahead to Romans 8:3-4 in Sermon 152, probably because he sees Romans 8 as the key to Romans 7, or, more precisely, sees the three meanings of the law (the law of works or the letter, the law of sin and death, and the law of the Spirit of life) as the key to the entire section. Then he moves back to deal with the intervening paragraphs in Sermons 153 and 154. There is no discussion of Romans 8:18-23 and 8:26-28.

Augustine had been accustomed to citing passages from this chapter to show that the effects of sin continue even in the Christian life. But now he specifically raises the question, "In whose person does Paul speak in this chapter?"--an issue raised with special intensity during the climactic phase of the controversy with Pelagius. It has generally been thought that the year would be 419. But one of the letters newly discovered by Divjak shows that Augustine was not in Carthage in October of 419, and the most likely year would be 417.[19]

Other surviving sermons were also preached during September and October in Carthage. Among them are sermons 163 and 26, based on texts in Galatians, which deal with themes that are treated at greater length in Sermons 151-156.

The three subsequent sermons, 157-159, do not discuss the same issue. They are thematic discussions of hope, referring to Romans 8 almost as though it illustrates a more philosophical theory of hope: its object is not yet experienced (Sermon 157), it is based upon divine promise (Sermon 158), and it is animated by delight in the invisible value of justice (Sermon 159). These sermons come from approximately the same time, and it is likely that Augustine, having started through these chapters, continued to discuss the themes raised--if not in Carthage, then back home in Hippo. This would not be unusual, for Augustine was beginning to complete his series of expository sermons on the Psalms and on the Gospel according to John, even dictating rather than preaching some of them.

Finally, in order to "complete the record" on Augustine's preaching on Romans 7, we should take note of two sermons (77/A [Guelferbytanus 33] and 154/A [Morin 4]) which use this text in conjunction with the pericope of the Canaanite woman (Mt 15:21-28).

Augustine will often use the psalm which had been chanted between the "apostle" and the "gospel" to confirm his interpretation of Paul: if the Pelagians will not acknowledge the continuing power of sin and the need for reliance upon grace, the psalm resolves the issue. In this way Augustine anticipates a point made a few decades later by his follower Prosper of Aquitaine, who originated the slogan Lex orandi lex credendi, "The rule of prayer is the rule of faith"--and in the same context of polemic against those who diminished the role of grace.[20]

The Situation

The sermons come from a moment of triumph in the Pelagian controversy. The bishop of Rome, Innocent, had sent a letter early in the year declaring his agreement with the two African councils of Carthage and Milevis in 416, which had condemned the "new heresy." At the end of one sermon, after mentioning those who are ignorant of God's justice and want to establish their own, Augustine exults:

> For already two councils on this question have written to the Apostolic See; rescripts have also come from there. The case is finished; would that error be finished sometime! Therefore we warn so that they might take heed; we teach so that they might be instructed; we pray so that they might be changed.[21]

In that mood Augustine set about refuting them, and the series of sermons interpreting Romans 7 was preached.

The situation, as Augustine knew, was not one of total victory. The Eastern synod of Diospolis had vindicated Pelagius in 415, and the two African councils in 416 had gone ahead with their condemnation in full knowledge of this other action. Thus it was necessary to use a combination of argument and diplomacy. And in a few months Augustine would learn that the new pope, Zosimus, had called two local councils which in succession declared first Caelestius and then Pelagius free of error; his letter reversing the actions of his predecessor was dated September 21, soon after the series of sermons was begun. After that the controversy would take on new earnestness and bitterness action. Thus it was necessary to use on both sides. The Africans would call upon the aid of the Emperor, who would condemn the Pelagians for their allegedly radical social views.[22] The pope would follow suit. But his doctrinal condemnation of the Pelagians, while declaring the necessity of baptism, would not affirm original sin as the Africans wished. Soon Julian of Eclanum, a young married bishop from southern Italy, would raise the controversy to a new level of intensity, provoking lengthy and detailed polemical treatises from Augustine. All of that was still to come.

At this time of cautious triumph, Augustine not only was able to take a firmer stand against Pelagius; he was under the necessity of doing so, not only to defend himself against a variety of attacks but to convince those who wavered, and even to strengthen-- or to correct--those who agreed with him. The immediate target was a work by Pelagius (probably entitled For Free Will) in which he answered Jerome's attacks.[23]

Jerome was always a problematical ally for Augustine. At least twenty years older, learned in Greek and Hebrew, enjoying a widespread reputation by the time Augustine became known to the Christian world, he treated Augustine disdainfully in their first rounds of correspondence. He was, furthermore, impulsive and inclined to overstatement, especially in the midst of controversy. During a dispute over the relative merits of marriage and celibacy during the 390s--which he essentially won, since the position of Jovinian was condemned by Pope Siricius--he so deprecated marriage as to shock his friends. They tried to keep the work out of circulation. Augustine's works on marriage and celibacy were written in 401 as a corrective to Jerome's violent polemic. The unknown Roman critic of Jerome during those years may well have been Pelagius himself, rehearsing, in effect, the later and better known controversy. Thus when Augustine takes pains to differentiate his views from those of the Manichaeans, he may be defending not only himself but Jerome--and at the same time correcting some of his more extreme utterances by offering a more adequate account of good and evil, spirit and flesh. As Schleiermacher would do later in his discussion of the two "natural heresies" of Christian anthropology,[24] Augustine tried to show how the "Catholic faith" is the mean between the errors of the Manichaeans and the Pelagians.[25]

Even more important, however, may have been Jerome's contribution to the interpretation of Romans 7. Earlier and more insistently than Augustine he cited it as one among many proofs that the struggle with sin continues after baptism.[26] Pelagius responded by explicitly raising the question "in whose person" Paul

was speaking in this passage.[27] Thus it was in large part to defend
Jerome, his strongest ally in the East, that Augustine began to
investigate Romans 7 more systematically.

Augustine's Theory of Willing

The sermons with which we are dealing represent a new stage in
Augustine's description of the affections and the process of
willing. He becomes even more insistent than before upon the
conflict within the self. "It is not what I will that I do, the
good; but what I hate, evil, this is what I do" (Rom 7:15). That
is the key passage. Augustine questions how someone under the law-
-which arouses fear--could say, "I delight in the law of God after
the inward person" (Rom 7:22). In this connection he emphasizes
the repeated use of "now": "Now then it is no longer I who do it"
(Rom 7:17), "There is therefore now no condemnation" (Rom 8:1).[28]
In order to understand Augustine's interpretation of Romans 7, let
us look at his analysis of willing as it developed through the
years. The basic observation is that it is not in our power to
control what will "occur to us," either from external events or
through the inward association of ideas. (In addition, it was a
common opinion among philosophers in the ancient world that angelic
or demonic powers could influence the human imagination--but not
the human mind--by commingling themselves with it and impressing
their own imaginings upon it.) What is in our power is how we
respond to these impressions that "come to mind."[29]
But it is not as simple as that, for these impressions can
arouse strong feelings and inclinations toward action. They can
even conflict with each other, so that we are drawn both this way
and that. The outcome seems to be determined by what most delights
us--or most terrifies us; or, if they equally attract or repel us,
then we waver between them.[30] In addition, our inclinations are
reinforced by "custom." When we become accustomed to certain
things our affections remain tied to them. It was a commonplace in
the ancient world to say that custom becomes "second nature," so
that what began as a free response to external stimuli becomes
hardened into necessity. Thus Augustine is not surprised to find
Paul talking about conflict within the will, and even about the
bondage of the will to its own disordered affections, for phenomena
like these, with varying intensity, are familiar in human
experience.
Augustine typically isolates three factors in willing.[31] First,
he says, comes the suggestion, which occurs to us either through
the senses or through our own free association of ideas. This in
turn arouses delight in what is presented to us. (In other
connections, Augustine can also talk about fear as the other
feeling which strongly motivates us.) But delight is only a
movement of the affections; it does not issue in action, either
inward or outward, until consent is freely given in the center of
the self. In consent we "cede to," give in to, ratify some

inclination that has already been aroused. Or perhaps we "resist" the inclination, do not cede to it, but consent to another inclination.

In this triple analysis Augustine sometimes emphasizes suggestion through external events or association of ideas; sometimes consent, for which we ourselves are responsible. But increasingly the middle factor of delight or inclination or desire seems to be the crucial one. And even after consent has been given, there can remain a conflict of inclinations, resisting each other and resisting what has been consented to.

The Problem of Desire

"Do not desire." That was the example Paul chose to illustrate the commands of the law (Rom 7:7). The word used in the ancient world (epithumein, concupiscere) must be translated "desire," not "covet." It is the same word used in the Platonist tradition to describe one of the basic human impulses (the other was anger, thumos, ira). While the tenth commandment speaks of coveting specific things, Paul, by abbreviating the commandment and removing the specific objects, gives it a kind of generality, focusing attention upon the subjective tendency itself.[32] This serves to remind us that desire, while it may be aroused by the specific things that we encounter, reaches out more broadly. It is always there to be aroused; it may spring forth even without being presented an object; one object of desire may suggest another that is not directly encountered. Does Augustine, in asking for the elimination of desire, demand something that is impossible and even inhuman? The point he is making is essentially a "theological transformation" of what he had learned much earlier from Cicero: all people desire happiness, but this does not mean that people should seek whatever delights them, or that happiness consists in having whatever one desires, for one cannot be happy in possessing something inappropriate to human fulfillment.[33]

Romans 7 was not the only Biblical text concerned with desire. "Do not go after your desires," said Sirach 18:30. "Each is tempted by one's own desire; . . . then desire, when it has conceived, brings forth sin," said James 1:13-15. Paul had said, "You shall not fulfill the desires of the flesh" (Gal 5:6), and, "Do not deliver your members to sin as weapons of iniquity" (Rom 6:13).[34] Augustine is much criticized for his concern about desire (it sounds especially awful when it goes under the name of "concupiscence"). But in what sense is desire a problem to him? Several different answers can be seen in the sermons under discussion here.[35]

First, desire often means sexual desire. Especially as the Pelagian controversy went on, there was extended discussion between Augustine and his opponents not only about original sin but about the means of its transmission, and it was easy to quote, at least as a shorthand explanation, the words of Psalm 51[50]:7, "I was conceived in iniquity." The virginal conception of Christ seemed not only appropriate but indispensable if there was this close connection between sexual activity and sin. If others are conceived through desire, Christ is conceived through faith, when Mary believes God's Word and says, "Let it be" (Lk 1:38).[36] Furthermore, if procreation is so closely linked with sin, other questions arise. Would there have been begetting at all apart from sin? If so, would it have been accompanied by sexual arousement? Such issues are debated at eye-glazing length in the polemics between Augustine and Julian of Eclanum--and the debate is reported in all its prurient details by modern scholars.

And yet, quite paradoxically, Augustine may come out better, despite the polemics of his ancient and modern opponents. Julian was even more concerned than Augustine with the physiology of reproduction, which in the ancient world included many now outdated notions about the biological necessity of sexual arousal. Augustine, while he shared some of these assumptions (they were a major reason for his theory that sin is transmitted through desire and his emphasis on the virginity of Mary), shifted the emphasis to psychology. By appropriating and internalizing erotic desire he not only brought it closer to the center of the person but traced in it, as elsewhere in human life, the limits of conscious will and the possibilities for evil. In the process he overcame the ancient assumption that the human person is simply a soul occupying a body--and with it the scapegoating of the body or sexuality as the primary cause of sin.[37] This is still not enough, of course, to bring Augustine fully into harmony with modern sensibilities, or to free him from the accusation of teaching shame and repression to Western culture. Precisely in "personalizing" sexual desire he also made it the central problem of the human person, the chief obstacle to spiritual freedom.[38]

In the second place, sexual desire can be an illustration of desire more generally, the primary example, the part which signifies the whole. The involuntary character of sexual desire (about which the congregation shouted out in recognition when he mentioned it at the end of one of his sermons[39]) was for Augustine a dramatic illustration of what desire is in general. It seemed unlikely to him that God would allow intelligent and free beings to be subjected to involuntary movements except as the result of a moral tragedy. The course of that tragedy could be traced, and he found in it a certain poetic justice. Humanity had voluntarily turned away from God, in whom it had its true life. In consequence it was subjected involuntarily to lower desires, and in the end to death as well. This does not mean that sexual desire is identical with sin; rather it is the consequence of sin, the expression or symbolization of sin, proof of a deeper reality of disobedience. Indeed, desire is the "contention of death" (I Cor 15:55, Old Latin), just what one would expect in the "body of death" (Rom 7:24): having deserted God, humankind dies a spiritual death and suffers disorder as a consequence.

Third, desire can be a metaphor for all the affections.[40] In one of the sermons[41] the point is made explicitly as Augustine warns against "the desire which is called avarice," calls it "the root of all evils" (I Tim 6:10), and gives numerous examples. Even more broadly, he often cites I John 2:16, which speaks of "the desire of the flesh [the manifold desire for sensible things], the desire of the eyes [curiosity, the desire of the mind], and the ambition of this world [anger, rivalry, desire for esteem]." The affections reach out indefinitely to all possible objects, sensible or intelligible, real or imaginary. The human heart is drawn in many directions. Augustine sees that when Paul speaks of "flesh" he often refers to "the human"--in other words, to any mode of acquiescence in human inclinations or reliance upon human capabilities, even the most spiritual.[42]

The Inner Struggle

Augustine thinks in terms of the sequence "suggestion-inclination-consent," which we have traced above. But the inward struggle dealt with in Romans 7 makes it much more complex--especially in the Christian believer, to whom Augustine is sure this passage applies--than this simple sequence would imply.

First of all, Romans 7 speaks of two conflicting inclinations or delights. On the one hand there is the pervasive role of desire, such that Paul says--twice, in slightly different form--that it is not what he wants, but what he does not want, that he does (Rom 7:15, 19), so that it is no longer he who does it but sin dwelling within him (Rom 7:20). Augustine interprets this to mean that the will is in bondage to its own misdirected affections, delighting wrongly or in the wrong things. These affections are summed up as desire, which is characterized as sin (Rom 7:8-11, 17) or the "law of sin" (Rom 7:23, 25b) in the flesh. On the other hand, there is the contrary factor of delighting in the law of God (Rom. 7:22) or with the mind serving the law of God (Rom 7:25b), even while this is resisted by desire in the flesh. As we shall see in a moment, Augustine became convinced that one cannot "delight in the good" through the law, since the law arouses only fear; thus the crucial role is played by the grace of the Holy Spirit in evoking delight in the good.

Second, one can consent to the good and yet not be totally untroubled and free of conflict. If it is uncertain what Paul means in saying, "I delight in the law of God after the inward person" (Rom 7:22)--is it merely delight but not yet consent?--he has already said, "I consent to the law, because it is good" (Rom 7:16),[43] or "I find that the law, when I will to act, is a good thing to me" (Rom 7:21).[44] The result of this consent to the good, however, is that the conflict of delights becomes even more intense.

How and why does one "consent"? This is at the center of Augustine's wrestling with Romans 7. Earlier his explanation had been in terms of the first phase, "suggestion" or "suasion": when one is called "congruously," in a way suited to one's condition, one will respond to that divine call.[45] Now he gives the crucial role to the second phase, delight or inclination-specifically, to the "law of grace," which is identified with the Holy Spirit.[46] Augustine was already accustomed to quoting Romans 5:5--"the love of God has been poured into our hearts by the Holy Spirit which has been given to us." Now he understands this verse to refer to God's infusing of delight in the good, overcoming the other delight in temporal things. This new delight "draws" or "leads" the will,[47] inviting consent and making it possible. This consent consists of faith, which Paul habitually contrasts with the law. Faith is a yielding or consenting to the authority and the appeal of God's call. And because faith is a looking beyond oneself, it can do what the law could not do through fear. What the law commands (imperat) faith seeks and obtains (impetrat), as Augustine often says,[48] in the continuing assistance of divine grace.

This consent in the center of the self intensifies the inner conflict. There arises a mutual resistance: the "law of sin" resists the law to which the mind gives consent (Rom 7:23), while consent to the good resists the law of sin in the flesh. Both sinful desire and consent to the good are spoken of as ways of "acting" or "doing," prior to any internal or external action. It is to these inward inclinations that Paul refers when he says, "I do not know"--meaning "I do not acknowledge" or "I do not approve"[49]--"what I do" (Rom 7:15), and "it is no longer I who do it but that which dwells in me, sin" (Rom 7:16).

Thus in every phase of willing there is conflict, for misdirected desire resists consent to the good and limits the accomplishment of what one wills. The struggle is understood eschatologically, as the beginning of resurrection; indeed, it is an inward resurrection which will reach fulfillment only in bodily resurrection.

The Nature of the Conflict

We may object to the adversarial imagery Augustine uses. He speaks of combat between opposing delights within oneself, of taking sides among delights, vanquishing or being vanquished, dominating or being dominated, even killing. Paul himself, of course, had already spoken of mortifying, putting to death, the actions of the flesh (Rom 8:13), whose members might otherwise be yielded to sin as weapons of iniquity (Rom 6:13).

We must be more precise, however, about this imagery of conflict.[50] In the Roman world, references to the military suggested loyalty and discipline and closed ranks, not the valor of single combat. Augustine's dominant metaphor, already suggested by Paul (especially I Cor 9:24-27) is the agon, an athletic competition in the stadium or theater. It was not gladiatorial combat. Augustine chooses the pancratium, the most popular entertainment in his culture; while it was fought without weapons, it was still brutal, because all blows were permitted. The Martyrdom of Perpetua, read every year on her "birth day" of March 7, authorized the use of this image. Condemned to fight the beasts in the arena, Perpetua dreamed that she was transformed into a male and defeated an Egyptian in a contest of exactly this sort. And while the violent Circumcellions in the countryside called themselves agonistici who "fought the good fight" (II Tim 4:7), Augustine emphasized that the Christian agon is in the stadium of the heart.[51] The pancratium, furthermore, was unlike the field of battle in that a judge was present--not to limit the blows but to declare the victor. Augustine gives the custom a new twist by making Christ a judge who not only watches but comes to the aid of the Christian lying on the ground.[52]

Augustine also uses the imagery of household conflict and assumes that, when it occurs, the husband should subdue the wife (this is the one inequality which Augustine thinks to be natural rather than the result of sin). To some it may look like a comical Taming of the Shrew, to others like spouse abuse. The imagery, while it may have been reinforced by social custom, was actually supplied by Ephesians 5:28, where husbands are told to love their wives as they love their own bodies[53]; in other words, male and female are related like mind and body, or Christ and the Church, and it is necessary to maintain, in a spirit of love, the proper subordination. Augustine does not remain bound, however, to the cultural values of his society. Just as easily he can use the examples of Susanna's chastity and Joseph's deference toward Mary as illustrations of what happens in "the theater of our hearts."[54]

And finally there is medical imagery. Augustine speaks of letting the disease grow worse so that it will fully manifest itself and treatment can begin. The treatment is surgical, without anesthesia; it hurts, but it is for one's eventual good.[55] In one way or another, then, he evokes the need for making tough choices, sacrificing one thing for the sake of something else.

And yet he does not want to be misunderstood. He denies that he is speaking of two different substances constantly at war with each other, as the Manichaeans suppose. He quotes with approval the statement that "no one hates one's own flesh" (Eph 5:29).

Augustine's metaphors are often those of combat between hostile parties. But he is referring, of course, to the conflict within an individual drawn in different directions. For this reason he prefers the image of a space that is already shared, but unhappily. Most often it is the stadium with its contestants, but sometimes it is the household, where we find not a friendly family discussion but disorder. Resolution of the conflict through compromise or moderation may be impossible. Decision will become inevitable. Even then--especially then--frustration, resistance, opposition will continue from one side or the other.

The conflict of "flesh and spirit" is finally resolved not by reconciling irreconcilable impulses but by framing the conflict in a new way. Augustine is able to <u>acknowledge</u> (rather than deny or exclude from awareness) the reality of inclinations against which he struggled, precisely because a <u>higher loyalty</u> has relativized them and set them in a different perspective. Mention has already been made of the philosophical point that he had learned from Cicero: when we say that all people desire happiness, this does not mean that they should seek whatever delights them, or that happiness consists in having whatever one desires, for one cannot be happy in possessing what is inappropriate.[56] In this way it becomes acceptable to make short-term sacrifices for the sake of fulfillment in the long run, frustrating the "desires of the flesh" for the sake of eventual harmony between flesh and spirit, negating the negation brought about by evil so that more positive features can be freed.

Fate or Freedom?

If later readers have had difficulty with Augustine's statements about desire and the ongoing conflict it causes, they have had even greater difficulty with his solution--that grace gives a delight in the good which, being stronger than desire, makes consent possible and indeed inevitable. If human willing is in bondage to its own misdirected affections, to such an extent that it cannot delight in or consent to or will the good, then it must be freed from that bondage. But is it really freed if it merely crosses from one sphere of influence to another, from the inevitability of wrong delight to the inevitability of correct delight? For that matter, once we begin thinking about inevitabilities it is not a foregone conclusion where our sympathies will lie. Popular culture more easily identifies with the overpowering but tragic love between Tristan and Isolde, Francesca da Rimini and Paolo, than with the delight in the good which claims to free the human spirit. This was already a tendency in ancient culture; Augustine mentions that people often say, "Venus made me do it" or "Mars made me do it."[57] In his own youth, he recalls, he mourned the death of Dido, who killed herself from love, but not his own spiritual death.[58]

Augustine believed in predestination--that is, God's election of some persons out of the lump of sinful humanity, all of whom deserve condemnation, to be offered an undeserved salvation. He came to that conviction in 396, while considering the problems raised by Romans 9. The only question was how God's purpose to save certain persons takes effect. His first theory was that it occurs through "congruous calling," ensuring that the elect are called in a way that is suited to their condition and will lead infallibly to a favorable response. In the sermons on Romans 7 and 8 we begin to see a rethinking. Because of the conflict of delights, he insists, one cannot will what is good unless one already takes delight in it. By the year 418 he came to the view that something more is needed, and he emphasized the role of a victorious delight in the good.[59]

Serious inquiry along these lines was resumed in the late sixteenth century by both Catholics and Protestants as they wrestled with the relation of grace and free will. During those years a metaphorical distinction was made between two ways of thinking about the action of grace. Does it act "physically," in the way one thing acts on another? The Dominicans and many of the Calvinists chose this model. Or does it act "morally," making an appeal through meanings and affects? The Jesuits, the Arminians, and the Amyraldians, moderate Calvinists who still held firmly to predestination, chose this model.[60] Obviously Augustine understands grace to operate in the second way, and this can mean that, even when we are "physically" capable of willing the good, we can still be "morally" unable to do so, bound by our own affections and desires until we are freed by delight in the good.

Under such circumstances, are we really free? Let us consider Augustine's answers to this challenge. First, he urges us to examine what our free choice really amounts to. There is a sort of underlying potentiality for affection, choice, loyalty, but it is situated "between" basic options for higher and lower values. Once it has chosen the lower values it cannot liberate itself; to be freed it must be drawn by a factor which is not its own, not under its control. In other words, we are never in a position to make a neutral and totally autonomous choice; or, if we were once in that position in the freshness of creation, we are in it no longer. In any event, Augustine would add, we can insist too strongly upon freedom of choice among alternatives, for true freedom, responsiveness to the good, is even more to be valued. We must avoid the mistake, then, of supposing that there is complete symmetry between lesser and greater values, or between delight in lesser values (which Augustine thinks will fragment our attention, distract our affections, and lead to bondage rather than freedom) and delight in higher values (which he thinks will unify the affections and give true freedom to the self and full consistency in its willing).[61]

But this is not the end of the matter. Even predestination and grace, as
Augustine understands them, take into account the role of human consent. He often thinks of God's adapting the call so that it will be "congruous" with the person's needs; at times he even imagines God looking ahead to what a person "would do" under this or that set of inducements, and applying those that will tilt the affections without fail.[62] Despite the indispensable role of "delight" in human willing, however, it is "consent" that makes it one's own. And yet consent, despite its decisive role, remains fragile. Congruous calling and victorious delight may lead "infallibly" to consent, but they are not "irresistible," for there is resistance both before and after consent.[63]

Therefore Augustine not only uses the "synchronic" conceptuality of suggestion-inclination-consent in analyzing the process of willing; he is also aware of a "diachronic" drama within the self, for past judgments, past affections, past choices, retain their power in the present.[64] Even the elect do not generally experience assurance or inevitability. They are aware of struggle and anxiety, and victory is achieved only because grace persists through time and supplies perseverance. Human beings still live "under grace"; they are not yet "in peace." The difference is that, while freedom in the latter state is the "happy necessity" of responding to the good,[65] in the former there remains a conflict between impulses, such that in consenting to the better impulses one must continue to resist the worse ones.

We may object that Augustine leaves us only "technically free." In a sense that is true, for the outcome not only is certain to God but is planned by God, who calls the person "congruously" or infuses a victorious delight. And yet Augustine would say that even "technical freedom" is not to be scorned, for consent has the irreducible role of ratifying, validating, appropriating. Even if there should be no difference in content between an attractive "suggestion," an overwhelming "inclination," and the "consent" that is given, there is a difference in meaning. Consent is our own personal resolution of all the factors impinging upon us, our own way of coming to terms with them and ranking their importance or relevance to us. One suggestion, one inclination, may be so dominant that consent seems inevitable. Yet there will be other suggestions, other inclinations, as a passage like Romans 7 indicates. They not only struggle for consent before the decision is made; they also resist the consent after it is given.

The meaning of freedom is a classic problem among modern philosophers. Ever since Locke's careful scrutiny of the meaning of free choice, emphasizing the constant flow of "preferences"--but also insisting in his second edition that freedom, in the sense of a kind of "uneasiness," intervenes between desiring and willing[66]-- there have been some who emphasize the aspect of inevitability. Jonathan Edwards, seeing that Locke's psychology could be used to buttress his own predestinarianism of the "moral influence" type, argued that freedom consists in following the greatest apparent good or the strongest inclination. Unlike Augustine, however, he did not differentiate between inclination and consent, and thus he did not leave room even for "technical" freedom of choice.[67]

There are those, of course, who insist that talk about freedom has meaning because we in fact experience it, if not in every aspect of our lives, at least in some aspects. When pressed they may even acknowledge the overwhelming presence of preconditions of all sorts--our bodies, our circumstances, experiences and conditioning, pressures and appeals from family or friends, government or the media--yet they will still insist that the experience of freedom is not without meaning.[68] At a minimum they will adopt the position called "compatibilism," the position, in other words, that there is not a forced choice between the theories called (perhaps too starkly) determinism and libertarianism, because both of them give helpful descriptions of our experience, dealing with distinct aspects of it and from contrasting points of view.[69]

On these terms, Augustine is a compatibilist, at least with respect to grace and free will (the theological term is "congruist"). But this makes it all the more important to keep in mind his distinction between suggestion, inclination, and consent--overlooked, I think, in most of the contemporary discussion--for he identifies several distinct "layers" of considerations that must be described and related to each other in any discussion of freedom. When one adds his awareness of continued resistance from other impulses, and thus an ongoing struggle within the self, it becomes evident that he does not imagine either sin or grace to operate in a simple and uncomplicated way.[70]

"I am the field upon which I labor," Augustine once said, "with difficulty and much sweat."[71] He found this to be the case over and over, as he dealt with many different problems, and in different tones of voice. It may help us, as we seek our own way, to learn how he set his questions concerning himself in the larger framework of relationships with other beings, with other persons--- and finally with the Other who, he was sure, is most intensely present.

1. For the "interpretation history" of Romans 7 see W.G. Kümmel, Römer 7 und die Bekehrung des Paulus (Leipzig: J.C. Hinrichs, 1929); K.H. Schelkle, Paulus: Lehrer der Väter (Düsseldorf: Patmos Verlag, 1956), pp. 236-48; Ulrich Wilckens, Der Brief an die Römer, Evangelisch-Katholischer Kommentar zum Neuen Testament 6 (Neukirchen-Vluyn: Neukirchener Verlag, 1978-1982) II:101-17; Peter Gorday, Principles of Patristic Exegesis: Romans 9-11 in Origen, John Chrysostom, and Augustine, Studies in the Bible and Early Christianity 4 (New York and Toronto: Edwin Mellen Press, 1983). Gerd Theissen, Psychological Aspects of Pauline Theology, Translated by John P.Galvin (Philadelphia: Fortress Press, 1987), pp. 177-265, champions the psychological interpretation on the basis of parallels with Greek philosophy and literary criticism. A challenge to the psychological approach, which sees Augustine's misreading of the chapter as a crucial factor in the history of interpretation, has been issued by Paula Fredriksen in "Paul and Augustine: Conversion Narratives, Orthodox Traditions, and the Retrospective Self," Journal of Theological Studies NS 37 (1986), 3-34, esp. 22-33, and "Beyond the Body/Soul Dichotomy: Augustine on Paul Against the Manichees and the Pelagians," Recherches Augustiniennes 23 (1988), 87-114.

2. For general discussions see my Augustine the Theologian (New York: Herder and Herder, 1970), pp. 156-65, 176-82, 258-66; Peter Gorday, Principles of Patristic Exegesis: Romans 9-11 in Origen, John Chrysostom, and Augustine (New York and Toronto: Edwin Mellen Press, 1983), pp. 137-87. The major shifts in Augustine's

thinking about Paul are traced in a subtle way in the two articles by Paula Fredriksen, note 1.

3. This period in Augustine's thought is discussed in Paula Fredriksen, Augustine's Early Interpretations of Paul (Ann Arbor: University Microfilms, 1979) and William S. Babcock, "Augustine's Interpretation of Romans (A.D. 394-396)," Augustinian Studies 10 (1979) 55-74.

4. The transition can be seen in De diversis quaestionibus ad Simplicianum. In answering the first question--which deals with Romans 7!--Augustine still assumes that the sinner seeks divine assistance. In answering the second, he becomes persuaded that grace has the initiating role.

5. De div. quaest. ad Simpl. I, q. 2,22.

6. This change in Augustine's thinking has been documented and traced with care by J. Patout Burns, The Development of Augustine's Doctrine of Operative Grace (Paris: Études Augustiniennes, 1980).

7. Rudolf Bultmann, Theology of the New Testament, Translated by Kendrick Grobel, I (New York: Charles Scribner's Sons, 1951), pp. 246-49; The Old and New Man in the Letters of Paul, Translated by Keith R. Crim (Richmond: John Knox Press, 1967), pp. 16, 24, 33-48. A recent discussion along Bultmannian lines is Paul W. Meyer, "The Worm at the Core of the Apple: Exegetical Reflections on Romans 7," The Conversation Continues: Studies in Paul and John in Honor of J. Louis Martyn (Nashville: Abingdon Press, 1990), pp. 62-84.

8. Serm. 103,8.

9. See Johannes Munck, Paul and the Salvation of Mankind, Translated by Frank Clarke (Atlanta: John Knox Press, 1959); Krister Stendahl, Paul among Jews and Gentiles and Other Essays (Philadelphia: Fortress Press, 1976); and the two articles by Paula Fredriksen, note 1 above.

10. Serm. 152,7; 155,3-6.

11. Serm. 155,6; 156,14.

12. Serm. 154/A [Morin 4],5.

13. These four stages are developed in Exp. prop. Rom. 13-18, and in De div. quaest. q. 61,7 and q. 66,3. Augustine reaffirms them many years later in Enchiridion xxxi,118-119. This fourfold classification is related to philosophical theories of moral development by James Wetzel, "The Recovery of Free Agency in the

Theology of St. Augustine," Harvard Theological Review 80 (1987), 112-118.

14. It could even be said that, for Augustine, human life is the cosmos writ small. Paul had said (Rom 8:18-20) that the whole creation "groans in travail," having been subjected to vanity. Augustine construes "the whole creation" to mean "the whole creature," the entire human being, which includes matter, soul, and mind, and in this sense is "all creation" (omnis creatura, not merely totus creatura). According to this interpretation, human being in its entirety is subjected to vanity, that is, to earthly change and vulnerability, but in hope of resurrection; the "first fruits of the spirit" is the human mind, offering itself to God through faith. See Exp. prop. Rom. 45; De div. quaest. q. 67.

15. This argument is stated in a programmatic way in Krister Stendahl, "The Apostle Paul and the Introspective Conscience of the West," Harvard Theological Review 56 (1960), 199-215, reprinted in Paul Among Jews and Gentiles, pp. 78-96. It is further developed in Paula Fredriksen, "Paul and Augustine," pp. 23-30.

16. "The Apostle Paul and the Introspective Conscience of the West," in Paul among Jews and Gentiles, pp. 93.

17. "Beyond the Body/Soul Dichotomy," p. 112.

18. Ibid., p. 113.

19. La Bonnardière, "La date," 129-130.

20. Jaroslav Pelikan, The Christian Tradition: A History of the Development of Doctrine, I. The Emergence of the Catholic Tradition (100-600) (Chicago: University of Chicago Press, 1971), p. 339, and The Melody of Theology: A Philosophical Dictionary (Cambridge: Harvard University Press, 1988), pp. 264-65.

21. Serm. 131,10. Roman Catholics have customarily seen in this papal endorsement of the African councils an early proof of the authority of the Pope. But even Catholic scholars caution that the African appeal has a large element of coalition-building through subtle flattery, and that the papal endorsement of the African councils may indicate not so much agreement with their doctrine in all details as an attempt to maintain the dignity of the Roman see and its right to intervene in the affairs of other churches, especially in the West.

22. The more widespread, and more cynical, view is that they appealed to the imperial court in order to go over the head of the pope. The more benign view, argued by J. Patout Burns,

"Augustine's Role in the Imperial Action against Pelagius," Journal of Theological Studies, NS 30 (1979), 67-83, is that the appeal to the court was made between September 23, when they learned of Innocent's action, and November 2, when the learned of Zosimus's suspension of that action. In the latter case, their appeal would be a "normal" request for imperial coercitio to back up a judgment by the church.

23. Augustine always cites the work as Pro libero arbitrio, perhaps to characterize its bias, perhaps because that was the title Pelagius gave it. The latter would not be unlikely, for Pelagius knew how to be assertive. He had earlier written a work De natura in response to Augustine's emphasis on the human need for grace; the work defending free will was issued in an even more polemical context. The expression "pro libero arbitrio" gained negative connotations as Augustine looked back over his own intellectual development, recalling, for example, how he had labored for free will but the grace of God prevailed (Retr. II,1 (CC 57,89-90).

24. Friedrich Schleiermacher, The Christian Faith, Translated by H.R. Mackintosh and J.S. Stewart (Edinburgh: T. & T. Clark, 1928) §22,2 (p. 98) and §80,4 (pp. 329-30).

25. De nupt. et conc. II,iii,9; C. du. ep. Pel. III,ix,25.

26. André Rétif, "A propos de l'interprétation du chapitre VII des Romains par saint Augustin," Recherches de science religieuse 33 (1946), 368-371, pointed out that Pelagius could not have been responding to Augustine, who had not taken a stand on the interpretation of Romans 7.

27. In Serm. 154,4 Augustine comments that this question had been raised by Pelagius, and his work Pro libero arbitrio did indeed raise it, as we learn from other passages in Augustine.

28. The emphasis on "now"--later mentioned in C. du. ep. Pel. I,x,22, written in 419--is first encountered in Serm. 154,11 and 155,2. See La Bonnardière, "La date," pp. 133-34.

29. See especially De div. quaest. ad Simpl. I, q. 2,10-13 and 21-22; De spir. et litt. xxxiv,60.

30. This is the position Augustine had already stated about the year 394 in his Exp. ep. ad Gal. 49 and 54. The struggle between inclinations is evoked with special power in Conf. VIII,ix, 21, where Augustine asks how it can happen that the human spirit

resists its own commands to itself, and answers that its willing is "half-hearted," inclined toward contrary things.

31. De <u>Gen. adv. Man.</u> II,xiv,20-21 and xiv, 28; <u>De serm. Dom. in mon.</u> I,xii,34. For a more thorough analysis of this theory of willing (which Augustine saw allegorized in the three figures of the Eden narrative) see Eugene TeSelle, "Serpent, Eve, and Adam: Augustine and the Exegetical Tradition," <u>Augustine: Presbyter Factus Sum</u>, Edited by Joseph T. Lienhard, S.J., Earl C. Muller, S.J., Roland J. Teske, S.J., <u>Collectanea Augustiniana</u> (New York: Peter Lang, 1994), pp. 341-361.

32. Paul has a similarly brief summary of the Decalogue in Rom 13:8-9, including "Do not desire." In Rom 7 he seems to makes desire the basic or general sin (as also in I Cor 10:6). It may be not only a summary of the Decalogue but a recollection of the Eden narrative (Gen 3:6). Backgrounds in Palestinian and Hellenistic Judaism are examined in Stanislaus Lyonnet, "'Tu ne convoiteras pas' (Rom. vii 7)," <u>Neotestamentica et Patristica. Eine Freundesgabe Herrn Professor Dr. Oscar Cullmann zu seinem 60. Geburtstag überreicht</u> (Leiden: E.J. Brill, 1962), pp. 157-65, and more briefly in Walter Schmithals, <u>Die Theologische Anthropologie des Paulus. Auslegung von Röm 7, 17-8, 39</u>, Kohlhammer Taschenbücher 1021 (Stuttgart: Verlag W. Kohlhammer, 1980), p. 26, and Theissen, pp. 204-5. Many centuries later, Calvin followed Augustine (explicitly acknowledging him) and interpreted the tenth commandment to prohibit not only the specific kinds of "coveting" which are listed--for most of these have already been prohibited in earlier commandments--but any motivation other than love grounded in God. In this respect, he felt, the tenth commandment made a transition to the twin commandment of love <u>(Institutio Christianae Religionis</u> II,viii,49-50).

33. <u>De mor. eccl. cath.</u> I,iii,4: <u>Ep.</u> 130,10; <u>De Trin.</u> XIII,v,8, quoting from Cicero's <u>Hortensius</u>.

34. Augustine uses these other passages to explicate the command "Do not desire" in <u>In Ev. Ioann.</u> tr. 41,12.

35. For a comprehensive discussion of the term, see Gerald Bonner, "<u>Libido</u> and <u>concupiscentia</u> in St Augustine," <u>Studia Patristica</u> 6 = <u>Texte und Untersuchungen</u> 81 (Berlin: Akademie-Verlag, 1962), pp. 303-314.

36. <u>De Trin.</u> XIII,xviii,23; <u>Ench.</u> x,34; <u>Serm.</u> 196,1; 215,4; 293,1.

37. Peter Brown, <u>The Body and Society: Men, Women and Sexual Renunciation in Early Christianity</u> (New York: Columbia University

Press, 1988), pp. 413-22; Paula Fredriksen, "Beyond the Body/Soul Dichotomy," p. 112.

38. The tension is brought out by Margaret R. Miles, "The Body and Human Values in Augustine of Hippo," Grace, Politics and Desire: Essays on Augustine, Edited by H.A. Meynell (Calgary: University of Calgary Press, 1990), pp. 61-62.

39. Serm. 151,8.

40. For a general survey of this theme, see Gerald W. Schlabach, "Friendship and Adultery: Social Reality and Sexual Metaphor in Augustine's Doctrine of Original Sin," Augustinian Studies 23 (1992), 125-147.

41. Serm. 77/A [Guelf.33],4. In De continentia Augustine shows that in many Biblical texts "living according to the flesh" means "living according to the human" (iv,10-11), and makes the point that "the flesh desires nothing except through the soul" (viii, 19).

42. Serm. 153,8.

43. Augustine's paraphrase of this verse in Serm. 154,10 indicates that he understands it to mean "consenting to the law," "willing what the law wills."

44. In De div. quaest. ad Simpl. I, q. 1,12 the verse is paraphrased, "Therefore the law, when I will, is a good thing to me, when I will to do what the law commands." Augustine's later interpretation of Rom 7:21 can be seen in Serm. 154,13 and in C. du. ep. Pel. I,x,19, where it is paraphrased, "The law is a good thing to one who wills to act, but evil lies near through desire, to which one does not consent," and De nupt. et conc. I,xxx,33, where the passage is applied to willing what the law wills, against one's own desires.

45. For the development of Augustine's theory of conversion, see my Augustine the Theologian, pp. 41-42, 178-79, and J. Patout Burns, The Development of Augustine's Doctrine of Operative Grace (Paris: Études Augustiniennes, 1980), pp. 141-58, 183-88.

46. Serm. 152,5-7.

47. Serm. 156,10-11. The locus classicus for this theme is In evang. Ioann. 26,4-5, where Augustine quotes Vergil's Eclogue II,65 to the effect that "each is drawn by one's own pleasure" and compares it with being "drawn" by the Father (Jn 6:44).

48. In the later writings, Ep. 196,6; C. du. ep. Pel. IV,v,10; Ench. xxxi,117.

49. <u>Serm.</u> 154,11.

50. This imagery of combat and victory is explored in Suzanne Poque, <u>Le langage symbolique dans la prédication d'Augustin d'Hippone. Images héroïques</u> (Paris: Études Augustiniennes, 1984), pp. 53-60.

51. Poque, pp. 83-84 and nn. 107-111.

52. <u>Serm.</u> 154/A [Morin IV],3. Poque (p. 96 and n. 169) notes the parallel with <u>Pius Aeneas</u>, who ends a combat between Entellus and Dares when the latter is endangered (<u>Aeneid</u> V:491-496).

53. <u>Serm.</u> 154,15.

54. <u>Serm.</u> 363,5-6.

55. For a discussion of the medical imagery see Poque, pp. 180-88; Rudolph Arbesmann, "Christ the <u>Medicus Humilis</u> in St. Augustine," <u>Augustinus Magister</u> II: 623-29, and Petrus Cornelis Josephus Eijkenboom, <u>Het Christus-Medicusmotief in de preken van Sint Augustinus</u> (Assen: Van Gorcum, 1960).

56. See note 33 above.

57. <u>Enn. Ps.</u> 40,6; 61,23.

58. <u>Conf.</u> I,xiii,21.

59. This notion of <u>delectatio victrix</u> or <u>vincens</u> is found in <u>De pecc. mer.</u> II,xix,32; <u>C. du. ep. Pel.</u> I,xii,27; <u>Ench.</u> xxii,81; <u>De cont.</u> 20; and <u>C. Iul. op. imp.</u> I, 107; II, 217; and II, 226.

60. There is a need for an "ecumenical" survey of the disputes of this period, for Catholics and Protestants learned much from each other--positively and not merely by way of provocation or bad examples to be spoken against. For general surveys one must still consult the classic histories of doctrine or theological encyclopedias. Beyond these, there are studies of particular figures, often quite narrow in scope.

61. For a contemporary statement along the same lines see Susan Wolf, "Asymmetrical Freedom," <u>Journal of Philosophy</u> 77 (1980), pp. 151-66, and the more extended discussion (more technical, but not adding basically new points) in <u>Freedom Within Reason</u> (New York: Oxford University Press, 1990). As she states it, we are free when we have good reasons for acting as we do, and our action can even be said to be "determined" by those considerations. What we ordinarily call free choice is a situation of psychological uncertainty about the definitive reasons to act. And actions that go against what we consider to

be true or good are not free except in a perverse sense. The theological tradition is aware of the additional complications introduced by sin and "carnal custom," so that one does not inevitably will what one knows to be right or good. This became an explicit issue at the University of Paris in 1270, when the bishop condemned the thesis that the will necessarily follows what the intellect sees to be good. Thomas Aquinas adjusted his own position about this time, increasing the tension in his thought between rational deliberation, which judges whether an act is "right or wrong," and motivation, which is "good or bad" because of caritas or the lack of it. The issues are discussed in James F. Keenan, S.J., Goodness and Rightness in Thomas Aquinas's Summa Theologiae (Washington: Georgetown University Press, 1992), and Daniel Westberg, "Did Aquinas Change His Mind About the Will?" The Thomist, 58 (1994), 41-60.

62. This is what the Jesuit theologians called God's "middle knowledge" of "futuribles" or "future possibles." The hypothesis is that God knows what persons "would do" if offered grace under this or that set of circumstances and plans accordingly. Augustine clearly considered this (Ep. 102, q. 2,14-15), for he was aware (like Origen earlier) of the passage in the gospels which speaks of what the people of Tyre and Sidon "would have done" (Mt 11:20-24=Lk 10:13-15).

63. James Wetzel, Augustine and the Limits of Virtue (Cambridge: Cambridge University Press, 1992), pp. 198-200, insists too strongly that grace cannot be "resisted." While that would become one of the essential doctrines of the strict Calvinists, Augustine used the word differently, speaking of wrong desires "resisting" consent to the good, and vice versa (e.g., C. Iul. VI,55).

64. This theme is traced, thoroughly and subtly, throughout Wetzel's The Limits of Virtue.

65. De perf. iust. hom. iv,9; C. Iul. op. imp. I,103.

66. John Locke, An Essay Concerning: Human Understanding, Edited with a Foreword by Peter H. Nidditch (Oxford: Clarendon Press, 1975), Book II, Chapter xxi, §§29-48 (pp. 249-265). The very different discussion in the first edition is printed in the footnotes.

67. Jonathan Edwards, Freedom of the Will, edited by Paul Ramsey (New Haven: Yale University Press, 1957) pp. 16-17, 156-62, 236-38, 328-33. While Edwards did speak of "consent," he meant by it not the act of consenting but the state of being in agreement or union of heart with God, or with God's providential ordering of the world. The subsequent discussion among the "Edwardsians" is

traced by Allen C. Guelzo, Edwards on the Will: A Century of American Theological Debate (Middletown: Wesleyan University Press, 1989). He shows that, just as Locke felt compelled to move from a "one-stage" to a "two-stage" theory of willing, many of the Edwardsians moved from a one-stage to a two-stage theory (pp. 55-59, 109-10) and some even to a three-stage theory (pp. 211, 100-105). In many ways it is a repetition of the ancient discussion, especially among the Stoics, which I have tried to trace in "Serpent, Eve, and Adam," 343-47.

68. The same issues even appear in public policy debates. Is it true (as the National Rifle Association argues) that "Guns do not kill people, people kill people"? or (as opponents of censorship or self-regulation argue) that "Television does not cause violence, people cause violence"? When the debate is framed in this way, the sole alternative is suggestion versus consent. Sociologists and psychologists are likely to emphasize the middle factor of inclination and ask about the many factors that intervene between the "suggestions" that come from society (ready access to guns, images of violence on television) and the final "consent" to acting in this or that way.

69. The analyses of contemporary philosophers are strong on logical complexity and often weaker on exploration of the range of human experience. For convenient summaries see Louis P. Pojman, "Freedom and Determinism: A Contemporary Discussion," Zygon, 22 (1987), 397-417 and the still-classic essay by Richard Taylor, "Determinism," Encyclopedia of Philosophy, Edited by Paul Edwards (New York: Macmillan Company and The Free Press, 1967), II, 359-73. The most Augustinian position is that of Susan Wolf, cited above--if one adds the complexities that come from inward struggle and resistance.

70. I have already criticized Edwards for too simplistic a conception of freedom, that it consists in following the greatest apparent good or the strongest inclination. Among Catholics, Jansenism has been similarly criticized for making the delectatio victrix a sort of "concupiscence in reverse." The alternative is to emphasize a constant interaction, such that only those who consent to the good can take delight in it, and delight in turn stimulates the next act of consent. Cf. my comments in "Serpent, Eve, and Adam," 354 and n. 48.

71. Conf. X,xvi,25.

What Has Jerusalem to Do with Beijing?
The Book of Revelation and Chinese Christians

Yeo Khiok-khng (K.K.)
Garrett-Evangelical Theological Seminary

Introduction

The paper is a revised chapter of the author's newly published work entitled *What Has Jerusalem to Do Beijing? Biblical Interpretation from Chinese Perspective* (Trinity Press International, 1998). The book reflects the range of biblical reading I have preferred to do over the last seven years in the light of a multi-faith, multi-textual, and multi-cultural context of Asia: a Chinese Christian reading of the biblical text from an Asian perspective.

The book begins with clarifying methodological issues of a cross-cultural reading from theological (rhetorical and contextual) and biblical basis (Galatians 3:1-20). Then eight scriptural texts are read with an Asian eye. The eight texts are divided into two main categories: one group of four texts falls into the area of dialoguing with perennial themes in Chinese cultures. These essays seek to express biblical truth in the language of my own people. The language of yin-yang philosophy and the Confucian understanding *of T'ien Ming* (Mandate of Heaven) as well as *li* (law/propriety) and *jen* (love) are used to convey the biblical notions of God, humanity, sabbath-rest, will of God and so forth.

The other group of four texts are read with intertextual theories of reading. Artificial limits are placed on the four texts on the significations of *li* (law), *jen* (love in the Spirit), *T'ien Ming* (Will of God), and *Tai-Chi* (rest) in my reading of the Analects and the biblical passages. For example, through the use of rhetorical criticism, Paul's preaching is heard as speaking not only to Athenian philosophers, but also to Chinese Taoists in Acts 17. The message of hope found in the book of Revelation is heard as speaking to the Chinese Christians who lived through the Cultural Revolution. Isaiah 5:1-7 and 27:2-6 offer a political and social message of restoration to those who felt betrayed in the June Fourth Event of national disgrace at Tienanmen Square. An analysis of 1 Corinthians 8 and 10 in view of the Malaysian "Vision 2020" put out by the Prime Minister suggests that the Pauline vision of mutuality between men and women is a better vision than that found in exclusively man or woman theologies which stop short of the wider transformation needed. This paper will focus on the book of Revelation and its appealing force for Chinese Christians during the Cultural Revolution.

Political Oppression and Spiritual Hope in Revelation and China

Although the book of Revelation has been subjected to many abuses over the centuries, and many First World Christians may not find Revelation illuminating, Revelation was meaningful to Chinese Christians who lived in the grim reality of overt and covert persecution and suffering during the Cultural Revolution. The abundant esoteric imagery found in Revelation had not deterred Chinese Christians from tapping the power of its faith and finding comfort in it.

The Context of Suffering for Christians in Revelation

The persecution of Christians in the book of Revelation arose from their resistance to emperor worship,[1] their exclusive loyalty to Christ without compromising with the synagogue, and their persistent adhering to a faith at odds with the syncretistic practices of pagan religions. Revelation depicts the religious, cultural, economic and political struggles of Christians at the end of the first century,[2] probably during the reign of the Roman Emperor Domitian. Barclay views the background of Revelation as that of Caesar worship. He sees the Roman Empire as the earthly body of Satan through which Satan exercises his power.[3] In the Roman period, the first Provincial temple of the Imperial cult in Asia was built at Pergamum in honor of Rome and Augustus (29 BC probably). The imperial cult, the worship of the spirit of Rome and of the emperor, was found at the center of the city. The one and only criterion recognized as loyalty to the country was a citizen's willingness to perform the ritual of the State religion, and to make an offering to the Imperial God, the Divine Emperor. During the reign of Domitian (81-96 CE), Christian martyrs emerged as victors in Roman persecution. "Throne" in Revelation is a political term. The usage perhaps indicates the political polemic in light of the Caesar cult. The repeated "Worthy art thou" (4:11; 5:9, 12) reflects the acclamation used to

---

[1] S. MacL. Gilmour, "Use and Abuse of the Book of Revelation," *Andover Newton Quarterly* 7 (1, 1966): 15-18.

[2] This date is found in Irenaeus, Adv. Haer. 5. 30. 3 and Eusebius, *EH* 3, 18. Cf. W. G. Kümmel, *Introduction to the New Testament,* trans. A. J. Mattill (London: SCM Press, 1966), pp. 327-329. My reconstruction basically agrees with Collins' and Thompson's research that Irenaeus' dating of Revelation to the reign of Domitian (ca. 90-95 CE) does not seem to rest on the tradition that Domitian was the second great persecutor of Christians. Furthermore, though internal evidence in Revelation is consistent with Irenaues' dating, there is no reliable external evidence that Domitian systematically persecuted Christians -- the first two centuries witnessed only sporadic repression of Christians. Cf. Leonard Thompson, "A Sociological Analysis of Tribulation in the Apocalypse of John," *Semeia* 36 (1986): 147-174.

[3] The power culminated in the return of Nero Redivivus. Cf. W. Barclay, "Great Themes of the New Testament: V. Revelation xiii," *Expository Times* 70 (9, 1959): 260-264; 292-296.

greet the emperor during his triumphal entrance.[4] The title "Lord and God" (4:8) is paralleled by the claims of Domitian and other emperors. It is even surmised that the twenty-four elders may be the twenty-four lictors who surrounded Domitian.[5]

John claims that history is under the control of God, and that the end of history is the defining point of both the past and the present. John conceives history as God's revelational activity. Jesus is the real anticipation of the final end of universal history; Jesus is, in Pannenberg's understanding, the "proleptic presence of the eschatological future of all history."[6] The book of Revelation does not set forth stages of world history, but a Christian philosophy of history with heavy orientation on eschatology. Eschatology involves "future history." The breaking-in of God's kingdom and the destruction of evil forces at the end-time have confirmed for believers their present reality. The present is subordinated to the future and confirmed partially by the past. The present receives its significance from the future. The book of Revelation is a Christian theology of history in terms of the Christ-event which defines the meaning of history in terms of eschatology.

The purpose of this chapter does not concern the chronological sequence of events in world history that coincide with history in Revelation. Instead, it concerns a particular view of history that gives birth to the rhetorical effect and imagery of the apocalypse, which in turn evoke hope and faith for Christians in the first century and during the Cultural Revolution.

The Chinese Context of Suffering

The persecution experienced by Chinese Christians during the Cultural Revolution had its ideological-political and religious-philosophical cause, as did the persecution suffered by Christians in Roman times. In Communist China, religious freedom as guaranteed in Article 88 of the 1954 constitution (viz., "Citizens of the People's Republic of China enjoy freedom of religious belief"[7]) and was in line with the Marxist dogma. According to this dogma, religion originated in primitive society as a way of dealing with the unexplainable forces of nature and with human tragedy. But as society developed, religion had become a tool of the upper class to

---

[4]M. E. Boring, *Revelation* (Louisville: John Knox Press, 1989), p. 103.

[5]D. E. Aune, "The Influence of Roman Imperial Court Ceremonial on the Apocalypse of John," *Biblical Research* 28 (1983): 13.

[6]Carl E. Braaten, "Wolfhart Pannenberg," in *A Handbook of Christian Theologians*, ed. Martin E. Marty & Dean G. Peerman (Nashville: Abingdon Press, 1984), p. 643.

[7]For more, see G. Thompson Brown, *Christianity in the People's Republic of China* (Atlanta: John Knox Press, 1986), pp. 76-77.

exploit and control the lower class by taking "the minds of the exploited off their present condition of misery."[8] The Chinese constitutional idea that religion must not become an exploiter of the people was thus in agreement with Marx's famous dictum that "religion is the opiate of the people."[9]

The Chinese communist has viewed religion (especially Christianity) as a foreign imperialist's ideological tool for the exploitation of common people.[10] Mao Tse-tung himself considered Christian missionary work in China to be a form of foreign cultural aggression. It is understandable that the Christian Manifesto[11] would agree with the Communist Party's view. As such, the Christian Manifesto states that, "missionaries who brought Christianity to China all came themselves from these imperialistic countries, Christianity consciously or unconsciously, directly or indirectly, became related with imperialism."[12] It is not surprising, then, that although religious freedom was guaranteed in Article 88 of the 1954 constitution, after 1949 and under the banner of Mao, pastors and Christians were harassed and placed under constant surveillance and suspicion. Many were persecuted, imprisoned and killed.[13] Many had to go through "accusation meetings," being suspected of "counter-revolutionary" activities. Few Christians escaped trial and death because they were accused of subscribing to, and being brainwashed by, the foreigner's religion.

In 1966 Mao approved the organizing of the Red Guards (1966-1967). Millions of teenagers indoctrinated with fanaticism ravaged the country and wrecked structures of orderly society, including religious institutions. Churches were closed and Christians suffered greatly. Many churches installed a large white statue of Mao at the center. Posters such as this one were common:

---

[8]Brown, *Christianity*, pp. 76-77.

[9]Robert C. Tucker, *Philosophy and Myth in Karl Marx* (Cambridge: University Press, 1972), p. 105.

[10]That view is understandable if one views Chinese history (prior to the Communist regime) through the eyes of the Chinese. Cf. Leslie Lyall, *God Reigns in China* (London: Hodder and Stoughton, 1985), p. 126 elaborates this point.

[11]In 1950 nineteen Protestant leaders, with the leading force of Y. T. Wu, met with Zhou Enlai to prepare a statement called Christian Manifesto concerning the difficulties the Churches faced in New China. The controversial document states specifically the political viewpoints of the Christian Church. It is therefore not a theological document. The full text of the document is published in *Tien Fung* 233-234 (Sep 1950): 146-147. Cf. Philip L. Wickeri, *Seeking the Common Ground. Protestant Christianity, the Three-Self Movement, and China's United Front* (Maryknoll, New York: Orbis, 1988), 127-133.

[12]*Documents of the Three-Self Movement* (hereafter *Documents*; ed. Wallace C. Merviwn, Francis P. Jones (New York: National Council of the Churches of Christ, 1963), pp. 19-20.

[13]Cf. C. Jones, *The Church in Communist China: A Protestant Appraisal* (New York: Friendship Press, 1962).

> There is no God; there is no Spirit; there is no Jesus; . . . How can
> adults believe in these things? . . . Protestantism is a reactionary
> feudal ideology, the opium of the people . . . We are atheists; we
> believe only in Mao Tsu-tung. We call on all people to burn Bibles,
> destroy images, and disperse religious associations.[14]

In the midst of the Great Leap Forward (1958-1960), the
consolidation of churches and worship services was required and
monitored by the Religious Affairs Bureau. All pastors were told to be
allied with the Socialist reconstruction of the mother land. Biblical
teaching concerning the Last Day was prohibited for preaching, being
considered poisonous thoughts.

The Thriving of Chinese Christians

During the ten catastrophic years of the Cultural Revolution (1966-
1976) when all the churches were closed, the house churches kept
functioning and blossoming. These "underground" Christians kept
meeting, praying, witnessing and studying in family and close-knit groups.
In the 1970s and 1980s these house congregations became the mainstream
of New China Christianity.

Most of these groups have loved to study the book of Revelation,
from which they derive strength, faith, and hope. They hold to this
apocalyptic hope in the midst of turmoil and danger. A high view of
Christology helps them to hold fast to their faith. The worship experiences
and preaching of such groups are often charismatic. The important
doctrines they hold dear center around the sacrificial death, resurrection
and second coming of Christ. All these doctrines grant hope and assurance
to these Christians.

The book of Revelation does not give Chinese Christians during the
Cultural Revolution merely the existential strength, the book also infuse
them with a view of history which differed from that of the communists.
Unlike the communists, Chinese Christians are able to see the world from
the transcendent perspective in the apocalyptic visions of Revelation.
Chinese Christians counter the communist, socialist, and human
construction of utopian society by opening the world to divine
transcendence and New Heaven. By way of the motifs of visionary
transportation to heaven, visions of God's throne-room in heaven, angelic
mediators of revelation, symbolic visions of political powers, coming
judgment and new creation, Chinese Christians see the final destiny of this
despaired world in the transcendent divine purpose.

The achievement of God's righteous rule over his world encourages
Chinese Christians to counter the communist world view which is anti-

---

[14]G. Thompson Brown, *Christianity in the People's Republic of China* (Atlanta:
John Knox Press, 1986), p. 125.

divine. The righteous suffer, the wicked flourish: the world seems to be ruled by evil, not by God. But that is only part of the picture then! The apocalyptic world view assures Chinese Christians that God's kingdom is about to reign, and that they should maintain their faith in the one, all-powerful and righteous God in the face of the harsh realities of evil in the world, especially the political evil of the oppression of God's faithful people by the pagan regime. God rules his creation and the time is coming soon when he will overthrow the evil empire and establish his kingdom. The theology of the lamb as one who suffers and the One who controls history speak to the Chinese Christians the assured victory of the faithful despite the apparent domination of the evil power. It is the hope portrayed in the book of Revelation that sustains Chinese Christians to endure to the end.

History has proven that such hope has worked miracles among Chinese Christians for the past 40 years. The number and faith of these Christians have not declined, but increased. Chinese Christians have seen the whole picture of God's revelation working itself out in history. For they have seen the end of history; and that grants them assurance of victory, comfort in suffering, and hope in the midst of dismay. They have learned to be open to God and to the future in an attitude of obedience and surrender. As a people oppressed, they have seen salvation emerge from hopelessness and death, for they have seen Christ as the End and the Hope in history.

The Three-Self Patriotic Movement in China and the Anti-Roman Ideology in Revelation

Despite the fact that the Christians of Revelation and of China both suffered for their faith because of political-religious causes, there is one church movement in China that is unique from what we can find in the book of Revelation. Unlike the stance taken by the book of Revelation in which separationists were commended, accommodationists accused, the TSPM (Three-Self Patriotic Movement)[15] held to political accommodation. The TSPM thrived despite its position.

Separation Strategy and Independent Result

In fact, separation was ordered by the Communist party stating that Chinese churches had to be loyal to none other than the Chinese government. The Religious Affairs Department was set up in Peking in 1950 and were commissioned to cut off all Christian bodies in China from their overseas ties, to expel foreign missionaries, and to promote an autonomous church movement. In the mid-1950s, Chou En-lai met

---

[15]Richard X. Y. Zhang, "The Origin of the 'Three Self'," *Jian Dao* 5 (1996): 175-202.

separately with Protestant and Catholic leaders, assuring them of the government's intention to protect freedom of religious belief, but requesting them to separate themselves from overseas imperialist control, and to express their patriotic sentiments by adapting to the new political situation in the New China. The new government officially launched the TSPM in 1951, calling for self-support, self-government, and self-propagation by the Protestant Christian bodies in China. However, this separation from outside contact provided a nursing bed for the healthy growth of the Chinese churches.

The three-self concept had originally been the idea of two American missionaries, S. L. Baldwin and V. Talmage, in the 1800's.[16] In the 1890 and the 1907 missionary conferences, the thematic emphasis of the Chinese churches was on self-support, leadership, and evangelism.[17] When the communist government came to power, they seriously adopted this policy and added a political twist. C. M. Chen, an official of the Religious Affairs Bureau, once said that the purpose of the government was not outright extermination but restriction, reformation and control. Chen pointed out that the TSPM had been created to make religion serve politics and to make the church politically harmless.[18]

The separation strategy of the Communists has also meant that the Chinese churches have had to work closer with the communist leadership. Wu Yao-tsung, a visionary and first president of TSPM, was influenced by the worldwide Christian socialist movement of the 1930's and became more and more sympathetic to Chinese Communist ideas.[19] He saw a crucial task neglected by Christians and the churches but fulfilled by communists.

The uniqueness of the TSPM is its willingness and courage to cooperate with the Communist party at least on the common ground of social issues. It is little wonder that the Christian Manifesto was prepared by Wu Yao-tsung and premier Chou En-lai.[20] By that time (1950) war had broken out in Korea, anti-American sentiment was high, and patriotic

---

[16]S. L. Baldwin, "Self-support of the native church," and J. V. N. Talmage, "Should the native Churches in China be united ecclesiastically and independent of foreign churches and societies," *Records of the General Conference of the Protestant Missionaries of China Held at Shanghai*, May 10-20, 1877 (Shanghai: Presbyterian Mission Press, 1878), pp. 283ff, 429ff.

[17]G. L. Mason "Methods of Developing Self-Support and Voluntary Effort," *Records of the General Conference of the Protestant Missionary of China Held at Shanghai*, May 7-20, 1890 (Shanghai: American Presbyterian Mission Press, 1890), pp. 415ff. And J. C. Gibson, "The Chinese Church," *Records: China Centenary Missionary Conference*, Held at Shanghai, April 25 to May 8, 1907 (Shanghai: Centenary Conference Committee, 1907), pp. 1ff.

[18]Lyall, *God Reigns*, p. 129.

[19]*Documents*, pp. 184-191. Cf. Brown, *Christianity*, p. 81.

[20]*Documents*, pp. 19-21.

fervor was rampant. A massive campaign was launched to get Christians all over China to sign the Manifesto.[21] The Manifesto called on Chinese Christians to heighten their "vigilance against imperialism, to make known the clear political stand of Christians in New China, to hasten the building of a Chinese Church whose affairs are managed by the Chinese themselves." It stated further that Christians should support the "common political platform under the leadership of the government."[22] It called upon churches relying on foreign personnel and financial aid to discontinue these relations and work toward self-reliance.[23] In October 1950, the biannual meeting of the Chinese National Christian Council was held for the purpose of adopting the Manifesto and implementing means to bring about the "three self reform."[24] In April 1951, the newly organized Religious Affairs Bureau of the government invited 151 Protestant leaders to a conference in Beijing. There, they voted

> . . . to thoroughly, permanently and completely sever all relations with American missions and all other missions, thus realizing self-government, self-support and self-propagation in the Chinese church.[25]

In order to carry out this policy, the Protestant TSRM (Three-Self Reform Movement)[26] was officially established.[27] In 1958 Wu wrote in *Tien Fung (Heavenly Wind)* that "without the Communist Party there would not have been the TSPM or the Christian Church . . . I love the Communist Party."[28] At that time, TSPM drafted a "message of respect" to Chairman Mao which had four main points: (1) To promote the greater unity of all Christian Churches by carrying out the three-self policy in response their love for both the country and the Christian religion; (2) To support the Draft Constitution of the People's Republic of China and to strive with the people of the whole nation to construct a socialist society; (3) To oppose imperialist aggression to safeguard the peace of the world; and, (4) To

---

[21] By 1952, at least 400,000 Christians signed it. Cf. Brown, *Christianity*, p. 83; *Tien Fung*, 233-234 (1950, Sept 30): 2-3.

[22] *Tien Fung* 423 (1954, July 7): 1 and 425-427; (1954, Sept 3): 3-10.

[23] Brown, *Christianity*, p. 84, and *Documents*, pp. 177-186.

[24] Donald MacInnis, *Religious Policy and Practice in Communist China* (New York: The Macmillan Co. , 1973), p. 99.

[25] MacInnis, *Religious Policy*, p. 99.

[26] In 1954 the name was changed to the Protestant Three-Self Patriotic Movement for the sake of unity. Cf. *Documents*, p. 4.

[27] Lyall critically observes that TSPM is not a spontaneous, free independent body of the Chinese Church, but an organization created by the Communist Party to carry out party policy. Lyall's point is that the late Wu Yao-tsung was pro-Communist and a serious student of Marxism.

[28] Lyall, *God Reigns*, p. 131; *Documents*, pp. 184-191.

encourage all Christians of the nation to seriously learn patriotism.[29] Most of the resistance to TSPM came from conservative preachers like Wang Ming-dao[30] and Watchman Nee,[31] some underground house-churches and the Roman Catholic Church,[32] who were reacting against the more 'liberal' theology of TSPM and its cooperation with the Communist Party. Obviously, the Roman Catholic Church in China could not break its ties to Rome.

Chinese Christianity in the Communist Context

A brief survey of the rise of TSPM within the context of the complex historical development of communist ideology is suffice to raise some crucial issues related to the Christian Church in the New China, even though these issues may raise more questions than answers. The issues are interrelated and must be thought through before one can talk about Chinese Christianity as a westernized or an indigenous faith in China.

Chinese Christians struggled with the issue of the Christian's ultimate loyalty, whether it should be to God or to the State. TSPM Christians declare,

We love our country, the People's Government and socialism. . . . The communists are atheistic, but they respect our faith,[33] . . . . Although we and the communists differ in faith, we are all Chinese,

---

[29]George N. Patterson, *Christianity in Communist China* (Texas, Waco: Word Books Publisher, 1969), pp. 88-89.

[30]Wang Ming-dao (1900-1988) is a militant preacher who independently organized his own church, the Christian Tabernacle in Beijing. He distributed *The Spiritual Food Quarterly*. See his two articles, "We, Because of Faith" and "Self-Examination," in *Documents*, pp. 99-113, 117-120 criticizing TSPM in the light of the Bible. Cf. Ng Lee Ming, "Christianity and Social Change: The Case of China" (Diss., Princeton Theological Seminary, 1970).

[31]Watchman Nee (1903-1972) is a prolific author and charismatic speaker who founded "Little Flock" (cf., Luke 12:32) or "Christian Assembly" in Fuzhou. He opposed denominational structure, which he believed to be a human construction. He preached the message of personal salvation and sanctification. He was arrested and charged with "counter-revolutionary activity" many times, even TSM and Protestant leaders denounced him, see *Tien Fung* 498 (Feb 6, 1956): 9-10. Cf. Brown, *Christianity*, pp. 82-85; Patterson, *Christianity in Communist China*, pp. 91-93, Wickeri, *Seeking the Common Ground*, pp. 162-164.

[32]See Brown, *Christianity*, pp. 86-88 for details.

[33]Zhou En-lai once remarked to a Christian delegation during a conference, "So we are going to go on letting you teach, trying to convert the people. . . . After all we both believe that truth will prevail; we think your beliefs untrue and false, therefore if we are right, the people will reject them, and your church will decay. If you are right, then the people will believe you, but as we are sure that you are wrong, we are prepared for that risk." See MacInnis, *Religious Policy*, p. 24.

and are one in our desire for the increasing prosperity and . . . building up of our country.[34]

That Chinese Christians love their country does not mean that they have ceased to love God or that they love God less. Like John's attitude toward the Roman government, Western Christians often have a deep prejudice or unjustified fear that because Communism allows less freedom than democracy, to cooperate with the Communist Party is to ally with the Devil. The question becomes, can Christianity survive only in a capitalistic society? Or, is one form of government more divinely ordained than another? In fact, the three-self principles should mean that the church is independent of foreign churches and also of the Communist Party within China. Brown rightly points out that TSPM is not China's "official church."[35] China has no official church. The Chinese Church is run by Chinese Christians.

Chinese Christians also struggled with the relation between God's creative work and God's redemptive work.[36] Is the Gospel of Christ concerned only with the reconciliation of people to God, or does it also have meaning for the state and society? After years of breaking off all relations with imperialism and gradually learning to rule, to support, and to propagate, the Chinese Christian Church has come to recognize communist government leadership as sincere in is its policy of freedom of religious belief, and its willingness to help the church in any difficulties it may meet. It has also come to recognize that to participate in the government is one way to bear witness for the Lord.[37] Bishop Ting, for example, has commented that Christians must learn to live with atheists in New China, not being seduced by them but learning how to present the gospel to them.[38] In his article "A Call for Clarity: Fourteen Points from Christians in the People's Republic China to Christians Abroad," K. H. Ting affirms the positive attitude TSPM has towards the New China. His point is that Chinese Christians' patriotism is "not without a prophetic and critical character."

By supporting the TSPM, the Chinese Christians have chosen the common ground between Christianity and communism instead of magnifying their difference. This does not compromise the Christian truth. No doubt these two competing "ideologies", each supremely sure of its own understanding of reality, have "compatible and partly convergent

---

[34]*Documents*, p. 172.

[35]Brown, *Christianity*, p. 213. Cf. K. H. Ting, "A Call for Clarity: Fourteen Points from Christian in the People's Republic China to Christians Abroad," *China Notes* 19 (Winter 1980-1981): 145-149.

[36]*Documents*, p. 171.

[37]*Documents*, p. 172.

[38]*Documents*, p. 156.

positions regarding the dignity and destiny of man and his call to transform the world."[39] Julia Ching calls this alternative way "that of collaboration in the humanist cause, . . . a faith in man which can be acceptable to Christians, in so far as it is open to God."[40] TSPM regards the policy of religious freedom to be "a reasonable one" but has no illusions about communism's atheist views.[41] TSPM therefore can and must work with the state on the "common ground" explained above for the sake of Christ and the benefit of the people.

Towards an Indigenous Chinese Faith

Chinese Christianity ought to be a product of reflection on the Chinese experience and culture as lived by the Chinese themselves, neither as interpreted by Westerners -- nor by a simple and linear application of the message of Revelation. Christians, wherever they live, ought not abandon their traditions. In fact, adding another "self," that is, "self-expression," to the three-self principle is appropriate in the context of the Chinese experience.

The hermeneutical implications of the whole chapter do not call for a simple application of the message of Revelation to the situation of the Chinese Christians. If they did, the Three-Self Movement would have to be deemed heretical according to the standard of Revelation. We have already pointed out the similarity of the Christians in both the book of Revelation and China going through suffering because of their faith. We have also seen a unique church movement in China that is unparalleled in Revelation.

As an historic movement the TSPM represents post-denominational unity in an unprecedented manner for the Chinese people. The divisions and denominations of Christianity in the West has long confused Chinese Christians. Ecumenical concern for unity in variety and for a pluralism of self-expression is characteristic of TSPM. During the last thirty years or so, it has held dialogues between the church and the state and between Christians and non-Christians. Today the vast majority of Chinese Christians are patriotic citizens and support the Three-Self Principles.[42]

This chapter does not seek to give the impression that TSPM is a perfect movement; it has its shortcomings and weaknesses. The chapter merely tries to point out that Christ, the End of history gives hope for the Chinese Christians under persecution, but that they seek in their own context to live the biblical message in some ways quite different from the

---

[39]Julia Ching, "Faith and Ideology in the Light of the New China," *Christianity and the New China* (California: Ecclesia Publications, 1976), p. 26.

[40]Ching, "Faith and Ideology," p. 26.

[41]Ting, "A Call for Clarity," pp. 145-149.

[42]Brown, *Christianity*, p. 213.

total intention of the writer of Revelation. TSPM is not a "communist" Christianity but a Chinese Christianity in the New Communist China. TSPM may be "the result of the leading of the Holy Spirit" in light of the complex historical and ideological situation of New China from which it has emerged, but without believing in Christ as its hope, TSPM will not thrive.

Hermeneutical Implications

These experiments with cross-cultural hermeneutics hope to achieve the transformation of both biblical reading and the Chinese culture. The paper and the monograph attempt to answer this question from different biblical texts and with different perspectives. The question of "What has Jerusalem to do with Beijing?" is meant not to seek an comprehensive answer; the intention of asking the question is to engender further experiment and dialogue.

As the monograph and this chapter have shown, a cross-cultural reading is also a contextual reading. A contextual reading of the Bible is difficult for me because "the historical tradition to which we all belong"[43] is predominantly a western philosophical and theological tradition. I include myself in this tradition because my theological training occurred in the United States of America (1984-1992). I have no pretense at all that the reading demonstrated in these essays is not "westernized." Their use of biblical material, exegetical method, as well as thought forms are all "westernized." Regarding exegetical method and the use of biblical research material, it is difficult to come up with a purely Chinese method or with purely Chinese research, if there is one. The use of the English medium is an audience-oriented issue.

Although the medium of expression is indicative of one's cultural mindset, it is not necessarily conditioned or limited by it. Just as Paul could convey Jewish thought through the medium of Greek, I have used English to express Chinese thought. What is intriguing and necessary is the transference of thought from one culture to another. In that sense, methods and material need to be multi-cultural. The cross-cultural reading done here is itself a Chinese perspective, with which I am experimenting. These are some of the factors that will increasingly shape and sharpen my critical reading of the Bible.

As much as I would like for a mutual transformation between the biblical text and the context in which I live, I have to admit that I have no control over the transformative process. I do admit that if the formative powers of the tradition, the text, world history, and the pre-understanding I bring to the process are neither universal nor unified, neither

---

[43]H.-G. Gadamer, *Truth and Method*, trans. Garrett Borden John Cumming (New York: Seabury Press, 1975), p. xxv.

Abrahamically rooted nor historically oriented, then my cross-cultural and interreligious hermeneutic needs to be articulated and not left in silence. Furthermore, the hermeneutic has to be open to a genuine on-going community dialogue which is transcultural and free. Interpretation involves not only speaking but also listening, and transposing oneself "out of one's own frame of mind."[44] Such interpretation is not only dialogical in a social context but also critical in intentionality.

If I were to attempt to read the biblical text without a critical eye, I would end up agreeing with the claim of the universality of the biblical texts. To question the legitimacy of authority or tradition in the distorted communication process is what I need and have begun to do. One cannot assume that one particular reading is the right one simply because it has been there for a long time. Neither can one assume that a particular person's reading is correct simply because of that person's authority within a community. One needs to assume that any reading is unavoidably a distorted process.

The cross-cultural reading in this paper also faces the issue of my own ideological reading. If "ideological reading of the biblical text" means letting a "system of ideas [express] a particular point of view"[45], then I must acknowledge my "ideology" which includes my cultural bias, certain ideological presuppositions, and a readerly orientation. However, if "ideological reading of the biblical text" means the rationalization of self-interest as well as the reinforcing of one's status quo, then I need to allow the ideological critique of a cross-cultural hermeneutics to challenge and transform my reading. One might cite the harmonization of Scripture as one of the best reading principles, but often such harmonization does not do justice to the cultural and authorial contexts. The biblical narratives of God's interaction with the people over the millennia, in different geographic, political, social, economic and cultural settings, calls for diversity in God's revelation and divine responses in the Bible. Biblical truth is transcendent only in the sense that it is from the divine (transcending the human realm and thought), but biblical truth is concretely and historically revealed to specific problems, needs, and opportunities of its various contexts.

The cross-cultural reading of biblical texts in this paper has shown my concern for the way the biblical narratives help to relate to our stories, diverse as they are in terms of racial, national, religious, educational, economic, gender factors. The biblical texts point to a larger narrative in which the Divine interacts with mankind's story to create meaningful and bountiful life. This is accomplished by the Messiah of Yahweh who

---

[44]F. D. E. Schleiermacher, *Hermeneutics: The Handwritten Manuscripts*, trans. J. Duke and J. Forstman (Missoula: Scholars Press, 1977), p. 109.

[45]Robert McAfee Brown, *Theology in a New Key* (Philadelphia: Westminster, 1978), pp. 78-80.

redeemed us from ambiguity and meaninglessness by giving us hope and the promise of eternal life through the unveiling of the End by His resurrection. He has redeemed us from alienation and loneliness by incarnating God's presence both in the Word narrated (Scripture) and in the Word celebrated (sacrament). He has redeemed us from evil and suffering by his own passionate suffering on the cross, thus transforming evil into good.

David M. Scholer
Fuller Theological Seminary

Introduction

This brief listing supplements the Q bibliographies that have appeared in the *Society of Biblical Literature Seminar Papers* volumes since 1986. This Supplement contains an additional one hundred two items. It is the plan to publish a comprehensive Q bibliography (through 1998; appearing in 2000) in connection with the work of James M. Robinson, John S. Kloppenborg, Paul Hoffmann and others (in the Documenta Q series published by Peeters). I wish to thank Susan Carlson Wood for her excellent help in the preparation of this manuscript.

Books and Reviews

Allison, D. C., Jr. *The Jesus Tradition in Q.* Harrisburg, PA: Trinity Press International, 1997. [This book is comprised of nine chapters, three of which are completely new; the remaining six chapters are significantly revised forms of previous articles. The only entry in this bibliography is the book.]

Carruth, S. and Garsky, A. *The Database of the International Q Project: Q 11:2b-4....*
Légasse, S. *Bulletin de Littérature Ecclésiastique* 97 (1996), 293.
McNichol, A. J. *Religious Studies Review* 24 (1998), 83.
Moore, A. *Religious Studies and Theology* 16 (1997), 91-93.

Carruth, S. and Robinson, J. M. *The Database of the International Q Project: Q 4;1-13, 16....*
See also Neirynck, F. "Note on Q 4,1-2...."

Catchpole, D. R. *The Quest for Q....*
Ellis, E. E. *Southwestern Journal of Theology* 38:3 (Summer 1996), 54-55.
Parker, D. C. *Scottish Journal of Theology* 50 (1997), 507-08.

Fleddermann, H. T. *Mark and Q....*
Ellis, E. E. *Southwestern Journal of Theology* 39:1 (Fall 1996), 69-70.
Maloney, E. C. *Catholic Biblical Quarterly* 59 (1997), 578-80.
Niemand, C. *Studien zum Neuen Testament und seiner Umwelt* 21 (1996), 237-41.
Tuckett, C. M. *Biblica* 78 (1997), 279-83.

Garsky, A.; Heil, C. Hieke, T.; and Amon, J. E. *The Database of the International Q Project: Q 12:49-59, Children against Parents—Judging the Time—Settling out*

of Court. Vol. Ed. S. Carruth. (Documenta Q.) Leuven: Peeters, 1997. [Not seen.]
Neirynck, F. Ephemerides Theologicae Lovenienses 73 (1997), 458-59.

Hoffmann, P. Tradition und Situation....
Kloppenborg, J. S. Critical Review of Books in Religion 1996 (1997), 231-33.
März, C.-P. Theologische Literaturzeitung 122 (1997), 673-74.

Hoffmann, P.; Amon, J. E.; Hieke, T.; Boring, M. E.; and Asgeirsson, J. M. The Database of the International Q Project: Q 12:8-12, Confessing or Denying— Speaking against the Holy Spirit—Hearings before Synagogues. Vol Ed. C. Heil. (Documenta Q.) Leuven: Peeters, 1997. [Not seen.]

Jacobson, A. D. The First Gospel....
Fuchs, A. Studien zum Neuen Testament und seiner Umwelt 21 (1996), 243-46.

Kloppenborg, J. S. Conflict and Invention....
Sweder, K. M. Toronto Journal of Theology 13 (1997), 108-09.

Kristen, P. Familie, Kreuz und Leben: Nachfolge Jesu nach Q und dem Markusevangelium. (Marburger Theologische Studien 42.) Marburg: N. G. Elwert, 1995.

Mack, B. L. The Lost Gospel....
Adams, A. C. Lexington Theological Quarterly 31 (1996), 147-54.

Neirynck, F. Q-Synopsis.... [1988]
Bonora, A. Rivista Biblica 37 (1989), 245-46.

Neirynck, F. Q-Synopsis.... [1995]
Fuchs, A. Studien zum Neuen Testament und seiner Umwelt 20 (1995), 208-09.
Poppi, A. Rivista Biblica 44 (1996), 367-68.

Piper, R. A. The Gospel Behind the Gospels....
Hunt, S. A. Journal for the Study of the New Testament 67 (1997), 123.
Malina, B. J. Biblical Interpretation 5 (1997), 220-21.

Tuckett, C. M. Q and the History of Early Christianity....
Bridges, L. M. Review and Expositor 94 (1997), 463.
Catchpole, D. R. Journal of Theological Studies 48 (1997), 191-94.
Frenschkowski, M. Theologische Literaturzeitung 122 (1997), 811-13.
Houlden, J. L. Theology 99 (1996), 470-71.
Neirynck, F. Ephemerides Theologicae Lovenienses 73 (1997), 173-77.
Telford, W. R. Expository Times 108 (1996/97), 305-06.

Uro, R. Symbols and Strata: Essays on the Sayings Gospel Q....
Burnett, F. W. Religious Studies Review 24 (1998), 197.

Morgan, R. *Expository Times* 109 (1997/98), 117-18.
Neirynck, F. *Ephemerides Theologicae Lovanienses* 73 (1997), 177-79.

Vaage, L. E. *Galilean Upstarts....*
Arnal, W. E. *Toronto Journal of Theology* 13 (1997), 121-23.
Kloppenborg, J. S. *Studies in Religion/Sciences Religieuses* 25 (1996), 504-05.
See Robinson, J. M. "*Galilean Upstarts:....*"

Zager, W. *Gottesherrschaft und Endgericht in der Verkündigung Jesu: Eine Untersuchung zur markinischen Jesusüberlieferung einschliesslich der Q-Parallelen.* (BZNW 82.) Berlin/New York: Walter de Gruyter, 1996.
Oehler, M. *Theologische Literaturzeitung* 122 (1997), 571-73.
Wenham, D. *Journal of Theological Studies* 48 (1997), 581-82.

Articles

Anonymous. "'Q'," *The Oxford Dictionary of the Christian Church* (ed. F. L. Cross; 3d ed., ed. E. A. Livingstone; Oxford/New York: Oxford University Press, 1997), 1354.

Arnal, W. E. "Why Q Failed: From Ideological Project to Group Formation," *AAR/SBL Abstracts 1997* (1997), 18.

Bauer, U. "Der Anfang der Endzeitrede in der Logienquelle (Q 17): Probleme der Rekonstruktion und Interpretation des Q-Textes," *Wenn drei das gleiche sagen—Studien zu den ersten drei Evangelien: Mit einer Werkstattübersetzung des Q-Textes* [Für Paul Hoffmann] (hrsg. S. H. Brandenburger und T. Hieke; Theologie 14; Münster: LIT-Verlag, 1998), 79-101.

Bjorndahl, S. G. "The Divorce that Spawned a War and the Reconstruction of Q 16:16-18," *AAR/SBL Abstracts 1997* (1997), 38.

Bjorndahl, S. G. "An Honor Map of Q," *Wenn drei das gleiche sagen—Studien zu den ersten drei Evangelien: Mit einer Werkstattübersetzung des Q-Textes* [Für Paul Hoffmann] (hrsg. S. H. Brandenburger und T. Hieke; Theologie 14; Münster: LIT-Verlag, 1998), 63-78.

Braun, W. "Greco-Roman 'Schools' and the Sayings Gospel Q," *AAR/SBL Abstracts 1997* (1997), 18.

Broadhead, E. K. "The Extent of the Sayings Tradition," *AAR/SBL Abstracts 1997* (1997), 38-39.

Broadhead, E. K. "On the (Mis)Definition of Q," *Journal for the Study of the New Testament* 68 (1997), 3-12.

Brodie, T. L. "Intertextuality and Its Use in Tracing Q and Proto-Luke," in *The Scriptures in the Gospels* (ed. C. M. Tuckett; BETL 131; Leuven: Leuven University Press/Peeters, 1997), 469-77.

Brown, R. E. "The Existence of 'Q,'" a section in *An Introduction to the New Testament* (Anchor Bible Reference Library; New York: Doubleday, 1997), 116-22.

Corley, K. E. "Mourners in the Marketplace: Q 7:31-32," *AAR/SBL Abstracts 1997* (1997), 39.

Cotter, W. "The Q Community in the Context of Popular First-Century Religious Trends: Locating the Appeal of a Prophetic Community," *AAR/SBL Abstracts 1997* (1997), 18.

Donahue, J. R. "Q," *The HarperCollins Encyclopedia of Catholicism* (ed. R. P. McBrien; San Francisco: HarperSanFrancisco, 1995), 1074.

Douglas, R. C. "A Jesus Tradition Prayer (Q 11:2b-4; Matt 6:9b-13; Luke 11:2b-4; *Didache* 8.2)," Chapter 36 in *Prayer from Alexander to Constantine: A Critical Anthology* (ed. M. Kiley et al.; London and New York: Routledge, 1997), 211-15.

Downing, F. G. "Word-Processing in the Ancient World: The Social Production and Performance of Q," *Journal for the Study of the New Testament* 64 (1996), 29-48.

Edwards, D. R. "Archaeology and the Quest for 'Q,'" *AAR/SBL Abstracts 1997* (1997), 97.

Ettl, C. "Der 'Anfang der ... Evangelien': Die Kalenderinschrift von Priene und ihre Relevanz für die Geschichte des Begriffs εὐαγγέλιον: Mit einer Anmerkung zur Frage nach der Gattung der Logienquelle," *Wenn drei das gleiche sagen— Studien zu den ersten drei Evangelien: Mit einer Werkstattübersetzung des Q-Textes* [Für Paul Hoffmann] (hrsg. S. H. Brandenburger und T. Hieke; Theologie 14; Münster: LIT-Verlag, 1998), 121-51.

Funk, R. W. and the Jesus Seminar. "The Sayings Gospel Q," in *The Acts of Jesus: The Search for the Authentic Deeds of Jesus* (San Francisco: HarperSanFrancisco, 1998), 41-50.

Goodman, D. E. "Renewing the Bodies of Israel: 'Kingdom of God' as a Symbolic Form in Q," *AAR/SBL Abstracts 1997* (1997), 39-40.

Heil, C. "'Πάντες ἐργάται ἀδικίας' Revisited: The Reception of Ps 6,9a LXX in Q and in Luke," *Von Jesus zum Christus: Christologische Studien: Festgabe für Paul Hoffmann zum 65. Geburtstag* (hrsg. R. Hoppe und U. Busse; BZNW 93; Berlin/New York: Walter de Gruyter, 1998), 261-76.

Heil, C. "Die Rezeption von Micha 7,6 LXX in Q und Lukas," *Zeitschrift für die neutestamentliche Wissenschaft* 88 (1997), 211-22.

Heil, C. "Das Spruchevangelium Q—Stand der Forschung," *Bibel und Liturgie* 71 (1998), 37-39.

Hieke, T. "Methoden und Möglichkeiten griechischer Synopsen zu den ersten drei Evangelien," *Wenn drei das gleiche sagen—Studien zu den ersten drei Evangelien: Mit einer Werkstattübersetzung des Q-Textes* [Für Paul Hoffmann] (hrsg. S. H. Brandenburger und T. Hieke; Theologie 14; Münster: LIT-Verlag, 1998), 1-36.

Hoffmann, P. "Betz and Q," *Zeitschrift für die neutestamentliche Wissenschaft* 88 (1997), 197-210.

Hoppe, R. "Das Gastmahlgleichnis Jesu (Mt 22,1-10/Lk 14,16-24) und seine vorevangelische Traditionsgeschichte," *Von Jesus zum Christus: Christologische Studien: Festgabe für Paul Hoffmann zum 65. Geburtstag* (hrsg. R. Hoppe und U. Busse; BZNW 93; Berlin/New York: Walter de Gruyter, 1998), 277-93.

International Q Project. "Der vom Internationalen Q-Projekt rekonstruierte Q-Text: Eine Werkstattübersetzung," *Wenn drei das gleiche sagen—Studien zu den ersten drei Evangelien: Mit einer Werkstattübersetzung des Q-Textes* [Für Paul Hoffmann] (hrsg. S. H. Brandenburger und T. Hieke; Theologie 14; Münster: LIT-Verlag, 1998), 103-20.

Jonge, H. J. de. "The Sayings on Confessing and Denying in Q 12:8-9 and Mark 8:38," *Sayings of Jesus: Canonical and Non-Canonical: Essays in Honour of Tjitze Baarda* (ed. W. L. Petersen, J. S. Vos and H. J. de Jonge; Supplements to Novum Testamentum 89; Leiden: E. J. Brill, 1997), 105-21.

Kee, H. C. "Jesus as God's Eschatological Messenger: The Q Document," Chapter Three in *Jesus in History: An Approach to the Study of the Gospels* (3d ed.; Fort Worth: Harcourt Brace College Publishers, 1996), 74-115.

Kirk, A. "A Socio-historical Location for Q: Second Temple Jewish Sectarianism," *AAR/SBL Abstracts 1997* (1997), 40.

Kirk, A. "Upbraiding Wisdom: John's Speech and the Beginning of Q (Q 3:7-9, 16-17)," *Novum Testamentum* 40 (1998), 1-16.

Knierim, R. P. "Excursus: On Q," in *The Task of Old Testament Theology: Substance, Method, and Cases* (Grand Rapids/Cambridge, UK: William B. Eerdmans, 1995), 456-59.

Koester, H. "The Sayings of Q and Their Image of Jesus," *Sayings of Jesus: Canonical and Non-Canonical: Essays in Honour of Tjitze Baarda* (ed. W. L. Petersen,

J. S. Vos and H. J. de Jonge; Supplements to Novum Testamentum 89; Leiden: E. J. Brill, 1997), 137-54.

Linnemann, E. "Det bortkomne Q-evangelium—fup eller fakta?" *IXΘΥΣ* 24 (1997), 15-29.

Linnemann, E. "Q—das verlorene Evangelium—Fantasie oder Faktum?" *Jahrbuch für evangelikale Theologie* 9 (1995), 43-61.

Loader, W. R. G. "Jesus' Attitude towards the Law according to Q," Chapter 4 in *Jesus' Attitude towards the Law: A Study of the Gospels* (WUNT 2/97; Tübingen: Mohr Siebeck, 1997), 390-431.

Luz, U. "Matthäus und Q," *Von Jesus zum Christus: Christologische Studien: Festgabe für Paul Hoffmann zum 65. Geburtstag* (hrsg. R. Hoppe und U. Busse; BZNW 93; Berlin/New York: Walter de Gruyter, 1998), 201-15.

Melzer-Keller, H. "Frauen in der Logienquelle und ihrem Trägerkreis: Ist Q das Zeugnis einer patriarchatskritischen, egalitären Bewegung?" *Wenn drei das gleiche sagen—Studien zu den ersten drei Evangelien: Mit einer Werkstattübersetzung des Q-Textes* [Für Paul Hoffmann] (hrsg. S. H. Brandenburger und T. Hieke; Theologie 14; Münster: LIT-Verlag, 1998), 37-62.

Merk, O. "Die synoptische Redenquelle im Werk von Werner Georg Kümmel— Eine Bestandsaufnahme—," *Von Jesus zum Christus: Christologische Studien: Festgabe für Paul Hoffmann zum 65. Geburtstag* (hrsg. R. Hoppe und U. Busse; BZNW 93; Berlin/New York: Walter de Gruyter, 1998), 191-200.

Moreland, M. C. "The Pharisees in the Market Places: The Archaeology of Roman Galilee and the Woes," *AAR/SBL Abstracts 1997* (1997), 97.

Moreland, M. C. and Robinson, J. M. "The International Q Project: Editorial Board Meetings 1-10 June, 16 November 1995, 16-23 August, 22 November 1996, Work Sessions 17 November 1995, 23 November 1996," *Journal of Biblical Literature* 116 (1997), 521-25.

Neirynck, F. "The Eschatological Discourse," Chapter 28 in F. Neirynck, *Evangelica II 1982-1991: Collected Essays* (BETL 99; Leuven: Leuven University Press/Peeters, 1991), 493-510.

Neirynck, F. "Goulder and the Minor Agreements," *Ephemerides Theologicae Lovanienses* 73 (1997), 84-93.

Neirynck, F. "Note on Q 4,1-2," *Ephemerides Theologicae Lovanienses* 73 (1997), 94-102.

Neirynck, F. "Q 6,20b-21; 7,22 and Isaiah 61," in *The Scriptures in the Gospels* (ed. C. M. Tuckett; BETL 131; Leuven: Leuven University Press/Peeters, 1997), 27-64.

Neirynck, F. "Q^Mt and Q^Lk and the Reconstruction of Q," *Ephemerides Theologicae Lovanienses* 66 (1990), 385-90.

Neirynck, F. "Q^Mt and Q^Lk and the Reconstruction of Q," Chapter 26 in F. Neirynck, *Evangelica II 1982-1991: Collected Essays* (BETL 99; Leuven: Leuven University Press/Peeters, 1991), 475-80.

Neirynck, F. "Response to the Multiple-Stage Hypothesis: III: The Eschatological Discourse," *The Interrelations of the Gospels: A Symposium Led By M.-É. Boismard—W. R. Farmer—F. Neirynck, Jerusalem 1984* (ed. D. L. Dungan; BETL 95; Leuven: Leuven University Press/Peeters, 1990), 108-24.

Neirynck, F. "Saving/Losing One's Life: Luke 17,33 (Q?) and Mark 8,35," *Von Jesus zum Christus: Christologische Studien: Festgabe für Paul Hoffmann zum 65. Geburtstag* (hrsg. R. Hoppe und U. Busse; BZNW 93; Berlin/New York: Walter de Gruyter, 1998), 295-318.

Öhler, M. "Die Logienquelle," §2.B; 3.B and "Elia in der Logienquelle," §6.A.3 in *Elia im Neuen Testament: Untersuchungen zur Bedeutung des alttestamentlichen Propheten im frühen Christentum* (BZNW 88; Berlin/New York: Walter de Gruyter, 1997), 48-69; 154-63; 292.

Reed, J. L. "'Israelite Village Communities' and the Sayings Gospel Q," *AAR/SBL Abstracts 1997* (1997), 98.

Robinson, J. M. "Galilean Upstarts: A Sot's Cynical Disciples?" *Sayings of Jesus: Canonical and Non-Canonical: Essays in Honour of Tjitze Baarda* (ed. W. L. Petersen, J. S. Vos and H. J. de Jonge; Supplements to Novum Testamentum 89; Leiden: E. J. Brill, 1997), 223-49.

Robinson, J. M. "The Jesus of Q as Liberation Theologian," *The Bible and Immigrant Theology: In Honor of Chan-Hie Kim* (ed. S. D. Kang and J. H. Chang; Claremont: Center for Pacific and Asian Ministries, 1995), 204-18.

Robinson, J. M. "The Real Jesus of the Sayings Gospel Q," *Princeton Seminary Bulletin* 18 (1997), 135-51.

Robinson, J. M. "The Sequence of Q: The Lament over Jerusalem," *Von Jesus zum Christus: Christologische Studien: Festgabe für Paul Hoffmann zum 65. Geburtstag* (hrsg. R. Hoppe und U. Busse; BZNW 93; Berlin/New York: Walter de Gruyter, 1998), 225-60.

Robinson, J. M. "Der wahre Jesus? Der historische Jesus im Spruchevangelium Q," *Protokolle zur Bibel* 6 (1997), 1-14.

Robinson, J. M. and Heil, C. "Zeugnisse eines schriftlichen, griechischen vorkanonischen Textes: Mt 6,28b ℵ*, P.Oxy. 655 I,1–17 (EvTh 36) und Q 12,27," *Zeitschrift für die neutestamentliche Wissenschaft* 89 (1998), 30-44.

Schlosser, J. "Q 11,23 et la christologie," *Von Jesus zum Christus: Christologische Studien: Festgabe für Paul Hoffmann zum 65. Geburtstag* (hrsg. R. Hoppe und U. Busse; BZNW 93; Berlin/New York: Walter de Gruyter, 1998), 217-24.

Schlosser, J. "L'Utilisation des Ecritures dans la Source Q," *"L'Evangile exploré": Mélanges offerts en hommage à Simon Legasse à l'occasion de ses soixante-dix ans* (éd. A. Marchadour; Lectio Divina 166; Paris: Éditions du Cerf, 1996), 123-46.

Scholer, D. M. "Q Bibliography Supplement VIII: 1997," *SBL 1997 Seminar Papers* (SBLSPS 36; Atlanta: Scholars Press, 1997), 750-56.

Schröter, J. "Between John the Baptist and the Coming Son of Man: A Perspective on Time in Q," *AAR/SBL Abstracts 1997* (1997), 40.

Schröter, J. "Erwägungen zum Gesetzverständnis in Q anhand von Q 16, 16-18," in *The Scriptures in the Gospels* (ed. C. M. Tuckett; BETL 131; Leuven: Leuven University Press/Peeters, 1997), 441-58.

Taylor, N. H. "Interpretation of Scripture as an Indicator of Socio-Historical Context: The Case of the Eschatological Discourses in Mark and Q," in *The Scriptures in the Gospels* (ed. C. M. Tuckett; BETL 131; Leuven: Leuven University Press/Peeters, 1997), 459-67.

Trimaille, M. "Jésus et la sagesse dans la 'Quelle,'" Chapter 13 in *La Sagesse biblique: De l'Ancien au Nouveau Testament: Actes du XVe Congrès de l'ACFEB* (Paris, 1993) (éd. J. Trublet; Lectio Divina 160; Paris: Cerf, 1995), 279-319.

Tuckett, C. M. "Scripture and Q," in *The Scriptures in the Gospels* (ed. C. M. Tuckett; BETL 131; Leuven: Leuven University Press/Peeters, 1997), 3-26.